The Inner Cohesion between the Bible and the Fathers in Byzantine Tradition

Towards a codico-liturgical approach to
the Byzantine biblical and patristic manuscripts

S.M. Royé

ORTHODOX LOGOS PUBLISHING

The Inner Cohesion between the Bible and the Fathers in Byzantine Tradition
Towards a codico-liturgical approach to the Byzantine biblical and patristic manuscript

by S.M. Royé

Front cover Illustration
The front cover illustration is taken from A. Džurova, *Byzantinische Miniaturen. Schätze der Buchmalerei vom 4. bis zum 19. Jahrhundert*, Regensburg, 2002.

Plate No 67: Johannes Chrysostomos, *Homilien*, Katharinenkloster, Berg Sinai, Ms. 364, Pergament, 33 x 25 cm, 1042-1050; f: 2 der Evangelist Matthäus und der hl. Johannes Chrysostomos.

Printed with kind permission of Professor A. Džurova.

© 2007, S.M. Royé

© 2008, Orthodox Logos Publishing, The Netherlands

www.orthodoxlogos.com

ISBN: 978-90-811555-3-3

This book is in copyright. No part of this publication may be reproduced, stored in a retrieval system or transmitted in any form or by any means without the prior permission in writing of the publisher, nor be otherwise circulated in any form of binding or cover other than that in which it is published without a similar condition, including this condition, being imposed on the subsequent purchaser.

†††

Distinguish, o man, what thou art reading! Can these things be known from ink? Or can the taste of honey be spread over the palate of the reader, from written documents?

Isaac the Syrian, *Mystic Treatises by Isaac of Nineveh* (trans. A.J. Wensinck, I, 41)

Acknowledgement

The dissertation at hand* is the result of a twelve year period of study which I have conducted in the area of biblical science and Byzantine patrology, in cooperation with my supervisor Professor Dr. C. Houtman, Professor emeritus of Old Testament Studies at the Protestant Theological University of Kampen. The result of this period of critical and honest exchange of opinion, developed, surprisingly for us both, in the direction of catalogue and manuscript studies. I would sincerely like to thank professor Houtman for his longstanding patience and ever supportive advice.

I am grateful to my second supervisor Professor Dr. R. Roukema, Professor of New Testament Studies and Patristics at the same university, for being a critical reader and for his help in correcting the text.

This dissertation was defended in Kampen on 19th October 2007 at the Protestant Theological University of Utrecht – Kampen – Leiden.

I must certainly also thank Dr. M. Welte for the hospitality he showed when I visited the Hs. Kartei during my working visit to the *Institut für Neutestamentliche Textforschung* (Münster), with regard to my research of the 'lectionary equipment' in the NT codices.

An orientation visit I paid to the *Patriarchal Institute of Patristic Studies* in Thessaloniki, where the Athos codices are collected on microfilm) shows how great the ignorance of the Western academic world still is (in the first place of this PhD student) with regard to a Greek Orthodox evaluation of the Byzantine Greek manuscripts, as well as of later Greek editions and secondary New Greek specialised literature. Deeper acquaintance and better academic communication with the above is of the greatest necessity for further research in this area.

Very inspirational were my two year long monthly weekend working visits to the *Institute of Orthodox Christian Studies* in Cambridge (UK), not only because of the possibility to learn about the international academic Orthodox world from within, but also because of the possibility to make use of the excellent resources of Cambridge University Library.

I must also thank H. Weeda for her help, not only for her expertise in editing the text of this dissertation, but also for her personal and longstanding support of the work. I also wish to thank Dr. L. Weeda for assisting me in the correction of the Greek text, for helping me in Münster (INTF), and for providing feedback on numerous aspects of this work. Naturally, the responsibility for any language or other errors remains entirely mine.

My friend C. Tsekrekos should be mentioned for the many lively discussions on the themes at hand, his close ties to modern Greek Orthodoxy and all the books he brought me from Athens. I wish also to recall the contributions of young student T. Huyts for his stimulating and kind help in the pioneering period of developing the framework for the *Catalogue of Byzantine Liturgical Codices*.

---

* Further research has led to corrections having been made in this publication, as compared to the earlier unpublished dissertation (which was printed in 50 copies only). Especially the references in the Tables in Chapter 3.4 have now been checked against the actual texts of the lessons in the Greek original of the Greek Orthodox editions of the liturgical books.

Table of Contents

	Page
Acknowledgement	5
Table of Contents	6
Introduction	9

1. The Byzantine Manuscripts and the Western Cataloguing Tradition — 21

    1.1 Preliminary Remarks to Codicological Study of the Byzantine Manuscripts
    1.2 Advantages and Disadvantages of Specialised Catalogues
    1.3 Existing Paradigms of Manuscript Classification
    1.4 Examples of Codicological Research of the Byzantine Manuscripts
    1.5 Recapitulation

2. The Byzantine Liturgy and the Biblical and Patristic Manuscripts — 53

    2.1 The Byzantine Ecclesiastical, Liturgical Manuscripts
    2.2 Scripture in the Byzantine Liturgical Manuscripts
    2.3 The Liturgical Impact of the Biblical Commentary Manuscripts
    2.4 The Byzantine Calendar and the Liturgical Lessons
    2.5 The Typikon: The Ruling Principle of the Byzantine Liturgical Calendar
    2.6 The Scriptural Foundation of Byzantine Hymnography
    2.7 Conclusions

3. The Byzantine Lection System – a Patristic, Liturgical Hermeneutics of Scripture — 87

    3.1 The Purpose of the Byzantine Lection System
    3.2 Sources of the Byzantine Liturgical Lessons
    3.3 The Cycle of the Eleven Resurrection Evangelia
    3.4 The Movable and Immovable Cycles of Lessons of the Byzantine Calendar
    3.5 The Byzantine Cycle of Psalmody
    3.6 The Nine (Biblical) Odes of the Byzantine Psalterion
    3.7 Concluding remarks

4. The Eastern Libraries and the Catalogues of Byzantine Manuscripts — 121

    4.1 The Value of the Eastern Libraries and their Manuscript Holdings
    4.2 The Present State of Byzantine Manuscript Holdings in East and West
    4.3 The Greek Libraries, their Catalogues and Manuscripts
    4.4 The Slavic, Romanian and Georgian Libraries, their Catalogues and Manuscripts
    4.5 Conclusion

5. The Contours of a Codico-Liturgical Model of Classification — 153

    5.1 The Setting up of a *Catalogue of Byzantine Manuscripts*
    5.2 The Proposed Classification of the Byzantine Manuscripts
    5.3 The Contours of a Typology of the Codification of the Byzantine Manuscripts
    5.4 Concluding remarks

6.	**The *Catalogue of Byzantine Manuscripts***	**167**
	6.1 The Tabular Specimens	
	6.2 Group I. Byzantine Biblical Codices (NT)	
	6.3 Group II. Byzantine Biblical Codices (OT)	
	6.4 Group III. Byzantine Composite Codices (OT/NT)	
	6.5 Group IV. Byzantine Composite Codices (Biblical/Liturgical)	

Final Conclusion and Perspective   **183**

Annexes   **185**

I.	Glossary of terms	**187**
II.	Bibliography	**193**
III.	Indices of the Byzantine Anagnosmata	**219**

Introduction

Contemporary research of the Scriptures and the fathers is characterised by pluriformity. Throughout the rich history of Bible research and patrology, a palet of different traditions has always existed. One of these, which is based on an abundant manuscript tradition of biblical and patristic interpretation, is the tradition of the Eastern Orthodox Church. It is to this tradition that this study is dedicated.

1. Main objective

In this dissertation I defend an approach to the Byzantine biblical and patristic manuscripts, which could adequately be called a *liturgico-codicological* approach, and which is closely related to modern manuscript studies and especially to codicology. This approach offers, in my view, a key to understanding the position of and opinion concerning the biblical and patristic writings in the Eastern Orthodox churches. It stems from what I call a 'liturgical hypothesis', which I will explain in more detail further in this introduction, and implies the necessity of a thorough reclassification of the extant manuscripts.
Before I present the liturgico-codicological approach and the liturgical hypothesis in more detail however, I will provide a short impression of how the Eastern Orthodox churches look upon the biblical and patristic manuscripts.

2. The hermeneutical context of Eastern Orthodox Bible interpretation

Characteristic of the Orthodox vision are: 1) the anchoring of the biblical writings in the liturgy of the church; and 2) the close connection between the Scriptures and the interpretative framework of the fathers. This first point will be discussed in depth in chapter 2: *The Byzantine Liturgy and the Biblical and Patristic Manuscripts*. The second point is treated succinctly in this introduction, in three short paragraphs about Bible interpretation from an Eastern Orthodox perspective.

It is a given that the overwhelming majority of Byzantine and later Eastern Orthodox church fathers, as well as modern Orthodox scholars keenly advocate that biblical research should not be separated from the interpretative framework of the fathers of the church. I do not intend to dwell on this subject. There is a whole body of literature of scholars from Greece, Russia and other Orthodox countries, as well as those living in the West who have identified and written on this issue in depth[1]. And also in Western scholarship is attention paid to the subject[2]. Here we will provide only a couple of examples of Eastern Orthodox opinion, to remind us of what we could call the "patristic" point of departure. The Russian scholar Alexander Schmemann, for example, describes how the isolated position of Scripture in modern biblical science, is something that has not rooted in Orthodox theology: 'Unchallenged by the Reformation with its emphasis on *Sola Scriptura*, Orthodox theology implicitly rather than explicitly rejects the isolation of Scripture into a closed and self-sufficient field of study...'[3]; and the Greek biblical scholar Theodore Stylianopoulos refers to the 'gradual fading away of the Orthodox awareness that the Fathers must function as an intermediary screen between the student and the Bible'[4].

---

[1] T. Athanasopoulos, Ἐκκλησία: ὁ αὐθέντικος φύλακας καὶ ἑρμηνεύτης τῆς Ἁγίας Γραφῆς, Athens, 1998; P.K. Chrestou, Ἑλληνικὴ Πατρολογία, T. I-V, Thessaloniki, 1976-1992, Idem, *Greek Orthodox Patrology. An Introduction to the Study of the Church Fathers*, Vol. I, Ed. and Trans: G.D. Dragas, Rollinsford, New Hampshire, 2005; H. Alfeyev, *St. Symeon the New Theologian and Orthodox Tradition*, Oxford, 2000; H. Alfeyev, *The Spiritual World of Isaac the Syrian*, Kalamazoo, Mich., 2000; T.G. Stylianopoulos, *The New Testament. An Orthodox Perspective, Volume One: Scripture, Tradition, Hermeneutics*, Brookline, Mass., 1999; G.V. Florovsky, *Bible, Church, Tradition: An Eastern Orthodox View*, Belmont, 1972; G.V. Florovsky, *The Eastern Fathers of the IVth Century*, Vaduz, 1987; Idem, *The Byzantine Fathers of the Vth Century*, Belmont, 1987; Idem, *The Byzantine Fathers of the VIth – VIIIth Centuries*, Belmont, Mass., 1987; Idem, *The Byzantine Ascetic and Spiritual Fathers*, Belmont, MA, 1987, translated and extended revisions of Византийские Отцы V-VIII [The Byzantine Fathers of the Vth–VIIIth Centuries], Paris, 1933 and Восточные Отцы IV-го Вѣка [The Eastern Fathers of the IVth Century], Paris, 1931; V. Lossky, *The Mystical Theology of the Eastern Church*, Cambridge & London, 1973.

[2] E.g. C. Kannengieser (Ed.), *Handbook of Patristic Exegesis*, 2 Vols., Leiden / Boston, 2004; P.M. Blowers, (Ed. and Trans.), *The Bible in Greek Christian Antiquity*, Notre Dame, Indiana, 1997.

[3] A. Schmemann, *Russian Theology 1920-1965. A Bibliographical Survey*, Crestwood, NY, 1969, 8-9.

[4] T.G. Stylianopoulos, "Historical Studies and Orthodox Theology or the Problem of History for Orthodoxy", in *The Greek Orthodox Theological Review*, 12.3 (1967), 406. Cf. Idem, *The New Testament: An Orthodox Perspective* (Vol. 1: Scripture, Tradition, Hermeneutics), Brookline, Mass., 1999, and J. Panagopoulos, Ἡ ἑρμηνεία τῆς Ἁγίας Γραφῆς τὴν Ἐκκλησία τῶν Πατέρων [The interpretation of Holy Scripture in the Church of the Fathers], t. 1 (Athens, 1991).

Three recent conferences held in the last decennium: the first, the *West-östlichen Neutestamentler/innen-Symposiums von Neamţ (Auslegung der Bibel in orthodoxer und westlicher Perspektive)* in Romania in 1998[5]; the second, *Zweiter Europäischer Orthodox-Westliche Exegetenkonferenz (Das Alte Testament als Christliche Bibel in Orthodoxer und Westlicher Sicht)* in Rila, Bulgaria in 2001[6]; and the *Third East-Western Symposium of European NT Scholars (Unity and Diversity in NT Ecclesiology)* in St. Petersburg by the newly founded Biblical Institute of the Philological Faculty of St. Petersburg State University in 2005[7], show very clearly how the topic of the place that the fathers and tradition in general receive in Eastern Orthodox theology is still very high on the agenda of biblical scholarship. We need only to look at the conference agenda of the Neamţ conference to confirm this: 1) the meaning of the church fathers for the interpretation of the Bible; 2) the authority of the Church and the interpretation of the Bible; 3) Western scientific methods of Bible exegesis and their reception through Orthodoxy; 4) the inspiration of the Bible and its interpretation.

3. Different approaches to the interpretation of the Bible

In his concluding resumé to the conference held in Rila, Bulgaria in 2001, K.W. Niebuhr suggested that: '… there is hardly any difference between Orthodox and non-Orthodox exegesis when it comes to the valuation and application of philological and historical methods, whilst the differences between the theological interpretations of exegetical findings continue to be considerable'[8] [trans: Ed.]. Niebuhr does not enter into the whole area of philological and historical research in more depth to explain his statement, but we feel that this should be nuanced somewhat. If one takes into account those aspects of biblical and patristic studies, such as palaeography & codicology[9], textual criticism & criticism of the canon[10], linguistic & literary research, then one can only but conclude that the differences in the practice and application of different approaches to the interpretation of the Bible in East and West are not to be neglected[11]. One is confronted with a complex phenomenon, which can be traced back to the differences in philological methodology and style that are closely linked to the theology and hermeneutics of the different backgrounds to which they belong. In the field of Western philology of the Bible[12], which was deeply influenced by classical philology since the Renaissance[13], research has led to a major focus on the biblical text, separated from patristic and liturgical frameworks, and the production of critical editions of the Bible[14]. In the East, where Byzantine philology persistently dominated the field of biblical studies, one generally speaking finds an adherence to ecclesiastical practices in the transmission of biblical and patristic texts, reflected

---

[5] J.D.G. Dunn et al. (Eds.), *Auslegung der Bibel in orthodoxer und westlicher Perspektive, (Akten des west-östlichen Neutestamentler/innen-Symposiums von Neamţ vom 4.-11. September 1998)* (Tübingen, 2000).

[6] I.Z. Dimitrov et al. (Eds), *Das Alte Testament als christliche Bibel in orthodoxer und westlicher Sicht: Zweite europäische orthodox-westliche Exegetenkonferenz, im Rilakloster vom 8-15 September 2001* (Tübingen, 2004).

[7] www.bibliothecabilica.unibe.ch/Petersburgspecial.htm (seen 1 June 2007).

[8] K.W. Niebuhr, 'Zu den Ergebnissen des Rila-Symposiums', in I. Dimitrov (Ed. et al.), *Op. Cit.* (Tübingen, 2004), 365.

[9] E.E. Granstrem, 'Zur byzantinischen Minuskel', in *Griechische Kodikologie und Textüberlieferung*, D. Harlfinger (Ed.) (Darmstadt, 1980), 77-78: 'Die Mehrzahl der angeführten Gelehrten (mit Ausnahme von B. de Montfaucon, V.K. Ernštedt, E.M. Thompson und G.F. Cereteli) betrachteten die Paläographie lediglich als Summe von Kenntnissen, die für das Lesen und die richtige Datierung von Texten notwendig sind. Viele Paläographen beschäftigten sich mit den paläographischen Gegebenheiten inhaltlich verwandter Texte, was eine Sichtung und den Vergleich der verschiedenen Schrifttypen miteinander, wie sie (...), beim Kopieren von Handschriften unterschiedlicher Bestimmung und verschienenen Inhalts gebraucht wurden, ausschloß'.; idem, "Greek Palaeography in Russia", in *Bulletin no 17 of the Institute of Classical Studies*, University of London (1970), 126-127.

[10] See § 4 and § 7 of this Introduction.

[11] A Greek introduction to Byzantine Philology can be found in N.B. Tomadakis, Κλεὶς τῆς Βυζαντινῆς Φιλολογίας (Thessaloniki, 1993); for the Slavonic philological tradition one can consult, A.A. Alexeev, Текстология Славянской Библии (St. Petersburg, 1999).

[12] For a general picture, see J.J. Pelikan, *The Reformation of the Bible. The Bible of the Reformation, Catalogue of the Exhibition by V. Hotchkiss and D. Price* (New Haven and London, 1996); J.C. Trebolle Barrera, *The Jewish Bible and the Christian Bible. An Introduction to the History of the Bible* (Leiden/New York/ Köln and Grand Rapids/ Cambridge, U.K., 1998); B.M. Metzger and B.D. Ehrman, *The Text of the New Testament. Its Transmission, Corruption and Restoration* (New York/Oxford, 2005); J.H. Bentley, *Humanists and Holy Writ. New Testament Scholarship in the Renaissance* (Princeton, 1983).

[13] E.E Granstrem, "Greek Palaeography in Russia", in *Bulletin no 17 of the Institute of Classical Studies* (1970), 124-135, esp. 126: 'The foundations of the nineteenth-century study of Greek palaeography in Russia were quite other than those on which the discipline rested in Western Europe. There – and especially in Latin countries – the revival of interest in Greek manuscripts was above all connected with the activities of the humanists who studied the works of classical authors and of the printers who published them, i.e. with the rise of classical philology'.

[14] T.H. Darlow and H.F. Moule (Eds.), *Historical Catalogue of the Printed Editions of Holy Scripture in the Library of the British and Foreign Bible Society*, vol. II: Polyglots and Languages Other Than English (New York, reprint, 1963): 'Ancient Greek'.

not only in the continuing manuscript tradition[15], but also in the forms of the printed editions based on these manuscripts[16].

4. Contemporary Orthodox position on philology of the Bible

Elucidating the contemporary Orthodox position on philology of the Bible is not easy. Conservative forces in Greece[17] and Russia[18] can be very strong, precisely in the areas of manuscript studies of Scripture, Bible edition or translation.[19] Eastern Orthodox biblical scholarship, both in Greece[20] as well as in Russia (in Russia palaeography and philology of the Bible[21] was occupied primarily with textual research of the Slavonic Bible and interest in the Byzantine text - the Greek manuscripts since the 9th century - in so far as the Slavonic translation was based on that text)[22] has only participated "moderately" in the critical branch of textual research, in so far as we are able to discern[23]. There has been a concentration first and foremost on exploration of the codices and their holdings and the cataloguing of these manuscripts (see chapter 4). It should be noted that critical editions of the Bible have not been produced by Eastern Orthodox themselves[24]. A well-organised editorial committee of Russian philologists was in an advanced stage of producing a critical edition of the Slavonic Bible at the end of the 19th and beginning of the 20th century, until the Russian Revolution interrupted

---

[15] Descriptions of Byzantine manuscripts since the 16th - 19th centuries have selectively been adopted in the catalogues of Aland, Rahlfs, Ehrhard and more completely in the catalogues at location of the individual libraries in East and West. This considerable group of later manuscripts have been less studied. Cf. D. Holton et al. (Eds.), Κωδικογράφοι, συλλέκτες, διασκευαστές, και εκδότες. Χειρόγραφα και εκδόσεις της όψιμης βυζαντινής και πρώιμης νεοελληνικής λογοτεχνίας. *Copyists, collectors, redactors and editors: manuscripts and editions of late Byzantine and early modern Greek literature* (Heraklaeion, 2005).

[16] Basic bio-bibliographical entries to these publications are: N.B. Tomadakis, Κλείς τῆς Βυζαντινῆς Φιλολογίας, (Thessaloniki, 1993); E.N. Fragkiskos, *La Bibliothèque de Patmos. Catalogue d' imprimés (XVe-XIXe s.): introduction, description des imprimés, annexes, index* (Athens, 1995-1996); P. Meyer, *Die Theologische Literatur der griechischen Kirche im sechzehnten Jahrhundert* (Leipzig, 1899); E. Legrand, *Bibliographie Hellénique ou Description raisonnée des ouvrages publiés par des Grecs aux dix-septième siècle*, 5 vols., (Paris, 1894-1903, repr. Paris, 1975); A. Papadopoulos-Vretos, Νεοελληνική Φιλολογία (Athens, 1854-1857).

[17] A. Delicostopoulos, 'Major Greek Translations of the Bible', in *The Interpretation of the Bible. The International Symposium in Slovenia*, Ed. J. Krašovec (Sheffield, 1998), 304: 'The Greek State, however, in conjunction with the Church of Greece, exercise a certain degree of control. Our state constitution (Article 3 § 3) mentions: "The text of the Holy Scriptures is kept unaltered (Ἀναλλοίωτον). Any rendering in any other official linguistic form of the Greek language is forbidden without the approval of the Church of Greece and the Ecumenical Patriarchate of Constantinople'"; E.G. Pantelakis, "Les Livres ecclésiastiques de l'Orthodoxie. Étude Historique", in *Irénikon*, 13.5 (1936), 537; cf. N. Milasch, *Das Kirchenrecht der morgenländischen Kirche. Nach den allgemeinen Kirchenrechtsquellen und nach den in den autokephalen Kirchen geltenden Spezial-Gesetzen* (Mostar, 1905).

[18] A. Ivanov, "К вопросу о восстановлении первоначального греческого текста нового завета" [Towards the Question about the Restoration of the Original Greek Text of the New Testament], in Журнал Московской Патриархии, 3 (1954), 38-50; cf. R.P. Casey, "A Russian Orthodox View of New Testament Textual Criticism", in *Theology*, 60.439 (1957), 51 [Ivanov is quoted in Casey's report]: 'In textual questions, as in other matters, the Orthodox theologian must be guided by the dictum: nihil aliud probamus nisi quod Ecclesia'.

[19] E. Bryner, "Bible Translations in Russia", in *The Bible Translator*, 25.3 (1974), 327 [in referring to one of the basic criteria for a translation of the Scriptures]: 'The translation, which is intended for Russian Orthodox readers, must be published with the blessing and under the direct control and supervision of the Russian Orthodox Church'.

[20] A. Delicostopoulos, 'Major Greek Translations of the Bible', in *Op. Cit.* (Sheffield, 1998), 297-316; J.D. Karavidopoulos, Ἑλληνικὴ βιβλικὴ βιβλιογραφία τοῦ 2000οῦ αἰῶνα (1900-1995) [Greek biblical bibliography of the 20th century (1900-1995)], Thessaloniki, 1997.

[21] E.E Granstrem, "Greek Palaeography in Russia", in *Bulletin no 17 of the Institute of Classical Studies*, University of London (1970), 124-135.

[22] R.K. Tsurkan, Славянский перевод Библии: Происхождение, история текста и важнейшие издания [The Slavonic Version of the Bible. Introduction to the history of the text and the most important editions] (St. Petersburg, 2001); M. Garzaniti, *Die altslavische Version der Evangelien: Forschungsgeschichte und zeitgenössische Forschung* (Köln-Weimar-Wien, 2001); A.A. Alexeev, Текстология Славянской Библии (St. Petersburg, 1999); F.J. Thomson, 'The Slavonic Translation of the Old Testament', in *The Interpretation of the Bible. The International Symposium in Slovenia*, by J. Krašovec (Ed.) (Sheffield, 1998), 605-920; cf. the articles by Logachev & Ivanov below.

[23] Russian criticism is articulated by, for instance: K.I. Logachev, 'Greek Lectionaries and Problems in the Oldest Slavonic Gospel Translations', in *New Testament Textual Criticism. Its Significance for Exegesis, (Essays in Honour of Bruce M. Metzger)*, Ed. E.J. Epp and G.D. Fee (Oxford, 1981), 345-348; Idem, "The Problem of the Relationship of the Greek Text of the Bible to the Church Slavonic and Russian Text", in *The Bible Translator* 25, 3 (July, 1974), 313-318; Idem, "Русский перевод Нового Завета (к 150-летию изданию)" [The Russian Translation of the NT], in Журнал Московской Патриархии, 11 (1969), 61-68; Idem, "Критические издания текстов Священного Писания" [Critical editions of the text of Holy Scripture], in Журнал Московской Патриархии, 6 (1971), I., 78ff; 2 (1972), II., 79ff; 9 (1972), III. 76-80 [discussed are: the edition of Rahlfs, 8th Ed. 1956; Kittel's Biblia Hebraica, 14th Ed., 1966; Nestle's Novum Testamentum Graece, 25th Ed., 1963; the Greek New Testament, Eds. Aland, Black, Martini, Metzger and Wigren, 2nd Ed., 1968]. And: A. Ivanov, "К вопросу о восстановлении первоначального греческого текста нового завета" [Towards the Question about the Restoration of the Original Greek Text of the New Testament]", in Журнал Московской Патриархии, 3 (1954), 38-50; Idem, "Новое критическое издание Греческого текста Нового Завета" [A New Critical Edition of the Greek text of the New Testament], in Журнал Московской Патриархии, 3 (1956), I-III, 49-58; 4 (1956), IV-VII, 49-58; 5 (1956), VIII-X, 43-52.

[24] This fact has been recently confirmed by the Greek NT scholar J. Karavidopoulos in a communication with us, in November 2006.

the endeavour[25]. It would be an interesting exercise indeed to retrace their principles and procedures, but this is beyond the scope of the present thesis. Critical textual research is remarkably also a lesser explored field by Orthodox scholarship in the West. Yet this area of biblical studies deserves major attention by Orthodox academia, especially where it Byzantine (and Church Slavonic) codicology and manuscript studies concerns.

5. The liturgical hypothesis as the basis of a liturgico-codicological approach

In the above two inferences were made to the position of and opinion concerning the biblical and patristic writings in the Eastern Orthodox churches, namely: 1) the anchoring of the biblical writings in the liturgy of the church; and 2) the close connection between the Scriptures and the interpretative framework of the fathers. These are two closely interrelated conclusions, two sides of one and the same coin. This becomes apparent when we revisit the primary sources; i.e. the extant Byzantine manuscripts and the Byzantine / Eastern Orthodox editions based thereon. Here we find evidence of an inherent cohesion between the Scriptures and the interpretative framework of the fathers, and we can ascertain that this is rooted in the Byzantine liturgy. In this dissertation we therefore advocate a new, namely a *liturgical*-codicological approach which can make this cohesion visible. Manuscript research of the biblical and patristic codices to date that is represented in the manuscript catalogues, provides us of course with a wealth of information, but does not provide a complete insight into the actual content and codex formation of the extant manuscripts. Thus, special attention will be paid to setting out a path of codicological research that could redirect study of the Byzantine codices to a system that allows for a more complete and inclusive picture of the original biotope in which the manuscripts were created and evolved. Once inside this biotope, the reasons for and choices behind the content and codex formation of the biblical and patristic manuscripts become apparent. Consequently, this leads to a suggested reclassification of the Byzantine manuscripts, in light of the above [26].

As already mentioned, the Byzantine manuscripts and the printed editions based thereon bear witness to the close cohesion between the Bible and the fathers as well as to their anchoring in the liturgy. This assumption forms the basis of what I call the liturgical hypothesis and leads to the liturgico-codicological approach - the revisiting of the codices themselves, as well as their places of origin, namely the Byzantine liturgy on the one hand which was responsible for their codicological forms (chapter 2) and the monasteries and libraries and holdings on the other, in which they were manufactured, stored and kept (chapter 4). The leading idea of this hypothesis is that the codex forms of the extant manuscript materials are the direct result of the liturgical needs of the Church, and that they have been generated in the course of an age-long liturgico-codicological process of evolution (indeed very gradually), in which the preservation and transmission of the most valued books of the Church was always assumed to be a task of primary importance[27]. The liturgical function of the Scriptures required a codification of a particular (with regard to the content) and practical (with regard to form) character and this led to the formation of a whole variety of basic codex forms or codicological patterns (see chapter 5). Once developed, such codicological patterns persisted for centuries, and they were even maintained in later printed editions. The lectionary manuscripts - the ecclesiastical reading books, to which much less philological attention has been paid than to the biblical text manuscripts, contain texts that are based on a very cautious and long established tradition of delivery[28]. And beside lectionary manuscripts, many text and commentary codices also have a liturgical imprint. A reassessment of the codicological status quo of these manuscripts, keeping this liturgical imprint in mind, could throw a new light on manuscript research. In the long term, detailed manuscript study is required, on the basis of large-scale autopsy along the lines set out in this thesis, to make the liturgical hypothesis binding. What we offer here, in anticipation of an intended reclassification of the extant codices, is some evidence to show that a thorough reassessment of manuscript research in the areas discussed previously is desirable.

---

[25] F.J. Thomson, 'The Slavonic Translation of the Old Testament', in *The Interpretation of the Bible. The International Symposium in Slovenia*, by J. Krašovec (Ed.) (Sheffield, 1998), 619-631.

[26] J. Karayannopoulos remarks in 'Bericht über Paläographie, Kodikologie und Diplomatik im Rahmen der Byzantinistik', in *Actes du XIVe Congrès International des Études Byzantines*, by M. Berza and E. Stănescu (Eds.) (Bucharest, 1976), III, 16: 'Hauptaufgabe der Kodikologie ist die Katalogisierung von Hss., ein höchst wichtiges ... Unterfangen. Wie H. Hunger bemerkt, ist sie "die schwierigste und zeitraubendste, aber wichtigste kodikologische Unternehmung"'.

[27] The critical opinion of Photius concerning 'textual exactness' is quoted in N.G. Wilson, *Scholars of Byzantium* (London, 1983), 117 [*Amphilochia* 1, PG 101, 84ff.].

[28] B.M. Metzger and B.D. Ehrman, *Op. Cit.* (New York/Oxford, 2005), 47; C.D. Osburn, 'The Greek Lectionaries of the New Testament', in *The Text of the New Testament in Contemporary Research. Essays on the Status Quaestionis*, Ed. B.D. Ehrman and M.W. Holmes (Grand Rapids, Mich., 1995), 61; B.M. Metzger, 'Greek lectionaries and a critical edition of the Greek New Testament', in *Die alten Übersetzungen*, by K. Aland (Ed.) (Berlin/New York, 1972), 479; A. Wigren, "Chicago Studies in the Greek lectionary of the New Testament", in *Biblical and Patristic Studies, (in Memory of Robert Pierce Casey)*, Ed. J.N. Birdsall and R.W. Thomson (Freiburg-Basel-Barcelona-New York-Roma-São Paulo-Wien, 1963), 121; C.R. Gregory, 'Griechische Liturgische Bücher', in *Textkritik des Neuen Testamentes* (Leipzig, 1900), I, 328-329.

In the following paragraphs of this introduction I will summarise the content and aims of the chapters that follow, provide information on the sources and the literature I have consulted and used and present some terminological clarifications.

6. Structure and content of the thesis

Chapter 1 is dedicated to the Byzantine manuscripts and the editions based upon these manuscripts, the underlying notion being that the manuscripts themselves express the implicit and explicit patristic hermeneutics of the biblical books: implicit, in so far as the biblical codices that do not possess commentaries, *do* show the clear choices made behind the selection of content and codex formation (for a great deal liturgically motivated); and highly explicit, in those codices that contain commentary texts. In chapter 1 I provide a critical analysis of the manner in which the manuscripts have been catalogued, described and presented to date and I make a plea for setting up a new categorisation, based on the manuscripts' codicological character and original environment.

Merely embarking on codicological research leads to my conclusion that the biblical and patristic manuscripts are anchored in the Byzantine liturgy, and that the liturgy is the domain that can well display the unity between the biblical and the patristic books. In *chapter 2* I lead the reader to the liturgy of the Orthodox Church and present the lectionary cycles and reading schemes which rule the manuscripts' use and function. I illustrate the way that the liturgical scriptures are 'used' in the data (the Byzantine lection system) that I provide in *chapter 3*. This data has the added function of also showing the hermeneutics that lies implicit in the manuscripts and that was responsible for their codex and textual forms. It is precisely this that makes codicology so important.

Codicological research implies the study of the manuscripts themselves and this brings us analogously to the places where they are housed and kept, in particular the Eastern libraries of the Middle East, Greece and Russia etc, where authentic collections can still be found that display the unity between biblical and patristic manuscripts. *Chapter 4* presents these locations and holdings, preparing the way for a re-evaluation of the state of affairs where the manuscripts are concerned.

Chapter 5 sets out the contours of the proposed codico-liturgical model of classification and *chapter 6* introduces the *Catalogue of Byzantine Manuscripts*. Detailed specimens are provided to give a flavour of the cataloguing system I advocate. This endeavour can be linked to other current manuscript research as well as the existing specialised catalogues. At the end of this dissertation, in the *Final conclusion and perspective*, I reflect on the sense and use of a new catalogue.

A chronological index of lessons (of the Movable and Immovable Cycles) - the *Indices of the Byzantine Anagnosmata*-, as presented in Chapter 3, completes the work.

7. Some preliminary clarifications

7.1 Editions of biblical books used in this thesis

Considering the aim of this thesis, I have opted to use side by side the Greek Orthodox editions of the text of Scripture, e.g. the Evangelion (Θεῖον καὶ Ἱερὸν Εὐαγγέλιον)[29], the Apostolos (Ἀπόστολος)[30], the Psalterion (Ψαλτήριον)[31] and the Prophetologion (Προφητολόγιον)[32], the latter today being spread over different liturgical books, i.e. the Triodion, the Pentekostarion and the Menaia, the writings of the Byzantine and later Greek fathers and the Byzantine liturgical books on the one hand, and the scientific editions of the Bible (Rahlfs / Hanhart, 2006[33]; Aland / Aland, 2006[34]), the Greek fathers and the Western editions of the Byzantine liturgical books on the other.

---

[29] Θεῖον καὶ Ἱερὸν Εὐαγγέλιον, κατὰ τὸ κείμενον τὸ ἐγκεκριμένον ὑπὸ τῆς Μεγάλης τοῦ Χριστοῦ Ἐκκλησίας, Ed. A. Androuses (Athens, second edition 1992) [1st edition 1982; on the basis of the "Patriarchal Edition" of 1904].
[30] Ἀπόστολος, Πράξεις καὶ Ἐπιστολαὶ τῶν ἁγίων Ἀποστόλων, αἱ καθ' ὅλον τὸ ἔτος ἐπ' Ἐκκλησίαις ἀναγιγνωσκόμεναι καθὼς καὶ τῶν ἱερῶν τελέτων, 5th ed. (Athens, 2002).
[31] Ψαλτήριον τοῦ προφήτου καὶ βασιλέως Δαυΐδ, μετὰ τῶν ἐννέα ᾠδῶν καὶ τῆς ἑρμηνείας ὅπως δεῖ στιχολογεῖσθαι τὸ Ψαλτήριον ἐν ὅλῳ τῷ ἐνιαυτῷ, 9th edition (Athens, 2002).
[32] There is a Prophetologion edition edited by the *Institute of Byzantine Musical Studies* in Copenhagen: C. Høeg, G. Zuntz, G. Engberg (Eds.), *Prophetologium I-II* (Monumenta Musicae Byzantinae. Lectionaria. Vol. I) (Copenhagen, 1939-1981).
[33] A new reprint edition by R. Hanhart is, *Septuaginta. It est Vetus Testamentum graece iuxta lxx interpretes edidit Alfred Rahlfs, Editio altera quam recognovit et emendavit Robert Hanhart*, (Duo volumina in uno) (Stuttgart, 2006).

The edition of the complete Greek Bible (OT and NT)³⁵ we have consulted is Ἡ Ἁγία Γραφή - Παλαιὰ Διαθήκη καὶ ἡ Καινὴ Διαθήκη, by P.I. Bratsiotis (Ed.), Athens, 1999 [15th edition]³⁶. In Byzantine tradition the OT used is the Septuagint (i.e. 'Εβδομήκοντα' or LXX = the 70 interpreters). In Eastern Orthodox academic opinion³⁷, the Septuagint represents the basic primary source of the Greek NT writings³⁸.

> This was the Bible of the Undivided Church of the first eight centuries, sanctified through the use of the apostles, the fathers of the church and the local and ecumenical synods, and remained, either completely or partially, as the basis of all other ancient ecclesiastical versions, and it is still the official *Bible of the Eastern Orthodox Church*.
> P. Bratsiotis (Ed.), Ἡ Ἁγία Γραφή - Παλαιὰ Διαθήκη καὶ ἡ Καινὴ Διαθήκη (Athens, 1999), 5³⁹

It appears, quite remarkably, that, as far as we know, Orthodox scholarship never made a scientific (critical) edition of the Bible (not of the Greek OT, nor of the Greek NT)⁴⁰. Besides the stream of practical, liturgical editions of Scripture (Venice, Constantinople, Athens), only re-editions of scientific publications produced in the West have been made; for instance, the 'Moscow edition' (1821) of the Greek Bible (OT and NT) was an adoption of the Oxford-Grabe edition of the LXX text, later re-edited by the Greeks (Athens, 1850). The same applies in the case of the Greek Bible edition of 1924, where very slight justification is given for the procedures used and textual decisions made, including only the short prefatory remark that the edition of Tischendorff was consulted⁴¹. This edition was reissued in 1950 with a short preface by Bratsiotis⁴², who, in his turn consulted Rahlfs (1935). The 'Patriarchal edition' of the NT, Ἡ Καινὴ Διαθήκη ἐγκρίσει τῆς μεγάλης τοῦ Χριστοῦ ἐκκλησίας, by B. Antoniadis [et al. Eds], Athens 2004 (first edition, Constantinople, 1904)⁴³, although

---

³⁴ A corrected reprint edition was recently published, *Novum Testamentum Graeca, post Eberhard et Erwin Nestle editione vicesima septima revisa, (Apparatum criticum novis curis elaboraverunt Barbara et Kurt Aland una cum Instituto Studiorum Textus Novi Testamenti Monasterii Westphaliae)*, Ed. K. and B. Aland, J. Karavidopoulos, C. M. Martini, B. M. Metzger, 27th revised edition (9. corrected printing) (Stuttgart, 2006).

³⁵ In anticipation of later discussions on the basic codex forms found in Byzantine manuscript tradition, it should be said that complete editions of the Greek Bible and separate editions of the Greek OT and NT, which are so characteristic for the Western printed edition-tradition, are uncommon for Byzantine and later Greek publications of the Scriptures, although 'whole' Bible codices do exist.

³⁶ The 1st edition appeared in Athens in 1928. The basis of the Greek OT is the edition of Tischendorf-Nestle, Vols. I-II (7th ed. 1887) (cf. A. Delicostopoulos, 'Major Greek Translations of the Bible', in *The Interpretation of the Bible. The International Symposium in Slovenia*, Ed. J. Krašovec (Sheffield, 1998), 309 [text of Σ and A]); the text of the Greek NT is based on the Patriarchal edition of Constantinople (1904) (cf. Preliminary to the NT part, 867).

³⁷ Philaret Drozdov (Metropolitan Philaret of Moscow), "О догматическом достоинстве и охранительном употреблении греческого семидесяти толковников и славянского переводов священного писания 1845 год" [On the dogmatic merit and conservative function of the Greek Septuagint commentators and the Slavonic translation of Holy Scripture], in Прибавления к изданию творений Святых Отцов Церкви в русском переводе [Supplements to the Editions of the Works of the Holy Fathers of the Church in Russian Translation], 17 (Moscow, 1858), 452-484. [Reprint in Metropolitan Philaret, Избранные Творения (Moscow, 2004), 355-373]; K. Oikonomos, Περὶ τῶν Ο' Ἑρμηνευτῶν τῆς παλαιᾶς θείας Γραφῆς (Athens, 1849).

³⁸ According to A. Delicostopoulos in 'Major Greek Translations of the Bible', in *Op. Cit.* (Sheffield, 1998), 307: 'we must emphasize the fact that in the New Testament we have 350 verses from the Old Testament, of which 300 at least agree with the LXX. During the centuries of the undivided Church in the East and West the LXX was used in all liturgical forms'.

³⁹ See the Prologue to the second edition of this edition, 5: 'αὕτη ὑπῆρξεν ἡ Βίβλος τῆς ἀδιαιρέτου ἐκκλησίας τῶν ὀκτὼ πρώτων αἰώνων, καθηγιάσθη διὰ τῆς χρήσεως αὐτῆς ὑπό τε τῶν ἀποστόλων καὶ τῶν ἐκκλησιαστικῶν πατέρων καὶ τῶν τοπικῶν καὶ οἰκουμενικῶν συνόδων, διετέλεσεν, εἴτε ἐν ὅλῳ εἴτε ἐν μέρει, ἡ βάσις πασῶν τῶν ἄλλων παλαιῶν ἐκκλησιαστικῶν μεταφράσεων καὶ ἐξακολουθεῖ νὰ εἶναι ἐπίσημος Βίβλος τῆς Ὀθοδόξου ἀνατολικῆς ἐκκλησίας'.

⁴⁰ A hint to the possible reasons for this is provided in a study of the Slavonic Bible/NT, H.P.S. Bakker, 'Historical Text and Text History', in *Towards a Critical Edition of the Old Slavic New Testament. A Transparent and Heuristic Approach* (Amsterdam, 1996), 9: 'It is understandable that most Palaeoslavists refuse to or refrain from making a construct the base text of a critical edition. Such an eclectic and normalised, 'Lachmannian' text never existed as such and is therefore ahistorical'.

⁴¹ Πρόλογος Α'. The editor(s) wrote: 'But in the case of each difference of 'written text' (orthography), or 'lines' or 'numbering of chapters and verses' we preferred the text of the critical edition of Tischendorf, since this edition is exact and much-elaborated'. It appears to be the 8th ed. rev. by E. Nestle (1887), which was a revision of the 'Sixtine edition' of the Septuagint (with the Codex Vaticanus as most prominent manuscript used). See A. Delicostopoulos, *art. cit.* (Sheffield, 1998), 309.

⁴² Πρόλογος Β'. It becomes clear that the Byzantine ecclesiastical/liturgical text was used, but what remains an open question is which OT Byzantine (lectionary?) text was provided, on what manuscript(s) and/or printed edition(s) it was based, and how the text was constituted. Only in general terms, it is said, were liturgical books consulted, both manuscripts (of Athenian libraries) as well as printed editions (those of Venice).

⁴³ Greek reviews: Gennadios of Heliopolis, "Πῶς οἱ Ἀμερικανοὶ Θεολογοὶ ἐκφράζονται περὶ τῆς Πατριαρχικῆς ἐκδόσεως τῆς Καίνης Διαθήκης", in Ὀρθοδοξία, 13 (1938), 74-76; D. Chatzedaniel, "Ἡ Καινὴ Διαθήκη (ἐγκρίσει τῆς μεγάλης τοῦ Χριστοῦ ἐκκλησίας)", in Ἐκκλησίας Ἀληθεία, ΚΕ/29 (1905), 458-461.

interesting in many aspects[44], can neither be qualified as a scientific 'critical' text in the strict sense, since the procedure of selecting manuscripts and the choice of variants[45] are not made explicit and cannot be verified[46].

7.2 Editions of Byzantine patristic literature used

J.P. Migne's *Patrologiae Cursus Completus: Series Graeca*, vols. 1-161 (Paris, 1857-1866) is the main source of works of the Greek and Byzantine fathers we have consulted[47] (Migne is also available in a Greek reprint edition[48]); together with the *Corpus Christianorum*, Series Graeca (Turnhout-Leuven, 1977-); *Die Griechischen Schriftsteller der ersten drei Jahrhunderte* (Berlin, 1887-), *Sources Chrétiennes* (Paris, 1941-); E.D. Moutsoula and K.G. Papachristopoulos (Eds.), Βιβλιοθήκη Ἑλλήνων Πατέρων καὶ Ἐκκλησιαστικῶν Συγγραφέων, t. 1-82 (Athens, 1955-); and P.K. Chrestou and others (Eds.), Ἕλληνες Πατέρες τῆς Ἐκκλησίας (Gr.-NGr., Thessaloniki, 1953-).

7.3 Editions of Byzantine liturgical books used

The Byzantine Greek liturgical books are the official books of the Orthodox church, used throughout the ages, without discontinuation and in use to the present day. They are of primary importance for this thesis, from a codicological and textual point of view and are discussed in chapters 2 and 3.
The many editions of liturgical books produced by the Propaganda Press in Rome under the auspices of the Vatican (for use in the Uniate Churches) are easier to consult in Western libraries and are generally used in scholarship in the West. Greek and Slavic editions are more difficult to acquire. Yet, for our purpose we have opted for the latter, even if the Roman editions are deemed better[49]. The reason for this is that, although both Roman and Greek editions were based on the Venetian editions, the Roman underwent certain changes[50], whilst the Greek editions continued to transmit the liturgical texts in line with Greek Orthodox tradition.[51]

7.4 Concerning the 'Byzantine manuscripts' and the 'Byzantine text'

Eastern scholars often understand the terms 'Byzantine manuscripts' or 'Greek manuscripts' in a broad scope, incorporating in its remit manuscripts from the 4/5th century onwards, including the period in which the uncials (the great codices A, B and S/א among others) were dominant (until the 9th century) and continuing into and including the period in which the minuscles[52] evolved (since the 9th century).[53] Moreover the term 'Byzantine text' is regarded as a family of related texts[54], rather than the 'one', standard Byzantine text ('Einheitstext'). The

---

[44] See the introduction, γ'- η' [Eng. J.M. Rife, 'The Antonides Greek New Testament', in *Prolegomena to the Study of the Lectionary Text of the Gospels*, Ed. E.C. Colwell and D.W. Riddle (Chicago, Illinois, 1933), 57-62]. D.W. Riddle, "The use of Lectionaries in critical editions and studies of the New Testament text", in *Op. Cit.* (Chicago, Illinois, 1933), 73: 'it will be remarked here merely that the Introduction not only stated the principles of the edition, but made penetrating remarks about the nature of the text of lectionary MSS.'

[45] The consulted manuscripts (116 Byzantine codices, 9th-16th c.) are enumerated in the short preface (γ'-η'). See reviews of R.D. Dedman, "Why the 'Patriarchal' Text of Greek New Testament?" (Web-site, Athos manuscripts, April 2005); J. Karavidopoulos, "L'Édition Patriarchale du Nouveau Testament (1904). Problèmes de Texte et de Traduction dans le monde Orthodoxe", in *Kleronomia*, 20 (1988), 197; J.M. Rife, 'The Antioniades Greek New Testament', in *Op.Cit.*, (Chicago, Illinois, 1933), 57-66.

[46] B. Antoniadis (Ed.), Ἡ Καινὴ Διαθήκη ἐγκρίσει τῆς μεγάλης τοῦ Χριστοῦ ἐκκλησίας, (Athens, 2004), ς', Transl: J.M. Rife: 'Such was the critical procedure, however, that, except in punctuation and orthography, no criticism was made of the authority of the text of the MSS. There was no transposition, substitution, addition, or excision, except in rare cases, and these with sufficient testimony elsewhere'.

[47] Entries to PG of Migne are: F. Cavallera, *Patrologiae cursus completus accurante J.P. Migne, Series graeca, Indices* (Paris, 1912); Dorotheos Scholarios, Κλεῖς Πατρολογίας καὶ Βυζαντινῶν συγγραφέων (Athens, 1879) (= Migne, PG, T. 162).

[48] Reprinted by the Center of Patristic Studies, Athens, 1987ff., with critical introductions and new biblical indices (cf. G.D. Dragas, *Op. Cit.*, (Rollinsford, NH, 2005, 209)).

[49] G. Pantelakis, "Les Livres ecclésiastiques de l'Orthodoxie. Étude Historique", in *Irénikon*, 13.5 (1936), 550: 'Dans son ensemble, l'édition de Rome est meilleure que celle de Venise'.

[50] G. Pantelakis, *Art. Cit.* (1936), 550: 'La base de travail choisie fut l'édition de Venise, dont furent éliminés les synaxaires et certains offices, par example celui de Grégoire Palamas'.

[51] Cf. K. Krumbacher (Ed.), *Geschichte der Byzantinischen Litteratur von Justinian bis zum Ende des oströmischen Reiches [527-1453]* (München, 1897), 658: 'In neuerer Zeit sind auch einzelne Ausgaben in Athen, Konstantinopel und Jerusalem erschienen. – Neben diesen offiziellen griechischen Ausgaben sind natürlich die von katholischer oder protestantischer Seite veranstalteten Drucke nur mit Vorsicht zu benützen. Das gilt selbst von der bedeutendsten abendländischen Leistung, dem *Εὐχολόγιον* sive Rituale Graecorum etc. opera Jacobi Goar, Paris 1647, Editio II. Expurgata et accuratior, Venedig 1730.' This remark is still valid.

[52] E.E. Granstrem, 'Zur byzantinischen Minuskel', in D. Harlfinger (Ed.), *Griechische Kodikologie und Textüberlieferung* (Darmstadt, 1980), 76; B.L. Fonkič, 'Griechische Kodikologie', in *Op. Cit.*, (Darmstadt, 1980), 14-21.

[53] Catalogues: E.E. Granstrem, "Каталог греческих рукописей ленинградских хранилищ" [Catalogue of Greek manuscripts in Leningrad holdings], in Византийский временник (1959 - 1971), who discusses manuscripts from the 4th to the 15th centuries; A.I. Papadopoulos-Kerameus, Ἱεροσολυμιτικὴ Βιβλιοθήκη (St. Petersburg, 1891-1915) [Repr., Bruxelles, 1963], who discusses manuscripts from the 7th to the 19th centuries; B.L. Fonkič, 'Griechische Kodikologie', in *Op. Cit.*, (Darmstadt, 1980), 16: 'Bis in unserer Zeit haben sich ca. 55 000 griechische Handschriften vom 4.-19. Jh. erhalten'.

[54] A. Delicostopoulos, 'Major Greek Translations of the Bible', in *Op. Cit.* (Sheffield, 1998), 305-306: 'For those studying the tradition of the Greek New Testament text there is much to be done in discovering and establishing the various groups of manuscripts that

study of the Byzantine text is still in an early stage of development. It includes different categories: a) Byzantine lectionary manuscripts; b) Byzantine text manuscripts; c) Byzantine commentary manuscripts.[55] In this dissertation I advocate codicological research of the manuscripts which could throw new light on the status of the Byzantine textual forms.

Another issue that requires clarification is the denotation 'koine edition' (ἡ κοινὴ ἔκδοσις[56]) or simply 'koine' (ἡ κοινὴ). The term 'koine edition' came into use among the early Byzantine fathers (Origen, Basil the Great, Gregory of Nazianz, Jerome), was used for later Byzantine editions of the Scriptures (resulting in the text form of Constantinople - Κωνσταντινοπολικόν at the end of the 15th and in the 16th centuries), was used for the printed editions of Scripture in Venice since the 16th century and later in Constantinople, and finally for recently published 'koine editions' by the Great Church of Constantinople and the Church of Greece. Although these different editions display the developments in textual history, and the diversity of underlying Byzantine text forms, the persistent use of the term 'koine edition' indicates an 'ecclesiastical (liturgical) consensus' of what was considered a common standard of scriptural text ('κατὰ πάντα σύμφωνον πρὸς τὸ παραδεδεγμένον ὑπὸ τῆς Ἐκκλησίας ἀρχέτυπον κείμενον'[57]). This implied both the text of the Greek OT books, as well as the Greek NT books, authorised by liturgical use and an age-long practice of reading and homiletic interpretation. Other denotations also came into being: the 'ecclesiastical' edition (ἐκκλησιαστικὴ ἔκδοσις[58]), the 'Constantinopolitan' edition, the 'Lucianic' edition (the latter especially with regard to the LXX), or the 'liturgical' edition[59]. This last denotation is especially interesting for our thesis. One of my overriding conclusions in studying the Eastern Orthodox tradition is that it does not presuppose the absolute maintenance by the Church of "one", "original", "uniform" Byzantine text/edition[60]. Since there were many different variations of the sacred texts[61], the corruption of manuscripts (the phenomenon of textual variants) since early stages in the textual history of the Greek Scriptures was regarded as a textual *reality*: ὅποιος γράφει παραγράφει ('he who writes miswrites')[62]. The notion of a completely "pure" and "authentic" text is unrealistic for textual reconstruction[63], both from a practical as well as from a scientific point of view[64]. This said, however, it was the 'common edition' (κοινὴ ἔκδοσις) of the Bible that was transmitted by the Church throughout its history (taking into account the difference between the transmission of Greek OT[65] and NT[66] corpora), basically unaltered and unmodified, in

---

constitute the "K" text (Κωνσταντινοπολικόν). Furthermore, they need to know better the history of the text of our Church, and also to find out the influence of the Byzantine text on the other texts'.

[55] B.M. Metzger and B.D. Ehrman, 'The Byzantine Text', in *Op. Cit.* (New York / Oxford, 2005), 279-280.

[56] E. Nestle, 'Septuagint: Printed Editions', in *A Dictionary of the Bible*, 4 (1906), 437-454: 'A frequent designation among the old Greek writers was also ἡ κοινὴ ἔκδοσις, or merely ἡ κοινὴ, 'the common, the Vulgate edition', in contradistinction to the Hebrew text and the later Greek versions; cf; for intance Basil, i. 447d, on Is. 2^{22}', 438.

[57] According to the Synod of the Church of Greece, in their word of recommendation to the Greek edition of Holy Scripture, Athens, 1928 (Prologos A), the edition was approved by the Holy Synod as being 'in agreement with the transmitted Archetype Text by the Church'.

[58] E. Nestle, *art. cit.* (1906), 438: Gregory of Nyssa, *In Psalm* 8.

[59] I.D. Karavidopoulos, "L'Édition Patriarchale du Nouveau Testament (1904). Problems de Texte et de Traduction dans le monde Orthodoxe", in *Kleronomia*, 20 (1988), 198: 'Si, en fin de compte, nous préférons la désignation du texte comme "ecclésiastique"ou "liturgique", c'est qu'elle s'approche d'avantage de la réalité'.

[60] K.I. Logachev, "The Problem of the Relationship of the Greek Text of the Bible to the Church Slavonic and Russian Text", in *The Bible Translator*, 25.3 (1974), 313-318, esp. 316-317: 'Today, Russian biblical scholarship takes a position which accepts, on the level of the whole church, all Greek forms of the biblical text, excluding of course only those which were the result of a known activity of heretics. Thus it questions the individual importance of any one form at national church level. This excludes a one-sided preference either for the late Greek forms or for the oldest forms of the biblical text. The concept of a "later corruption of the original text" is likewise excluded'.

[61] R. Devreesse, *Introduction à l'Étude des Manuscrits Grecs* (Paris, 1954), 85-86: 'Il n'existe probablement pas de manuscrits sans corrections, et l'on peut retenir que la très grande majorité ont été relus et amendés. Certaines portent mention expresse de collation-révision (Δ = διώρθωσεν)'. Cf. B.D. Ehrman, "The Text of Mark in the Hands of the Orthodox", in *Lutheran Quarterly*, 5.1 (1991), 143: 'while we have literally thousands of biblical manuscripts, none of them is an autograph and all of them contain mistakes'; A.A. Alexeev, 'Holy Scripture and its Translation', in *The Interpretation of the Bible. The International Symposium in Slovenia*, by J. Krašovec (Ed.), (Sheffield, 1998), 1394: 'The text of the Scripture is not yet fixed in its final form. In fact there are more than 5,000 Greek witnesses of the NT from the 2nd to 16th centuries that differ more or less'.

[62] An ancient scribe's proverb, quoted in I. Ševčenko, I. Chernukhin, and N. Cherkas'ka, Грецькі рукописи у зібраннях Києва. Каталог (Greek Manuscripts in the Collections of Kiev. Catalogue) (Kiev-Washington, 2000), 382.

[63] H.P.S. Bakker, 'Corruption is Rife in Old Slavic Manuscripts', in *Towards a Critical Edition of the Old Slavic New Testament. A Transparent and Heuristic Approach* (Amsterdam, 1996), 6: 'Corruption of the transmitted text occurs inevitably and is attested in other traditions as well'; and the reference in n. 3 on page 9: 'The anti-Lachmann schools therefore claim that a text comprising words taken now from one partly corrupt manuscript, now from another - i.e. a composite critical text – is in fact merely an example of composite corruption'.

[64] B.M. Metzger and B.D. Ehrman, *Op. Cit.* (New York/Oxford, 2005), Ch. 8 'Complications in Establishing the Original Text', 272-274, and especially the complication remarked upon with regard to the collection of Paul's writings, 274 n. 5.

[65] Exact and concise information on this issue can be found in E. Nestle, 'Early History of the Septuagint', in *A Dictionary of the Bible*, 4 (1906), 442. With regard to the LXX is said: 'This variety of texts, strange as it may appear, is not difficult to account for. (1) 𝔊 was liable to all the dangers connected with transmission to which literary works were exposed in the days before the invention of the printing-press. (2) These dangers were increased in the case of works which were frequently copied and used not only privately but also in public service. (3) 𝔊 is not an original text, but a translation, or rather a series of translations, and therefore much more exposed to alterations than an original text; for every reader possessed of some knowledge of Hebrew, or of a different exegetical tradition from that embodied in 𝔊, might change his text (cf. the changes introduced in many MSS of the OT from the quotations in the NT, e.g. in Ps 13^3 from

other words, "uncorrupted". If the original text is a problematic issue[67], then the origin and measure of "corruption" (either heterodox or orthodox) is problematic too.

This Eastern Orthodox concept of 'koine text' can not immediately be equated with the *textus receptus* (NT), which was based, as is well-known, on a limited group of Byzantine manuscripts (reflected in editions of Erasmus, Stephanus, Elzevir) adopted in the West as the original text until far into the 19th and even the 20th century ('*textum ergo habes, nunc ab omnibus receptum: in quo nihil immutatum aut corruptum damus*'[68]). The *textus receptus* did not evolve from a common ecclesiastical practice, as the 'koine text' used in the Greek Orthodox churches did[69], but from a printed text tradition[70]. One could say that the concept of a 'critical edition' evolved during the making of the *textus receptus*, in striving for an original textual form, which could be reconstructed by conjectural emendation and other philological aids.[71] The many editions produced since the 16th century ('*No one knows exactly how many separate edtions of the Greek Testament have come from the press since 1514...*')[72] are sufficient evidence indeed to re-evaluate the search for the original text. In my conviction, the evaluation of the Byzantine 'koine text' of Scripture is a task that should be set up afresh, in the context of codicological research of the manuscripts.

7.5 The Eastern Orthodox Canon of Holy Scripture

In Eastern Orthodoxy, the Scriptures are divided into three groups: the books known as canonical books (κανονιζόμενα), the books that are recommended by the Church 'to be read' (ἀναγινωσκόμενα) and the apocrypha (ἀπόκρυφα)[73]. The New Testament comprises only canonical books. The 'ἀναγινωσκόμενα' (non-canonical – in the strict sense of the word) of the OT[74], i.e. *1 Esdras, Tobit, Judith, 1-3 Maccabees, Wisdom of Solomon, Ecclesiasticus/Sirach, Baruch, the Letter of Jeremias*, additional parts to *Daniel [The Story of Susanna, The Song of the Three Children, The Idol Bel and the Dragon]*, and such texts as the *Prayer of Manasse* and other smaller variations), were acknowledged for reasons of elementary catechetical teaching and private study since the early days of Christianity and have been maintained in Orthodox tradition.[75] These books have a high status in Orthodox patristic tradition which comes close to that of canonical.[76] The inclusion of this

---

Ro 3[10-18]). (4) If the situation was bad enough before, it became worse when other Greek versions of the OT, especially those of Aquila, Symmachus, Theodotion, appeared and began to influence 𝔊.'

[66] E. Nestle, 'Early History of the Septuagint', *Ibid.*, 442: 'Even the *New Testament*, with its great number of quotations, does not permit of any very definite statements, except that it proves again that textual corruption had already found its way into the copies used by the writers of the NT (cf. He 3⁹ ἐν δοκιμασίᾳ, 12⁵ ἐνοχλῇ). Cf. Origen, 'A Letter from Origen to Africanus', in *The Writings of Origen*, Trans: F. Crombie, Vol 1 (Edinburgh, 1868); M. Harl and N. de Lange (Eds.), *Origène: Philocalie, 1-20 sur les écritures, introd., texte, trad. [du grec] et notes. La lettre à Africanus sur l'histoire de Suzanne, introd., texte, trad. [du grec] et notes* (Paris, 1983).

[67] E.J. Epp, 'The multivalence of the term "original text" in New Testament textual criticism", in *Perspectives on New Testament Textual Criticism. Collected Essays, 1962-2004* (Leiden / Boston, 2005), 551-593.

[68] That is: '[the reader has] the text which is now received by all, in which we give nothing changed or corrupted', quoted in B.M. Metzger and B.D. Ehrman, *Op. Cit.*, (New York/Oxford, 2005), 152. These words come from the Preface to the second Elzevir edition of the NT (1633), cf. n.36 on p. 152.

[69] Textual differences are indicated in the preface to the The "Patriarchal edition" of the NT, Ἡ Καινὴ Διαθήκη ἐγκρίσει τῆς μεγάλης τοῦ Χριστοῦ ἐκκλησίας, by B. Antoniadis [et al. Eds] (Athens, 2004, first edition, Constantinople, 1904), ζ': 'The text of the present edition, prepared and printed as above described, differs from the Textus Receptus distributed by the Bible societies in about 2000 readings and 1400 passages, specifically: Mt. 150, Mk. 175, Lk. 260, Jn. 100, Acts 125, Pauline Epistles 165, Catholic Epistles 65, and the remainder in the Apocalypse' [Transl. Rife].

[70] E.g. the recent edition by the Trinitarian Bible Society, Ἡ Καινὴ Διαθήκη. *The New Testament, the Greek Text underlying the English Authorised Version of 1611* (London, 1991), which is a reprint edition of Beza (1598) and Scrivener (1894 and 1902).

[71] E.J. Epp, "The Multivalence of the Term 'Original Text' in New Testament Textual Criticism", in *Harvard Theological Review*, 42 (1999), 245-281.

[72] B.M. Metzger and B.D. Ehrman, *Op. Cit.*, (New York/Oxford, 2005), 194.

[73] Nicodemos' Handbook of Orthodox Canon Law, the Πηδάλιον, Ed. by Agapios the Peloponnesian and Nicodemos the Hagiorite (Leipzig, 1800), 585 for this threefold division (with regard to Athanasius the Great, Festival Letter 39): 'Εἰς τρία διαιρεῖ ὁ Ἅγιος τὰ Βιβλία ἐν τῇ Ἐπιστολῇ ταύτῃ, εἰς ἀπόκρυφα, εἰς κανονιζόμενα καὶ εἰς ἀναγινωσκόμενα'.

[74] See Cyril of Jerusalem and Athanasius, plus the later synodal decisions of the Councils of Jassy (1642) and Jerusalem under Patriarch Dositheus (1672), where the books were declared to be 'genuine parts of Scripture'. The denotation 'apocrypha' with regard to this particular category, stems from the Latin Church father Jerome ('inter apocrypha esse ponendum', in the *prologus galeatus* to the Books of Samuel [MPL 28, 601ff.]) and *praef. in Iudith* ('apud Hebraeos liber Iudith inter apocrypha legitur').

[75] Cf. E. Oikonomos, 'Die Bedeutung der deuterokanonischen Schriften in der orthodoxen Kirche', in *Die Apokryphen-Frage im ökumenischen Horizont*, Ed. S. Meurer (Stuttgart, 1989), 26-40; H.B. Swete and R.R. Ottley, 'Books not Included in the Hebrew Canon', in *An Introduction to the Old Testament in Greek* (Peabody, Mass., 1989), Ch. III, 265-288, but consult also Ch. II, 'Books of the Hebrew Canon', 231-264, for differences of titles, arrangement and contents between the Hebrew Massoretic Bible and the Greek Version of the Seventy (O').

[76] See with regard to the question of the canonical status of the 'anaginoskomena' in Eastern Orthodoxy, H.P. Scanlin, "The Old Testament Canon in the Orthodox Churches", in *New Perspectives on Historical Theology: Essays in Memory of John Meyendorff*, Ed. B. Nassif (Grand Rapids, 1996), 300-312; E. Oikonomos, 'Die Bedeutung der deuterokanonischen Schriften in der orthodoxen Kirche', in *Op. Cit.* (Stuttgart, 1989), 26-40; T. Mitrevski, "Die kanonische Geltung der deuteronomische Bücher. Der heilige Schrift in der orthodoxen Kirche nach den Konzilsentscheidungen", in *Kyrios*, 13 (1973), 49-77.

category of Scriptures as books of the Church is clearly demonstrated in the Byzantine Greek manuscript tradition of the Old Testament.[77]

The apocrypha comprise a group of books that was clearly determined non-canonical and that is generally known as the pseudepigraphical books of the Old Testament.

7.6 Eastern Orthodox patristic literature

The Eastern Orthodox concept of the patristic period does not end with John of Damascus[78], nor with the Fall of Constantinople[79], but runs into the present day[80]. The Greek patrologist Panagiotes Chrestou formulates this sharply in his five volume work on Greek patrology[81]. A special role in the Eastern Orthodox approach to patrology is fulfilled by the so-called startsi (elders), such as Elders of Optina (Staretz Leonid, Staretz Makarij, Staretz Ambrosij), Ignatius Brianchaninov, Theophan the Recluse, Serafim of Sarov[82] and of the 20th century, Silouan the Athonite, Archimandrite Ioann (Krestjankin), Nikolai Gurjanov, Kirill Pavlov, Serafim Tjapochkin, and Samson Sivers in Russian tradition; Hadji-Georgis the Athonite, Nikephorus of Chios, Arsenios of Paros, Nectarios of Aegina, Savvas the New, Philotheos Zervakos, Philaretos of the Holy Mountain, Gabriel Dyonysiatis, Iakovos of Epiros, Joseph the Hesychast, Paisios the Athonite, Amphilochius of Patmos, Epiphanius of Athens, Porphyrius of Kavsokalyvia, George of Drama in Greek tradition.[83]

7.7 Concerning the primary language of the Eastern Orthodox Church

Greek (κοινή) is, of course, the "first language" of the Christian Church and in Greece this language has been maintained until this present day for official use in the Church (the liturgy). For Eastern Orthodox, Greek is the original language of the Scriptures, of the Old (Septuagint) and New Testament[84]. Greek was also the language for ecclesiastical documents, such as synodal decisions, acts and letters and the whole Byzantine patristic literature[85]. This linguistic continuity is an important factor for textual transmission and codex formation[86] (Byzantine codicology[87]). But it should be added that translations (ἑρμηνεῖαι)[88] belong intrinsically to the

---

[77] A. Rahlfs, *Verzeichnis der griechischen Handschriften des Alten Testaments für das Septuaginta Unternehmen*, in *Nachrichten der koeniglichen Gesellschaft der Wissenschaften zu Göttingen, Philolologisch Historische Klasse*, (Beiheft) (Berlin, 1914), 1-443, *passim*.

[78] C. Kannengieser, *Handbook of Patristic Exegesis* (Leiden / Boston, 2004); M. Geerard and J. Noret (Eds.), *Clavis Patrum Graecorum* (Turnhout, 1974-1998); R. Drobner, *Lehrbuch der Patrologie* (Freiburg/Basel/Vienna, 1994); B. Altaner and A. Stuiber, *Patrologie. Leben, Schriften und Lehre der Kirchenväter* (Freiburg/Basel/Wien, 1980); J. Quasten, *Patrology* (Utrecht, 1962-1986); O. Stählin, 'Christliche Schriftsteller' in *Wilhelm von Christs Geschichte der Griechischen Litteratur* (München, 1924).

[79] A. Ehrhard, 'Theologie', in *Geschichte der byzantinischen Litteratur von Justinian bis zum Ende des oströmischen Reiches (527-1453)*, Ed. K. Krumbacher (München, 1897), 37-218; H.G. Beck, *Kirche und Theologische Literatur im byzantinischen Reich*, (München, 1959).

[80] H. Alfeyev, *St. Symeon the New Theologian and Orthodox Tradition* (Oxford, 2000), 278-279: 'Symeon became one of the most widely read Byzantine authors in Russia. In contrast to the situation in late Byzantium (cf. Palamas), in Russia they did not distinguish between ancient and later church Fathers, and Symeon was for them as authoritative a writer as the great Fathers of the first Christian centuries and enjoyed the same popularity'. C. Karakolis, 'Erwägungen zur Exegese des Alten Testaments bei den griechischen Krichenvätern', in I.Z. Dimitrov et al. (Eds), *Das Alte Testament als christliche Bibel in orthodoxer und westlicher Sicht: Zweite europäische orthodox-westliche Exegetenkonferenz, im Rilakloster vom 8-15 September 2001* (Tübingen, 2004), 21 n.1: 'Nach orthodoxen Verständnis gibt es im Gegensatz zum westlichen Kriterium der *antiquitas* keine zeitliche Begrenzung für die "Periode der Kirchenväter". Ein *Kirchenvater* ist eine kirchliche Persönlichkeit, deren Orthodoxie und Heiligkeit durch die Kirche anerkannt wurde. Dieses Kriterium gilt zweifellos auch für Gestalten der neueren Zeit, wie z.B. für die heiligen Nektarios von Pentapolis (1847-1920) und Silouan vom Berg Athos (1866-1938)'. Cf. G. Florovsky, *Bible, Church, Tradition: An Eastern Orthodox View* (Belmont, 1972), 110-113.

[81] P.K. Chrestou, Ἑλληνικὴ Πατρολογία (t. I-V, Thessaloniki, 1976-1992), t. I (Tr. G.D. Dragas, *Greek Orthodox Patrology. An Introduction to the Study of the Church Fathers*, Rollinsford, NH, 2005, 15-16): 'The Church has never excluded the appearance of renowned teachers in her bosom, who are outstanding bearers of the divine grace of the divine spirit, and she has never restricted this appearance to any particular period of her history. Orthodox ecclesiastical conciousness , which attributes the title of father in every epoch to elect vessels of grace that lived in previous epochs, has already pushed the patristic period to the end of the Byzantine era and is pushing forward it more and more'.

[82] I. Smolitsch, *Leben und Lehre der Starzen* (Wien, 1936).

[83] G. Mantzaridis, "Universality and Monasticism", in *Precious Vessels of the Holy Spirit. The Lives and Counsels of Contemporary Elders of Greece*, Ed. H.A. Middleton (Thessalonica & Asheville, NC, 2004), 25-36; T. Ware (Bishop Kallistos of Diokleia), "The Spiritual Guide in Orthodox Christianity", in *The Inner Kingdom* (Crestwood, New York, 2004), 127-151 [see Lit. in n. 1]; Idem, "The Spiritual Father in Saint John Climacus and Saint Symeon the New Theologian", in I. Hausherr, *Spiritual Direction in the Early Christian East* (Kalamazoo, MI., 1990), vii-xxxiii (Forword).

[84] A. Delicostopoulos, 'Major Greek Translations of the Bible', in *The Interpretation of the Bible. The International Symposium in Slovenia*, Ed. J. Krašovec (Sheffield, 1998), 297: 'The Greek nation has the rare privilege of having as it mother tongue the language of the New Testament as well as of the Septuagint (LXX). The validity of the Septuagint was verified by the Lord and the Apostles and the 'consensus ecclesiae' through the official use throughout the centuries'.

[85] P.K. Chrestou, Ἑλληνικὴ Πατρολογία, Vol. I-V (Thessaloniki, 1976-1992), v. I., Β΄. Η Γλῶσσα, 77-90.

[86] P.K. Chrestou, *Op. Cit.*, 'Χειρόγραφος Παράδοσις', 249-301.

[87] We will use the expression 'Byzantine Codicology' analogously to 'Byzantine Palaeography'. Cf. E.E. Granstrem, 'Zur byzantinischen Minuskel', in *Griechische Kodikologie und Textüberlieferung*, D. Harlfinger (Ed.) (Darmstadt, 1980), 76, esp. note 4.

[88] With regard to the ancient as well as modern translations represented in printed editions, see T.H. Darlow and H.F. Moule (Eds.), *Historical Catalogue of the Printed Editions of Holy Scripture in the Library of the British and Foreign Bible Society*, in 2 volumes,

phenomenon of the Bible's manifestation and distribution[89]. Indeed, the *Translation of the Seventy* itself (ἡ τῶν Ο' ἑρμηνεία) is the best example to demonstrate this given. In this dissertation the Slavic manuscript and edition tradition, which developed from the late Byzantine manuscript tradition, will also receive due attention[90].

8. Use of quotations in this thesis

All quotations in this thesis are in English. Bible quotations are taken from *The Holy Bible, containing the Old and New Testaments and the Books called Apocrypha, Appointed to be read in churches, Authorised King James Version*, edited with an introduction and notes by Robert Carroll and Stephen Prickett (Oxford University Press, 1997). Quotations from the fathers and Orthodox theologians of later days are taken from available translations. On rare occasions, when there was no English translation known, some quotations in the text have been translated into English by the writer of this dissertation.

9. Technical terminology

With regard to the Byzantine Greek terminology used in biblical, patristic and other ecclesiastical books (manuscripts as well as printed), as well as in later Greek interpretative literature, we follow the Greek and Slavic/Russian practices as consistently as possible. A *Glossary of Terms* is provided at the end of the thesis.

Vol. II: Polyglots and Languages Other Than English (New York, reprint, 1963). [1st ed. London, 1903-1911], Introduction, ix ('Thus the whole Catalogue comprises editions in a total number of 628 languages and dialects').

[89] A.A. Alexeev, 'Holy Scripture and Its Translation', in *The Interpretation of the Bible. The International Symposium in Slovenia*, Ed. J. Krašovec (Sheffield, 1998), 1389: 'The languages that were the mother-languages for the Scripture are not the mother-languages for Christian peoples today. However, even now the original Bible texts keep their importance as primary sources for theology; besides, being the base of new translations, they exist as an integral part of religious life, more as a symbol than as a real agent. Today Bible translations are more popular among Christians than the original texts. Thus a paradoxical need arises to distinguish Holy Scripture from its translations. Indeed in Christian communities there are some tendencies towards removing distinctions of principle that divide the former from the latter'.

[90] A.A. Alexeev, 'Holy Scripture and Its Translation', in *Op. Cit.* (Sheffield, 1998), 1396: 'Thus we come to the next distinction of principle between Holy Scripture and its translation. Holy Scripture is by its very nature an omni-confessional text. It means that every Christian denomination can find and does find support for its teaching in the existing text without recourse to text criticism devices and strained interpretation. Plurality of meanings is an immanent characteristic of Holy Scripture. As for translation, a direct dependence on a given Christian community is among the primary conditions of its existence, and a uni-confessional text is a typical form of translation. Confessional orientation of translation may manifest itself in the choice of a base text (...). Thus, the natural omni-confessionalism of Holy Scripture is opposed to the practical uni-confessionalism of translation'.

Chapter 1

The Byzantine Manuscripts and the Western Cataloguing Tradition

In this chapter I will provide an analysis of the manner in which the extant Byzantine manuscripts have been collected, studied, catalogued, described and presented to date. When using the term 'Byzantine manuscripts', I am referring to the ecclesiastical manuscripts. I start with some preliminary remarks on a codicological approach to the Byzantine manuscripts looking at the various edition forms of the printed Greek Bibles and highlighting how the tradition of Byzantine manuscript delivery was maintained in the East. I then turn to the disciplines of palaeography and codicology to show how these can bring a new perspective in understanding the edition practices of the East. I proceed to look at the pros and cons of specialised manuscript categorisation and the existing paradigms of manuscript classification. I end with a short explanation of the necessity to visit the ecclesiastical books of the Byzantine liturgy, where one can find the justification for setting up a new manuscript categorisation. Finally I provide some examples of modern codicological manuscript research of liturgical books, which could be regarded as precursors of the codicological research here advocated.

1.1 Preliminary Remarks to Codicological Study of the Byzantine Manuscripts

As we have already pointed out in the Introduction, Eastern Orthodox scholars have to date never made a critical edition of the Bible. Byzantine Bible editions, one could say, can be characterised by their liturgical functionality - they are editions that were intended for ecclesiastical practice[91] - think of the Psalterion[92], the Evangelion[93], the Apostolos[94], the Prophetologion[95], and the other liturgical codices[96]. The Western academic editions of the Greek Bible, such as the Complutensian Polyglot[97], the New Testament of Erasmus, the Aldine Greek Bible, the Sixtine Septuagint etc.[98] (which served as paradigms for later reprints and critical editions), do not have obvious, scholarly counterparts in the East. In our view, however, it is of utmost interest to study precisely this Eastern liturgical, printed, edition practice, academic or not, because it provides profound insight into the Byzantine manuscript tradition, from a codicological as well as a textuological point of view.[99]

---

[91] E. Legrand, *Bibliographie Hellénique des XVe et XVIe siècles ou Description raisonnée des ouvrages publiés en Grec [ou] par des Grecs aux XVe et XVIe siècles* (Paris, 1885-1906; repr. 1962); Idem, *Bibliographie Hellénique ou Description raisonnée des ouvrages publiés par des Grecs aux dix-septième siècle* (Paris, 1894-1903 ; repr. Paris, 1975), I. Nos. 1-364bis (année 1601-1644) – 1894 ; II. Nos. 365-639 (année 1645-1690) – 1894; III. Nos. 640-715 (année 1691-1700) Notices biographiques – 1895; IV. Notices biographiques – 1896; V. Supplement. Notices biographiques – 1903]; E. Legrand and H. Pernot, *Bibliographie Ionienne. Description raisonnée des ouvrages publiés par des Grecs des sept-îles ou concernant ces îles du XVe siècle à l'année 1900* (Paris, 1910); E. Legrand, *Bibliographie Hellénique ou Description raisonnée des ouvrages publiés par des Grecs aux dix-huitième siècle* (Paris, 1918-1928; repr. Paris, ca. 1975), [I. Nos. 1-562 (année 1701-1760) – 1918; II Nos. 563-1260 (année 1761-1790) – 1928]; P. Meyer, *Die theologische Litteratur der griechischen Kirche im sechzehnten Jahrhundert. Mit einer allgemeinen Einleitung* (Leipzig, 1899); A. Papadopoulos Vretos, Νεοελληνικὴ Φιλολογία ἤτοι κατάλογος τῶν ἀπὸ πτώσεως τῆς βυζαντινῆς αὐτοκρατορίας μέχρι ἐνκαθιδρύσεως τῆς ἐν Ἑλλάδι βασιλείας τυπωθέντων βιβλίων παρ' Ἑλλήνων εἰς τὴν ὁμιλουμένην, ἢ εἰς τὴν ἀρχαίαν ἑλληνικὴν γλῶσσαν συνεθεὶς, Vol. I (Athens, 1854-1857).

[92] Editio princeps: Ψαλτήριον, Ed. Alexander of Crete (Venice, 1486).

[93] Editio princeps: Θεῖον καὶ Ἱερον Εὐαγγέλιον, Ed. ? (Venice, 1539).

[94] Editio princeps: Ἀπόστολος, Ed. ? (Venice, 1534).

[95] Editio princeps: Ἀναγνωστικόν, Ed. E. Glyzonios (Venice 1596). [= Προφητολόγιον]

[96] Chapter 2 provides more detailed information about these editions.

[97] Bible editions in other languages than Latin, were made for scholarly ends. For instance, the Complutensian Polyglot – including first editions of the Greek NT and OT – was a joint publication of the professors of the University of Alcalá in Spain. Desiderius Erasmus, the most influential NT editor of the time lectured at Cambridge University, etc. cf. J.H. Bentley, *Humanists and Holy Writ. New Testament Scholarship in the Renaissance* (Princeton, 1983).

[98] For a chronological overview of the history of editions of the Greek Bible [NT & OT] see T.H. Darlow and H.F. Moule (Eds.), *Historical Catalogue of the Printed Editions of Holy Scripture in the Library of the British and Foreign Bible Society* (New York, reprint, 1963), Part II, 'Polyglots', 1-36, 'Ancient Greek', 573-679.

[99] See further chapter 2.

1.1.1 The printed Bible editions

Printed editions of the Bible since the Renaissance, which started with the publication of a Byzantine text form, later called the *Textus Receptus*, were focused on the plain Greek biblical text of the manuscripts, with a view, on the one hand, to providing the uncorrupted (primary) text, often leaving out of consideration other secondary texts (patristic commentaries/scholia/catena), or liturgical equipment (lectionary or hymnographical) which were to be found in the very same codices. The biblical text would be "extracted", one could say, from its liturgical or patristic context, in an eclectic approach, and reconstructed according to a process of comparison of variant readings[100]. On the other hand, editors were interested in the Greek text in order to "criticise" the authority of the Latin Vulgate[101], and not primarily in the Greek text itself, or the Byzantine manuscripts themselves.

The Polyglot Psalters (diglots or triglots) were the first printed editions, which included the Greek text of the OT (LXX version)[102]. A salient characteristic of the publication forms of the Bible since the Renaissance was the grouping together of all biblical books into one edition, the so-called Pandect-Bibles[103], or at least into larger comprehensive text units. These complete Bibles were: the Polyglot edition forms of the whole Bible[104], which were multilingual Bibles, including the OT in Latin-Hebrew-Greek, and the NT in Greek and Latin Vulgate); the Greek New Testaments (often bilingual: Gr.-Lt.); the Greek Old & New Testaments (the complete Greek Bible); and the Greek Old Testaments (Septuagint). Interesting is, that these edition forms were actually quite unusual in Byzantine manuscript tradition and also in later Greek printed editions, which displayed a practice of delivery of smaller compartments of the Bible.

> In the Byzantine period the Greek Bible was usually produced in small and convenient sections of the Old (Septuagint) and New Testaments, such as the Octateuch (the eight books from Genesis to Ruth), the Psalter (the Psalms with the Canticles), and the Four Gospels. The Prophets formed another practical unit of text of this type. It seems to have been a rarity to produce a complete Bible, whether in one or more volumes, and the number of surviving manuscripts show that the demand of Byzantines for the Psalter and the Gospels far exceeded that for the other sections. This is understandable, since those were the texts most widely needed for private study and liturgical devotion.
> J. Lowden, *Illuminated Prophet Books. A Study of Byzantine Manuscripts of the Major and Minor Prophets* (University Park and London, 1988), 5

The publication of the "complete" Greek Bible (OT & NT), which became known in the West through the Complutensian Polyglot Bible (Ed. Diego López de Zuñiga, et al.)[105] and the Aldine Edition of the Greek Bible

---

[100] K.H. Jobes and M. Silva, *Invitation to the Septuagint* (Grand Rapids, Michigan, 2001), 74: 'Instead of printing the entire text of one manuscript, an editor or editorial committee examines the textual variants and decides which reading is most likely original. This approach produces a reconstructed text often referred to as eclectic, because the resulting printed text is not identical to any manuscript in its entirety.'; B.M. Metzger and B.D. Ehrman, *Op. Cit.* (New York/Oxford, 2005), Preface xv: 'The textual critic seeks to ascertain from the divergent copies which form of the text should be regarded as most nearly conforming to the original'.

[101] B.M. Metzger and B.D. Ehrman, *The Text of the New Testament. Its Transmission, Corruption and Restoration*, 4th edition (New York/Oxford, 2005), 138: 'the publication of the Greek Testament offered to any scholar acquainted with both languages a tool with which to criticize and correct the official Latin Bible of the Church'.

[102] The first diglot liturgical Psalter is mentioned in T.H. Darlow and H.F. Moule (Eds.), *Op. Cit.* (New York, reprint, 1963), No 4590, 574: a Psalter in Greek and Latin, with appended Canticles, Ed. J. Crastonus (Chrestonus?), Milan, 1481. After several other psalter editions, a polyglot psalter followed, cf. T.H. Darlow and H.F. Moule (Eds.), *Op. Cit.* (New York, reprint, 1963), No 1411, 1-2: *Psalterium Hebraeum, Graecum, Arabicum, et Chaldaeum, cum tribus latinis interpretationibus et glossis*, Ed. A. Giustiniani, Genoa, 1516 [in eight columns it gives the Hebrew text, a literal Latin version of the Hebrew, the Latin Vulgate, the Greek Septuagint, the Arabic, the Chaldee, (in Hebrew characters), a literal Latin version of the Chaldee, and *Scholia*]; cf. J.J. Pelikan, *The Reformation of the Bible. The Bible of the Reformation, Catalogue of the Exhibition by V. Hotchkiss and D. Price* (New Haven and London, 1996), Item I. 26, 111-113.

[103] The editions of the Latin Bible, since the first *Biblia Latina* (Ed. J. Gutenberg, Mainz, 1454-1455), later called shortly *Biblia* (Ed. R. Estienne, Paris, 1528) and *Biblia Sacra* (Official edition of the Vulgate under the auspices of Clement VIII, Rome, 1592, the "Sixtine-Clementine" or "Clementine Bible"), were already such Pandects. These printed edition forms, which can be retraced in the Latin manuscript tradition (cf. J. Pelikan, *Op. Cit.*, (New Haven and London, 1996), 90: Item I.9 and B. Fischer, *Lateinische Bibelhandschriften im frühen Mittelalter* (Freiburg im Breisgau, 1985), 246-250: 'Die Idee des Pandekten', served probably as paradigms for the Polyglot and Complete Greek-Latin Bibles. There was a considerable printing history of Latin Bibles before the publication of the first Greek Bible edition started up. cf. B.M. Metzger and B.D. Ehrman. *Op. Cit.*, (New York/Oxford, 2005) 137: 'During the next 50 years [since the editio princeps of Gutenberg], at least 100 editions of the Latin Bible were issued by various printing houses').

[104] The idea of a polyglot Bible emerged in Caesarea in the 3rd century with the Hexapla edition of the whole OT, including the Hebrew and Greek texts in parallel columns, an enormous task, which had been undertaken by Origen and the calligraphers at his disposal. Origin also endeavored to create a Tetrapla edition of the Psalterion. These 'patristic' polyglot editions, the Hexapla and Tetrapla, disappeared over the ages, but several parts and fragments remained and were re-collected and edited (Montfaucon, Field). Cf. N.F. Marcos, 'Origins Hexapla', *The Septuagint in Context. Introduction to the Greek Versions of the Bible* (Leiden/Boston/Köln, 2000), 204-222; E. Würthwein, 'Die Hexapla des Origenes', in *Der Text des Alten Testaments* (Stuttgart, 1973), 58-61; H.B. Swete and R.R. Ottley, 'The Hexapla, and the Hexaplaric and other Recensions of the Septuagint', in *An Introduction to the Old Testament in Greek* (Peabody, Mass., 1989 [reprint 1914]), 59-86.

[105] The whole 6 volume edition was produced at Complutum (Alcalá) in Spain during the years 1514-1517 [and only published in 1520] : *Biblia Sacra Polyglotta complectentia V.T. Hebraico Graeco et Latino idiomate, N.T. Graecum et Latinum*); cf. J.J. Pelikan, 'Biblia Polyglotta', in *Op. Cit.* (New Haven and London, 1996), Item I. 25, 109-110; B.M. Metzger and B.D. Ehrman, *Op. Cit.* (New York/Oxford,

(Ed. A. Asolanus, Venice, 1518)[106], was quite uncommon in the East it seems - there is only a very small number of extant manuscripts that contain the more or less complete Greek Bible (11 codices correspond to this type)[107], and not all of these contain an identical set of books or a uniformly established text.

The first edition of the complete Greek New Testament was included in the Complutensian Polyglot (1514). Separate editions incorporating the whole Greek New Testament commenced with the *Novum Instrumentum omne*[108], which was followed by four revised editions (renamed *Novum Testamentum omne* with the 2nd ed., Basel, 1519). The characteristic title *Novum Testamentum Graecum* as it was called in the West, retained to the present day in the Nestle/Aland editions, appeared for the first time in an edition of N. Gerbelius, (Hagenau, 1521)[109]. This edition form of the complete Greek New Testament was similarly rare in Byzantine manuscript tradition (there are circa 45 extant manuscripts of the whole Greek NT)[110]. Such a complete New Testament (Τῆς Καινῆς Διαθήκης ἅπαντα) was not generally used as a basic textual unit in Byzantine tradition[111], or in the Greek church, which explains the relatively small number of extant manuscripts of this type. It was the Apostolo-Evangelion form (without the Apocalypse), both lectionary as well as text form, of which we have a considerable number of extant manuscripts. Yet it was, paradoxically, the complete Greek NT form that Western editors chose as a publishing unit. Instead of 'back to the sources', a new tradition of delivery commenced.

The printed edition of the Greek Old Testament (the O', or LXX)[112], which was published separately for the first time by A. Carafa (Ed. et al.), Ἡ Παλαιὰ Διαθήκη κατὰ τοὺς Ἐβδομήκοντα. *Vetus Testamentum iuxta Septuaginta ex auctoritate Sixti V. Pont. Max. editum*, Rome, 1586 (1587), and which is known as the "Sixtine Edition" of the LXX (under the auspices of Sixtus V)[113], was neither a common codex form in the ancient church[114], as one can conclude from the extant Byzantine manuscripts. Rahlfs lists only *one* manuscript that contains the entire Greek Old Testament separately, but this codex is incomplete as the Psalter is lacking[115]. So there is, in fact, not one extant separate integral Greek Old Testament.

Textual research was thus based on compiled editions. From here, scholars set out to search for the "original text". Codicological research will decompile these forms, as we shall see.

1.1.2 From Montfaucon's *Palaeographia Graeca* to modern codicology

Bernard de Montfaucon's monumental *Palaeographia Graeca* (Paris, 1708) and his *Bibliotheca bibliothecarum manuscriptorum nova* (Paris, 1739, 2 vols. folio)[116], placed scientific research of the Byzantine manuscripts in a new perspective. The *Palaeographia Graeca*[117] is a first systematic introduction to the study of Greek manuscripts (palaeographical phenomena induced from Byzantine classical as well as ecclesiastical codices),

---

2005), 137-142; J.H. Bentley, 'The Complutensian New Testament', in *Humanists and Holy Writ. New Testament Scholarship in the Renaissance* (Princeton, 1983), 70-111.

[106] The Aldine Bible, the first complete printed edition of the Greek Bible (OT and NT) was published in Italy: Πάντα τὰ κατ᾽ἐξοχὴν καλούμενα Βιβλία θείας δηλαδὴ Γραφῆς παλαιᾶς τε, καὶ νέας. Sacrae Scripturae veteris, novaeque ominia (Venice, 1518-1519), the OT part (1) Gen.-Ps.; (2) Prov.-3 Macc. on the basis of Bessarion's collection of codices, preserved in St. Mark' s Library at Venice (Mss. 29, 68, 121); (3) the NT, on the basis of Erasmus' first edition 1516. Cf. T.H. Darlow and H.F. Moule (Eds.), *Op. Cit.*, 576-577; cf. H.B. Swete, 'Printed texts of the Septuagint', in *An Introduction of the Old Testament in Greek*, Ed. R.R. Ottley, (Peabody, Mass., 1989), 173-174.

[107] Paragraph **6.4** Tabular Specimens from the *Catalogue*: Group III. Specimen VII: 'OT and NT Byzantine Greek Codices'.

[108] Greek and Latin, and annotations by Erasmus of Rotterdam, 2 parts, Basel, 1516, f°; cf. J.J. Pelikan, 'Novum instrumentum omne', *Op. Cit.* (New Haven and London, 1996), Item I. 16, 100; B.M. Metzger and B.D. Ehrman, *Op. Cit.* (New York/Oxford, 2005), 142-149; J.H. Bentley, *Op. Cit.* (Princeton, 1983), 112-193, esp. 114: 'the methods, principles and reasoning that governed its preparation'; T.H. Darlow and H.F. Moule (Eds.), *Op. Cit.* (New York, reprint, 1963), No 4591, 574-575.

[109] T.H. Darlow and H.F. Moule (Eds.), *Op. Cit.* (New York, reprint, 1963), No 4598, 578. This edition was the earliest separate edition of the New Testament in Greek.

[110] Paragraph **6.2** Tabular Specimens from the *Catalogue*: Group I. Specimen III: 'NT Byzantine Greek Codices'.

[111] P. Meyer, *Op. Cit.* (Leipzig, 1899), 161, mentions a Greek NT published in Venice 1538 in the context of other printings of biblical books by the Greeks in Venice. The editor, however, was Melchior Sessa and the edition, Τῆς Καινῆς Διαθήκης ἅπαντα. Novi Testamenti Omnia, 2 vols., Venice, 1538, has nothing to do with the Greek printing tradition. Cf. W.H.P. Hatch, "An Early Edition of the New Testament in Greek", in *Harvard Theological Review*, 34.2 (1941), 69-78.

[112] E. Nestle, 'Septuagint: Printed Editions', in *A Dictionary of the Bible*, 4 (1906), 437-454. Eastern scholarship prefers the Greek designation ἑβδομήκοντα, abbreviated to O', in accordance with the tradition of the Byzantine fathers; cf. K. Oikonomos, Περὶ τῶν Ο' Ἑρμηνευτῶν τῆς παλαιᾶς θείας Γραφῆς (Athens, 1849).

[113] This edition of the Greek LXX was considered the *textus ab omnibus receptus* in Western scholarship (E. Nestle, *Septuagintastudien* (Ulm, 1886), I, 1); cf. T.H. Darlow and H.F. Moule (Eds.), *Op. Cit.* (New York, reprint, 1963), No 4647, 597-598; J.J. Pelikan, 'Vetus Testamentum iuxta Septuaginta', in *Op. Cit.* (New Haven and London, 1996), Item I. 24, 108-109;

[114] The Sixtine Edition was based on the OT part of the 4th century *Codex Vaticanus Graecus 1209* [B] (Vatican Library), and the choice of this ancient codex was highly remarkable, considering editions were usually based on Byzantine minuscules. For other consulted and used manuscripts see G. Pani, "Un centenaire à rappeler: l'édition Sixtine des Septante", in *Théorie et pratique de l'exegèse*, Eds. I. Backus and F. Higman (Geneve, 1990), 413-428; H.B. Swete, 'Printed texts of the Septuagint' (Peabody, Mass., 1989), 174-182.

[115] Codex 46 (Paris, Bibl. Nat., Coisl. 4 [381]), which represents an "incomplete" complete Greek OT; cf. A. Rahlfs, 'Verzeichnis der griechischen Handschriften des Alten Testaments für das Septuaginta Unternehmen' (Berlin, 1914), 184-185.

[116] H. Leclercq, 'Montfaucon (Dom Bernard de)', in *Dictionnaire d'Archéologie Chrétienne et de Liturgie*, 11 (1934), 2608-2672.

[117] H. Leclercq, *Art. Cit.*, 2628-2636 (La << Palaeographia Graeca >>).

which laid the foundations for a more integral approach to the manuscripts[118]. The *Bibliotheca bibliothecarum manuscriptorum nova*[119] includes a catalogue of catalogues of Greek and other manuscripts of major European libraries (the Vatican and other libraries in Italy, France, Great Britain, Germany and Austria etc.). In the *Bibliotheca Coisliniana*[120] Montfaucon contributed to the scientific description of Byzantine manuscripts in their actual locations (monasteries, museums, private collections). Together with Montfaucon and the other Maurist erudites[121], the Greek manuscript collections in the West and later also in the East were further explored[122], inventories were made of the codices[123], and they were catalogued[124], described, edited.

Since the Renaissance manuscript studies and collations were made by biblical scholars for editions that were primarily focused on the text. A new editing tradition of the Greek NT developed, marked by such scholars as: Erasmus (five editions since Basel, 1516), Stephanus (3rd Ed., Paris, 1550, the "Editio Regia"), Beza ([Geneva] 1565), Elzevir (Leiden, 1624), Wettstein (2 vols., Amsterdam, 1751-1752), Scholz (2 vols., Leipzig, 1830-1836), Lachmann (2 vols., Berlin, 1842-1850), Tischendorff (Editio octava critica maior, 3 vols., v. 3, Prolegomena by C.R. Gregory, Leipzig, 1869-1872), Scrivener (Cambridge, 1881), von Soden (I. Teil : Untersuchungen, Berlin, 1902-1910, II. Teil : Text mit Apparat, Göttingen, 1913), Nestle/Aland (Stuttgart, 1898-2006 [27. revidierte Auflage])[125]. In parallel, editors of the LXX started to produce large series of OT editions, in which scholars such as A. Carafa (et al., Rome, 1587, the Sixtine edition), Morinus (Paris, 1628), Grabe/Lee/Wigan (Oxford, 1707-1720), Stroth [started with a independent catalogue of LXX manuscripts] (1779-1782), Holmes-Parsons (5 vols., Oxford, 1798-1827.), Von Tischendorf (6th ed. rev. by E. Nestle, 2 vols., Leipzig, 1880), Swete (3 vols., Cambridge, 1909-1922), Brooke/McLean (Cambridge, 1906-1940), Rahlfs (2 vols., Stuttgart, 1935), Rahlfs/Hanhart (2 in one vol., Stuttgart, 2006) were involved[126]. Stimulated by generations of extensive and exclusive textual scholarship, research of the Byzantine manuscripts (4th-15th/16th century) resulted in specialised catalogues, culminating towards the end of the 19th and the beginning of the 20th century in the rich catalogues of Gregory, Karo/Lietzmann, von Soden, Rahlfs, Ehrhard, and reflected in the lists of manuscripts that are briefly described in the editions of the Greek OT and NT, the Greek/Byzantine fathers, the Byzantine liturgical books, the homiletic and hagiographical collections and the corpora of Byzantine Canon Law. Important for codicological research of the Byzantine manuscripts is to know which manuscripts were used in the editions and how they were used[127].

---

[118] Montfaucon was not a biblical scholar, but an expert in Byzantine patristic studies and (co)editor of the works of Athanasius, Origen and John Chrysostom; cf. V. Gardthausen, *Griechische Palaeography*, 2nd ed. (Leipzig, 1911), I, 5-8.

[119] H. Leclercq, *Art. Cit.*, 2661-2662.

[120] H. Leclercq, *Art. Cit.*, 2636-2640.

[121] D.-O. Hurel, 'The Benedictines of the Congregation of St. Maur and the Church Fathers', in I. Backus (Ed.), *Reception of the Church Fathers in the West. From the Carolingians to the Maurists* (Leiden, 1997), II, 1009-1038.

[122] Historical references of Eastern and Western Byzantine manuscript studies, palaeography and codicology are provided in N.B. Tomadakis, Κλεὶς τῆς Βυζαντινῆς Φιλολογίας ἤτοι Εἰσαγωγή εἰς τήν Βυζαντινήν Φιλολογίαν (Thessaloniki, 1993), Part III, Ch. 5: 'Αἱ εἰς τὴν Εὐρώπην βυζαντιναὶ σπουδαὶ' (including Russia, the Balkans and Greece).

[123] Further information is given concerning the library of manuscripts, especially those in Eastern Libraries in chpater 3. Cf. M. Richard and J.M. Olivier, *Répertoire des Bibliothèques et des Catalogues de Manuscrits Grecs* (Turnhout, 1995).

[124] The historical background of Western and Eastern libraries containing holdings of Greek manuscripts and their (ancient) catalogues is indicated in V. Gardthausen, *Sammlungen und Cataloge Griechischer Handschriften* (Leipzig, 1903) - an old work, but interesting in many aspects, especially for the ancient catalogues.

[125] The number of consulted and used Byzantine manuscripts in Greek NT editions (the first generation of editors) may be found in von Soden's *Die Schriften des Neuen Testaments in ihrer ältesten erreichbaren Textgestalt hergestellt auf Grund ihrer Textgeschichte* (Göttingen, 1911²), Liste III, 81-94.

[126] For the number and identity of the used Byzantine manuscripts in Greek Bible (LXX) editions, one may consult A. Rahlfs, *Op. Cit.* (Berlin, 1914), 335-372, '1) Holmes-Parsons, 2) Lagarde, 3) Swete, 4) Brooke-McLean, 5) Rahlfs)'.

[127] Lit. For both the Polyglots as well as the Greek NT and OT editions since the Renaissance: T.H. Darlow and H.F. Moule (Eds.), *Historical Catalogue of the Printed Editions of Holy Scripture in the Library of the British and Foreign Bible Society* (New York, reprint, 1963). [1st ed. London, 1903-1911]; Cf. J.J. Pelikan, *The Reformation of the Bible. The Bible of the Reformation* (New Haven and London, 1996); J.H. Bentley, *Humanists and Holy Writ. New Testament Scholarship in the Renaissance* (Princeton, New Jersey, 1983). ‖ For the manuscripts used in Greek NT editions: B.M. Metzger and B.D. Ehrman, *The Text of the New Testament. Its Transmission, Corruption and Restoration* (New York/Oxford, 2005), Part II, 137-204; H. von Soden, *Die Schriften des Neuen Testaments in ihrer ältesten erreichbaren Textgestalt hergestellt auf Grund ihrer Textgeschichte* (Göttingen, 1911), v.1, Liste III, 81-94 [editions 1-10]; C.R. Gregory, *Textkritik des Neuen Testamentes* (Leipzig, 1900-1909), v. 2, 'Geschichte der Kritik: Der ganze Text'; F.H.A. Scrivener, *A Plain Introduction to the Criticism of the New Testament for the Use of Biblical Students* (London, 1894), 'Early Printed Editions', 175-195, 'Critical Editions', 196-243; S.P. Tregelles, *An Account of the Printed Text of the Greek New Testament with Remarks on Its Revision upon Critical Principals: Together with a Collation of Critical Texts of Griesbach, Scholtz, Lachmann and Tischendorf, with That in Common Use* (London, 1854). ‖ For the used manuscripts in Greek OT editions: K.H. Jobes and M. Silva, *Invitation to the Septuagint* (Grand Rapids, Michigan, 2001), 'Printed Editions', 70-75; E. Würthwein, *Der Text des Alten Testaments* (Stuttgart, 1973), 'Die Septuaginta: Ausgaben', 77-80; A. Rahlfs, *Verzeichnis der griechischen Handschriften des Alten Testaments für das Septuaginta Unternehmen* (Berlin, 1914), '1) Holmes-Parsons, 2) Lagarde, 3) Swete, 4) Brooke-McLean, 5) Rahlfs', 335-372; H.B. Swete and R.R. Ottley, 'Printed Texts of the Septuagint', in *An Introduction to the Old Testament in Greek* (Peabody, Mass., 1989 [repr. 1914]), 171-194; E. Nestle, 'Septuagint: IV. Printed Editions of the Septuagint', in *A Dictionary of the Bible*, 4 (1906), 437-454.

Generally speaking biblical and patristic manuscript research developed into different disciplines. Research of the patristic texts included in or related to biblical manuscripts ('commentary manuscripts' and 'homiletic commentary manuscripts') was separated from research of the pure biblical text codices (the textual value of patristic texts was primarily taken into account for reasons of textual criticism). Catena research also evolved separately; lectionary manuscripts (in uncial and minuscule script) were set aside; liturgical elements in biblical manuscripts were considered of secondary importance or were neglected; connections with other liturgical and patristic manuscripts were not made. Specialisation, then, led to the isolation of certain pieces of content from a given codex, whereby the full codicological richness of such a codex, based on its history of transmission, was somewhat lost.

Greek palaeography developed in the 19th – 20th century[128]. Besides the use of manuscripts for textual studies, attention was paid to individual, integral codices (facsimile and diplomatic editions)[129], not only in the context of preparatory textual studies for editions of the Bible, but also for the publication of individual Byzantine iconographical and hymnographical manuscripts. Besides palaeography, codicology[130] and library history[131] became disciplines in which manuscripts were studied in accordance with the milieu of the manuscripts themselves and analysed in their integral forms[132]. Manuscript iconography[133] resulted in new insights into the integral state, form and heritage of the Byzantine manuscripts[134], and the latter were presented and discussed in a manner new to the departments of Old and New Testament textual criticism[135]. Attention was now also paid to

---

[128] J. Karayannopoulos, 'Bericht über Paläographie, Kodikologie und Diplomatic im Rahmen der Byzantinistik', in *Actes du XIVe Congrès International des Études Byzantines*, by M. Berza and E. Stănescu (Eds.) (Bucharest, 1976), III, 13-21; V. Gardthausen, *Griechische Palaeographie*, Vol.I: Das Buchwesen im Altertum und im Byzantium, Vol. II: Die Schrift, Unterschriften und Chronologie im Altertum und byzantinischen Mittelalters (Leipzig, 1911-1913); S.P. Lambros (Trans.), Ἐγχειρίδιον ἑλληνικῆς καὶ λατινικῆς παλαιογραφίας, by E. Thompson (Athens, 1903 [reprint 1973]). Representative of the discipline are also the compilars of catalogues of Byzantine manuscripts H.O. Coxe (Oxford), E. Miller and C. Graux (Spain), H. Omont (France, Belgium, Holland, Spain, and other places in Europe), S. Lambros (Athos), I. Sakkelion (Patmos and Athens), A. Papadopoulos-Kerameus (Jerusalem), Archimandrite Vladimir (Moscow) etc.

[129] For instance, O. Mazal (ed.), *Jozua-Rolle. Vollständige Faksimile-Ausgabe im Original-format des Codex Vaticanus Palatinus Graecus 431 der Biblioteca Apostolica Vaticana* (Graz, 1983-4). Cf. B.M. Metzger, 'Collections of Facsimiles of Greek Manuscripts', in *Manuscripts of the Greek Bible. An Introduction to Greek Palaeography* (New York and Oxford, 1981), 142-143.

[130] Codicology, as the study of the ancient codex within the book milieu to which it belonged, is today a well-established branch of manuscript research. The introduction of the term is accredited to A. Dain: Cf the review of Dain's book *Les manuscrits* (Paris, 1949) by F. Masai, "La paléographie et la codicologie", in *Scriptorium*, 4 (1950), 270-293; and the later discussions on the topic by A. Dain in 'Rapport sur la codicologie byzantine', in *Berichte zum XI. Internationalen Byzantinisten-Kongreß* (München, 1958). Lit. : B.L. Fonkič, 'Griechische Kodikologie', in *Griechische Kodikologie und Textüberlieferung*, Ed. D. Harlfinger, (Darmstadt, 1980); D. Harlfinger and G. Prato (Eds), *Paleografia e Codicologia Greca* (Atti del II Colloquio internazionale [Berlino-Wolfenbüttel, 17-21 ottobre 1983]) (Allesandria, 1991); J. Bompaire and J. Irigoin (Eds.), *La paléographie grecque et byzantine (Paris, 21-25 octobre 1974)*. (Actes du Colloque international sur la paléographie grecque et byzantine organisé dans le cadre des colloques internationaux du Centre National de la Recherche Scientifique à Paris du 21 au 25 octobre 1974) (Paris, 1977); L. Politis, *Paléographie et littérature byzantine et néo-grecque : recueil d'études* (London, reprint 1975); J. Lemaire, 'La Codicologie', in *Introduction à la Codicologie* (Louvain-la-neuve, 1989), 1-9, esp. 1-2 ('Les définitions de la codicologie') and n.1.

[131] O. Mazal, *The Keeper of Manuscripts* (Turnhout, 1992); E. Plümacher, 'Bibliothekswesen', in *Theologische Realenzyklopädie*, 6 (1980), 413-426; A. Hobson, *Große Bibliotheken der Alten und der Neuen Welt* (München, 1970); H.J. de Vleeschauwer, "Encyclopaedia of Library History", in *Mousaion* 2 (1955), 1-44, 46-95; C. Wendel, 'Das griechisch-römische Altertum', in *Handbuch der Bibliothekswissenschaft*, Ed. F. Milkau and G. Leyh, (Leipzig, 1931-1940) [1. Schrift und Buch, bearb. v. Hans Schnorr v. Carolsfeld u.ä., 1931; 2. Bibliotheksverwaltung, bearb.v. Gustva Abb u.ä., 1933; 3. Geschichte der Bibliotheken, bearb.v. Aloys Bomer u.ä., Bd. 3, 1940, 1-63.]; H. Leclercq, 'Bibliothèques', in *Dictionnaire d'Archéologie Chrétienne et de Liturgie*, 2(1925), 842-904.

[132] See K. Treu, "Zu den neutestamentlichen Handschriften in der UdSSR" in *Forschungen und Fortschritten*, 38.4 (1964), 118, 'In den letzten Jahrzehnten, besonders seit dem zweiten Weltkrieg, ist ein neues Forschungsgebiet zu selbstständigen Rang und namen gelangt: die Kodikologie, die Lehre vom Buch in der Form des Kodex, der seit der späteren Antike die klassische Schriftrolle verdrängt hat und uns heute allein geläufig ist (...). War die Paläographie im herkömmlichen Sinne immer mehr oder weniger die Hilfsdisziplin der Philologie geblieben, als die sie entstanden war, so erhebt sich mit dem neuen Namen Kodikologie auch ein neuer Anspruch. Das handschriftliche Buch soll nun ein Forschungsgegenstand sein, der um seiner selbst willen Aufmerksamkeit verdient. Nicht mehr allein der Text und die Schrift, sondern auch das äußere Gewand und seine materiell-technische Seite sollen berücksichtigt werden'.

[133] K. Weitzmann and G. Galavaris, *The Monastery of Saint Catherine at Mount Sinai. The Illuminated Greek Manuscripts*, Volume I (Princeton, New Jersey, 1990); K. Weitzmann and H.L.K. Essler, *The Cotton Genesis: British Library Codex Cotton Otho B. VI.* (Princeton, 1986); K. Weitzmann, *Illustrations in Roll and Codex. A Study of the origin and method of text illustration* (Princeton 1970); T. Uspenskij, *L' Octateuch de la Bibliothèque du Sérail à Constantinople* (Sofia, 1907); J. Strzygowski, *Der Bilderkreis des griechischen Physiologus des Kosmas Indikopleustes und Oktateuch nach Handschriften der Bibliothek zu Smyrna* (Leipzig, 1899); N.P. Kondakov, *Histoire de l'art byzantin considéré dans les miniatures* (New York, reprint 1970).

[134] J. Lowden, 'A codicological approach to description', in *The Octateuchs. A Study in Byzantine Manuscript Illustration* (University Park, Pennsylvania, 1992), Ch. 2, 'The term (Fr. *Codicologie*) was coined by Alphonse Dain in 1944 as a translation of the German *Handschriftenkunde*, and at its broadest means the study of the book (codex) in all its aspects. On the face of it, all students of illustrated manuscripts might therefore be considered codicologists'.

[135] B.D. Ehrman and M.W. Holmes (Eds.), *The Text of the New Testament in contemporary research: essays on the status questionis* (Grand Rapids, Mich., 1995); J.N. Birdsall, 'The Recent History of New Testament Textual Criticism (from Westcott and Hort, 1881, to the Present)', in *Aufstieg und Niedergang der römischen Welt*, Part II: Principate, Vol. 26.1 (Berlin / New York, 1992). This type of textual research is especially advocated in Germany at Das Septuaginta Unternehmen, Akademie der Wissenschaften in Göttingen, and at the Institut für neutestamentliche Textforschung, Münster i. W., Westfälische Wilhelms-Universität.

secondary textual elements and iconographic ornamentation[136], whereby the codex in its integral entirety was placed central stage. Illuminated manuscripts from Constantinople (the Octateuch of the Old Serail)[137], Smyrna (the perished Octateuch)[138], Sinai[139], Athos[140] and Athens[141] and also codices dispersed throughout Western Europe and the US, have been intensively studied and edited from this iconographical point of view[142]. According to the same principles, the hymnographical literature of the church was catalogued, described and published[143].

It was in these branches of palaeography that first serious scholarly attention was paid to the integral edition forms of the individual codices, e.g. the Octateuch, the Psalterion, the Evangelion, the Tetraevangelion, the Apostolos[144] etc, in Russia (2nd half of the 19th century) and then in Western Europe[145] and the USA (since the beginning of the 20th century). Palaeographers were no longer solely fixated on the text, but developed interest in other aspects of the transmission of the biblical and patristic books and their textual history, such as the art of making Byzantine codices and the copying process as such: iconographic decoration, lectionary design and equipment, internal arrangement and selection of texts, the scribes and their ateliers[146], the monastic background. Codicology can help a student of the Byzantine manuscripts (be they biblical, patristic, liturgical, ascetical or hagiographic) and the Byzantine text, to rediscover the full richness of the Byzantine codices and their synthetic interdependence, as well as their functional and historical value[147]. Since the biblical text was delivered in set 'edition forms', which crystallised into stereotyped codex forms, codicological research can throw new light onto the textual history of the Bible text, and even, we dare to state, can contribute to forming a more complete picture of the "original" text.

1.1.3 A codicological model of manuscript description

The form of any given codex is primarily defined by its content[148] - meaning the books/texts that are included and the arrangement in which they are placed together in the codex (the composition). In the case of the Scriptures, the contents clearly reflect their function: the reason for which the codex was produced and the manner in which it was used in the church. In addition to this, an awareness of the heritage and the conditions under which the codex was formed, throw highly interesting historical light on the choices behind the content and thus the form of the codex. The time and place of copying are important parameters to take in account, as are the textual presentation and configuration (how the text is placed on the page and in which order); the textual form of the included books (recension); the status of the additional texts that follow or precede the body of text, maybe in another script, or in the margins (commentaries, lectionary equipment, tables etc.); the format of the

---

[136] B.M. Metzger, 'Special Features of Biblical Manuscripts: Miniatures', in *Manuscripts of the Greek Bible. An Introduction to Greek Palaeography* (New York and Oxford, 1981), 44-46; K. Weitzmann, *Op. Cit.* (Princeton 1970); N.P. Kondakov, *Op. Cit.* (New York, reprint 1970); H.I. Bordier, *Description des peintures et autres ornaments contenu dans les Manuscrits Grecs de la Bibliothèque Nationale* (Paris, 1883).

[137] T. Uspenskij, *Op. Cit.* (Sofia, 1907); J. Strzygowski, *Op. Cit.* (Leipzig, 1899).

[138] J. Strzygowski, *Op. Cit.* (Leipzig, 1899).

[139] K. Weitzmann and G. Galavaris, *Op. Cit.* (Princeton, New Jersey,1990).

[140] S.M. Pelekanides, P.C. Christou, C. Mavropoulos–Tsioumis, S.N. Kadas (Eds.), *The Treasures of Mount Athos: Illuminated Manuscripts* (Athens, 1973, 1875, 1979, 1991).

[141] A. Marava–Chatzinicolaou and C. Toufexi–Paschou, *Catalogue of Illuminated Byzantine Manuscripts of the National Library of Greece. Vol II: Manuscripts of New Testament Texts 13th – 15th Century* (Athens, 1985); Idem, *Op. Cit., Vol I: Manuscripts of New Testament Texts 10th – 12th Century* (Athens, 1978); P. Buberl, *Die Miniaturenhandschriften der Nationalbibliothek in Athen* (Vienna, 1917).

[142] G. Vikan (Ed.), *Illuminated Greek Manuscripts from American Collections* (Princeton, 1973); P. Buberl, *Die byzantinischen Handschriften I: Die Wiener Dioskurides und die Wiener Genesis. Beschreibendes Verzeichnis der illuminierten Handschriften in Österreich* (Leipzig, 1937-1938); P. Buberl and H. Gerstinger, *Die byzantinischen Handschriften II: Die Handschriften des X bis XVIII Jahrhunderts. Die illuminierten Handschriften und Inkunabeln der Nationalbibliothek in Wien* (Leipzig, 1938).

[143] Catalogues: *Monumenta Musicae Byzantinae: Collection of Microfilms and Photographs*, Ed. C. Troelsgerd [Website publication: www.igl.ku.dk/MMB/mmb.html], Institute for Greek and Latin, University of Copenhagen; G.T. Stathis, Τὰ χειρόγραφα Βυζαντινῆς μουσικῆς Ἅγιον Ὄρος. Κατάλογος περιγραφικὸς τῶν χειρογράφων κωδίκων Βυζαντινῆς μουσικῆς τῶν ἀπὸ κείμενων ἐν ταῖς βιβλιοθήκαις τῶν ἱερῶν μονῶν καὶ σκητῶν τοῦ Ἁγίου Ὄρους, τ. 1-3 (Athens, 1975, 1976, 1993); A. Jakovljevič, *Catalogue of Byzantine Chant Manuscripts in the Monastic and Episcopal Libraries of Cyprus*, (Publications of the Cyprus Research Centre, 15) (Nicosia, 1990); A. Gastoué, *Introduction a la Paléographie Musicale Byzantine. Catalogue des Manuscrits de Musique Byzantine de la Bibliothèque Nationale de Paris et des Bibliothèques Publiques de France* (Paris, 1907).

[144] See paragraph **1.4** *Examples of Codicological Research of the Byzantine Manuscripts* where recent interest in these edition forms is discussed.

[145] Forerunners were H. Brockhaus, 'Die Miniaturmalereien', in *Die Kunst in den Athos-Klöstern* (Leipzig, 1891), 167-242; H. Bordier, *Op. Cit.* (Paris, 1883). In the area of Byzantine chant manuscripts: A. Gastoué, *Op. Cit.* (Paris, 1907): Ie Partie, Classement & Catalogue des Manuscrits, 59-99 and Appendice: Plance I-VII.

[146] H. Buchthal and H. Belting, *Patronage in Thirteenth-Century Constantinople: An Atelier of Late Byzantine Book Illumination and Calligraphy* (Washington, 1978).

[147] O. Mazal, *Op. Cit.* (Turnhout, 1992), 'General Prerequisites for the Processing of Manuscripts', 9-15.

[148] H. von Soden, *Op. Cit.* (Göttingen, 1911), v.1, 94 and A. Rahlfs, *Op. Cit.* (Berlin, 1914), XVIII-XIX already stipulated the contents as central items in their descriptions.

codex (folio, half folio, quarto, octavo); the script form (uncials, minuscules and their derivatives); the scope of the codex (the number of folio's); the size of the page, the writing material etc. A codicological approach to the Byzantine ecclesiastical manuscripts that takes all these parameters into account[149], demands in the first place, then, a complete description of the content and form of the individual codices, with attention for:

1) [the contents]. The content of the main text of the codex, whether the codex is complete or fragmented, and if it includes texts that were copied in at a later date; the registration of those texts or textual elements, which do not seem to be of immediate relevance for biblical studies - patristic, liturgical, hymnographical or hagiographical, and even classical.

2) [the apparatus[150]]. The secondary texts of the codex: a) the commentaries/scholia (following or alternating with the main text, in the margins); b) the liturgical elements (lectionary equipment); c) the hymnographic elements (ecphonetic notation above the texts); d) introductory and auxiliary materials (short description of contents, kephalaia, hypotheseis, prologues, Eusebian and Euthalian tables of canons, etc.).

3) [the design]. The age (date), the script form (uncial, minuscule), the folio's, format, writing materials, size, columns, lines, etc.

4) [the iconography]. The iconographic furbishment of the codex (contents of the icons, their number, their style, their position in the overall composition, their function in the manuscripts).

5) [technical condition]. The technical condition of the manuscript (codicology in the specific sense), the ornamentation and artistic design of the cover and the internal aesthetic arrangements and illustrations.

6) [the provenance]. The scribe and place of origin (if known), the current possessor, the religious or secular purpose/function (destined/intended for liturgical ends, for a church or monastery, for private use of secular devotes (Byzantine emperors or their family, magistrates or rich citizens), for a skeuophilakion or library, for private study of an erudite).

7) [the size and format]. Details concerning the size and format to analyse the manner in which the materials (contents) in the codex were incorporated and presented.

The existing catalogues of manuscripts are a major point of departure, to gather codicological data and trace the manuscripts' whereabouts. But the existing catalogues have been set up according to specialised needs: Aland, von Soden, Gregory, Scrivener for the New Testament; Stroth, Holmes/Parsons, Rahlfs, Fraenkel for the Old Testament; Karo/Lietzman, Faulhaber, Mühlenberg for the Catenae; and Ehrhard for the homiletic/hagiographic manuscripts. In the following paragraphs we will explore the advantages and shortcomings of these specialised catalogues, in our view. In chapter 2 we will set out the liturgical hypothesis that will lead us to redistribute the manuscripts in these catalogues according to new liturgico-codicological parameters in support of the thesis.

---

[149] O. Mazal, *Op. Cit.* (Turnhout, 1992), 'Guidelines for the Cataloguing of Manuscripts', 16-34.

[150] The patristic apparatus could comprise: 1) aids for public reading of the Scriptures (ἀνάγνωσις) according to the Byzantine calendar, including a complex system of textual divisions (ἀναγνώσεις or ἀναγνώσματα), the sequences of lessons and the tables belong to this (C.R. Gregory, *Textkritik des Neuen Testaments* (Leipzig, 1900), I, 'Griechische Liturgische Bücher', 327-342); 2) explicit hermeneutical aids, including scholia (σχόλια) and comments (ἑρμηνεῖαι) of scribes and fathers (H. von Soden, *Die Schriften des Neuen Testaments in ihrer ältesten erreichbaren Textgestalt hergestellt auf Grund ihrer Textgeschichte* (Göttingen, 1911), 'Die gelehrte Bearbeitungen der neutestamentlichen Schriften', 525-704); 3) textual-hermeneutical elements such as the super/subscriptions to the books (ἐπιγραφαί/ὑπογραφαί), the arrangement of the text in chapter divisions (κεφάλαια), the titles of chapters (τίτλοι), the number of verses (στοιχεῖαι), the Eusebian canons, the hypotheses (ὑποθέσεις), lives of the evangelists (βιοί), Euthalian apparatus, musical signs above the text (ecphonetic notation), biblical references in the margins (μαρτυρίαι). B.M. Metzger and B.D. Ehrman, *Op. Cit.* (New York/Oxford, 2005), '"Helps for readers" in New Testament Manuscripts', 33-47; C.R. Gregory, *Op. Cit.* (Leipzig, 1900), v.2, 'Geschichte der Kritik: Äussere Form des Textes', 849-906; H. von Soden, *Op. Cit.* (Göttingen, 1911), 293-485: 'Die in den neut. Handschriften vorkommenden textlichen Beigaben zu dem Wortlaut der neut. Schriften'. For patristic apparatuses in Greek OT manuscripts, see H.B. Swete and R.R. Ottley, *An Introduction to the Old Testament in Greek* (Peabody, Mass., 1989), 'Titles, Grouping, Number, and Order of the Books', 197-230; 'Text divisions: *Stichi*, Chapters, Lections, *Catenae*, &c.', 342-366. Cf. B.M. Metzger, *Manuscripts of the Greek Bible. An Introduction to Greek Palaeography* (New York and Oxford, 1981), 'Special Features of Biblical Manuscripts', 33-48.

1.2 Advantages and Disadvantages of Specialised Catalogues

The Byzantine manuscripts that are dispersed over the many local and national libraries in East and West are (more or less adequately) represented in the catalogues of these libraries, in so far as they are known to us at all.[151] In some specialised catalogues, i.e. in 1) the *Kurzgefasste Liste der griechischen Handschriften des Neuen Testaments* by K. Aland et al. (Berlin / New York, 1994²)[152], 2) the *Verzeichnis der griechischen Handschriften des Alten Testaments für das Septuaginta Unternehmen* by A. Rahlfs (Berlin, 1914)[153] and up-dated by D. Fraenkel (Göttingen, 2004, only part I), 3) the descriptive catalogue of homiletic (and hagiographic) codices in *Überlieferung und Bestand der hagiographischen und homiletischen Literatur der griechischen Kirche, von den Anfängen bis zum Ende des 16. Jahrhunderts, I-III* by Ehrhard (Leipzig / Berlin, 1937-52) and 4) the *Catenarum Graecorum Catalogus* compiled by Karo und Lietzmann (Göttingen, 1902), the Byzantine manuscripts have been extracted from the individual library catalogues and reorganized in clearly defined, separate, categories (NT, OT, Hagiography/Homiletics, Catena etc). When studying these catalogues, a clear overview of the (number of) extant collected and selected codices of any group of manuscripts is reached.

One major consequence, however, of such specific categorisation is that the full codicological information of any given codex falls away (completely or in part), and one loses the overview of the codex forms in their entirety. The specialised catalogues are monuments of research without which it would have been impossible for the present researcher to have gained a picture at all of the extent, whereabouts and nature of the extant manuscripts. In this chapter, however, we pay attention to certain aspects of each of the catalogues which we encountered as "obstacles" when trying to develop a codicological overview of the material at hand. This we do without in any way intending to do injustice to the intrinsic value of the catalogues. Below we point out some of the choices made in the catalogues of Aland, Rahlfs, von Soden, Ehrhard and Karo and Lietzmann, which illustrate our difficulty.

1.2.1 Aland's *Kurzgefasste Liste*

Aland's *Liste*, which was the continuation of Gregory's *Die Griechischen Handschriften des Neuen Testaments* (Leipzig, 1908)[154], in its turn based on Gregory's voluminous *Textkritik des Neuen Testamentes* (Leipzig, 1900-1909, Bd. I-III), being a formal enumeration of an accumulating series of manuscripts, and presenting information based on his specifically selected parameters, does not present all the concrete codicological information found in the manuscripts[155]. The lectionary equipment especially was omitted from the indexed series of codices[156]. To our mind, lectionary data is of far-reaching consequence for the determination of the manuscripts.

From Aland's *Liste* one receives the impression that there existed certain standard codex forms: e (= evangelion), ap (= apostolos), eap (= apostolo-evangelion), eapr (= apostolo-evangelion and revelation). Parallel to these basic text codex forms, the lectionaries are distinguished as: *l (*evangelion-lectionary*)*, *l*a (apostolos-lectionary), *l*+a (apostolo-evangelion-lectionary). However, because beside the standard codex forms, a great variety of additional materials intrinsically belonging to these codices was not made visible in the *Liste*, it is not possible to gain a full codicological picture of these forms. For example, Aland omitted to mention which NT codices contained OT texts (he does this only very incidentally and inconsistently), focusing entirely on the NT text. He similarly made no mention of patristic texts, liturgical texts (only incidentally), or texts of classical literature. To supplement this should be a first task of the *Catalogue* that is proposed in this thesis. A second task would be to attempt to rediscover original 'edition forms' of the Scriptures as transmitted in the Byzantine manuscripts, to show how they evolved from their use in the Byzantine liturgy. These standard forms (e, a, ap …), considered from a codicological point of view, could be a new point of departure of textual research in the narrower sense of the word, since it is the codex forms that provide the actual criteria (determinative factors) for the textual evaluation of the manuscripts. Such a criteria would be, for example, to study different related codex forms together: the [continuous] text Evangelion codices (e) should be researched together with the Evangelion

---

[151] See chapter 4.

[152] Built on the Lists of Wettstein, Scholz, Scrivener, Gregory and von Soden.

[153] On the basis of the Lists of Stroth, Holmes-Parsons, Lagarde, Tischendorf.

[154] K. Aland adopted not only the model and Gregory's enumeration of manuscripts, but also the title from this undertaking: 'Die Grund für die sofortige Herausgabe dieser kurzgefasste Liste…'., p. 20.

[155] The codicological information of the Byzantine NT codices, which was collected by the INTF in Münster (Germany), brought together on card-files and which forms the basis of the *Kurzgefasste Liste*, can be consulted on location. Moreover, micro-films are attainable and there is an internet site with reproductions of integral manuscripts.

[156] By kind permission we were able to consult the card-files in order to check the information concerning the lectionary equipments in the INTF. In von Soden's *Die Schriften des Neuen Testaments in ihrer ältesten erreichbaren Textgestalt hergestellt auf Grund ihrer Textgeschichte* (Göttingen, 1911²) one can find precise data concerning the lectionary equipment and other essential information with regard to the contents of the codices in which the NT books were compiled.

lectionaries (*l*) and the Evangelion commentaries (eK and *l*K), to which the homiletic manuscripts inherently belong (the last category having been omitted by Aland).

Aland included the commentary manuscripts[157] of the Greek NT in the main body of the *Liste* (distinguishing them with the letter K [eK etc.], and when referring to the lectionary manuscripts, with the symbol *l*K etc.). No distinction, however, was made by Aland between "catena" and "commentary" manuscripts, as does Rahlfs. Aland gave all the Greek NT commentary manuscripts a K serial number, and so implicitly agreed with their homogeneity. Interesting is that he placed the commentaries in the same list as the biblical text manuscripts, thus placing them on the same line, whereas the lectionaries he placed in a separate list (including *l*K). The major 'homiletic commentary' group was not adopted at all.

1.2.2 H. von Soden's *Die Schriften des Neuen Testaments*

The work of von Soden, *Die Schriften des Neuen Testaments in ihrer ältesten erreichbaren Textgestalt hergestellt auf Grund ihrer Textgeschichte*, I (Göttingen, 1911, 2nd edition) launched a new complicated system of classification[158] according to content and manuscript age[159]. Byzantine terminology was 're-introduced' (the δ -, ε - and α- codices).[160] The commentary codices were given serious attention and analysis[161]. In the first place the manuscripts are listed according to their codex formations: tetraevangelion-commentaries, praxapostoloscommentaries, and then according to smaller textual units or to single biblical books. Of great value is von Soden's registration of lectionary equipment[162] [Lect, Lect^{Text}, Lect^{Tab}][163] in the 'pure text' manuscripts[164], and also in the group of commentary manuscripts. However, von Soden did not, for practical and principal reasons, incorporate the lectionary manuscripts in his research plan.[165] Other contents than only the NT biblical texts[166] in one and the same manuscript were registered (liturgical, patristic etc.).[167]

1.2.3 Rahlfs' *Verzeichnis*

The *Verzeichnis der griechischen Handschriften des Alten Testaments* (Berlin, 1914) of Rahlfs is based on the earlier study of the Greek OT manuscripts by Stroth[168] (catalogue research), and the extensive edition of the

---

[157] The division of the different categories of commentaries can be deduced from the *Sigelkonkordanz II. v. Soden: Gregory 4.-20.*, in Aland's *Liste*, 401-405. Von Soden's division is: Kommentarcodices zu den Evangelien (a–g); Kommentarcodd zum Praxapostolos (a – d) including the Apocalypse commentaries [= d].

[158] B.M. Metzger and B.D. Ehrman, *Op. Cit.* (New York/Oxford, 2005), 186.

[159] H. von Soden, 'Gruppierung des in Liste I nachgewiesenen Gesamtbestandes an neu. Codd nach Inhalt und Alter', in *Die Schriften des Neuen Testaments in ihrer ältesten erreichbaren Textgestalt hergestellt auf Grund ihrer Textgeschichte* (1911), 94-95.

[160] The terminology was derived from the Greek titles 'διαθήκη', 'τετραευαγγέλιον' (simply εὐαγγέλιον and 'πραξαπόστολος' (or plainly ἀπόστολος). Of importance is especially the 'codex unit' of the Apostle, here correctly represented in contrast to the incorrect text unit a = Acts + Cath. Epist. (without Epist. of Paul). See the remark of von Soden on page 42 concerning the Greek terminology.

[161] H. von Soden, *Op. Cit.* (Göttingen, 1911), 'Kommentarcodices zu den Evangelien', 249-270; 'Kommentarcodd zum Praxapostolos', 270-289 [Statistischer Überblick: Kommantarhandschriften, 290-292]; Die gelehrten Bearbeitungen der neutestamentlichen Schriften', 525-704.

[162] H. von Soden, *Op. Cit.* (Göttingen, 1911), 99: 'Dagegen ist für die Frage nach der Art des Gebrauchs der neut. Schriften im Mittelalter die Feststellung wertvoll, in wie grossem Umfang die sie enthaltenden Codd durch entsprechende Ausstattung zur Benutzung als Lectionare eingerichtet waren'.

[163] See the descriptive system of von Soden, *Op. Cit.* (Göttingen, 1911), 101-102, Lect = Lektionenvermerk am Rande; Lect^{text}= Lektionsanfänge rot im text; Lect^{tab}= Listen der Lektionen (in the beginning or at the end) and justification on pages 99-100 [Lektionen Listen are indicated by syn= synaxarion and men= menologion.

[164] There is no such dividing line or gap between 'pure text' and 'lectionary text' as is often assumed. If one considers the 'lectionary equipment' of the pure text manuscripts, then it appears, that a considerable part of all Byzantine manuscripts could be called 'lectionaries'. See the descriptive system of von Soden, *Op. Cit.* (Göttingen, 1911), 101-102, Lect = Lektionenvermerk am Rande; Lect^{text}= Lektionsanfänge rot im text; Lect^{tab}= Listen der Lektionen (in the beginning or at the end) and justification on pages 99-100.

[165] H. von Soden, *Op. Cit.* (Göttingen, 1911), 19-20, 'Auf die L e k t i o n a r i e n ist nach langem Schwanken verzichtet worden. Erstlich schien das Material der Volltexte doch reichlich genug. Sodann war zu besorgen, dass die Textgeschichte der Lektionarien unter Umständen ihre eigenen Wege ging, und so ihre Herbeiziehung ebenso leicht das Bild verwirren als aufhellen könnte. Andrerseits schien es leichter, wenn erst die Wandlungen des Schrifttextes klar waren, von hier aus auch die Geschichte der Lesetexte zu entwirren. Freilich war nicht zu verkennen, dass von ihnen aus auch ein Einfluss auf die Abschriften des Gesamttextes sich geltend gemacht haben konnte, sodass für diese oder jene Etappe von dem Lektionartext aus auf ihren Ursprung Licht fallen dürfte'.

[166] H. von Soden, *Op. Cit.* (Göttingen, 1911), 95: (...)'sollen die Handschriften nach der buchtechnischen Seite charakterisiert werden. Dazu gehört es auch, wenn neut. Schriften etwa mit Schriften anderen Charakters verbunden worden sind'. Cf. also p. 102.

[167] In many Byzantine manuscripts are contained, in addition to the NT and/or OT books (or parts of these books or liturgical compilations), other works of the fathers, liturgical texts and hagiographical materials of great variety and quantity.

[168] F.A. Stroth, "Versuch eines Verzeichnisses der Handschriften der LXX", in *Repertorium für Biblische und Morgenländische Litteratur*, 5 (1779), 94-134; 8 (1781), 177-205; 11 (1782), 45-72. Stroth's work was a first endeavour to put together a catalogue of the OT manuscripts. He ordered the catalogue around its contents.

Septuagint by Holmes and Parsons[169]. Rahlfs distinguishes three main groups: a) plain Bible texts (Einfache Bibeltexte), b) catena (Catenen) and c) commentaries (Commentare). By discussing and registering all three, he implicitly indicates the close affinity between these distinct groups of biblical text and patristic commentaries. He presents a great number of the Greek OT manuscripts, but certainly not "all" relevant codices, since he omitted the main group of homiletic commentary manuscripts.[170] A synoptic overview of the commentary manuscripts of the Greek OT was provided by Rahlfs in '*Übersicht über das handschriftliche Material für die einzelnen Teile des A.T*'[171], brought together under the headings of 'Catenen' or 'Commentare', according to their categories (Octateuch, etc.) and in chronological order of the codices[172]. The short references in the *Übersicht* inform us about the libraries where the manuscripts are "presently" housed (in 1914) and their main contents; the catena manuscripts received serial numbers, but the commentary manuscripts did not, thus in the end excluding them significantly from the main group of text codices.[173]

1.2.4 Rahlfs/Fraenkel' *Verzeichnis*

Compared to Rahlfs, an important change in the *Verzeichnis* brought about by Fraenkel[174] is the demarcation line that Fraenkel introduces to separate the manuscripts of the period up until the $8^{th}/9^{th}$ century, from the period running from the 8th to the 16th centuries. Part 1 appeared in 2004 and part 2 is still under development. The latter is more relevant for our goal, because it concerns the period ($8/9^{th}$-16th centuries) from which the extant codex forms stem, whilst from the preceding period we have primarily fragments or parts of codices from which the form cannot be clearly deduced. This of course does not imply that these codex forms did not exist during this early period. Part 2 will also describe the Prophetologion manuscripts, which are highly interesting for our purpose, because the roots of this type of OT lectionary manuscript are regarded to be very deep in the textual and lesson tradition of the church. Of especial interest are the detailed descriptions of the uncial codices of the $4^{th}/5^{th}$ centuries.

1.2.5 Ehrhard's *Überlieferung und Bestand*

The homiletic commentaries, which Ehrhard[175] collected and classified in the context of his hagiographic manuscript research, are the Panegyrica homilies (festival orations) and later Kyriakodromia (Sunday orations). These are in fact commentaries on the Festival and Sunday lessons (Evangelion and Apostolos) which follow the main thread of the liturgical calendar. Ehrhard demonstrates the close connection between the hagiographic and homiletic codices. Yet, Ehrhard did not note all the homiletic codices, only those (and these are considerable indeed), which in his opinion were related to the hagiographic manuscript materials. He set up a classification of both categories.

1.2.6 Karo/Lietzmann's *Catenarum Graecorum Catalogus*

Karo and Lietzmann and in their footsteps later catena manuscript investigators (for example, Petit, Doreval, Mühlenberg, Krikonis, Devreesse[176]) brought by means of their inventory, the *Catenarum Graecorum Catalogus*

---

[169] R. Holmes and J. Parsons, *Vetus Testamentum Graecum cum variis lectionibus*, I-V (Oxford, 1798-1827); H.B. Swete and R.R. Ottley, *An Introduction to the Old Testament in Greek* (Peabody, Mass., 1989), 184-187.

[170] A. Rahlfs, *Op. Cit.* (Berlin, 1914), xii.

[171] A. Rahlfs, *Op. Cit.* (Berlin, 1914), 373-439.

[172] The main part of Rahlfs' *Verzeichnis* is alphabetical and provides a full description of the manuscripts. This section of the *Übersicht*, however, is conjectural, since the dating of manuscripts is, as is commonly known, difficult or controversial in many cases. There is a communis opinion about the age of most manuscripts [the dated manuscripts are, of course, less problematic]. The same can be said of the NT and other categories of Byzantine Greek manuscripts.

[173] A. Rahlfs, *Op. Cit.* (Berlin, 1914), xii: '... und die Hss. Die nur als Zeugen für den Tekst der Commentare, nicht als direkte Zeugen für den LXX-Tekst System gelten können'.

[174] D. Fraenkel, *Verzeichnis der griechischen Handschriften des Alten Testaments von Alfred Rahlfs. Die Überlieferung bis zum VIII Jahrhundert*, Bd. 1, 1, (Septuaginta Supplement) (Göttingen, 2004).

[175] A. Ehrhard, *Überlieferung und Bestand der hagiographischen und homiletischen Literatur der griechischen Kirche, von den Anfängen bis zum Ende des 16. Jahrhunderts* (Leipzig-Berlin, 1937-1952).

[176] F. Petit, *La chaîne sur la Genèse. Édition intégrale* (Louvain, 1991-1993); G. Doreval, *Les Chaines exegetiques greques sur les Psaumes: contributions à l'étude d'une forme littéraire* (Leuven, 1986-1995); F. Petit, *Catenae graecae in Genesim et in Exodum. II: Collectio Coisliniana in Genesim* (Turnhout / Louvain, 1986); F. Petit, *Catenae graecae in Genesim et in Exodum. I: Catena Sinaitica* (Turnhout / Louvain, 1977); E. Mühlenberg, *Psalmenkommentare aus der Katenenüberlieferung* (Berlin, 1975-1978). C.T. Krikonis, Συναγωγὴ Πατέρων εἰς τὸ κατὰ Λουκᾶν Εὐαγγέλιον ὑπὸ Νικῆτα Ἡρακλείας (κατὰ τὸν κώδικα Ἰβήρων 371) (Thessaloniki, 1973); R. Devreesse, *Les anciens commentateures grecs de l' Octateuque et des Rois. Fragments tirés des chaînes* (Cité du Vatican, 1959).

(Göttingen, 1902)[177], research of this particular group of commentary manuscripts to scholarly attention. In fact, these Σεῖραι or catena, compilations of selected passages from the commentaries of well-known Byzantine fathers (see the List of Lemmata in Krikonis for example[178]), are "annotated" collective commentaries of many different fathers. This huge group of Byzantine catena manuscripts underlines that the biblical interpretation of an individual is only of interest, if it can be placed in the Byzantine patristic tradition of biblical exegesis. By regrouping the catena contents into (in this catalogue artificially remodelled) groups of NT writings (catena to Matthew etc.), the editors passed over the codicological contexts and paradigms, in which the catena commentaries were fashioned.

Box 1:

Overview of the specialised catalogues

[1] **Aland** (in 1968 and the second edition in 1994) made an inventory of and selected Greek NT manuscripts, and this NT List was constantly up-dated; it contains not only the text codices, but also the commentary codices (including the results of **Gregory**) and lectionary codices (including the results of von Soden and Karo/Lietzmann).

[2] **Rahlfs** (1914) made an inventory of and selected Greek OT manuscripts, not only the text codices, but also the commentary codices (catena, as well as commentaries in the strict sense) and lectionary codices. His catalogue was reworked by **Fraenkel** (2004) and to date only Part I, i.e., the codices of the first eight centuries has been published. For our study the huge mass of Greek manuscripts starting in the 9th century (Part II) will be of great interest.

[3] **Ehrhard** (in 1937-1952) made an inventory of and selected a great deal of the biblical commentaries of a homiletic character (but not all homiletic categories were included, since his manuscript investigations were concentrated on the hagiographic materials), filling the gap, which was left open by Rahlfs and Aland. An updated inventory of the used codices and their libraries/holdings was compiled by L. Perria, *I Manoscritti Citati da Albert Ehrhard, Indice di; A. Ehrhard, Überlieferung und Bestand der hagiographischen und homiletischen Literatur der griechischen Kirche, I-III, Leipzig-Berlin, 1937-1952* (Roma 1979).

[4] **Karo/Lietzmann** (1902) made an inventory of and selected (a considerable group of) the catena commentary manuscripts, both of the OT and NT. The editors, however, did not escape "atomisme", in selecting their materials according to self-construed sections, forcing them into systematic arrangement of the biblical books, moving away from the codex formations in which the catena were transmitted.

1.3 Existing Paradigms of Manuscript Classification

There are two basic paradigms of classified Greek biblical manuscripts, one for NT and another for OT research. These paradigms were developed independently and are unconnected in approach. In addition, the classification paradigms of the homiletic and catena manuscripts were also elaborated independently from the other departments of biblical & patristic studies. In this paragraph we will analyse these four paradigms (NT, OT, homiletic and catena) in content and form, in order to assess in how far they could contribute to, or are removed from a codicological approach, with a view also to the construction of a new catalogue and reclassification of the manuscripts.

1.3.1. The paradigm of classifying Byzantine NT manuscripts [Gregory/Aland]

The first specialised catalogue-model and the implied classification of manuscripts we will discuss is the one produced to classify the New Testament manuscripts[179]. It was set up by Wettstein[180], later adopted by

---

[177] G. Karo und H. Lietzmann, 'Catenarum Graecorum Catalogus', in *Nachrichten der Gesellschaft der Wissenschaften zu Göttingen, Philol.hist. Klasse* (Göttingen, 1902), 1-66; 299-350; 559-620.

[178] C.T. Krikonis, *Op. Cit.* (Thessaloniki, 1973), 'κατάλογος λήμματων κατὰ συγγραφεῖς', 521-530 [№ 1-70, of which the more important commentators are: Chrysostom (συν. 859); Cyril of Alexandria (συν. 556); Basil of Caesarea (συν. 244); Gregory of Nyssa (συν. 189); Gregory of Nazianz (συν. 129); Titus of Bostra (συν. 128); Eusebius of Caesarea (συν. 126); Athanasius of Alexandria (συν. 121); Origen (συν. 112); Isodore of Pelusium (συν. 98); Severus of Antiochia (συν. 57); Maximus Confessor (συν. 49); John Geometris (συν. 47); Symeon Metaphrastes (συν. 46); Theodoret of Cyrrhus (συν. 44); Photius (συν. 37); Macarius the Egyptian (συν. 32) etc. There are, moreover: ἀνεπίγραφα (συν. 46) and ἀνώνυμος (συν. 75)].

[179] The list provides the current Gregory-Aland number assigned to each manuscript [Hss.-Nr.], with details in parallel columns about: its contents [Inhalt], age [Jh.], writing material [Beschr.stoff], the number of extant pages [Blatt-zahl], the number of columns [Spalten] and lines per page [Zeilen], the format [Format] and the library classification where the manuscript is housed [Aufbewahrungsort].

[180] The edition of J.J. Wettstein (Ed.), 'Η Καινὴ Διαθήκη. *Novum Testamentum Graecum editionis receptae cum lectionibus variantibus Codicum MSS* (...), (Amsterdam, 1751-1752) contained a critical apparatus, in which the practice of indicating the uncial manuscripts with Roman letters and the cursive manuscripts with Arabic numerals was introduced. In the Gospels his list includes the uncials A to O, and the cursives 1 to 112; in the Acts and Catholic Epistles, A to G, 1 to 58; in the Pauline Epistles, A to H, 1 to 60; in Revelation, A to C, 1 to 28; besides 24 Evangeliaria and 4 Apostoli. Cf. T.H. Darlow and H.F. Moule (Eds.), *Op. Cit.* (New York, 1963), II, 629-630.

Gregory[181] and elaborated by Aland and resulted in the *Kurzgefasste Liste der griechischen Handschriften des Neuen Testaments* (Berlin / New York, 1994²).[182] The catalogue was developed by the INTF (Münster) in the context of the NT edition-project, to support the undertaking of producing critical editions of the Greek NT[183] and thus primarily served textual research ends. In this catalogue one can find all known available NT manuscripts and manuscript fragments numbered in continuous series: papyri: P^1- P^{99}; uncials: 01 (א) – 0306; minuscules: 1-2856 (note that there is a large number of open serial numbers – because manuscripts were lost over time, or merged with other codices etc)[184]. Not only were the (more or less) complete codices registered according to their codex forms (e, ap etc.), but also incomplete manuscripts and fragments. Commentary codices were arranged in the same manner according to their codex formation (eK, apK etc.), continuous text and commentary/catena codices were placed in the same listing. The lectionaries (Lektionare) were numbered separately, comprising No 1-2403. The papyri manuscripts were also enumerated separately and comprise No P^1- P^{99}. The NT manuscripts were listed according to different classes, based on a) writing material (papyrus, parchment, and paper) and b) the age assigned to the script form, *uncials* and *minuscules*[185].

Already in the Wettstein edition (Amsterdam, 1751-1752), the NT manuscripts were grouped into collection units on the grounds of their content, i.e. the four Gospels together (= e); the Acts and Catholic Letters (= a); the Letters of Paul (fourteen Epistles, including Hebrews) (= p); and the Revelation of John (= r). Composite manuscripts were indicated by the use of combined symbols (ea, ap, eap etc.). Beside these categories another group was created, which was set sharply apart from the afore-mentioned (pure) text manuscript groups - namely the 'lectionary manuscripts' (*l*). The sign *l* was used for the whole group of lectionary manuscripts, including particular groups such as the Gospel lectionaries (the lessons from the four Gospels according to the schedule of the Byzantine ecclesiastical year); the Apostle lectionaries (l^a) (the lessons from the Acts, the Catholic Epistles and the Pauline Epistles); lectionaries in which the Gospel and Apostle lessons were combined (l^{+a}); lectionaries with commentary (*l*K).[186]

Each category (Evangelion, Apostolos, Apostolo-evangelion) was again subdivided into various types of lectionary codices[187], distinguished according to lessons for the Sundays (κυριακαί), for the Saturdays and Sundays (σαββατο-κυριακαί) and for the weekdays (καθημεριναί). The adopted sigla *l*, l^a, l^{+a} signify either a) the whole Evangelion or Apostolos codex, or b) series of lessons incorporated in other codices (liturgical, patristic etc.). They are registered and characterised in the following manner[188]:

1) a first group of codices containing complete series of lessons, for every day of the whole year according to the movable [κινητός] and immovable [ἀκινητός] cycles of the Byzantine calendar (Pascha to Pascha and September to August), indicated by the symbol *l*e = ἑβδομάδες [ἐβδ], that is, lessons for all days of all the weeks of the Byzantine liturgical calendar;
2) a second group of codices containing less complete series of NT lessons, every day for the period between Easter and Pentecost, but for the rest of the ecclesiastical year for Saturday-Sunday lessons only (*l*esk = ἐβδ + σαββατο-κυριακαί);
3) a third group of codices providing series of NT lessons, for the whole year only the Saturday-Sunday lessons (*l*sk = σαββατο-κυριακαί);
4) a fourth group of codices providing only series of lessons for the Sundays (*l*k = κυριακαί);
5) a fifth group of codices containing a compilation of selected NT lessons for particular days (*l*sel);

---

[181] The modern generally accepted classification is that of C.R. Gregory in *Op. Cit.* (Leipzig, 1908), 20: 1. Grosschriften; 2. Papyri; 3. Kleinschriften; 4. Lesebücher (with *l* and l^{+a} and l^a). Here the terminology of 'Kurzgefasste Liste' was coined. The contents of the manuscripts were indicated as follows: e (the four Gospels); a (the Acts and the Catholic Epistles); p (the Pauline Epistles); r (Revelation).

[182] The structure of the work is as follows: 1) Vorwort with statistical remarks, VII-IX; 2) Erläuterungen und Abkürzungen, XIII-XIX; 3) Papyri: P^1- P^{99}. [ms/items]; 4) Majuskeln: 01 (א) – 0306; 5) Minuskeln: 1 – 2856; 6) Lektionare: *l* 1 – *l* 2403; 7) Sigelkonkordanzen: I. Tischendorf: Gregory; II. von Soden: Gregory; III. Gregory: von Soden; 8) Bibliotheksverzeichnis, 431-507.

[183] K. Aland (and others), *Op. Cit.* (Berlin / New York, 1994), Foreword, 7.

[184] Updates can be found in J.K. Elliott, *A Bibliography of Greek New Testament Manuscripts* (Cambridge, 2000): Introduction, 1-12. The status quo in 1998 was: Papyri: P^{100}- P^{115}; Majuskeln: 0307 – 0309; Minuskeln: 2857 – 2862; Lektionare: *l* 2404 – 2412. That is circa 5700 NT manuscript items.

[185] The preference for uncial codices in textual criticism dominates NT and OT research until the present day. The approach of many biblical scholars since the Renaissance, in their search for the most ancient manuscripts, could be called historico-philological (implying the objective assessment of individual manuscripts), rather than codico-philological.

[186] K. Aland (et al.), *Op. Cit.* (Berlin / New York, 1994), XIV. Cf. K. and B. Aland, *The Text of the New Testament* (Leiden, 1987), 128. For an extensive scheme of the classified description of the NT manuscripts see also, K. Aland, "Zur Liste der Neutestamentliche Handschriften. V.", in *Zeitschrift für die neutestamentliche Wissenschaft*, 45.1-2 (1954), 181-182.

[187] C.R. Gregory, in *Op. Cit.*, I (Leipzig, 1900), 339-340, gives a useful and elucidative scheme for a detailed description of lectionary manuscripts.

[188] The distinctions used by Aland were basically adopted from C.R. Gregory, *Op. Cit.*, I (Leipzig, 1900), 335-339, in which the contents of the lectionary manuscripts are discussed and explained in their diverse fashions. Interesting is the historical excursion in which Gregory illustrates these different fashions: stage I only lessons for the Sundays (κυριακαί); stage II also lessons for the Saturday (σαββατο-κυριακαί); stage III lessons for all week-days (καθημεριναί).

6) a sixth group of codices containing NT lessons incorporated in liturgical manuscripts like the Triodion, Pentecostarion, Menaia and others (*l*Lit);
7) finally, a last group of codices comprising unspecified series of NT lessons (*l*unsp).

Not indicated in the *Kurzgefasste Liste* are other in our view essential components of the lectionaries, for example different sorts of tables of lessons at the beginning and/or the end of the codex: συναξάρια and μηνολόγια, or musical signs. Gregory did, in his *Textkritik des Neuen Testamentes* (Leipzig, 1900-1909) include a scheme of lectionary contents[189], but this did not find its way into Aland's *Kurzgefasste Liste,* nor into Gregory's own *Die Griechischen Handschriften des Neuen Testaments* of 1908.

In box 2 below we systematically present Gregory/Aland's subdivision of the whole group of lectionaries, in order to provide a quick overview of the complex variety of the different codex forms found among the body of Byzantine NT manuscripts. Moreover, the divers liturgical functions of the lectionaries are highlighted.

Box 2:
Tables *l* : Lectionaries [Lektionarien] (Gregory/Aland)

I. A Byzantine Lectionary Codices

l : Εὐαγγέλια

*l*e : ἑβδομάδες [ἑβδ]
Evangelion with lessons of all seven days of the week (ἑβδομάδες = καθημεριναί and σαββατο-κυριακαί)

*l*esk : ἑβδ + σαββατο-κυριακαί
Evangelion with lessons of all seven days of the week between Easter and Pentecost/ and lessons (the rest of the year) of the Saturday/Sunday (ἑβδομάδες and σαββατοκυριακαί)

*l*sk : σαβ.-κυρ.
Evangelion with lessons of the Saturday/Sunday only (σαββατοκυριακαί)

*l*k : κυρ.
Evangelion with lessons of the Sunday only (κυριακαί)

*l*sel : ἐκλ.
Evangelion with lessons for particular days (ἐκλόγαι)

*l*Lit : Λειτ.
Evangelion lessons included in a Liturgical codex, i.e. Euchologion (Λειτουργικόν)

*l*Unsp : ἄδηλ.
Evangelion with lessons which cannot be specified (ἄδηλοι)

*l*ᵃ : Ἀπόστολοι

*l*ᵃe : ἑβδ
Apostolos with lessons of all seven days of the week (ἑβδομάδες)

*l*ᵃesk : ἑβδ + σαββατο-κυριακαί
Apostolos with lessons of all seven days of the week between Easter and Pentecost/ and lessons (the rest of the year) of the Saturday/Sunday (ἑβδομάδες and σαββατοκυριακαί)

*l*ᵃsk : σαβ.-κυρ.
Apostolos with lessons of the Saturday/Sunday only (σαββατοκυριακαί)

*l*ᵃk : κυρ.
Apostolos with lessons of the Sunday only (κυριακαί)

*l*ᵃsel : ἐκλ.
Apostolos with lessons for particular days (ἐκλόγαι)

*l*ᵃLit : Λειτ.
Apostle lessons included in a Liturgical codex, i.e. Euchologion (Λειτουργικόν)

*l*ᵃUnsp : ἄδηλ.
Apostoloi lessons which cannot be specified (ἄδηλοι)

---

[189] C.R. Gregory, *Op Cit.* I (Leipzig, 1900), 339-340.

l⁺ᵃ : Ἀποστολοευαγγέλια

l⁺ᵃe : ἐβδ
Apostolo-evangelion with lessons of all seven days of the week (ἐβδομάδες)

l⁺ᵃesk : ἐβδ + σαββατο-κυριακαί
Apostolo-evangelion with lessons of all seven days of the week between Easter and Pentecost/ and lessons
(the rest of the year) of the Saturday/Sunday (ἐβδομάδες and σαββατοκυριακαί)

l⁺ᵃsk : σαβ.-κυρ.
Apostolo-evangelion with lessons of the Saturday/Sunday only (σαββατοκυριακαί)

l⁺ᵃk : κυρ.
Apostolo-evangelion with lessons of the Sunday only (κυριακαί)

l⁺ᵃsel : : ἐκλ.
Apostolo-evangelion with lessons for particular days (ἐκλόγαι)

l⁺ᵃLit : Λειτ.
Apostle-evangelion lessons included in a Liturgical codex, i.e. Euchologion (Λειτουργικόν)

l⁺ᵃUnsp : ἄδηλ.
Apostle-evangelion lessons which cannot be specified (ἄδηλοι)

Sources:
K. Aland (et al.), 'Sigelkonkordanzen', in *Op. Cit.*, II. von Soden: Gregory, (Berlin / New York, 1994), 401-405
C.R. Gregory, *Die Griechischen Handschriften des Neuen Testaments* (Leipzig, 1908)
C.R. Gregory, *Textkritik des Neuen Testamentes*, I-III (Leipzig, 1900-1909)

Commentary manuscripts (= K) were initially not registered as a separate group by Gregory (Leipzig, 1908), but were listed together with the text manuscripts. They were, however, thoroughly studied by von Soden and his collaborators in *Die Schriften des Neuen Testaments in ihrer ältesten erreichbaren Textgestalt hergestellt auf Grund ihrer Textgeschichte* (Gottingen, 1911), who classified them as a separate group[190] and later incorporated in Aland's *Kurzgefasste Liste* (Berlin / New York, 1994).[191] They were distinguished according to their contents, as respectively eK, apK etc. in parallel to the text manuscripts, but without separating or sub-dividing the group into '[text] commentaries' and 'catena commentaries', as did Rahlfs for the Greek OT codices, which we shall see later.

In box 3 we have brought together the NT commentary codices as subdivided by von Soden and adopted by Aland, to draw attention to the connection between the biblical text and the interpretative tradition of the fathers and to make this visible, since relatively little attention has been paid in textual and hermeneutic research to the commentary codices. One will observe that the commentary codices are set up analogously to the text commentary codices (e – eK, ap – apK, r – rK, eap – eapK, eapr – eaprK).

Box 3:

Tables K: NT commentary codices (Aland / von Soden)

K. I[192] : **Tetraevangelion Commentary Codices [eK]**

1. Tetraevangelion Commentary Codices

- Anonymous Evangelion commentary codd [eK[Anon A]], originating between the 5th and 8th/9th centuries;[193]
this commentary edition with scholia in the margins is identified as comprising the commentaries of Chrysostom for
M and J; of Victor of Antioch for Mk and for L Titus of Bostra, referred to as Antiochian commentary codex;
(von Soden: **A**);[194] [Aland: 105 codd; von Soden: 103 codd]

---

[190] H. von Soden, *Op. Cit.*, (Göttingen, 1911), 39: 'Die Kommentare bietenden Codd sind bisher promiscue mit den blossen Textcodices registriert worden. Dies ist falsch. Sie sind ihrem wesen nach Zeugen von Kommentarwerken und als solche zunächst zu untersuchen. Ihre erste Verwendung finden sie bei der diplomatischen Rekonstruktion des betreffenden Kommentars. Und erst der Text, der daraus als von dem Kommentator zu Grund gelegt sich ergiebt, rückt als Zeuge für die Geschichte des Textes ein. Darum müssen sie auch getrennt gebucht werden oder wenigstens ihre eigene Signatur erhalten'.

[191] K. Aland (et al.), 'Sigelkonkordanzen', in *Op. Cit.*, II. von Soden: Gregory, (Berlin / New York, 1994), 401-405.

[192] The numbering K I through K V is ours, in order to mark the order of the whole group of classified K manuscripts.

[193] H. von Soden, *Op.Cit.*, II (Göttingen, 1911), 612.

[194] Compiled by an unknown editor, probably living in the Justinian age.

- Theophylact tetraevangelion commentary codd [eK[Theoph]], (von Soden: **Θ**);
  [Aland: 133 codd; von Soden: 115 codd]

- Zigabenus tetravangelion commentary codd [eK[Zig]], (von Soden: **Z**);
  [Aland: 13 codd; von Soden.: 10 codd]

- An Anonymous Evangelion commentary of unknown origin [eK[Anon B]], (von Soden: **E**ᵉ);
  [Aland: 1 codd; von Soden: 1 cod]

2. Separate Evangelion commentaries

- Nicetas' commentaries to John, Luke and Matthew [ePK: J[Nic], L[Nic], Mt[Nic]], (von Soden: **N**μ, **N**λ, **N**ι);
  [Aland: 32 codd, von Soden: 32 codd → Aland / von Soden: Nμ 7, 6 codd, Nλ 19, 17 codd, Nι: 6, 6 codd]

- Cyril of Alexandria's commentary to John [ePK: J[Cyr]], (von Soden: **K**ι);
  [Aland: 5 codd, von Soden: 5 codd]

- Anonymous catena scholia to Matthew and John [ePK: Mt[Anon], J[Anon]], (von Soden: **C**μ, **C**ι);
  [Aland: John: 13 codd, Mt: 3 codd; von Soden: John: 13 codd, Mt: 3 codd]

K. II: Praxapostolos Commentary Codices [apK]

1. The praxapostolos commentary (Acts, General and Pauline Epistles)

- Oecumenius commentary to the Praxapostolos [apK[Oec]], (von Soden: **O**: APK or PK/KP or PAp);
  [Aland: 25 codd; von Soden: 26 codd]
- Oecumenius' commentary to the Acts and General Epistles combined with Theodoretus' commentary
  to the Pauline Epistles [apK[Oec + Theod]], (von Soden: **OΘδ**); [Aland: 1 cod; von Soden: 2 codd]
- Oecumenius' commentary to the Acts and General Epistles combined with Theophylacts' commentary
  to the Pauline Epistles [apK[Oec + Theoph]], (von Soden: **OΘ**); [Aland: 8 codd; von Soden: 7 codd]
- Anonymous commentary to the Praxapostolos [apK[Anon A]], (von Soden: **E**ᵅ); [Aland: 1 cod; von Soden: 1 cod]

2. The praxapostolos with the Apocalypse commentary

- Oecumenius commentary to the Praxapostolos and the Apocalypse, (von Soden: **O**: APKAp); [Aland:-; von Soden: 8 codd]
- Oecumenius commentary to the AK and Theophylacts' commentary to Paul and the Apocalypse, (von Soden: **OΘ**);
  [Aland: - ; von Soden: 2 codd.]

3. Separate commentaries to parts of the Praxapostolos

Separate commentaries to the Acts and the Seven General Epistles of the Apostles (aK)
- Andreas' commentary to the Acts and the Seven General Epistles, (von Soden: **A**πρ: AK or A or K);
  [Aland: 11 codd; von Soden: 10 codd]
- Oecumenius' commentary to the Acts and the Seven General Epistles, (von Soden: **O**πρ);
  [Aland: 6 codd; von Soden: 6 codd.]

Separate commentaries to the Pauline Epistles (incl. Hebrews) (pK)
- Chrysostom (von Soden: **X**); [Aland: 11 codd; von Soden: 11 codd]
- Theodoret (von Soden: **Θδ**); [Aland: 7 codd; von Soden: 6 codd]
- John of Damascus (von Soden: **I**); [Aland: 2 codd; von Soden: 2 codd]
- Niketas (von Soden: **N**); [Aland: 3 codd; von Soden: 3 codd.]
- Zigabenus (von Soden: **Z**); [Aland: 3 codd; von Soden: 3 codd.]
- Theophylact (von Soden: **Θ**); [Aland: 42 codd; von Soden: 42 codd]
- Oecumenius (von Soden: **O**π); [Aland: 47 codd; von Soden: 47 codd]
- Anonymous catena commentary (von Soden:, **C**π); [Aland: 6 codd; von Soden: 6 codd.]
- Anonymous commentary (von Soden: **E**π); [Aland: 1 cod; von Soden: 1 cod]

K. III: Apocalypse Commentary Codices (rK)

Separate commentaries to the Apocalypse
- Andreas' commentary to the Apocalypse (von Soden: **Aν**); (Aland: 62 codd; von Soden: 57 codd]
- Arethas' commentary to the Apocalypse (von Soden: **Aρ**); (Aland: 1 cod; von Soden: 2 codd]
- Oecumenius' commentary to the Apocalypse (von Soden: **O**ᵅ); (Aland: 5 codd; von Soden: 5 codd]
- Maximus' commentary to the Apocalypse (von Soden: **M**); (Aland: 1; von Soden: 3 codd]
NB. See above: The praxapostolos with the Apocalypse commentary

K. IV: Apostolos-Evangelion Commentary Codices (eapPK)

- an Apostolos-Evangelion Commentary ("incomplete") codex (without comm. to Acts); [Aland: 1 cod; von Soden -]

K. V: Evangelion-Apostolos-Apocalypse Commentary Codices [NT commentary] (eaprK)

> - a Complete Apostolos-Evangelion-Apocalypse Commentary codex; [Aland: 4 codd; von Soden -]
>
> Sources:
> K. Aland (et al.), 'Sigelkonkordanzen', in *Op. Cit.*, II. von Soden: Gregory, (Berlin / New York, 1994), 401-405
> H. von Soden, *Op. Cit.* (Göttingen, 1911), 249-292.

There a some aspects of presentation of the *Kurzgefasste Liste* which demand attention.

1) If one peruses the lists of manuscripts, which have all been given a serial number, one notices that complete codices and incomplete codices are interspersed. A) Often Aland gives the total number of pages of a given codex, from its beginning to its end, but does not describe the contents of the whole codex, concentrating only on the NT part and thus leaving the impression that the whole codex contains NT books.

> **Example**: see Aland 33 [δ 48], a codex including eap, 143 f., but without mention of the OT Prophets on f. 1-50 (cf. von Soden).

B) For the complete manuscripts, Aland often gives a number of folios which registers only the NT components and not the number of folios of the whole codex, with the consequence that it remains unknown which other books the codex contains.

> **Example**: see serial number Aland ℵ 01, 148 f. (Blattzahl) < Rahlfs S [259], 393 f. ('Im ganzen sind jetzt 393 Bl. (darunter 4 fragmentarisch) vorhanden', *Verzeichnis*, p. 227).

C) For incomplete codices, Aland uses the sign † to indicate that small parts of a codex are missing. Many manuscripts with a serial number are single folia items, or have only a limited number of folia, or are mere fragments. Thus, of the total number of NT items (complete and incomplete) registered by Aland, it is impossible, for a large part, to determine what kind of codex forms these actually had, because they are fragments.

2) Commentary manuscripts in catena form are not distinguished from the authentic patristic commentary manuscripts (as Rahlfs does).

3) The main body of the *Liste* comprises the uncials and minuscules, showing the preference in NT research for text codices; lectionaries are presented towards the end of the *Liste*. The papyri are placed at the beginning.

4) Because this catalogue focuses on NT materials, complete Bibles (Πανδέκται)[195] are indexed arbitrarily, sometimes OT parts are registered, sometimes not.

> **Examples**: of the complete bibles (10 codices), comprising more or less all the books of the Greek OT and NT, the OT is mentioned only in three cases (Aland 205, 205^{abs}, 218)[196]. In the other cases the OT is not mentioned at all (Aland ℵ 01, A 02, B 03, C 04, 582, 664, of two codices [Rahlfs V II-I, 55] the NT part is lost)[197]. Of the 3 combined codices including the complete NT and the Psalterion (Ps./Od.) none of the included Ps. is mentioned (Aland 18, 242, 339[198]). Of the 22 Apostolo-evangelion codices with Psalterion[199] (one of which is not registered[200]), the inclusion of the Psalterion is not taken into account, although the total number of folios is given in many of these cases, e.g. Aland 1521 [δ 477] (see example 3 in the last paragraph of this chapter). Relevant information is further omitted in other groups, e.g. Aland 1718 [Athos, Vatopediou 851, 192 f.], comprising an Apostolos and Psalterion with Nine Odes, not only ap and 124 f.; or Aland *l* 751 [Athos, Philotheou 49] an Apostolo-evangelion lectionary combined with a Prophetologion part, not only *l*$^{+a}$esk, etc.

5) There are no reports concerning the catalogues of the libraries and their holdings from which Aland drew his material (as Rahlfs and Ehrhard do). Aland provides a library index, but the catalogues

---

[195] A Pandect is a manuscript copy of the whole Bible. Gr. πανδέκτης: 'all-receiver'. Lt. Pandecta. In Greek catalogues of manuscripts the expression is also used for other great compilations.

[196] Rahlfs, *Op. Cit.* (Berlin, 1914), 341-342, gives both OT and NT parts in his descriptions, also in the case of lost components; in a corresponding sequence they are: 68, 122, 130.

[197] Rahlfs, *Op. Cit.* (Berlin, 1914), 339-341, in a corresponding sequence they are: S, A, B, C, 106/107, 44.

[198] Cf. H. von Soden, *Op.Cit.*, I (Göttingen, 1911), 113 [δ 411], 106-107 [δ 206], 108-109 [δ 303].

[199] Aland 142, 491, 712, 1505, 2127, 2191, 57, 1448, 1358, 365, 823, 941, 1141, 1404, 393, 1382, 1240, 1521, 1609, 2225, 252 [cf. von Soden, in a corresponding sequence: δ 151, δ 152, δ 160, δ 165, δ 202, δ 250, δ 255, δ 256, δ 262, δ 367, δ 368, δ 369, δ 370, δ 384, δ 393, δ 1382, δ 1240, δ 1521, δ 1609, δ 2255 (Aland 252 not in von Soden).

[200] Istanbul, Πατριαρχικὴ Βιβλιοθήκη, Παν. Καμαρ. 133 (130); cf. Tsakopoulos I, 185 (Catalogue title: Ψαλτήριον καὶ Καινὴ Διαθήκη, 461 f.).

consulted are not mentioned, thus checking or looking for arguments and data behind the choices made by Aland is difficult.

6) Lectionary equipment and liturgical ecphonetic/musical signs in the text manuscripts are not registered.

> **Examples**: Of the selected tetraevangelion codices (1.323), 843 include lectionary equipments (= Lect)[201]; see the list of majuscule manuscripts <u>with Lect</u> (not registered) in Aland F 09, G 010, K 017, M 021, S 028, V 031, λ 039 + 566, Ω 045, 047 (cf. von Soden, in corresponding sequence: ε 86, 87, ε 71, ε 72, ε 89, ε 75, ε 77, ε 61, ε 95).

7) The groupings of the NT manuscripts are useful for codicological divisions, except the 'a' category (= Acts and the Seven General Epistles), for which there is no basis in the manuscript tradition, since there is only one manuscript, which can be identified as such[202].

What should also be mentioned is the disappearance of the original Greek names from the '*Bibliotheks-Verzeichnis* of the second edition of Aland's *Liste*. Missing is also an index containing an overview of the different categories of manuscripts (e, ap, etc) discriminated in the *Liste*.
Of great practical utility are the refined discriminations made for the lectionaries, as are the *Sigelkonkordanzen*. The library index provides insight into the locations in which the manuscripts can be found at present. Aland's *Liste* will be laid at the basis of our reclassification of the NT manuscripts, in particular Aland's groupings which are an important point of departure for a codicological approach.

1.3.2 The paradigm of classifying Byzantine OT manuscripts [Rahlfs/Fraenkel]

The basic catalogue of Greek OT codices is Rahlfs' *Verzeichnis der griechischen Handschriften des Alten Testaments für das Septuaginta Unternehmen* (Berlin, 1914). Despite its age, the *Verzeichnis* is still of high value, in structure and detail, but should be consulted together with the up-dated and revised edition by Fraenkel (*Septuaginta Unternehmen der Akademie der Wissenschaften*[203]), of which Part I was published in 2004 (Göttingen)[204]. In the introductions to critical editions of the individual OT books published under the auspices of the *Septuaginta Unternehmen* (Rahlfs, Ziegler, Wevers, Hanhart), mention is also made of the used and consulted manuscripts.

Rahlf's classification model sprung from text critical approaches, in the context of editions of the Greek OT Scriptures (on the basis of previous editions of among others Holmes/Parsons; de Lagarde; Brooke/McLean; Swete)[205]. The *Verzeichnis* was created on the basis of:

1) manuscript catalogues of the different libraries;
2) concrete descriptions of the manuscripts as they were maintained in the library holdings, alphabetically arranged after their locations[206];
3) a grouping / classification of the manuscripts on the basis of their contents[207]. These groups are given the following abbreviations: 1) Oct., 2) Reg., Par., Esdr, 3) Est., Idt., Tob., 4) Mac. I-IV, 5) Ps. Od, 6) Libri sapientiales incl. Ps. Sal., 7) XVI prophetae (the 'twelve' and the 'four' prophets).

OT lectionary manuscripts were registered separately.[208] The palaeographic condition of the manuscripts was, of course, taken into consideration, but not distinctions of script form, obviously not being opportune for the classification[209] (Rahlfs differs from Aland in this respect). Commentary manuscripts (subdivided into 'Catenen'

---

[201] See paragraph **6.2**: Tabular Specimens from the Catalogue: Group I, specimen II, Tetraevangelion.
[202] The one codex is: Athens, Ἐθν. Βιβλ. 105, X., [f. 1-8: XIV], 86 f. + f. 87-295: Πράξεις τῶν Ἀποστόλων, τὰς Ζ' Καθολικὰς ἐπιστολὰς Ἰακώβου, Πέτρου, Ἰωάννου, καὶ Ἰούδα + Ις' Ὁμιλίας τοῦ Χρυσοστόμου εἰς τὰς Πράξεις τῶν Ἀποστόλων. But even this one can be considered as a commentary manuscript, since there is a close approximity of the text of Acts and the homiletic commentary of Chrysostom to Acts. Excluded according to our norm are 52 of the 53 ms. items (Aland). From the list of von Soden (the 'α-Codices, die nur AK enthalten' [or A, or K or fragments]) 24 of the 25 ms. are excluded.
[203] www.septuaginta-unternehemen.gwdg.de
[204] D. Fraenkel, *Verzeichnis der griechischen Handschriften des Alten Testaments von Alfred Rahlfs. Die Überlieferung bis zum VIII Jahrhundert*, Bd. 1, 1, (Septuaginta Supplement) (Göttingen, 2004).
[205] K.H. Jobes and M. Silva, *Invitation to the Septuagint* (Grand Rapids, Michigan, 2001), 242-247.
[206] A. Rahlfs, *Op. Cit.* (Berlin, 1914), 'Anordnung des Verzeichnisses', XIV-XV.
[207] A. Rahlfs, *Op. Cit.* (Berlin, 1914), XVIII [Inhalt]: 'Bei der Angabe des Inhalts wurde auf möglichste Kürze und Übersichtlichkeit gesehen. Daher sind nicht alle Bücher einzeln aufgezählt, sondern die Gruppen, welche eine regelmäßig wiederkehrende Anordnung aufweisen, zusammengefaßt'. In the first place pragmatical not codicological considerations were the criteria for grouping.
[208] A. Rahlfs, *Op. Cit.* (Berlin, 1914), 'Verzeichnis der Lectionar-Handschriften', 440-443.
[209] A. Rahlfs, *Op. Cit.* (Berlin, 1914), XXIV: 'Es gibt in den Hss. selbst keine scharfe Scheidelinie zwischen Majuskel und Minuskel. Eine Reihe von Hss., besonders Catenen, enthalten beide Schriftarten nebeneinander'. And one can add, that the same is true in the

and 'Commentare') were differentiated from pure text manuscripts ('Einfache Bibeltexte') and registered on an equal level. Only catena manuscripts were judged to be useful for text critical edition[210] and only the text and catena codices received serial numbers.

Box 4 shows how Rahlfs subdivided the manuscripts over groups and the terminology he used to name the subdivisions. Besides the fixed main groupings (Psalterion, Octateuch etc.) one observes a diversity of concrete extant codex formations.

Box 4:

Byzantine OT Codices: Classification Rahlfs

Byzantine OT Text Codices

1) Octateuch Codices
Octateuchus (Oct.): Genesis (Gen.), Exodus (Exod.), Leviticus (Lev.), Numeri (Num.), Deuteronomium (Deut.), Iosue (Ios.), Iudicum (Iud.), Ruth

    a) Einfache Bibeltexte: 374 - 377
    b) Catenen   : 377 - 378
    c) Commentare   : 378 - 382

2) Historical Codices
Regnorum I-IV (Reg.), Paralipomenon I-II (Par.), Esdrae I-II (Esdr.)
[NB. Esdr. I-II = apogryphes Esdrasbuch und kanonisches Buch Esdr.-Neh.]

    a) Einfache Bibeltexte : 382 - 385
    b) Catenen   : 385
    c) Commentare   : see above 379 - 382

3) Historical Codices
Esther (Est.), Iudith (Idt.), Tobit (Tob.)

    a) Einfache Bibeltexte : 385 - 387
    [b and c are absent]

4) Historical Codices
Machabaeorum I-IV (Mac.)

    a) Einfache Bibeltexte : 387 - 390
    [b and c are absent]

5) Psalms and Odes
Psalmi, Odae (Ps.Od.)

    a) Einfache Bibeltexte : 390 - 399
    b) Catenen   : 399 - 401
    c) Commentare   : 402 - 410

6) Libri sapientiales incl. Ps.Sal.
Iob (Iob), Proverbia (Prov), Ecclesiastes (Eccl.), Canticum (Cant), Sapientia (Sap), Siracides (Sir), Psalmi Salomonis (Ps Sal)

    a) Einfache Bibeltexte : 410 - 414
    b) Catenen   : 415 - 420
    c) Commentare   : 420 - 4424

7) XVI Prophetae

    a) Einfache Bibeltexte : 424 - 428
    b) Catenen   : 428 - 430
    c) Commentare   : 430 - 438

[8)] Verzeichnis der Lectionar-Handschriften : 440 - 443

Additional Compilations
Octateuch and Historical Codices

---

lectionary manuscripts. Again Rahlfs: 'Auch hinsichtlich der Textform pflegt zwischen den jungen Majuskelhss. und den alten Minuskelhss. kein wesentlicher Unterschied zu bestehen. Daher habe ich die Majuskelhss. im großen und ganzen ebenso mit arabischen Ziffern bezeichnet wie die Minuskelhss'.

[210] A. Rahlfs, *Op. Cit.* (Berlin, 1914), xxvi: ,'Mit Sigeln versehen sind die Hss. des einfachen Bibeltextes und der Catenen (vgl. § 1), aber n i c h t d i e H s s. d e r C o m m e n t a r e, da diese nicht als direkte Zeugen für den LXX-Text, sondern nur als Zeugen für den Text der Commentare in Betracht kommen. Zwischen Cat. und Comm. ist allerdings die Grenze oft schwer zu ziehen (§ 1); vorläufig habe ich zweifelhafte Hss. meist zu den Catenen gerechnet'.

> Historical and Poetic Codices
> Historical and Prophet Codices
> Poetic and Prophets Codices
> All OT books in one Codex [Psalms excluded]
>
> * Excluded from this category are commentaries in the form of Σειραί, are the deutero-canonical books (Faulhaber, 1909, 387)
> ** There are many Σειραί or Catena manuscripts compiled by anonymous editors (see Athens/Ethn.Bibl./Sakkelion: Index)
> *** There are extensive manuscript materials, see Swete III, 811-834 (Faulhaber, 1909, 387)
>
> Source:
> A. Rahlfs, *Op. Cit.* (Berlin, 1914), 373; cf. XVIII-XIX.
> References are given from Rahlfs' *Verzeichnis* (1914): 'Übersicht über das handschriftliche Material für die einzelnen Teile des A.T.', 373-439, and 'Verzeichnis der Lectionar-Handschriften', 441-443.

Rahlfs registered the codex contents that served his purpose, which was to research the textual base of individual OT works (Septuaginta Unternehmen): 'Der Inhalt der Hss. ist in der Regel nur soweit angegeben, als er für uns in Betracht kommt'[211] and: 'Andrerseits habe ich aber bei Hss. die mehrere biblische Bücher oder Buchgruppen oder außer den biblischen Büchern auch andere Werke enthalten, aus praktischen Gründen stets, soweit ich konnte, angegeben, auf welchen Seiten die einzelnen Stücke der Hs. Anfangen, und nötigenfalls auch, wo sie enden'.[212] A complete description of the contents of the integral codices was not deemed useful and although, in contrast to Aland, Rahlfs did register the total number of folios in the majority of cases, and did indicate which other books beside the OT were included in the codex, albeit unsystematically.

> **Examples**:
> - Athos, Iberon 382 (4502). 996 f. 13a Alttest. Geschichte von Adam bis zum Auftreten des Isaias, 45b Ruth, 47b-69b Reg. I-IV, 468b-526a Andreae comm. in Apoc.)[213]
> - Sometimes Rahlfs indicates only what is included with "unter anderen", e.g.: Athos, Dionysiou 65 [3599]: Ps. u.a. [In fact the codex has 26 items, of which item 1 is a Psalterion. The other items are of patr. & lit. nature. See Lambros I (Cambridge, 1895-1900), 324].
> - Or he gives merely one "item number", e.g.: Athos, Dionysiou 54 [3588]: 9) Mac. IV. [In fact the codex has 13 items, primarily hagiographical works. Item 13 is even a commentary to the Prophet Hoseia (OT). See Lambros I (Cambridge, 1895-1900), 323].
> - Or he mentions that NT materials were included, e.g.: Athos, Vatopediou 610 [762 Spyridon/Eustratiades] 18-88 Ps.Od., dann folgt das N.T. (ohne Apoc.).
> - In the same manner, he refers to liturgical materials, e.g.: Athos, Dionysiou 432 [3966], Liturgische Werke: 7) Lect. [In fact this codex has 10 items, liturgical texts, including the Octoechos, Triodion, Pentecostarion, Menologion. See Lambros I (Cambridge, 1895-1900), 424].
> - Sometimes he passes over all references to other parts of the codex, e.g.: Athos, Lavra 145 [B25]. XV. 328 f. 1-195 Euthymii Zigabeni comm. in Ps., [omitting the liturgical part of the codex, i.e. Horologion].

Rahlfs' interest was primarily concentrated on the Old Testament text. The descriptions Rahlfs gave of the OT manuscripts are highly detailed, and moreover, he provided an overview of the manuscript contents in an index.[214] Rahlfs worked with a fixed number of basic groups (7), in order to bring some order into the variety of different types of form and content, and pragmatic as they are, not all groups are adequate from a codicological point of view, because the groupings are not all based on the actual, that is, complete state of affairs of the manuscripts themselves.

With regard to the classification of some groups the formation is immediately evident, as in the case of the Octateuch, the Psalterion, the Prophetologion. The sub-groups of the section of the historical books, however, [2] Reg., Par., Esdr., [3] Est., Idt. Tob., [4] Mac. I-IV, seem to be based on meagre codicological support; they are only substantiated by one or a few codices[215], i.e. they lack a clearly defined, independent codex formation, or are incorporated in other codex formations. The proposed groups, however, can function as a starting point for more detailed codicological research, on the basis of 'contents data' delivered in Rahlfs' *Verzeichnis*[216].

Here we would like to make a few remarks about the nature of the catalogue.
1) A considerable number of libraries/holdings were not taken into consideration, or were insufficiently investigated by Rahlfs and his co-operators. The catalogues of manuscripts used were sometimes

---

[211] A. Rahlfs, *Op. Cit.* (Berlin, 1914), XVIII.

[212] A. Rahlfs, *Op. Cit.* (Berlin, 1914), XIX

[213] A. Rahlfs, *Op. Cit.* (Berlin, 1914), 13.

[214] This index is practical for a global overview, but offers insufficient data for a codicological approach.

[215] Of group [3] Est., Idt., Tob., are presented as a separate category and 55 ms. items are recorded, but only one (538: Paris, Bibl. Nat., Gr. 1087, XIV, 178 f.), is probably an appropriate codex form of group [3], corresponding to the three books which should be contained in it. Cf. A. Rahlfs, *Op. Cit.* (Berlin, 1914), 385-387. But even the contents of this codex is not completely described and contains other materials.

[216] A. Rahlfs, *Op. Cit.* (Berlin, 1914), 373-443. For a quick overview see the 'Verzeichnis der Sigeln', for more specific information see the 'Übersicht über das handschriftliche Material für die einzelnen Teile des A.T.' and for extensive descriptions in the main part 'Die griechischen Handschriften des A.T., alphabetisch nach Orten und Bibliotheken geordnet'.

incomplete or deficient in many aspects (as Rahlfs frequently indicated). The reports concerning the consulted catalogues and other entries to the manuscripts at the head of each library/holding are useful and informative to check sources.

2) Some departments of the *Verzeichnis* remain incomplete, since many data and sources are based on materials from before 1914, as for instance research of the Prophetologia codices and the catena and commentary manuscripts show.

3) Save the catena manuscripts, Rahlfs excluded the commentary and/or homiletic manuscripts for principal and practical reasons, since homilies on OT books or themes were not considered as relevant for the primary study of the OT text[217]. For example, a manuscript such as Athos, Iberon, 73 (4193), a commentary to the Psalms of John Chrysostom[218], does not feature in Rahlf's catalogue. A sharp demarcation line between 'catena/commentary' and 'one-author/commentary' or between '(continuous) text/commentary' and 'homiletic/commentary.' is, however, in many cases difficult and unjustified, as Rahlfs observed[219].

4) Although Rahlfs acknowledged the liturgical factor of the OT manuscripts[220], he did not register the liturgical manuscripts that include OT texts for practical reasons[221].

5) Only commentary manuscripts since 400 A.D were registered. The biblical codices since the XVIIth c. were completely omitted.[222]

Finally we will look at the manner in which Rahlfs gave serial numbers to the OT manuscripts that were adopted in his catalogue. Excluded from sigla were commentary (homiletical), lectionary and liturgical manuscripts.[223] Rahlfs 'Serial List' is still in use today, and is currently in a process of revision and up-dating, see Fraenkel, *Op. Cit.* I, (Göttingen, 2004). From this 'Serial List' one finds quick information as to whether a manuscript item is complete or incomplete, composite or singular, a whole codex or an isolated fragment.

In box 5, we show how Rahlfs designed groups to number the manuscripts. These groups are different from those described in the previous paragraph, which Rahlfs developed for his index. Rahlfs thus left us two systems of grouping the OT manuscripts. The box below provides fast insight in the total number of manuscript items registered by Rahlfs in their groups.[224]

---

[217] A. Rahlfs, *Op. Cit.* (Berlin, 1914), XII: 'Neben den Sammelwerken, welche die Erklärungen verschiedener Kirchenväter miteinander verbinden [i.e. the Catena manuscripts], stehen die Commentare, welche die Auslegung eines einzelnen Autors enthalten. Obwohl auch sie Bibeltexte einschließen, wird man sie doch nicht, wie HoP in einigen Fällen getan haben, mit den einfachen Bibel-hss. und den Catenen auf gleiche Stufe stellen, da bei ihnen Text und Auslegung aufs engste zusammengehören, ja oft ineinander übergehen, und die Hss. hier nur als Zeugen für den Text der Commentare, nicht als direkte Zeugen für den LXX-Text gelten können. Eine vollständige Aufführung aller Commentarhss., die sehr viel Raum in Anspruch genommen haben würde, schien mir nicht nötig (...)'. Cf. *Op Cit.* (1914) XXVI: 'Mit Sigeln versehen sind die Hss. des einfachen Bibeltextes und der Catenen (vgl. § 1) aber nicht die Hss. der Commentare, da diese nicht als direkte Zeugen für den LXX-Text, sondern nur als Zeugen für den text der Commentare in Betracht komen'.

[218] Lambros, *Op. Cit.*, II (Cambridge, 1895-1900), 7. Cf. *Verzeichnis*, 12 (codices of OT contents at Iberon monastery).

[219] A. Rahlfs, *Op. Cit.* (Berlin, 1914), XII: 'Die Grenze ist hier allerdings oft nicht scharf zu ziehen. Und ebenso ist der Unterschied zwischen Commentar und Catene bei den durchweg unselbständigen Machwerken der jüngeren Zeit oft ein fließender: die Commentare sind hier oft nur gekürzte Catenen, in welchen die Namen der excerpierten Kirchenväter fortgelassen und ihre ursprünglich lose nebeneinander gestellten Erklärungen zu einer fortlaufenden Auslegung zusammengeschweißt sind. Auch wird die Unterscheidung der Commentare von den Catenen durch die Ungenauigkeit mancher Kataloge so erschwert, daß ich durchaus nicht sicher bin (...), hier immer das Richtige getroffen zu haben'. Cf. p. XXVI 'Zwischen Cat. und Comm. ist allerdings die Grenze oft schwer zu ziehen (§ 1); vorläufig habe ich zweifelhafte Hss. meist zu den Catenen gerechnet'.

[220] A. Rahlfs, *Op. Cit.* (Berlin, 1914), XIII.

[221] A. Rahlfs, *Op. Cit.* (Berlin, 1914), XXVI: 'Nicht mit Sigeln versehen sind auch die liturgischen Bücher, da ihre Erforschung kaum begonnen hat, und ich daher nicht aufs Geratewohl Sigeln einführen mochte, die sich später vielleicht als unpraktisch erweisen. Ich spare mir also ihre Bezeichnung für später auf' (...).

[222] A. Rahlfs, *Op. Cit.* (Berlin, 1914), XIII.

[223] A. Rahlfs *Op. Cit.* (Berlin, 1914), XXVI: 'Mit Sigeln versehen sind die Hss. des einfachen Bibeltextes und der Catenen (vgl. § 1) aber nicht die Hss. der Commentare, da diese nicht als direkte Zeugen für den LXX-Text, sondern nur als Zeugen für den text der Commentare in Betracht komen'.

[224] A. Rahlfs, *Op. Cit.* (Berlin, 1914), 'Verzeichnis der Sigeln', 335-372.

> Box 5:
> ## Rahlfs' serial numbering of manuscripts (sigla)
>
> Rahlfs used the list of Holmes/Parsons as a basis on which to build his catalogue, and proceeded to number the manuscripts as of serial number 312. We have given the first group of Holmes/Parsons, the group number [0].
>
> [0] **The Revised List of Holmes/Parsons** (see for mutations/alterations 'Verzeichnis der Sigeln': n. 1Holmes-Parsons, p. 335-337) including Psalterion manuscripts (Ps.Od.), p. 339-345.
>   The letters/numbers of this group are:
>   a) letter code: A B C D F G K L M Q R S T U V W Z $^{I-VI}$ = <u>22</u> manuscript items
>   b) number code: 13 – 311   [299 numbers – 61 open numbers = <u>238</u> manuscript items
>   Total a + b = **<u>260</u> manuscript items**
>
> Note: there are respectively <u>4</u> (a) and <u>109</u> (b) separate Psalterion ms. items (Ps.Od.) in this group (see further Psalterion codices), besides the ones included in larger codex formations (OT+NT codices).
>
> [1] **The OT codices without Psalterion manuscripts (Ps. Od.)**, p. 345-355.
> The numbers of this group are: 312 – 769 [458 numbers – 19 open numbers = **<u>439</u> manuscript items**]
>
> Note: there are nevertheless several Ps.Od. in this group, due to their belonging to larger codex formations [508, 603, 613, 728 and 769 Od.]; Ps.Od. were also included in the so-called Complete Bible codices (OT and NT).
>
> [2] **Fragments of OT codices without Psalterion manuscripts (Ps. Od.)**, p. 355-356.
> The numbers of this group are: 901 – 951 [51 numbers – 5 open numbers = **<u>46</u> manuscript items**]
>
> [3] **Psalterion manuscripts (Ps. Od.) of the IX – XII c.**, p. 356-361.
> The numbers of this group are: 1001 – 1229 [1229-1001+1= **<u>229</u> manuscript items**; 0 open numbers]
>
> Note: 1190 (XIII/IX), 1208 (VIII), 1219 (IV/V).
>
> [4] **Psalterion manuscripts (Ps. Od.) of the XIII – XVI c.**, p. 361-371.
> The numbers of this group are: 1401 – 1916 [516 numbers – 10 open numbers = **<u>506</u> manuscript items**]
>
> [5] **Psalterion (Ps. Od.) fragments until the VIII c.**, p. 371-372.
> The numbers of this group are: 2001 – 2048 [2048-2001+1= **<u>48</u> manuscript items**; 0 open numbers]
>
> Sum Total: 260 [0]   Sum Total: Psalterion (Ps. Od.): 113 [0]
>   439 [1]   229 [3]
>   46 [2]   506 [4]
>   229 [3]   48 [5]
>   506 [4]   ======
>   48 [5]
>   ======   **896 Ps/ms. items**
>
>   **<u>1.528</u>** OT manuscript items [- Ps. Od. manuscript items = **<u>632</u>** OT manuscript items]
>
> Sources:
> A. Rahlfs, *Op. Cit.* (Berlin, 1914), 'Allgemeine Vorbemerkungen: § 4. 'Sigeln', p. XXI-XXVI and 'Verzeichnis der Sigeln', 335-372.

The *Verzeichnis* provides a valuable contribution for further codicological research and will be laid at the basis of our reclassification where the Greek OT manuscripts are concerned (see chapter 5).

1.3.3 The paradigm of classifying the Byzantine homiletic (hagiographic) manuscripts [Ehrhard]

Rahlfs and von Soden (and Aland who adopted his results) were already engaged in the making of inventories and the evaluation of commentary manuscripts in the context of their edition projects (respectively the Septuaginta Unternehmen and INTF). However, research of the Greek OT and NT commentary codices was reduced to: a) catena manuscripts and b) individual commentary manuscripts. Rahlfs excluded the large and central group of homiletic biblical commentaries, as we saw above. Von Soden did not make a clear distinction between catena, individual commentary and homiletic commentary manuscripts. He did distinguish the Byzantine edition forms of the commentary manuscripts ('Editionen') – see box 3 above. Aland, in his turn, took over von Soden's distinctions in his *Liste*, but at the same time placed all the commentary manuscripts in one list together with the text manuscripts (distinguishing them with K), making the commentaries less visible than they in fact were before. However, by placing the commentaries and the text manuscripts together in the same list, Aland displays the congruence of their edition forms, thus indicating that there may be a greater kinship between the text and commentary manuscripts that one may have thought.

Rahlfs, von Soden and Aland excluded from their investigations the liturgical and other patristic codices. This gap was partly filled by the enormous research programme of Ehrhard, who worked for 40 years in Western and Eastern libraries. His autopsies of the codices and other observations were of great importance for the methodology he developed concerning the identification and classification of manuscripts in the libraries, which he visited on location[225]. The presentation of the Byzantine Greek homiletic codices by Ehrhard in his *Überlieferung und Bestand der hagiographischen und homiletischen Literatur der griechischen Kirche, von den Anfängen bis zum Ende des 16. Jahrhunderts*, I-III (Leipzig / Berlin, 1937-1952 [repr. 1965]) is based on one important assumption: the intertwined incorporation of both hagiographic and homiletic compositions, a thesis which is made evident on the basis of a huge number of investigated manuscript materials (a total of 2750 manuscripts, p. XVII[226]). Ehrhard introduced the awareness that the hagiographic and homiletic manuscripts find their roots in the Byzantine liturgy[227]. At times Ehrhard refers to the so-called lectionaries (e.g. 'Evangeliarien und der Praxapostolos'), indicating the liturgical function of these biblical books, but he does not highlight the concrete reading cycles in which these books were used[228] (see paragraph **3.4**, where these reading cycles are presented). Indeed, he also identifies hagiographic and homiletic materials as being liturgical, but Ehrhard does not connect these materials to the biblical readings to which they correspond, neither does he treat these biblical books. What Ehrhard does provide is a transparent exposition of the Byzantine liturgical calendar and its underlying systems ('Einleitung: Das griechische Kirchenjahr und der byzantinische Festkalender', *Op. Cit.* (Leipzig-Berlin, 1937-1952), 25-35), with a discussion of the relevant liturgical books (Triodion, Pentekostarion, Typikon, Menaia, Synaxarion) which regulate the calendar[229] or organise the complicated celebrations and services. This is further explored in chapter 2.

Ehrhard designated the following "codicological" categories: 1) collective collections ('Jahressammlungen'), with the distinctions - annual, semi-annual, or monthly - compiled by known or anonymous editors; and 2) collections of individual patristic preachers ('Spezialpanegyriken und homiliarien'), panegyrics/homilies of individual authors[230].
Ehrhard applied codico-liturgical (calendaric) criteria for the differentiation and classification of the manuscripts. He identified three main groups of manuscripts: the hagiographic, the homiletic and the mixed group, comprising both hagiographical and homiletic writings. Distinctions were made between manuscripts which were employed in the organisation of the Byzantine liturgical calendar, and those of a more private character, auxiliaries to the liturgical programme (for individual use by the monks).
Ehrhard divided the available material into chronologically defined groups, configured around the dominant Metaphrastic edition: 1. compilations comprising the period up to Symeon Metaphrast or Pre-Metaphrastic (IV-IXth c.); 2. Menologion compilations of the Metaphrast (Xth c.); 3. compilations comprising the period after the Metaphrast or Post-Metaphrastic (XIth – XVIth c.). An important and large group of independent codices ('Vom Metaphrast Unabhängigen späten Menologien und Panegyriken') was presented separately.

For the first time, beside the activities of the Bollandists[231], a philologically trained scholar was seriously engaged in the study and classification of a huge collection of homiletic manuscripts. Ehrhard provided points of entry to this important group of Byzantine commentary manuscripts. What Ehrhard disregarded were all 'unorderly' codices, those without position in the calendar scheme. The decision to exclude these was, probably, justifiable from a calendaric (and systematic) point of view, but not from a codicological point of view. Great compilations [Πανδέκται[232]] and disorderly compositions [Σύμμικτα[233]] are characteristic of Byzantine codex

---

[225] J.M. Hoeck, "Der Nachlass Albert Ehrhards und seine Bedeutung für die Byzantinistik", in *Byzantion*, 21.1 (1951), 171-178.

[226] J.M. Hoeck, *Art cit.* (1951), 176, speaks of ca. 3000 manuscripts; not all these manuscripts, however, are adopted (or mentioned) in Ehrhard's work.

[227] A. Ehrhard, *Op. Cit.* (Leipzig/Berlin, 1937-1952), I, Vorwort, vii-viii. See for a lucid review of the Byzantine Typikon, A. Ehrhard, *Op. Cit.* (Leipzig/Berlin, 1937-1952), I, Hilfsmittel, 35-51.

[228] A. Ehrhard, *Op. Cit.* (Leipzig/Berlin, 1937-1952), I, 23-24, '(...) die hagiographische und die homiletische Literatur der griechischen Kirche in eine innige Verbindung gebracht worden war. Der Grund dafür springt in die Augen, sobald man sich des Charakters dieser Sammlungen als liturgischer Bücher bewuß wird, die für den Gebrauch im Gottesdienst bestimmt waren, gleichwie die sog. Evangeliarien und der Praxapostolos. Es entsprach einem praktischen Bedürfnis, nicht nur Sammlungen zu besitzen, die entweder nach der Heiligenfest-ordnung oder nach dem beweglichen Kirchenjahr geordnet waren, sondern auch solche, in denen Lesungen für den Morgengottesdienst bereitgetellt waren, sowohl für die auf bestimmte Tage fallenden Herrn- und Heiligenfeste als für die Sonn- und festtage des beweglichen Kirchenjahres'.

[229] A. Ehrhard, *Op. Cit.* (Leipzig/Berlin, 1937-1952), I, Hilfsmittel, 35-53.

[230] For the period IVth-Xth c.: Gregory of Nazianz, Gregory of Nyssa, John Chrysostom, Theodor of Studion, Photios of Constantinople, Imperator Leo VI the Wise, Niketas the paphlagonier, Ephrem the Syrian; for the period XIth- IVth-Xth c.XVIth c.: John Xiphilinos, Patriarchs of Constantinople - John IX Agapetos [of Chalcedon], Germanos II, John XIII Glykys, John XIV Kalekas, Philotheos; (Italo-Greek; Neophytos Enkleistos, Antonios of Larissa, Markarios of Chrysokephalos, Gregorios Palamas, Patriarch Neilos of Constantinople, Isidoros of Thessaloniki, Archbishop Gabriel of Thessaloniki, Unknown Bishop of Berrhoia).

[231] Bollandists, *Acta Sanctorum*, 67 vols. (Brussels, Venice, Paris, 1643-1940).

[232] I. Sakkelion and A.I. Sakkelion, Κατάλογος τῶν χειρογράφων τς Ἐθνικς Βιβλιοθήκης τς Ἑλλάδος (Athens, 1892): Codd. 650. 652. 656-657.

[233] I. Sakkelion, *Op. Cit.* (Athens, 1892), Codd. 1062. 1098.

formation and contain many homiletic works. Ehrhard did not always describe or mention their complete contents, only those parts that took his interest.

A complex aspect in the work of Ehrhard is the tendency towards over-systematisation. Through extensive differentiation, one gains the impression that the manuscripts were the result of conscious scientific elaboration and scribal strategies. Finally, some criticism is necessary where terminology is concerned. Too much systematisation leads a scholar to apply sharp denotations and terminological refinements to the discriminated material, where these do not exist. Thus, a sharp distinction between "Panegyrica" and "Homiliaria" for example, as introduced by Ehrhard, is unnecessary to our mind. In the Byzantine codices themselves such sharp distinctions do not exist (panegyrica and homilies, logoi, katecheseis, hermeneiai etc.). The books in their different codex formations are used beside one another and supplement each other. The same is true for the sharply coined distinction between Synaxaria and Menologia, introduced by Delehaye and adopted by Ehrhard.

Ehrhard's monumental work has an extremely complicated structure, which does not make it highly accessible. In box 6 we provide an overview of its structure, to aid transparency. With an eye to the importance of Ehrhard's catalogue, the work was updated and verified by L. Perria, *I Manoscritti Citati da Albert Ehrhard, Indice di: A. Ehrhard, Überlieferung und Bestand der hagiographischen und homiletischen Literatur der griechischen Kirche, I-III, Leipzig-Berlin, 1937-1952* (Roma 1979).

Box 6:

Structural overview of Ehrhard's *Überlieferung*

Total manuscripts [Hagiographic and Homiletic]: ca. 2.750. [ca 3000, Hoeck 1951, p.176]
(See Vorwort, p. VIII-XIII)

The rating of the consulted manuscripts and the number of codices per category are given by E. in I (1937), VIII-IX.

Bd. I: Abschn. II: p. 154 – 325. Alten Jahressammlungen [**Hag/Hom**]

Bd. I: Abschn. III: p. 326 – 437. Alten Jahresmenologien. [**Hag**]

Bd. I: Abschn. IV: p. 438 – 701. Alten Monatsmenologien. [**Hag**] [**72 manuscripts**]

Bd. II: Abschn. V: Alten Panegyriken und Homiliarien p. 1 – 305. [**Hom**]

[**280 manuscripts** = Alten Panegyriken und Homiliarien + Jahressammlungen.+ Monatsmenologien.]

Bd. II: Abschn. VI: p. Menol. Sym. Des Metaphr. [**Hag**] [**700 manuscripts** + 112 fragmenten]

Total: ca 1.160 manuscripts [I, p. IX] [= 72 manuscripts + 280 manuscripts + 700 manuscripts + 112 (fragments)]

Bd. III: Abschn. VII: p. 201 – 341. Verkürzte, Erweiterte, Vermischte Metaphrast [**Hag/Hom**]
[**230 manuscripts**]

        [+ zwei kaiserlichen Menologien; **10 manuscripts**]

Bd. III: p. 463 – 519. Vom Metaphrast Unabhängigen späten Menologien und Panegyriken [**Hag/Hom**]
[**49 manuscripts**]   [Menologien; Panegyriken: 11. – 15. Jahrh.]

Bd. III: p. 520 – 722. Späten Spezialpanegyriken und Homiliarien [**Hom**]
[**ca 253 manuscripts**]

Total: ca. 545 manuscripts [I, p. XI] [= Groups I 230 manuscripts + II ca 10 manuscripts + III ca 49 manuscripts + IV ca 253 manuscripts]

Bd. III: p. 723 – 1033. Abschn. VIII. Nebenwege der Überlieferung.

I. Nichtmenologische Sammlungen: Privatsammlungen [**Hag/Hom: without calendaric-liturgical order**]
  (1) Alte Texte [**140 manuscripts**]
    (2) Mischung von alten und von metphrastischen Texten [**130 manuscripts**]
      (3) alte und junge Texte (without Metaphrast) [**24 manuscripts**]

Total: ca 300 manuscripts.

> II. Spezialsammlungen
> ~ Apostel
> ~ Märtyrer- und Heiligenfeste
> ~ Feste weiblicher Heiliger
> ~ Mönchsleben
>
> **Total: ca 100 manuscripts** [Mönchsleben: ca 50]
>
> III. Einzelüberlieferung [ein einziger hagiographischer Text]
>   Total (umfangreichere Texte): **152 manuscripts** [alte Texte 105 mss]
>
> IV. Akoluthien mit hagiographischen Texten [**105 manuscripts**]
>
> V. Manuscripts of Church fathers and Byzantine theologians [**150 manuscripts**, but John Climakos **240 manuscripts**]
>
> **Total: I 300 mss + II 100 mss + III 152 mss + IV 105 mss + V 150+240 = 1.047 manuscripts.**
>
> **Sum Total: ca 1160 + ca 545 + ca 1047 = ca 2.752 manuscripts.**
>
> Sources:
> A. Ehrhard, *Op. Cit.*, (Leipzig-Berlin, 1937-1952); L. Perria, *Op. Cit.*, (Rome, 1979)

1.3.4 The paradigm of classifying the Byzantine catena manuscripts [Karo/Lietzmann]

Beside the large group of homiletic commentary manuscripts classified by Ehrhard, we have the large group of catena codices, known as Σειραί (chains), classified by Karo/Lietzmann in a concise and important catalogue (G. Karo und H. Lietzmann, *Catenarum Graecorum Catalogus*, in *Nachrichten der Gesellschaft der Wissenschaften zu Göttingen, Philol. hist. Klasse* (Göttingen, 1902), 1-66 [Pars I]; 299-350 [Pars II]; 559-620 [Pars III]. This catalogue was updated in part in the course of the 20th century and several catena editions of the manuscripts were published. Rahlfs adopted the results of Karo/Lietzmann's catena research in his *Verzeichnis* (Berlin, 1914). The Karo/Lietzmann catena catalogue is characterised by far-reaching categorical differentiations and sub-divisions. M. Geerard and J. Noret (Eds.) did adopt the basic Karo/Lietzmann classification system in their *Clavis Patrum Graecorum* (Turnhout, 1974-1998), IV, 'Catenae', 185-259 [Index Alphabeticus, 273] and updated and extended it up until 1980. Karo/Lietzmann's catalogue brings together the various groups of catena manuscripts, ca 450 codices were identified and classified (see Index Codicum[234])[235] under the main headings of OT [I-II] and NT [III].

> Box 7:
>
> **Catena Divisions of Karo/Lietzmann's *Catenarum Graecorum Catalogus***
>
> **Total of the inventarised manuscripts: ca. 450 ms. items [Faulhaber 1909, p. 386]**
> **Cf. the Index Codicum, Pars III, 615-618.**
>
> **Pars I**
>
> Catenae in Octateuchum et Regnorum Libros : p. 2 – 17 [items I-III]
>
> Catena in Regnorum Libros : p. 17 – 20
>
> Catenae in Psalterium : p. 20 – 66 [items I- XXVII]
>
> **Pars II**
>
> Catenae in Proverbia : p. 299 – 310 [items I-V]
>
> Catenae in Ecclesiasten : p. 310 – 312 [items I-II]
>
> Catenae in Canticum : p. 312 – 319 [items I-V]
>
> Catenae in Iob : p. 319 – 331 [items I-II]
>
> Catenae in XII Prophetas : p. 331 – 334 [items I-II]

---

[234] G. Karo und H. Lietzmann, 'Catenarum Graecorum Catalogus', in *Op. Cit.* (Göttingen, 1902), Pars Tertia, 615-618.
[235] Additional materials were provided by M. Faulhaber, "Die Katenenhandschriften der spanischen Bibliotheken", in *Biblische Zeitschrift*, 1 (1903), 151-159, 246-255, 351-371 added 39 manuscripts from Spanish libraries. The consultancy of the Eastern libraries is especially minimal; Cf. A.I. Papadopoulos-Kerameus, (St. Petersburg, 1891-1915) [Repr., Bruxelles, 1963].

Catenae in Isaiam : p. 334 – 342 [items I-V]
Catenae in Ieremiam Baruch Threnos : p. 343 – 346 [items I-II]
Catenae in Ezechielem : p. 346 – 348 [items I-II]
Catenae in Danielem : p. 348 – 350 [items I-II]
Pars III
Catenae in Matthaeum : p. 559 – 571 [items I-VI]
Catenae in Marcum : p. 571 – 572
Catenae in Lucam : p. 572 – 583 [items I-VI]
Catenae in Iohannem : p. 583 – 591 [items I-VII]
Catenae in Acta Apostolorum : p. 592 – 595
Catenae in Epistulas Catholicas : p. 595 – 597
Catenae in Epistulas S. Pauli : p. 597 -610 [items I-IX]

Some remarks on the assessment of this catalogue will suffice: 1) beside the usefulness of the inventarisation and its categorisation of the extant catena codices (one may note that especially the manuscripts of Eastern libraries are incomplete and under-represented), certain groups of catena are omitted, i.e. catena to the Nine Odes, to the Salomonica [Song of Songs, Proverbs, Ecclesiastes], to the Tetraevangelion, the Praxapostolos and other combinations, to the Apocalypse, the anonymous catena, catena with introductory biblical matters[236]; 2) the catena manuscripts were sharply hived off from the whole group of commentary manuscripts[237]. This sharp distinction is not common in Byzantine Greek tradition, which one can observe in the Greek manuscript catalogues (Sakkelion, Lambros etc.), in which the Σειραί are often brought under the common headings of 'Ἑρμηνεῖαι', 'Ἐξηγήσεις' or 'Σχόλια'; 3) the sub-divisions set up within the categories are highly differentiated and split into minor groups and sub-groups, sometimes in extreme (for instance, in the case of the catena of the Psalms: items I-XXVII). Such schematic categorisations, how praiseworthy they are in themselves, may be useful for textual research, and in general, the classification do not correspond to the codicological structure of the catena manuscripts. It would be interesting to research whether the edition forms as found in the text and individual commentary manuscripts, are also to be found in the catena manuscripts.

1.3.5 Existing Greek and Russian catalogues

It has become evident that, in order to obtain a more adequate picture of the complete contents of the extant codices, it is desirable to revisit the manuscripts catalogues of the libraries on location, since none of the specialised catalogues discussed above will provide such completeness of information. In chapter 4 we list the updated bibliographical information of the Greek and Russian catalogues that are regarded as important sources for the study of the Eastern Orthodox approach to the Byzantine manuscripts. They display at a glance the cohesion between biblical, patristic and liturgical manuscripts; not only through the manner in which they are presented on location, but also through the manner in which the contents are described. Many references can be found concerning the *provenance* and *calligraphic milieu* of the manuscripts. Important are also the used *termini technici*. Although the older catalogues display manifold imperfections[238] when compared to modern catalogisation[239], these catalogues of Byzantine manuscripts are highly interesting for new codicological research for the descriptions and terminology connected to this that stems from a longstanding tradition.

---

[236] M. Faulhaber, "Katenen und Katenenforschung", in *Byzantinische Zeitschrift*, 18 (1909), 383-395.

[237] A. Rahlfs, *Op Cit.* (Berlin, 1914), 'Einleitung', XXVI, 'Mit Sigeln versehen sind die Hss. des einfachen Bibeltextes und der Catenen (vgl. § 1), aber nicht die Hss. der Commentare, da diese nicht als direkte Zeugen für den LXX-Text, sondern nur als Zeugen für den Text der Commentare in Betracht kommen. Zwischen Cat. und Comm. ist allerdings die Grenze oft schwer zu ziehen (§ 1); vorläufig habe ich zweifelhafte Hss. meist zu den Catenen gerechnet'.

[238] Rahlfs, Ehrhard, Gregory and von Soden and others frequently refer to the imperfections of the catalogues of manuscripts on which their research was based. Rahlfs, for instance, remarks in his *Verzeichnis* (Berlin, 1914), XII: 'Auch wird die Unterscheidung der Commentare von den Catenen durch die Ungenauigkeit mancher Kataloge so erschwert, daß ich durchaus nicht sicher bin, hier immer das Richtige getroffen zu haben'.

[239] The criteria as applied in modern catalogues are exposed, in O. Mazal, *The Keeper of Manuscripts* (Turnhout, 1992).

1.4 Examples of Codicological Research of the Byzantine Manuscripts

The overview of the data included in the catalogues discussed above and an analysis of their construction results in two conclusions, which contain, at the same time, pointers in the direction of future catalogue and manuscript research. The first conclusion concerns the codicological factor, the second the liturgical. Both are intrinsically related.

To begin with, the very process of cataloguing and classification as developed by Aland, Rahlfs etc and the attention for exact and extensive descriptions (the external and internal status quo) of whole or parts of any given codex is exemplary of the interest in the codices, in their content and form. But, since this attention was born from specialised needs, serving the purpose of particular research aims, different in the case of each catalogue, those catalogues we have at our disposal today still do not give us a complete picture of the actual, full contents of the manuscripts and their forms.

Secondly, although the liturgical nature of many codices was acknowledged by several catalogue compilers (Scrivener, Gregory, Metzger, Rahlfs, Engberg), it did not receive the attention it deserves, as the main focus in compiling the catalogues was determined by textual research aims and the use of the manuscripts in the constitution of new printed editions. If we acknowledge, however, that certain codex forms, think only of the Evangelion, were modelled according to their liturgical function, and that the services of the church demanded the need for a whole plethora of codex forms, we can ascertain that the liturgical factor is of utmost importance in assessing the why's and wherefore's of the forms of the extant codices.

There are some more recent studies that pay due attention to both the codicological as well as the liturgical factor. These include studies of the individual Byzantine codex forms: an Evangelion codex, Octateuch codices[240], a Psalterion codex[241], a (composite) codex of the Psalterion + Apostolo-evangelion, Prophetologion codices, Prophets codices[242], Prophets Commentary codices and the (composite) codices of the whole Greek Bible. These studies, conducted either from an artistic, philological, iconographical or hymnographical perspective, touch indeed upon the liturgical aspects of the codices, but for the time being they remain isolated examples, led by specialised research aims. Below we will elaborate some of these studies.

The first four examples we provide concern Byzantine lectionary codices. The next examples are dedicated to the so-called Byzantine text/catena manuscripts. The last example is the study of the Pandect OT/NT codices, which shows other facets of interest from the point of view of codicology.

1.4.1 A Byzantine Evangelion codex

G. Vikan has described the Evangelion codex now maintained in Baltimore/Maryland, Walters Art Gal., Ms. W. 535 (Aland *l*1029)[243] in some detail. His main interest lay in the manuscript's iconography. It is a large deluxe Greek manuscript (about 40 x 27 cm.), dated 1594 A.D., comprising in total 420 folios and includes numerous iconographic paintings (some elaborate portraits and fifty-seven framed marginal miniatures). The manuscript belonged to the Greek Orthodox Patriarchate of Jerusalem until ca 1918 and was finally acquired by H. Walters in the 1920s in Paris. It was copied and illuminated in Wallachia (Romania), illustrated in Moscow in ca 1596 and was sent as a gift to a church or monastery in Palestine. It was described by A. Papadopoulos-Kerameus in 1897 as codex 4 (title: Λειτουργικὸν εὐαγγέλιον) in his 'Catalogue of the Greek manuscripts maintained in the Skeuophylakion of the Church of the Anastasia', which can be found in T. III of his Ἱεροσολυμιτικὴ Βιβλιοθήκη (5 vols., St. Petersburg, 1891-1915 [Repr., Bruxelles, 1963]), 199-200. The liturgical nature of the manuscript and its particular function as reading book of the Byzantine liturgy is singled out by Vikan ('such service books continued to play a central role in the liturgy of the Orthodox – as the embodiment of Christ's divine wisdom in the "Little Entrance", and as an ever-present, often luxuriously bound altar implement –')[244].

The codex contains a full Evangelion lectionary (*le*), with complete lessons for all days of the Byzantine ecclesiastical movable year, from Easter to Easter [f. 9^r – 379^r], arranged in the order of lessons according to the

---

[240] K. Weitzmann and M. Bernabò, *The Byzantine Octateuchs* (Princeton, 1999); J. Lowden, *The Octateuchs. A Study in Byzantine Manuscript Illustration* (University Park, Pennsylvania, 1992).

[241] A. Cutler, *The Aristocratic Psalters in Byzantium* (Paris, 1981).

[242] J. Lowden, *Illuminated Prophet Books. A Study of Byzantine manuscripts of the Major and Minor Prophets*, (University Park and London, 1988); H. Belting and G. Cavallo, *Die Bibel des Niketas, Ein Werk der höfischen Buchkunst in Byzanz und sein antikes Vorbild* (Wiesbaden, 1979).

[243] G. Vikan, 'Walters Lectionary W.535 (A.D. 1594) and the Revival of Deluxe Greek Manuscript Production after the Fall of Constantinople', in *The Byzantine Tradition after the Fall of Constantinople*, Ed. J.J. Yiannias (Charlottesville / London, 1991), 181-222, with Plates 268-268 [Fig. 3.1-3.61].

[244] G. Vikan, *Op. Cit.* (Charlottesville / London, 1991), 181-182.

Gospels of John, Matthew, Luke and Mark), and with a full series of lessons for the fixed part of the Byzantine calendar [f. 380ᵛ – 421ᵛ]. The relevance of Vikan's particular study is the attention given to: a) the codex in its integral state (contents as well as form); b) the provenance and the scribe ('The Scribe')[245] of the codex; c) the broader codicological framework (comparison with other, similar and comparable Gospel lectionaries, such as Dionysiou 587, Morgan Library M 639, San Giorgio dei Greci 2, Vatican Library, Gr. 1156 and Jerusalem, Patriarchal Library, Anastaseos 5)[246]; and d) the liturgical function of the manuscript and organisation of the lesson cycles, in combination with the many detailed iconographic paintings (p. 207-209) compared with a similar Gospel lectionary of the same Jerusalem Patriarchal Library, Anastaseos 5 (p. 213-215)

1.4.2 A Byzantine Psalterion codex

L. Nees' article, "An Illuminated Byzantine Psalter at Harvard University" (1975)[247], concerns one particular Byzantine Psalter codex (including the Nine Odes appended to the 150 [+1] psalms), which stemmed from Constantinople and was purchased by E. Everett in 1819, who brought it to Harvard. This interest in an individual manuscript, with attention for all contents and its specific scribal and codicological features is characteristic for the approach. The Harvard Psalter, dated 1105 A.D., is written on parchment in minuscule script and in single columns (21 or 22 lines on a page), comprises 289 folios measuring 22.5 x 17.8 cm, and contains three full-page miniatures and three ornamental headpieces, two of which have figures. It is interesting that Nees was fully aware of the liturgical impact of the manuscript ('like the lectionary, the Psalter is a liturgical manuscript')[248] and that the contents of the Psalterion are not only linked to the Byzantine liturgy, but are completely imbued in it. In other words, the Psalterion plus Odes is primarily a lectionary manuscript and not a text manuscript[249]. Nees provided the following short description of the manuscript's contents.

Contents

f. 1 – 7v	Psellus' introduction to the Psalms
f. 8v	full-page miniature of the Deesis
f. 9r	ornamental headpiece to Psalm 1
f. 9r – 112v	Psalms 1 – 76
f. 113r	headpiece to Psalm 77
f. 113r – 215r	Psalms 77 – 151
f. 215v	full-page miniature of David and Goliath
f. 216v	full-page miniature of the Crossing of the Red Sea
f. 217r	headpiece to the first Ode of Moses
f. 217r – 232v	Odes
f. 232v	verses of an unidentified monk Gregory on the Last Judgement
f. 233r – 261v	various prayers
f. 262r – 279v	Synaxarion
f. 279v – 281v	Troparion
f. 282r – 289v	Easter tables

The integration of the Psalterion in the whole Byzantine liturgical repertoire explains why other patristic and liturgical textual elements are included in the codex, for instance, Psellus' introduction to the Psalms at the head of the codex. Moreover, Nees indicates existing relationships with other Psalterion codices and the codex forms of Evangelia and Praxapostoloi etc., with regard to the iconography in the manuscript.

1.4.3 A Byzantine Psalterion & Apostolo-evangelion codex

Another Byzantine codex form is the Psalterion & Apostolo-evangelion, which received the attention of S. Der Nersessian, "A Psalter and New Testament Manuscript at Dumbarton Oaks" (1965)[250]. It concerns Washington, Dumbarton Oaks Ms. 3 [Aland 1521], a manuscript which was acquired in 1962 and formerly belonged to the Athos Pantokrator Monastery. It was previously described by S.P. Lambros in his Κατάλογος τῶν ἐν ταῖς

---

[245] G. Vikan, *Op. Cit.* (Charlottesville / London, 1991), 186-190: the scribe is Luke the Cypriot. Cf. n.13 on p. 211 with a list of 'Luke's Manuscripts' (22).

[246] G. Vikan, *Op. Cit.* (Charlottesville / London, 1991), 190-194.

[247] L. Nees, "An Illuminated Byzantine Psalter at Harvard University", in *Dumbarton Oaks Papers*, 29 (1975), 207-224. Pl. 1-56.

[248] L. Nees, *Art. Cit.* (1975), 211.

[249] The differences in approach were already manifested in the editions of E.T. De Wald, *Psalms and Odes, 1. Vaticanus graecus 1927; 2. Vaticanus graecus 752* (The Hague, 1941-1942) and A. Rahlfs, *Psalmi cum Odis* (Göttingen, 1931 [repr. 1967 and 1979¹]).

[250] S. Der Nersessian, "A Psalter and New Testament Manuscript at Dumberton Oaks", in *Dumberton Oaks Papers*, 19 (1965), 153-183.

βιβλιοθήκαις τοῦ Ἁγίου Ὄρους ἑλληνικῶν κωδίκων, I, Pantokratoros, 49[251] [von Soden δ 477, Rahlfs 1031], XIV, as comprising 369 folios, but this figure should be rectified to 364 f. Another rectification is its age: 1084 A.D. Der Nersessian's *Description of the Manuscript* and *Contents of the Manuscript and Description of the Miniatures* is very precise, and provides excellent insight in the present state and contents of the codex [Psalms 1-151, Nine Odes, the four Gospels, Acts, Epistles of the Apostles and Pauline Epistles][252]. The title of the article "A Psalter and New Testament" is apparently used in a broad sense, since the mentioned NT part of the codex is, in fact, only the Apostolo-evangelion. The Nine Odes are placed between the Psalterion and the NT part of the codex. It is interesting that this manuscript combines different OT and NT contents, transcending the current boundaries between the two. As already stated, in biblical scholarship, this type of codex (and many other combined codex forms) were catalogued, but passed over as not being very relevant, save their iconography[253]. The contribution of Der Nersessian is therefore extremely welcome. Moreover, the combination of Psalter annex Apostolo-evangelion, as well as the other included contents (e.g. 'Tables of Gospel and Epistle lessons for the various liturgical cycles') clearly identifies the codex as a liturgical manuscript.

1.4.4 Byzantine Prophetologion codices

The most neglected, although characteristic OT codex form of the Byzantine liturgy is the Prophetologion. From a hymnographical point of view, attention was paid to the Byzantine Prophetologia in the context of the Copenhagen edition programme *Monumenta Musicae Byzantinae*. Although the musical factor expressed in the notation systems of Byzantine music manuscripts (ecphonetic notation) was the main research aim of the editors, they spent a lot of energy in collecting, collating and studying the liturgical background of the available materials. The programme was executed by a team of scholars of different generations, C. Høeg, G. Zuntz, G. Engberg (Eds.), *Prophetologium. I Pars prima: Lectiones anni mobilis continens (Fasc. I-VI)* (Copenhagen, 1939-1970); *Prophetologium. Pars altera: Lectiones anni immobilis (Fasc. I-II)*, (Monumenta Musicae Byzantinae. Lectionaria. Vol. I), Copenhagen, 1980-1981 [Indices][254]. The last editor, S. Engberg, who worked on the lessons of the fixed feasts of the Byzantine liturgical calendar in the Prophetologion codices (C. Høeg and G. Zuntz were engaged with the movable part of the Byzantine ecclesiastical year), wrote some interesting articles in which the liturgical aim and embedding of this type of Byzantine codex form was emphatically brought to the attention of the academic world (resp. in 2005, 2003, 1987)[255]. The edition was based initially on a small group of codices, but with Engberg the group was extended to 71 Prophetologion manuscripts of the 9th – 14th c.[256].

The full contents of both cycles of lessons are provided in an overview in the indices of the edition, the lessons of the movable part in *Prophetologium*, Vol. I, . Ed. C. Høeg and G. Zuntz (Copenhagen, 1970), Fasc. 6, 'Index Lectionum' [L 1 – L 47], 600-604 and 'Index Locorum', 605-609; completed with the lessons of the fixed part of the Byzantine Calendar in *Prophetologium, Vol. I, Pars Altera* (Copenhagen, 1980-1981), 'Index lectionum' [L 48 – L 76], 163-165 and 'Index Locorum Veteris Testamenti', 166-170 and 'Index Locorum Novi Testamenti', 171-173 and also an 'Index Psalmorum', 174-183. These give insight in the biblical substrata of the Byzantine Prophetologion and the sequences and extension of OT lessons in the context of the Byzantine liturgical order.

1.4.5 Byzantine Octateuch-Catena codices

Of the OT text manuscripts one codex form, comprising the first eight books of the Greek Bible (the Octateuch), had already been discussed in its "Octateuch form" in the context of art historical scholarship, early in the 20th century by T. Uspensky in 1907[257] and D.C. Hesseling in 1909[258]. The Octateuch was studied again and more

---

[251] S.P. Lambros, *Catalogue of the Greek Manuscripts on Mount Athos*. Κατάλογος τῶν ἐν ταῖς βιβλιοθήκαις τοῦ Ἁγίου Ὄρους ἑλληνικῶν κωδίκων, Vol 1 (Cambridge, 1895): Παντοκρ., 49, 98 [items 1-13].

[252] S. Der Nersessian, *Art. Cit.* (1965), 156- 164.

[253] Der Nersessian, *Art. Cit.* (1965), 156, remarks that even in manuscript iconography 'the miniatures have not been considered in their entirety and, strangely enough, those which accompany the New Testament have hardly ever been recorded'.

[254] A.A. Alexeev, 'The Old Testament Lections in Orthodox Worship', in *Op. Cit.* (Tübingen, 2004), 91-117, esp. 92-94.

[255] S.G. Engberg, "Les lectionnaires grecs", in *Les manuscrits liturgiques, cycle thématique 2003-2004 de l'IRHT* (Paris, 2005), 1-20; idem, "Prophetologion Manuscripts in the << New Finds >> of St. Catherine's at Sinai", in *Scriptorium*, 57.1 (2003), 94-109; idem, "The Greek Old Testament Lectionary as a Liturgical Book", in *Cahiers de l'Institut du Moyen Âge grec et latin*, 54 (1987), 39-48; and Engberg's forthcoming publication *Profetie-anagnosmata-prophetologion*.

[256] S.G. Engberg, 'Conspectus Codicum', in *Prophetologium. Pars altera: Lectiones anni immobilis (Fasc. I-II)* (Copenhagen, 1980-1981), Fasc.II, 307-308 [71 ms. items].

[257] T. Uspenskij, *L'Octateuch de la Bibliothèque du Sérail à Constantinople* (Sofia, 1907). [Title also in Russ.: 255p + 6 pl. and un Album avec 47 pl. in folio].

[258] D.-C. Hesseling, *Miniatures de l'Octateuque Grec de Smyrne manuscrit de l'école évangélique de Smyrne, édition phototypique* (Leiden, 1909).

intensively by J. Lowden, *The Octateuchs: A Study in Byzantine Manuscript Illustration* in 1992[259], and more recently in 1999 in the monumental joint publication of K. Weitzmann and M. Bernabò, *The Byzantine Octateuchs*[260].

The Byzantine Octateuchs survived in their complete codicological form since the 10th century. Lowden describes and discusses: Vaticanus Graecus 747 (XI), 260 f. [Rahlfs, 255, Cat. Oct.]; Smyrna, Evangelical School A.1 (XII, lost), 262 f. [Rahlfs, 293-294, Cat. Oct.]; Istanbul, Torkapi Sarayi Müzesi, Gr.8 (XII), 568 f. [cf. Rahlfs, 90, Cat. in Oct.]; Vaticanus Graecus 746 (XII), 508 f. [Rahlfs, 254-255, Cat. Oct.]; Mount Athos, Vatopedi 602 (XIII) [Rahlfs, 8-9, Lev. – Ruth, Scholia; cf. Spyridon/Eustratiades]. He provided an exact description of each of these codices, all of which are catena Octateuchs. We present here the first of the group, the Codex Vaticanus Graecus 747, to give an indication of the content of the codex form discussed (Lowden, Appendixes, 125).

Contents

1r – 11v	Letter of Aristeas
12r	Theodoret to Hypatius
12v	blank
13r – 71v	Genesis
72r – 122v	Exodus
123r – 146v	Leviticus
147	blank
148r -151v	Deuteronomy 4, 41-9, 2
152r-186v	Numbers 3, 13-34, 29
187r-215r	Deuteronomy (lacking Dt. 1, 1-3, 4, 41-12, 3)
215v – 236v	Joshua
237r – 255v	Judges
256r – 259r	Ruth
259r – 260v	On the Seven Translations
260r	On the Dispersals of the Israelites
260r – 260v	On the Oscurity of Holy Scripture
260v	On the Ten Names of God

It was not the Pentateuch form (there are only two Pentateuch codices known)[261], which served as the basic Byzantine OT unit, but the Octateuch (in text, commentary and catena codex forms).

Lowden and other investigators of the Octateuch indicate that pure forms existed. But, an investigation of the manuscript materials (see Rahlfs, *Verzeichnis*, 'Octateuchus', 374-382 [sub-divided in: a) Einfache Bibeltexte, b) Catenen, c) Commentare]) reveals that many "free combinations" were also produced, within the group and in combination with other OT (and NT) groups of books.

1.4.6 Byzantine Prophets-Catena codices

Clearly distinguished from the Prophetologion codices, which are lectionaries, are the Prophet codices in their basically threefold formation - text/catena/commentary. The dividing lines between the types of Byzantine manuscripts often seem to be less sharp than commonly supposed. This can be seen in the group of Prophet-catena codices (the XII minor and IV major Prophets). J. Lowden underlined that this particular codex form, of which several designations were in use, was not intended to be the "only" edition form[262]. He discussed the codices first individually: Vaticanus Chisianus R. VIII. 54; Turin, Biblioteca Nazionale Cod. B. I.2 and Florence, Biblioteca Medicea-Laurenziana, Cod. Plut. 5.9; Vaticanus Graecus 755; Oxford, Bodleian, Laudianus Graecus 30A; Oxford, New College 44; Vaticanus Graecus 1153 + 1154[263]. In fact, within the group of Prophet codices, a whole range of varieties of codices were produced; some combining for example Prophets and other OT books; others containing only the Minor Prophets. Lowden's studies of the Prophet codices provided not only factual descriptions and analyses of the discussed manuscripts, but also new observations concerning the more "well-known" codices[264].

---

[259] J. Lowden, *The Octateuchs. A Study in Byzantine Manuscript Illustration* (University Park, Pennsylvania, 1992).
[260] K. Weitzmann and M. Bernabò, *The Byzantine Octateuchs*, 2 vols. (Princeton, 1999).
[261] See Rahlfs' *Verzeichnis* (Berlin, 1914): Patmos, John the Theol. 411 and Rome, Bibl. Vat. Pii II. Gr. 20; note also two Pentateuchs with catena: Athos, Lavra, 189 and Patmos, John the Theol., 216.
[262] J. Lowden, *Op. Cit.* (University Park and London, 1988), 6-7.
[263] J. Lowden, *Op. Cit.* (University Park, Pennsylvania, 1992), 'Analysis of the Prophet Books', 9-38 and Appendices: Catalogue of manuscripts, 109-119.
[264] J. Lowden, *Op. Cit.* (University Park, Pennsylvania, 1992), 2.

1.4.7 The Pandect codex form of the Ancient Greek Bibles

T.S. Pattie's article "The Creation of the Great Codices"[265], discussing afresh the three famous codices of the 4th and 5th centuries; the first kept in Vatican City, Biblioteca Apostolica Vaticana, Ms. Vat. Gr. 1209 [IV], 1536 f. and the other two in London, British Library: Cod. Alexandrinus, BL, Royal MSS, I D v-viii [V], 279+238+118+144 f.; and Cod. Sinaiticus, Add. Ms 43725 [St. Petersburg, Imperial Public Library, Cod. Gr. 259], [IV], 393 f.[266]. These ancient codices (B, A, and א)[267] are considered from a technical/historical (codicological) point of view, in contrast to the longstanding discussion on the textual value of these codices. A codicological approach demands, as Pattie presupposes[268], a precise description of the whole codex and all its contents. This approach resulted in the following observations: 1) both parts (OT and NT) of the codices are treated together and on an equal basis (biblical scholars tend to study OT and NT parts, or the text of individual books, separately); 2) a complete enumeration of all the incorporated books is necessary for a complete picture of the codex; 3) the actual arrangement of the books is registered; 4) the organic inclusion of the anaginoskomena (OT) in the group of canonical books is a given; 5) the patristic and liturgical apparatuses/elements[269] are considered to be of decisive importance for the codicological and textual evaluation of the manuscripts.

Considered from this point of view, the question as to which codex entities (Evangelion, Praxapostolos, Psalterion, Octateuch etc.) can be identified as having been used by copyists as archetypes in the compilation and scribal production process should be explored, before textual issues can be solved. In our view, this is a challenging undertaking.

1.5 Recapitulation

The Byzantine manuscripts - the primary sources, and the editions based thereon, are the concrete material expression of the theological and liturgical tradition of the Eastern Orthodox church. There exists, one could say, a codicological "network" of manuscripts, an arrangement of interconnected liturgically motivated books, that developed since the 4th century and runs to the 16th century. This arrangement was continued in the printed editions from the 16th century onwards. Since the founding of the printing press, the Bible was published in a great diversity of editions (in book form, in translation, with and without commentary…), but, remarkably, the ecclesiastical-liturgical Byzantine codex forms were not published avidly, and neither were the Byzantine patristic commentaries. In Eastern printing tradition (after the Fall of Constantinople Greek printing houses and editors were primarily active in Venice and other locations in Italy, as well as in Jerusalem, Constantinople, Alexandria, Kiev, Moscow, St. Petersburg, etc.), the numerous codex forms of the manuscripts were reduced to, in fact, a select representation of only the most used liturgical, biblical, patristic and other ecclesiastical (and classical) books. If one leafs cursorily through the bibliographies of the later Byzantine and neo-Hellenic printed

---

[265] T.S. Pattie, 'The Creation of the Great Codices', in *The Bible as Book: the Manuscript Tradition* (London / Newcastle, 1998), 61-72.

[266] See for details respectively: Rahlfs, 258-260 (B), 114-116 (A), 226-229 (א); up-dated by D. Fraenkel, *Verzeichnis der griechischen Handschriften des Alten Testaments von Alfred Rahlfs. Die Überlieferung bis zum VIII Jahrhundert*, Bd. 1, 1, (Septuaginta Supplement) (Göttingen, 2004).

[267] See paragraph **6.4**: Tabular Specimens from the Catalogue: Group III, specimen VII, OT and NT Byzantine Greek codices.

[268] Editions: Codex Vaticanus Graecus 1209: G. Cozza–Luzi (ed.), *Vetus Testamentum iuxta LXX interpretum versionem e codice omnium antiquissimo Graeco Vaticano 1209 phototypice repraesentatum* (Rome, 1890); G. Cozza–Luzi (ed.), *Novum Testamentum e codice Vaticano 1209 nativi textus graeci primo omnium* (Rome, 1889); C. Vercellone et G. Cozza–Luzi (Eds.), *Bibliorum Sacrorum.Graecus: codex Vaticanus, auspice Pio IX. Pontifice Maximo collatis studiis* etc.,6 tom., (Rome, 1868-1881): v. 1: Pentateuchum et Librum Iosue (1869); v. 2: Libros Iudicum, Ruth, Regnorum (1870); v. 3: Paralipomenon et Esdrae (1871); v. 4: Libros Psalmorum, Proverbiorum, Ecclesiastes, Cantici, Iob, Sapientiae Salomonis et Sirachi; v. 5 Novum Testamentum (1868); v. 6: Prologomena, Commentarii et tabulae (1881)]; Codex Alexandrinus BL, Royal MSS, I D V-VIII: Ed. M. Thompson (Ed.), *Facsimile of the Codex Alexandrinus* (London, 1879-1883): v. 1: Genesis – 2 Chronicles (1881); v. 2: Hosea – 4 Maccabees (1883); v. 3: Psalms – Ecclesiastes (1883); v. 4: New Testament and Clemetine Epistles (1879); Codex Sinaiticus, Add. Ms 43725: H. and K. Lake (Eds.), *Codex Sinaiticus Petropolitanus. The Old Testament preserved in the public library of Petrograd, in the library of the Society of Ancient Literature in Petrograd, and in the Library of the University of Leipzig, now reproduced in facsimile from photographs, with a description and introduction to the history of the Codex* (Oxford, 1922); H. and K. Lake (Eds.), *Codex Sinaiticus Petropolitanus: the New Testament, the Epistle of Barnabas and the Shepherd of Hermas* (Oxford, 1911).

[269] H.B. Swete and R.R. Ottley, *An Introduction to the Old Testament in Greek* (Peabody, Mass., 1989 [repr. 1914]), 358: 'Such traces of adaptation to liturgical use are found even in cod. B, though not *prima manu*. Whether any of the larger chapters which appear in certain MSS. (e.g. the later system in cod. B) are of the nature of lections, must be remain doubtful until the whole subject has received the fuller treatment which it demands'.

editions since the Fall of Constantinople[270], a considerable edition history indeed, a decrease of the diversity and pluriformity of literary forms can be observed. Although the Byzantine manuscript tradition continued to produce new codices until far into the 19th century and even until the beginning of the 20th century, the great variety of codex forms is not represented in the editions published.

In order to recover the original codicological forms, we will proceed to look at the homeland of the Byzantine manuscripts, at liturgical practice and the climate of Eastern Orthodox tradition. In the following chapter we will set out what we referred to earlier as the 'liturgical hypothesis'. By revisiting the Byzantine liturgy, we can discover how the codex forms and the contents of the manuscripts were actually shaped by liturgical practice and how the (patristic) choices behind their form and content were crucial for their development. Recognition of the liturgical heritage of the codex formations leads us to want to regroup the extant codices in a manner different to the way in which they have been grouped to date. Thus the liturgical hypothesis eventually leads to the suggested outline of a codico-liturgical model of classification, which could lay at the basis of a future catalogue of the Byzantine manuscripts.

---

[270] E. Legrand, *Bibliographie Hellénique des XVe et XVIe siècles ou Description raisonnée des ouvrages publiés en Grec [ou] par des Grecs aux XVe et XVIe siècles* (Paris, 1885-1906; repr. 1962); Idem, *Bibliographie Hellénique ou Description raisonnée des ouvrages publiés par des Grecs aux dix-septième siècle* (Paris, 1894-1903 ; repr. Paris, 1975), I. Nos. 1-364bis (année 1601-1644) – 1894 ; II. Nos. 365-639 (année 1645-1690) – 1894; III. Nos. 640-715 (année 1691-1700) Notices biographiques – 1895; IV. Notices biographiques – 1896; V. Supplement. Notices biographiques – 1903]; E. Legrand and H. Pernot, *Bibliographie Ionienne. Description raisonnée des ouvrages publiés par des Grecs des sept-îles ou concernant ces îles du XVe siècle à l'année 1900* (Paris, 1910); E. Legrand, *Bibliographie Hellénique ou Description raisonnée des ouvrages publiés par des Grecs aux dix-huitième siècle* (Paris, 1918-1928; repr. Paris, ca. 1975), [I. Nos. 1-562 (année 1701-1760) – 1918; II Nos. 563-1260 (année 1761-1790) – 1928]; P. Meyer, *Die theologische Litteratur der griechischen Kirche im sechzehnten Jahrhundert. Mit einer allgemeinen Einleitung* (Leipzig, 1899); G.I. Zabiras, Νέα Ἑλλὰς ἢ Ἑλληνικὸν Θέατρον (Athens, 1872; repr. Athens, 1972); A. Demetrakopoulos, Προσθῆκαι καὶ διορθώσεις εἰς τὴν Νεοελληνικὴν Φιλολογίαν Κ. Σάθα (Leipzig, 1871); K.N. Sathas, Νεοελληνικὴ Φιλολογία. Βιογραφίαι τῶν ἐν τοῖς γράμμασι διαλαμψάντων Ἑλλήνων ἀπὸ τῆς καταλύσεως τῆς Βυζαντινῆς Αὐτοκρατορίας μέχρι τῆς ἐθνεγερσία (Athens, 1868); A. Papadopoulos Vretos, Νεοελληνικὴ Φιλολογία ἤτοι κατάλογος τῶν ἀπὸ πτώσεως τῆς βυζαντινῆς αὐτοκρατορίας μέχρι ἐνκαθιδρύσεως τῆς ἐν Ἑλλάδι βασιλείας τυπωθέντων βιβλίων παρ' Ἑλλήνων εἰς τὴν ὁμιλουμένην, ἢ εἰς τὴν ἀρχαίαν ἑλληνικὴν γλῶσσαν συνεθεὶς (Athens, 1854-1857).

Chapter 2

The Byzantine Liturgy and the Biblical and Patristic Manuscripts

In this chapter we will explore how the biblical and patristic manuscripts[271] are anchored in the Byzantine liturgy[272] (the 'liturgical hypothesis'), and that the liturgy is the domain that can well display the unity between the biblical and the patristic books. We will set the landscape of the Byzantine ecclesiastical and liturgical manuscripts, providing an overview of the main liturgical books that are still in use today. We will present the lectionary cycles and reading schemes which rule the manuscripts' use and function in the services. The lessons are scriptural, and they are based on the calendar of the Byzantine church, which is liturgical.

In the liturgy one can observe the way in which the fathers interpreted the Bible, which they laid at the base of liturgical rituals, images, lessons, psalmody, hymnology, to form a ritualised/visualised *interpretation* of Holy Scripture. Both liturgical practice and the reading from Scripture lie at the base of a complex historical process of simultaneous growth (symbiosis). We also look at the patristic, homiletic codices as a basic form of biblical exegesis, as here the hand of the Byzantine fathers is particularly visible.

We illustrate the way that the liturgical scriptures are 'used' in the data that we provide in chapter 3, i.e. the reading cycles of the Byzantine lection system. This data has the concrete function of showing the hermeneutics of the fathers that lies implicit in the manuscripts and that was responsible for their codex and textual forms. It is precisely this that makes codicology so important.

2.1 The Byzantine Ecclesiastical, Liturgical Manuscripts

It is not an easy task to subdivide the large group of Byzantine ecclesiastical manuscripts (τὰ ἐκκλησιαστικά)[273], comprising biblical, liturgical and patristic material into appropriate categories, or to set aside the liturgical codices (τὰ λειτουργικά)[274] from the larger group of codices in order to produce a representative list of codices of this nature[275]. When making distinctions one should be aware of the many codices which combine biblical, liturgical and patristic components. The Scriptures, for example, were not only interpreted in biblical commentary codices, but also in other categories of patristic books[276], such as the ascetical writings[277] and works

---

[271] 'Patrististic manuscripts' are, roughly defined: all biblical homilies and the whole arsenal of commentaries of the Byzantine fathers.

[272] For reading on the liturgy, and in particular, the Byzantine liturgy: M. Prokurat, A. Golitzin, M.D. Peterson (eds.), *Historical Dictionary of the Orthodox Church* (Lanham, MD, 1996), 413-426 ('Bibliography: Liturgy'); R. Taft, *The Byzantine Rite: A Short History* (Collegeville, 1992); H.J. Schulz, *The Byzantine Liturgy: Symbolic Structure and Faith Expression* (New York, 1986); G. Dix, *The Shape of the Liturgy* (San Francisco, 1982); K Kucharek, *The Byzantine-Slav Liturgy of Saint John* Chrysostom (Ontario, 1971); R. Bornert, *Les commentaires byzantines de la divine liturgie du VIIe au XVe siècle* (Paris, 1966); A. Schmemann, *Introduction to Liturgical Theology* (London/Portland, 1966); O. Casel, *The Mystery of Christian Worship and other Writings* (Westminster., Md., 1962); H.G. Beck, *Kirche und Theologische Literatur im byzantinischen Reich* (München, 1959); A. Baumstark, *Liturgie comparée* (Prieuré d'Amay, 1939); P. De Meester, 'Grecques (Liturgies)', in *Dictionnaire d'Archéologie Chrétienne et de Liturgie*, 6 (1925), 1643-1644; A. Baumstark, *Die Messe im Morgenland* (Kempten und München, 1906); F.E. Brightman, *Liturgies Eastern and Western*. Vol. I. Eastern Liturgies (Oxford, 1896); J.M. Neale, *A History of the Holy Eastern Church, Part 1: General Introduction*, 2 vols (London, 1850).

[273] Although the Byzantine manuscripts of Greek classical & philosophical works (the "κλασικοὶ συγγραφεῖς καὶ φιλοσοφικά") are excluded from the present investigation, they nevertheless belong to the all-embracing category of Byzantine manuscripts (Cf. P.K. Chrestou, Ἑλληνικὴ Πατρολογία, Τ. Α', Εἰσαγωγή (Thessaloniki, 1976), 58-66: 'Ἡ Φιλοσοφία). Excluded also are manuscript of Byzantine patristic literature such as church histories (ἱστορικά), canon law (κανονικὰ καὶ συνοδικά), and so on. The reason for this limitation is a practical one, not one of lack of evidence.

[274] O.G. Rigas, Τυπικόν, (Liturgica Vlatadon I), (Thessaloniki, 1994), 24-25: 'Λειτουργικὰ βιβλία: Τὸ *Εὐαγγέλιον*, Ὁ *Ἀπόστολος*, Τὸ *Εὐχολόγιον*, Τὸ *Ὡρολόγιον*, Τὸ *Ψαλτήριον*, *Μηναῖα* (τὰ δώδεκα), Τὸ *Τριῴδιον*, Τὸ *Πεντηκοστάριον*, Ἡ *Παρακλητική* and *Ὀκτώηχος*, Τὸ *Θεοτοκάριον*, Τὸ *Ἐκλογάριον*, Τὸ *Εἱρμολόγιον*, *Λειτουργικόν*, *Ἁγιασματάριον*, Τὸ *Τυπικόν*.

[275] P.K. Chrestou, *Op. Cit.* (Thessaloniki, 1976): ' Ἡ Ἑλληνικὴ Χριστιανικὴ [Πατερικὴ] Γραμματεία : Τὰ λογοτεχνικὰ εἴδη', 125-174: Εὐαγγέλια, Ἀποκαλύψεις, Ἀποστολικαὶ Πράξεις, Ἐπιστολαί, Ὁμιλίαι, Δογματικὰ Κείμενα, Λειτουργικὰ Κείμενα, Ποιήματα, Ἐκκλησιαστικαὶ Διατάξεις, Ἑρμηνευτικὰ Κείμενα, Ἱστοριογραφία, Πραγματεῖαι.

[276] For the Byzantine fathers (including the Pre- or Palaeo Byzantine fathers of the first centuries) up to the 15th c. and their works one may consult the Greek Index to the works of the Byzantine fathers (with full titles and contents) collected in Migne's PG, provided by Dorotheos Scholarios, Κλεὶς Πατρολογίας καὶ Βυζαντινῶν συγγραφέων (Athens, 1879, [Repr. in Migne, PG, T. 162]).

of spiritual guidance of, for instance, John Climacus, Makarius of Egypt, Ephrem the Syrian or Isaac the Syrian[278]. Furthermore, scriptural texts are included in the service codices, and liturgical instructions have been placed in the manuscripts of Scripture.

One cannot speak of systematic classification where the Byzantine scribes were concerned, diversity being one of the main characteristics of Byzantine booklore. This does not imply that there were no clearly separated categories of books and no systematisation at all, but there is a pluriformity of handwritten texts of Byzantine literature and, from the point of view of philologists of later times, their transmission at times seems highly chaotic[279].

What we identify in this thesis as the clear unifying factor of the Byzantine ecclesiastical codices is the given that all codices, which were used in the undivided church, and of which the immediate descendants are still in use today, are deeply rooted in the liturgy and in fact governed by its laws. We presuppose that all these codices, biblical or patristic, are liturgical, some more than others[280], and that many received their forms and names from their liturgical function and content.[281] In this thesis the study of the Byzantine liturgy, and in particular the *liturgical manuscripts*[282], is the area of research where biblical and patristic studies meet[283].

---

[277] See the Triodion, *passim*. Cf. Archimandrite Ephrem (Lash), 'Saint Ephrem the Syrian: Ascetical and other Writings extant only in Greek' and 'Theodore the Studite: Catecheses to his monks' [web.ukonline.co.uk/ephrem/ephrem.htm]. Cf. L. Politis, Ὁδηγὸς καταλόγου χειρογράφων (Athens, 1961), 52-53.

[278] For the edition of the writings of John Scholasticus, also called "Climacus", see Dorotheos Scholarios, *Op. Cit.* (Athens, 1879), 369-371 [Migne, PG 88]; Makarios the Egyptian, 100-103 [PG 34]. Concerning the writings of the Syrian fathers in Byzantine tradition, Isaac of Niniveh and Ephrem the Syrian, see H. Alfeyev, *The Spiritual World of Isaac the Syrian* (Kalamazoo, Mich., 2000) and the contributions of S. Brock, 'The Changing Faces of St Ephrem as Read in the West', and E. Lash, 'The Greek Writings Attributed to Saint Ephrem the Syrian', in J. Behr, A. Louth, D. Conomos (Eds.), *Abba. The Tradition of Orthodoxy in the West* (Crestwood, New York, 2003), resp. 65-80 and 81-98. || Translations: John Climacus, *The Ladder of Divine Ascent* (Boston, Mass., 1991); Isaac of Nineveh, *Mystic Treatises* (Amsterdam, 1923); Makarius the Great, *Fifty Spiritual Homilies* (Willits, Cal., 1974); [Ephrem the Syrian] *A Spiritual Psalter or Reflections on God, excerpted by Bishop Theophan the Recluse from the works of our Holy Father Ephraim the Syria*, (St. John of Kronstadt Press, 1997).

[279] J.M. Neale, *A History of the Holy Eastern Church, Part 1: General Introduction* (London, 1850), Book IV, Ch. III, 819: 'The Office-Books of the Orthodox Eastern Church, for to that alone I shall confine myself, present a field for investigation of very great difficulty. This arises from several causes, which it may be well to particularize. The variety, bulk, and intricacy of the volumes themselves; the number and obscurity of the rubrics; the unwritten tradition which guides and adjusts all, and a knowledge of which is a prerequisite, scarcely to be gained but by oral teaching; the abbreviations of diction, the extraordinary contractions of words, the technicalities in quotation of Psalms or versicles; the shifting backwards and forwards from book to book; the absence of any one general rule for concurrences of festivals; these things form one great source of difficulty'.

[280] L. Politis, Ὁδηγὸς καταλόγου χειρογράφων (Athens, 1961), 49: 'With regard to the great number of theological manuscripts we can make a distinction into two sub-divisions: (1) the manuscripts, which are used in worship, the liturgy of the church and its services; and (2) other manuscripts, which are used with an eye to this purpose.' ('εἰς τὸν μέγαν αὐτὸν ἀριθμὸν τῶν θεολογικῶν χειρογράφων δυνάμεθα νὰ διακρίνομεν δύο ὑποδιαιρέσεις, 1) τὰ χειρόγραφα, τὰ ὁποῖα χρησιμεύουν διὰ τὴν λατρείαν, τὴν ἐν τῇ ἐκκλησίᾳ λειτουργίαν καὶ τὰς ἀκολουθίας, καὶ 2) τὰ ἄλλα τὰ ὁποῖα δὲν χρησιμοποιοῦνται πρὸς τὸν σκοπὸν αὐτόν'). Politis makes a distinction has been made between 'theological' (τὰ θεολογικά) and 'ecclesiastical/liturgical' (τὰ ἐκκλησιαστικά/λειτουργικά) books. To the category of 'theological codices' belong (L. Politis, Ὁδηγὸς καταλόγου χειρογράφων (1961), 49-59): α') τὰ βιβλία τῆς Π. Διαθήκης; β') τὰ βιβλία τῆς Κ. Διαθήκης; γ') οἱ λόγοι Πατέρων (κυριακοδρόμια, πανηγυρικά); δ') βίοι καὶ μαρτύρια ἁγίων; ε') πατερικὰ καὶ γεροντικά. To the 'ecclesiastical/liturgical codices' belong (*Ibid.*, 61-69): Ψαλτήριον, Προφητεῖαι, Εὐαγγελιστάρια, Ἀπόστολος/Πραξαπόστολος, Μηναῖον, Συναξάρια, Τριῴδιον, Πεντηκοστάριον, Παρακλητική /Ὀκτώηχος, Ὡρολόγιον, Τυπικόν, Εὐχολόγιον, Αἱ θεῖαι λειτουργεῖαι, Ἀκολουθίαι, Πανδέκτη. Closely connected with the last group of codices are the 'codices of Byzantine music' (Μούσικα, *ibid.*, 70-72): Στιχηράριον, Παπαδική, Μαθηματάριον, Εἱρμολόγιον, Ἀναστασιματάριον, Δοξαστάριον, Ἀνθολόγιον.

[281] The designation Εὐαγγέλιον is used in the manuscripts for the whole group of Gospel codices (either 'continuous' or 'lectionary' text). Cf. I. Karavidopoulos, "The Origin and History of the Terms >>Evangelistarion<< and >>Evangeliarion<<", in *Orthodox Forum*, 7.2 (1993), 177-183. Consult for the terminology used for the Byzantine manuscripts in general (focused on codicological evidence) P.K. Chrestou, *Op. Cit.* (Thessaloniki, 1976), III στ'; L. Politis, *Op. Cit.* (Athens, 1961), 50 and 61-62.

[282] Particularly important for the study of the Byzantine liturgical manuscripts are the classical works of the Russians: A.A. Dimitrievsky, Описание литургическихъ рукописей хранящихся въ библиотекахъ православнаго востока [Description of the liturgical manuscripts kept in Eastern Orthodox Libraries], I-III (I. Kiev, 1895; II. Kiev, 1901; III. Petrograd, 1917); N.F. Krasnoseltsev, Материалы для истории чинопоследования литургии св Иоанна Златоустаго [Material for the History of the Order of the Liturgy of St. John Chrysostom] (Kazan, 1889); I.A. Karabinov, Тріодъ постная [The Lenten Triodion] (St. Petersburg, 1910); N.F. Krasnoseltsev, Сведения о некоторыхъ литургическихъ рукописяхъ Ватиканской библиотеки [Witnesses of some Liturgical Manuscripts of the Vatican Library] (Kazan, 1885). || Other literature concerning the study of liturgical (and chant) manuscripts: R.F. Taft, *A History of the Liturgy of St. John Chrysostom: The Precommunion Rites*, Vol. V (Rome, 2000), 'Index of manuscripts'; G.T. Stathis, Τὰ χειρόγραφα Βυζαντινῆς μουσικῆς, Ἅγιον Ὄρος. Κατάλογος περιγραφικὸς τῶν χειρογράφων κωδίκων Βυζαντινῆς μουσικῆς τῶν ἀποκείμενων ἐν ταῖς βιβλιοθήκαις τῶν ἱερωνύμων καὶ σκητῶν τοῦ Ἁγίου Ὄρους, τ. 1-3 (Athens, 1975, 1976, 1993); R.F. Taft, 'Chronological List of Manuscripts' and 'Index of Manuscripts', in *The Great Entrance* (Rome, 1978), 435-446 and 447-453; M. Arranz, "Les grandes etapes de la liturgie byzantine: Palestine - Byzance - Russie. Essai d'aperçu historique", in *Liturgie de l'Église Particulière et Liturgie de l'Église Universelle* (1976); D.E. Conomos, *Byzantine Trisagia and Cheroubika of the Fourteenth and Fifteenth Centuries: A Study of Late Byzantine Liturgical Chant* (Thessaloniki, 1974), 47-49; A. Jacob, 'La Tradition Manuscrite de la Liturgie de Saint Jean Chrysostome', in *Eucharisties d'orient en d'occident* (Paris, 1970), 109-138; A. Jacob, *Histoire du formulaires grecs de la liturgie de Saint Jean Chrysostome* (Louvain, 1968); P.N. Trempelas (Ed.), Αἱ τρεῖς λειτουργίαι κατὰ τοὺς ἐν ἀθήναις κώδικας (Athens, 1935); P. De Meester, 'Grecques (Liturgies)', in *Dictionnaire d'Archéologie Chrétienne et de Liturgie*, 6 (1925), 1643-1644; A. Gastoué, *Introduction à la paléographie musical byzantine. Catalogue du MSS. de musique byzantine* (Paris, 1907); A. Jacob, "Les euchologes du fonds Barberini grec de la Bibliothèque Vaticane", in *Didaskalia*, 4 (1974), 131-222; D.N. Moraitis, "Οἱ ἐν τῇ Ἐθνικῇ

How is the liturgical fundament to be demonstrated? The Byzantine scriptural codices of the OT & NT have been differentiated into two types: codices that contain continuous 'text manuscripts'; and codices that contain series of scriptural lessons in a (moderately) re-arranged form - 'lectionary manuscripts'.[284] Both have in common that they are "used" in the Byzantine Liturgy i.e. they are read publicly. The Fourfold Gospel Codex (Τετραευαγγέλιον, including Matthew, Mark, Luke and John), as well as the Apostle Codex (Απόστολος or Πραξαπόστολος, including Acts, the Pauline and General Epistles) for example, are essentially liturgical, since a serious number[285] of these codices contain lectionary equipment[286] and tables (συναξάρια and/or μηνολόγια) of Gospel, Apostolic and Prophetic lessons.[287] A considerable number of text and commentary codices are similarly provided with lectionary equipment[288]. An additional liturgical aspect is the ecphonetic notation[289] in the scriptural codices (indicating recitation or chanted form of reading - 'ekphonesis'[290]). Such evidence dispels any doubts as to the original liturgical context in which these manuscripts developed.

The rearrangement of the Bible by the fathers into codex units, in both text form (with lectionary equipment) as well as in lectionary form for use in the services had far-reaching theological and interpretative consequences. The grouping together of the four Gospels (τὰ τέσσαρα εὐαγγέλια) had a protective (by canonical decision) as well as a hermeneutical impact, emphasising on the one hand the inner harmony between the four Gospels and on the other hand the exclusion of all non-canonical gospels (ἀπόκρυφα and ψευδεπίγραφα)[291]. The grouping of the Acts and the Pauline and Catholic Epistles into the Praxapostolos was also a practical (an act of canon formation) and interpretative choice; by bringing these books together in one codex, they could be read in the liturgy and studied together. Thus the Apostolos was codicologically clearly differentiated from the Evangelion (Εὐαγγέλιον), through their very codex forms, whilst the liturgical unity was maintained in the practice of

---

Βιβλιοθήκη τῶν Παρισίων ῾Ελληνικοὶ λειτουργικοὶ κώδικες", in Θεολογία, 24 (1953), 536-542; F.E. Brightman, *Liturgies Eastern and Western*. Vol. I. Eastern Liturgies (Oxford, 1896), lxxxviii-xci 'Manuscripts'.

[283] The study of the liturgy is a discipline in its own right, almost completely isolated from biblical research. Byzantine liturgics, which should be a pillar of patrology, is not always fairly represented in patristic handbooks and studies. Nevertheless, in P.K. Chrestou, *Op. Cit.* (Thessaloniki, 1976-1992); G. Florovsky, *The Byzantine Fathers of the VIth – VIIIth Centuries* (Belmont, Mass, 1987), Ch 1; J. Meyendorff, *Byzantine Theology. Historical Trends and Doctrinal Themes* (Oxford, 1983); B. Altaner and A. Stuiber, *Patrologie. Leben, Schriften und Lehre der Kirchenväter* (Freiburg/Basel/Wien, 1980); L. Politis, *Op. Cit.* (Athens, 1961); H.G. Beck, *Kirche und Theologische Literatur im byzantinischen Reich* (München, 1959); A. Ehrhard, 'Theologie', in *Geschichte der Byzantinischen Litteratur von Justinian bis zum Ende des oströmischen Reiches (527-1453)*, Ed. K.Krumbacher (München, 1897), the subject was considered important enough to be discussed as part of patristic studies.

[284] In Byzantine tradition this category of liturgical books was not called 'lectionaries'. Cf. C.R. Gregory, *Textkritik des Neuen Testamentes* (Leipzig, 1900), 333; B.M. Metzger, 'Greek lectionaries and a critical edition of the Greek New Testament', in *Die alten Übersetzungen*, by K. Aland (Ed) (Berlin/New York, 1972). The Greek equivalent 'τὰ ἀναγινωσκόμενα' [i.e. βιβλία] is but rarely used or used in the form of a description, see L. Politis, *Op. Cit.* (Thessaloniki, 1961), 61: 'οἱ ἐπ᾽ ἐκκλησίᾳ ἀναγινωσκόμεναι περικοπαὶ τῶν βιβλίων τῆς Παλαιᾶς καὶ τῆς Καινῆς Διαθήκης'. Names of the Byzantine liturgical books were derived from the contents of these books and standardised.

[285] F.H.A. Scrivener, *A Plain Introduction to the Criticism of the New Testament for the Use of Biblical Students* (London, 1894), I, 74-77; esp. 76: 'they are more frequently found than the contrary in later manuscripts [i.e. minuscules] of every kind; while there are comparatively few copies that have not been accommodated to ecclesiastical use either by their original scribe or a later hand, by means of noting the proper days for each lesson (often in red ink) at the top or bottom or in the margin of the several pages. Not only in the margin, but even the text itself is perpetually interpolated, mostly in vermilion or red ink, the beginning (ἀρχή or αρχ) and ending (τέλος or τελ) of each lesson, and the words to be inserted or substituted in order to suit the purpose of public reading'. See also C.R. Gregory, *Op. Cit.*, I (Leipzig, 1900), 339: '...die in den vielen Handschriften der Vier-Evangelien und der Apostel-geschichte und Briefe stehen' (i.e. said of Synaxaria and Menologia of lessons).

[286] See chapter 1, box 2.

[287] Lit: L. Politis, *Op. Cit.* (Thessaloniki 1961), 50: 'πολλάκις εἰς τὸ τέλος ἐπιτάσσεται ἐν εἴδει εὑρετηρίου πίναξ τῶν ἐπ᾽ ἐκκλησίᾳ ἀναγινωσκομένων περικοπῶν κατὰ τὴν χρονολογικὴν σειρὰν (ἀπὸ τῆς Κυριακῆς τοῦ Πάσχα μέχρι τοῦ Μεγάλου Σαββάτου καὶ ἀπὸ τοῦ Σεπτεμβρίου μέχρι τοῦ Αὐγούστου); Cf. H. von Soden, *Op. Cit.* (Göttingen, 1911), I, 19-20; 99-100 and 101-102. Lectionary equipment is registered minutely in Liste IV, 102-248 (Codices mit neut. Text geordnet nach Inhalt und Alter), 249-289 (Kommentarcodices). The following abbreviations are used: Lect. = Lektionenvermerk am Rande; Lect[text] = Lektionsanfänge rot im Text; Lect[tab] = Listen der Lektionen. See for a transposition of von Soden's classification into the current Gregory-Aland system the 'Sigelkonkordanzen' in K. Aland (et al.), *Op. Cit.* (Berlin / New York, 1994); C.R. Gregory, *Op. Cit.* (Leipzig, 1900), I, in the descriptions of the manuscripts; F.H.A. Scrivener, *Op. Cit.* (London, 1894), in the descriptions of the then available manuscripts in vol. I; cf. abbr. on pages 189-190 (with regard to the cursive manuscripts).

[288] H. von Soden, *Op. Cit.* (Göttingen, 1911), I, 249-289 (Kommentarcodices), *passim*.

[289] A considerable number of service codices – such as the Horologion or the Pentecostarion - also contain 'ecphonetic' signs.

[290] The introduction of the expression 'ecphonetic' in scholarly literature ('den durch diese Zeichen geregelten Vortrag aus den Lesebüchern der byzantinischen Kirche") is attributed to J. Tzetzes (1874) and J. Thibaut (1899); cf. E. Wellesz, "Die byzantinischen Lektionszeichen", in *Zeitschrift für Musikwissenschaft*, 11 (1929), 513, quoting Tzetzes in translation: 'Da Psalmen und Gebete mit lauter Stimme (ἐκφώνως) gelesen wurden'; J. Thibaut, "Etude de Musique byzantine: Le chant ekphonétique", in *Byzantinische Zeitschrift*, 8 (1899), 122-147.

[291] See the judgement of Bishop Melito of Sardis (2nd C.) with regard to the so-called Gospel of Peter, mentioned in Eusebius of Caesarea, *The Ecclesiastical History* II (Cambridge, Mass. & London, 1980), VI 12, 41: 'For our part, brethren, we receive both Peter and the other apostles as Christ, but the writings which falsely bear their names we reject, as men of experience (ἔμπειροι), knowing that such were not handed down to us'.

reading from both codices in close proximity to one another in the liturgy (see the Liturgy of John Chrysostom²⁹²).

As we saw previously, it was Ehrhard, who became convinced of the deep liturgical roots of also the Byzantine Greek hagiographic-homiletic codices and who made the liturgical hypothesis convincible by means of an enormous research programme, based to a large extent on autopsy of the manuscripts: 'The transmission of the writings of the Church fathers of the first five ages and the early Byzantine theologians is for the greatest part not dominated by academic interests, but, exceptions excluded, primarily by liturgical'²⁹³. Ehrhard developed a large group of classification categories in order to make the main characteristics of the manuscripts belonging to this, a prima facie, huge group transparent (manuscripts of the 8/9th to the 16th c.)²⁹⁴. One of his conclusions was that the patristic collections of the Lives of Saints and panegyrica/homilies were based on the *biblical* substrata of the daily, weekly and yearly lessons of the Orthodox Liturgy²⁹⁵.

> Finally I acknowledged that both the Menologia, as well as all these hagiographic-homiletic Mss were nothing else than liturgical books, in which the lessons were prepared, and which according to the rules of the so-called Typika, i.e. the arrangements of worship, should be performed during the morning service, and that the different types of their collections corresponded to the different liturgical needs.
> A. Ehrhard, *Op. Cit*, (Leipzig-Berlin, 1937-1952), Vorwort, vii-viii [Trans Ed]

This was a first step towards re-identifying the principle of "inner cohesion" between bible research and patristic studies in Byzantine tradition.

We might discriminate cautiously and subdivide the whole group of Byzantine ecclesiastical/liturgical manuscripts and printed editions under main headings that correspond to their contents.²⁹⁶ The following overview is adopted from the indices of Greek manuscript catalogues.

A. Ἁγιαγραφικά or Ἁγίαι Γραφαὶ: codices including complete books or partial compilations of the Scriptures, which are roughly subdivided in Παλαιὰ Διαθήκη and Νέα Διαθήκη (Greek OT and NT manuscripts);
B. Ἑρμηνεῖαι Γραφῶν / Ἐξηγητικά: codices including the biblical commentaries, homilies and catecheses on the Scriptures, but especially on the Evangelion (Four Gospels) and on the lessons of the liturgical year (see C and D); they appear in different forms: Ὑπομνήματα, Σχόλια, Σειραί, Ἐρωτήσεις καὶ Ἀποκρίσεις (Ἀπορίαι καὶ Λύσεις);
C. Ὁμιλίαι and Πανηγυρικά: liturgical homilies and festival orations on the feasts and saints (both genres based on liturgical biblical lessons);
D. Κυριακοδρόμια: codices including patristic commentaries on the Sunday lessons (collections of Sunday/Kyriake homilies);
E. Λειτουργικά: liturgical or service codices, e.g. Euchologia, Horologia, Menaia, and so on, composed of prayers of the Divine Liturgies and offices, litanies, doxologies and including a great variety of hymnographical compositions;
F. Ἑρμηνεῖαι τῆς Λειτουργίας: codices with commentaries on the Byzantine liturgies;
G. Ἐκκλησιαστικὴ μουσική: codices including hymnographical materials collected according to the musical needs of the Church;
H. Συναξάρια καὶ Μαρτυρολόγια: codices consisting of Synaxaria²⁹⁷ and Martyrologia, that are the accounts of the lives of the Saints (Βίοι ὁσίων) and martyrs as celebrated in the course of the Byzantine liturgical year;

---

²⁹² Edition: Εὐχολόγιον τὸ Μέγα τῆς κατὰ Ἀνατόλας Ὀρθοδόξου Ἐκκλησίας, Ed. S. Zervos (Athens, 1992), 52-53. Translation: The Stavropegic Monastery of St. John the Baptist, Essex (Ed.), *The Orthodox Liturgy being The Divine Liturgies of S. John Chrysostom and S. Basil the Great and the Divine Office of the Presanctified Gifts* (Oxford, 1982), 46-50.
²⁹³ A. Ehrhard, *Op. Cit.*, Vol. II (Leipzig-Berlin, 1937-1952), 209
²⁹⁴ A. Ehrhard, *Op. Cit.* (Leipzig-Berlin, 1937-1952), I, xv: 'Ich mache darauf aufmerksam, daß die Grenze, bis zu welcher ich die Hss heranzog, das Ende des 16. Jahrhunderts ist. In die Bibliotheken des Ostens befinden sich allerdings manche einschlägige Hss, die aus dem 17. und 18. Jahrhundert stammen. In der Regel sind es aber Abschriften älterer Hss ohne selbständigen Wert. Diejenigen, die für die Kenntnis der älteren Sammlungen von Wichtigkeit sind, habe ich berücksichtigt'.
²⁹⁵ Ehrhard, however, underlined these underlying and connecting factors, but did not pay much attention to the biblical lessons (only here and there), which were read in the same liturgical context and according to the same cycles (movable and unmovable) of the Byzantine calendar on which the homilies and panegyrica were built. Neither did he discuss the liturgical place of the hagiographic and homiletic materials in more detail within the Byzantine services, besides what was presented in the Einleitung and the calendaric aspect.
²⁹⁶ For a quick overview of the later (printed) Byzantine Greek ecclesiastical literature and literary categories, see A.P. Vretos, Νεοελληνικὴ Φιλολογία ἤτοι κατάλογος τῶν ἀπὸ πτώσεως τῆς βυζαντινῆς αὐτοκρατορίας μέχρι ἐνκαθιδρύσεως τῆς ἐν Ἑλλάδι βασιλείας τυπωθέντων βιβλίων παρ' Ἑλλήνων εἰς τὴν ὁμιλουμένην, ἢ εἰς τὴν ἀρχαίαν ἑλληνικὴν γλῶσσαν συνεθεὶς (Athens, 1854-1857), vol. I.
²⁹⁷ F. Halkin, *Catalogue des manuscrits hagiographiques de la Bibliothèque Nationale d'Athènes* (Brussels, 1983), F. Halkin, *Manuscrits grecs de Paris. Inventaire hagiographique* (Brussels, 1968); H. Delehaye, *Synxarium ecclesiae Constantinopolitanae* (Leuven, 1954); H. Delehaye, "Catalogus codicum hagiographicorum graecorum bibliothecae Scholae theologicae in Chalce insula", in *Analecta Bollandiana*, 44 (1926), 5-63; A. Ehrhard, 'Theologie', in *Geschichte der byzantinischen Litteratur von Justinian bis zum Ende des oströmischen Reiches (527-1453)*, Ed. K. Krumbacher, 2nd ed (München, 1897). For a general introduction, see Makarios (Hieromonk) of Simonos Petra, *The Synaxarion. The Lives of the Saints of the Orthodox Church* (Ormylia / Chalkidike, 1998), Introduction, vii-xxiii, General Bibliography, xxv-xxxvii.

I. Ἀσκητικά: ascetical codices (Ἀποφθέγματα τῶν ὁσίων πατέρων, πατερικά, γεροντικά, λαυσαϊκά, παράδεισος, φιλοκαλία), some of them used to support the lessons and homilies read during the liturgical year (e.g. the Κατηχήσεις of Theodore of Studios, the Κλίμαξ τοῦ Παραδείσου of John Climacus[298]);

J. Διδασκαλίαι τῶν Πατρῶν καὶ τῶν ἐκκλησιαστικῶν συγγράφεων: codices with dogmatic and anti-heretical materials.

K. Κανονικὰ καὶ Συνοδικά: codices containing the documents of the Ecumenical and Local Synods and other relevant materials for the study of Canon Law or Nomokanon (Νομοκανων).

L. Ἐκκλησιαστικαὶ ἱστορίαι: Church historical codices (including historical notes to Byzantine literature).

Sources of Greek nomenclature: Papadopoulos-Kerameus[299]; Sakkelion/Sakkelion[300]; Politis[301]; Dorotheos Scholarios[302].

All these codices have in common their heritage in the services of the undivided church. They share the aspect of being rooted not only in the liturgy, but also in Byzantine biblical tradition.[303] They are, for this reason, closely related to each other, and form, in fact, one codicological family, which is profoundly scriptural in essence.[304]

The majority of biblical scholars have tended to set aside the Byzantine liturgical manuscripts from the group of so-called 'text manuscripts' [i.e. the continuous or plain text manuscripts][305]. Some scholars have asked for attention to be paid to the textual value of the lectionary manuscripts (Osburn, Metzger, Colwell, Rahlfs, Antoniades, Gregory, Scrivener, Matthaei), but to date these have not yet been given adequate attention.[306] The link between the Byzantine liturgy (in the evolution of which the fathers were intensively engaged)[307], the biblical manuscripts (in the formation of which the fathers intervened not a little) and the patristic commentary manuscripts, has rarely been taken as point of departure for manuscript or textual research. Thus we are now faced with the difficulty of positioning the Byzantine liturgical books correctly in the field of manuscript research. The Scriptures and other liturgical codices are still used today in the Eastern Orthodox churches, and they have been printed and reprinted throughout the ages with only marginal codicological or textual changes, as

---

[298] Τριῴδιον κατανυκτικόν, περιέχον ἄπασαν τὴν ἀνήκουσαν αὐτῷ ἀκολουθίαν τῆς ἁγίας καὶ μεγάλης τεσσαρακοστῆς. ἀπὸ τῆς κυριακῆς τοῦ τελώνου καὶ τοῦ φαρισαίου μέχρι τοῦ ἁγίου καὶ μεγάλου σαββάτου (2003), 175 (during Great Lent the catecheses of Theodor of Studios are read), 176 (the Klimaka are read).

[299] A.I. Papadopoulos-Kerameus, Ἱεροσολυμιτικὴ Βιβλιοθήκη, 5 vols. (St. Petersburg, 1891-1915 [Repr., Bruxelles, 1963]).

[300] I. Sakkelion and A.I. Sakkelion, Κατάλογος τῶν χειρογράφων τῆς Ἐθνικῆς Βιβλιοθήκης τῆς Ἑλλάδος (Athens, 1892).

[301] L. Politis, Op. Cit. (Athens, 1961).

[302] Dorotheos Scholarios, Op. Cit. (Athens, 1879).

[303] See A. Ehrhard, Op. Cit. (Leipzig / Berlin, 1937-1952), 27: 'Um so ausgiebiger sind sie, vor allem die Homiliarien, mit Lesungen für die ersten zwei Teile versehen. Maßgebend für diese Lesungen selbst sind durchwegs die Evangelienperikopen, die an den betreffenden Sonn- und Wochentagen gelesen wurden. Das Perikopensystem, das in den meisten Fällen vorausgesetzt wird, ist kein anderes als das byzantinische, das vom 9. Jahrhundert an die Allein herrschaft im oströmischen Reiche besaß'.

[304] Mother Mary and Archimandrite K. Ware, *The Festal Menaion* (London, 1977), 16: 'The material in the Orthodox service books falls into two clearly defined categories. First, there is a Scriptural 'stratum' – readings from the Psalter and other parts of the Old Testament, from the Epistles and the Gospels. Alongside this, there is a non-Scriptural 'stratum', consisting in religious poetry – canons, stichera, kontakia, sessional hymns, and the like. (...) Yet even this second 'stratum' is in its deeper reality profoundly Scriptural, being everywhere permeated with Biblical images and phraseology: indeed, the Orthodox service books as a whole are in the last analysis little else than one vast and extended meditation upon Holy Scripture.'

[305] For instance, Aland, Metzger, von Soden, Nestle, Westcott/Hort (Greek NT) and Marcos, Hanhart, Wevers, Ziegler, Swete, (Greek OT), Rahlfs (Greek OT). A rare exception is C.R. Gregory, 'Griechische Liturgische Bücher', in Op. Cit. (Leipzig, 1900), I, 327-342, who presented an introduction to the list of lectionaries. 331-332: 'Oder wir könnten umgekehrt vom Gottesdienst und von Liturgien oder gottesdienstlichen Ordnungen reden und von da aus zu den Lesestücken gelangen. Man weiss überhaupt wenig, viel zu wenig, über die kirchlichen Bücher der Griechen. (...) Wenn ich Zeit hätte hier näher auf diese Bücher einzugehen, so wären, ausser den „Evangelien" und den „Aposteln", hauptsächlich folgende sechs ins Auge zu fassen: μηναῖον, μηνολόγιον, τριώδιον, τυπικόν, εὐχολόγιον, und ἀνθολόγιον. Sie fassen das zusammen, was für den Gottesdienst nötig ist, von verschiedenen Seiten ausgehend und unter jeweiliger betonung der erzählenden, erbauenden, gesanglichen, oder betenden Bedürfnisse des Geistlichen und der Gemeinde. In alle diese Bücher ist es möglich, dass die Hersteller gelegentlich Lesestücke aus dem Alten und aus dem Neuen Testamente aufnehmen'. But in the same introduction (p. 333) he accepted separation of the categories. B. Metzger also pointed towards the importance of the 'NT lectionary codices' and their liturgical background.

[306] A concise research history of lectionary manuscripts can be found in C.D. Osburn, 'The Greek Lectionaries of the New Testament', in *The Text of the New Testament in Contemporary Research* (Grand Rapids/ Mich, 1995), 61-74 and B.M. Metzger, 'Greek lectionaries and a critical edition of the Greek New Testament', in *Die alten Übersetzungen*, by K. Aland (Ed) (Berlin/New York, 1972).

[307] Contributors in the evolution process of the Byzantine liturgy (liturgies) were John Chrysostom, Basil the Great and Gregory Dialogos (cf. E. Wellesz, 'Byzantine Liturgy', in *A History of Byzantine Music and Hymnography* (Oxford, 1971), 123-124), and later, with regard to the development of the Byzantine office, some generations of hymnograhers: Andreas of Crete, Sophronios of Jerusalem, Kosmas of Maiuma, John of Damascus, Theodoros the Studite and Joseph the Studite (cf. E. Wellesz, Op. Cit. (Oxford, 1971), 204, 206, 229, 234, 236-237; 'List of Hymnographers from the fifth to the fifteenth centuries', 442-444; T. Ware (Bishop Kallistos of Diokleia), 'The Liturgical Hymnography', in *The Lenten Triodion* (London & Boston, 1977), 40-43); H.J.W. Tillyard, *Byzantine Music and Hymnography* (London, 1923) [repr. New York, 1976], Ch. III-V. ‖ Lit. R.F. Taft, *The Byzantine Rite. A Short History* (American Essays in Liturgy) (Collegeville, 1992); A. Schmemann, *Introduction to Liturgical Theology* (London/Portland, 1966); A. Baumstark, *Die Messe im Morgenland* (Kempten und München, 1906); F.E. Brightman, *Liturgies Eastern and Western.* (Vol. I. Eastern Liturgies) (Oxford, 1896).

far as we can oversee³⁰⁸, a fact which demands that they should also be studied in their own context, namely as part of the Byzantine liturgy.

A complicating factor in the setting of the landscape of the Byzantine liturgical codices, is that a comprehensive catalogue of the Byzantine liturgical codices, which is a basic must for our investigations, does not seem to exist³⁰⁹. It would certainly be welcome if such a catalogue were drawn up in the near future, however complex the task may be. There are several past and future research initiatives in the field of the liturgical manuscripts which need mentioning. Especially valuable, although less known in the West (beyond a small group of experts), is a group of Russian liturgists (Dimitrievsky, Krasnoseltsev, Karabinov, Skabalanovich, Mansvetov, Nikolsky, Mirkovich, Bishop Uspensky, Golubtzov, Muretov), which operated around the end of the 19th and beginning of the 20th century. This group studied the Byzantine sources of the Orthodox liturgy extensively. In Western academic circles, first steps have been taken in the study of this branch of Byzantine studies (Goar, Allatius, Pitra, Brightmann, Baumstark, Wellesz, de Meester, Jacob, Mateos, Arranz, Taft and others), but these studies took place independently from biblical and patristic studies.

In the following we advocate that biblical research be re-positioned on a liturgical and patristic frame of reference, and broadened to include not only pure text manuscripts but lectionaries and liturgical books as well. The Byzantine liturgical manuscripts, be they scriptural, service books or commentaries, are literary products in which the scribal hand of the Byzantine fathers is evident. The fathers not only modelled the Scriptures into forms appropriate for their liturgical functions, they also modelled the liturgy according to Scripture. Acknowledgement of this liturgical and patristic frame of reference leads to the recognition of the interrelationship between the different groups of manuscripts. Our research endeavours will be concentrated on repositioning the Byzantine liturgical manuscripts in their original context, which will have repercussions on the integration of the different isolated disciplines, such as Byzantine liturgical studies, hymnography, biblical science and patrology. The Byzantine liturgy is advocated to be the common denominator of all the Byzantine ecclesiastical books.

2.2 Scripture in the Byzantine Liturgical Manuscripts

> The exceptional importance of the liturgical approach to Biblical studies is evident, since the sacred status of Scripture is at the same time the groundwork and expression of its public presentation in office. As for catechetical instructions, they depend entirely on liturgical use of the Scriptures.
> **A. Alexeev**, 'The Old Testament lections in Orthodox Worship', in *Das Alte Testament als christliche Bibel in orthodoxer und westlicher Sicht* (Tübingen, 2004) 91-92.

2.2.1 Scripture in the liturgy

It is within the framework of the liturgy that the Scriptures were and are still read and explained.³¹⁰ In fact, the Scriptures are liturgical books κατ'ἔξοχεν³¹¹, and any dividing line between biblical and liturgical is, from the point of view of Byzantine tradition, unjustified on the ground of manuscript evidence. It was in the context of the early Christian liturgy that the Prophets and other OT books³¹², and later the Gospels and the Letters were

---

³⁰⁸ E.G. Pantelakis, "Les Livres ecclésiastiques de l'Orthodoxie. Étude Historique", in *Irénikon*, 13.5 (1936), 521- 557, esp. 538.

³⁰⁹ C.R. Gregory, in *Op. Cit.* (Leipzig, 1900) already underlined the necessity of new research (I, p. 331): 'Man weiss überhaupt wenig, viel zu wenig, über die kirchlichen Bücher der Griechen', cf. n.1 on the same page, and p. 332; with reference to a catalogue of liturgical books he says on p. 333: 'Da wir aber unmöglich eine eigene Liste für jede Art von Buch aufstellen können, so wäre es richtig und praktisch, meine ich, drei Abteilungen zu machen: Evangelien, Apostel, und andere liturgische Bücher. Die ersten zwei wären die Hauptteile, da die betreffenden Bücher ausgesprochener Massen den neutestamentlichen Text enthalten und fast nichts sonst. Die dritte Abteilung hätte dann die Menäen, Euchologien, und andere liturgische Bücher aufzunehmen (...)'. However, at that time it was not yet possible to set up a catalogue of this category (p. 333: 'So begnügen wir uns für heute mit den zwei Teilen, und beschränken unsere weitere Bemerkungen auf sie, auf die Lesebücher des Neuen Testaments'). In 1900 this chapter was given the remarkable title 'Griechische Liturgische Bücher'; in 1909 he changed this to 'Lesebücher' (already in Gregory's concept of the 'Kurzgefasste Liste' in 1908: Handschriften des NT).

³¹⁰ D. Constantelos, "The Holy Scriptures in Greek Orthodox Worship (A Comparative and Statistical Study)", in *The Greek Orthodox Theological Review*, 12.1 (1966), 7-9: 'The starting point in every service is a phrase from the Holy Scriptures and almost every Liturgy, Sacrament, and service includes readings from the Bible. (...) The worship and the liturgical books of the Church abound in Scriptural Elements. This is clear from the evidence found in the hymnology and the prayers, the ethical, the doctrinal, and liturgical life of the Church (...). But the claim of the Orthodox Church for the Scriptural character is not based exclusively on the aforementioned readings, but rather on the evidence that her various liturgical acts and her prayer life, hymns, and services are imbued, one might almost say immersed, with Scriptural verses and allusions.'

³¹¹ O.G. Rigas, Τυπικόν (Thessaloniki, 1994), 24-25, enummerates the Scriptures used in the Greek Orthodox Church under the heading 'Λειτουγικὰ βιβλία'.

³¹² H.B. Swete and R.R. Ottley, *An Introduction to the Old Testament in Greek* (Peabody, Mass., 1989 [Repr. 1914]), 356-358.

read and interpreted³¹³. Christ's words, which were handed down to us in the biblical codices – the *Evangelion* and the *Apostolos*, were also adopted in liturgical codices such as the *Euchologion* (Εὐχολόγιον)³¹⁴ – the priest's handbook comprising the texts for the liturgical celebrations and other mysteries and prayers for a wide spectrum of occasions³¹⁵ - just think of the scriptural text: [ἐγὼ γὰρ παρέλαβον ἀπὸ τοῦ Κυρίου ὃ καὶ παρέδωκα ὑμῖν...]: 'λάβετε φάγετε· τοῦτό μού ἐστι τὸ σῶμα τὸ ὑπὲρ ὑμῶν κλώμενον· τοῦτο ποιεῖτε εἰς τὴν ἐμὴν ἀνάμνησιν...τοῦτο τὸ ποτήριον ἡ καινὴ διαθήκη ἐστὶν ἐν τῷ ἐμῷ αἵματι· τοῦτο ποιεῖτε ὁσάκις ἂν πίνητε, εἰς τὴν ἐμὴν ἀνάμνησιν' (I Cor. 11, 23-26):

> ['Ο δὲ Ἱερεὺς ἐπεύχεται μυστικῶς]: ...λαβὼν ἄρτον ἐν ταῖς ἁγίαις αὐτοῦ καὶ ἀχραντοῖς, καὶ ἀμωμήτοις χερσὶν, εὐχαριστήσας, καὶ εὐλογήσας, ἁγιάσας, κλάσας, ἔδωκε τοῖς ἁγίοις αὐτοῦ Μαθηταῖς καὶ Ἀποστόλοις, εἰπών· ['Εκφώνως]: Λάβετε, φάγετε, τοῦτό μού ἐστι τὸ Σῶμα, τὸ ὑπὲρ ὑμῶν κλώμενον, εἰς ἄφεσιν ἁμαρτιῶν.
> ['Ο Χορός·]: Ἀμήν.
> [Εἶτα μυστικῶς ὁ Ἱερεύς]: Ὁμοίως καὶ τὸ Ποτήριον μετὰ τὸ δειπνῆσαι, λέγων· ['Εκφώνως]: Πίετε ἐξ αὐτοῦ πάντες, τοῦτο ἐστι τὸ Αἷμα μου, τὸ τῆς καινῆς διαθήκης, τὸ ὑπὲρ ὑμῶν, καὶ πολλῶν ἐκχυνόμενον, εἰς ἄφεσιν ἁμαρτιῶν.
> ['Ο Χορός·]: Ἀμήν.
>
> Divine Liturgy of St. John Chrysostom, in the *Great Euchologion*³¹⁶

The *Propheteia* (Προφητεία)³¹⁷ or *Prophetologion* (Προφητολόγιον)³¹⁸ was an archetypal Byzantine liturgical book, containing series of OT lessons (prophetical, historical, sapiential)³¹⁹. Another OT liturgical book, read integrally in the church, is the *Psalterion* (Ψαλτήριον)³²⁰, otherwise called 'the Psalms of David' (Ψαλμῶν Δαυίδ). For liturgical reasons it is divided into 20 sections ('kathismata' and three 'staseis')³²¹. The Psalterion is supplemented with the Nine (Biblical) Odes (Αἱ ἐννέα ᾠδαί), a select series of OT and NT Chants stemming from ancient liturgical practice. This book was, and in fact, still is the prayer book of the Orthodox church. The Psalterion is used in all Byzantine liturgical services. According to the *Typikon* (Τυπικὸν)³²², the Psalterion should be read independently throughout the whole programme of daily offices (the weekly psalmodic cycle), and it also lies at the basis of hymnography.

The apostolic witnesses concerning the Gospel of Christ were brought together in the *Apostolos*³²³, that is the 'Messenger'. The denotation is in the singular, indicating the intrinsic unity of three distinguished groups contained therein: the Acts of the Apostles (Πράξεις τῶν Ἀποστόλων); the Fourteen Epistles of Paul (Αἱ ιδ΄

---

[313] E. Werner, 'The Churches and their Lessons: Sources', in *The Sacred Bridge. The Interdependence of Liturgy and Music in Synagogue and Church during the First Millennium* (London / New York, 1959), 58-63; C.R. Gregory, 'Griechische Liturgische Bücher', in *Op. Cit.* (Leipzig, 1900-1909), Vol. I, 327-342.

[314] Greek edition: Εὐχολόγιον τὸ Μέγα τῆς κατὰ Ἀνατόλας Ὀρθοδόξου Ἐκκλησίας (Athens, 1992). Translation: *Service Book of the Holy Orthodox-Catholic Apostolic Church, compiled, translated, and arranged from the Old Church-Slavonic service books of the Russian Church and collated with the service books of the Greek Church*, Ed. I.F. Hapgood (Englewood / New Jersey, 1983).

[315] The Εὐχολόγιον τὸ Μέγα (Athens, 1992), demonstrates a profound representation of adopted biblical texts. Added are, for instance, the Aposteloi and Evangelia [lessons] of the Feasts of the Lord and the Mother of God and the celebrated saints for the whole year [Sept.-Aug.], 613-663.

[316] Εὐχολόγιον τὸ Μέγα (Athens, 1992), 63.

[317] A. Rahlfs, *Op. Cit.* (Berlin, 1914), xx: 'Die Lectionare werden in den Hss. oft als προφητεία bezeichnet (z.b. Petersburg, K. öff. Bibl., Graec. 217); genauer sagt die Hs. Athen, Nat.-Bibl., 24: βιβλίον ὃ τὰς προφητείας τῶν προφητῶν περιέχει. Die griechischen Katalogschreiber brauchen gewöhnlich den terminus προφητολόγιον'. Probably the Russian Archimandrite Antonin Kapustin (19th century) introduced the expression in his catalogue of St. Catharina's monastery's library. See note S. Engberg, "Prophetologion Manuscripts in the << New Finds >> of St. Catherine's at Sinai", in *Scriptorium*, 57.1 (2003), 94 ('He may, of course, have used a term current in the Monastery itself'). The Russian liturgical tradition uses the term 'паремийникъ' (see Moscow, Syn. Libr. Cod. 8, = Vladimir, I, 7); it means, 'proverbs' (derived from the selected lessons, which should be read from the OT books during the ecclesistical year; among these are lessons of the book Proverbs (Παροιμίαι). Cf. K. Onasch, *Das Weinachtsfest im orthodoxen Kirchenjahr. Liturgie und Ikonographie* (Berlin, 1958), 'Das Lesebuch des AT, das sog. Paroimienbuch, "Parimejnik", wird gewiß auch von Konstantin oder Method hergestellt worden sein. Der älteste Parimejnik ist der Grigorovičev Parimejnik aus dem 12.-13. Jhdt'. See also F.J. Thomson, "The Slavonic Translation of the Old Testament", in *The Interpretation of the Bible. The International Symposium in Slovenia*, by J. Krašovec (Ed.) (Sheffield, 1998), 719-728.

[318] There exists an edition of the Prophetologion edited by the Institute of Byzantine Musical Studies in Copenhagen: C. Høeg, G. Zuntz, G. Engberg (eds.), *Prophetologium I-II* (Monumenta Musicae Byzantinae. Lectionaria. Vol. I) (Copenhagen, 1939-1981). Translation: *Prophetologion/The Lectionary*, Ed. Archimandrite Ephrem (Lash), http://web.ukonline.co.uk/ephrem/prophetologion.htm.

[319] Today the Propheteia/Prophetologion is incorporated in and spread over three liturgical books: the Triodion, the Pentekostarion and the (twelve) Menaia; cf. A. Alexeev, 'The Old Testament lections in Orthodox Worship', in *Das Alte Testament als christliche Bibel in orthodoxer und westlicher Sicht* (Tübingen, 2004), 91-117.

[320] Greek edition: Ψαλτήριον τοῦ προφήτου καὶ βασιλέως Δαυὶδ, μετὰ τῶν ἐννέα ᾠδῶν καὶ τῆς ἑρμηνείας ὅπως δεῖ στιχολογεῖσθαι τὸ Ψαλτήριον ἐν ὅλῳ τῷ ἐνιαυτῷ, 9th ed., (Athens, 2002). Translation: *The Psalter According to the Seventy, of St. David, the Prophet and King, together with the Nine Odes and an Interpretation of how the psalter should be recited throughout the whole year*, Trans: Holy Transfiguration Monastery (Boston, Mass., 1987).

[321] H.B. Swete and R.R. Ottley, *Op. Cit.* (Peabody, Mass., 1989 [Repr. 1914]), 359.

[322] O.G. Rigas, 'Στιχολογία τοῦ Ψαλτηρίου', in Τυπικόν (Thessaloniki, 1994), 31-37.

[323] Greek edition: Ἀπόστολος, Πράξεις καὶ Ἐπιστολαὶ τῶν ἁγίων Ἀποστόλων αἱ καθ' ὅλον τὸ ἔτος ἐπ' Ἐκκλησίαις ἀναγιγνωσκόμεναι καθὼς καὶ τῶν ἱερῶν τελετῶν, 5th ed., (Athens, 2002). Translation: *The Apostolos. The English New Testament Text is based on The Orthodox New Testament*, Ed. Holy Apostles Convent and Dormition Skete (Buena Vista, Colorado, 2000).

ἐπιστολαὶ Παύλου)³²⁴ and the Seven General Epistles (Αἱ ἑπτὰ καθολικαὶ ἐπιστολαί). The Apostolos was read in preparation of the reading from the Evangelion. The *Evangelion*³²⁵, that is, the 'Message' [of Jesus Christ] (Εὐαγγέλιον [i.e. ᾽Ιησοῦ Χριστοῦ]), containing the four canonical Gospels [in the order of John, Matthew, Luke, Mark or Matthew, Marc, Luke, John] in one book, grew out of and was used for liturgical practice.

2.2.2 The biblical substratum of the Byzantine liturgical codices

Just as the Scriptures and writings of the fathers are rooted in the liturgy, the Byzantine liturgical books in their turn have their foundation in Scripture and were conceived in patristic tradition.³²⁶ Both the Scriptures and the liturgical books were modelled and remodelled by the hands of the Byzantine fathers over the course of many ages³²⁷. In particular, the names of John Chrysostom, Basil the Great, Andrew of Crete, John of Damascus, Theodor the Studite are associated to the creative and editorial liturgical process. The fathers were, in other words, the *scribes* of the biblical books, and at the same time, the editors and commentators of the biblical texts. Quite remarkably the liturgical books can be studied in their most recent and up to date stage of evolution³²⁸, as they are used today in Greek speaking Orthodox churches. One can revisit their evolution in the earlier stages of their development via earlier printed editions back to the manuscript forms. In our opinion, the continuing interpretative framework of the liturgy is an essential factor to understanding the transmission of these texts, as the liturgy is not a dead artefact. The liturgical books were brought together into separate volumes of diverse contents and formats through a long, historical process. It is exactly in these liturgical testimonies that one will find the inner cohesion between Scripture and the writings of the fathers most clearly demonstrated. In order to expose the argument in more detail we will give a short overview of the main Byzantine liturgical books (Λειτουργικὰ βιβλία) in use today³²⁹ and show how these reveal the interconnectedness of the biblical texts and the interpretative framework of the fathers.

Of prime importance are the *Divine Liturgies* (Αἱ θεῖαι λειτουργεῖαι³³⁰), which include the three Liturgies of John Chrysostom and Basil the Great and the Liturgy of the Pre-sanctified Gifts. Next to this small compilation there is the afore-mentioned thick codex of the *Euchologion*, literally the 'Book of Prayer', which comprised the texts for liturgical celebrations used by the serving hierarch or priest. Constantelos reminds us that: 'All these services bear the influence of the Holy Scriptures. All include readings from the Holy Bible, both the Old and the New Testaments'.³³¹

The daily communal prayer book, the *Horologion* (῾Ωρολόγιον)³³² - the 'Book of Hours' – is intended for the readers and singers and comprises the biblical and liturgical texts of the "prayer hours" of the church (evening

---

[324] The Epistle to the Hebrews is codicologically included in the corpus of Pauline letters.

[325] <u>Greek edition</u>: Θεῖον καὶ ᾽Ιερὸν Εὐαγγέλιον κατὰ τὸ κείμενον τὸ ἐγκεκριμένον ὑπὸ τῆς Μεγάλης τοῦ Χριστοῦ ᾽Εκκλησίας, 2ⁿᵈ ed. (Athens, 1992). <u>Translation</u>: *The Evangelion. The English New Testament Text is based on The Orthodox New Testament*, Ed. Holy Apostles Convent and Dormition Skete (Buena Vista, Colorado, 2000).

[326] D.E. Conomos, 'Introduction' to *Byzantine Trisagia and Cheroubika of the Fourteenth and Fifteenth Centuries: A Study of Late Byzantine Liturgical Chant* (Thessaloniki, 1974); E. Wellesz, *A History of Byzantine Music and Hymnography* (Oxford, 1971), Ch. V; K. Kucharek, *The Byzantine-Slav Liturgy of Saint John Chrysostom* (Ontario, 1971); A. Schmemann, *Op. Cit.* (London/Portland, 1966); A. Baumstark, *Op. Cit.* (Kempten und München, 1906); F.E. Brightman, *Op. Cit.* (Oxford, 1896).

[327] R.F. Taft, *Op. Cit.* (Collegeville, 1992); H.J. Schulz, *The Byzantine Liturgy: Symbolic Structure and Faith Expression* (New York, 1986); R. Bornert, *Les commentaires byzantines de la divine liturgie du VIIe au XVe siècle* (Paris, 1966); P. De Meester, 'Grecques (Liturgies)', in *Dictionnaire d'Archéologie Chrétienne et de Liturgie* (1925).

[328] For a regressive approach of the study of liturgical books and their content (OT lessons), see A. Rahlfs, 'Die alttestamentlichen Lektionen der griechischen Kirche', in *Mitteilungen des Septuaginta-Unternehmens*, Heft V (Berlin, 1915), 146: 'Die alttestamentlichen Lektionen finden sich nicht nur in den Lektionaren, sondern auch in anderen liturgischen Büchern, besonders im Triodion, Pentekostarion und den Menäen, sowie im Anthologion. Hier sind sie allerdings mehr in der großen Masse des liturgischen Materials versteckt, weshalb ich diese werke in mein Verzeichnis der griechischen Hss. des A.T. nicht aufgenommen habe. Aber für den ersten Anfang der Arbeit auf diesem Felde bieten gerade diese größeren Werke einen unverkennbaren Vorteil darin, daß sie öfter gedruckt und daher ziemlich leicht zugänglich sind. Daher habe ich seinerzeit die Arbeit mit der exzerpierung jener größeren Werke begonnen und will auch hier kurz über ihr Verhältnis zu den Lektionaren berichten, da sie anderen, die sich mit diesen Studien beschäftigen wollen, gleichfalls als Ausgangspunkt dienen können'.

[329] For a concise overview, see O.G. Rigas, Τυπικόν (Thessaloniki, 1994): Λειτουργικὰ βιβλία, p. 24-25. There are fifteen books summarized in the following sequence: Τὸ Εὐαγγέλιον; ῾Ο ᾽Απόστολος; Τὸ Εὐχολόγιον; Τὸ ῾Ωρολόγιον; Τὸ Ψαλτήριον; Μηναῖα (τὰ δώδεκα); Τὸ Τριῴδιον; Τὸ Πεντηκοστάριον; ῾Η Παρακλητικὴ or ἡ ᾽Οκτώηχος; Τὸ Θεοτοκάριον; Τὸ ᾽Εκλογάριον; Τὸ Εἱρμολόγιον; Τὸ Λειτουργικόν; Τὸ ᾽Αγιασματάριον; and Τὸ Τυπικόν. Besides this work I will use L. Politis, *Op. Cit.* (Athens, 1961) in the following.

[330] <u>Greek edition</u>: Αἱ τρεῖς λειτουργίαι κατὰ τοὺς ἐν ἀθήναις κώδικας, Ed. P.N. Trempelas (Athens, 1935). <u>Translation</u>: *The Orthodox Liturgy being The Divine Liturgies of S. John Chrysostom and S. Basil the Great and The Divine Office of the Presanctified Gifts*, Ed. The Stavropegic Monastery of St. John the Baptist, Essex (Oxford, 1982).

[331] D.J. Constantelos, "The Holy Scriptures in Greek Orthodox Worship (A Comparative and Statistical Study)", in *The Greek Orthodox Theological Review*, 12.1 (1966), 8-9.

[332] <u>Greek edition</u>: ῾Ωρολόγιον τὸ Μέγα, περιέχον ἅπασαν τὴν ἀνήκουσαν αὐτῷ ἀκολουθίαν κατὰ τὴν τάξιν τῆς ᾽Ανατολικῆς ᾽Εκκλησίας καὶ τῶν ὑποκειμένων αὐτῇ εὐαγῶν Μοναστηρίων, 15ᵗʰ ed., (Athens, 2003). <u>Translation</u>: *The Unabbreviated Horologion*, Ed. rassaphor-monk Laurence (n.l., 1984).

and morning offices, the first, third hours etc.). Beside the above mentioned books, which are needed for the performance of the daily liturgy and offices, we have the books that prescribe the feasts and comemmorations for the different periods of the movable cycle of the Byzantine calendar: the *Triodion* (Τριῴδιον)[333] for the period of Great Lent; the *Pentekostarion* (Πεντηκοστάριον, 'Book of Fifty Days')[334] for the Easter period until Pentecost; and the *Oktoechos* ('Οκτώηχος[335], 'Book of Eight Modes (Tones)'), incorporating the hymnographical material for the liturgical period between Pentecost and the next Lenten Fast, weeks which are ruled by the recurring 'mode of the week'. This last book in an extended form (also including hymns for the weekdays) is called the *Parakletike* (Παρακλητική)[336], which could be translated as the 'Book of Comfort' (or Consolation). A parallel set of books for the choir /chanters is called the *Menaia* (Μηναῖα)[337], edited in twelve volumes (τὰ δώδεκα), comprising the hymnological material for the dated feasts and commemorations. The *Typikon* (Τυπικόν)[338], the liturgical 'Book of Order (Rule)', is the book that organizes and coordinates the different services in the course of the Byzantine ecclesiastical year and its liturgical cycles.

Ceremonial performance of public readings in the Liturgy of the Orthodox Church

The reading from Scripture (ἡ ἀνάγνωσις) in the Byzantine liturgy is a multi-layered ritual, which is described in minute detail in the liturgical books[339]. It embraces (a) the ceremonial handling of the Scriptures (how the Evangelion Codex is carried in procession from the Altar to the Katholikon of the Church during the Little Entrance (Μικρὰ Εἰσόδος) and its lifting up before the Iconastasis in sight of the congregation); (b) the chanted reading/recitation ("ekphonesis") of one of the selected lessons (τὸ ἀνάγνωσμα) from the series of inter-connected lessons: from the Psalterion, Prophetologion, Apostolos and the Evangelion; (c) the explanation of the lesson read (ἡ ἐξήγησις) or homily (ὁμιλία) by the celebrating hierarch (an archbishop, bishop or priest), in the liturgical context of the Sundays, feasts and commemorations.

Instructions concerning liturgical ceremonies and the role of Scripture therein

The Scriptures are represented in the liturgical codices in the instructions or rubrics in the Typikon and other service books, indicating how to handle and when and how to read from the Evangelion, Apostolos, Psalterion and Prophetologion. They are differentiated from the main text by the use of red ink. But not everything was written down. An interesting example of an unwritten instruction with regard to the liturgical role of the Evangelion in the Divine Liturgy, is the instruction to lift up the Evangelion Codex by the celebrant, and make the sign of the cross with it above the Holy Table, as he pronounces the opening words of the Divine Liturgy. These instructions, be they written or orally transmitted, connect the group of scriptural codices explicitly with the tradition of which they are the witnesses This tradition is set down in the liturgical books. The fact that Scripture is so incorporated in the liturgical books, points in the direction of their liturgical function and hermeneutical worth.

---

[333] Greek edition: Τριῴδιον κατανυκτικὸν, περιέχον ἅπασαν τὴν ἀνήκουσαν αὐτῷ ἀκολουθίαν τῆς ἁγίας καὶ μεγάλης τεσσαρακοστῆς, ἀπὸ τῆς κυριακῆς τοῦ τελώνου καὶ τοῦ φαρισαίου μέχρι τοῦ ἁγίου καὶ μεγάλου σαββάτου, 2nd ed. (Athens, 2003). Translation: *The Lenten Triodion*, Trans. Mother Mary and Archimandrite K. Ware (London & Boston, 1978).

[334] Greek edition: Πεντηκοστάριον χαρμόσυνον τὴν ἀπὸ τοῦ Πάσχα μέχρι τῆς τῶν ἁγίων πάντων κυριακῆς ἀνήκουσαν αὐτῷ ἀκολουθίαν, 2nd edition (Athens, 2002. [1st ed. 1994]). Translation: *The Pentecostarion*, Trans. Holy Transfiguration Monastery (Boston, Mass., 1990).

[335] Greek edition: Ὀκτώηχος τοῦ ἐν ἁγίοις πατρὸς ἡμῶν Ἰωάννου τοῦ Δαμασκηνοῦ, περιέχουσα τὴν ἐν ταῖς Κυριακαῖς τοῦ Ἐνιαυτοῦ Ψαλλομένην Ἀναστάσιμον Ἀκολουθίαν, by N.P. Papadopoulos (Ed.) (Athens and Thessaloniki, n.d. [1947]). Translation: *The Octoechos. Saturday and Sunday Offices Tones 1 – 8*, Trans. Orthodox Monastery of the Veil of Our Lady (Bussy-en-Othe, n.d).

[336] Greek edition: Παρακλητικὴ ἤτοι Ὀκτώηχος ἡ Μεγάλη, περιέχον ἅπασαν τὴν ἀνήκουσαν αὐτῷ ἀκολουθίαν, 3rd ed. (Athens, 1992).

[337] Greek edition: Μηναῖον τοῦ [Month: Σεπτεμβρίου etc.], περιέχον ἅπασαν τὴν ἀνήκουσαν αὐτῷ ἀκολουθίαν, διορθωθὲν τὸ πρίν ὑπὸ Βαρθολομαίου Κουτλουμουσιανοῦ τοῦ Ἰμβρίου καὶ πάρ'αὐτοῦ αὐξηθέν τῇ τοῦ τυπικοῦ προσθήκῃ κατὰ τὴν διάταξιν τῆς ἁγίας τοῦ Χριστοῦ Μεγάλης Ἐκκλησίας, Τ. I-XII , 6th ed. (Athens, 1990-2003). Translation: *The Festal Menaion*, Trans. Mother Mary and Archimandrite K. Ware (London, 1977); *The Complete Menaion, providing the services for the feasts of Our Lord Jesus Christ, of the Most Holy Theotokos, and of the Saints for Every Day of the Year, set to the meter of the original Byzantine melodies*, Trans. I.E. Lambertsen, (Holy Transfiguration Monastery), vols. 1-12 (Boston, Mass, 2005).

[338] Greek edition: Τυπικὸν τῆς τοῦ Χριστοῦ Μεγάλης Ἐκκλησίας, ὅμοιον καθ' ὅλα πρὸς τὴν ἐν Κωνσταντινουπόλει ἐγκεκριμένην ἔκδοσιν ἥτις δὶς ἐξεδόθη ὑπὸ Κωνσταντίνου πρωτοψάλτου μὲ πολλὰς προσθήκας καὶ ἐπιδιορθώσεις, revised ed. by G. Violakis (Protopsaltes) [on the basis of the edition of Protopsaltes Constantine] (Athens and Thessaloniki, n.d. [Repr. of the edition of M. Saliveros, Athens, 1915]) Translation: Ed. F.S. Kovalchuk, *Abriged Typicon* (South Canaan, 1985).

[339] See for the exact rules, O.G. Rigas, Τυπικόν (Thessaloniki, 1994), 123-126.

Biblical lessons in the Byzantine liturgical books

The liturgical codices abound with literal biblical lessons, the inclusion of texts and "off-texts" (rubrics), for example:

- the Apostle and Gospel lessons of the Great Feasts of the Lord and the Mother of God[340], included at the end of the Euchologion[341];
- the integration of scriptural lessons from the Prophetologion in the Triodion, the Pentecostarion and the Menaia[342];
- the adoption of the Eleven Anastasima Lessons for the Morning Service placed at the end of the Pentecostarion;[343]
- the Twelve Passion Gospels read on Good Friday referred to in the Triodion[344].

> See § 3.3 **The Cycle of the Eleven Resurrection Evangelia,** for an example of a series of Gospel lessons focused on the central theme of the Resurrection, that were selected by the fathers to be adopted in lection system of the liturgy.

Reception of particular biblical passages in Byzantine liturgical texts

There are many literal scriptural quotations interspersed throughout the service books. For instance, the Beatitudes (οἱ Μακαρισμοί[345]) at the beginning of the liturgy; the *Trisagion* (Τὸ Τρισάγιον[346]); Our Father (Πάτερ ἡμῶν)[347]; or the words of Christ spoken to His disciples at the Last Supper, which were transmitted in liturgical and scriptural form (as found in the Gospels and with the apostle Paul)[348].

Combined biblical and liturgical materials in certain codices

For example an Euchologion with OT lessons as well as Apostoloevangelia (Gregory Evl 52, Aland *l* 52 indicated as *l*⁺ᵃLit); or an Euchologion with NT lessons (Gregory Evl 54 = Aland *l* 54); or Menaia Sept – Febr with OT and NT lessons here and there etc. This domain of research is completely unexplored.

Byzantine liturgical books containing homiletic, hagiographic and ascetical readings

There are many prescriptions in the liturgical books that homilies, orations, encomia, lives of saints and panegyrics (which are based on the scriptual lesson of the day or feast), but also ascetical writings of the fathers should be read in the morning service of the Sundays and of feasts, especially during Lent.[349]

The Byzantine liturgical codices are vehicles for the transmission of Scripture, in a whole scala of rich and varied manners. These scriptural texts can be worthwhile for text researchers. These ancient layers in the

---

[340] See the List of feasts and commemorations in paragraph **2.5.2**.

[341] Εὐχολόγιον τὸ Μέγα τῆς κατὰ Ἀνατόλας Ὀρθοδόξου Ἐκκλησίας, Athens (1992), 613-666: Ἀπόστολοι καὶ Εὐαγγέλια τῶν τοῦ ὅλου ἐνιαυτοῦ etc.

[342] These OT lessons especially may stem from a very ancient date in the evolution of the biblical text, since the Apostolic Church commenced with OT readings, before the Gospels were written. A. Rahlfs, 'Die alttestamentlichen Lektionen der griechischen Kirche', in *Mitteilungen des Septuaginta-Unternehmens* (Berlin, 1915): Kap. II. 'Die alttestamentlichen Lektionen in den gedruckten Ausgaben des Triodion, des Pentekostarion, der Menäen und des Anthologion', 146-153 and S.G. Engberg, 'Les lectionnaires grecs', in *Les manuscrits liturgiques, cycle thématique 2003-2004 de l'IHRT*, by O. Legendre and J.B. Lebigue (Paris, 2005).

[343] Πεντηκοστάριον χαρμόσυνον, 2nd edition (Athens, 2002), 587-594: Εὐαγγέλια Ἀναστάσιμα Ἑωτινᾶια'; cf. also Εὐχολόγιον τό Μέγα (Athens, 1992), 667-676, where these Eleven Resurrection Morning lessons can be found. These lessons are read during the morning service of the Kyriake according to an independent recurring cycle of eleven readings [See Appendix 2.1].

[344] Τριῴδιον κατανυκτικὸν, 2nd edition (Athens, 2003), 895 f. with only the instruction (with reference to the name of the Evangelion to be read, with the ἀρχὴ (first words) and τέλος (the end of the passage), not the text in full. See for the full text, Θεῖον καὶ Ἱερὸν Εὐαγγέλιον, 2nd edition, Athens (1992), 193-206: Εὐαγγέλια Δώδεκα τῶν Ἁγίων καὶ Ἀχράντων Παθῶν. These included (concordant) series of Evangelion lessons, read at the Office of the Holy and Redeeming Passion of our Lord Jesus Christ, are: [1.] John 13, 31 – 18, 1; [2.] John 18, 1 – 28; [3.] Matt 26, 57 – 75; [4.] John 18, 28, 28 – 19, 16; [5.] Matt 27, 3 – 32; [6.] Mark 15, 16 –32; [7.] Matt 27, 33 – 54; [8.] Luke 23, 32 – 49; [9.] John 19, 25 – 37; [10.] Mark 15, 43 – 47; [11.] John 19, 38 – 42; [12.] Matt 27, 62 – 66. Cf. Mother Mary and Archimandrite K. Ware (Transl), *The Lenten Triodion* (London and Boston, 1978), 565-600.

[345] Cf. Matt 5, 3-12. Euchologion, p. 50. The text can be found in the Horologion, p. 122-123. The Evangelion is carried from the Altar to the middle of the Church when the Trisagion is sung. This prayer is said/sung many times in other services.

[346] Cf. Euchologion, 51-52.

[347] Cf. Matt 6, 9-13. Euchologion, 95. Text: Horologion, 1. The prayer is also said many times in other services.

[348] Cf. Matt 26, 26-30; Mark 14, 22-24; Luke 22, 14-20; and I Cor. 11, 23-26. Euchologion, p. 88.

[349] O.G. Rigas, Τυπικόν (Thessaloniki, 1994), 41: Ἀναγνώσεις.

transmission of the text of Scripture were maintained in the liturgical documents and they should therefore be given serious scholarly attention. They could also be interesting for research of the history of the biblical text.[350]

2.3 The Liturgical Impact of the Biblical Commentary Manuscripts

> It is required of the leaders of the Church on each day and especially on Sundays to instruct the clergy and the people in the words of piety out of Holy Scripture, relating to them the thoughts and judgements of truth. They are not to neglect the established canons or the tradition of the God-bearing Fathers. And if a certain passage of Scripture is even placed in question, it should never be interpreted differently from the teachers and Fathers of the Church in their writings. At the same time the people become familiar with what is important and what is not, so that they can reform their lives for the better.
> The Sixth Ecumenical Council, Nineteenth Canon, in Nicodemos of the Holy Mountain, *A Handbook of Spiritual Counsel*, Trans: P. A. Chamberas (New York, Mahwah, 1989), 191[351]

The importance of the Byzantine biblical commentary manuscripts lies in the fact that they reveal the authentically preserved background of the ancient biblical interpretation of the Church[352]. In delivering the transmitted exegesis, the biblical commentaries are deeply rooted in Byzantine liturgical practice, as deeply as the Scriptures that they complement. A considerable number of commentary codices (including κείμενον and ἑρμηνεία of the biblical books) contain lectionary equipment (added text elements in the margins, ἀρχ[ὴ] and τέλ[ος], or interlinear, marking the beginning and the end of lessons; tables of series of lessons at the beginning and/or at the end of the codex), codicological evidence of the liturgical heritage of these manuscripts. They demonstrate:

1) that the Scriptures are read and commented in accordance with the interpretation tradition of the church;
2) how the Scriptures are commented upon in a liturgical context and which interpretative keys/parameters were used;
3) in which forms the Byzantine fathers practiced biblical interpretation.

The exegetical oeuvre of the Byzantine Greek fathers in its totality is enormous and exceptional[353], moreover it is still accumulating steadily[354]. It is much more extensive than usually thought, since it includes the whole history of Byzantine exegesis up to the present day. All various forms and arrangements of text and commentary should, to our mind, be taken into consideration when studying this group (see the restrictions to the "pure" NT commentary codices by H. von Soden, in *Die Schriften des Neuen Testaments in ihrer ältesten erreichbaren Textgestalt hergestellt auf Grund ihrer Textgeschichte* (Göttingen, 1911), II, 525-529 and with regard to the OT commentary codices, by Rahlfs, in *Verzeichnis der griechischen Handschriften des Alten Testaments für das Septuaginta Unternehmen* (Berlin, 1914), XII. One of the most remarkable facts in the whole history of textual edition of the Scriptures (of both NT and OT books), is the omission from published Bibles of the ancient patristic commentary texts, which were originally transmitted together with the text of Scripture[355]. The isolation of biblical from patristic texts, when they were once part of the same manuscript, is to our mind quite unjustified from a codicological point of view. There are, of course, exceptions. As early as 16th century editions of Theophylact's Commentaries on the Four Gospels and the Epistles of Paul were published in Latin translation by I. Oecolampadius, *In quatuor Evangelia enarratione* (Basel, 1524) and *In omnes D. Pauli epistolas enarrationes* by C. Porsena (Cologne, 1528). In 1631 the Gospel commentary of Theophylact of Bulgaria in Greek and Latin

---

[350] C.R. Gregory, *Op. Cit.*, I (Leipzig, 1900), 332: 'Man darf aber nicht vergessen, dass gerade diese liturgischen Schriften uns bisweilen einen sicheren Halt bieten werden für die Festlegung der Zeit und des Ortes des von ihnen mitgebrachten Textes, und dass wir sie deswegen nicht übersehen dürfen'.

[351] Edition: G.A. Rallis–M. Potlis, Σύνταγμα τῶν Θείων καὶ Ἱερῶν Κανόνων τῶν τε ἁγίων καὶ πανευφήμων Ἀποστόλων καὶ τῶν ἱερῶν Οἰκουμενικῶν καὶ Τοπικῶν Συνόδων καὶ τῶν κατὰ μέρος ἁγίων Πατέρων (...), ἐκδοθὲν μετὰ τῶν ἀρχαίων ἐξηγητῶν, t. I-VI (Athens, 1852-1859), t. II, 346-349 [text of canon 19 with commentaries].

[352] See the opinion of two recent Greek biblical scholars: T. Athanasopoulos, Ἐκκλησία: ὁ αὐθέντικος φύλακας καὶ ἑρμηνεύτης τῆς Ἁγίας Γραφῆς (Athens, 1998) and J. Panagopoulos, Ἡ ἑρμηνεία τῆς Ἁγίας Γραφῆς στὴν Ἐκκλησία τῶν Πατέρων· Οἱ τρεῖς πρῶτα αἰῶνες καὶ ἡ ἀλεξανδρινὴ ἐξηγητικὴ παράδοση ὥς τὸν πέμπτο αἰώνα, t. 1 (Athens, 1991).

[353] If one only leafs through Dorotheos' Scholarios' Κλεὶς Πατρολογίας καὶ Βυζαντινῶν συγγραφέων (Athens, 1879), representing the contents of Migne's *Patrologia Graeca*, t.1-161, one will gain easy insight in the measure of the Byzantine biblical commentary tradition.

[354] To mention only one, the Greek Elder Ephraim of Mount Athos, *Counsels from the Holy Mountain. Selected from the Letters and Homilies of Elder Ephraim* (Florence, Arizona, 1999).

[355] Interesting is a comparison with Jewish editions of the Hebrew Bible, in which, in most cases, the Bible text is accompanied by Rabbinical commentaries (e.g. Rashi, Kimchi and others). See C.D. Ginsburg, 'History of the Printed Text of the Hebrew Bible', in *Introduction to the Massoretico-Critical Edition of the Hebrew Bible* (London, 1897 [repr. New York, 1966]), 782; 797, 806, 810, 820; 958 [the second edition of the Rabbinic Bible (Venice, 1524-25)].

(biblical text interspersed with commentary) was published for the first time in the West, *Theophylacti Archiepiscopi Bulgariae Commentarii in quatuor Euangelia. Opus nunc primum Graece et Latine editum* (Paris, 1631). Later all the commentaries of Theophylact where published by F. Foscari (Ed. e.a., in Greek and Latin, 4 vols., Venice, 1754-1763 [Migne, PG 123-126]). Also known to Western scholarship became the "Scholia Gregoriana" (Joh. Gregorius), *Novum Testamentum una cum scholiis Graecis e Graecis scriptoribus tam ecclesiasticis quam exteris maxima ex parte desumptis*, Ed. C. Grabe (Oxford, 1703). In the NT edition of C.F. Matthaei, *Novum Testamentum, XII. Tomis distinctum Graece et Latine* (Riga, 1782-1788) many (anonymous) scholia from Byzantine Greek codices with patristic commentary materials were included.[356] The Σειρὰ ἑνὸς καὶ πεντήκοντα ὑπομνηματιστῶν εἰς τὴν Ὀκτάτευχον καὶ τὰ τῶν Βασιλειῶν was published in Germany by Nikephoros Theotokos Ieromonachos (Leipzig, 1772-1773), and the anonymous scholia on the Four Gospels, Σχόλια παλαιὰ εἰς τοὺς Εὐαγγελιστάς, Ed. A. Mai, in *Classici Auctores*, 10 vols. (Rome, 1828-1838), vol. vi, 379-500 and vol. ix, 431-512 (Reprint in Migne, PG, 106, 1077-1290). These, however, are isolated examples.

2.3.1 The homily as the basic form of biblical exegesis

According to Byzantine[357] and the later Eastern Orthodox tradition, scriptural commentaries (ἑρμηνεῖαι τῶν Γραφῶν) stem from the earliest days of Christianity.

> The homily is a witness to the hearing of the Word of God, its reception and understanding. Therefore it is organically connected to the reading of Scripture and, in the early Church, constituted a necessary part of the "synaxis", an essential liturgical act of the Church.
> A. Schmemann, 'The Sacrament of the Word', in *The Eucharist. Sacrament of the Kingdom* (Crestwood, New York, 1988), 76

Alongside the public reading from Scripture and the homiletic explanation of lessons in the liturgy, the scribes were engaged in collecting and organising the relevant materials into compilations appropriate for liturgical use.[358] Different forms of commentary, comprising homiletic, hymnological, hagiographical, ascetical and doctrinal works were composed. In the first place there are the spoken words or *homilies* (Λόγοι, Ὁμιλίαι, and Πανηγυρικά)[359], which were linked to the prescribed lesson(s) of the feast of the day. Homilies explaining the series of Sunday lessons were collected in the *Kyriakodromia* (Κυριακοδρόμια). Homiletic reading moments in the context of the offices were (a) in the morning office and (b) in the liturgy following the scriptural lessons. Moreover, other patristic texts (catecheses, synaxaria, menologia) were also read in church (not only in the refectory), as part of the annual liturgical programme.

One can safely state that in Orthodox tradition the homily and the homiletic function of biblical exegesis was and still is the most important of all the types of interpretation. There is a huge number of codices of this group, of a great variety of authors and in many forms, stemming from a wide range of different ages and countries. It is not easy to form a comprehensive overview of the homiletic materials. There are homiletic collections of individual fathers, anonymous collections, collections of different homiletic forms depending on their liturgical function, separate homilies. They are dispersed and can be found in many and different sources[360]. The homily is the more

---

[356] Cf. G. Heinrici, 'Catenen', in *Realencyklopädie für protestantische Theologie und Kirche*, 3 (1897), 740, where the places of these scholia in the different volumes can be found.

[357] F.E. Brightman, *Liturgies Eastern and Western*. Vol. I. Eastern Liturgies (Oxford, 1896).

[358] This longstanding tradition of explaining the Evangelion (and Apostle) lessons in the Liturgy (ἑρμηνεία), by means of an oration (λόγος), homily (ὁμιλία), panegyrikon (πανηγυρικόν), catechesis (κατήχησις), or didaskalia (διδασκαλία), can be indicated by means of three categories of sources: (1) canonical (canon XIX of the Synod of Laodicea; canon XVIII of the Synod in Trullo); (2) liturgical typika (Jerusalem-Sabas typikon no 1096). Cf. A.A. Dimitrievsky, *Op. Cit.*, (Petrograd, 1917), III, p. 25 and this tradition in printed form III, p. 497; cf. P. Meyer, *Die Theologische Literatur der griechischen Kirche im sechzehnten Jahrhundert* (Leipzig, 1899), 151-152; (3) liturgical hermeneutics (patristic references in Liturgy commentaries, Justin Martyr, Origen, Apostolic Constitutions, Cyril of Jerusalem, John Chrysostom, Dionysius the Areopagite, Maximos Homologetes). However, any official mentioning of this item, *preaching*, is omitted in present day Typikon prescriptions, and also cannot be find in the rubrics of the Euchologion. Cf. F.S. Kovalchuk (Ed.), *Abridged Typicon* (South Canaan, 1985), 100 and A. Schmemann, *Op. Cit.* (London/Portland, 1966). Beside readings in the liturgy (on Sundays and week days) readings are also prescribed at other services: in the Orthros (the Resurrection Morning Evangelia; also the homilies and lives); in the Esperinos (the OT prophecies); at the Hours and Midnight service by occasion.

[359] Concerning the broad field of liturgical homiletics, from the point of view of the forms maintained in the manuscripts, see L.Politis, *Op. Cit.* (Athens, 1961): 'Λόγοι Πατέρων', 51-55 : 'In many forms appear in the manuscripts the writings, which contain the orations of the fathers of the Church' (πολλὰ σχετικῶς εἶναι ἐπίσης τὰ χφφ τὰ περιέχοντα συγγράμματα καὶ λόγους τῶν πατέρων τῆς Ἐκκλησίας).

[360] One may consult the index to the Migne PG series by F. Cavallera's, *Patrologiae cursus completus accurante J.P. Migne, Series graeca* (Paris, 1912) and the Greek Index by Dorotheus Scholarios (Athens, 1879); see also the *Clavis Patrum Graecorum* by M. Geerard and J. Noret (Eds.) (Turnhout, 1974-1998); P.K. Chrestou, Ἑλληνικὴ Πατρολογία (Thessaloniki, 1976-1992); A. Ehrhard, 'Theologie', in *Op. Cit.* (München, 1897); H.G. Beck, *Kirche und Theologische Literatur im byzantinischen Reich* (München, 1959); F. Halkin, *Bibliotheca Hagiographica Graeca* (Brussels, 1957); A. Ehrhard, *Op. Cit.*, I-III (Leipzig / Berlin, 1937-1952).

authentic commentary form in the ancient church in comparison with the commentaries on the continuous texts of biblical books (NB such commentaries were also developed in homily form), which are of more recent date. In the homily new and old interpretations were combined and transformed into encouraging and inspiring words, spoken by bishops and priests, indicating the permanent relevance of scriptural exegesis.

Many biblical manuscripts contain commentaries of the Byzantine fathers, far into the post-Byzantine epoch (15th/16th c.) and beyond. It is in these manuscripts that contain patristic commentaries, that the inner cohesion can be demonstrated most concretely and visibly. This cohesion is extrinsic in character, but the interpretative and editorial hand of the fathers is evident. In other words, the outward forms help to explain the inner purposes of those who composed the biblical manuscripts.

See the plate on the next page (commentary around biblical text)
Taken from A. Džurova, *Byzantinische Miniaturen. Schätze der Buchmalerei vom 4. bis zum 19. Jahrhundert* (Regensburg, 2002).

Plate No. 60, Tetraevangelion mit Kommentaren, Sofia, D. gr. 177, Pergament, 246 Folien, 35 x 28 cm, 11 Jh; f.14: Titelbalken in *Blütenblattstil* und B-Initiale zu Beginn des Matthäusevangeliums.

Printed with kind permission of Professor A. Džurova.

However, the fact that NT & OT books have appended commentaries is in itself not evidence of an inner connection between the two. Commentaries could have been placed around a biblical text quite arbitrarily. Works of completely differing content and character were often placed together in codices (including classical works). Codicological togetherness alone is not a sure basis to demonstrate the inner coherence of the incorporated works. One should take into consideration the liturgical embedding and function of biblical texts and the added commentaries and homilies in that framework. Then one can understand the adoption of biblical and patristic texts in liturgical codices, or biblical and patristic texts together in mixed codices. This will be explored below.

2.3.2 Typology of the Byzantine commentary codices

The Byzantine commentaries of Scripture are manifold and divers; one again observes a great diversity of forms and editions.[361] A typology should be set up very cautiously and should only be seen as a paradigmatic framework, in which main lines are sketched. The commentaries can roughly be brought under the following headings: 1) manuscripts classified according to their codicological scope and arrangements[362]; 2) manuscripts classified according to their contents; 3) manuscripts classified according to their literary forms and liturgical functions. The scribes arranged the commentaries around or in close proximity to the biblical texts. Both scriptural (OT and NT) text (divided into *commata*) and commentary segments (*lemmata*)[363], were brought together in one manuscript. Sometimes commentaries and scholia were written in the margins and sometimes they followed upon text sections or verses (alternating text and commentary). Groups of similar commentaries can be distinguished.

---

[361] General entries: F. Cavallera, *Patrologiae cursus completus accurante J.P. Migne, Series graeca, Indices* (Paris, 1912), Index Methodicus: IV. Scriptura Sacra, 143-156, V. Homiliae et Libri, 156-167; Dorotheos Scholarios, *Op. Cit.* (Athens, 1879); M. Geerard and J. Noret (Eds.), *Clavis Patrum Graecorum*, 6 vols. (Turnhout, 1974-1998), Vol. V, II: Index Biblicus-Liturgicus, 115-159. Special entries: For research of Byzantine NT commentary manuscripts: H. von Soden, *Op. Cit.* (Göttingen, 1911); for OT commentary manuscripts: A. Rahlfs, *Op. Cit.* (Berlin, 1914). For research of Byzantine homiletic commentary manuscripts: A. Ehrhard, *Op. Cit.*, Vol. I-III (Leipzig-Berlin, 1937-1952). For research of the catena manuscripts: G. Karo und H. Lietzmann, 'Catenarum Graecorum Catalogus', in *Op. Cit.* (Göttingen, 1902), 1-66; 299-350; 559-620.

[362] The codex form (the biblical and commentary contents) and the arrangement of the text in the codex are determinative. H. von Soden gives indications how the commentary text is arranged in the described codices. See, for instance, the division with regard to the catena in M. Faulhaber, "Katenen und Katenenforschung", in *Byzantinische Zeitschrift*, 18 (1909), 388: 'Formales in der Anlage der Katenen'. Four types are distinguished: 1) Column catena: the biblical text and scholia explanations are written in two columns beneath and besides each other; 2) Framework catena: the biblical text is written in the center of the page (larger script) and enframed with commenting scholia (smaller script); 3) Width catena: the biblical text is written out continuously over the whole width of the page, mixed with exegetical scholia; 4) Marginal catena: short additional notes or/and excerpts from other commentators are written in plain text manuscripts in the margins.

[363] N.F. Marcos, *The Septuagint in Context. Introduction to the Greek Versions of the Bible* (Leiden/Boston/Köln, 2000), 274-286 ('*Aporiai* and Biblical Commentaries'), 287-301 ('The Literature of the *Catenae*'); C.T. Krikonis, "Περὶ ἑρμηνευτικῶν σειρῶν (Catenae)", in *Byzantina*, 8 (1976), 91-139 [Πιν.1-26]; B.M. Metzger, *Manuscripts of the Greek Bible. An Introduction to Greek Palaeography* (New York and Oxford, 1981), 46-48 [Plates]; H.B. Swete and R.R. Ottley, *Op. Cit.* (Peabody, Mass., 1989 [repr. 1914]), 361-364; R. Devreesse, *Introduction à l'Étude des Manuscrits Grecs* (Paris, 1954); M. Faulhaber, "Katenen und Katenenforschung", in *Byzantinische Zeitschrift*, 18 (1909), 383-395.

† τοῦ ἐν ἁγίοις π(ατ)ρ(ὸ)ς ἡμῶν Ἰω(άννου) τοῦ χρυσοστό(μου) ἑρμ(ηνεία)
ἐκ τοῦ κατὰ Ματ(θαῖον) ἁγίου εὐαγγελίου :

† ΕΥΑΓΓΕΛΙΟΝ ΚΑΤΑ ΜΑΤΘΑΙΟΝ †

Type A: those manuscripts in which the full text of Scripture was explained verse by verse, i.e. the continuous commentary of a biblical book or group of books (NT or OT). This type focused on the content of a biblical book in its authentic textual arrangement, and appeared both in the form of homilies as well as commentaries. This type has its origin in the continuous reading of a biblical book during a certain period of the liturgical year; see, for example, the biblical commentaries of John Chrysostom: Ὁμιλίαι εἰς τὴν Γένεσιν; Ἑρμηνεῖαι εἰς τοὺς Προφήτας; Ὑπόμνημα εἰς Ματθαῖον.

Type B: those manuscripts in which the interpretation was more a paraphrased explanation of the biblical text (more freely selecting texts for the support of homiletic and catechetical instructions). This second type of commentary was directly linked to particular feasts or commemorations (according to the liturgical calendar). They were collected into comprehensive collections of homilies. The group can be found in the *Panegyrical orations* (Πανηγυρικοὶ λόγοι) and the *Homilies* (Ὁμιλίαι), which were transmitted in "collective" or in "individual" collections (the first represented in ancient *Panegyrical books* (Πανηγυρικὰ Βιβλία), the second in smaller collections of the fathers (Gregory of Nazianz, Gregory of Nyssa, John Chrysostom, Theodor of Studios, Photius of Constantinople, Imperator Leo VI the Wise, Niketas the Paphlagonic etc.).

Type C: those manuscripts in which an *x* number of biblical books were interpreted, for instance the Tetraevangelion (the four Gospels interpreted together as one codex) or the Oktoechos by one commentator/editor or anonymous.

Type D: those manuscripts in which different commentaries of different authors from various times and places are collected. These concern the interpretation of a biblical book or group of books (Ἑρμηνευτικαὶ Σειραί) by a patristic editor, or are anonymous.

The Byzantine commentary codics can also be grouped according to their liturgical function:

1) Λόγοι / Ὁμιλίαι / Πανηγυρικά
To this category belong the discourses and homilies preached during the liturgical services (thematic or verse-by-verse exegesis), explaining the lesson of the day, which could be a feast or commemoration of a saint. Sometimes they take the form of a connected series of explanations of the text of Scripture read in church, according to the scheme of the liturgical calendar. These discourses and homilies can be biblical (practical/devotional scriptural exegesis), liturgical (exegesis of liturgical days and feasts according to the calendar and the prescribed lessons), ascetical (practical interpretation with regard to ascetical life), doctrinal/dogmatic (instructions according to the teaching of the Church). A sharp distinction is impossible, since the different discourses are closely connected and the contents overlap[364].

2) Ὑπομνήματα / Ἐξηγητικά / Ἑρμηνεῖαι
To this category should be reckoned the elaborated biblical interpretations of individual fathers. Sometimes they took the form of continuous commentaries of an individual biblical book and sometimes a systematic discussion of a group of related books into volumes (τομοί)[365].

3) Σχόλια / Σημειώσεις, i.e. short notes to biblical phrases or sentences (in the margins or in the text)[366].

---

[364] Lit. Λόγοι/Ὁμιλίαι/Πανηκυρικά: M. Fiedrowicz, 'Homily', in *Dictionary of Early Christian Literature* (New York, 2000), 290; H.O. Old, *The Reading and Preaching of the Scriptures in the Worship of the Christian Church* (Grand Rapids, Mich./Cambridge, U.K, 1998-1999) [1: The Biblical period; 2: The Patristic Age; 3: The Medieval Church]; É. Junod, 'Wodurch unterscheiden sich die Homilien des Origenes von seiner Kommentaren?', in *Predigt in der Alten Kirche*, Ed. E. Mühlenberg (Kampen, 1993), 50-81; R. Grégoire, 'Homéliaires orientaux', in *Dictionnaire de Spiritualité* (Paris, 1969), 606-617; H. Hennephof, *Das Homilar des Patriarchen Neilos und die chrysostomische Tradition. Ein beitrag zur Quellengeschichte der spätbyzantinischen Homiletik* (Leiden, 1963); A. Ehrhard, *Op. Cit.* (Leipzig, Berlin, 1937-1952).

[365] Lit. N. F. Marcos, 'Aporiai and Biblical Commentaries', in *Op. Cit.* (Leiden/Boston/Köln, 2000), Ch. 18, 274-286; T.F. Fuhrer, 'Commentary', in *Dictionary of Early Christian Literature* (New York, 2000), 138-139; R.E. Heine, 'The Introduction to Origen's Commentary on John compared with the Introductions to the ancient philosophical commentaries on Aristotle', in *Origeniana Sexta: Origène et la Bible/Origen and the Bible* (Leuven, 1995), 3-12; É. Junod, 'Wodurch unterscheiden sich die Homilien des Origenes von seiner Kommentaren?', in *Op. Cit.* (Kampen, 1993), 50-81; J.P. Bouhot, 'Pentateuque chez les Pères', in *Dictionnaire de la Bible, Supplément*, 7 (Paris, 1966), 687-708; R. Devreesse, *Les anciens commentateures grecs de l'Octateuque et des Rois. Fragments tirés des chaînes* (Cité du Vatican, 1959); C.H. Turner, "Patristic Commentaries on the Gospel of St. Matthew", in *The Journal of Theological Studies*, 12 (1910-1911), 99-112; C.H. Turner, 'Greek Patristic Commentaries on the Pauline Epistles', in *A Dictionary of the Bible, Extra Volume* (Edinburgh, 1906), 484-531.

[366] Lit. É. Junod, 'Que savons-nous des <<Scholies>> (ΣΧΟΛΙΑ - ΣΗΜΕΙΩΣΕΙΣ) d'Origène', in *Origeniana Sexta: Origène et la Bible/Origen and the Bible* (Leuven, 1995), 133-149; P. Géhin, *Evagre le Pontique, Scholies aux Proverbes* (Paris, 1987); N.G. Wilson, 'Scholia', in *Scholars of Byzantium* (London, 1983), 33-36; N.G. Wilson, "A Chapter in the History of Scholia" in *Classical Quarterly* 17

4) Ἐρωτήσεις καὶ ἀποκρίσεις (Ἐρωταποκρίσεις), i.e. questions and answers; questions on obscure biblical phrases, with offered answers³⁶⁷.

5) Σειραί / Ἐκλόγαι (or Catena), i.e. an arrangement of selected biblical passages in the form of "chains" (Σειραί) from different commentators, of various times and places, or anonymous³⁶⁸.

There is no strict order, nor conformity in these commentary forms. All have the similar purpose of explaining the text of Scripture. The commentary manuscripts were produced and transmitted together with the NT writings. They contain Scripture and help us to understand Scripture; sure evidence of their importance when it comes to studying the biblical text.

2.4 The Byzantine Calendar and the Liturgical Lessons

An understanding of the Byzantine ecclesiastical calendar is conditional for insight in the function and purpose of the different Byzantine ecclesiastical manuscripts, which can only be properly understood in the context of the calendar systems.³⁶⁹ The Typikon directs the calendaric cycles³⁷⁰ and gives insight in the series of lessons ('αἱ προφητεῖαι', 'οἱ ἀπόστολοι', and 'τὰ εὐαγγέλια')³⁷¹, which move synchronically through the Byzantine liturgical year³⁷². In another liturgical book, the Euchologion, are presupposed (by means of references) the books, which were composed for lesson series in the Byzantine church. Through the Typikon, Euchologion and other liturgical books (written in red rubrics), one knows, where and when the scriptural books are to be used and in what manner.

(1967), 244-256; A. von Harnack, *Der Scholien-Kommentar des Origenes zur Apokalypse Johannis* (Leipzig, 1911); G. Heinrici, 'Scholien', in *Realencyklopädie für protestantische Theologie und Kirche*, 3.17 (1906), 732-741.

³⁶⁷ Lit. N. F. Marcos, 'Aporiai and Biblical Commentaries', in *Op. Cit.* (Leiden/Boston/Köln, 2000), Ch. 18, 274-286; L. Perrone, 'Perspectives sur Origène et la literature patristique des 'Quaestiones et Responsiones'', in *Origeniana Sexta: Origène et la Bible* (Leuven, 1995); G. Bardy, "La littérature patristique des 'Questiones et responsiones' sur l'Écriture sainte", in *Revue Biblique* 41 (1932), 210-236; 341-369; 515-537; 42 (1933), 14-30; 211-229; 328-352; G. Heinrici, "Zur Patristischen Aporienliteratur", in *Abhandlungen der philologisch-historischen Klasse der königlichen sächsischen Gesellschaft der Wissenschaften*; Bd. XXVII, No xxiv (Leipzig, 1909), 843-860.

³⁶⁸ Lit. N. F. Marcos, 'The Literature of the Catenae', in *Op. Cit.* (Leiden/Boston/Köln, 2000), Ch. 18, 287-301; K. Uthemann, 'Was verraten die Katenen über die Exegese ihrer Zeit?', in *Stimuli: Exegese und ihre Hermeneutik in Antike und Christentum* (Münster Westfalen, 1996), 284-296; E. Mühlenberg, 'Katenen', in *Theologische Realenzyklopädie*, 18 (1989), 14-21; G. Florovsky, 'Florilegia', in *The Byzantine Fathers of the Sixth to Eighth Centuries* (Belmont, Mass., 1987), 31-34; G. Doreval, 'Des Commentaires de l'Écriture aux les chaînes', in *Le monde grec ancien et la Bible* (Paris, 1984), 361-386; C.T. Krikonis, "Περὶ ἑρμηνευτικῶν σειρῶν (Catenae)", in *Byzantina*, 8 (1976), 91-139 [Πιν.1-26]. R. Devreesse, 'Les Chaînes Exégétiques et les Florilèges Dogmatiques', in *Introduction à l'Étude des Manuscrits Grecs* (Paris, 1954), 176-189; R. Devreesse, 'Chaines Exégétiques Grecques', in *Dictionnaire de la Bible*, Supplément, I (Paris, 1928), 1096-1099; H.B. Swete and R.R. Ottley, *Op. Cit.* (Peabody, Mass., 1989), 361-366. [Lit. 366, important for Mss.]; M. Faulhaber, "Katenen und Katenenforschung", in *Byzantinische Zeitschrift*, 18 (1909), 383-395; G. Heinrici, 'Catenen', in *Realencyklopädie für protestantische Theologie und Kirche*, 3 (1897), 754-767; A. Ehrhard, "Katenen", in 'Theologie', in *Geschichte der byzantinischen Litteratur von Justinian bis zum Ende des oströmischen Reiches (527-1453)* (München, 1897), 206-216; H. Lietzmann, *Catenen. Mitteilungen über ihre Geschichte und handschriftliche Überlieferung* (Freiburg/Leipzig/Tübingen, 1897); J.A. Cramer, *Catenae Graecorum Patrum in Novum Testamentum* (Oxford, 1838-1844).

³⁶⁹ Ehrhard saw this as an essential postulate for the integrated study of the hagiographic and homiletic manuscripts and provided a thorough introduction to the structure of the Byzantine Calendar: 'Das griechische Kirchenjahr und der byzantinische Festkalender', in *Op. Cit.*, I (Leipzig-Berlin, 1937), 25-35 and A. Rahlfs, 'Die alttestamentlichen Lektionen der griechischen Kirche', in *Mitteilungen des Septuaginta-Unternehmens*, Heft V (Berlin, 1915), 146-148.

³⁷⁰ Τυπικὸν τῆς τοῦ Χριστοῦ Μεγάλης Ἐκκλησίας, ὅμοιον καθ᾽ ὅλα, πρὸς τὴν ἐν Κονσταντινουπόλει ἐγκεκριμένην ἔκδοσιν ἥτις δὶς ἐξεδόθη ὑπὸ Κωνσταντίνου πρωτοψάλτου μὲ πολλὰς προσθήκας καὶ ἐπιδιορθώσεις, Ed. G. Violakis (Protopsaltes), revised edition on the basis of the edition Protopsaltes Constantine, Athens and Thessaloniki, [n. d.] [Reprint of the edition of M. Saliveros, Athens, 1913]

³⁷¹ Ed. G. Violakis, *Op. Cit.* (Thessaloniki, n.d.), 55 (Evangelion Resurrection lesson in the Orthros); 59-60 (Apostolos and Evangelion lesson in the Liturgy). Cf. O.G. Rigas, Τυπικόν, (Liturgica Vlatadon I) (Thessaloniki, 1994), 41: (General: 'Ἀναγνώσεις), 59-60 (Esperinos: 'Ἀναγνώσματα), etc.

³⁷² One manuscript example is preserved in codex Patmos Mon. of John the Theol., 266, X, 241 f.; a short description is found in the catalogue of I. Sakkelion, Πατμιακὴ βιβλιοθήκη (Athens, 1890), 136. The text is edited in A.A. Dimitrievsky, *Op. Cit.*, I. (Kiev, 1895), 1-110 (immov.) and 110-152 (mov.), a Typikon of the Great Church of Constantinople, in which the three cycles of normative lessons can be found (προφητεῖαι, ἀπόστολοι, and εὐαγγέλια) together and a comprehensive presentation of the Byzantine calendar.

We can state that the liturgical books are constant pointers to Scripture, i.e. to the Gospel codex - Εὐαγγέλιον; the Apostle codex - 'Απόστολος; the Psalter codex - Ψαλτήριον codex and to the "Prophetologion codex - Προφητολόγιον" (as adopted in the Triodion, Pentekostarion and Menaia). These books are treated below.

The calendar then, structures the system of biblical lessons (what is read on which day). Ehrhard refers to the pivotal role of the scriptural lessons (from the Evangelion) with regard to the hagiographical and homiletic manuscripts, as follows: 'Determinative for these readings [Lives of the Saints and Panegyrica and Homilies] are foremost the Evangelion Lessons, which were read on the intended Sundays and weekdays. The system of pericopes, that is in most cases presupposed, is nothing more than the Byzantine Calendar...'[373]. What is true of the hagiographical and homiletic manuscripts, is equally true of other codices of the same provenance. The liturgical calendar and the biblical lesson cycles it regulates, are constitutive for the Apostolos, Evangelion, Prophetologion, Psalterion, Panegyricon, Synaxarion and Menologion codices, as well as Asketica, Gerontica, Paterica and the Lausaicon.

2.4.1 The liturgical structure of the Byzantine calendar and the inclusion of scriptural lessons

The reading of passages of Scripture, containing the acts and words of Christ in the liturgy were gradually fixed on recurring days and dates, and collected into a refined system of corresponding lections, considered appropriate for these particular occasions.[374] In fact, a double (concurrent) annual series of lessons was created, one following the lunar cycle of the year with the movable date of Easter as point of departure, another following the solar cycle of fixed dates of the feasts of the church and the commemorations of saints according to the Byzantine liturgical calendar (running from 1 Sept to the end of August). There are three classes of *biblical* lessons: prophecies, apostolos and evangelion lessons[375] (we will discuss the homiletic lessons later).

The cycles of lessons in the next chapter serve to demonstrate the intrinsic ties between the different cycles of scriptural lessons and the particular feasts and commemorations of the saints and martyrs of the church in the course of the liturgical year. These ties are expressed by:

1) the parallel, yet independent cycles of lessons belonging to different systems:

   a. the Eleven Morning Resurrection Gospels (Eothina);
   b. the lessons of the movable liturgical year (Apostolos, Evangelion, Prophetologion);
   c. the cycle of psalm-readings (Kathismata)
   d. the lessons of the fixed liturgical year (Menaia);

---

[373] A. Ehrhard, *Op. Cit.*, I-III (Leipzig-Berlin, 1937-1952), I, Einleitung, 25-35, esp. 27: 'Maßgebend für diese Lesungen selbst sind durchwegs die Evangelienperikopen, die an den betreffenden Sonn- und Wochentagen gelesen wurden. Das Perikopensystem, das in den meisten Fällen vorausgesetzt wird, ist kein anderes ls das byzantinische, das vom 9. Jahrhundert an die Alleinherrschaft im oströmischen Reiche besaß'.

[374] For presentations, analyses and theories concerning the lection practices, see H.O. Old, *The Op. Cit.* (Grand Rapids, Mich./Cambridge, U.K., 1998-1999); D.M. Petras, "The Gospel Lectionary of the Byzantine Church", in *St Vladimir's Theological Quarterly*, 41.2-3 (1997), 113-140; C. Renoux, 'The Reading of the Bible in the Ancient Liturgy of Jerusalem', in *The Bible in Greek Christian Antiquity* (Notre Dame, Indiana ,1997), 389-414; Y. Burns, 'The Lectionary of the Patriarch of Constantinople', in *Studia Patristica*, 15 (1984), 515-520; Y. Burns, 'The Historical Events that Occassioned the Inception of the Byzantine Gospel Lectionaries', in *Jahrbuch der österreichischen Byzantinistik*, 32.4 (Vienna, 1982), 119-127; J. Mateos, *La célébration de la parole dans la liturgie byzantine* (Rome, 1971); A. Kniazeff, 'La lecture de l'Ancien et du Nouveau Testament dans le rite byzantin', in *La Prière des Heures* (Paris, 1963), 201-251; M. Tarchnischvili (ed.), *Le Grand Lectionnaire de l'Église de Jérusalem (Ve-VIIIe siècle)* (Louvain, 1959-60); A. Baumstark, *Op. Cit.* (Kempten und München, 1906); A. Rahlfs, *Art. Cit.* (Berlin, 1915); C.R. Gregory, *Op. Cit.*, I (Leipzig, 1900); N. Nilles, *Kalendarium Manuale* (Innsbruck, 1896-97); F.H.A. Scrivener, *Op. Cit.* (London, 1894); J.M. Neale, *Op. Cit., Part 1: General Introduction* (London, 1850).

[375] How the Byzantine biblical lessons are distributed over the NT and OT Scriptures in their authentic textual arrangement is demonstrated in **Annex III**: *Indices of the Byzantine Anagnosmata*. These Indices also show which passages/verses were *not* adopted for the liturgical practice of public readings (Evangelion and Apostolos), except in the case of the OT lessons, where there are too many lacunae. For the OT only the selected passages of the Prophetologion (as provided in the Triodion, Pentekostarion and the twelve Menaia) are indexed.

The reading cycles of the Byzantine Calendar

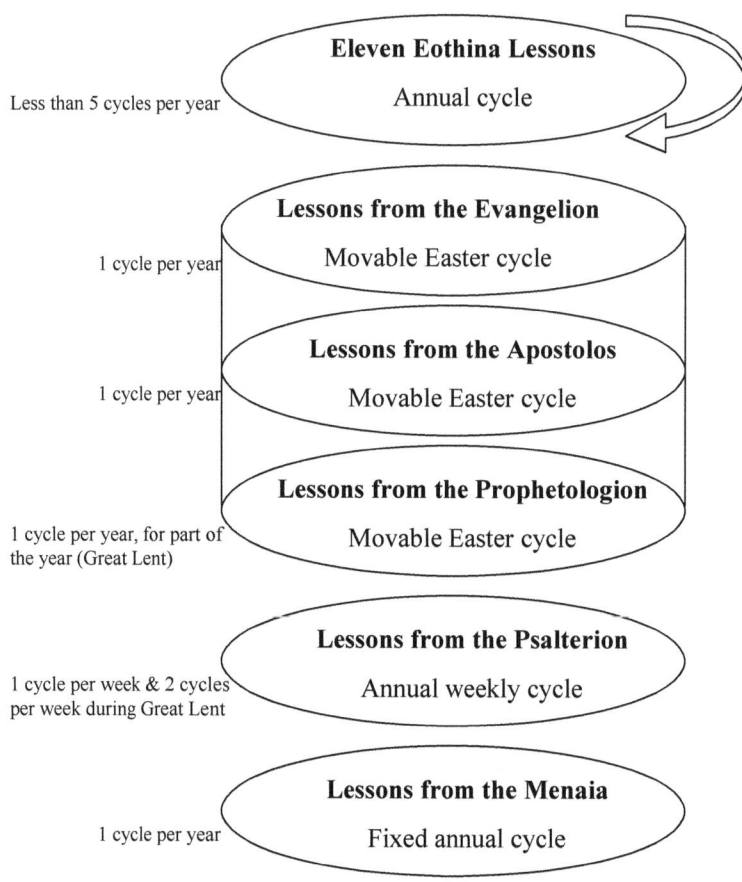

2) the periods in which the feasts and commemorations are prescribed (Triodion, Pentecostarion, Octoechos);
3) the particular feasts and commemorations for which the lessons (indicated by numbers) are intended;
4) the kind of service in which the lesson should be read (and explained), in the Liturgy or the orthros or the esperinos;
5) the hymnographical background and musical embedding of the feasts/commemorations and the lessons belonging to these is expressed by the cycle of Eight Tones (Octoechos), which repeats itself after eight weeks.

The lessons, which are scriptural, are based on the calendar, which is liturgical.

2.4.2 The books containing the scriptural lessons

Ἱερὸν Εὐαγγέλιον

The scriptural lessons (lections) were initially noted in the margins of the continuous Fourfold Gospel codex, by means of lectionary equipment[376]. Later the Gospels were re-arranged according to the order of prescribed lessons (ἀναγνώσεις)[377] for the Byzantine ecclesiastical year (a lectionary). Two basic Gospel codex forms thus

---

[376] See, for instance, the minute analyses of lectionary equipment in uncial manuscripts (Codex Macedonianus) by W.C. Braithwaite, "The Lection-System of the Codex Macedonianus", in *The Journal of Theological Studies*, 5 (1904), 265-274.

[377] Other denotations in the manuscripts are: 'ἀναγνώσματα' (passages selected for reading), or 'περικοπαί', 'τμήματα', 'κεφάλαια' ("segmented passages"), but also 'εὐαγγέλια', 'ἀποστολοί', 'προφητεῖαι' (passages taken from respectively the Evangelion, Apostolos and/or Prophetologion codex), indicating the contents of the lessons. Cf. C.R. Gregory, *Op. Cit.* (Leipzig, 1900-1909), Vol. I, 330-331.

developed: text and lectionary. Greek printing tradition chose the lectionary type of the Evangelion. The parallel Russian edition tradition of the Slavonic Evangelion preferred the text type of the Evangelion (also Tetraevangelion), whereby a lectionary apparatus necessary for the liturgical practice is included.

From these Evangelion codices (the lectionary form or ἀναγνωστικά)[378] one can see how the fathers re-arranged Gospels passages to give them a meaningful place in the liturgy. The public reading from the Evangelion, that takes place every day during the first part of the liturgy, be it from an Evangelion in lectionary form, or in text form, is selected according to the Byzantine lection system that is dependent on the movable or immovable cycles of the ecclesiastical year. The order of readings in the Evangelion are (according to the movable cycle): John, Matthew [Marc], Luke [Marc] and Marc. These are followed by the Twelve Resurrection Evangelia and the lessons of the Great Feasts and fixed dates of the saints, according to the order of the immovable cycle of the ecclesiastical year (Sept. – Aug.). Other lessons are also found in the Evangelion, for special occasions such as weddings, burial, sickness, etc.

Structure of a recent Greek edition of the Evangelion

ΘΕΙΟΝ ΚΑΙ ΙΕΡΟΝ ΕΥΑΓΓΕΛΙΟΝ

Εὐαγγέλια κατὰ Ἰωάννην
ἀρχόμενα ἀπο τοῦ ἁγίου Πάσχα, ἕως τῆς Πεντηκοστῆς, 13-42

Εὐαγγέλια κατὰ Ματθαῖον
ἀρχόμενα ἀπο τῆς Δευτέρας τῆς Πεντηκοστῆς, 47-95

Εὐαγγέλια κατὰ Λουκᾶν
ἀρχόμενα ἀπο τῆς Δευτέρας μετὰ τὴν Ὕψωσιν τοῦ Σταυροῦ, 101-161

Εὐαγγέλια εἰς τὰς παννυχίδας τῆς Α' ἑβδομάδος τῶν Νηστειῶν, 162-164

Εὐαγγέλια κατὰ Μᾶρκον
ἀρχόμενα ἀπο τοῦ Α' Σαββάτου τῶν Νηστειῶν, 169-176

Εὐαγγέλια τῆς Μεγάλης Ἑβδομάδος, 177-215

Εὐαγγέλια Ἑωθινὰ, 216-222

Εὐαγγέλια ἀκινήτων ἑορτῶν [Μηνολογίου], 223-291

Εὐαγγέλια Θ. Λειτουργίας εἰς μνήμας Ἁγίων, 292-293

Εὐαγγέλια εἰς διαφόρους περιστάσεις, 294-300

Ed. Apostolike Diakonia of the Greek Church: Θεῖον καὶ Ἱερὸν Εὐαγγέλιον, κατὰ τὸ κείμενον τὸ ἐγκεκριμένον ὑπὸ τῆς Μεγάλης τοῦ Χριστοῦ Ἐκκλησίας, 2nd edition, Ed. A. Androuses (Athens, 1992). [the 'Patriarchal Edition']

Ἀπόστολος

The Fathers deliberately placed the lessons from the Apostle before the reading from the Gospel Codex, the Apostle reading working as a 'Gospel proclamation'. The Apostolos[379], or, with a slight variation, the Praxapostolos (Πραξαπόστολος)[380], is formally related to the Evangelion (the Ἱερὸν Εὐαγγέλιον) and in every liturgical celebration one can note how the reading (and interpretation) of the Apostle passage is connected to the particular Gospel lesson. The selected lessons were chosen after an age-long process of crystallisation and are attuned to the particular religious celebrations. Apostle and Gospel readings were placed in the same liturgical

---

[378] Edition used: Θεῖον καὶ Ἱερὸν Εὐαγγέλιον κατὰ τὸ κείμενον τὸ ἐγκεκριμένον ὑπὸ τῆς Μεγάλης τοῦ Χριστοῦ Ἐκκλησίας, 2nd ed. (Athens, 1992).

[379] Edition used: Ἀπόστολος, Πράξεις καὶ Ἐπιστολαὶ τῶν ἁγίων Ἀποστόλων, αἱ καθ' ὅλον τὸ ἔτος ἐπ' Ἐκκλησίαις ἀναγιγνωσκόμεναι καθὼς καὶ τῶν ἱερῶν τελέτων, 5th ed. (Athens, 2002).

[380] The designation Ἀπόστολος is a combined abbreviation of the title of the series of included books in the one codex, the first, Πράξεις τῶν Ἀποστόλων, and the Ἐπιστολαὶ τῶν ἁγίων Ἀποστόλων, i.e. the corpora of the Seven General and Fourteen Pauline Epistles, which was indicated according to the epiteton ornans 'the Ἀπόστολος' of the writers, the apostles James, John, Peter, Jude, and Paul. See for this and other appellations as Πραξαπόστολος or Βιβλίον ἀποστολικόν, cf. L. Clugnet *Dictionnaire grec-français des noms liturgiques en usage dans l'église grecque* (London, 1971), s.v.

system, i.e. to accompany the (movable and immovable[381]) components of the ecclesiastical year. The Apostle Codex is kept in the church on the reader's analoy and is part of the small library of liturgical books in the choir.

Ψαλτήριον

What can be said of the Apostolos is equally true of the Psalterion[382]. If one disregards the "place" of the psalm readings in the liturgy, one misses the key to the Byzantine Christian interpretation of the psalms, namely their christological and typological significance.[383] The Psalterion or the 'Psalms and Odes Codex'[384] has been an important liturgical book of the Church since ancient times[385], intended to structure communal prayer in both the daily liturgy as well as in the offices (in combination with the Horologion, the Parakletike and other books).[386] The Byzantine church is distinguished by its liturgical chant and hymnography, that builds on psalmody as the basis of all liturgical and poetic expression.[387] Additional biblical-hymnographical material, the so-called Nine Odes[388], was added to the collection of 150 psalms in the Byzantine Psalterion. The Psalterion is arranged according to 20 kathismata, sessions of psalm-readings, in which fixed groups of psalms (stases) are distributed for recitation on particular prayer hours throughout the week. In Byzantine monastic practice the entire Psalterion is recited once each week and twice during Great Lent. Usually the director of the choir or one of the singers acts as psalmist (ψάλτης).

Προφητολόγιον

The Prophetologion or Paroimiarion (Паримийник, in Russian tradition)[389] is a liturgical codex containing selected passages from the Law (Genesis and Exodus), the Prophets (Isaiah and Ezekiel) and the Poetic books (Proverbs and Job)[390]. It was most opportune to read from this book on the Great Feasts and especially during Lent, a period in which the church revisits its OT roots. At first sight it may appear to many that the OT only played a minor role in the books of the Byzantine liturgy and works of the fathers. Of course there was a tendency to minimize the number of lessons from the Law and the Prophets and to replace them with Gospel and Apostle readings in the early church[391]. The church began to select, to change and transform existing lesson traditions from the Jewish liturgical year. This process of selection of OT readings finally resulted in the construction of the Prophetologion, which implied the reduction of OT lessons to an absolute minimum. The Prophetologion codex is divided basically into two parts: 1. lessons for the period of Great Lent and lessons for the eves of Christmas, Theophany, Easter and some other days; 2. lessons for the immovable part of the ecclesiastical year (beginning on Sept. 1st), in particular for some twenty-five fixed Feasts.[392] The reading of OT lessons for the rest of the year (the long period between Pentecost and Great Lent) were consequently replaced by Apostle and Gospel lessons. The Prophetologion also contained the lessons for the immovable part of the ecclesiastical year, with readings for the main feasts of the Church and commemorations.

---

[381] See § **2.5**

[382] Edition used: Apostolike Diakonia of the Greek Church: Ψαλτήριον τοῦ προφήτου καὶ βασιλέως Δαυὶδ μετὰ τῶν ἐννέα ᾠδῶν καὶ τῆς ἑρμηνείας, ὅπως δεῖ στιχολογεῖσθαι τὸ Ψαλτήριον ἐν ὅλῳ τῷ ἐνιαυτῷ, ninth edition (Athens, 2002), 9-177 [Kathisma 1-20], 179-195 [Nine Odes + 1]. See further § **3.5 and 3.6**

[383] A. Schmemann, 'The Sacrament of the Word', in *The Eucharist. Sacrament of the Kingdom* (Crestwood, New York, 1988), 66: 'In order to understand the prokeimenon, we must first recall the special place the psalms held in the early Church. Without exaggeration it could be said that in the early Church the psalms were not only one of the prophetic or liturgical 'highpoints' of the Old Testament, but a kind of special 'revelation inside the revelation'. If all Scripture prophesies about Christ, the exceptional significance of the psalms lies in the fact that in them Christ is revealed as though from 'within'.

[384] For the expression, see L. Clugnet, *Dictionnaire grec-français des noms liturgiques en usage dans l'église grecque* (London, 1971), s. v.

[385] This system of division of the Psalterion can already be found at the end of the 7th century; cf. Werner, *Op. Cit.* (London/New York, 1959), 149: 'For St. Theodore of Studios knew both terms and divisions' (i.e. stasis and kathisma).

[386] The Holy Synod of Nicea II, Canon II, in H. Percival (Ed.), *The Seven Ecumenical Councils of the Undivided Church, their Canons and Dogmatic Decrees* (Grand Rapids, Michigan, 1977), 556: 'Therefore we decree, that every one who is raised to the rank of the episcopate shall know the psalter by heart, so that from it he may admonish and instruct all the clergy who are subject to him'.

[387] See E. Wellesz, *Op. Cit.* (Oxford, 1971) and E. Werner, *Op. Cit.* (London / New York, 1959).

[388] H. Schneider, "Die Biblischen Oden .... ", I-IV, in *Biblica*, 30 (1949).

[389] Ed. [Greek-Slavonic]: Паримийник, си есть собрание паримий на все лето, Ed. Synodal Press of the Russian Patriarchate, T. I-II (St. Petersburg, 1890-1893); cf. A.A. Alexeev, 'The Old Testament Lections in Orthodox Worship', in *Das Alte Testament als christliche Bibel in orthodoxer und westlicher Sicht: Zweite europäische orthodox-westliche Exegetenkonferenz, im RilaKloster vom 8-15 September 2001*, Ed. I. Dimitrov (et al.) (Tübingen, 2004), 91-117, esp. 93: 'Among the various liturgical books that emerged in the period of great liturgical reforms in Constantinople in the 7th-8th centuries one finds a miscellany of the OT lections; it is known under the name of Prophetologion or Paroimiarion. The former term is used by the Greek Church and European scholarly tradition, the latter being the principal appellation in the Slavonic tradition, both Church and scholarly. Both titles stress the significance of two elements that compose the miscellany – the Prophets and Proverbs'.

[390] The most detailed presentation and discussion of the OT lection system is still, A. Rahlfs, 'Die alttestamentlichen Lektionen der griechischen Kirche', in *Mitteilungen des Septuaginta-Unternehmens*, Heft V, (Berlin, 1915), 120-230 [20-136].

[391] See A.A. Alexeev, *Op. Cit.* (Tübingen, 2004), 113-114.

[392] S. Antoniades observed that in the text of the Byzantine Liturgies the OT passages are represented more fully in the first part of the service and the NT passages in the second part of the liturgy, in *Place de la liturgie dans la tradition des lettres grecques* (Leiden, 1939).

The Prophetologion ceased to be used in the Orthodox Church in the 17th century (the manuscripts date from the 9th to the 17th c.[393]), and it was printed only once as a separate liturgical book[394], yet the selections of OT lessons (in the manuscripts referred to as Προφητεῖαι) remained in liturgical use, spread over the Triodion[395], Pentekostarion[396] and the Menaia[397]. These texts form the oldest layer of Byzantine biblical textual transmission (OT texts were the first "lectionaries" of the church and remained so for centuries)[398] and it is interesting to compare texts from the Prophetologion with those from other complete OT manuscripts.

Parallel to the process of reduction of OT readings in the liturgy, one finds the augmentation of individual OT books into larger and even mega collections (corpus-formation), such as the great codices of the 4th and 5th centuries, in which the hand of the Byzantine fathers can be recognised. The place of the OT in the Byzantine tradition of the fathers should be judged against the background of the following considerations: that the Evangelia and the entire NT became the first 'commentary on the Old Testament' of the church and gained primacy to be read regularly and extensively in the Sunday liturgy and later also in the Saturday[399] and weekday liturgies (instead of the lessons from the Law and the Prophets on the Sabbath); that the Psalterion became the first book of liturgical prayer and the basis for all services throughout the whole year; that OT lessons (from the books of the Law, the Prophets and Wisdom) were retained on essential moments throughout the liturgical year; that Byzantine hymnography is largely based on OT sources (the Great Canon of Andreas of Crete is a good example);[400] that great weight is ascribed in the Byzantine calendar to the saints of the Old Testament (all the Prophets and most of the eminent righteous men are revered in Orthodoxy);[401] that large collections of OT commentaries and commentary chains emerged and the editions of many OT books were provided with these commentaries.

Ὁμιλίαι, Πανηγυρικά

The biblical lessons, as represented in the Prophetologion, Apostolos and Evangelion[402] are profoundly connected with the patristic lessons, which unfolded according to the same liturgical-biblical practices underlying Orthodox worship and its calendar. The basic unity, the inner cohesion between the biblical and patristic reading strata is expressed most clearly in the liturgical reading prescriptions (ἡ ἀνάγνωσις) in the Typikon, for selected biblical and patristic-homiletic passages. Consult, for instance, the Slavonic Евангелие учительное, *The Gospel Commentary*[403], which is a recent example of how the composite series of patristic homilies are preserved and read in parallel to the prescribed biblical lessons (the pericope is mentioned first and

---

[393] A.A. Alexeev, *Op. Cit.* (Tübingen, 2004), 93. Cf. F.J. Thomson, "The Slavonic Translation of the Old Testament", in *The Interpretation of the Bible. The International Symposium in Slovenia*, by J. Krašovec (ed.) (Sheffield, 1998), 728.

[394] Ed. E. Glynzounios, Βιβλίον λεγόμενον Ἀναγνωστικόν. Περιέχον πάντα τὰ ἀναγνώσματα τὰ ἐν τοῖς ἑσπερινοῖς τοῦ ὅλου ἐνιαυτοῦ. τά τε εὑρισκόμενα, ἐν τοῖς βιβλίοις τῶν δώδεκα μηνῶν, καὶ τὰ ἐν τῷ τριῳδίῳ, καὶ ἐν τῷ πεντηκοσταρίῳ. Προσετέθησαν δὲ καὶ αἱ ἀκολουθίαι τῶν ὡρῶν τῆς παραμονῆς τῆς χῦ γεννήσεως. καὶ τῶν φώτων μετὰ τοῦ ἁγιασμοῦ, καὶ τῆς ἁγίας καὶ μεγάλης παρασκευῆς σὺν πάσῃ τῆς ἀκολουθίᾳ τοῦ ἑσπερινοῦ (Venice, 1595-1596). It was the first printed edition and remained a one off edition of the Prophetologion issued by the Greeks. A Russian edition, in Greek with the Slavonic version, compiled from the Menaia, Triodion, Pentekostarion and Hagiasmatarion, was published in two volumes in St. Petersburg, 1890-1893. Cf. F.J. Thomson, "The Slavonic Translation of the Old Testament", in *Op. Cit.* (Sheffield, 1998), 728 n. 602.

[395] Greek Church Ed. Τριῴδιον κατανυκτικόν, περιέχον ἅπασαν τὴν ἀνήκουσαν αὐτῷ ἀκολουθίαν τῆς ἁγίας καὶ μεγάλης τεσσαρακοστῆς. ἀπὸ τῆς κυριακῆς τοῦ τελώνου καὶ τοῦ φαρισαίου μέχρι τοῦ ἁγίου καὶ μεγάλου σαββάτου, 2nd edition (Athens, 2003).

[396] Greek Church Ed. Πεντηκοστάριον χαρμόσυνον τὴν ἀπὸ τοῦ Πάσχα μέχρι τῆς τῶν ἁγίων πάντων κυριακῆς ἀνήκουσαν αὐτῷ ἀκολουθίαν, 2nd edition, Ed. B. Koutloumousios (Athens, 2002).

[397] Μηναῖον τοῦ [Month: Σεπτεμβρίου etc.], περιέχον ἅπασαν τὴν ἀνήκουσαν αὐτῷ ἀκολουθίαν, διορθωθὲν τὸ πρὶν ὑπὸ Βαρθολομαίου Κουτλουμουσιανοῦ τοῦ Ἰμβρίου καὶ πάρ' αὐτοῦ αὐξηθέν τῇ τοῦ τυπικοῦ προσθήκῃ κατὰ τὴν διάταξιν τῆς ἁγίας τοῦ Χριστοῦ Μεγάλης Ἐκκλησίας, T. I-XII, 6th ed. (Athens, 1990-2003).

[398] E. Werner, 'The Churches and their Lessons: Sources', in *Op. Cit.* (London / New York, 1959), 58-71, esp. 60: 'The Eastern Churches have preserved a great deal more of the old type of continuous lessons to the present day (...) and the Byzantine Church follows the old Jewish principle of naming the Sundays after the (evangelic) lesson read on these days'.

[399] The Synod of Laodicea (A.D. 343-381), Canon XVI: 'The Gospels are to be read on the Sabbath [i.e. Saturday], with the other Scriptures'. Cf. H.R. Percival (Ed.), *The Seven Ecumenical Councils of the Undivided Church, their Canons and Dogmatic Decrees, together with the canons of all the local synods which have received ecumenical acceptance* (Grand Rapids, Michigan, 1977. [Repr. 1899]), 133.

[400] E. Wellesz, *Op. Cit.* (Oxford, 1971), 204.

[401] J.M. Neale, *Op. Cit.* (London, 1850), 766: 'One characteristic that distinguishes the Eastern from the Western Calendar, is the far greater importance that the former attaches to the Saints of the Old Testament. Thus, all the Prophets and most of the eminent righteous men in the old dispensation find a distinguished place in the Eastern hagiology; and there is, indeed, a *common* of Prophets, as well as of Apostles'.

[402] See § 3.4

[403] We consulted a fresh translation published by Hieromonk German Ciuba based on the Slavonic edition, *The Gospel Commentary. In Which Are Contained Lessons Taken from the Holy Gospel and from Many of the Divine Writings of Our Father among the Saints, John Chrysostom*, translated from the Slavonic into English (Erie, Pennsylvania, 2002).

then the homily follows; a Gospel sentence alternates with the 'explanation').[404] These readings are congruent: the biblical reading forms the basis for the homiletic, panegyric and ascetical explanation and interpretation. Both categories of lessons together structure the feasts and commemorations of the Byzantine calendar.

- ~ Categories of Lessons [ἀναγνώσεις, ἀναγνώσματα]
- ~ Propheteia [OT] lessons [προφητεῖαι]
- ~ Evangelia Morning Resurrection lessons [εὐαγγέλια ἀναστάσιμα ἑωτινὰ τὰ ια']
- ~ Apostolos lessons ['ἀπόστολοι]
- ~ Evangelion lessons [εὐαγγέλια]
- ~ Homiletic, Panegyric or Hagiographic lessons [λόγοι, ὁμιλιαι, πανηγυρικά, ἐγκώμια, βίοι ἁγίων]

The Typikon directs that homilies of the fathers might be read at the morning service (Orthros). This ancient practice is still maintained today. In Greek ecclesiastical and monastic practice, the patristic homiletic commentaries (catecheses and ascetical writings) are read during Lent and other periods of the liturgical year, which can be seen in recent editions of the Triodion and the Pentekostarion.

Examples from the Triodion

- Sunday of the Publican and the Pharisee [at the end of the Esperinos]: the Great Reading, p. 8.
- Sunday of the Prodigal Son [at the end of the Orthros]: the catecheses are read (Theodoros the Studite) p. 34.
- Meat-Fare Sunday [after the Agrypnia/Complines]: reading of [a commentary to] the Praxapostolos, p. 58; [in the Orthros] reading of a Sermon of the Theologian (Gregory of Nazianz), p. 58; [at the end of the Orthros (after the firat hour)] Reading from the catechesis of Theodor the Studite, p. 73.
- Cheese-fare Sunday: [on the third day: Orthros], a sermon of Basil the Great, p. 82; [on the fourth day: after the Orthros and first hour], catecheses of Theodor the Studite, p. 98; [on the fifth day: Orthros], a sermon of Anastasios the Hegoumen of the Sinai, p. 103; [on Friday: Orthros], a sermon of Basil the Great (from the Ethia) and one of Dorotheos, p. 110; [on Friday: Orthros], reading of the catecheses of Theodor the Studite, p. 121; [on Saturday: Orthros], reading of sermons of Ephraim – in three sections, p. 129 (after 2nd Kathisma); [on Sunday: Orthros], reading of the hexaemeron commentary of Chrysostom, p. 148 and reading of the sermon, p. 151; [on Sundays: Orthros], reading of the catecheses of Theodor the Studite, p. 160.
- Second day of the First Week of the Great Fast: [Orthros], reading of Ehrem (after 2nd kathisma), p. 166; second reading of Ephrem (after 3rd kathisma), p. 166 and a reading from the Lausaicon, p. 167; [Orthros, after first hour], reading of catecheses of Theodor the Studite, p. 175; [Third hour], reading of John of the Ladder, p. 176 [continuous for the whole of Lent]; [Sixth hour], after the reading of Isaiah follows again Climacos, p. 180; [Nineth hour], again a reading from Climacos, p. 182.

Ed: Τριῴδιον κατανυκτικὸν, περιέχον ἄπασαν τὴν ἀνήκουσαν αὐτῷ ἀκολουθίαν τῆς ἁγίας καὶ μεγάλης τεσσαρακοστῆς, ἀπὸ τῆς κυριακῆς τοῦ τελώνου καὶ τοῦ φαρισαίου μέχρι τοῦ ἁγίου καὶ μεγάλου σαββάτου (Athens, 2003)

The main reasons we advocate that biblical researchers study the Byzantine calendar is that the codicological choices behind the development of the ecclesiastical books can only be understood in their liturgical context. Some examples will suffice in anticipation of further treatment:

- the Gospel Codex (the Evangelion/Tetraevangelion) was generally used as an archetype in the Byzantine Church, rather than the whole NT[405];

- the text of the Gospel lectionary codices and other scriptural codices used in the liturgy, as has been suggested by several scholars (Osburn, Metzger, Riddle, Scrivener)[406], is expected in all probability to

---

[404] It is an anonymous collection, probably based on the collection of Patriarch Philotheos of Constantinople and other such collections. See Hieromonk German Ciuba's introduction, *Op. Cit.* (Erie, Pennsylvania, 2002), XVIII-XIX.

[405] C.R. Gregory, 'Griechische Liturgische Bücher', in *Op. Cit.*, I (Leipzig, 1900), 327: 'Liturgische Bücher sind die Hauptbücher der Gemeinden gewesen. Es kam für eine Gemeinde, für ein Kloster, weniger darauf an, Handschriften der neutestamentlichen Bücher zu haben, denn solche fanden eben keine Verwendung in dem öffentlichen Gottesdienst; sie konnten höchstens den Geistlichen oder den Gelehrten von Interesse sein. Was die Gemeinde brauchte, waren die Lesebücher, die Bücher, die die täglich vorzulesenden Abschnitte enthielten. Und diese Bücher als die Hauptbücher der Gemeinde mussten dann schön, und das will auch archaisirend sagen, hergestellt werden'.

[406] C.D. Osburn, 'The Greek Lectionaries of the New Testament', in *The Text of the New Testament in Contemporary Research* (Grand Rapids, Mich., 1995), 61-74; B.M. Metzger, 'Greek lectionaries and a critical edition of the Greek New Testament', in *Op. Cit.* (Berlin/New York, 1972), 479; D.W. Riddle, 'The Use of Lectionaries in Critical Editions and Studies of the New Testament Text', in *Prolegomena to the Study of the Lectionary Text of the Gospels* (Chicago / Illinois, 1933), 67-77, esp 74-75; C.R. Gregory, *Op. Cit.* (Leipzig, 1900), I, 327-329; F.H.A. Scrivener, *Op. Cit.*, Ed. E. Miller (London, 1894), I, 75.

be more archaic and pure (generally spoken) than continuous text manuscripts,[407] since they were copied and transmitted with much care and scribal attention;[408]

- the primacy of the Gospel of John in the lesson cycles[409], denoting the importance of the "spiritual Gospel" for the understanding of the biblical exegesis of the fathers during Eastertide, and for the biblical approach of the Church in general;

- homiletic interpretation of Scripture is an ancient custom, which is practiced permanently in Orthodox churches until this day.[410]

Critical study of the Byzantine liturgical year and calendar should commence with an analysis of present day practice (NB Greek and Russian applications of the liturgical typikon differ)[411]. Present editions of the liturgical books currently in use can be consulted to answer questions concerning the liturgical calendar and chronology. Earlier systems (derived from the liturgical manuscripts) can be taken into account to understand the earliest stages of the Byzantine liturgical year, whereby additional historical data can help.

2.5 The Typikon: The Ruling Principle of the Byzantine Liturgical Calendar

> The Ecclesiastical Typikon has been accepted by the Holy Church and has been in effect for more than a thousand years. All priests and deacons at ordination take an oath to observe it. All Orthodox bishops at their consecration in the rite of the "Profession of Faith" take a solemn oath in the presence of bishops, clerics, and people faithfully to observe the Church Typikon. The Typikon acquired the strength of the law in the Church for the externals of Divine worship of Almighty God. The Church looks upon it not as an ordinary work of man's mind, but as a holy book, obligatory in the celebration of divine services for all Orthodox Catholic Christians (…).
> F. Kovalchuk (Ed.), *Abridged Typicon*, 2nd edition (South Canaan, 1985), 10

Fundamental for insight in the liturgical-codicological arrangements of the biblical, service and commentary manuscripts is a comprehensive and experienced knowledge of Orthodox liturgical practice and the way it is structured over the year. This practice is laid down in the Typikon[412].

The Byzantine liturgical year is a complex phenomenon, not easily grasped and not unambiguously defined in the extant sources. Fundamental questions remain: how did the Feast of Easter take shape and how exactly was the cycle of other feasts and Sundays built around it? When was the Byzantine civil calendar introduced? When did the process of transformation of the Roman/Byzantine calendar into the calendar of the Byzantine Church - called the churchification of time by Russian liturgists - start? How was the movable part of the Byzantine calendar (centred around Easter) attuned to the fixed part of the calendar (with Christmas/Theophany as focal points)? What was the actual influence of the Jewish calendar of feasts and cycles of lessons (of the Law and the Prophets) on the Byzantine system of the liturgical year and the cycles of scriptural lessons? What was the idea behind the introduction of continuous readings from Scripture (Prophetic, Apostle and Gospel lessons)?[413]

---

[407] C.R. Gregory, *Op. Cit.* (Leipzig, 1900), 328: 'Die oben unter a. verzeichnete Beobachtung, dass liturgische Bücher konservativ sind, führt uns doch zu dem Gedanken, dass diese Bücher immer wieder ältere Texte der Bibel fortleben lassen, obschon die Handschriften des fortlaudenden Textes längst andere Formen angenommen hatten. (...) Deswegen sowohl theoretisch, wie auch durch einige Beispiele praktisch geleitet, erwarte ich, dass viele der Lesebücher wertvolles Zeugnis ablegen werden nicht für den jüngeren sondern für den älteren Text'.

[408] C.R. Gregory, *Op. Cit.* (Leipzig, 1900), 328: 'Sie mussten auf schönem Pergament, in zwei Spalten, in grossen Buchstaben geschrieben werden. Ihre Anfangsbuchstaben, hauptsächlich T E und A, mussten mit farbe und womöglich mit den feinsten Malkünsten verziert werden. Und der Buchbinder rief den Silberschmied und den Steinschneider zu Hilfe um den Einband mit dem Kreuze und dem Bilde des Gekreuzigten, und mit den kostbarsten Edelsteinen zu schmücken. Wenn dann im Gottesdienst der Priester aus dem Altarthor hervortrat, das „Evangelium" das heisst „das Buch der Lesestücke aus den Evangelien" and laut rief: Σοφία ὀρθοί ! [corr. R.] dann sah das Volk in diesem Lesebuch die Verkörperung des ganzen Wortes Gottes, das Edelste, was die Gemeinde an Schriften besass'.

[409] Nicodemos of the Holy Mountain, *A Handbook of Spiritual Counsel* (New York, Mahwah, 1989) for a patristic interpretation.

[410] A. Schmemann, 'The Sacrament of the Word', in *Op. Cit.* (Crestwood / New York, 1988), 76-80; A. Ehrhard, *Op. Cit.*, I (Leipzig/Berlin, 1937), 39.

[411] See for the differences J. von Gardner, *Russian Church Singing, Volume 1: Orthodox Worship and Hymnography* (Crestwood, NY, 1980) and the bibliographical references of Russian liturgists in this work.

[412] O.G. Rigas, Τυπικόν (Thessaloniki, 1994). A fine introduction from a Russian point of view is F.S. Kovalchuk (Ed.), *Abridged Typicon* (South Canaan, 1985); cf. also Mother Mary and Archimandrite K. Ware, *The Festal Menaion* (London, 1977), Appendix II, No 11. 'The Typikon', 541-543.

[413] Lit. T.J. Talley, *The Origins of the Liturgical Year*, Second, Emended Edition (Collegeville, Minnesota, 1991).

The Typikon does not answer these historical and philological questions, but it does continue to provide the structure fo the Orthodox calendar[414] and it has has actual significance, since it is still in use today.

In the Typikon, the Byzantine liturgical year is expressed in its twofold liturgical chronological system of movable (lunar) and immovable (solar) cycles. This twofold system is mirrored in parallel cycles of scriptural lessons, one starting with Easter (organised around the changing date of Easter) and the other commencing on September 1st (running from 1 Sept until 31 August). Both parts of the Byzantine calendar are to a certain degree independent of each other, but are at the same time closely connected. The fathers did not try to merge both systems into one harmonised system, because this would disturb the independence of each system and its specific characteristics. Therefore one can find in the liturgical scriptural codices (Prophetologion, Apostolos and Evangelion) lessons presented in two separate series, one series for the movable and one series for the immovable part of the liturgical year. Even the Typikon, where guidelines for the combination of both systems can be found, is structured according to the distinction between them. One can discriminate between both systems in their present integral and definite form.

> *(1) The Movable Annual Cycle (κίνητον)*
> The movable annual cycle (starting with Easter), adhering to the reading of the Gospel books in chronological order, combined with *selected* readings from both the OT and the NT in the Prophetic, Apostle and Gospel lessons for the movable feasts and seasons belonging to the Easter cycle;
>
> *(2) The Fixed Annual Cycle (ἀκίνητον)*
> The fixed annual cycle (starting on 1 September, the beginning of the Indiction) with a series of *selected* readings of Scripture, of the OT and NT for the fixed days of feasts, commemorations of Saints and martyrs of the Church (Christmas/Theophany are the main feasts around which the others were configured).

The celebration of the feasts is performed within the cycle of the movable calendar, as well as the fixed Byzantine calendar, creating chains of feasts and commemorations linked to a particular day (or to a fixed date).

The immovable calendar is, one can say, the counterpart of the movable liturgical year, but also its complement. Both systems are connected and yet, in some way, independent from each other, and ruled by different laws. It is, however, clear that the movable cycle is considered dominant. From a practical point of view this Byzantine calendar is called the 'weeks' before and after Easter. Easter is the leading theme and everything is attuned to it, so that it connects all liturgical days, individual feasts and seasons into one coherent year. This characteristic is lacking in the immovable calendar (despite its official character), which is in itself composed of individual and isolated feasts and days of commemoration, determined by their fixed dates. In the movable year the choice of lessons is guided by the principle of the *continuous reading* of Scripture, supplemented by *selected readings* for the Great Feasts (as for Palm Sunday, Ascension, Pentecost, All Saints) and some other particular days. The process of chosing lessons for the immovable feasts can be characterised as *eclectic* and *specific*.[415] There are influences between the two, however. The main liturgical motive of the movable calendar - the Pascha of the Lord - did influence its fixed counterpart. Not only do the Feasts of Theophany and the Nativity of Christ (with its preceding forty day fast) echo the Easter Cycle, there are also similarities in the choice of OT lessons[416]. In the chronological structure of the liturgical year one can observe two poles: one with feasts centred around the coming of the Lord into the world (Feasts of the Mother of God, Christmas/ Theophany) in Autumn and Winter; and another with feasts centring around the Resurrection of the Lord in Spring and Summer. The first liturgical pole is also called 'Little Easter' and it prepares in many aspects the Church for the second greater pole - Great and Holy Easter. If one can perceive in the movable cycle an emphasis on the heavenly work of Christ, then one can associate the immovable cycle with the earthly work of the Saviour, the establishing of His Body in the Church and in the lives of the Saints. Heaven and earth cooperate in the two calendars, to become, in fact, one.

---

[414] Two different editions of typikons of the Church are in use at present: the **Hagiopolitical-Hagioritical Typikon**, in use in the Russian Orthodox Church (in Slavonic: Типiконъ, сіесть уставъ, Moscow: at the Synodal Press, 1906 and several later reprints), in the Holy City (Patriarchate of Jerusalem), on Mount Athos and on Patmos (St. John the Theologian Monastery), and the **Constantinople Typikon** now in use by the Ecumenical Patriarchate and the Greek-speaking Orthodox Churches and the Bulgarian Orthodox Church (based on the revised edition of protopsaltis George Violakis, Τυπικὸν κατὰ τὴν τάξιν τῆς τοῦ Χριστοῦ Μεγάλης Ἐκκλησίας, Constantinople, 1888 (reprint: Τυπικὸν τῆς τοῦ Χριστοῦ Μεγάλης Ἐκκλησίας, ὅμοιον καθ'ὅλα, πρὸς τὴν ἐν Κωνσταντινουπόλει ἐγκεκριμένην ἔκδοσιν ἥτις δὶς ἐξεδόθη ὑπὸ Κωνσταντίνου πρωτοψάλτου μὲ πολλὰς προσθήκας καὶ ἐπιδιορθώσεις, revised edition by G. Violakis (Protopsaltes) [on the basis of the edition Protopsaltes Constantine], Athens and Thessaloniki, n. d. [Repr. of the edition of M. Saliveros, Athens, 1915].

[415] See § **3.4.4**

[416] K. Onasch, *Das Weinachtsfest im orthodoxen Kirchenjahr. Liturgie und Ikonographie* (Berlin, 1958).

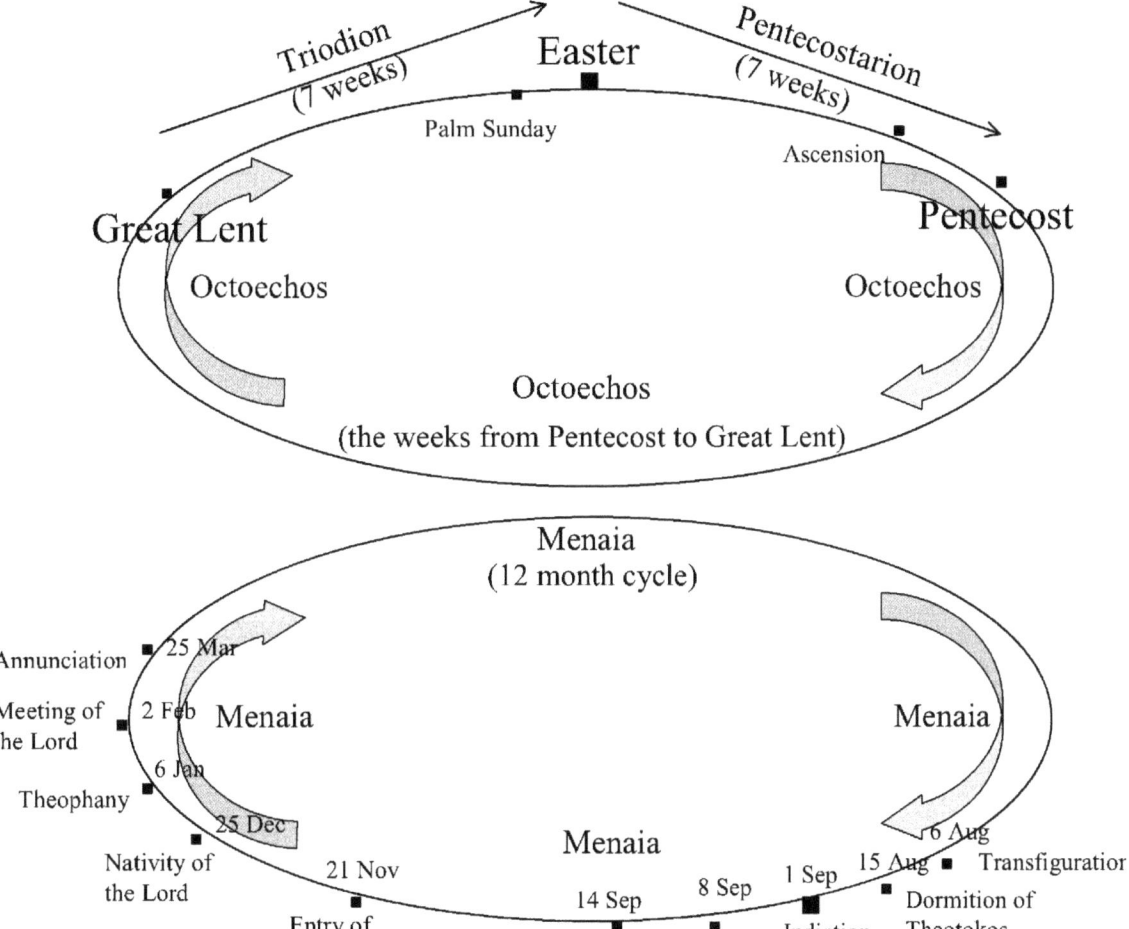

In the Typikon governing principles are laid down that show how these parallel systems of the movable and immovable cycles should be combined and practised. The Russian theologian Georges Florovsky speaks of a 'Book of models'.[417] All categories of Byzantine manuscripts are governed by the laws of the liturgical model (the typikon) and have a place in these movable/immovable cycles.

From the very first, two different styles emerged in the codices, stemming from the liturgical practice of the Church[418]: that of primary texts of the services, what to pray or sing (the prayers, litanies, doxologies, psalms,

---

[417] G. Florovsky, 'Hymnographers', in *Op. Cit.* (Belmont, Mass., 1987), 22: 'Thus is composed the 'regulations' – the *Typikon*. The Greek title expresses not only the motif of a norm or order but first of all a model. The *Typikon* is not so much a book of rules as a book of examples or models'.

[418] The basic principles of the Byzantine lection practices are codified in the liturgical Typikon. Since the Typikon is not delivered in a mono-typical edition form, it seems extremely important to study the exstant Typika in order to obtain adequate insight in the organisation of the lessons. Edition of Manuscript Sources: J. Mateos (Ed), *Le Typicon de la grande Église: ms. Saint-Croix no. 40, Xe siècle* (introd., texte critique, trad.), v. I-II (Rome, 1977 [reprint, 1962-1963]); A.A. Dimitrievsky, *Op. Cit.* (Kiev, 1895; 1901; Petrograd, 1917); A.I. Papadopoulos-Kerameus, Ἱεροσολυμιτικὴ Βιβλιοθήκη, 5 vols. (St. Petersburg, 1891-1915 [Repr., Bruxelles, 1963]). Different types of the liturgical Typikon: 1) the *Typikon of the Hagia Sophia in Constantinople*, Ed. A. Dimitrievsky, I (Kiev, 1895), 1-152, according to Patmos, Monastery of John the Theol., Cod. 266 [IX/X, f. 241, lost title]; 2) the *Typikon of the Evergetis Monastery in Constantinople* (τῆς Εὐεργέτιδος), Ed. A. Dimitrievsky, I (Kiev, 1895), 256-614, according to Athens, Ethn. Bibl., Cod. 788, [XI, f. 222], with the exact title Συναξάριον σὺν θ(ε)ῷ ἤτοι τυπικὸν ἐκκλησιαστικῆς ἀκολουθίας τῆς εὐαγοῦς μονῆς τῆς ὑπεραγίας Θεοτόκου ΤΗΣ ΕΥΕΡΓΕΤΙΔΟΣ; 3) the *Typikon of the Anastasis Church in Jerusalem (Typikon for Lent and Easter)*, Ed. A. Papadopoulos-Kerameus, Τυπικὸν τῆς ἐν Ἱεροσολύμοις ἐκκλησίας, on the basis of Holy Cross Monastery, Cod. 43, [1122 A.D., f. 155], (cf. Idem, the Catalogue of the Patriarchal Library in Jerusalem, III, 98-101), in Ἀνάλεκτα Ἱεροσολυμιτικῆς Σταχυολογίας (St. Petersburg, 1894), II, 1-254; 4) the *Typikon of the St Sabas-Lavra Monastery (near Jerusalem)*, Ed. A. Dimitrievsky, III (Petrograd, 1917), 1-508 (different recensions and

odes, hymns), but also that of the ceremonial texts, how to perform and organize the liturgy and the offices (the prescriptions/ instructions for the ceremonies).[419] Most liturgical codices contain this twofold distinction - the ceremony texts are marked in red ink, and the primary texts in black ink.

The paradigmatic function of the Typikon can also be found in the 'instructive parts' of other Byzantine liturgical codices, in the scriptural as well as the service codices. The significance of the Typikon for our subject is, that apart from it being the present and generally accepted 'model order' for the services, it coordinates and harmonizes both systems. It provides a synthetic overview and insight (often extremely detailed) of divers materials and practices. Thus, for example, what is contained in the Evangelion and Apostolos (when, in what order and how the lessons should be read) can only be understood adequately in the context of the paradigm of the Typikon. Moreover, a longstanding historical experience of the Orthodox church as to how the services and offices should be organized and performed is consolidated in the Typikon.

2.5.1 The movable cycle of the Byzantine calendar

The Byzantine liturgical cycles in their concurrent twofold form express the manner in which the fathers interpreted the Bible. This can be illustrated by looking at how the fathers' biblical exegesis was given liturgical form in the calendaric cycles and in the liturgical books that represent the cycles in the Liturgy: the Pentekostarion, Oktoechos, Triodion for the movable cycle and the Menaia for the immovable cycle.

The period from Easter until Pentecost (Pentecostarion)

The period from Easter until Pentecost (the paschal cycle) is ruled by the Pentecostarion.
In an early stage of the Byzantine liturgy, and even further back to the liturgy of the apostles and their disciples, the Sundays (κυριακαί) after Easter were celebrated in the light of the Feast of Feasts - Easter Sunday (the Holy and Great Day of the Resurrection of the Lord). This resulted in an Easter cycle, running from Easter Sunday until Pentecost Sunday, the fiftieth day (7 x 7 days plus 1 day), and formed a Pentecontade.[420] Pentecost (the fiftieth day) was the eighth Sunday, the day of the completion of the work of salvation. The Byzantine church fathers who formed the liturgy chose the period of the Pentecostarion to carry the Resurrection theme. The 'spiritual Gospel' of John is read from beginning to end during the period of the Pentecostarion, because it expresses the idea of the Resurrection profoundly. Each Sunday in this period recalls the Resurrection by its theme and is placed in a specific tone from the Octoechos. For example the first Sunday after the Bright Week is called 'Antipascha'.[421] The second Sunday is called after the Myrrh-Bearers, Joseph of Arimatea and Nicodemos.[422] Thus both biblical text and liturgical chant in the Pentecostarion were inspired by the Resurrection motives.

The period of the weeks after Pentecost (Octoechos)

> It is important to note that the long series of the Sundays after Pentecost, which bridges one calendar year over to the next from All Saints to Zacchaeus Sunday, does not indicate a break away from the Paschal Cycle, which somehow is extended indefinitely through the weekly recurrence of the 'Day of the Lord', its vigil with the Resurrection Gospel, and the weekly hymns of the eight tones, the Oktoechos.
> G. Barrois, *Scripture Readings In Orthodox Worship* (Crestwood, New York, 1977), 12.

What did the Octoechos model contribute to the liturgical profiling of Paschal-Pentecostal theme? The Octoechos is, in fact, the fundament and *moving factor* of the whole movable Byzantine liturgical year, because it covers not only the greatest part of the ecclesiastical year (the 32 weeks after Pentecost until Great Lent), but also underlies the period of Great Lent (included in the Triodion) as well as the Paschal Cycle (included in the

---

maintained in many manuscripts); the *Typikon of Constantinople*, Ed. J. Mateos, *Le Typicon de la grande Église: ms. Saint-Croix no. 40, Xe siècle* (introd., texte critique, trad.), v. I-II (Rome, 1977 [reprint, 1962-1963]). Cf. A. Papadopoulos-Kerameus, *Op. Cit.*, , III, 89-90.

[419] An early example in which the combination of liturgical text and ceremony text is shown, is the codex known as Apostolical Constitutions, an ecclesiastical/liturgical compilation of the 4th century. See F.E. Brightman, *Op. Cit.. Vol. I. Eastern Liturgies* (Oxford, 1896).

[420] E. Wellesz, *Op. Cit.* (Oxford, 1971), 69-70.

[421] 'When the tomb was sealed, Thou, the Life, O Christ our God, didst rise up from the grave; and when the doors were closed, Thou, the Resurrection of all, didst stand among the disciples, and through them renew a right spirit in us, according to Thy mercy'. Sunday of Antipascha, Troparion, tone 7.

[422] 'Noble Joseph took Thy immaculate Body down from the Tree, wrapped It in a clean shroud and spices, and having embalmed It laid It in a new sepulchre. But on the third day Thou didst rise, O Lord, granting to the world great mercy. To the myrrh bearing women at the sepulchre an Angel appeared and cried: Myrrh is fit for the dead, but Christ has shown Himself a Stranger to corruption. So cry: The Lord has risen, granting to the world great mercy'. Sunday of the Myrrhbearers, Troparion, Tone 2.

Pentecostarion). Even the particular 'echoi' of the feasts and commemorations of saints have their heritage in the Octoechos, because the 'mode' (melody pattern) for these feasts is adopted from there.

> According to the rules set down in the Typikon, the services of each week of the liturgical year are governed alternately by one of the eight tones. This governance begins at Saturday evening Vespers and extends through the Ninth Hour of the following Saturday. In this way there arises a rotating eight-week-long cycle of tones, the so-called 'Pillar of Tones' (Slav. гласовой столб).[423] The Pillar begins with the first tone on the second Sunday after Pentecost, and ends with Vespers of the last Saturday before Great Lent. The end of the cycle applies only to the weekdays of Great Lent, however. For Sundays the cycle continues until the fifth Sunday of Great Lent. Thus, the liturgical year contains approximately six Pillars.
> The cycle can be interrupted by the occurrence of Great Feasts. The services of these feasts have their own combination of tones, which have precedence over the prevailing tone of the week. Also, at various times hymns that are governed by the tone of the week may be supplemented or supplanted by hymns from the monthly cycle, the Menaion, for which there may be specified tones other than the prevailing tone of the week.
> J. von Gardner, *Russian Church Singing, Volume 1: Orthodox Worship and Hymnography* (Crestwood/NY, 1980), I, 58.

The central idea of the Octoechos Cycle is pneumatological. The system of Eight Tones on Eight Sundays during the weeks after Pentecost carries the fulfilment of the feast of Pentecost to all liturgies, throughout the whole year, until the next period of the Church's preparation for Pascha. The Octoechos contains only the Sundays. The texts for the other days of the week are found in the Parakletike, the Book of the Comforter, the Holy Ghost.

The question now is, what does the Octoechos mean in the Byzantine Tradition? To explain this, one should be conscious of the fact that the Octoechos Cycle is a very complex religious idea and that several factors worked together in establishing it historically and practically. These factors can be distinguished as *liturgical*, *biblical*, *calendaric*, and *hymnographical*. For our purpose it is important to realise that all liturgical feasts have a biblical foundation. The way in which the Liturgy is infused with the biblical word can be made clear through the following points: (a) by means of the biblical passage on which the liturgical feast or day is based; (b) by the prescribed reading of biblical passages (Prophetic, Apostle and Gospel lessons) in the Byzantine Liturgy and offices; (c) by the hymnographical reworking of the biblical theme and motives. And the Octoechos cycle is biblical, because it provides the liturgical framework for the weekly lessons, centred around the Lord's Day and the inherent Resurrection theme.

The period of the Forty Days of Great Lent (Triodion)

The Great Fast is the period preceding the Feast of Easter and comprises seven weeks, analogous to the seven weeks of Pascha.[424] Each Sunday is characterised by a special name: Sunday of Orthodoxy, Sunday of St. Gregory Palamas, Sunday of the Adoration of the Holy Cross, Sunday of St. John of the Ladder, Sunday of St. Mary of Egypt, Sunday of the Entry of the Lord into Jerusalem. The Triodion is the liturgical book which describes what is celebrated during this period (including three weeks of preparation). The Gospel-Apostle lessons are ceased during the five weekdays (retained on the Saturday and Sunday Liturgy) and OT readings replace the NT, indicating the inner harmony between the Testaments. The Lenten Triodion is not only a time of return to the biblical sources of the church (the Great Canon of St. Andrew of Crete is a thoroughly developed scriptural composition), but at the same time also to its patristic sources: the Sunday of Orthodoxy; the Sunday of St. Gregory Palamas; the Commemoration of St. Mary of Egypt.[425] The intensity of liturgical celebrations and lessons is brought to an absolute culmination in the Great and Holy Week. There are the Twelve Gospel Readings of the Passion of Christ on the Morning Service of Great Friday. There are OT and NT readings in the Holy Week, at the Royal Hours and the Vespers of Great Saturday. The hymnography of the Holy Week is extremely rich and inspired by the biblical lessons.[426] Both the Triodion and the Pentecostarion were edited in their final form, as is generally accepted, in the Studion Monastery, whereby the hegoumen Theodore of Studion was greatly involved in the work.[427]

---

[423] J. Von Gardner, *Op. Cit.* (Crestwood/NY, 1980), I, Note 58 on page 58 reads: 'There is also an eleven-week Pillar consisting of the eleven Resurrection Gospel readings at Matins and the corresponding exaposteilaria and Gospel stichera. To distinguish it from the Pillar of Eight Tones, it is termed the 'Gospel Pillar' (evangelskij stolp). The Gospel Pillar can never exactly coincide with the Pillar of Eight Tones'.

[424] A. Schmemann, 'Preparation for lent', in *Op. Cit.* (Crestwood, N.Y., 1974), Ch. 1, 17-30.

[425] A. Schmemann, 'The Lenten Journey', in *Op. Cit.* (Crestwood, N.Y. 1974), 63-85.

[426] For a conspicuous overview, see Mother Mary and Archimandrite K. Ware, 'The Liturgical Hymnography', in *Op. Cit.* (London & Boston, 1978), 40-43.

[427] E. Wellesz, 'The Liturgical Books', in *Op. Cit.* (Oxford, 1971), 141.

> See § 3.4.3 Selection and arrangement of lessons: **Movable cycle**, in which we present the lessons read in the services on each day of the week, from the Prophetologion, Apostolos and Evangelion, in the Pentekostarion, Oktoechos and Triodion periods, to demonstrate how the fathers focused on biblical themes (e.g. Pascha, Thomas Sunday) in the context of the liturgical calendar and attuned their selections of biblical readings to these themes. The reintegration of the lessons, by presenting them in one table, aims to undo the disintegration of the OT research (Prophetologion) from NT research. This reintegration is further underlined by the system of serial numbers introduced (A).

2.5.2 The immovable annual cycle

The history of development of the liturgy and the resulting liturgical books was a (long), gradual process, not marked by one significant moment or any one sole historical figure.[428] Many contributors to these developments remained anonymous. From the beginning of Christianity, incidental feasts and seasons developed slowly into liturgical and ecclesiastical realities, focused on the redemptive subjects (Easter, Ascension, Pentecost, Great Lent). These were repeated every year in a movable cycle as we saw above. But the Mother of God, the apostles, the martyrs and saints of the Church also became – with regard to their contribution to redemptive history – subjects of veneration and commemoration. The comemmoration of these subjects was, at a certain moment, repeated in the oral tradition of the Church year after year, written down and integrated in the whole complex of feasts and commemorations, and eventually fixed in the calendar - a process, which never stops. Even today, new names are added to the long chain of saints[429]. These dynamics are important. The fixed cycle of ecclesiastical feasts is not pure historical fact.

The selection of particular readings (from the OT and NT) for these feasts and commemoration days took place against the background of the liturgical feasts and was, although indirectly, a sure evidence of the "commentary" of the fathers. Their "choices" determined which should be the lessons for the particular feast and on what day should it be celebrated? From an early stage onwards the fathers elaborated the feasts and lives of the saints into lessons to be read during the services (at matins, after the sixth ode of the canon, the synaxarion of the Menaion is read with explanation of the feast and/or commemoration of the day).

The immovable calendar starts on Sept 1 and ends on 31 August and is structured according to the twelve months, which is why the liturgical books accompanying this cycle are called *Menaia* (Μηναῖα, month books)[430]. The Menaia include biblical, hymnographical, hagiographical and homiletic material, distributed over twelve volumes. A more condensed version includes only hagiographic/homiletic materials and is called the *Synaxarion* (Συναξάριον)[431] or *Menologion* (Μηνολόγιον).[432] An immense quantity of material (with regard to the immovable feasts and commemorations) is contained in the twelve Menaia[433]. They are rich volumes, which comprise a great deal of the treasures of Byzantine hymnography, hagiography and homiletic literature, collected and arranged during a process of many ages.[434] The final edition of the vast corpus is accredited to the monks of the Studion Monastery in Constantinople.[435] The full text of the scriptural lessons (except from the Evangelion) is incorporated in the Menaia. This is especially important with regard to the OT readings, since a separate Prophetologion no longer exists.[436] Instructions are also given with regard to the lessons (also for Gospel readings).

---

[428] E. Werner, *Op. Cit.* (London / New York, 1959), 72.

[429] See recent Calendars of the Greek or Russian Orthodox Churches.

[430] Manuscript Menaia date from the 9th century onwards. Since the 16th century (since 1526) the books were printed in twelve separate volumes, but sometimes also in two volumes (as can be found in the manuscripts as well as in the editions). The practical principal was apparently to have the necessary materials bundled per month in one book. A. Ehrhard, *Op. Cit.* (Leipzig / Berlin, 1937), 51-53.

[431] See for instance the edition of H. Delehaye, *Synxarium ecclesiae Constantinopolitanae* (Leuven, 1954).

[432] The term 'menologion' is confusing, since it means different things: (1) the menologia of Evangelia, Apostoloi and Prophetologia, including *Tables of Biblical Lessons* to be read during the twelve months of the ecclesiastical year; (2) the menologia of the Menaia, including Hagiographic and Homiletical materials for the Liturgy and offices on the proper days, existing in a manifold of codex and edition forms. For a concise overview, see E. Wellesz, *Op. Cit.* (Oxford, 1971), 135-136; a thoroughly elaborated work of manuscript study is A. Ehrhard, 'Einleitung', in *Op. Cit.* (Leipzig / Berlin, 1937).

[433] <u>English translation</u>: I. E. Lambertsen (Trans.), *The Complete Menaion. Providing the Services for the Feasts of Our Lord Jesus Christ, of the Most Holy Theotokos, and of the Saints for Every Day of the Year, Set to the Meter of the Original Byzantine Melodies* (Boston, Mass., 2005).

[434] The editing process of the Menaia, and in connection to it, of the Menologia, Synaxaria and Panegyria, was extremely complicated. Preparatory manuscript research has been conducted by Delehaye, Ehrhard, Halkin. How the lives of the saints and the Feasts of the Church were integrated is not known. It is interesting that more ancient Menaia have far more, and partly different, material. This means, that the present printed Menaia, which are not small books, are, comparatively, only minor (reduced) collections. See Archimandrite T. Themeles, Τὰ Μηναῖα ἀπὸ τοῦ ΙΑ΄- ΙΓ΄ αἰῶνος (Alexandria, 1931); A. Papadopoulos-Kerameus, "Σχεδίασμα περὶ τῶν λειτουργικῶν Μηναίων", in Βυζαντινὰ Χρονικά [= Византийский Временникъ], 1 (1894), 341-388; on the basis of this article the short report of K. Krumbacher (Ed), *Geschichte der Byzantinischen Litteratur von Justinian bis zum Ende des oströmischen Reiches (527-1453)* (München, 1897), 685-689.

[435] A. Ehrhard, *Op. Cit.* (Leipzig / Berlin, 1937), 21.

[436] J.M. Neale, *A History of the Holy Eastern Church, Part 1: General Introduction* (London, 1850), I iv, 766: 'One characteristic that distinguishes the Eastern from the Western Calendar is the far greater importance that the former attaches to the Saints of the Old

If one reviews the list of fixed feasts[437], then one gets the impression of a pendulum, that moves from the feasts of the Mother of God (beginning with the Birth of the Virgin) to those of the Lord and from there onwards to the saints and back to the Mother of God (the Feast of her Dormition). The following schedule illustrates the connection between the two calendars.

1 Sept	Beginning of the Indiction or the New Year of the Church
8 Sept	The Nativity of Our Most Holy Lady the Mother of God
14 Sept	The Universal Exaltation of the Precious and Life-giving Cross
21 Nov	The Entry of the Most Holy Theotokos into the Temple
25 Dec	The Nativity according to the Flesh of our Lord, God and Saviour Jesus Christ
6 Jan	The Holy Theophany of Our Lord, God, and Saviour Jesus Christ
2 Febr	The Meeting of our Lord, God and Saviour Jesus Christ
25 March	The Annunciation of Our Most Holy lady, the Theotokos and Ever Virgin Mary
[Movable]	Beginning of Great Lent (40 days before Easter)
	Palm Sunday (7 days before Easter)
	Easter Sunday
	Ascension (40 days after Easter)
	Pentecost (50 days after Easter)
6 Aug:	The Holy Transfiguration of Our Lord, God and Saviour Jesus Christ.
15 Aug:	The Dormition of Our Most Holy Lady the Theotokos and Ever-Virgin Mary

> **See § 3.4.4 Selection and arrangement of lessons: Immovable cycle** in which we present the lessons read in the services on each day of the month (only there where readings are prescribed), from the Prophetologion, Apostolos and Evangelion, according to the Menaia, to demonstrate how the fathers focused on biblical and ecclesiastical figures (saints, prophets, martyrs, ascetics, etc) and events in the context of the liturgical calendar and attuned their selections of biblical readings to them. The reintegration of the lessons, by presenting them in one table, aims to undo the disintegration of hagiographical research from biblical research. This reintegration is further underlined by the system of serial numbers introduced (B). A particular characteristic of this list is its extension to the modern day. Besides the Menaia, we included saints and events of more recent date from the most recent Church calendars in use today.

2.6 The Scriptural Foundation of Byzantine Hymnography

All Byzantine hymnology[438] is rooted in Scripture, particularly in the Evangelion and in the Psalterion.[439] Evangelion readings (the cycle of *Eleven Resurrection Evangelia*) are the basis for the Eothina Stichira (ἐωθινά στιχηρά)[440] sung on the Orthros of the Sunday and other hymnographical forms ('psalms and hymns and spiritual songs', of which the apostle Paul spoke [Eph. 5, 19])[441], and the Psalter is the basis for other types of Stichira. The liturgical tradition of the Orthodox Church, in Greece and the Slavic speaking countries, has produced an enormous quantity of diverse hymnographical compositions,[442] for the greatest part of the daily and seasonal services.

Testament. Thus, all the Prophets and most of the eminent righteous men in the old dispensation find a distinguished place in the Easter hagiology; and there is, indeed, a *common* of Prophets, as well as of Apostles'.
The commemoration days of the Prophets, Righteous men and Saints of the OT times are embedded in the chronological setting of the Byzantine calendar. They are adopted side by side with the NT Saints, martyrs, fathers and confessors and incorporated within the over-all structure of the feasts and commemorations of the Orthodox church. The patriarchs, Prophets and sages of the OT era found in the Byzantine calendar were received in a similar manner as OT text passages, which were integrated in the reading cycles. We found that there are lessons prescribed for a select number of Prophets (in retrograde chronological order, for: Samuel, Seven Maccabees, Elias, Elisha, Isaiah, [Job], Jeremiah, Daniel and the three Youths, Zephaniah, Habbakuk, Nahum, Joel, Hosea, Moses). For some there is only an Apostolos lesson; for others there are lessons from both the Apostolos and Evangelion. The commemorations/dates are distributed over the whole ecclesiastical year in order to be conscious of the prophetical foundations of the Christian Church and its liturgical expression of that fact. The commemorations are placed side by side with the apostles and the fathers and saints of later days. There are general Epistle lessons for services to the Prophets: I Cor. 14, 20 – 25 or Hebr. 6, 13 – 20 or James 5, 10 – 20; and Evangelion lessons: Matt. 23, 29 – 39 or Luke 11, 47 – 54

[437] J. Manley, 'The Major Fixed Feasts', in *The Bible and the Holy Fathers for Orthodox. Daily Scripture Readings and Commentary for Orthodox Christians* (Crestwood/ New York, 2003), Appendix II, 949-1035; Mother Mary and Archimandrite K. Ware, *Op. Cit.* (London, 1977); G. Barrois, *Scripture Readings In Orthodox Worship* (Crestwood, New York, 1977); J.M. Neale, *Op. Cit.* (London, 1850).

[438] See for lists of specific hymnographical names and forms, M. Prokurat, A. Golitzin, M. D. Peterson, *Historical Dictionary of the Orthodox Church* (Lanham, MD, 1996); P.D. Day, *The Liturgical Dictionary of Eastern Christianity* (Collegeville, MN., 1991); L. Clugnet, *Op. Cit.* (London, 1971); E. Wellesz, *Op. Cit.* (Oxford, 1971); E. Werner, *Op. Cit.* (London / New York, 1959); J. von Gardner, *Op. Cit.* (Crestwood, NY, 1980).

[439] E. Werner, 'Hymns and Cognate Forms. Byzantine Hymnody', in *Op. Cit.* (London / New York, 1959), Ch. 7.

[440] H.J.W. Tillyard, "'ΕΩΘΙΝΑ ΑΝΑΣΤΑΣΙΜΑ. The Morning Hymns of the Emperor Leo", in *Annual of the British School at Athens*, Part I, vol. xxx, 86-108; and Part II, vol. xxxi, 115-147.

[441] E. Wellesz, *Op. Cit.* (2nd ed., Oxford, 1971), 32-35.

[442] J. von Gardner, 'Types of Hymns', in *Op. Cit.* (Crestwood, NY, 1980), 34-53 (No 1-12).

2.6.1 Byzantine psalmody

The Psalterion forms the basis of a differentiated scale of psalms, psalm groups and psalm verses used in the daily liturgy and offices. This book, fundamental for all services, is closely connected with the Horologion, in which many psalms and clusters of psalms were incorporated for the daily prayer hours. The Psalterion is used in the liturgy in conjunction with the Apostolos and the Evangelion. The manner in which the Psalterion is used in the liturgy is in itself an "interpretation" of Scripture. It could be called a biblical hymnography containing hymns, odes, spiritual songs, prayers and praises.[443]

Besides the singing of psalms (psalmody), i.e. the recitation of the 150 Psalms of the Psalterion, the use of psalms and psalm-groups in Byzantine liturgical tradition is very rich and extensive.[444] Verses from the psalms are recited and sung as antiphon, stichos or prokeimenon and psalms have a fixed position in the daily services and on feasts.[445] For instance, the Psalm of the Creation (Ps. 103) is sung at the beginning of the Evening service, the Vesper Psalms (140, 141, 129 and 116), sung in one of the tones of the Octoechos, follow the recitation of one of the kathismas. Psalms 19 and 20 are sung in the morning service, and later the cluster of six psalms (the hexapsalm) - 3, 37, 62, 87, 102 and 142. Matins also contain two or three kathismas of the Psalter (according to the day of feast in the year), Psalm 50, and in the last part of the matins the Psalms of Praise, 148, 149 and 150 are sung in the tone of the week or the feast. In the Liturgy the psalms are represented mainly in the 'Liturgy of the catechumens', in the form of the three Antiphons. The lessons are introduced through prokeimena and psalm verses between the lessons (Alleluia).[446]

> **See § 3.5 The Byzantine Cycle of Psalmody**, in which we present the 150 psalms, grouped into 20 subgroups (kathismata), distributed over the week, according to a strict reading scheme. The reading scheme from the psalterion is a very important factor for the whole of liturgical practice, the selection of the lessons most clearly reflecting the psalm interpretation of the fathers. Psalms are used not only as lessons in their own right, but verses are also used as introductions to other readings, and they lie at the basis of hymnography.

The Psalterion is divided into twenty sections, called 'kathismas' (καθίσματα: one sits during recitation) and each of these kathismas is again divided into three 'staseis' (στάσεις: one may stand between the kathismas) with the inserted trinitarian doxology after the first and second stasis.

2.6.2 Byzantine hymnography

We will discuss here only two central hymnographical compositions: the Stichera (στιχηρά)[447] and the Canon (κανών) as they are central hymnographical poems of the morning service.

> Stichera as a whole are extremely important from a hymnographical and liturgical standpoint. They communicate the main theme of a given day – an event from the New Testament or the life of a saint. They are the hymns that serve the most to direct the thoughts of the worshippers in a particular direction. Sung, for the most part, to relatively simple melodies of a syllabic or neumatic character with only an occasional melismatic passage, stichera display a tight connection between the music and the text, and thus are more easily memorized by the listener.
> J. Von Gardner, *Russian Church Singing, Volume 1: Orthodox Worship and Hymnography* (Crestwood, NY, 1980), 37.

The Stichera,[448] which are explicitly scriptural, are the Eleven Resurrection Stichera of the Morning Office (incorporated at the end of the Octoechos), hymnographically paraphrasing and explaining the Eleven Resurrection lessons.

---

[443] A. Schmemann, 'Lent: Journey to Pascha', in *Great Lent* (Crestwood, N.Y., 1974), 39: 'Psalms have always occupied a central and indeed unique place in Christian worship. The Church sees in them not only the best, the most adequate and perfect expression of man's prayer, repentance, adoration, and praise, but a true verbal icon of Christ and the Church, a revelation within the Revelation.'

[444] E. Werner, 'The Psalmodic Forms and their Evolution', in *Op. Cit.* (London / New York, 1959), Ch. 5.

[445] Lit. J. Manley (Ed.), *Grace for Grace: The Psalter and the Holy Fathers* (Menlo Park, CA, 1992); K. Weitzmann, *Byzantine Liturgical Psalters and Gospels* (London, 1980); J. Mateos, "La psalmodie dans la rite byzantin", in *Periodica Orientalia Christiana*, 15 (1965), 107-126; K. Onasch, "Der Psalter in der byzantinisch-slavischen Orthodoxie", in *Wissenschaftliche Zeitschrift der Martin-Luther-Universität Halle-Wittenberg*, 7.1 (1957), 145-168; E. Werner, "The Origin of Psalmody", in *Hebrew Union College Annual*, 25 (1954), 327-345; K. Kallinikos, Ὑπόμνημα εἰς τὸν ἱερὸν ψαλτῆρ (Alexandria, 1929); K. Kallinikos, Εἰσαγωγὴ εἰς τὸν ἱερὸν ψαλτῆρ (Alexandria, 1927).

[446] K. Onasch, *Art. Cit.* (1957), 149-151: 'Der Psalter im orthodoxen Kirchenjahr'.

[447] J. Von Gardner, *Op. Cit.* (Crestwood, NY, 1980), 35: 'Stichera are poetic verses of varying content and length, having usually between 8 and 12 lines, set to a corresponding number of melodic lines. In performance a group of stichera is commonly inserted between the verses of a psalm in such a way that the psalm verse precedes the sticheron; less often, the psalm verse follows the sticheron'.

[448] See the overview of the different types of Stichera and their use in the services in J. Von Gardner, *Op. Cit.* (Crestwood, NY, 1980), 35-37: Types A.G. In note 22 on page 37 Von Gardner explains the creation of the separate liturgical book called Sticherarion as follows: 'Stichera were originally collected separately in a book called the Sticherarion (Στιχηράριον). With time, however, the stichera for

The Canon is a relatively late Byzantine hymnographical composition, but one which is rooted profoundly in Scripture. Werner describes how the Canon had a psychological function to connect Scripture to the calendar: 'The Kanon, which emerged as a seemingly new form, intends to attain, within the framework of liturgy, an ancient ideal: the psychological association which, in the mind of the faithful, would connect the sacred text with the specific season or occasion. The method, used by the poets of the Kanon, likewise employed two ancient principles that pervade the history of sacred poetry: the paraphrase or variation of Sacred Writ, and the principle of free poetic intercalation between the scriptural passages. These are two concepts dominant in the hymnic literature and music of the Near East. Thus, extended variations and meditations on a scriptural text are built up in a series of stanzas, which surround or pervade the individual sentences of the biblical text.'[449]

With the introduction of the Canon in the Morning Service (Orthros) at the end of the 7th century an interesting internal correction within Byzantine patristic tradition was made manifest: a radical change was made from the free-style, non-biblical Kontakia (κοντάκια), to explicit biblical Canons.[450]

The Canon is a complex poetical composition, a series of Nine Odes complemented by hymns, sung within the Octoechos system - that is, the Canon is performed in changing standard melodies (one of the eight tones). Each Ode is based on a scriptural text. There are Nine Odes (Αἱ ἐννέα ᾠδαί), selected poetical passages from Scripture (eight from the OT and one from the NT). Each Ode is composed of a model stanza, the Irmos (εἱρμός), that sets the melody for the other stanzas called troparia (τροπάρια), which should be sung in the track of the Irmos. Interesting is the focus on the inclusion of OT texts.[451]

> Each ode of the kanon consists of an initial stanza, the *heirmos* (εἱρμός), lit. 'link', and a set of two, three, or occasionally more troparia-stanzas, which in meter, number of syllables (in the Greek original) and melody are identical to the heirmos. By its content the heirmos serves as a connecting link between the theme of the Old Testament canticles and the New Testament theme that is developed in the troparia of the given ode.
> J. Von Gardner, *Op. Cit.* (Crestwood, NY, 1980), 40.

The Nine Odes of Scripture which stem from an ancient liturgical tradition, were originally sung in the morning service,[452] and are retained in full only in the period of Great Lent and between Easter and Pentecost.[453] In a second stage the Odes of Scripture were combined with the sung stanzas (irmos and troparia).[454]

The Canons, with the hirmoi and troparia, were incorporated in the Octoechos, the Triodion and the Pentecostarion. In the Canons for the Great Feasts of the Church, the Canons for the Lord, the Mother of God, the angels and the saints, the same poetical standard models are applied. The *Hirmologion* (Εἱρμολόγιον) is a compilation containing only the Hirmoi, isolated from the context of the canon for historical or pragmatic reasons (the volumes became too bulky). The Resurrection Canon (also called the Golden Canon, ascribed to John of Damascus) is a fine example of Byzantine poetical biblicism. It is exemplary for the whole cycle of Canons during the ecclesiastical year, illustrating the inner structure of the Resurrection Scriptures and the interpretation the fathers on the basis of the transmitted nine odes.

---

various occasions were regrouped according to the order of service and included alongside other hymns (troparia, kanons, etc. in other liturgical books, such as the Oktoechos, Menaion, and Triodion'. A facsimile edition of a complete Sticherarion was published in Mon. Mus. Byz., vol. 1 (1935), Cod. Theol. Gr. 181 of the National Library in Vienna, written in 1221 by John Dalasenos. See for an overview, E. Wellesz, *Op. Cit.* (Oxford, 1971), 244-245.

[449] E. Werner, *Op. Cit.* (London / New York, 1959), 227-228.

[450] See E. Wellesz, *Op. Cit.* (Oxford, 1971), 203-204.

[451] G. Bebis, 'Introduction', in *Nicodemos of the Holy Mountain. A Handbook of Spiritual Counsel* (NY, Mahwah, 1989), 35: 'St. Nikodemos makes also the point that the first eight odes are from the Old Testament and the ninth is from the New Testament. This proves the interconnection and the absolute eternal unity of the Old Testament with the New Testament. Each one is connected to the other. Because most of the verses of the odes come from the Old Testament, the holy Fathers put them together in order to show that the Old Testament preceded as an icon and a shadow, and the New Testament followed as the prototype and the truth'.

[452] J. Von Gardner, *Op. Cit.* (Crestwood, NY, 1980), 43: 'The kanon, which occupies a central position in matins, is divided into three sections separated one from another by Little Litanies and other short hymns – sedalen, hypakoe, and kontakia with oikos. The odes are grouped as follows: (a) 1, [2], 3; (b) 4, 5, 6; and (c) 7, 8, 9. The Ninth Ode is usually preced by the singing of the magnificat ('My soul magnifies the Lord...', Luke 1, 46-55) with the refrain 'More honorable than the Cherubim', while on Great Feasts special refrains to the Mother of God replace the magnificat'.

[453] J. Von Gardner, *Op. Cit.* (Crestwood, NY, 1980), 43:'both the heirmos and troparia of a given ode were sung in alternation with verses from the corresponding Old Testament canticle. This practice is still followed occasionally during Great Lent'. E. Wellesz, *A History of Byzantine Music and Hymnography* (1971), 198.

[454] See Mother Mary and Archimandrite K. Ware (Trans.), 'The Contents of the Triodion', in *The Lenten Triodion* (London & Boston, 1978), 38: 'During the Canon itself a particular prominence is likewise given to the Scriptures of the Old Covenant; for the Old Testament Canticles are sung in full on weekdays in Lent, instead of being greatly abbreviated or omitted altogether, as at other times of the year. This serves as a reminder of the original form of the Canon, which in the early period consisted of Scriptural Canticles with no more than a short refrain between the verses from the Bible'.

> See § 3.6 **The Nine Biblical Odes of the Byzantine Psalterion**, in which we present the odes, to indicate implicit biblical foundation of the liturgical hymnography. In the Lenten period this biblical layer is made explicit when the odes are sung in full. Byzantine hymnography is basically rooted in biblical hymnography (the odes are all songs from the OT and NT).

2.6.3 Specific examples of patristic formation of scriptural liturgical text

Some appropriate biblical and liturgical texts, which can help to demonstrate the inner cohesion in more detail are:

1) **Euchologion**: The passage from the Divine Liturgy of John Chrysostom (Liturgy of the Catechumens), in which the ceremonial role of the Evangelion is described, embedded in the context of the readings from the Apostolos and the Evangelion. This passage gives liturgical instructions, as well as the texts to be sung by the celebrants, the reader and the choir. [Ed.: Εὐχολόγιον τὸ Μέγα τῆς κατὰ Ἀνατόλας Ὀρθοδόξου Ἐκκλησίας (Athens, 1992), 50-53]

2) **Psalterion**: The nine biblical odes (Αἱ ἐννέα ᾠδαί), eight from the OT and one from the NT, indirectly indicating the Byzantine fathers' selection processes. The series was eventually published separately as an annex to the 150 psalms of David in the Psalterion. The hand of the fathers is visible in: a) the selection of the biblical texts to form a coherent series of lessons – from the Pentateuch, the Historical books, Prophets, Wisdom; b) the order in which biblical texts are transmitted in the services and how they are grouped; c) the prescriptions indicating in which service they should be read or sung; d) the (christological/typological) interpretation of the hymnographical compositions, inherent in these poetical passages. [Ed.: Ψαλτήριον τοῦ προφήτου καὶ βασιλέως Δαυὶδ, μετὰ τῶν ἐννέα ᾠδῶν καὶ τῆς ἑρμηνείας ὅπως δεῖ στιχολογεῖσθαι τὸ Ψαλτήριον ἐν ὅλῳ τῷ ἐνιαυτῷ, 9th edition (Athens, 2002), 179-196]

3) **Triodion**: The Great Canon - the Canon of St. Andreas of Crete - which is based on the nine biblical odes, together with many other OT and NT quotations and allusions and which is read during the period of the Great Fast (Genesis, Proverbs, Isaiah). [Ed.: Τριῴδιον κατανυκτικὸν, περιέχον ἄπασαν τὴν ἀνήκουσαν αὐτῷ ἀκολουθίαν τῆς ἁγίας καὶ μεγάλης τεσσαρακοστῆς, ἀπὸ τῆς κυριακῆς τοῦ τελώνου καὶ τοῦ φαρισαίου μέχρι τοῦ ἁγίου καὶ μεγάλου σαββάτου (Athens, 2003), I. 196-206, II. 217-226; III. 237-246; IV. 256-266 (Monday-Thursday of the First Week of the Great Fast; and 626-663 (repeated on the Fifth Day of the Fifth Week)]

4) **Pentecostarion**: The Golden Canon – the Canon of John of Damascus, revealing the mystery of the Resurrection, which is also based on the nine odes, and linked to the twelve Resurrection Gospels. [Ed.: Πεντηκοστάριον χαρμόσυνον, τὴν ἀπὸ τοῦ Πάσχα μέχρι τῆς τῶν ἁγίων πάντων κυριακῆς ἀνήκουσαν αὐτῷ ἀκολουθίαν, new and revised edition by B. Koutloumousios, 2nd edition (Athens, 2002), 17-24]

5) **Triodion**: The Twelve Gospel Passion lessons (on the Orthros of Good Friday), demonstrating the fathers' liturgical compilation of interconnected lessons (with overlaps) taken from the four Gospels. [Ed.: Τριῴδιον κατανυκτικὸν, περιέχον ἄπασαν τὴν ἀνήκουσαν αὐτῷ ἀκολουθίαν τῆς ἁγίας καὶ μεγάλης τεσσαρακοστῆς, ἀπὸ τῆς κυριακῆς τοῦ τελώνου καὶ τοῦ φαρισαίου μέχρι τοῦ ἁγίου καὶ μεγάλου σαββάτου (Athens, 2003), 193-206 (see for liturgical embedding the Triodion)]

6) **Oktoechos**: The Stichira of the Resurrection (Στιχηρὰ Ἀναστοτάσιμα), connected to the Gospel readings of the Resurrection (together with the stichoi of psalms). [Ed.: Ὀκτώηχος τοῦ ἐν ἁγίοις πατρὸς ἡμῶν Ἰωάννου τοῦ Δαμασκηνοῦ, περιέχουσα τὴν ἐν ταῖς Κυριακαῖς τοῦ Ἐνιαυτοῦ Ψαλλομένην Ἀναστάσιμον Ἀκολουθίαν, by N. P. Papadopoulos (Ed.) (Athens and Thessalonike, n.d. [1947]), 39 (ἦχος Α'); 61-62 (ἦχος Β'); 83(ἦχος Γ'); 107-108 (ἦχος Δ'); 132 (ἦχος πλ. Α'); 157 (ἦχος πλ. Β'); 181 (ἦχος πλ. Γ'); 206-207 (ἦχος πλ. Δ')].

2.7 Conclusions

In the foregoing paragraphs we have shown how the inner cohesion between biblical & patristic studies comes to light against the background of Byzantine liturgical studies. Below the main indicators of this hypothesis are summarised.

1) **the annual cycles of scriptural lessons are embedded in liturgical feasts and commemorations.** Independent cycles of lessons were compiled from the Evangelion, Apostolos, Psalms, Prophets, that are attuned to one another. These emerged gradually from the liturgical practice of the Byzantine Greek Church. The choice of the lessons and their arrangement for each feast and commemoration, are, implicitly, choices of *patristic interpretation.*

2) **the forms of the biblical codices / editions are determined by their liturgical use.** The edition forms of the Byzantine scriptural manuscripts (Evangelion, Apostolos, Apostolo-Evangelion, Psalterion, Prophetologion) came about as a result of the liturgical choices made by the fathers, when maintaining and distributing the sacred writings.

3) **the Byzantine liturgy is infused with biblical text and symbolism.** That is visible not only in the texts recited, but also in the liturgical ceremonies, their ritual forms (for instance, the Little Entrance), attributes and instruments, the vestments of the hierarchs and clergy, the arrangements of the Church building, icons and frescoes .

4) **the contents of Scripture are unfolded and visualised during liturgical ceremonies, through the service books.** The edition forms of the Byzantine liturgical books (both of the Scriptures and the service books) demonstrate the explicit (incorporating liturgical or biblical texts) and implicit relationships (quotations and allusions in the celebration texts) between Scripture and the choices made by the fathers.

5) **the panegyrica, homilies and other patristic texts (lives of saints, synaxaria, catecheses, ascetical works) are scripturally incorporated in the liturgy, through the biblical lessons assigned them in the Byzantine calendar.** The collections of patristic commentaries of individual Byzantine fathers, from the 4th to the 16th centuries are rooted in the Byzantine liturgy, but have not been physically incorporated in "liturgical collections". They should be defined as 'para-liturgical' and should be collected up until the present day.

6) **the hymnographical compositions of the Byzantine fathers pervade Scripture.** Byzantine hymnography is based on scriptural passages, sometimes implicitly (the Nine Odes presupposed in the Canons of the Morning Service), sometimes explicitly (the full reading of the Nine Odes in the Triodion period).

7) **The Euchologion contains a vast evidence of biblical and patristic texts**, adopted and integrated in all Byzantine services.

8) **the connection between Old Testament and New Testament.** The hand of the fathers is made visible and maintained in their contributions to the "inner cohesion" between the OT ("Propheteiai") and the NT books and texts, which were interwoven/interconnected in the ancient ecclesiastical ceremonies and liturgical practices.

9) **the ceremonial role given to Scripture in the celebration of the Byzantine liturgy and its offices.** In particular the Evangelion Codex is treated utmost ceremonially (mystagogy), which reflects the importance attached by the fathers to the preservation of the "sacred" (and "mystical") character of Scripture in the ritual. The patristic hermeneutic implication being that Scripture is interpreted as a "sacred" text.

Chapter 3

The Byzantine Lection System - a Patristic, Liturgical Hermeneutics of Scripture

3.1 The Purpose of the Byzantine Lection System

In chapter 2 we introduced the Byzantine biblical and patristic codices that make up part of an elaborate cycle of liturgical practice. The liturgical aspect is manifested in the lessons, or readings from these codices, and the manner in which biblical and patristic texts are "used" as part of the liturgy. In this context we have presented the basic structure and characteristics of the Byzantine lection system.
In this chapter we will demonstrate how the "inner cohesion" between the Bible and fathers is concretely expressed in the Byzantine lection system, by presenting data from the system. The cohesion we aim to show, is reflected in the selection and grouping of lessons, in their positioning in the liturgy, and in the whole organisation of the reading cycles, eventually incorporated in the structure of the Byzantine ecclesiastical calendar. It is here that the patristic hermeneutics of the church and the exegetical choices and principles implied in Byzantine theology is demonstrated most clearly.

All the reading cycles from all the liturgical books, make up part of the same liturgical, Byzantine calendar system[455]. Thus Evangelion, Apostolos and Prophetologion (and also the Homiletic and Panegyrica) lessons belong to one and the same frame of reference and should be presented as belonging intrinsically together (see § 3.4). We base our presentation on data from the printed Byzantine liturgical books (see § 3.2.2), since it is in these printed editions that the lection system is represented in a near complete stage of evolution[456]. Gregory and Rahlfs used a select group of resp. Evangelion, Apostolos[457] and Prophetologion[458] codices as a basis[459]. The presentation of the system of 'anagnosmata' was continued in the printed liturgical books, as Rahlfs[460] and Gregory pointed out. In these books are preserved, is supposed, the ancient traditions of biblical reading practice. In the course of a longstanding historical selection process (there is unfortunately little information about the manner in which the selections developed)[461], the Byzantine lection system developed a refined and elaborate, yet highly condensed form, in which series of lessons from the NT and OT, homilies, catecheses and ascetics are connected and interwoven. This system is still practiced to the present day.

---

[455] According to A. Ehrhard, 'Das griechische Kirchenjahr und der byzantinische Festkalender', in *Op. Cit.* (Leipzig-Berlin, 1937-1952), I, 32-34, the calendar system of the Byzantines acquired its main construction at the end of the 7th century, Constantinople being its liturgical formative centre. An equal chronological dating was reached and argumented by A. Rahlfs, 'Alter und Ursprung der dem konstantinopolitanischen Lektionssystem zugrunde liegenden Fastenpraxis', in 'Die alttestamentlichen Lektionen der griechischen Kirche', in *Mitteilungen des Septuaginta-Unternehmens*, Heft V (Berlin, 1915), 205: 'Hiermit haben wir zugleich eine terminus post quem für das konstantinopolitanische Lektionssystem der Fastenzeit gewonnen. In seiner jetzigen Ausgestaltung kann es frühestens um 630 n. Chr. Entstanden sein'. As terminus ante quem was 900 A.D. (Rahlfs, 'Herkunft des in Kap. I und II vorgeführten Lektionssystems aus Konstantinopel', in *Op. Cit.* (Berlin, 1915), 164-165 [70-71].)

[456] A. Rahlfs, *Op. Cit.* (Berlin, 1915), 146 [52] states: 'Aber für den ersten Anfang der Arbeit auf diesem Felde bieten gerade diese größeren Werke einen unverkennbaren Vorteil darin daß sie öfter gedruckt und daher ziemlich leicht zugänglich sind. Daher habe ich seinerzeit die Arbeit mit der Exzerpierung jener größeren Werke begonnen und will auch hier kurz über ihr Verhältnis zu den Lektionarien berichten, da sie anderen, die sich mit diesen Studien beschäftigen wollen, gleichfalls als Ausgangspunkt dienen können'. Rahlfs consulted the editions of the Triodion (Venice, 1636 and Rome, 1879), the Pentecostarion (Venice, 1634 and Rome 1883), the Menaia (Venice, 1612-1648 and Rome 1888-1901, the Anthologion (Rome, 1630).

[457] C.R. Gregory, 'Die kirchlichen Lesestücke aus dem Neuen Testament', in *Textkritik des Neuen Testamentes*, 3 vols. (Leipzig, 1900-1909), I, 343-364 ['Synaxarion: Das bewegliche Jahr', i.e. Evangelion lessons]; I, 365-386 ['Μηνολόγιον', i.e. Apostolos lessons]. The evangelion lessons are based on Evl 32 [= Matthaei], Evv KM 262, 264 [= Scholz] and added Evl 292 (Gregory) and some other mss; the apostolos lessons on Evl 33 and Evl 44.

[458] A. Rahlfs used the codd.: Cod. S. Simeonis, Trier, Domschatz 143. F; Paris, Bibl. Nat. Gr. 272 and 273, Gr. 308, Suppl. Gr. 805; two other prophetologion types are consulted: Paris, Bibl. Nat., Gr. 275 and Messina, Bibl. Univ., Salv. 102 in 'Die alttestamentlichen Lektionen der griechischen Kirche', in *Mitteilungen des Septuaginta-Unternehmens*, Heft V (Berlin, 1915), 120-230.

[459] See § 3.2

[460] A. Rahlfs, 'Die alttestamentlichen Lektionen der griechischen Kirche', in *Op. Cit.*, Heft V (Berlin, 1915), 148 [54], 'Da diese Werke in ihren Lektionen im großen und ganzen mit den Hss. Des Lektionars übereinstimmen, ist es nicht nötig, hier nochmals alle Lektionen aufzuzählen'. Rahlfs indicates only the differences and deviations from his manuscript evidences in overview (148-153 [54-59]).

[461] C.R. Gregory, *Op. Cit.* (Leipzig, 1900-1909); B.M. Metzger, 'Greek lectionaries and a critical edition of the Greek New Testament', in *Die alten Übersetzungen*, by K. Aland (Ed) (Berlin/New York, 1972), 479-497; Y. Burns, 'The Historical Events that Occasioned the Inception of the Byzantine Gospel Lectionaries', in *Jahrbuch der österreichischen Byzantinistik 32/4* (Akten II/4, XVI Internationaler Byzantinistenkongress Wien, 4-9 Oktober, 1981) (Vienna, 1982), 119-127.

Another important reason for interest in the Byzantine lection system is that this reading system connects the lectionary manuscripts with the text and commentary manuscripts (those that contain lectionary equipment). Thus, according to the Byzantine calendar, the four gospels are always read in the order of John, Matthew, Luke, Marc, be it from an Evangelion (a lectionary manuscript), or a Tetraevangelion (text manuscript + lect). The Acts and Epistles of the Apostles (subdivided into the seven General + fourteen Pauline Epistles, or vice-versa) are always read in the same order, be it from an Apostolos (a lectionary manuscript), or a Praxapostolos (text manuscript + lect).

The Prophetologion manuscripts display well how the biblical text is 'shared' between a lectionary (Prophetologion) and the liturgical books (Triodion, Pentekostarion, Menaia). The Prophetologion contains roughly the same OT text as do the three liturgical codices. Lessons from the Prophetologion are performed firstly during Great Lent, as well as in the fixed calendar cycle (especially on the Great Feasts of the Lord and the Mother of God). Incorporated in the Triodion, Pentekostarion and the twelve Menaia, the Prophetologion is completely immersed in liturgical reality. Together with the Psalterion and the Nine Odes, the Prophetologion constitutes the OT fundament of Byzantine reading practice. This does not imply that other OT books were not used in the liturgy. There are lection (liturgical) elements in other OT codices (Genesis, Proverbs, Wisdom) – as the Greek catalogues demonstrate -, and the hymnographical reception of the OT historical, prophetical and sapiential materials (Canon of Andrew of Crete).

Ehrhard observed that the codex formation was ruled by the liturgical function of the materials used (panegyrica and homilies) and insight in their composition depends on knowledge of the Byzantine lection system[462]. Not only the contents of the homilies depended on these lesson-series, but also the corpora of patristic collections of homilies, which were organised according to the Byzantine liturgical calendar. In this Ehrhard was a forerunner of a codico-liturgical approach.

The liturgical reading practices have, of course, hermeneutic consequences. One could speak of a liturgico-biblical context of interpretation. The liturgical 'sense' of Scripture is reflected in the whole organisation of the reading cycles. The intriguing question remains, whether the biblical texts in the liturgical, biblical manuscripts have retained traces of the "authentic" text and whether this can be recovered with evidence.

The Byzantine liturgical lessons ('Αναγνώσματα), their sources, their arrangement and the way that they are included in manuscript as well as printed editions, is determined then, by the Byzantine calendar. The tables presented in this chapter will provide an integrated picture of the reading cycles, to demonstrate how the fathers incorporated biblical themes (e.g. Pascha, Thomas Sunday) in the context of the liturgical calendar and attuned their selections of biblical readings to these themes. As we said earlier, the liturgical calendar and the biblical lesson cycles it regulates, contributed greatly to the codicological formation of the liturgical manuscripts. It was not only constitutive for the Apostolos, Evangelion, Prophetologion, Psalterion manuscripts, but also for the Homiletic[463], Panegyricon, Synaxarion and Menologion codices. Although it was not possible here to present also the liturgical homiletic and ascetical lessons in the following tables (we provided some examples from the Triodion in § **2.4.2**), we should accentuate that they are ruled by the same calendar system as the series of biblical lessons to which we confine ourselves[464].

We presume that the evolution of the Byzantine lection system is the common, hermeneutical editorial work of Byzantine patristic tradition, a shared heritage of ancient readings system[465].

---

[462] A. Ehrhard, *Op. Cit.* (Leipzig-Berlin, 1937-1952), II, 209-210 (a 'Spezialpanegyrikum' of Gregory of Nazianz), 215-216 (John Chrysostom): 'Es ist eine bekannte Tatsache, daß die Überlieferung der Schriften des Johannes Chrysostomus († 407) die reichste der patristische Zeit ist. Weniger bekannt ist, daß sie wesentlich im Dienste liturgischer Interessen steht. Wenn seine alt- und neutestamentlichen Kommentare in einer Unzahl von Hss vorliegen, so ist das in erster Linie auf die Vorschriften der Typika zurückzuführen, denen zufolge sie in bestimmten Abschnitten des Kirchenjahres während des Morgengottesdienstes gelesen wurden'. Cf. p. 289 ('Spezialhomiliarien').

[463] For an overview of Eastern Homiletics, see H.O. Old, *The Reading and Preaching of the Scriptures in the Worship of the Christian Church*, 3 vols. (Grand Rapids, Mich./Cambridge, U.K., 1998-1999), Vol. II, Ch. I-IV ('The Flourishing of Greek Preaching in the Christian Empire – the School of Alexandria', 'The Jerusalem Lectionary in the Fifth Century', The Flourishing of Greek Preaching in the Christian Empire – the School of Antioch', The Syriac Church'); Vol. III, Ch. I ('Byzantine Preaching').

[464] Beside the lections tabulated there are, during the first three days of the Passion Week, lections of the entire Four Gospels (to John 13, 30), which are divided into nine parts (two for each Gospel and three for Luke) and read at the Third, Sixth, and Ninth Hours. Moreover, the Four Gospels are read continually, in the middle of the Church besides the Tomb of Christ, after the Orthros of Good Friday, during the whole night until the next morning; and before the Orthros of Pascha the reading of the Acts of the Apostles by members of the congregation is prescribed.

[465] H.O. Old, *Op. Cit.* (Grand Rapids, Mich./Cambridge, U.K., 1998-1999), II, 135-166 ('The Jerusalem Lectionary in the Fifth Century'); C. Renoux, 'The Reading of the Bible in the Ancient Liturgy of Jerusalem', inP.M. Blowers (Ed. and Trans.), *The Bible in Greek Christian Antiquity* (Notre Dame, Indiana, 1997), 389-414.

3.2 Sources of the Byzantine Liturgical Lessons

The subject of the Byzantine lection system has an extensive research history, that has concentrated on the ruling laws and other technicalities of the Byzantine calendar. Certainly, the importance of the lections for the study of the biblical and homiletic/hagiographic manuscripts was acknowledged (by Gregory, Rahlfs and Ehrhard, Metzger, the Chicago school of NT lectionary research, for example), yet this area of research has remained somewhat isolated from the main stream of manuscript research. Moreover, research of the lections was limited to either the NT or OT branches of biblical studies to which it belonged. In the present thesis the reintegration of the results of these separate disciplines is foreseen. In the following we will present a short overview of research of the lessons.

The tables provided in **§ 3.3 to 3.6**, of different series of biblical lessons, are based firstly on the Byzantine printed editions of the liturgical books [the tables of lessons are compiled from these sources], and only in the second instance on manuscript evidence as represented in printed editions (Gregory, Rahlfs, Engberg), including the indexes (Synaxaria/Menologia) of the Byzantine manuscripts[466]. Western printed editions and studies of the Byzantine lection system have also been consulted. In fact, the present series of tables of biblical lessons is a *Synaxarion / Menologion*.

3.2.1 Greek Printed editions of the Liturgical books

- Θεῖον καὶ Ἱερὸν Εὐαγγέλιον, κατὰ τὸ κείμενον τὸ ἐγκεκριμένον ὑπὸ τῆς Μεγάλης τοῦ Χριστοῦ Ἐκκλησίας, 2nd edition (Athens, 1992).

- Ἀπόστολος, Πράξεις καὶ Ἐπιστολαὶ τῶν ἁγίων Ἀποστόλων, αἱ καθ' ὅλον τὸ ἔτος ἐπ' Ἐκκλησίαις ἀναγιγνωσκόμεναι καθὼς καὶ τῶν ἱερῶν τελετῶν, 5th ed. (Athens, 2002).

- Ψαλτήριον τοῦ προφήτου καὶ βασιλέως Δαυΐδ, μετὰ τῶν ἐννέα ᾠδῶν καὶ τῆς ἑρμηνείας ὅπως δεῖ στιχολογεῖσθαι τὸ Ψαλτήριον ἐν ὅλῳ τῷ ἐνιαυτῷ, 9th edition (Athens, 2002).

- Πεντηκοστάριον χαρμόσυνον, τὴν ἀπὸ τοῦ Πάσχα μέχρι τῆς τῶν ἁγίων πάντων κυριακῆς ἀνήκουσαν αὐτῷ ἀκολουθίαν, new and revised edition by B. Koutloumousios, 2nd edition (Athens, 2002).

- Τριῴδιον κατανυκτικόν, περιέχον ἅπασαν τὴν ἀνήκουσαν αὐτῷ ἀκολουθίαν τῆς ἁγίας καὶ μεγάλης τεσσαρακοστῆς, ἀπὸ τῆς κυριακῆς τοῦ τελώνου καὶ τοῦ φαρισαίου μέχρι τοῦ ἁγίου καὶ μεγάλου σαββάτου (Athens, 2003).

- Μηναῖα [12 tom. according the months Sept-Aug], revised edition of B. Koutloumousios (Athens, 1990-2003).

- Τυπικὸν τῆς τοῦ Χριστοῦ Μεγάλης Ἐκκλησίας, ὅμοιον καθ' ὅλα, πρὸς τὴν ἐν Κωνσταντινουπόλει ἐγκεκριμένην ἔκδοσιν ἥτις δὶς ἐξεδόθη ὑπὸ Κωνσταντίνου πρωτοψάλτου μὲ πολλὰς προσθήκας καὶ ἐπιδιορθώσεις, revised edition by G. Violakis (Protopsaltes) [on the basis of the edition Protopsaltes Constantine] (Athens and Thessaloniki, n.d. [repr. of the edition of M. Saliveros, Athens, 1913]).

3.2.2 Separate Printed editions of *Synaxaria* and *Menologia*

Greek Evangelistarion

- ΒΙΒΛΙΟΝ ἤτοι ΕΥΑΓΓΕΛΙΣΤΑΡΙΟΝ, περιέχον τὴν τῶν Εὐαγγελιστῶν διαδοχήν, πόθεν ἄρχονται καὶ ποῦ καταλήγουσι. Ἔτι δὲ καὶ κανόνια ἐν οἷς εὑρίσκονται τὸ Εὐαγγέλιον καὶ ὁ Ἀπόστολος τῶν Κυριακῶν τοῦ ὅλου ἐνιαυτοῦ, καθὼς καὶ τὸ Ἑωθινὸν καὶ ὁ Ἦχος ἑκάστης Κυριακῆς· προσέτι δὲ καὶ ἑρμηνεία περὶ τοῦ εὑρίσκειν τὴν ἡμέραν τοῦ ἁγίου Πάσχα, Ed. E. Glyzonios. = Incorporated at the end of the Edition of the Evangelion, Θεῖον καὶ Ἱερὸν Εὐαγγέλιον, κατὰ τὸ κείμενον τὸ ἐγκεκριμένον ὑπὸ τῆς

---

[466] Synaxaria and/or menologia: the indices of lessons are sometimes placed at the beginning, sometimes at the end, and sometimes both at the beginning and the end of a codex. For example, in the 12th century Gospel Lectionary Sin. 2090, the menologion is on f. 259v-323r. In the Four Gospel codex Sin. 157, A.D. 1127-1157/58, a Synaxarion is on f. 1r-4v and a Menologion on f. 265v-269r. And in the 12th century Gospel Lectionary Sin. 208, a Menolgion is on f. 182r-251r. The examples come from, K. Weitzmann and G. Galavaris, *The Monastery of Saint Catherine at Mount Sinai. The Illuminated Greek Manuscripts*, Volume I: From the ninth to the twelfth century (Princeton, New Jersey, 1990), resp. No 49, 59 and 60. Further, see C.R. Gregory, *Op. Cit.* (Leipzig, 1900-1909), I, 343-344 and 365; III, 1219.

Μεγάλης τοῦ Χριστοῦ ᾽Εκκλησίας, 2nd edition (Athens, 1992), separately numbered, 1-59 [revised edition by G.G. Bekatoros].

- Εὐαγγελιστάριον (Venice, 1614).

- Εὐαγγελιστάριον, Ed. Emmanuel Glyzonios (Venice, 1588).

NB. The Evangelistarion should be sharply distinguished from the Evangelion, since it contains only the tables of Sunday Gospel lessons, *not* the text of these lessons. Later were added to this book the table of Sunday Apostle lessons. The lessons of the other days are not included.

Western Editions of Synaxaria and Menologia

- F.H.A. Scrivener, *A Plain Introduction to the Criticism of the New Testament for the Use of Biblical Students*, 4th ed. Ed. E. Miller, 2 Vols. (London, 1894), 80-89 ('Appendix to Chapter III: Synaxarion and Eclogadion of the Gospels and Apostolic writings daily throughout the year', 80-85; 'on the menology, or calendar of immovable festivals and saints days', 87-89)

- J.M.A. Scholz, *Novum Testamentum Graece*, I-II (Leipzig, 1830-1836), Vol. I, 'Synaxarium et Menologium codicum KM 262. 274', 453-473 and 474-493. On the basis of Cod. Cyprius (K) = Paris, Bibl. Nat. Gr. 63, IX [U], f. 269, fol. 1-9; Cod. Campianus (M), Paris, Bibl. Nat. Gr. 48, IX [U], f. 257, fol. 1-8. Vol II: 'De synaxariis et menologiis quae reperiuntur in codicibus Parisiensibus Act. et Ep., Codd. 205, 199', 456-469.

- S.A. Morcelli, Μηνολόγιον τῶν εὐαγγελίων ἑορταστικόν *sive Kalendarium ecclesiae Constantinopolitanae. Accedunt quattuor evangeliorum lectiones in codice variantes*, 2 vols. (Rome, 1788). [Publication of the Menologion of Evl 33 (*l* 563): Cod. Vat. Gr. 2144, Unc. IX. 306 f 2 c.]

- C.F. Matthaei, *Novum Testamentum Graece… Iterum recensuit, sectiones maiores et minores Eusebii, Euthalii et Andreae Caesariensis notavit, primum quoque lectiones ecclesiasticas ex usu Ecclesiae Graecae designavit ac synaxaria Evangeliarii et Praxapostoli addidit et criticis interpositis animadversionibus edidit*, Ed. Hof (Ronneburg, 1803-1807), Vol I: Synaxarium evangeliarii et praxapostoli, 723-768 [Evl 32]; Vol. III: Menologium, 1-24 [Evl 47 and 50].

References
- T. Ware, 'Lectionary, in *The Orthodox Study Bible (New Testament and Psalms* (Nashville, Tennessee, 1993), 771-780, [Eng: E, A, P]
- I.M. De Vries, "The Epistles, Gospels and Tones of the Byzantine Liturgical Year [I-IV]", in *The Eastern Churches Quarterly*, 10 (1953-1954), 41-49; 85-95; 137-149; 192-195, [Eng : E, A].
- E. Lash, Archimandrite (Ed.), *Prophetologion/The Lectionary*, on http://web.ukonline.co.uk/ephrem/prophetologion.htm.

3.2.3 The lectionary apparatuses in the Slavonic Bible codex of Gennadius (1499 A.D.)

- Библия 1499 года и Библия в синодальном переводе. Библия книги священного писания ветхого и нового завета: Господа нашего Иисуса Христа Святое Евангелие от Матфея, Марка, Луки, Иоаннна,Том 7, Ed. Moscow Patriarchate, Moscow, 1992, 390-398 (Столпы Евангельские).
- Библия 1499 года и Библия в синодальном переводе. Библия книги священного писания ветхого и нового завета: Деяния святых Апостолов. Послания святых Апостолов Иакова, Петра, Иоанна, Иуды. Послания святого Апостола Павла. Апокалипсис Том 8, Ed. Moscow Patriarchate, Moscow, 1992, 406-417 (Столпы Апостольские).

3.2.4 Recent Orthodox calendars (Greek & Russian)

- Greek Orthodox Calendar [published annually] (Ecumenical Patriarchate)
- Russian Orthodox Calendar [published annually] (Moscow Patriarchate)
- Троицкій Православный Русскій Календарь на годъ (Holy Trinity Monastery, USA)
- Calendar and Lectionary for 2005 according to the revised Julian (new style) calendar (The Orthodox Fellowship of Saint John the Baptist, Essex, GB)
- Saint Herman Calendar 2005. The year 7513 from the creation of the world. (St. Herman of Alaska Brotherhood, USA)
- Saint Herman Calendar 2006. The year 7514 from the creation of the world. (St. Herman of Alaska Brotherhood, USA)
- Orthodoxe Kalender Oude Stijl 2006 met Lezingen en Heiligen voor elke dag (Russisch-Orthodoxe Kerk Heilige Nikolaas van Myra te Amsterdam)

3.2.5 Byzantine calendar nomenclature

1) *The Byzantine Daily order of services* [ἡμερονύκτιος, day-night division]

Ἑσπερινὸς	[Early Evening service or Vesper]
Ἀπόδειπνον	[Evening service or Compline]
Μεσονυκτικόν	[Midnight service]
Ὄρθρος	[Sunday Morning service]
Ὧραι	[Hours]
α′ ὥρα	[First Hour]
γ′ ὥρα	[Third Hour]
ς′ ὥρα	[Sixth Hour]
θ′ ὥρα	[Ninth Hour]
Λειτουργία	[Liturgy]

NB. In the Byzantine calendar the Ἑσπερινὸς on the eve of the Sunday (Day of the Lord) is considered the beginning of the week. The Liturgy is normally celebrated between the Sixth and the Ninth Hour.

References:
- O.G. Rigas, *Op. Cit*, (Thessaloniki, 1994), 52-132.
- J. von Gardner, *Op. Cit.* (Crestwood, NY, 1980), 70-73.
- Mother Mary and K. Ware (Trans.), 'The Orthodox Services and their Structure', in *The Festal Menaion* (London, 1977), 38-80.
- L. Clugnet, *Dictionnaire grec-français des noms liturgiques en usage dans l'église grecque* (London, 1971 [Repr. 1895]).

2) *The Byzantine Weekly order* [the ἑβδομάς or seven-day division]

Κυριακή (Πρωτή ἡμέρα) [Day of the Lord]
Δευτέρα (ἡμέρα) [Second day]
Τρίτη [Third day]
Τετάρτη [Fourth day]
Πέμπτη [Fifth day]
Παρασκευή [Day of Preparation]
Σάββατον [Sabbath]

NB. In the Byzantine names of the days are preserved ancient biblical expressions. The first day is the Κυριακή, since it is the day of the Resurrection (cf. O.G. Rigas, *Op. Cit*, (Thessaloniki, 1994), 25). The days of the week are numbered. The Friday and Saturday are characteristically called Παρασκευή and Σάββατον.

Ref.: O.G. Rigas, *Op. Cit*, (Thessaloniki, 1994), 25-26.

3.2.6 References

- O.G. Rigas, Τυπικόν (Thessaloniki, 1994).
- T.J. Talley, *The Origins of the Liturgical Year*, second edition (Collegeville, Minnesota, 1991).
- J. von Gardner, *Russian Church Singing, Volume 1: Orthodox Worship and Hymnography* (Crestwood, NY, 1980).
- T. Ware (Bishop Kallistos), *The Orthodox Church* (n.l., 1997).
- G. Barrois, *Scripture Readings In Orthodox Worship* (Crestwood, New York, 1977).
- A. Schmemann, *Introduction to Liturgical Theology* (London/Portland, 1966).
- K. Onasch, *Das Weinachtsfest im orthodoxen Kirchenjahr. Liturgie und Ikonographie* (Berlin, 1958).
- A. Ehrhard, *Überlieferung und Bestand der hagiographischen und homiletischen Literatur der griechischen Kirche, von den Anfängen bis zum Ende des 16. Jahrhunderts*, 1 (Leipzig-Berlin, 1937).
- A. Rahlfs, 'Die alttestamentlichen Lektionen der griechischen Kirche', in *Mitteilungen des Septuaginta-Unternehmen*, Heft V (Berlin, 1915), 120-230.
- C.R. Gregory, *Textkritik des Neuen Testamentes*, 3 volumes, (Leipzig, 1900-1909).
- J.M. Neale, *A History of the Holy Eastern Church, Part 1: General Introduction*, 2 vols (London, 1850).

3.3 The Cycle of the Eleven Resurrection Evangelia

3.3.1 Liturgical purpose/function

In this reading cycle are included a series of eleven Gospel lessons, based on the Resurrection theme: the Εὐαγγέλια Ἀναστάσιμα Ἑωτινὰ τὰ ια′. This individual cycle of readings, in Russian characteristically termed the 'Gospel pillar' (евангельский столп) are read in the morning service (Ὄρθρος), on the eve of Sunday, the day of Resurrection. The cycle repeats itself every eleven weeks. The order of lessons is: 1 lesson according to Matthew; 2 lessons according to Mark; 3 lessons according to Luke; and finally 5 lessons according to John. The traditional chronological order of Gospels is reflected in this series of Resurrection lessons.

The centrality of the Resurrection theme in the Byzantine calendar is evident. This reading cycle shows how the fathers focused on the Resurrection theme and selected and systemised readings accordingly. All biblical passages relating to the Resurrection, were divided over 11 readings (pericopes).

The 11 readings are to be found in the:
- Evangelion (sometimes twice, in the relevant biblical book (e.g. Matt. 28, 16-10), as well as in the special section 'Eothina' at the end of the Evangelion);
- Euchologion (written in full).
- Pentekostarion, for the Paschal cycle (written in full, but in a different order).

For biblical scholars, this implies different sources of comparative material.

3.3.2 Sources Used

- Ἐυαγγέλια Ἑωτινὰ Ἀναστάσιμα ἀναγινωσκόμενα εἰς τοὺς Ὄρθρους ἑκάστης Κυριακῆς', in Θεῖον καὶ Ἱερὸν Εὐαγγέλιον, 2nd edition (Athens, 1992), 216-222.

- "Ἐυαγγέλια Ἑωτινὰ Ἀναγινωσκόμενα ἐν τῷ Ὄρθρῳ ἑκάστης Κυριακῆς καὶ Δεσποτικῆς Ἑορτῆς ἀπὸ τοῦ Πάσχα μέχρι τῶν Ἁγίων Πάντων', in Πεντηκοστάριον χαρμόσυνον, 2nd edition (Athens, 2002), 587-594.

- Ἐυαγγέλια Ἑωτινὰ Ἀναστάσιμα ΙΑ'', in Εὐχολόγιον τὸ Μέγα, 4th ed. (Athens, 1992), 667-676.

3.3.3 Selection and arrangement of lessons

Ἑωθινὸν Α' : Matt 28, 16-20
Ἑωθινὸν Β' : Mark 16, 1-8
Ἑωθινὸν Γ' : Mark 16, 9-2
Ἑωθινὸν Δ' : Luke 24, 1-12
Ἑωθινὸν Ε' : Luke 24, 12-35
Ἑωθινὸν ς' : Luke 24, 36-53
Ἑωθινὸν Ζ' : John 20, 1-10
Ἑωθινὸν Η' : John 20, 11-18
Ἑωθινὸν Θ' : John 20, 19-31
Ἑωθινὸν Ι' : John 21, 1-14
Ἑωθινὸν ΙΑ' : John 21, 15-25

3.3.4 The cycle

There are five 'Resurrection-Evangelia Pillars', i.e. the cycle of eleven lessons is repeated 5 times successively during the whole Byzantine ecclesiastical year. The first (Eastertide) and the last (Great Lent) pillars are, however, incomplete. From Easter up to and including Pentecost an alternative series is prescribed, with a different arrangement of lessons including the following Εὐαγγέλια Ἀναστάσιμα Ἑωτινὰ (see the Pentekostarion, 587-594)[467].

Sunday of Easter: Ἑωθινὸν Β'
Sunday of Anti-Pascha: Ἑωθινὸν Α'
Sunday of the Myrrhbearers: Ἑωθινὸν Δ'
Sunday of the Paralytic: Ἑωθινὸν Ε'
Sunday of the Samaritan Woman: Ἑωθινὸν Ζ'
Sunday of the Blind man: Ἑωθινὸν Η'
Feast of the Ascension: Ἑωθινὸν Γ'
Sunday of the Holy Fathers: Ἑωθινὸν Ι'
Sunday of Pentecost: Ἑωθινὸν Θ' [NB John 20, 19-23 omitting vs. 24-31]

---

[467] C.R. Gregory, *Op. Cit.* (Leipzig, 1900-1909), I, 364 refers to Evl 402, Athen, Nat. Sakk. 180, vom Jahre 1089, f. 393 and provides the note in Greek concerning the reading of the 'τὰ ἀναστάσιμα εὐαγγέλια τὰ ἑωτινὰ' in this manuscript.

In the Easter Pillar, Ἑωθινὸν VI and XI fall away.
During Great Lent the Resurrection Gospels (Ἑωθινὸν IV-VIII) are read, but the cycle breaks off before Psalm Sunday (see the Triodion). Omitted are Ἑωθινὸν IX-XI.
The regular cycle starts with the Sunday of All Saints (Ἑωθινὸν I).

The cycle of Resurrection Gospel lessons covers approximately the whole Byzantine ecclesiastical year and sets a liturgical tone on every Sunday morning service. Connected to the Morning Resurrection Gospel lessons are the corresponding exapostilaria and Gospel stichera. Immediately following the lessons, the hymn Ἀνάστασιν Χριστοῦ is sung. Finally, patristic interpretations are preserved in *Homilies on the Morning Evangelia*[468].

References
- O.G. Rigas, *Op. Cit*, (Thessaloniki, 1994), 52-132;
- J. von Gardner, *Op. Cit.* (Crestwood, NY, 1980), 70-73.
- C.R. Gregory, 'εὐαγγέλια ἑωτινὰ ἀναστάσιμα', in *Op. Cit.* (Leipzig, 1900-1909), I, 364.

3.4 The Movable and Immovable Cycles of Lessons of the Byzantine Calendar

3.4.1 Liturgical function

In the following four tables we offer a presentation of readings from the Prophetologion, Apostolos and Evangelion, for:

- Period I of the movable cycle: Pentekostarion (from Pascha until Pentecost)
- Period II of the movable cycle: Octoechos/Parakletiki (from Pentecost until Great Lent)
- Period III of the movable cycle: Triodion (the Great and Holy Forty Days/Great Lent)
- The immovable cycle for the whole ecclesiastical year.

We have compiled this form of presentation to show the calendar cohesion of the Byzantine lection system. All four tables have in common three parallel columns of respectively Prophetologion, Apostolos and Evangelion lessons, even for periods where a series of readings is absent (for example from the Prophetologion). In this case the column is empty. However, the absence of readings in a column tells us just as much about the hermeneutic choices behind the incorporated lessons, as the full columns do. Especially revealing is the absence of Prophetologion readings in periods I and II. Similarly, the absence of Apostolos and Evangelion readings on the weekdays of Great Lent (save the Great Week).

By presenting the lessons together in one table, we also demonstrate how OT and NT readings are related. Apostolos and Evangelion readings are integrally connected; this we can see visibly, either thematically (lessons related to feasts or commemorations chosen eclectically), or systematically (continuous lessons, not immediately linked to a theme or event). Formally, we could say, the one does not exist without the other; Evangelion readings are preceded by Apostolos readings. To reinforce this integration we have allocated the readings of the day 1 serial number (A..).

The movable and immovable cycles move in parallel and are supplementary to one another, as we described in chapter 2. This implies that there are in fact two reading cycles for every day of the year. The Typikon determines which reading cycle is dominant for whichever day of the week, and whether lessons from both cycles are read, or whether one reading from one of the cycles falls away.
In chapter 2 we noted that the Prophetologion no longer exists as an edition form, and that the OT prophet readings have been incorporated in the Pentekostarion and Triodion (for the movable cycle) and the Menaia (for the immovable cycle). The original Prophetologion was composed of a section with the movable cycle readings, and a section with the immovable cycle readings – evidence of cohesion between the two cycles, in one codex. For the purpose of our tables, we have revitalised the Prophetologion codex. It is, codicologically, a manuscript form, based on some 132 extant manuscripts (see **§ 5.6**). Not all Prophetologia codices comprise both sections, movable and immovable.
This tabular presentation reveals the inner cohesion between the different liturgical books, and the hermeneutic hand of the fathers in shaping their usage. It also hints at the necessity, therefore, of combined codicological research of the codices that lie at the base of these tables, since they intrinsically belong together.

---

[468] These homilies can be found, e.g. in a codex of various materials (διάφορα), Athos, Lavra 1206 [I 122], XIV. f. 1a-56b, item 1 [Spyridon/Eustratiades, 202]: Ὁμιλίαι εἰς τὰ ἑωθινὰ εὐαγγέλια.

3.4.2 Sources Used

The editions listed here are given above, in § **3.2.2 and 3.2.3**:
a) For the movable cycle:
    1) Evangelion Greek edition
    2) Apostolos Greek edition
    3) Prophetologion [Triodion and Pentekostarion Greek edition]

b) For the immovable cycle:
    4) Evangelion Greek edition
    5) Apostolos Greek edition
    6) Prophetologion [Twelve Menaia Greek edition]

c) Manuscript evidence:
    7) Gregory: Evangelion + Apostolos lessons
    8) Rahlfs: Prophetologion lessons
    9) Engberg: Prophetologion lessons [Indices]

d) English Tables
    10) Ware
    11) De Vries

e) Calendars
    12) Saint Herman Calendar 2006. The year 7514 from the creation of the world. (St. Herman of Alaska Brotherhood, USA)
    13) Троицкій Православный Русскій Календарь на годъ (Holy Trinity Monastery, USA)

3.4.3 Selection and arrangement of lessons: Movable cycle

Period I: Pentekostarion (from Pascha until Pentecost)

In this cycle we present the lessons read on each day of the week from the Apostolos, the Evangelion[469] and the Prophetologion if there is an OT reading, (these lessons are written in full in the Pentekostarion)[470], in the Pascha period, demonstrating how the fathers focused on exclusive biblical themes (e.g. Pascha, Thomas Sunday) in the context of the liturgical calendar and attuned their selections of biblical readings to these themes, besides the practice of continuing daily readings following (more or less) the chronological order of the chosen (prescribed) books. During the whole Easter period (7 weeks + 1 day) emphasis is placed on the Sunday (the day of Resurrection), the first day of the seven following weeks. This calendaric paradigm and rhythm changes at Pentecost (the day of the Descent of the Holy Spirit).

From the Sunday of Easter (Midnight-Office) until the Sunday of Pentecost (the Fiftieth Day)

Weeks 1-7 (Eastertide)

Anagnosis	Synaxarion	Prophetologion	Apostolos	Evangelion
	Week of the Renewing			
A 1	Holy and Great Sunday of Pascha		Liturgy Acts 1, 1-8[471]	Morning office Eothina II Liturgy John 1, 1-17
A 2	Second day of the Renewing		Acts 1, 12-17, 21-26	John 1, 18-28
A 3	Third day of the Renewing		Acts 2, 14-21	Luke 24, 12-35
A 4	Fourth day of the Renewing		Acts 2, 22-36	John 1, 35-52
A 5	Fifth day of the Renewing		Acts 2, 38-43	John 3, 1-15
A 6	Friday of the Renewing		Acts 3, 1-8	John 2, 12-22
A 7	Saturday of the Renewing		Acts 3, 11-16	John 3, 22-33

---

[469] Greek sources: Θεῖον καὶ Ἱερὸν Εὐαγγέλιον, κατὰ τὸ κείμενον τὸ ἐγκεκριμένον ὑπὸ τῆς Μεγάλης τοῦ Χριστοῦ Ἐκκλησίας, 2nd edition (Athens, 1992); Ἀπόστολος, Πράξεις καὶ Ἐπιστολαὶ τῶν ἁγίων Ἀποστόλων, αἱ καθ'ὅλον τὸ ἔτος ἐπ'Ἐκκλησίαις ἀναγιγνωσκόμεναι καθὼς καὶ τῶν ἱερῶν τελέτων, 5th ed. (Athens, 2002). Cf. C.R. Gregory, 'Die kirchlichen Lesestücke aus dem Neuen Testament', in *Textkritik des Neuen Testamentes* (Leipzig, 1900), I, 343-364, 'Synaxarion: Das bewegliche Jahr', i.e. Evangelion lessons, on the basis of Evl 32 / *l* 32esk [Gotha, Forsch und Landesbibl. Memb. I 78, 273 f, 2, XI] and 3 other mss.

[470] The basis of the selected passages of the "Prophetologion" are the editions of the Pentekostarion and the Triodion (Ed. Apostolike Diakonia); see **3.2.1** above. Cf. C. Høeg, G. Zuntz, (Eds.), *Prophetologium I* (Monumenta Musicae Byzantinae. Lectionaria. Vol. I) (Copenhagen, 1970), Fasc. 6, Index Lectionum [Movable], 600-604, = L 1-47.

[471] The references have been checked against Ἡ Ἁγία Γραφή - Παλαιὰ Διαθήκη καὶ ἡ Καινὴ Διαθήκη, Ed. P. Bratsiotis, 15th edition, (Athens, 1999).

Anagnosis	Synaxarion	Prophetologion	Apostolos	Evangelion
	Second Week of Pascha			
				Morning office Eothina I
			Liturgy	**Liturgy**
A 8	Sunday of Antipascha		Acts 5, 12-20	John 20, 19-31
	H. Apostle Thomas			
A 9	Second day of the second week		Acts 3, 19-26	John 2, 1-11
A 10	Third day of the second week		Acts 4, 1-10	John 3, 16-21
A 11	Fourth day of the second week		Acts 4, 13-22	John 5, 17-24
A 12	Fifth day of the second week		Acts 4, 23-31	John 5, 24-30
A 13	Friday of the second week		Acts 5, 1-11	John 5, 30-47; 6, 1-2
A 14	Saturday of the second week		Acts 5, 21-32	John 6, 14-27
	Third Week of Pascha			
				Morning office Eothina III
			Liturgy	**Liturgy**
A 15	Third Sunday of the Myrrhbearing Women Joseph of Arimathea and Nicodemos		Acts 6, 1-7	Mark 15, 43-47; 16, 1-8
A 16	Second day of the third week		Acts 6, 8-15; 7, 1-5, 47-60	John 4, 46-54
A 17	Third day of the third week		Acts 8, 5-17	John 6, 27-33
A 18	Fourth day of the third week		Acts 8, 18-25	John 6, 35-39
A 19	Fifth day of the third week		Acts 8, 26-39	John 6, 40-44
A 20	Friday of the third week		Acts 8, 40; 9, 1-18	John 6, 48-54
A 21	Saturday of the third week		Acts 9, 19-31	John 15, 17-27; 16, 1-2
	Fourth Week of Pascha			
				Morning office Eothina IV
			Liturgy	**Liturgy**
A 22	Fourth Sunday of the Paralytic		Acts 9, 32-42	John 5, 1-15
A 23	Second day of the fourth week		Acts 10, 1-16	John 6, 56-69
A 24	Third day of the fourth week		Acts 10, 21-33	John 7, 1-13
A 25	Fourth day of the fourth week (Mid-Pentecost)	**Evening office** (1) Mic 4, 2-3, 5; 5, 2-5, 8; 5, 3 (2) Is 55, 1-3, 6-13 (3) Prov 9, 1-11	Acts 14, 6-18	John 7, 14-30
A 26	Fifth day of the fourth week		Acts 10, 34-43	John 8, 12-20
A 27	Friday of the fourth week		Acts 10, 44-48; 11, 1-10	John 8, 21-30
A 28	Saturday of the fourth week		Acts 12, 1-11	John 8, 31-42
	Fifth Week of Pascha			
				Morning office Eothina VII
			Liturgy	**Liturgy**
A 29	Fifth Sunday of the Samaritan Woman		Acts 11, 19-30	John 4, 5-42
A 30	Second day of the fifth week		Acts 12, 12-17	John 8, 42-51
A 31	Third day of the fifth week		Acts 12, 25; 13, 1-12	John 8, 51-59
A 32	Fourth day of Mid-Pentecost		Acts 13, 13-24	John 6, 5-14
A 33	Fifth day of the fifth week		Acts 14, 20-28; 15, 1-4a	John 9, 39-41; 10, 1-9
A 34	Friday of the fifth week		Acts 15, 5-12	John 10, 17-28
A 35	Saturday of the fifth week		Acts 15, 35-41	John 10, 27-38
	Sixth Week of Pascha			
				Morning office Eothina VIII
			Liturgy	**Liturgy**
A 36	Sixth Sunday of the Blind Man		Acts 16, 16-34	John 9, 1-38
A 37	Second day of the sixth week		Acts 17, 1-9	John 11, 47-54
A 38	Third day of the sixth week		Acts 17, 19-28	John 12, 19-36
A 39	Fourth day of the sixth week		Acts 18, 22-28	John 12, 36-47
A 40	Fifth day of the sixth week Ascension of the Lord	**Evening office** (1) Is 2, 2-3 (2) Is 62, 10-12; 63, 1-3, 7-9 (3) Zech 14, 1, 4, 8-11	**Liturgy** Acts 1, 1-12	**Morning office** Mark 16, 9-20 **Liturgy** Luke 24, 36-53
A 41	Friday of the sixth week		Acts 19, 1-8	John 14, 1-11
A 42	Saturday of the sixth week		Acts 20, 7-12	John 14, 10-21

Anagnosis	Synaxarion	Prophetologion	Apostolos	Evangelion
	Seventh Week of Pascha			Morning office Eothina X
A 43	Sunday of the 318 Holy Godbearing Fathers assembled in Nicea I	Evening office (1) Gen 14, 14-20 (2) Deut 1, 8-11, 15-17 (3) Deut 10,14-18, 20-21	Liturgy Acts 20, 16-18, 28-36	Liturgy John 17, 1-13
A 44	Second day of the seventh week		Acts 21, 8-14	John 14, 27-31; 15, 1-7
A 45	Third day of the seventh week		Acts 21, 26-32	John 16, 2-13
A 46	Fourth day of the seventh week		Acts 23, 1-11	John 16, 15-23
A 47	Fifth day of the seventh week		Acts 25, 13-19	John 16, 23-33
A 48	Friday of the seventh week		Acts 27, 1-44; 28, 1	John 17, 18-26
A 49	Saturday of the seventh week		Acts 28, 1-31	John 21, 14-25
A 50	**Sunday of Holy Pentecost Descent of the Holy Spirit on the Disciples-Trinity Sunday**	Evening office (1) Num 11, 16-17, 24-29 (2) Joel 2, 23-32; 3, 1-5 (3) Ezek 36, 24-28 Liturgy Acts 2, 1-11		Morning office Eothina IX Liturgy John 7, 37-52; 8, 12

Period II: Octoechos/Parakletiki (from Pentecost until Great Lent)

In this table we present the lessons read on each day of the week from the Apostolos and the Evangelion (and the Prophetologion lessons, except those of All Saints and in the last week before Great Lent, only in the parallel series **B** of the immovable cycle), in the Octoechos/Parakletike period, to demonstrate how the fathers focused not so much on biblical themes in the context of the liturgical calendar, prefering the continuous reading of Scripture. From Pentecost to Easter Saturday of the next year, during all the weeks 'after Pentecost' (and also in the Triodion period), commencing with the Sunday of All Saints, the Sunday follows 'at the end' of the week; this is reflected in the weekly prescription of lessons, running from the Monday until the Sunday inclusive.

From the 2nd day of Pentecost to the Exaltation of the Cross (14 Sept) and from there to Great Lent

Weeks 1-17 and 18-32 (after Pentecost)

Anagnosis	Synaxarion	Prophetologion	Apostolos	Evangelion
	First Week after Pentecost		Liturgy	Liturgy
A 51	Second day of the first week		Eph 5, 8-19	Matt 18, 10-20
A 52	Third day of the first week		Rom 1, 1-7, 13-17	Matt 4, 23-25; 5, 1-13
A 53	Fourth day of the first week		Rom 1, 18-27	Matt 5, 20-26
A 54	Fifth day of the first week		Rom 1, 28-32; 2, 1-9	Matt 5, 27-32
A 55	Friday of the first week		Rom 2, 14-28	Matt 5, 33-41
A 56	Saturday of the first week		Rom 1, 7-12	Matt 5, 42-48
A 57	**Sunday of All Saints**	Evening office (1) Is 43, 9-14 (2) Wis 3, 1-9 (3) Wis 5, 15-6, 3	 Liturgy Heb 11, 33-40; 12, 1-2	Morning office Eothina I Liturgy Matt 10, 32-33, 37-38; 19, 27-30
	Second Week after Pentecost		Liturgy	Liturgy
A 58	Second day of the second week		Rom 2, 28-29; 3, 1-18	Matt 6, 31-34; 7, 9-11
A 59	Third day of the second week		Rom 4, 4-12	Matt 7, 15-21
A 60	Fourth day of the second week		Rom 4, 13-25	Matt 7, 21-23
A 61	Fifth day of the second week		Rom 5, 10-16	Matt 8, 23-27
A 62	Friday of the second week		Rom 5, 17-21; 6, 1-2	Matt 9, 14-17
A 63	Saturday of the second week		Rom 3, 19-26	Matt 7, 1-8
A 64	**Sunday of the second Week**		Rom 2, 10-16	Morning office Eothina II Matt 4, 18-23
	Third Week after Pentecost		Liturgy	Liturgy
A 65	Second day of the third week		Rom 7, 1-13	Matt 9, 36-38; 10, 1-8
A 66	Third day of the third week		Rom 7, 14-25; 8, 1-2	Matt 10, 9-15
A 67	Fourth day of the third week		Rom 8, 2-13	Matt 10, 16-22
A 68	Fifth day of the third week		Rom 8, 22-27	Matt 10, 23-31
A 69	Friday of the third week		Rom 9, 6-19	Matt 10, 32-36; 11, 1
A 70	Saturday of the third week		Rom 3, 28-31; 4, 1-3	Matt 7, 24-29; 8, 1-4
A 71	**Sunday of the third Week**		Rom 5, 1-10	Morning office Eothina III Matt 6, 22-33

Anagnosis	Synaxarion	Prophetologion	Apostolos	Evangelion
	Fourth Week after Pentecost		Liturgy	Liturgy
A 72	Second day of the fourth week		Rom 9, 18-33	Matt 11, 2-15
A 73	Third day of the fourth week		Rom 10, 11-21; 11, 1-2	Matt 11, 16-20
A 74	Fourth day of the fourth week		Rom 11, 2-12	Matt 11, 20-26
A 75	Fifth day of the fourth week		Rom 11, 13-24	Matt 11, 27-30
A 76	Friday of the fourth week		Rom 11, 25-36	Matt 12, 1-8
A 77	Saturday of the fourth week		Rom 6, 11-17	Matt 8, 14-23
				Morning office Eothina IV
A 78	**Sunday of the fourth Week**		Rom 6, 18-23	Matt 8, 5-13
	Fifth Week after Pentecost		Liturgy	Liturgy
A 79	Second day of the fifth week		Rom 12, 4-5, 15-21	Matt 12, 9-13
A 80	Third day of the fifth week		Rom 14, 9-18	Matt 12, 14-16, 22-30
A 81	Fourth day of the fifth week		Rom 15, 7-16	Matt 12, 38-45
A 82	Fifth day of the fifth week		Rom 15, 17-29	Matt 12, 46-50; 13, 1-3
A 83	Friday of the fifth week		Rom 16, 1-16	Matt 13, 3-9
A 84	Saturday of the fifth week		Rom 8, 14-21	Matt 9, 9-13
				Morning office Eothina V
A 85	**Sunday of the fifth Week**		Rom 10, 1-10	Matt 8, 28-34; 9, 1
	Sixth Week after Pentecost		Liturgy	Liturgy
A 86	Second day of the sixth week		Rom 16, 17-24	Matt 13, 10-23
A 87	Third day of the sixth week		I Cor 1, 1-9	Matt 13, 24-30
A 88	Fourth day of the sixth week		I Cor 2, 9-16; 3, 1-8	Matt 13, 31-36
A 89	Fifth day of the sixth week		I Cor 3, 18-23	Matt 13, 36-43
A 90	Friday of the sixth week		I Cor 4, 5-8	Matt 13, 44-54
A 91	Saturday of the sixth week		Rom 9, 1-5	Matt 9, 18-26
				Morning office Eothina VI
A 92	**Sunday of the sixth Week**		Rom 12, 6-14	Matt 9, 1-8
	Seventh Week after Pentecost		Liturgy	Liturgy
A 93	Second day of the seventh week		I Cor 5, 9-13; 6, 1-11	Matt 13, 54-58
A 94	Third day of the seventh week		I Cor 6, 20; 7, 1-12	Matt 14, 1-13
A 95	Fourth day of the seventh week		I Cor 7, 12-24	Matt 14, 35-36; 15, 1-11
A 96	Fifth day of the seventh week		I Cor 7, 24-35	Matt 15, 12-21
A 97	Friday of the seventh week		I Cor 7, 35-40; 8, 1-7	Matt 15, 29-31
A 98	Saturday of the seventh week		Rom 12, 1-3	Matt 10, 37-42; 11, 1
				Morning office Eothina VII
A 99	**Sunday of the seventh Week**		Rom 15, 1-7	Matt 9, 27-35
	Eighth Week after Pentecost		Liturgy	Liturgy
A 100	Second day of the eighth week		I Cor 9, 13-18	Matt 16, 1-6
A 101	Third day of the eighth week		I Cor 10, 5-12	Matt 16, 6-12
A 102	Fourth day of the eighth week		I Cor 10, 12-22	Matt 16, 20-24
A 103	Fifth day of the eighth week		I Cor 10, 28-33; 11, 1-8	Matt 16, 24-28
A 104	Friday of the eighth week		I Cor 11, 8-23	Matt 17, 10-18
A 105	Saturday of the eighth week		Rom 13, 1-10	Matt 12, 30-37
				Morning office Eothina VIII
A 106	**Sunday of the eighth Week**		I Cor 1, 10-17	Matt 14, 14-22
	Ninth Week after Pentecost		Liturgy	Liturgy
A 107	Second day of the ninth week		I Cor 11, 31-34; 12, 1-6	Matt 18, 1-11
A 108	Third day of the ninth week		I Cor 12, 12-26	Matt 18, 18-22; 19, 1-2, 13-15
A 109	Fourth day of the ninth week		I Cor 13, 4-13; 14, 1-5	Matt 20, 1-16
A 110	Fifth day of the ninth week		I Cor 14, 6-19	Matt 20, 17-28
A 111	Friday of the ninth week		I Cor 14, 26-40	Matt 21, 12-14, 17-20
A 112	Saturday of the ninth week		Rom 14, 6-9	Matt 15, 32-39
				Morning office Eothina IX
A 113	**Sunday of the ninth Week**		I Cor 3, 9-17	Matt 14, 22-34
	Tenth Week after Pentecost		Liturgy	Liturgy
A 114	Second day of the tenth week		I Cor 15, 12-19	Matt 21, 18-22
A 115	Third day of the tenth week		I Cor 15, 29-38	Matt 21, 23-27
A 116	Fourth day of the tenth week		I Cor 16, 4-12	Matt 21, 28-32
A 117	Fifth day of the tenth week		II Cor 1, 1-7	Matt 21, 43-46
A 118	Friday of the tenth week		II Cor 1, 12-20	Matt 22, 23-33
A 119	Saturday of the tenth week		Rom 15, 30-33	Matt 17, 24-27; 18, 1-4
				Morning office Eothina X
A 120	**Sunday of the tenth Week**		I Cor 4, 9-16	Matt 17, 14-23

Anagnosis	Synaxarion	Prophetologion	Apostolos	Evangelion
	Eleventh Week after Pentecost		Liturgy	Liturgy
A 121	Second day of the eleventh week		II Cor 2, 3-15	Matt 23, 13-22
A 122	Third day of the eleventh week		II Cor 2, 14-17; 3, 1-3	Matt 23, 23-28
A 123	Fourth day of the eleventh week		II Cor 3, 4-11	Matt 23, 29-39
A 124	Fifth day of the eleventh week		II Cor 4, 1-12	Matt 24, 13-28
A 125	Friday of the eleventh week		II Cor 4, 13-18	Matt 24, 27-33, 42-51
A 126	Saturday of the eleventh week		I Cor 1, 3-9	Matt 19, 3-12
				Morning office Eothina XI
A 127	**Sunday of the eleventh Week**		I Cor 9, 2-12	Matt 18, 23-35
	Twelfth Week after Pentecost		Liturgy	Liturgy
A 128	Second day of the twelfth week		II Cor 5, 10-15	Mark 1, 9-15
A 129	Third day of the twelfth week		II Cor 5, 15-21	Mark 1, 16-22
A 130	Fourth day of the twelfth week		II Cor 6, 11-16	Mark 1, 23-28
A 131	Fifth day of the twelfth week		II Cor 7, 1-10	Mark 1, 29-35
A 132	Friday of the twelfth week		II Cor 7, 10-16	Mark 2, 18-22
A 133	Saturday of the twelfth week		I Cor 1, 26-31; 2, 1-5	Matt 20, 29-34
				Morning office Eothina I
A 134	**Sunday of the twelfth Week**		I Cor 15, 1-11	Matt 19, 16-26
	Thirteenth Week after Pentecost		Liturgy	Liturgy
A 135	Second day of the thirteenth week		II Cor 8, 7-15	Mark 3, 6-12
A 136	Third day of the thirteenth week		II Cor 8, 16-24; 9, 1-5	Mark 3, 13-21
A 137	Fourth day of the thirteenth week		II Cor 9, 12-15; 10, 1-7	Mark 3, 20-27
A 138	Fifth day of the thirteenth week		II Cor 10, 7-18	Mark 3, 28-35
A 139	Friday of the thirteenth week		II Cor 11, 5-21	Mark 4, 1-9
A 140	Saturday of the thirteenth week		I Cor 2, 6-9	Matt 22, 15-22
				Morning office Eothina II
A 141	**Sunday of the thirteenth Week**		I Cor 16, 13-24	Matt 21, 33-42
	Fourteenth Week after Pentecost		Liturgy	Liturgy
A 142	Second day of the fourteenth week		II Cor 12, 10-19	Mark 4, 10-23
A 143	Third day of the fourteenth week		II Cor 12, 20-21; 13, 1-2	Mark 4, 24-34
A 144	Fourth day of the fourteenth week		II Cor 13, 3-13	Mark 4, 35-41
A 145	Fifth day of the fourteenth week		Gal 1, 1-3, 20-24; 2, 1-5	Mark 5, 1-20
A 146	Friday of the fourteenth week		Gal 2, 6-10	Mark 5, 22-24, 35-43; 6, 1
A 147	Saturday of the fourteenth week		I Cor 4, 1-5	Matt 23, 1-12
				Morning office Eothina III
A 148	**Sunday of the fourteenth Week**		II Cor 1, 21-24; 2, 1-4	Matt 22, 1-14
	Fifteenth Week after Pentecost		Liturgy	Liturgy
A 149	Second day of the fifteenth week		Gal 2, 11-16	Mark 5, 24-34
A 150	Third day of the fifteenth week		Gal 2, 21; 3, 1-7	Mark 6, 1-7
A 151	Fourth day of the fifteenth week		Gal 3, 15-22	Mark 6, 7-13
A 152	Fifth day of the fifteenth week		Gal 3, 23-29; 4, 1-5	Mark 6, 30-45
A 153	Friday of the fifteenth week		Gal 4, 8-21	Mark 6, 45-53
A 154	Saturday of the fifteenth week		I Cor 4, 17-21; 5, 1-5	Matt 24, 1-13
				Morning office Eothina IV
A 155	**Sunday of the fifteenth Week**		II Cor 4, 6-15	Matt 22, 35-46
	Sixteenth Week after Pentecost		Liturgy	Liturgy
A 156	Second day of the sixteenth week		Gal 4, 28-31; 5, 1-10	Mark 6, 54-56; 7, 1-8
A 157	Third day of the sixteenth week		Gal 5, 11-21	Mark 7, 5-16
A 158	Fourth day of the sixteenth week		Gal 6, 2-10	Mark 7, 14-24
A 159	Fifth day of the sixteenth week		Eph 1, 1-9	Mark 7, 24-30
A 160	Friday of the sixteenth week		Eph 1, 7-17	Mark 8, 1-10
A 161	Saturday of the sixteenth week		I Cor 10, 23-28	Matt 24, 34-37, 42-44
				Morning office Eothina V
A 162	**Sunday of the sixteenth Week**		II Cor 6, 1-10	Matt 25, 14-30
	Seventeenth Week after Pentecost		Liturgy	Liturgy
A 163	Second day of the seventeenth week		Eph 1, 22-23; 2, 1-3	[Mark 10, 46-52][472]
A 164	Third day of the seventeenth week		Eph 2, 19-22; 3, 1-7	[Mark 11, 11-23]
A 165	Fourth day of the seventeenth week		Eph 3, 8-21	[Mark 11, 23-26]
A 166	Fifth day of the seventeenth week		Eph 4, 14-17	[Mark 11, 27-33]
A 167	Friday of the seventeenth week		Eph 4, 17-25	[Mark 12, 1-12]
A 168	Saturday of the seventeenth week		I Cor 14, 20-25	Matt 25, 1-13
				Morning office Eothina VI
A 169	**Sunday of the seventeenth Week**		II Cor 6, 16- 18; 7, 1	Matt 15, 21-28

---

[472] These lessons are not found in the Greek source; see the 2nd to the 5th days of the *Thirty Second Week after Pentecost*.

Anagnosis	Synaxarion	Prophetologion	Apostolos	Evangelion
	Eighteenth Week after Pentecost		Liturgy	Liturgy
A 170	Second day of the eighteenth week		Eph 4, 25-32	Luke 3, 19-22
A 171	Third day of the eighteenth week		Eph 5, 20-25	Luke 3, 23-38; 4, 1
A 172	Fourth day of the eighteenth week		Eph 5, 25-33	Luke 4, 1-15
A 173	Fifth day of the eighteenth week		Eph 5, 33; 6, 1-9	Luke 4, 16-22
A 174	Friday of the eighteenth week		Eph 6, 18-24	Luke 4, 22-30
A 175	Saturday of the eighteenth week		I Cor 15, 39-45	Luke 4, 31-36
				Morning office Eothina VII
A 176	**Sunday of the eighteenth Week**		II Cor 9, 6-11	Luke 5, 1-11
	Nineteenth Week after Pentecost		Liturgy	Liturgy
A 177	Second day of the nineteenth week		Phil 1, 1-7	Luke 4, 38-44
A 178	Third day of the nineteenth week		Phil 1, 8-14	Luke 5, 12-16
A 179	Fourth day of the nineteenth week		Phil 1, 12-20	Luke 5, 33-39
A 180	Fifth day of the nineteenth week		Phil 1, 20-27	Luke 6, 12-19
A 181	Friday of the nineteenth week		Phil 1, 27-30; 2, 1-4	Luke 6, 17-23
A 182	Saturday of the nineteenth week		I Cor 15, 58; 16, 1-3	Luke 5, 17-26
				Morning office Eothina VIII
A 183	**Sunday of the nineteenth Week**		II Cor 11, 31-33; 12, 1-9	Luke 6, 31-36
	Twentieth Week after Pentecost		Liturgy	Liturgy
A 184	Second day of the twentieth week		Phil 2, 12-16	Luke 6, 24-30
A 185	Third day of the twentieth week		Phil 2, 16-23	Luke 6, 37-45
A 186	Fourth day of the twentieth week		Phil 2, 24-30	Luke 6, 46-49; 7, 1
A 187	Fifth day of the twentieth week		Phil 3, 1-8	Luke 7, 17-30
A 188	Friday of the twentieth week		Phil 3, 8-19	Luke 7, 31-35
A 189	Saturday of the twentieth week		II Cor 1, 8-11	Luke 5, 27-32
				Morning office Eothina IX
A 190	**Sunday of the twentieth Week**		Gal 1, 11-19	Luke 7, 11-16
	Twenty First Week after Pentecost		Liturgy	Liturgy
A 191	Second day of the twenty first week		Phil 4, 10-23	Luke 7, 36-50
A 192	Third day of the twenty first week		Col 1, 1-3, 6-11	Luke 8, 1-3
A 193	Fourth day of the twenty first week		Col 1, 18-23	Luke 8, 22-25
A 194	Fifth day of the twenty first week		Col 1, 24-29; 2, 1	Luke 9, 7-11
A 195	Friday of the twenty first week		Col 2, 1-7	Luke 9, 12-18
A 196	Saturday of the twenty first week		II Cor 3, 12-18	Luke 6, 1-10
				Morning office Eothina X
A 197	**Sunday of the twenty first Week**		Gal 2, 16-20	Luke 8, 5-15
	Twenty Second Week after Pentecost		Liturgy	Liturgy
A 198	Second day of the twentysecond week		Col 2, 13-20	Luke 9, 18-22
A 199	Third day of the twenty second week		Col 2, 20-23; 3, 1-3	Luke 9, 23-27
A 200	Fourth day of the twenty second week		Col 3, 17-25; 4,1	Luke 9, 44-50
A 201	Fifth day of the twenty second week		Col 4, 2-9	Luke 9, 49-56
A 202	Friday of the twenty second week		Col 4, 10-18	Luke 10, 1-15
A 203	Saturday of the twenty second week		II Cor 5, 1-10	Luke 7, 1-10
				Morning office Eothina XI
A 204	**Sunday of the twenty second Week**		Gal 6, 11-18	Luke 16, 19-31
	Twenty Third Week after Pentecost		Liturgy	Liturgy
A 205	Second day of the twenty third week		I Thes 1, 1-5	Luke 10, 22-24
A 206	Third day of the twenty third week		I Thes 1, 6-10	Luke 11, 1-10
A 207	Fourth day of the twenty third week		I Thes 2, 1-8	Luke 11, 9-13
A 208	Fifth day of the twenty third week		I Thes 2, 9-14	Luke 11, 14-23
A 209	Friday of the twenty third week		I Thes 2, 14-20	Luke 11, 23-26
A 210	Saturday of the twenty third week		II Cor 8, 1-5	Luke 8, 16-21
				Morning office Eothina I
A 211	**Sunday of the twenty third Week**		Eph 2, 4-10	Luke 8, 27-39
	Twenty Fourth Week after Pentecost		Liturgy	Liturgy
A 212	Second day of the twenty fourth week		I Thes 2, 20; 3, 1-8	Luke 11, 29-33
A 213	Third day of the twenty fourth week		I Thes 3, 8-13	Luke 11, 34-41
A 214	Fourth day of the twenty fourth week		I Thes 4, 1-12	Luke 11, 42-46
A 215	Fifth day of the twenty fourth week		I Thes 4, 18; 5, 1-10	Luke 11, 47-54; 12, 1
A 216	Friday of the twenty fourth week		I Thes 5, 9-13, 24-28	Luke 12, 2-12
A 217	Saturday of the twenty fourth week		II Cor 11, 1-6	Luke 9, 1-6
				Morning office Eothina II
A 218	**Sunday of the twenty fourth Week**		Eph 2, 14-22	Luke 8, 41-56

Anagnosis	Synaxarion	Prophetologion	Apostolos	Evangelion
	Twenty Fifth Week after Pentecost		**Liturgy**	**Liturgy**
A 219	Second day of the twenty fifth week		II Thes 1, 1-10	Luke 12, 13-15, 22-31
A 220	Third day of the twenty fifth week		II Thes 1, 10-12; 2, 1-2	Luke 12, 42-48
A 221	Fourth day of the twenty fifth week		II Thes 2, 1-12	Luke 12, 48-59
A 222	Fifth day of the twenty fifth week		II Thes 2, 13-17; 3, 1-5	Luke 13, 1-9
A 223	Friday of the twenty fifth week		II Thes 3, 6-18	Luke 13, 31-35
A 224	Saturday of the twenty fifth week		Gal 1, 3-10	Luke 9, 37-43
				Morning office Eothina III
A 225	**Sunday of the twenty fifth Week**		Eph 4, 1-7	Luke 10, 25-37
	Twenty Sixth Week after Pentecost		**Liturgy**	**Liturgy**
A 226	Second day of the twenty sixth week		I Tim 1, 1-7	Luke 14, 1, 12-15
A 227	Third day of the twenty sixth week		I Tim 1, 8-14	Luke 14, 25-35
A 228	Fourth day of the twenty sixth week		I Tim 1, 18-20; 2, 8-15	Luke 15, 1-10
A 229	Fifth day of the twenty sixth week		I Tim 3, 1-13	Luke 16, 1-9
A 230	Friday of the twenty sixth week		I Tim 4, 4-8, 16	Luke 16, 15-18; 17, 1-4
A 231	Saturday of the twenty sixth week		Gal 3, 8-12	Luke 9, 57-62
				Morning office Eothina IV
A 232	**Sunday of the twenty sixth Week**		Eph 5, 8-19	Luke 12, 16-21
	Twenty Seventh Week after Pentecost		**Liturgy**	**Liturgy**
A 233	Second day of the twenty seventh week		I Tim 5, 1-10	Luke 17, 20-25
A 234	Third day of the twenty seventh week		I Tim 5, 11-21	Luke 17, 26-37; 18, 8
A 235	Fourth day of the twenty seventh week		I Tim 5, 22-25; 6, 1-11	Luke 18, 15-17, 26-30
A 236	Fifth day of the twenty seventh week		I Tim 6, 17-21	Luke 18, 31-34
A 237	Friday of the twenty seventh week		II Tim 1, 1-2, 8-18	Luke 19, 12-28
A 238	Saturday of the twenty seventh week		Gal 5, 22-26; 6, 1-2	Luke 10, 19-21
				Morning office Eothina V
A 239	**Sunday of the twenty seventh Week**		Eph 6, 10-17	Luke 13, 10-17
	Twenty Eighth Week after Pentecost		**Liturgy**	**Liturgy**
A 240	Second day of the twenty eighth week		II Tim 2, 20-26	Luke 19, 37-44
A 241	Third day of the twenty eighth week		II Tim 3, 16-17; 4, 1-4	Luke 19, 45-48
A 242	Fourth day of the twenty eighth week		II Tim 4, 9-22	Luke 20, 1-8
A 243	Fifth day of the twenty-eight h week		Tit 1, 5-14	Luke 20, 9-18
A 244	Friday of the twenty eighth week		Tit 1, 15-16; 2, 1-10	Luke 20, 19-26
A 245	Saturday of the twenty eighth week		Eph 1, 16-23	Luke 12, 32-40
				Morning office Eothina VI
A 246	**Sunday of the twenty eighth Week**		Col 1, 12-18	Luke 14, 16-24
	Twenty Ninth Week after Pentecost		**Liturgy**	**Liturgy**
A 247	Second day of the twenty ninth week		Heb 3, 5-11, 17-19	Luke 20, 27-44
A 248	Third day of the twenty ninth week		Heb 4, 1-13	Luke 21, 12-19
A 249	Fourth day of the twenty ninth week		Heb 5, 11-14; 6, 1-8	Luke 21, 5-7, 10-11, 20-24
A 250	Fifth day of the twenty ninth week		Heb 7, 1-6	Luke 21, 28-33
A 251	Friday of the twenty ninth week		Heb 7, 18-25	Luke 21, 37-38; 22, 1-8
A 252	Saturday of the twenty ninth week		Eph 2, 11-13	Luke 13, 19-29
				Morning office Eothina VII
A 253	**Sunday of the twenty ninth Week**		Col 3, 4-11	Luke 17, 12-19
	Thirtieth Week after Pentecost		**Liturgy**	**Liturgy**
A 254	Second day of the thirtieth week		Heb 8, 7-13	Mark 8, 11-21
A 255	Third day of the thirtieth week		Heb 9, 8-23	Mark 8, 22-26
A 256	Fourth day of the thirtieth week		Heb 10, 1-18	Mark 8, 30-34
A 257	Fifth day of the thirtieth week		Heb 10, 35-39; 11, 1-7	Mark 9, 10-15
A 258	Friday of the thirtieth week		Heb 11, 8-16	Mark 9, 33-41
A 259	Saturday of the thirtieth week		Eph 5, 1-8	Luke 14, 1-11
				Morning office Eothina VIII
A 260	**Sunday of the thirtieth Week**		Col 3, 12-16	Luke 18, 18-27
	Thirty First Week after Pentecost		**Liturgy**	**Liturgy**
A 261	Second day of the thirty first week		Heb 11, 17-31	Mark 9, 42-50; 10, 1
A 262	Third day of the thirty first week		Heb 12, 25-27; 13, 22-25	Mark 10, 2-12
A 263	Fourth day of the thirty first week		James 1, 1-18	Mark 10, 11-16
A 264	Fifth day of the thirty first week		James 1, 19-27	Mark 10, 17-27
A 265	Friday of the thirty first week		James 2, 1-13	Mark 10, 23-32
A 266	Saturday of the thirty first week		Col 1, 1-6	Luke 16, 10-15
				Morning office Eothina IX
A 267	**Sunday of the thirty first Week**		I Tim 1, 15-17	Luke 18, 35-43

Anagnosis	Synaxarion	Prophetologion	Apostolos	Evangelion
	Thirty Second Week after Pentecost		**Liturgy**	**Liturgy**
A 268	Second day of the thirty second week		James 2, 14-26	Mark 10, 46-52
A 269	Third day of the thirty second week		James 3, 1-10	Mark 11, 11-23
A 270	Fourth day of the thirty second week		James 3, 11-18; 4, 1-6	Mark 11, 23-26
A 271	Fifth day of the thirty second week		James 4, 7-17; 5, 1-9	Mark 11, 27-33
A 272	Friday of the thirty second week		I Pet 1, 1-25; 2, 1-10	Mark 12, 1-12
A 273	Saturday of the thirty second week		I Thes 5, 14-23	Luke 17, 3-10 **Morning office Eothina X**
A 274	**Sunday of the thirty second Week (Sunday of Zacheus)**		I Tim 4, 9-15	Luke 19, 1-10
	Thirty Third Week after Pentecost		**Liturgy**	**Liturgy**
A 275	Second day of the thirty third week		I Pet 2, 21-25; 3, 1-9	Mark 12, 13-17
A 276	Third day of the thirty third week		I Pet 3, 10-22	Mark 12, 18-27
A 277	Fourth day of the thirty third week		I Pet 4, 1-11	Mark 12, 28-37
A 278	Fifth day of the thirty third week		I Pet 4, 12-19; 5, 1-5	Mark 12, 38-44
A 279	Friday of the thirty third week		II Pet 1, 1-10	Mark 13, 1-9
A 280	Saturday of the thirty third week		II Tim 2, 11-19	Luke 18, 2-8 **Morning office Eothina XI**
A 281	**Sunday of the thirty third Week (Sunday of the Publican and the Pharisee)**		II Tim 3, 10-15	Luke 18, 10-14
	Thirty Fourth Week after Pentecost		**Liturgy**	**Liturgy**
A 282	Second day of the thirty fourth week		II Pet 1, 20-21; 2, 1-9	Mark 13, 9-13
A 283	Third day of the thirty fourth week		II Pet 2, 9-22	Mark 13, 14-23
A 284	Fourth day of the thirty fourth week		II Pet 3, 1-18	Mark 13, 24-31
A 285	Fifth day of the thirty fourth week		I John 1, 8-9; 2, 1-6	Mark 13, 31-37; 14, 1-2
A 286	Friday of the thirty fourth week		I John 2, 7-17	Mark 14, 3-9
A 287	Saturday of the thirty fourth week		I Tim 6, 11-16	Luke 20, 46-47; 21, 1-4 **Morning office Eothina I**
A 288	**Sunday of the thirty fourth Week (Sunday of the Prodigal Son)**		I Cor 6, 12-20	Luke 15, 11-32
	Thirty Fifth Week after Pentecost		**Liturgy**	**Liturgy**
A 289	Second day of the thirty fifth week		I John 2, 18-29; 3, 1-8	Mark 11, 1-11
A 290	Third day of the thirty fifth week		I John 3, 9-22	Mark 14, 10-42
A 291	Fourth day of the thirty fifth week		I John 3, 21-24; 4, 1-11	Mark 14, 43-72; 15, 1
A 292	Fifth day of the thirty fifth week		I John 4, 20-21; 5, 1-21	Mark 15, 1-15
A 293	Friday of the thirty fifth week		II John vers 1-13	Mark 15, 20.22.25, 33-41
A 294	Saturday of the thirty fifth week		I Cor 10, 23-28	Luke 21, 8-9, 25-27, 33-36 **Morning office Eothina II**
A 295	**Sunday of the thirty fifth Week (Sunday of the Last Judgement)**		I Cor 8, 8-13; 9, 1-2	Matt 25, 31-46
	Thirty Sixth Week after Pentecost		**Liturgy**	**Liturgy**
A 296	Second day of the thirty sixth week		III John vers 1-15	Luke 19, 29-40; 22, 7-39
A 297	Third day of the thirty sixth week		Jude vers 1-10	Luke 22, 39-42, 45-71; 23, 1
A 298	Fourth day of the thirty sixth week	**Sixth Hour** Joel 2, 12-26 **Evening Office** Joel 4, 12-21	[no liturgy]	[no liturgy]
A 299	Fifth day of the thirty sixth week		Jude vers 11-25	Luke 23, 1-31, 33, 44-56
A 300	Friday of the thirty sixth week	**Sixth Hour** Zech 8, 7-17 **Evening Office** Zech. 8, 19-23	[no liturgy]	[no liturgy]
A 301	Saturday of the thirty sixth week		Rom 14, 19-23; 16, 25-27	Matt 6, 1-13 **Morning office Eothina III**
A 302	**Sunday of the thirty sixth Week (Sunday of the Forgiveness)**		Rom 13, 11-14; 14, 1-4	Matt 6, 14-21

Period III: Triodion (the Great and Holy Fourty Days/Great Lent)

In this table we present the lessons read in the services on each day of the week, now also from the Prophetologion as incorporated in the Triodion[473] (during the 5 week days), the Apostolos and the Evangelion (on Saturdays and Sundays), in the period of Great Lent (in the Triodion commencing with the Sunday of the

---

[473] Ed. Apostolike Diakonia, Τριῴδιον κατανυκτικὸν (Athens, 2003).

Publican and the Pharisee), to demonstrate how the fathers focused on: 1) continuous readings from the OT books (propheteia); 2) select lessons on biblical themes in the context of the liturgical calendar; and 3) the attuning of their (greatly enhanced) selections of biblical readings to the events and mysteries of the Great Week.

From the Beginning of the Period of Forty days until Pascha (including the Holy and Great Week)

Anagnosis	Synaxarion	Prophetologion	Apostolos	Evangelion
	First Week of Great Lent			
A 303	Second day of the first week	**Sixth Hour** Is 1, 1-20 **Evening Office** Gen 1, 1-13 Prov 1, 1-20		
A 304	Third day of the first week	**Sixth Hour** Is 1, 19-31; 2, 1-3 **Evening Office** Gen 1, 14-23 Prov 1, 20-33		
A 305	Fourth day of the first week	**Sixth Hour** Is 2, 3-11 **Evening Office** Gen 1, 24-2, 3 Prov 2, 1-22		
A 306	Fifth day of the first week	**Sixth Hour** Is 2, 11-21 **Evening Office** Gen 2, 4-19 Prov 3, 1-18		
A 307	Friday of the first week	**Sixth Hour** Is 3, 1-14 **Evening Office** Gen 2, 20-3, 20 Prov 3, 19-34		
A 308	Saturday of the first week		**Liturgy (St. Chrysostom)** Heb 1, 1-12	**Liturgy (St. Chrysostom)** Mark 2, 23-28; 3, 1-5
A 309	**Sunday of the first week** **Sunday of Orthodoxy**		**Liturgy (St. Basil)** Heb 11, 24-26; 32-40	**Liturgy (St. Basil)** John 1, 43-52

Anagnosis	Synaxarion	Prophetologion	Apostolos	Evangelion
	Second Week of Great Lent			
A 310	Second day of the second week	**Sixth Hour** Is 4, 2-6; 5, 1-7 **Evening office** Gen 3, 21- 4, 7 Prov 3, 34-4, 22		
A 311	Third day of the second week	**Sixth Hour** Is 5, 7-16 **Evening office** Gen 4, 8-15 Prov 5, 1-15		
A 312	Fourth day of the second week	**Sixth Hour** Is 5, 16-25 **Evening office** Gen 4, 16-26 Prov 5, 15-6, 3		
A 313	Fifth day of the second week	**Sixth Hour** Is 6, 1-12 **Evening office** Gen 5, 1-24 Prov 6, 3-20		
A 314	Friday of the second week	**Sixth Hour** Is 7, 1-14 **Evening office** Gen 5, 32-6, 8 Prov 6, 20-7, 1		
A 315	Saturday of the second week		**Liturgy (St. Chrysostom)** Heb 3, 12-16	**Liturgy (St. Chrysostom)** Mark 1, 35-44
A 316	**Sunday of the second week** **Sunday of Gregory Palamas**		**Liturgy (St. Basil)** Heb 1, 10-14; 2, 1-3	**Liturgy (St. Basil)** Mark 2, 1-12

Anagnosis	Synaxarion	Prophetologion	Apostolos	Evangelion
	Third Week of Great Lent			
A 317	Second day of the third week	**Sixth Hour** Is 8, 13-9, 7 **Evening office** Gen 6, 9-22 Prov 8, 1-21		
A 318	Third day of the third week	**Sixth Hour** Is 9, 9-10, 4 **Evening office** Gen 7, 1-5 Prov 8, 32-9, 11		
A 319	Fourth day of the third week	**Sixth Hour** Is 10, 12-20 **Evening office** Gen 7, 6-9 Prov 9, 12-18		
A 320	Fifth day of the third week	**Sixth Hour** Is 11, 10-12, 2 **Evening office** Gen 7, 11-8, 3 Prov 10, 1-22		
A 321	Friday of the third week	**Sixth Hour** Is 13, 2-13 **Evening office** Gen 8, 4-21 Prov 10, 31-11, 12		
A 322	Saturday of the third week		**Liturgy (St. Chrysostom)** Heb 10, 32-38	**Liturgy (St. Chrysostom)** Mark 2, 14-17
A 323	**Sunday of the third week** **Veneration of the Holy Cross**		**Liturgy (St. Basil)** Heb 4, 14-16; 5, 1-6	**Liturgy (St. Basil)** Mark 8, 34-38; 9, 1

Anagnosis	Synaxarion	Prophetologion	Apostolos	Evangelion
	Fourth Week of Great Lent			
A 324	Second day of the fourth week	**Sixth Hour** Is 14, 24-32 **Evening office** Gen 8, 21-9, 7 Prov 11, 19-12, 6		
A 325	Third day of the fourth week	**Sixth Hour** Is 25, 1-9 **Evening office** Gen 9, 8-17 Prov 12, 8-22		
A 326	Fourth day of the fourth week	**Sixth Hour** Is 26, 21-27, 9 **Evening office** Gen 9, 18-10, 1 Prov 12, 23-13, 9		
A 327	Fifth day of the fourth week	**Sixth Hour** Is 28, 14-22 **Evening office** Gen 10, 32-11, 9 Prov 13, 19-14, 6		
A 328	Friday of the fourth week	**Sixth Hour** Is 29, 13-23 **Evening office** Gen 12, 1-7 Prov 14, 15-26		
A 329	Saturday of the fourth week		**Liturgy (St. Chrysostom)** Heb 6, 9-12	**Liturgy (St. Chrysostom)** Mark 7, 31-37
A 330	**Sunday of the fourth week** **Sunday of John Klimacos**		**Liturgy (St. Basil)** Heb 6, 13-20	**Liturgy (St. Basil)** Mark 9, 17-31

Anagnosis	Synaxarion	Prophetologion	Apostolos	Evangelion
	Fifth Week of Great Lent			
A 331	Second day of the fifth week	**Sixth Hour** Is 37, 33-38, 6 **Evening office** Gen 13, 12-18 Prov 14, 27-15, 4		
A 332	Third day of the fifth week	**Sixth Hour** Is 40, 18-31 **Evening office** Gen 15, 1-15 Prov 15, 7-19		
A 333	Fourth day of the fifth week	**Sixth Hour** Is 41, 4-14 **Evening office** Gen 17, 1-9 Prov 15, 20-16, 9		
A 334	Fifth day of the fifth week	**Sixth Hour** Is 42, 5-16 **Evening office** Gen 18, 20-33 Prov 16, 17-17, 17		
A 335	Friday of the fifth week	**Sixth Hour** Is 45, 11-17 **Evening office** Gen 22, 1-18 Prov 17, 17-18, 5		
A 336	Saturday of the fifth week		**Liturgy (St. Chrysostom)** Heb 9, 24-28	**Liturgy (St. Chrysostom)** Mark 8, 27-31
A 337	**Sunday of the fifth week** **Sunday of Mary of Egypt**		**Liturgy (St. Basil)** Heb 9, 11-14	**Liturgy (St. Basil)** Mark 10, 32-45

Anagnosis	Synaxarion	Prophetologion	Apostolos	Evangelion
	Sixth Week of Great Lent			
A 338	Second day of the sixth week	**Sixth Hour** Is 48, 17-49, 4 **Evening office** Gen 27, 1-41 Prov 19, 16-25		
A 339	Third day of the sixth week	**Sixth Hour** Is 49, 6-10 **Evening office** Gen 31, 3-16 Prov 21, 3-21		
A 340	Fourth day of the sixth week	**Sixth Hour** Is 58, 1-11 **Evening office** Gen 43, 25-30; 45, 1-16 Prov 21, 23-22, 4		
A 341	Fifth day of the sixth week	**Sixth Hour** Is 65, 8-16 **Evening office** Gen 46, 1-7 Prov 23, 15-24, 5		
A 342	Friday of the sixth week	**Sixth Hour** Is 66, 10-24 **Evening office** Gen 49, 33-50, 26 Prov 31, 8-31		
A 343	**Saturday of the sixth week** **Commemoration of Lazarus the Righteous**	**Evening office** (1) Gen 49, 1-2, 8-12	**Liturgy** Heb 12, 28-29; 13, 1-8	**Liturgy** John 11, 1-45 **Morning office** Matt 21, 1-11, 15-17
A 344	**Sunday of the of the sixth week** **Entry of the Lord into Jerusalem (Palm Sunday)**	(2) Zeph 3, 14-19 (3) Zech 9, 9-15	**Liturgy** Phil 4, 4-9	**Liturgy** John 12, 1-18

Anagnosis	Synaxarion	Prophetologion	Apostolos	Evangelion
	Holy and Great Week			
A 345	Holy and Great Second Day	Sixth Hour Ezek 1, 1-20 Evening office Ex 1, 1-20 Job 1, 1-12		Morning office Matt 21, 18-43 Liturgy of the Presanctified Gifts Matt 24, 3-35
A 346	Holy and Great Third Day	Sixth Hour Ezek 1, 21-28 Evening office Ex 2, 5-10 Job 1, 13-22		Morning office Matt 22, 15-48; 23, 1-39 Liturgy of the Presanctified Gifts Matt 24, 36-51; 25, 1-46; 26, 1-2
A 347	Holy and Great Fourth Day	Sixth Hour Ezek 2, 3-10; 3, 1-3 Evening office Ex 2, 11-23 Job 2, 1-10		Morning office John 12, 17-50 Liturgy of the Presanctified Gifts Matt 26, 6-16
A 348	Holy and Great Fifth Day (Last Supper of the Lord)	First Hour Jer 11, 18-23; 12, 1-5, 9-11, 14-15		Morning office Luke 22, 1-39
A 349		Office of the Washing of the Feet Evening office (1) Ex 19, 10-19 (2) Job 38, 1-21; 42, 1-5 (3) Is 50, 4-11	Evening office I Cor 11, 23-32	First Lesson John 13, 3-11 Second Lesson John 13, 12-17 Liturgy (St. Basil) Matt 26, 2-20; John 13, 3-17; Matt 26, 21-39; Lk 22, 43-44; Matt 26, 40-75; 27, 1-5
A 350	Holy and Great Fifth Day			Great Evening office (The Twelve Passion Evangelia) (1) John 12, 31-18, 1 (2) John 18, 1-28 (3) Matt 26, 57-75 (4) John 18, 28-19, 16 (5) Matt 27, 3-32 (6) Mark 15, 16-32 (7) Matt 27, 33-54 (8) Lk 23, 32-49 (9) John 19, 25-37 (10) Mark 15, 43-47 (11) John 19, 38-42 (12) Matt 27, 62-66
A 351	Holy and Great Friday (Holy Passion of the Lord)	The Royal Hours First Hour Zech 11, 10-13 Third Hour Is 50, 4-11 Sixth Hour Is 52, 13-54, 1 Ninth Hour Jer 11, 18-23; 12, 1-5, 9-11, 14-15	The Royal Hours First Hour Gal 6, 14-18 Third Hour Rom 5, 6-10 Sixth Hour Heb 2, 11-18 Ninth Hour Heb 10, 19-31	The Royal Hours First Hour Matt 27, 1-56 Third Hour Mark 15, 16-41 Sixth Hour Lk 23, 32-49 Ninth Hour John 19, 23-37
A 352		Evening office (1) Ex 33, 11-23 (2) Job 42, 12-17 (3) Is 52, 13-54, 1	Evening office I Cor 1, 18-31; 2, 1-2	Evening office Matt 27, 1-38; Luke 23, 39-43; Matt 27, 39-54; John 19, 31-37; Matt 27, 55-61
A 353	Holy and Great Saturday	Morning office Ezek 37, 1-14	Morning office I Cor 5, 6-8; Gal. 3, 13-14	Morning office Matt 27, 62-66
A 354	Holy and Great Saturday Evening office 1) Gen. 1, 1-13 (2) Is 60, 1-16 (3) Ex 12, 1-11 (4) Jona [ch. 1-4] (5) Josh 5, 10-15 (6) Ex 13, 20-22; 14, 1-31; 15, 1-19 (7) Zeph 3, 8-15 (8) III Kgs 17, 8-24	Evening office (9) Is 61, 10-11; 62,1-5 (10) Gen 22, 1-18 (11) Is 61, 1-10 (12) IV Kgs 4, 8-37 (13) Is 63, 11-19; 64, 1-5 (14) Jer 38, 31-34 (15) Dan 3, 1-23 (and the Hymn of the Holy Children, 1-33)	Liturgy (St. Basil) Rom 6, 3-11	Liturgy (St. Basil) Matt 28, 1-20

3.4.4 Selection and arrangement of lessons: Immovable cycle

In this table we present the lessons read in the services on each day of the month (only there where readings are prescribed), from the Prophetologion (according to the Menaia)[474], the Apostolos and the Evangelion[475], to demonstrate how the fathers focused on biblical and ecclesiastical figures (saints, prophets, apostles, martyrs, ascetics, fathers, etc) and events in the context of the liturgical calendar and attuned their selections of biblical readings to them. The reintegration of the lessons, by presenting them in one table, counters the disintegration of hagiographical research from biblical research. This reintegration is further underlined by the system of serial numbers introduced [B], indicating the cohesion between the OT (Prophetologion)[476] and NT (Evangelion and Apostolos) lessons. A particular characteristic of this list is its dynamic extension to the modern day (e.g. the repose of Elder Epiphanios Theodoropoulos of Athens in 1989), which resulted in lessons for each day of the calendar. Besides from the Menaia, saints and events of more recent date from the most recent calendars in use today are included. In the following a selection of the more important feasts and commemorations is provided[477]. The Prophetologion (OT) passages are written out in full in the Menaia with references (in the rubrics) only to the Apostle and Gospel readings, of which the complete text was adopted in the Apostolos and Evangelion.

Anagnosis	Menologion	Prophetologion	Apostolos	Evangelion
	I. The Month September			
B 1	1 Sept Beginning of the Indiction, the New Ecclesiastical Year. Commemoration of Our Holy Father Symeon the Stylite	Evening office (1) Is 61, 1-10 (2) Lev 26, 3-5, 7b-8a, 9-12, 14-16a, 16c-17, 19-20, 22, 33b, 23b-24a, (3) Wis 4, 7-15	Liturgy I Tim 2, 1-7	Liturgy Luke 4, 16-22
B 2	8 Sept The Nativity of Our Most Holy Lady the Theotokos and Ever-Virgin Mary	Evening office (1) Gen 28, 10-17 (2) Ezek 43, 27-44, 4 (3) Prov 9, 1-11	Liturgy Phil 2, 5-11	Morning office Luke 1, 39-49 Liturgy Luke 10, 38-42; 11, 27-28
B 3	13 Sept: Commemoration of the Founding of the Church of the Resurrection at Jerusalem (the Holy Sepulchre)	Evening office (1) III Kgs 8, 22-23a, 27-30 (2) Prov 3, 19-34 (3) Prov 9, 1-11	Liturgy Heb 3, 1-4	Liturgy Matt 16, 13-19
B 4	14 Sept The Universal Exaltation of the Precious and Life-giving Cross	Evening office (1) Ex 15, 22-16, 1a (2) Prov 3, 11-18 (3) Is 60, 11-16	Liturgy I Cor 1, 18-24	Morning office John 12, 28-36 Liturgy John 19, 6-11, 13-20, 25-28, 30-35
B 5	23 Sept: The Conception of the Honourable, Glorious Prophet, Forerunner and Baptist John	[No Prophecy lessons]	Liturgy Gal 4, 22-27	Liturgy Luke 1, 5-25
B 6	26 Sept Repose of the Holy Apostle and Evangelist John the Theologian	Evening office (1) I John 3, 21-4, 6b (2) I John 4, 11-16 (3) I John 4, 20-5, 5	Liturgy I John 4, 12-19	Morning office John 21, 15-25 Liturgy John 19, 25-27; 21, 24-25

---

[474] Selected have been the 'Prophetologion lessons' from the complete series of Greek Menaia (Ed. Apostolike Diakonia). Cf. G. Engberg, *Prophetologium I* (Monumenta Musicae Byzantinae. Lectionaria. Vol. I), 2 vols., (Copenhagen, 1980-1981), I, Index Lectionum [Immovable], 163-165 = L 48-76; A. Rahlfs, 'Die alttestamentlichen Lektionen der griechischen Kirche' (Berlin, 1915), 126 [32]-127 [33], 139 [45]-146 [52]. For an English version of the Prophetologion texts (incl. the movable and immovable cycles), see the internet publication by E. Lash, Archimandrite (Ed.), *Prophetologion/The Lectionary*, on http://web.ukonline.co.uk/ephrem/prophetologion.htm.

[475] The basis of the Greek text of the selected lessons, of both the Apostolos and the Evangelion, are the editions of the Apostolike Diakonia, see **3.2.1** above.

[476] A considerable number of lessons are composite texts, configurations of freely combined verses and passages, e.g. B 1, also called 'cento', a piece of patchwork; the latter does not express well the intention of the calendar-lesson compilers.

[477] A specialised study of the lessons of the immovable cycle is required; which lessons precisely belong to it, in the Byzantine and later Greek Orthodox Calendar, also compared with Slavic calendar systems, as laid down and reflected in the manuscripts, as well as in printed editions. Moreover, the exact text forms of these lessons should be analysed, since one is faced with different use and functions of the text, varying from strict use of the original to more free combinations of texts and even far-reaching transformation of text forms.

Anagnosis	Menologion	Prophetologion	Apostolos	Evangelion
	II. The Month October			
B 7	6 Oct Holy and Glorious Apostle Thomas	**Evening office** (1) I John 1, 1-7 (2) James 1, 1-12 (3) Jude 1, 1-7, 17-25 [Not in Menaion]	**Liturgy** I Cor 4, 9-16	**Morning office** John 21, 15-25 **Liturgy** John 20, 19-31
B 8	9 Oct Holy Apostle James, son of Alphaeus	**Evening office** (1) I John 1, 1-7 (2) James 1, 1-12 (3) Jude 1, 1-7, 17-25 [Not in Menaion]	**Liturgy** I Cor 4, 9-16	**Morning office** John 21, 15 – 25 **Liturgy** Matt 9, 36-38; 10, 1-8
B 9	11 Oct Holy Fathers of the Council of Nicea II	**Evening office** (1) Gen 14, 14-20 (2) Deut 1, 8-11; 15-17 (3) Deut 10, 14-21	**Liturgy** Tit 3, 8-15	**Liturgy** Luke 8, 5-15
B 10	18 Oct Holy Apostle and Evangelist Luke	**Evening office** (1) I John 1, 1-7 (2) James 1, 1-12 (3) Jude 1, 1-7, 17-25 [Not in Menaion]	**Liturgy** Col 4, 5-11, 14-18	**Morning office** John 21, 15-25 **Liturgy** Luke 10, 16-21
B 11	20 Oct Righteous John Wonder-worker of Kronstadt	**Evening office** (1) Joel 2, 12-27 (2) Joel 2, 27-32 (3) 1 John 4, 20-5, 5	**Liturgy** 1 John 4, 7-11	**Morning office** Luke 6, 17-23 **Liturgy** Luke 6, 31-36
B 12	On the same day Holy Gerasimos the New ascetic of Kephalonia	**Evening office** (1) Wis 3, 1-9 (2) Wis 5, 15-6, 3 (3) Wis 4, 7-15	**Liturgy** Gal 5, 22-26; 6, 1-2	**Morning office** Luke 6, 17-23 **Liturgy** Matt 11, 27-30
B 13	23 Oct Holy Apostle James the Brother of the Lord	[No Prophecy lessons]	**Liturgy** Gal 1, 11-19	**Liturgy** Matt 13, 54-58
B 14	26 Oct Holy and Glorious Great-martyr Demetrius the Myrrh-gusher of Thessalonica. The Great Earthquake of Constantinople in A.D. 740	**Evening office** (1) Is 63, 15-19; 64, 1-5a, 8-9 (2) Jer 2, 1-12 (3) Wis 3, 1-9	**Liturgy** II Tim 2, 1-10 [Heb 12, 6-29]	**Morning office** Luke 21, 12-19 **Liturgy** John 15, 17-27; 16, 1-2
B 15	28 Oct The Protecting Veil of Our Most Holy Lady the Theotokos and Ever-Virgin Mary	**Evening office** (1) Num 9, 15-23 (2) Ex 40, 15-32 (3) Ezek 43, 27; 44, 1-4	**Liturgy** Heb 9, 1-7	**Morning office** Luke 1, 39-49, 56 **Liturgy** Luke 10, 38-42; 11, 27-28

Anagnosis	Menologion	Prophetologion	Apostolos	Evangelion
	III. The Month November			
B 16	**8 Nov** Synaxis of the Archangel Michael and the other Bodiless Powers [the Archangels Gabriel, Raphael, Uriel, Salaphiel, Jegudiel, Barachiel, and Jeremiel]	**Evening office** (1) Josh 5, 13-15 (2) Judg 6, 2, 7, 11-24 (3) Dan 10, 1-21	**Liturgy** Heb 2, 2-10	**Morning office** Luke 18, 10-20 **Liturgy** Luke 10, 16-21
B 17	**9 Nov** Commemoration of Our Holy Father Nektarios the Wonderdower, Metropolitan of Pentapolis	**Evening office** (1) Prov 10, 7, 6; 3, 13-15a, 15c, 16c; 8, 6a, 34a, 35, 4, 12, 14, 17, 5-9; 22, 21a, 19a; 15, 4c (2) Wis 4, 7-15 (3) Prov 10, 31a, 32a; 11, 2b, 6, 7, 19; 13, 2, 9; 8, 17b; 15, 2a; 14, 33a; 22, 11a; Eccl. 8, 1b; Wis 6, 13, 12b, 14a, 15b-16a; 7, 30b; 8, 2b, 2a, 3b-4, 7b-8, 9b, 17b, 18, 21c; 9, 1-5a, 10, 11, 14.	**Liturgy** Heb 10, 32-38	**Morning office** John 10, 1-9 **Liturgy** John 10, 9-16
B 18	**13 Nov** Commemoration of Our Holy Father John Chrysostom, Archbishop of Constantinople	**Evening office** (1) Prov 10, 7, 6; 3, 13-15a, 15c, 16c; 8, 6a, 34a, 35, 4, 12, 14, 17, 5-9; 22, 21a, 19a; 15, 4c (2) Prov 10, 31a, 32a; 11, 2b, 6, 7, 19; 13, 2, 9; 8, 17b; 15, 2a; 14, 33a; 22, 11a; Eccl. 8, 1b; Wis 6, 13, 12b, 14a, 15b-16a; 7, 30b; 8, 2b, 2a, 3b-4, 7b-8, 9b, 17b, 18, 21c; 9, 1-5a, 10, 11, 14. (3) Prov 29, 2a; Wis 4, 1b-c, 14a; 6, 11, 17a, 18a, 21b, 22b; 7, 15b, 16, 21b-22a, 26, 27, 29; 10, 9, 10, 12; 7, 30; 1, 8; 2, 1, 10-11, 12, 13-16, 17, 19-21, 22, 23; 16, 13; Eccles. 2, 11; Wis 16, 8; Eccles 2, 11; Prov 3, 24	**Liturgy** Heb 7, 26-28; 8, 1-2	**Morning office** John 10, 1-9 **Liturgy** John 10, 9-16
B 19	**21 Nov** The Entry of the Most Holy Theotokos into the Temple	**Evening office** (1) Ex 40, 1-5, 7, 9, 14, 28-29 (2) III Kgs 8, 1, 3, 9, 10-11 (3) Ezek 43, 27-44, 4	**Liturgy** Heb 9, 1-7	**Morning office** Luke 1, 39-49, 56 **Liturgy** Luke 10, 38-42; 11, 27-28
B 20	**25 Nov** Commemoration of the Great Martyr in Christ Catherine of Alexandria	**Evening office** (1) Is 43, 9-14a (2) Wis 3, 1-9 (3) Wis 5, 15-6, 3	**Liturgy** Gal 3, 23-29; 4, 1-5	**Liturgy** Mark 5, 24-34
B 21	**30 Nov** Commemoration of the Holy All-praised Apostle Andrew the First-called	**Evening office** (1) I Pet 1, 1-2, 6 (2) I Pet 2, 21-3, 9 (3) I Pet 4, 1-11	**Liturgy** I Cor 4, 9-16	**Morning office** Matt 4, 18-23 **Liturgy** John 1, 35-52

Anagnosis	Menologion	Prophetologion	Apostolos	Evangelion
	IV. The Month December			
B 22	**4 Dec** Commemoration of the Holy Great Martyr Barbara, Our Holy Father John of Damascus and the Holy Martyr Seraphim, Bishop of Phanarion	Evening office (1) Is 43, 9-14a (2) Wis 3, 1-9 (3) Wis 4, 7-15	Liturgy Gal 3, 23-29; 4, 1-5	Morning office Matt 25, 1-13 Liturgy Mark 5, 24-34
B 23	**5 Dec** Commemoration of Our Holy God-bearing Father Sabbas the Sanctified	Evening office (1) Wis 3, 1-9 (2) Wis 5, 15-6, 3 (3) Wis 4, 7-15	Liturgy Gal 5, 22-26; 6, 1-2	Morning office Luke 6, 17-23 Liturgy Matt 11, 27-30
B 24	**6 Dec** Commemoration of Our Holy Father Nicholas the Wonderdoer, Archbishop of Myra in Lycia	Evening office (1) Prov 10, 7, 6; 3, 13-16; 8, 6, 32, 34, 4, 12, 17, 5-9; 1, 23; 15, 4 (2) Prov 10, 31-11, 12 (3) Wis 4, 7-15	Liturgy Heb 13, 17-21	Morning office John 10, 1-9 Liturgy Luke 6, 17-23
B 25	**[11 Dec] Second Sunday before the Nativity of Christ** Commemoration of the Holy Forefathers (NB. The date is linked to the day of the Nativity)	[No Prophecy lessons]	Liturgy Col 3, 4-11	Liturgy Luke 14, 14-24
B 26	**Sunday before the Nativity of Christ** Commemoration of all the Righteous who pleased God, from Adam down to Joseph the Betrothed of the Theotokos (NB. The date is linked to the day of the Nativity)	Evening office (1) Gen 14, 14-20 (2) Deut 1, 8-11; 15-17 (3) Deut 10, 14-21	Liturgy Heb 11, 9-10, 32-40	Liturgy Matt 1, 1-25
B 27	**23 Dec** Preparation day of the Nativity of Jesus Christ	Great (Royal) Hours First Hour Mic 5, 1-3 Third Hour Bar 3, 35-4, 4 Sixth Hour Is 7, 10-16a; 8, 1-4, 9-10 Ninth Hour Is 9, 6-7	Great (Royal) Hours First Hour Heb 1, 1-12 Third Hour Gal 3, 23-29; 4, 1-5 Sixth Hour Heb 1, 10-14; 2, 1-3 Ninth Hour Heb 2, 11-18	Great (Royal) Hours First Hour Matt 1, 18-25 Third Hour Luke 2, 1-20 Sixth Hour Matt 2, 1-12 Ninth Hour Matt 2, 13-23
B 28	**24 Dec** The Eve of the Nativity according to the flesh of Our Lord and Saviour Jesus Christ	Evening office (1) Gen 1, 1-13 (2) Num 24, 2b-3a, 5-9, 17b-18 (3) Mic 4, 6-7; 5, 1-3 (4) Is 11, 1-10 (5) Bar 3, 35-4, 4 (6) Dan 2, 31-36, 44b-45 (7) Is 9, 6-7 (8) Is 7, 10-16; 8, 1-4, 9-10	Liturgy on the Eve (St. Basil) Heb 1, 1-12; 2, 1-3	Liturgy (St.. Basil) Luke 2, 1-20
B 29	**25 Dec** The Nativity according to the flesh of Our Lord and Saviour Jesus Christ		Liturgy (St. John Chrysostom) Gal 4, 4-7	Morning office Matt 1, 18-25 Liturgy (St. John Chrysostom) Matt 2, 1-12

Anagnosis	Menologion	Prophetologion	Apostolos	Evangelion
	V. The Month January			
B 30	**1 Jan** The Circumcision according to the flesh of Our Lord and Saviour Jesus Christ. Commemoration of St. Basil the Great.	**Evening office** (1) Gen 17, 1-2, 4b-7, 3a, 9-12a, 14 (2) Prov 8, 22-30 (3) Prov 10, 31a, 32a; 11, 2b, 6, 7, 19; 13, 2, 9; 8, 17b; 15, 2a; 14, 33a; 22, 11a; Eccl. 8, 1b; Wis 6, 13, 12b, 14a, 15b-16a; 7, 30b; 8, 2b, 2a, 3b-4, 7b-8, 9b, 17b, 18, 21c; 9, 1-5a, 10, 11, 14.	**Liturgy** Col 2, 8-12	**Morning office** John 10, 1-9 **Liturgy** Luke 2, 20-21, 40-52
B 31	**5 Jan** Preparation day of Theophany	**Great (Royal) Hours** **First Hour** Is 35, 1-10 **Third Hour** Is 1, 16-20 **Sixth Hour** Is 12, 3-6 **Ninth Hour** Is 49, 8-15	**Great (Royal) Hours** **First Hour** Acts 13, 25-32 **Third Hour** Acts 19, 1-8 **Sixth Hour** Rom 6, 3-11 **Ninth Hour** Tit 2, 11-14; 3, 4-7	**Great (Royal) Hours** **First Hour** Matt 3, 1-6 **Third Hour** Mark 1, 1-8 **Sixth Hour** Mark 1, 9-11 **Ninth Hour** Luke 3, 1-18
B 32	**5 Jan** Eve of the Holy Theophany of Our Lord and God and Saviour Jesus Christ	**Evening office** (1) Gen 1, 1-13 (2) Ex 14, 15-18, 21-23, 27-29 (3) Ex 15, 22-27; 16, 1 (4) Josh 3, 7-8, 15-17 (5) IV Kgs 2, 6-14 (6) IV Kgs 5, 9-14 (7) Is 1, 16-20 (8) Gen 32, 1-10 (9) Ex 2, 5-10 (10) Judg 6, 36-40 (11) III Kgs 18, 30-39 (12) IV Kgs 2, 19-22 (13) Is 49, 8-15 **Office of the Great Blessing of the water** (1) Is 35, 1-10 (2) Is 55, 1-13 (3) Is 12, 3-6	**Liturgy** (St. Basil) I Cor 9, 19-27 **Office of the Great Blessing of the water** I Cor 10, 1-4	**Liturgy** (St. Basil) Luke 3, 1-18 **Office of the Great Blessing of the water** Mark 1, 9-11
B 33	**6 Jan** The Holy Theophany of Our Lord and God and Saviour Jesus Christ. Baptism of the Lord (After the Liturgy the *Office of the Great Blessing of the water* is repeated)		**Liturgy** Tit 2, 11-14; 3, 4-7	**Morning office** Mark 1, 9-11 **Liturgy** Matt 3, 13-17
B 34	**7 Jan** The Synaxis of the Holy Glorious Prophet, Forerunner and Baptist John	[No Prophecy lessons]	**Liturgy** Acts 19, 1-8	**Liturgy** John 1, 29-34
B 35	**11 Jan** Commemoration of Our Holy Father Theodosius the Cenobiarch	**Evening office** (1) Wis 3, 1-9 (2) Wis 5, 15-6, 3 (3) Wis 4, 7-15	**Liturgy** II Cor 4, 6-15	**Morning office** Luke 3, 1-15 **Liturgy** Matt 11, 27-30
B 36	**17 Jan** Commemoration of the Holy and God-bearing Father Anthony the Great	**Evening office** (1) Wis 3, 1-9 (2) Wis 5, 15-6, 3 (3) Wis 4, 7-15	**Liturgy** Heb 13, 17-21	**Morning office** Matt 11, 27-30 **Liturgy** Luke 6, 17-23

Anagnosis	Menologion	Prophetologion	Apostolos	Evangelion
B 37	18 Jan Commemoration of Our Holy and Great Fathers, Archbishops of Alexandria, Athanasius and Cyril	Evening office (1) Deut 1, 8-11; 15-17a (2) Deut 10, 14-21 (3) Wis 3, 1-9	Liturgy Heb 13, 7-16	Morning office John 10, 9-16 Liturgy Matt 5, 14-19
B 38	25 Jan Commemoration of Our Holy Father Gregory the Theologian, Archbishop of Constantinople	Evening office (1) Prov 10, 7, 6; 3, 13-15a, 15c, 16c; 8, 6a, 34a, 35, 4, 12, 14, 17, 5-9; 22, 21a, 19a; 15, 4c (2) Wis 4, 7-15 (3) Prov 10, 31a, 32a; 11, 2b, 6, 7, 19; 13, 2, 9; 8, 17b; 15, 2a; 14, 33a; 22, 11a; Eccl. 8, 1b; Wis 6, 13, 12b, 14a, 15b-16a; 7, 30b; 8, 2b, 2a, 3b-4, 7b-8, 9b, 17b, 18, 21c; 9, 1-5a, 10, 11, 14.	Liturgy Heb 7, 26 –28; 8, 1-2	Morning office John 10, 1-9 Liturgy John 10, 9-16
B 39	27 Jan Translation of the Relics of St. John Chrysostom, Archbishop of Constantinople	(1) Prov 10, 7, 6; 3, 13-15a, 15c, 16c; 8, 6a, 34a, 35, 4, 12, 14, 17, 5-9; 22, 21a, 19a; 15, 4c (2) Prov 29, 2a; Wis 4, 1b-c, 14a; 6, 11, 17a, 18a, 21b, 22b; 7, 15b, 16, 21b-22a, 26, 27, 29; 10, 9, 10, 12; 7, 30; 1, 8; 2, 1, 10-11, 12, 13-16, 17, 19-21, 22, 23; 16, 13; Eccles. 2, 11; Wis 16, 8; Eccles 2, 11; Prov 3, 24 (3) Prov 10, 31a, 32a; 11, 2b, 6, 7, 19; 13, 2, 9; 8, 17b; 15, 2a; 14, 33a; 22, 11a; Eccl. 8, 1b; Wis 6, 13, 12b, 14a, 15b-16a; 7, 30b; 8, 2b, 2a, 3b-4, 7b-8, 9b, 17b, 18, 21c; 9, 1-5a, 10, 11, 14.	Liturgy Heb 7, 26-28; 8, 1-2	Morning office John 10, 1-9 Liturgy John 10, 9-16
B 40	30 Jan Commemoration of Our Holy Fathers and Ecumenical Teachers, Basil the Great, Gregory the Theologian and John Chrysostom	Evening office (1) Deut 1, 8-11, 15-17 (2) Deut 10, 14-21 (3) Wis 3, 1-9	Liturgy Heb 13, 7-16	Morning office John 10, 9-16 Liturgy Matt 5, 14-19

Anagnosis	Menologion	Prophetologion	Apostolos	Evangelion
	VI. The Month February			
B 41	**2 Febr:** The Meeting of Our Lord and God and Saviour Jesus Christ	Evening office (1) Ex 12, 51-13, 3b; 22, 29; 13, 10-12, 14-16; Lev 12, 2-4, 6-8; Num 8, 16-17; Gen 14, 20; Is 30, 12 (2) Is 6, 1-12 (3) Is 19, 1, 3-5, 12, 16, 19-21	Liturgy Heb 7, 7-17	Morning office Luke 2, 25-32 Liturgy Luke 2, 22-40
B 42	**6 Febr:** Commemoration of Our Holy Father, Confessor and Equal-to-the-Apostles Photius, Patriarch of Constantinople	Evening office (1) Prov 10, 7, 6; 3, 13-15a, 15c, 16c; 8, 6a, 34a, 35, 4, 12, 14, 17, 5-9; 22, 21a, 19a; 15, 4c (2) Prov 29, 2a; Wis 4, 1b-c, 14a; 6, 11, 17a, 18a, 21b, 22b; 7, 15b, 16, 21b-22a, 26, 27, 29; 10, 9, 10, 12; 7, 30; 1, 8; 2, 1, 10-11, 12, 13-16, 17, 19-21, 22, 23; 16, 13; Eccles. 2, 11; Wis 16, 8; Eccles 2, 11; Prov 3, 24 (3) Prov 10, 31a, 32a; 11, 2b, 6, 7, 19; 13, 2, 9; 8, 17b; 15, 2a; 14, 33a; 22, 11a; Eccl. 8, 1b; Wis 6, 13, 12b, 14a, 15b-16a; 7, 30b; 8, 2b, 2a, 3b-4, 7b-8, 9b, 17b, 18, 21c; 9, 1-5a, 10, 11, 14.	Liturgy Heb 7, 26-28; 8, 1-2	Morning office John 10, 1-9 Liturgy John 10, 9-16
B 43	**10 Febr:** Commemoration of the Hieromartyr Haralambos, the Wonderworker	Evening office (1) Is 43, 9-14a (2) Wis 3, 1-9 (3) Wis 5, 15-6, 3	Liturgy II Tim. 2, 1-10	Liturgy John 15, 12-13, 18-19 Morning office Matt 6, 19-21
B 44	**19 Febr:** Commemoration of the Saint and Martyr Philothei of Athens	Evening office (1) Prov 31, 10-20, 25 (2) Wis 3, 1-9 (3) Wis 5, 15-6, 3	Liturgy Acts 9, 36-42	Liturgy John 15, 12-13, 18-19

Anagnosis	Menologion	Prophetologion	Apostolos	Evangelion
	VII. The Month March			
B 45	**9 March:** Commemoration of the Holy Forty Martyrs of Sebaste	Evening office (1) Is 43, 9-14a (2) Wis 3, 1-9 (3) Wis 5, 15-24 [Not in Menaion]	Liturgy Heb 12, 1-10	Liturgy Matt 20, 1-16
B 46	**25 March:** The Annunciation of Our Most Holy Lady, the Theotokos and Ever-Virgin Mary	Evening office (1) Gen 28, 10-17 (2) Ezek 43, 27-44, 4 (3) Prov 9, 1-11	Liturgy Heb 2, 11-18	Morning office Luke 1, 39-49, 56 Liturgy Luke 1, 24-38

Anagnosis	Menologion	Prophetologion	Apostolos	Evangelion
	VIII. The Month April			
B 47	10 Apr: Commemoration of the Holy Martyr Gregory V, Patriarch of Constantinople	Evening office (1) Prov 10, 7, 6; 3, 13-15; 22, 19, 21; 15, 4 (2) Is 43, 9-14 (3) Wis 3, 1-9	Liturgy Heb 7, 26-28; 8, 1-2	Liturgy John 10, 9-16
B 48	23 Apr: Commemoration of the Holy Glorious Great-martyr, Victory-bearer and Wonderworker George	Evening office (1) Is 43, 9-14a (2) Wis 3, 1-9 (3) Wis 5, 15-6, 3	Liturgy Acts 12, 1-11	Morning office Luke 21, 12-19 Liturgy John 15, 17-27; 6, 1-2
B 49	25 Apr: Commemoration of the Holy Apostle and Evangelist Mark	Evening office (1) James 1, 1-12 (2) James 1, 13-27 (3) James 2, 1-13 [Not in Menaion]	Liturgy I Pet 5, 6-14	Liturgy Luke 10, 16-21
B 50	30 Apr: Commemoration of the Holy Apostle James, the brother of St. John the Theologian	Evening office (1) James 1, 1-12 (2) James 1, 13-27 (3) James 2, 1-13 [Not in Menaion]	Liturgy Acts 12, 1-11	Morning office John 21, 15-25 Liturgy Luke 9, 1-6

Anagnosis	Menologion	Prophetologion	Apostolos	Evangelion
	IX. The Month May			
B 51	8 May: Commemoration of the Holy Glorious Apostle and Evangelist John	Evening office (1) I John 3, 21-4,6 (2) I John 4, 11-16 (3) I John 4, 20-5, 5	Liturgy I John 1, 1-7	Liturgy John 19, 25-27; 21, 24-25
B 52	11 May: Office of the holy Glorious Equal-to-the-Apostles Methodius and Cyril Lights of the Slavs and whole Europe	Evening office (1) Prov 10, 7, 6; 3, 13-15a, 15c, 16c; 8, 6a, 34a, 35, 4, 12, 14, 17, 5-9; 22, 21a, 19a; 15, 4c (2) Prov 10, 31-32; 11, 1-2, 3 [cod. A], 11, 3-12 (3) Wis 5, 15-6, 3a	Liturgy Rom 10, 11-21; 11, 1-2	Morning office Luke 9, 1-6 Liturgy Matt 5, 14-19
B 53	21 May: Commemoration of the Holy Glorious and Great Equal-to-the-Apostles Constantine and Helen	Evening office (1) III Kgs 8, 22-23, 27-30 (2) Is 61, 10-11; 62, 1-5 (3) Is 60, 1-16	Liturgy Acts 26, 1, 12-20	Morning office John 10, 9-16 Liturgy John 10, 1-9
B 54	27 May: Office of Our Holy and God-bearing Father John the Russian, the New Confessor	Evening office (1) Wis 3, 1-9 (2) Wis 5, 15-6, 3a (3) Wis 4, 7-16	Liturgy II Tim 2, 1-10	Liturgy Luke 6, 17-23

Anagnosis	Menologion	Prophetologion	Apostolos	Evangelion
	X. The Month June			
B 55	11 June: Commemoration of the Holy Apostles Bartholomeus and Barnabas	**Evening office** (1) I Pet 1, 3-9 (2) I Pet 1, 13-19 (3) I Pet 2, 11-24 [Not in Menaion]	Liturgy Acts 11, 19-30	Liturgy Luke 10, 16-21
B 56	24 June: The Nativity of the All-praised Glorious Prophet, Forerunner and Baptist John	**Evening office** (1) Gen 17, 15-17, 19; 18, 11-14; 21, 1-2, 4-8 (2) Judg 13, 2-8, 13-14, 17-18, 21a (3) Is 40, 1-5, 9c; 41, 17-18; 45, 8; 48, 20b-21a; 54,1	Liturgy Rom 13, 11-14; 14, 1-4	**Morning office** Luke 1, 24-25, 57-68, 76, 80 Liturgy Luke 1, 1-25, 57-68, 76, 80
B 57	29 June: Commemoration of the Holy Glorious and All-praised Leaders of the Apostles, Peter and Paul	**Evening office** (1) I Pet 1, 3-9 (2) I Pet 1, 13-15 (3) I Pet 2, 11-24	Liturgy II Cor 11, 21-33; 12, 1-9	**Morning office** John 21, 15-25 Liturgy Matt 16, 13-19
B 58	Same Day: Commemoration of the Holy Glorious All-praised and First Leader (Protocoryphee), the Apostle Paul	**Evening office** (1) Acts 9, 1-22 (2) Acts 17, 16-34 (3) II Tim 4, 1-8; 16-18	Liturgy II Cor 11, 21-33; 12, 1-9	Liturgy Luke 10, 16-21
B 59	30 June: Synaxis of the Holy, Glorious and All-praised Twelve Apostles: Peter, Andrew, James and John the sons of Zebedee, Philip, Bartholomew, Thomas, Matthew, James the son of Alphaeus, Jude the brother of James, Simon Zelotes, and Matthias	[No Prophecy lessons]	Liturgy I Cor 4, 9-16	Liturgy Matt 9, 36; 10, 1-8

Anagnosis	Menologion	Prophetologion	Apostolos	Evangelion
	XI. The Month July			
B 60	1 July: Commemoration of the Holy and Wonderworking Unmercenaries Cosmas and Damian, Martyrs at Rome	**Evening office** (1) Is 43, 9-14a (2) Wis 3, 1-9 (3) Wis 5, 15-6, 3	Liturgy I Cor 12, 27-31; 13, 1-8	Liturgy Matt 10, 1, 5-8
B 61	5 July: Commemoration of Our Holy and God-bearing Father Athanasius of Mount Athos	**Evening office** (1) Wis 3, 1-9 (2) Wis 5, 15-6, 3 (3) Wis 4, 7-15 [not in Menaion]	Liturgy Gal 5, 22-6, 2	**Morning office** Luke 1, 24-25, 57-68, 76, 80 Liturgy Luke 6, 17-23

Anagnosis	Menologion	Prophetologion	Apostolos	Evangelion
B 62	11 July: Commemoration of the Holy Great-martyr Euphemia, the All-praised	Evening office (1) Is 43, 9-14a (2) Wis 3, 1-9 (3) Wis 5, 15-6, 3	Liturgy II Cor 6, 1-10	Liturgy Luke 7, 36-50
B 63	13 July: Sunday of the 630 Holy and God-bearing Fathers of the Fourth Holy Ecumenical Synod (if it is on a Sunday, otherwise on the first Sunday after the 13th)	Evening office (1) Gen 14, 14-20 (2) Deut 1, 8-11, 15-17b (3) Deut 10, 14-18, 20-21	Liturgy Tit 3, 8-15	Liturgy Matt 5, 14-19
B 64	20 July: Commemoration of the Holy Glorious Prophet Elias the Thesbite	Evening office (1) III Kgs 17, 1-24 (2) III Kgs 18, 1, 17-46; 19, 1-6 (3) III Kgs 19, 19-21; IV Kgs 2, 1, 6-14	Liturgy James 5, 10-20	Morning office Luke 4, 22-30 Liturgy Luke 4, 22-30
B 65	25 July: Commemoration of the Dormition of Holy Anna, Mother of the Most Holy Theotokos	Evening office (1) Wis 5, 15-6, 3 (2) Wis 3, 1-9 (3) Wis 4, 7-15	Liturgy Gal 4, 22-27	Liturgy Luke 8, 16-21
B 66	27 July: Commemoration of the Holy Great-martyr and Healer Panteleimon	Evening office (1) Is 43, 9-14a (2) Wis 3, 1-9 (3) Wis 5, 15-6, 3	Liturgy II Tim 2, 1-10	Liturgy Luke 21, 12-19

Anagnosis	Menologion	Prophetologion	Apostolos	Evangelion
	XII. The Month August			
B 67	6 Aug: Commemoration of the Holy Metamorphosis	Evening office (1) Ex 24, 12-18 (2) Ex 33, 11-23; 34, 4-6, 8 (3) III Kgs 19, 3-9, 11-13, 15-16	Liturgy II Pet 1, 10-19	Morning office Luke 9, 28-36 Liturgy Matt 17, 1-9
B 68	15 Aug: Commemoration of the Dormition of Our Most Holy Lady the Theotokos and Ever-virgin Mary	Evening office (1) Gen 28, 10-17 (2) Ezek 43, 27- 44, 4 (3) Prov 9, 1-11	Liturgy Phil 2, 5-11	Morning office Luke 1, 39-49, 56 Liturgy Luke 10, 38-42; 11, 27-28
B 69	24 Aug: Commemoration of the Holy Glorious Martyr and Equal-to-the-Apostles Kosmas of Aetoli	Evening office (1) Prov 10, 7, 6; 3, 13-15; 22, 19, 21; 15, 4 (2) Is 43, 9-14 (3) Wis 3, 1-9	Liturgy Eph 4, 7-13	Liturgy Matt 10, 1, 5-8
B 70	27 Aug: Commemoration of the Holy Glorious Martyr Phanurius the Newly Appeared [of Rhodos]	Evening office (1) Is 43, 9-14a (2) Wis 3, 1-9 (3) Wis 5, 15-6, 3	Liturgy Eph 6, 10-17	Liturgy Matt 17, 24-18, 4
B 71	29 Aug: Commemoration of the Beheading of the precious Head of the Holy Glorious Prophet, Forerunner and Baptist John	Evening office (1) Is 40, 1-3, 9; 41, 17- 18; 45, 8; 48, 20-21; 54,1 (2) Mal 3, 1-3, 5-7, 12, 18; 4, 4-6 (3) Wis 4, 7, 16-17, 19-20; 5, 1-7	Liturgy Acts 13, 25-32	Morning office Matt 14, 1-13 Liturgy Mark 6, 14-30

3.5 The Byzantine Cycle of Psalmody

3.5.1 Liturgical function

In this table we present the Byzantine Cycle of Psalmody, the 150(+1) psalms, grouped into 20 subgroups (kathismata), distributed over the week, according to a strict reading scheme. See the detailed instructions in Pinax 1-5 below. The Roman numerals indicate the groups of psalm lessons read on a particular day (3 readings in the Orthros and 1 in the Esperinos [not on Sundays]). See **§ 3.5.5** for an overview of the psalms comprising each group.

Leaving aside the frequent singing of psalms in all liturgical services, we are here concerned with actual readings from the Psalterion. The compact distribution of Psalterion readings (in a week all the psalms are read) indicates the importance the fathers attached to the OT Psalms for public worship. The selection of the lessons (the daily prayer ours, see below) reflects the deliberate psalm interpretation of the fathers.

3.5.2 Editions

1) Ed. Apostolike Diakonia of the Greek Church: Ψαλτήριον τοῦ προφήτου καὶ βασιλέως Δαυὶδ μετὰ τῶν ἐννέα ᾠδῶν καὶ τῆς ἑρμηνείας, ὅπως δεῖ στιχολογεῖσθαι τὸ Ψαλτήριον ἐν ὅλῳ τῷ ἐνιαυτῷ, ninth edition (Athens, 2002), 9-177 [Kathisma 1-20].

2) Ed. E.T. De Wald, *Psalms and Odes, 1. Vaticanus graecus 1927; 2. Vaticanus graecus 752* (The Illustrations in the Manuscripts of the Septuagint; v. 3) (The Hague, 1941-1942).

3) Ed. A. Rahlfs, *Psalmi cum Odis*, (Septuaginta Societatis Scientiarum Gottingensis auctoritate) (Göttingen, 1931).

4) Ed. H.B. Swete, *The Old Testament in Greek according to the Septuagint*, 4th ed., 3 vols., Cambridge, 1909-1922. [1st ed. 1887-1894]

3.5.3 Translation

The Psalter According to the Seventy, Of St. David, the Prophet and King, Together with the Nine Odes and An Interpretation of How the Psalter Should be Recited Throughout the Whole Year, Translated from the Septuagint Version of the Old Testament by the Holy Transfiguration Monastery (Boston, Massachusetts, 1987. [1st ed. 1974]).

3.5.4 Numbering of the Psalms

Greek LXX	Hebrew Masoretic (KJ)
1-8	1-8
9	9-10
10-112	11-113
113	114-115
114	116 v. 1-9
115	116 v. 10-19
116-145	117-146
146	147 v. 1-11
147	147 v. 12-20
148-150	148-150

3.5.5 Table of Kathismata and Staseis

Each kathisma contains three recitations (staseis). Each stasis contains a select number of psalms belonging to the group (sometimes 3, sometimes 2 or 1); in the case of psalm 118 the whole psalm is divided in three staseis. After each stasis follows a short doxology: 'Glory to the Father, and to the Son, and to the Holy Spirit, both now and ever, and to the ages of ages. Amen. Alleluia, Alleluia, Alleluia. Glory to Thee, O God. (*thrice*) Lord have mercy. (*thrice*) Glory to the Father, and to the Son, and to the Holy Spirit, both now and ever, and to the ages of ages. Amen' [after the third stasis at the end of the whole kathisma: 'Glory to the Father, and to the Son, and to the Holy Spirit, both now and ever, and to the ages of ages. Amen. Alleluia, Alleluia, Alleluia. Glory to Thee, O God. (*twice*). Alleluia, Alleluia, Alleluia. Glory to Thee, o God our Hope, o Lord, Glory be to Thee'].

Kathisma	Psalms	**stasis 1**	**stasis 2**	**stasis 3**
I	1 – 8	**1, 2, 3**	**4, 5, 6**	**7, 8**
II	9 – 16	**9, 10**	**11, 12, 13**	**14, 15, 16**
III	17 – 23	**17**	**18, 19, 20**	**21, 22, 23**
IV	24 – 31	**24, 25, 26**	**27, 28, 29**	**30, 31**
V	32 – 36	**32, 33**	**34, 35**	**36**
VI	37 – 45	**37, 38, 39**	**40, 41, 42**	**43, 44, 45**
VII	46 – 54	**46, 47, 48**	**49, 50**	**51, 52, 53, 54**
VIII	55 – 63	**55, 56, 57**	**58, 59, 60**	**61, 62, 63**
IX	64 – 69	**64, 65, 66**	**67**	**68, 69**
X	70 – 76	**70, 71**	**72, 73**	**74, 75, 76**
XI	77 – 84	**77**	**78, 79, 80**	**81, 82, 83, 84**
XII	85 – 90	**85, 86, 87**	**88**	**89, 90**
XIII	91 – 100	**91, 92, 93**	**94, 95, 96**	**97, 98, 99, 100**
XIV	101 – 104	**101, 102**	**103**	**104**
XV	105 – 108	**105**	**106**	**107, 108**
XVI	109 – 117	**109, 110, 111**	**112, 113, 114**	**115, 116, 117**
XVII	118	**118 v. 1-72**	**118 v. 73-131**	**118 v. 132-176**
XVIII	119 – 133	**119, 120, 121,122, 123**	**124, 125, 126, 127, 128**	**129, 130, 131, 132, 133**
XIX	134 – 142	**134, 135, 136**	**137, 138, 139**	**140, 141, 142**
XX	143 – 150	**143, 144**	**145, 146, 147**	**148, 149, 150**

3.5.6 The Psalmodic recitation scheme

Presented are the distribution of the psalm recitations spread over the week. The entire Psalterion is read once a week, and twice a week during Lent. The beginning of the week according to Byzantine practice is the evening service on the eve of Sunday.

<u>Pinax 1</u>

1. From 22 September to the Nativity of Christ and
2. From 15 Januari to Meat-Fare Saturday.

Week day	Kathismata of the Orthros			Kathismata of the Hesperinos
	Kathisma A'	Kathisma B'	Kathisma C'	
Sunday	II	III	XVII or Polyeleos	-
Second day	IV	V	VI	XVIII
Third day	VII	VIII	IX	XVIII
Fourth day	X	XI	XII	XVIII
Fifth day	XIII	XIV	XV	XVIII
Friday	XIX	XX		XVIII
Saturday	XVI	XVII		I

Source: Ψαλτήριον (Athens, 2002), 198-199.

<u>Pinax 2</u>

1. From the Nativity of Christ to 14th Januari.
2. From Meat-Fare Sunday to Cheese-Fare Sunday, and
3. From the Sunday of Anti-Pascha to 22 September

Week day	Kathismata of the Orthros			Kathismata of the Hesperinos
	Kathisma A'	Kathisma B'	Kathisma C'	
Sunday	II	III	XVII or Polyeleos	-
Second day	IV	V	-	VI
Third day	VII	VIII	-	IX
Fourth day	X	XI	-	XII
Fifth day	XIII	XIV	-	XV
Friday	XIX	XX	-	XVIII
Saturday	XVI	XVII	-	I

Pinax 3

During the I, II, II, IV and VI weeks of the Holy and Great Fast

Week day	Kathismata of the Orthros			Kathismata of the Hours				Kathismata of the Hesperinos
	Kathisma A'	Kathisma B'	Kathisma C'	1	3	6	9	
Sunday	II	III	XVII	-	-	-	-	-
Second day	IV	V	VI	-	VII	VIII	IX	XVIII
Third day	X	XI	XII	XIII	XIV	XV	XVI	XVIII
Fourth day	XIX	XX	I	II	III	IV	V	XVIII
Fifth day	VI	VII	VIII	IX	X	XI	XII	XVIII
Friday	XIII	XIV	XV	-	XIX	XX	-	XVIII
Saturday	XVI	XVII	-	-	-	-	-	I

Pinax 4

During the V week of the Great Fast

Week day	Kathismata of the Orthros			Kathismata of the Hours				Kathismata of the Hesperinos
	Kathisma A'	Kathisma B'	Kathisma C'	1	3	6	9	
Sunday	II	III	XVII	-	-	-	-	-
Second day	IV	V	VI	-	VII	VIII	IX	X
Third day	XI	XII	XIII	XIV	XV	XVI	XVIII	XIX
Fourth day	XX	I	II	III	IV	V	VI	VII
Fifth day	VIII	-	-	-	IX	X	XI	XII
Friday	XIII	XIV	XV	-	XIX	XX	-	XVIII
Saturday	XVI	XVII	-	-	-	-	-	I

Pinax 5

During the Holy and Great Week

Week day	Kathismata of the Orthros			Kathismata of the Hours				Kathismata of the Hesperinos
	Kathisma A'	Kathisma B'	Kathisma C'	1	3	6	9	
Sunday	II	III	**Polyeleos**	-	-	-	-	-
Second day	IV	V	VI	-	VII	VIII	VIII	XVIII
Third day	IX	X	XI	-	XII	XIII	XIII	XVIII
Fourth day	XIV	XVI	XVI	-	XIX	XX	XX	XVIII
Great Saturday	XVII							

References

- Τυπικὸν τῆς τοῦ Χριστοῦ Μεγάλης Ἐκκλησίας, revised edition by G. Violakis (Protopsaltes).
- O.G. Rigas, Τυπικόν (Thessaloniki, 1994).
- Mother Mary and Archimandrite K. Ware (Transl.), *The Festal Menaion* (London, 1977), Appendix I: The Psalter, 529-533.
- J. Mateos, *La célébration de la parole dans la liturgie byzantine*, (OCA 191) (Rome, 1971).
- J. Mateos, "La psalmodie dans la rite byzantin", in *Periodica Orientalia Christiana*, 15 (1965), 107-126.
- E. Werner, 'The Psalmodic Forms and their Evolution', *The Sacred Bridge* (London & New York, 1959), Ch. 5.
- K. Onasch, "Der Psalter in der byzantinisch-slavischen Orthodoxie", in *Wissenschaftliche Zeitschrift der Martin-Luther-Universität Halle-Wittenberg*, 7.1 (1957), 145-168.
- E. Werner, "The Origin of Psalmody, in *Hebrew Union College Annual*, 25 (1954), 327-345.
- H. Schneider, "Die biblischen Oden im Christlichen Altertum", in *Biblica* (1949).

3.6 The Nine (Biblical) Odes of the Byzantine Psalterion.

3.6.1 Liturgical purpose/function

The importance of the Nine (biblical) Odes of the Byzantine Psalterion reflects the ancient practice of selecting OT (odes 1-8) and NT (ode 9 and the prayer of Zacharias) texts from the Scriptures and collecting them for liturgical practice. This ancient *biblical chant* repertoire, together with the hundred and fifty psalms, were gathered together in the liturgical book the Psalterion. The synthesis of these independent components of the Psalterion codex, the psalmodic system [divisions of psalm reading] and the hymnodic system [divisions of the odes] represents the deliberate patristic choices and arrangements concerning the use of these biblical texts in the liturgical practice.

3.6.2 Edition

Ed. Apostolike Diakonia: Ψαλτήριον τοῦ προφήτου καὶ βασιλέως Δαυὶδ μετὰ τῶν ἐννέα ᾠδῶν καὶ τῆς ἑρμηνείας, ὅπως δεῖ στιχολογεῖσθαι τὸ Ψαλτήριον ἐν ὅλῳ τῷ ἐνιαυτῷ, ninth edition (Athens, 2002), 179-196.

3.6.3 Translation

The Psalter According to the Seventy, trans. by the Holy Transfiguration Monastery (Boston, Mass.), 1974, 262-287.

3.6.4 The hymnodic divisions

Στιχολογία τῶν ἐννέα ᾠδῶν

ᾠδὴ α'   ᾠδὴ Μωσέως ἐν τῇ Ἐξόδῳ
ᾠδὴ β'   ᾠδὴ Μωσέως ἐν τῷ Δευτερονομίῳ
ᾠδὴ γ'   προσευχὴ Ἄννης τῆς μητρὸς Σαμουὴλ τοῦ Προφήτου
ᾠδὴ δ'   προσευχὴ Ἀββρακοὺμ τοῦ Προφήτου
ᾠδὴ ε'   προσευχὴ Ἡσαΐου τοῦ Προφήτου
ᾠδὴ ϛ'   προσευχὴ Ἰωνᾶ τοῦ Προφήτου
ᾠδὴ ζ'   προσευχὴ τῶν ἁγίων τριῶν Παίδων
ᾠδὴ η'   ὕμνος τῶν ἁγίων τριῶν Παίδων
ᾠδὴ θ'   ᾠδὴ τῆς Θεοτόκου
   -     προσευχὴ Ζαχαρίου τοῦ πατρὸς προδρόμου

3.6.5 Biblical sources of the Nine (+ One) Odes

First Ode	The Ode of Moses (Ex. 15, 1-19 and 21)
Second Ode	The Ode of Moses (Deut. 32, 1-43)
Third Ode	The Prayer of Hannah the mother of Samuel the Prophet (I Kings 2, 1-10)[478]
Fourth Ode	The Prayer of Habakkuk the Prophet (Hab. 3, 1-19)
Fifth Ode	The Prayer of Isaiah the Prophet (Is. 26, 9-19)
Sixth Ode	The Prayer of Jonah the Prophet (Jon. 2, 1-9)
Seventh Ode	The Prayer of the Three Holy Young men (Dan. 3, 26-51a)
Eighth Ode	The Hymn of the Three Holy Young men (Dan. 3, 51b-88)
Ninth Ode (a)	The Ode of the Mother of God (Luke 1, 46-55
-	The Prayer of Zacharias, the father of the Forerunner (Luke 1, 68-79)

3.6.6 An ancient number of biblical odes (Codex Alexandrinus)

Ode 1-7	are idem.
Ode 8	The Prayer of Azariah (Dan. 3)
Ode 9	The Prayer of Hezekiah (Is. 38)
Ode 10	The Prayer of Manasseh (Apogryphal)
Ode 11	The Prayer of Zacharias (Luke 1, 68-79)
Ode 12	The Ode of the Mother of God (Luke 1, 46-55)
Ode 13	The Hymn of Simeon (Luke 2, 29-32)

---

[478] = I Samuel

Ode 14   The Hymn of Praise (Doxa) [an ancient liturgical hymn]

Source:
Codex Alexandrinus (H.B. Swete and R.R. Ottley, *An Introduction to the Old Testament in Greek* (Peabody, Mass., 1989 [repr. 1914]), 253-254.

References:
- J. Von Gardner, *Op. Cit.* (Crestwood, NY, 1980), 40-44
- E. Wellesz, *Op. Cit.* (Oxford, 1971), 38-40, 214-216
- E. Werner, *Op. Cit.* (London / New York, 1959), 139-142.
- H. Schneider, "Die biblischen Oden im Christlichen Altertum", in *Biblica* (1949).
- H.B. Swete and R.R. Ottley, *An Introduction to the Old Testament in Greek* (Peabody, Mass., 1989 [repr. 1914]).

For the liturgical use of the Biblical Odes (Canticles) in the Period of Great Lent, see Mother Mary and Archimandrite Kallistos Ware, *Op. Cit.* (London & Boston, 1978): 'The Structure of the Lenten Offices', 75-79. N.B. The biblical Odes are sung during Lent on weekdays and on Saturdays at Matins, when the canons are sung in a particular sequence and with some restrictions.

3.7   Concluding remarks

In this concluding summary we will sum up and underline, once again, the relevance of presenting in full the foregoing Tables of Lessons of the Movable and Immovable cycles of the Byzantine (and later Eastern Orthodox) calendar. The fundamental significance of these lesson series, in their threefold structure of Prophetologion, Apostolos and Evangelion readings throughout the year, constitute in their final form, the liturgical basis of: a) the public reading of the Scriptures (OT and NT); b) the public homiletic commentaries of the Church; and, at the same time, they provide the biblical basis and framework of the liturgical feasts and commemoration days of the Byzantine Orthodox calendar. Liturgical and biblical structuring go hand in hand. In addition to this, anagnostico-liturgical and calendaric studies are presupposed for any further codico-liturgical research of the Byzantine manuscripts. Finally, the recent lists of lessons, as transmitted and performed in modern Orthodoxy, should be the foundation stone of any further research in both the *anagnostico-liturgical* as well as the *codico-liturgical* directions.[479]

---

[479] Further critical research should explore and refine already existing studies, paying special attention to Greek and Russian liturgical and agnostico-calendaric studies. This should be conducted in the context of the codico-liturgical approach presented in this thesis, including both the study of manuscripts, as well as printed editions. The following research aims will be essential: (1) the precise selection of lessons; (2) the composition of the lessons into two series of anagnosmata; (3) the exact confines of the lessons; (4) the two applied principles of constituting serial lessons (namely the continous reading of lessons following more or less the chronological order of Scriptures and the eclectic compilation of lessons following the themes of the liturgical calendar); (4) the precise textual form and synthesis of the lessons.

Chapter 4

The Eastern Libraries and the Catalogues of Byzantine Manuscripts

In this chapter we attempt to sketch the authentic backdrop of the Byzantine Greek manuscripts, by visiting the Eastern libraries and their catalogues. The libraries and holdings of ecclesiastical Byzantine manuscripts in the East make the cohesion between the different types of manuscripts, as well as the liturgical hypothesis we set out previously, visible. This is particularly evident when we look at: 1) the location of the holdings and library, near to, or even in the church; 2) the position and arrangement of books on the shelves; 3) the classification (or non-classification) of the codices; 4) the codex catalogues; and 5) the terminology used for titles and other technical denotations concerning Byzantine books (scribes, catalogues, indices and holdings). The collections of Byzantine Greek manuscripts were originally housed in Orthodox churches and monasteries in the Katholikon or Skeuophylakion, or in libraries on the upper floor of the Narthex (in Tower buildings close by), near to the church were the liturgy was held. The ecclesiastical manuscripts directly or indirectly originated in the Byzantine liturgy, as we saw in chapter 2. This factor is of enormous importance to understand the provenance and the codicological formation of the Byzantine Greek manuscripts.

4.1 The Value of the Eastern Libraries and their Manuscript Holdings

When visiting the libraries or catalogues of the libraries of the East one is invited to look upon a rich history of Byzantine and Eastern Orthodox booklore[480], which is traditionally, but not exclusively, linked to Eastern monasticism. In general there are four types of Byzantine and Eastern Orthodox libraries that include manuscript holdings of different size and importance: monastic, ecclesiastical (patriarchal/synodal), imperial/national and private collections. Many of the monastic and smaller collections have now been incorporated in national museums and scientific libraries, but originally, the Eastern libraries of monasteries, churches and of the Patriarchates[481] were distinguished by their huge holdings of biblical, patristic (ascetical), hagiographic and liturgical works[482]. Parallel to this, the imperial libraries in Byzantium also paid great attention to the upkeep and acquisition of the classics of ancient Greece[483].

Revisiting the sources and/or resources of the Church (ἐπὶ τὰς πήγας, *ad fontes*), since many liturgical books are both, at one and the same time, as we saw in chapter 2, primarily implies the study of the Byzantine biblical and patristic (liturgical) manuscripts[484] in their original environments[485], the authentic places of production of the manuscripts, i.e. the Eastern libraries and their scriptoria.[486] It was in the library milieu of the Eastern Orthodox

---

[480] H.Y. Gamble, 'Early Christian Libraries', in *Books and Readers in the Early Church. A History of Early Christian Texts* (New Haven and London, 1995), Ch. IV; H. Hunger, 'Buch und Gesellschaft. Bibliotheken', in *Schreiben und Lesen in Byzanz. Die byzantinische Buchkultur* (München, 1989), 130-136; T.M. Tanner, "A History of Early Christian Libraries from Jesus to Jerome", in *The Journal of Library History, Philosophy and Comparative Librarianship*, 14.1 (1979), 407-435; N.G. Wilson, "The Libraries of the Byzantine World", in *Greek, Roman, and Byzantine Studies*, 8.2 (1967), 53-80; H.J. de Vleeschauwer, "The Byzantine Library to Justinian", in *Mousaion*, 74 (1964), 187-220; O. Volk, *Die byzantinischen Klosterbibliotheken von Konstantinopel, Thessalonike und Kleinasien* (München, 1954); C. Wendel, "Die erste kaiserliche Bibliothek in Konstantinopel", in *Zentralblatt für das Bibliothekswesen*, 5 (1942), 193-209; C. Wendel, 'Das griechisch-römische Altertum', and V. Burr, 'Byzantiner und Araber', in *Handbuch der Bibliothekswissenschaft* (Leipzig, 1940), resp 1-63, 64-89.

[481] As Archbishop Aristarchos of Constantina ((librarian of the Jerusalem Patriarchal library, of the Greek Orthodox Patriarchate of Jerusalem) recently remarked, in "The Mission of the Greek Orthodox Patriarchate of Jerusalem Today", on www.jerusalem-patriarchate.org/ (seen 2003): 'Along with the educational activity it is worthwhile to mention the maintenance by the Patriarchate of a great library with many valuable books and two thousand manuscripts, which witness to the spiritual standard of the Church through the centuries'.

[482] K.S. Staikos, *The Great Libraries. From Antiquity to the Renaissance (3000 B.C. to A.D. 1600)* (Newcastle DE/London, 2000), Ch. IX, 137-187 ('Byzantium'); K.S. Staikos (Kotinos), "Libraries: History (Byzantine)", seen December 2005 on www.libraries.gr/nonmembers/en/history_bizadinos.htm.

[483] N.G. Wilson, *Scholars of Byzantium* (London, 1983).

[484] The common codicological heritage of both departments of ecclesiastical literature (distinguished from classical Greek literature) is keenly exposed in L. Politis, 'Β'. Περιεχόμενον', in 'Ὀδηγὸς καταλόγου χειρογράφων (Athens, 1961).

[485] B.L. Fonkič, 'Griechische Kodikologie', in *Griechische Kodikologie und Textüberlieferung* (Darmstadt, 1980), 14-21. Consult also the other contributions and the bibliography by the editor D. Harlfinger in this work ('Ausgewählte bibliographische Hinweise', 657-678) and H. Hunger, 'Schriftträger und ihre Formen', in *Op. Cit.* (München, 1989), Ch. II.

[486] See for bibliographical information concerning 'scribe and scriptoria-research', Richard/Olivier, 'Copistes', in *Répertoire des Bibliothèques et des Catalogues de Manuscrits Grecs* (Turnhout, 1995), 26-27.

monasteries and churches that the Byzantine manuscripts were, manufactured and housed[487], and it was the ecclesiastical and monastic climate of the East, which determined not only the outer (codicological) fashion of the manuscripts, but also their content and textual form[488].

Today a considerable number of manuscripts has survived the test of time (about 60.000 Byzantine manuscripts according to Delicostopoulos, or 55.000 according to Fonkič, containing, beside biblical writings, a whole scala of ancient Greek authors[489], both Christian and classical)[490], and these are scattered all over the world.[491] Well known were the monasteries of St. Sabas (Palestine), St. Catherine (Sinai), Stoudios (Constantinople), St. John the Theologion (Patmos), and the Athos monasteries (Greece) as centres of learning and writing manuscripts[492]. There was no artificial halt to the process of continuing creation, and the transmission of books (in printed as well as in manuscript form) continues until the present day[493].

In Russia, interest for Greek manuscripts was awakened in the 17th century.

> Russians appear to have been reasonably familiar with Greek literature during the seventeenth century. This is evident from the expertise shown by the Muscovite monk Arseny Sukhanov when selecting Greek manuscripts at Mount Athos. Among those which he brought back to Moscow were both classical and Byzantine texts. It is clear that he was himself well-informed in the matter and that he had been clearly and carefully briefed as to the type of manuscripts which were required in connection with the preparations for the establishment of the Slavonic-Greek-Latin School in Moscow at that time. Sukhanov brought back 498 manuscripts from Athos. These were for the library of the Patriarch of Moscow and represent the first major collection of Greek manuscripts in Russia.
> E.E Granstrem, "Greek Palaeography in Russia", in *Bulletin no 17 of the Institute of Classical Studies*, (University of London, 1970), 126

In the last part of the 19th century, visits of Russian palaeographers to libraries in the Levant (the Patriarchal library at the Phanar in Constantinople, the monastic libraries at Athos, the Patriarchal Library in Jerusalem, Sinai, Athens, Alexandria, Cairo, Patmos etc) was quite normal and they contributed to cataloguing the Byzantine manuscripts (A. Kapustin, P. Uspensky, V. Benesevič) and to editing facsimiles and reproductions of these manuscripts[494]. In particular we should mention the work of A. Dimitrievsky, who travelled extensively to the Eastern libraries and contributed greatly to Byzantine manuscript research in the context of liturgical studies[495].

---

[487] O. Mazal, 'Describing Medieval Manuscripts', in *The Keeper of Manuscripts* (Turnhout, 1992), 21: 'It is therefore a matter of mentioning all references to the use of the manuscript (such as remarks by the reader, glossing, borrowing ect.), references to the libraries in which the manuscript was housed (ownership marks, entries regaring purchase or donation, ex-libris or supra libros, old shelf marks, and even when these are not ascribable to particular libraries); here also is the place for references to mention of the manuscript in old library catalogues'.

[488] B.L. Fonkič, 'Griechische Kodikologie', in *Op. Cit.* (Darmstadt, 1980), 14-21.

[489] A. Delicostopoulos, 'Major Greek Translations of the Bible', in *The Interpretation of the Bible. The International Symposium in Slovenia* (Sheffield, 1998), 298: 'Referring to the history of the Greek manuscripts, I must mention that the New Testament by itself accounts for 13% of ancient manuscripts, while the remaining 87% represents more than 2.100 ancient writers'.

[490] Included in this number are the Byzantine manuscripts of classical Greek literature. Cf. A. Delicostopoulos, 'Major Greek Translations of the Bible', in *Op. Cit.* (Sheffield, 1998), 298: 'In the world today there exist about 60.000 Greek manuscripts. Of these 7.300 belong to the Bible. No other pre-Christian or Christian book has reached such a high number. The classical Greek writers are represented by 1 to 10 mss each, and only Homer is preserved in 190 mss'.

[491] B. Fonkič, 'Griechische Kodikologie', in *Op. Cit.* (Darmstadt, 1980), 16: 'Till our days approximately 55.000 Greek manuscripts from the 4th to the 19th century have been preserved. The greatest part of these codices, which originated in the relatively small region of the Balkan Peninsula and the Western shore of Asia Minor, are today scattered over the manuscript holdings all over the world'.

[492] A. Papadopoulos–Kerameus pays attention to the lost and former manuscripts of the ancient Library of St. Sabas Monastery in Ἱεροσολυμιτικὴ Βιβλιοθήκη, ΙΙ, παράρτημα Ι' (Brussels, 1963); and V.N. Benešević to those of St. Catherine's Monastery at Sinai in Описаніе греческихъ рукописей монастыря Святой Екатерины на Синаѣ Томъ I (St. Petersburg, 1911 [repr. Hildesheim, 1965]), the Appendix 605-651. For those of the Monasteries of Mount Athos, J. Duplacy, 'Manuscrits grecs du Nouveau Testament émigrés de la Grande Laure de l'Athos', in *Studia Codicologia* (Berlin, 1977), 159-178.

[493] D. Holton et al. (Eds.), Κωδικογράφοι, συλλέκτες, διασκευαστές, και εκδότες. Χειρόγραφα και εκδόσεις της όψιμης βυζαντινής και πρώιμης νεοελληνικής λογοτεχνίας. *Copyists, collectors, redactors and editors: manuscripts and editions of late Byzantine and early modern Greek literature* (Papers given at a Conference held at the Danish Institute at Athens, 23-26 May 2002, in honour of H. Eideneier and A. van Gemert) (Heraklaeion, 2005).

[494] E.E Granstrem, "Greek Palaeography in Russia", in *Bulletin no 17 of the Institute of Classical Studies* (University of London, 1970), 127-129.

[495] A.A. Dimitrievsky travelled throughout the whole Middle East, investigating the libraries and the many manuscripts kept there, in Constantinople, Jerusalem, Athos (several times), Athens, Sinai, Patmos. He later also visited the great Western libraries in Naples, Grottaferrata, Rome, Florence, Milan, Vienna, Dresden. His results were mainly published in his three-part Описаніе литургическихъ рукописей, хранящихся въ библиотекахъ православнаго востока [Description of the liturgical manuscripts kept in Eastern Orthodox Libraries] (T. I. Τυπικά, Kiev, 1895; T. II. Εὐχολόγια, Kiev, 1901; T. III. Τυπικά, Petrograd, 1917), but also in other works. Cf. M. Arranz, "Les archives de Dmitrievsky dans la bibliothèque d'Etat de Leningrad", in *Orientalia Christiana Periodica*, 40 (1974), 61-83; G. van Aalst, "Die Bibliographie des russischen Liturgisten A.A. Dmitrievskij", in *Orientalia Christiana Periodica*, 26 (1960), 108-140; G. van

Since the 18th century, Western scholarly interest received a new impulse to study the Byzantine manuscripts stored in Western libraries (Montfaucon and many other scholars) and during the 19th and 20th centuries, more and more attention was paid also to the libraries in the East[496] (by Tischendorf, Gregory, Clark, von Soden, Ehrhard, Halkin from the West; by Barski, Sevastianov, Uspensky, Kapustin, Dimitrievsky from Russia; and by Lambros, Papadopoulos-Kerameus, Sakkelion, Bees from Greece)[497]. Without losing sight of the Western libraries and the importance of their manuscript holdings[498], we will restrict ourselves in this chapter to presenting primarily the Eastern libraries (a selection of the Greek libraries, together with some representative Slavic libraries) for the following reasons:

- to reawaken, as far as possible, an awareness of the birth places of the Byzantine manuscripts, of their original provenance, that is, the Orthodox monasteries and churches that are still in function today;
- to remind us of the integral position of the many orphaned biblical and patristic codices in the library holdings of Byzantine ecclesiastical literature;
- to strengthen the awareness of the common heritage of different categories of manuscripts - liturgical, biblical, ascetical, and patristic, which are currently subdivided over different specialised branches of academic study;
- to manage the phenomenon of the great number of unexplored Byzantine manuscripts[499];
- to emphasise the continuous and ongoing flow of Byzantine literature - that there has been no break since the Fall of Constantinople and that all demarcation lines are artificial[500];
- to contribute to a general broadening of the knowledge of Eastern Orthodox scholarship relating to Byzantine (and Slavonic) manuscript studies[501];
- to stimulate further research on and to participate in library history and manuscript cataloguing, and the related branches of Byzantine palaeography and codicology.

4.1.1 The authentic library milieu of the Byzantine Greek manuscripts

The founding of any monastery usually connotes the establishment of a library that will house the manuscripts-codices needed primarily for the liturgical needs of the monastic brotherhood. According to monastic tradition the manuscripts are housed in the upper floor of the outer narthex of the "Katholikon" (the main church of the monastery). Often though, we find the library in other locations, such as in the central

---

Aalst, "Alexius Afanasevič Dmitrievskij (1856-1929): Biographische gegevens, zijn leer over het liturgisch typikon", in *Het Christelijk Oosten en Hereniging*, 7 (1955), 29-37, 212-225; 8 (1956), 163-176.

[496] For an exhaustive alphabetical list of places of libraries in East and West that preserve Byzantine Greek manuscripts, see M. Richard and J.M Olivier, *Op. Cit.* (Turnhout, 1995), IX-XVI: 565 places are enumerated.

[497] E.W. Saunders, "Operation Microfilm at Mt. Athos", in *The Biblical Archaeologist*, 18.2 (1955), 22-41, esp. 27-28: 'Russian scholars were among the earliest visitors to Athos. In 1726 and 1744 V.G. Barski travelled among the monasteries, reporting later on the treasures he saw. He was followed in 1842 by Archimandrite Uspensky, who compiled and published the first catalogue of documents, and by P.I. Sevastianov, who did the earliest photographing of manuscripts during 1857 and 1859-60. German scholars, alert to this opportunity to study Byzantine culture, ecclesiastical art and the textual history of the Bible began to come to the Holy Mount in the 19th century: J.J. Fallmerayer (1840); the jurist C.E. Zachariae v. Lingenthal (1840); the art historian H. Brockhaus (1888), and C.R. Gregory (1886, 1902, 1906). At the turn of the century (1899) K. Lake visited these libraries and photographed some of the earliest manuscripts. During and immediately after World War I the renowned art historian, Professor C. Millet of Paris, worked at Athos and later presented to the scholarly world his matchless photographs of the most important frescoes of Athonite churches and refectories. A definitive study of Byzantine book illustrations has been the product of Princeton's K. Weitzmann's several extended visits to Athos. More recently a Rosenberg-sponsored German expedition under the leadership of the eminent Byzantinologist F. Doelger of Munich spent several months at Athos in 1942 compiling some 1800 photographs of the buildings, frescoes, ikons, art objects, manuscripts and other documents'.

[498] See the enumeration of Western libraries (with their collections of Byzantine Greek manuscripts, biblical, patristic, liturgical) as presented in the specialised catalogues of Byzantine manuscripts § 4.2.6.

[499] B.L. Fonkič, *'Griechische Kodikologie'*, in *Op. Cit.* (Darmstadt, 1980), 16: 'daß die mehr als die Hälfte aller griechischen Handschriften umfassende Bestände des Athos, Jerusalems, und des Sinai für langwierige und sorgfältige Untersuchungen heute noch fast völlig unzugänglich sind'.

[500] This insight is breaking through into modern scholarship. See the joint publication of C. Conticello and V. Conticello (Eds.), *La Théologie Byzantine et sa Tradition XIIIe-XIXe s.* (Turnhout, 2002), in which a select group of Byzantine fathers (ancient and new) are presented from the 13th to the 19th centuries.

[501] Political circumstances and ecclesiastical schisms have been the cause of the independent evolution of the different churches and the relative isolation of academic activities and book production. In addition to this language and cultural barriers may have contributed to difficulties in understanding each others backgrounds. Cf: E. Granstrem, "Greek Palaeography in Russia", in *Bulletin no 17 of the Institute of Classical Studies*, (University of London, 1970), 125: 'Western European scholars, when treating the history of mediaeval Greek palaeography, neglect Russian developments; they normally refer to contributions by only a handful of Russian scholars, and they restrict themselves to individual bibliographical references (in particular to collections of reproductions from manuscripts) and to providing information about only the most outstanding manuscripts in Russian collections'. The contribution of Eastern scholars to manuscript research should not be underestimated: Bishop Savva, Archimandrite Amphilochy, Porfiry Uspensky, Archimandrite Antonin Kapustin, V.K. Ernstedt, V.G. Vasilevsky, G.F. Tsereteli, K.I. Uspensky, V.N. Beneshevich, Archimandrite Vladimir, E.E. Granstrem, B.L. Fonkich, I.N. Lebedeva, A. Džurova, Jakovljevic, S.P. Lambros, A. Papadopoulos-Kerameus, S. Eustratiades, G. Kremos, N. Bees, L. Polites, E. Lamberz, E. K. Litsas.

> building of a monastery or even in adjacent buildings. This is for security reasons or, as in the case of Great Lavra, most probably because the upper floor of the outer narthex was not big enough to hold the increased number of books acquired by the library.
> The study of the history of Mount Athos libraries is difficult. Relevant information either does not exist or is limited, dispersed and in most cases obtained accidentally. Medieval library catalogues – as is the case with the libraries of the medieval monasteries in Western Europe - probably never existed or at least have not survived. Current, systematic cataloguing of the manuscripts that could be sufficient for research on the history of the libraries is not at all progressing easily, due both to the huge number of manuscripts and also to the tedious nature of the work required for such a task.
> E. Litsas, "Libraries and manuscripts in Mount Athos. A survey", *Mount Athos Manuscripts Digital Library* (2001).

The collection, preservation and studying of the manuscripts in the Eastern libraries served the practical needs of the liturgical life of a particular monastery (or group of monasteries) and/or a particular church. There was a large need for handwritten texts and books.

- for the daily liturgical cycles and services (Scriptures, service books, chant books, homiletic materials);
- for the guidance of the ascetical life in the monasteries and churches (ascetical and spiritual books);
- for the practical organisation of the monasteries and churches (typika);
- for the universal organisation of monasteries and churches (synodika and dogmatic books, canon law);
- for the veneration of the saints and martyrs of the Eastern Orthodox Church (hagiography, synaxaria, menologia).

The ancient libraries of the East that held and hold the Byzantine Greek manuscripts, also housed codices in the languages of other Orthodox countries, such as Georgian, Armenian, Syrian, Coptic, Arabic, Slavic, Russian, Bulgarian, Serbian, and Romanian[502]. They were situated in the churches and monasteries, where the books were used in the liturgy and in other services, where they were made, prayed, studied and stored[503].

> Most important, however, is the fact that many of these libraries have been intact for half a millennium or more. Unlike museum collections, where manuscripts have been collected as bearers of text or art, many of their manuscripts may be organically related to the life of the monastery itself, not only because they were written there, but also because they are books commissioned or purchased in order to meet particular needs or interests in the monastery. Cataloguers must take this possibility seriously and incorporate into their catalogues the data necessary to establish those relationships.
> R. Allison, 'The Libraries of Mt. Athos: the Case of Philotheou', in *Mount Athos and Byzantine Monasticism* (Variorum, 1996), 135-136

Divers church books, biblical commentaries and theological works were stored in a room close to the church, in the treasury (Skeuophylakion) or in the library, and often the different codices were simply placed side by side, without much bibliographical arrangement[504]. This can be deduced from the local catalogues of these libraries and from manuscript inventories and card files[505]. The proximity of the library to the church (often situated on the upper floor of the narthex) is of key importance. The church itself (the "katholikon") is also a holding, housing codices for daily usage in the liturgy and other services[506]. Apart from the central position of the

---

[502] See the Jerusalem catalogues, K.W. Clark, *Checklist of Manuscripts in the Libraries of the Greek and Armenian Patriarchates in Jerusalem* (Washington, 1953), viii; Sinai, M. Kamil, *Catalogue of all manuscripts in the Monastery of St. Catherine on Mount Sinai* (Wiesbaden, 1970), Introduction, 1-2: the Arabic, Armenian, Coptic, Ethiopian, Georgian, Greek, Latin, Persian, Polish, Slavonic, Syrian manuscripts, and the Palestinian Syrian Collections, Arabic and Turkish scrolls, and *passim*.

[503] A. Papadopoulos–Kerameus, Ἱεροσολυμιτικὴ Βιβλιοθήκη, I, 'βιβλιοθῆκαι καὶ κτήτορες' (Brussels, 1963), 532-537. Cf. H.Y. Gamble, 'Early Christian Libraries', in *Op. Cit.* (New Haven and London, 1995), Ch. 4, 144: 'These various libraries constitute a significant aspect of the history of early Christian literature: on the one hand, they were an important result of the publication and circulation of Christian literature, and on the other they were themselves part of that process, stimulating and furnishing resources for the further dissemination of texts. At the same time, their immediate purpose was to enable and promote the use of Christian texts, and in that role they shed light on the literary culture of the ancient church. Although studies have occasionally been devoted to this or that Christian library, the subject as a whole has not been adequately explored'.

[504] In discussing the ancient inventories of the library of St. John's Monastery on Patmos, Wilson remarked with regard to the list of 1201 A.D., 'There does not seem to be any other principle of arrangement, and there are no shelf-marks. Apart from this division into categories (i.e. 'the parchment and paper volumes') it looks as if the books were not kept in any fixed positions, and when the monks made the inventory they probably went through the books as they happened to be on the shelves at the time', in N.G. Wilson, "The Libraries of the Byzantine World", in *Greek, Roman, and Byzantine Studies*, 8,2 (1967), 70.

[505] See, for instance, the catalogue of the manuscripts, which are preserved in the Patriarchal Library in Jerusalem by A. Papadopoulos-Kerameus, *Op. Cit.* (Brussels, 1963), *passim*. Of particular interest are the handwritten catalogues and card files of the monastic and ecclesiastical libraries, which were collected in this catalogue (see *ibid.*, (Brussels, 1963), t. I, Κατάλογοι, Codd. 505, 506, 507; t. V, Βιβλίων κατάλογοι, Codd. 93, 123). Not only is the history of the Eastern libraries of importance for manuscript research, the history of handwritten catalogues is also of great interest, those of Sinai, Patmos, Mount Athos, cf: M. Richard and J.M Olivier, *Op. Cit.* (Turnhout, 1995).

[506] In the Hagia Sophia of the Byzantine epoch, - the Cathedral of the Ecumenical Patriarchate for more than thousand years and known as the Great Church - two Gospel codices were maintained in the Cathedral itself and seven Gospel codices in the Skeuophylakion or

liturgical Evangelion Codex (Εὐαγγέλιον[507]), which is placed eminently on the holy table in the altar (in all Eastern Orthodox churches and monasteries), there is a select number of other liturgical books that are also kept in the church, placed on stands in the altar or in the choir[508], or stored away in rooms that annex the church. The latter include books of Scripture: the Apostolos, Psalterion and in earlier days also the Prophetologion; service books such as the Euchologion, Horologion, Parakletike, Oktoechos and so on[509]; and chant books, Hirmologion, Sticherarion, etc.

An interesting trait of the Eastern monastic libraries, is that the early cataloguers (e.g. Lambros and Bees) encountered, if one can believe their catalogues and their descriptions of the libraries[510], a remarkable disorder of piles of codices (printed editions and manuscripts heaped together), apparently "unsystematic", that is, an arrangement of different categories of codices, according to their formats and not to their contents or classes etc.[511]

Example: The Athos Monasteries
'In den meisten Klöstern aber wurden die Handschriften in den Theken in folgender Weise aufgestellt: Vorangestellt wurden die Pergamente, die nach dem Formate geordnet wurden; hierauf folgten die Papier-Handschriften, die weder nach ihrem Inhalt in kirchliche, liturgische, klassische und weltliche, auf Gesetzgebung und Musik bezughabende eingeteilt wurden, bei welcher Unterabtheilung wieder das Format als Norm festgehalten wurde'.
S. Lambros, *Die Bibliotheken der Klöster des Athos* (Bonn, 1881), 18

A particular problem in the cataloguing process was the a-typical form of many codices[512], the group of so-called *miscellanei* (Κουβαράδες)[513]. But this apparent disorder is telling: for the original owners of the holdings, the manuscripts belong together as one body. What one finds side by side on the shelves, one also finds side by side inside the codices themselves.

The holdings of the Eastern libraries demonstrate the richness of the Byzantine ecclesiastical, liturgical and theological literature. They reveal the permanent interest in liturgical, biblical and patristic subjects, which is clearly expressed in the high quantities of extant manuscripts. The libraries were surely plundered in preceding ages, yet a considerable part of their treasures were maintained. A common feature of all Eastern libraries is the presence of many handwritten books from the 16th to the 19th/20th centuries. This demonstrates the continuing practice of the copying tradition. Finally, the Eastern libraries show the great interest in classical letters, a phenomenon that is characteristic of the tradition of Byzantine Christianity[514]. This interest surely contributed to the survival of many classical books of antiquity.

4.1.2 Byzantine Greek manuscripts in Russian libraries

Apart from the libraries of Greece (including Mount Athos)[515], Israel (formerly Palestine), Lebanon, Syria, Egypt (including the Sinai) and Turkey (Istanbul/Constantinople)[516], we should pay due attention to the libraries

---

Treasury House. See the article on the web-site of the Ecumenical Patriarchate, 'Hagia Sophia. Little Chronicle of the Great Church' (www.patriarchate.org) with references to Millosich-Muller II.

[507] In the 'synoptic index' of A. Papadopoulos–Kerameus, *Op. Cit.* (Brussels, 1963), referred to as Εὐαγγέλιον λειτούργικον.

[508] Liturgical books, such as the Apostle codex, the Psalterion, the Prophetologion, the Euchologion etc. were also maintained in the church, in the choir or in annex rooms.

[509] In the 'synoptic index' of A. Papadopoulos–Kerameus, *Op. Cit.* (Brussels, 1963), referred to as Λειτουργικά.

[510] In the catalogue of A. Papadopoulos–Kerameus, *Op. Cit.* (Brussels, 1963), codices with quite different contents are placed beside each other and numbered, apparently organised according to their format, or by other unknown criteria; the manuscripts are only brought under common headings and "classified" in an appended 'synoptic index' (συνοπτικὸς πίναξ). There are, interestingly, differences in the 'synoptikos pinax' of the separate volumes (I-V). The observer receives the impression that the cataloguer noted the material as he found it, and the concrete peculiarities of each codices, rather than adhering to a predetermined cataloging scheme.

[511] See the telling comments of S. Lambros in his efforts to reorganize and systematicize the Athos monastery libraries, in *Die Bibliotheken der Klöster des Athos* (Bonn, 1881).

[512] In Greek catalogi (e.g. I. Sakkelion and A.I. Sakkelion, Κατάλογος τῶν χειρογράφων τῆς Ἐθνικῆς Βιβλιοθήκης τῆς Ἑλλάδος (Athens, 1892) also indicated as Ἄδηλοι or Ἀνθολόγια Ἐκκλησιαστικὰ or Σύμμικτα.

[513] S. Lambros, *Die Bibliotheken der Klöster des Athos* (Bonn, 1881), 18-19: 'Wie Allen bekannt ist, die mit hellenischen Handschriften des Mittelalters sich beschäftigt haben, enthalten diese entweder von Anfang bis zum Ende einen und denselben Stoff von demselben Autor als einheitliche Composition, oder sie sind Sammel-Codices (miscellanei), in welchen die Bücherschreiber allerlei Abhandlungen eines oder vieler Autoren zusammenschrieben. Die Beschreibung der Codices erster Art ist leicht genug und kann mit Wenigem erledigt werden; anders aber ist es mit den Sammel-Codices, die vom mittelalterlichen Hellenismus Κουβαράδες (etwa >> Knäuel <<) genannt worden'.

[514] A. Džurova, *Op. Cit.* (Regensburg, 2002), 'Einleitung', 7: 'Die reich bestückten Bibliotheken des Kaiserhofs, der Aristokratie und der Klöster enthielten natürlich auch viele nicht-liturgische Bücher. Die entsprechenden Werke hatten die Byzantiner aus der griechischen Antike geerbt, sie waren also mit jener klassischen Tradition verknüpft, auf die Europa im Laufe seiner Geschichte immer wieder zurückgreifen wird'.

[515] Richard/Olivier, *Op. Cit.* (Turnhout, 1995): 'Hellas', 39-45.

[516] Richard/Olivier, *Op. Cit.* (Turnhout, 1995): 'Türkiye', 60-63.

of Russia, other Slavic speaking countries, Romania[517] and Georgia. There were close ties and particular relations between the Slavic and the Byzantine Greek Orthodox churches since the Christening of the former[518]. The continuation of Byzantine literary culture after the Fall of Constantinople in Greece, and, connected to this, the Slavic fashioning of the Byzantine literary heritage[519], was adequately typified by the Romanian scholar Jorga as '*Byzance après Byzance*'.[520]

The Russian and Slavic branches of Byzantine manuscript research (cataloguing, palaeography and codicology) are of particular interest[521], since many Greek manuscripts were collected and preserved in Russia[522] and Russian scholars developed a very own approach in selecting and analysing codicological and textual data, a fact that has only recently become known to the wider circle of academics[523]. The Russian approach concentrated on the 'whole body' of Byzantine ecclesiastical & theological manuscripts. Because Russian academic interest primarily encompassed the whole Byzantine literary heritage, the Russians upheld, more than elsewhere, the ancient connections between the biblical and the patristic manuscripts. Russian interest in the Greek manuscripts was born from linguistic and historical reasons. The 20th century Russian catalogue compiler, Evkaterina Granstrem, points out the different roots of Western and Russian palaeography, drawing attention to the Russian historico-linguistic fundament.

> The foundations of the nineteenth-century study of Greek palaeography in Russia were quite other than those on which the discipline rested in Western Europe. There – and especially in Latin countries – the revival of interest in Greek manuscripts was above all connected with the activities of the humanists who studied the works of classical authors and of the printers who published them, i.e. with the rise of classical philology. Numerous codices containing the works of classical authors began to reach Italy and France after 1453 and the libraries of a certain number of Greek monasteries survived in Southern Italy. During the following four centuries travellers and collectors of antiquities (and of the exotic) journeyed to the Levant – once the lands of the Byzantine Empire – specifically to search out and acquire manuscripts. (…) Interest in Greek literature was aroused in Russia primarily for religious reasons, but also in connection with the rise of the study of Old Russian literature. Here we are concerned not only with translations from the Greek, but with the fact that Old Russian literature was primarily edifying and, as such, greatly under the impress of Greek homiletic and instructive literature: so much so, indeed, that many native Russian literary works of the period were fathered on Greek authors. Thus the earliest contributions to Greek Palaeography in Russia in the nineteenth century owe nothing to classical philology: they are connected with the rising interest in Russian historical documents and in the history of Russian and the other Slavonic languages.
> E. Granstrem, Greek Palaeography in Russia", in *Bulletin no 17 of the Institute of Classical Studies*, University of London (1970), 126-127.

---

[517] Richard/Olivier, *Op. Cit.* (Turnhout, 1995): 'România', 56-58.

[518] V. Gardthausen, *Sammlungen und Cataloge Griechischer Handschriften* (Leipzig, 1903), 2: 'Mit einen Worte sei auch noch Rußland erwähnt, das durch seine Kirche von den ältesten Zeiten an mit dem byzantinischen reiche verbunden war. Hier war das Studium des Griechischen wenigstens in der Theorie ebenso unerläslich, wie im Abendlande die Pflege der lateinischen Sprache, obwohl man sich in der Praxis meistentheils durch Übersetzungen der griechischen Originale zu helfen pflegte. Wenn schon in den meisten griechischen Bibliotheken die theologischen Handschriften ganz bedeutend überwiegen, so gielt dies in noch höherem Maße für die älteren Sammlungen Rußlands'

[519] The Moscow Patriarchate was established in the 15th century.

[520] After the first publication of N. Jorga's book, *Byzance après Byzance: Continuation de l'Histoire de la vie Byzantine* (Bucharest, 1935/1971), there was much dispute about the subject, with arguments for and against the term. Cf. A.M. Hakkert (E.), *Byzanz après Byzanz: Aufsätze Symposion Byzantinon* (Amsterdam, 1991). The expression 'Post-Byzantine Literature', for instance, is, although commonly used (also in Greece), less correct from this point of view.

[521] See the interesting historical overview by E.E. Granstrem, "Greek Palaeography in Russia", in *Bulletin of the Institute of Classical Studies*, 17 (1970), 124-135; and idem, 'Zur byzantinischen Minuskel', in *Griechische Kodikologie und Textüberlieferung* (Darmstadt, 1980), 76-119, esp. 76–79 with an aperçu of Byzantine palaeography from the Russian point of view. Bibliographical information in concise form is provided in an earlier publication of E.E. Granstrem, "Греческие рукописи в собраниях Советского Союза (дополнительные сведения)"[Greek manuscripts in collections of the Soviet Union (additional testimonies)], in Византийский временник, 11 (1956), 285-291, with a list of recent publications and less known bibliographical materials about Greek manuscript collections in Russia. A general aperçu of the Byzantine Greek manuscripts in Russian libraries one can also find in B. Fonkič, 'Греческие рукописи советских хранилищ' [Greek manuscripts in Soviet holdings], in *Studia Codicologica*, Ed. K. Treu (Berlin, 1977), 189-195.

[522] As early as the 17th century the Muscovite monk Arseny Sukhanov was sent to Athos and other libraries in the East searching for Byzantine Greek manuscripts. He was very successful and brought with him to Russia 498 codices. These were intended for the library of the Patriarch of Mocow and they still form the basis of the Byzantine Greek manuscript holdings in Moscow. See E.E. Granstrem, *Art. cit.* (1970), 126. See also page 125: 'Greek manuscripts became known in Russia at the time of the acceptance of Christianity in the ninth century. Greek priests brought manuscripts with them to Russia and Russians acquired others during the course of their visits to the Holy Places. In Constantinople, on Mount Athos, and in Sinai Russians read and translated Greek Manuscripts'.

[523] Especially valuable with regard to Western interests in Russian collections of Byzantine Greek manuscripts were the visits of Marcel Richard to Russia in 1960 (reported in 1961), "Rapport sur une mission d'étude en U.R.S.S. (5 octobre-3 novembre 1960)", in *Bulletin d'information de l' Institut de recherche et d' histoire des textes*, 10 (1961), 43-56, and K. Treu, resulting in the article, "Zu den neutestamentlichen Handschriften in der UdSSR", in *Forschungen und Fortschritte*, 38 (1964), 118-122 and the catalogue of NT text manuscripts, *Die griechischen Handschriften des Neuen Testaments in der UdSSR. Eine systematische Auswertung der Texthandschriften in Leningrad, Moskau, Kiev, Odessa, Tbilissi und Erevan* (Berlin, 1966). Finally, the *Répertoire des Bibliothèques et des Catalogues de Manuscrits Grecs*, by Richard/Olivier (Turnhout, 1995) is a fine example of expert knowledge of Slavonic sources and resources in Russia and the other Slavic speaking countries. See for a detailed general bibliographical p. 65-69: 'Catalogues régionaux: Ex-U.R.S.S.'

Consequently, Russian scholars focused their interest on the study of both the uncial and the minuscule manuscripts[524], as well as their artistic, iconographic furnishing[525] (akin to codicology). The latter can be deduced from the style of production of the Russian Greek manuscript editions (diplomatic and in facsimile) and from their exploration of Byzantine palaeographic and codicological studies[526]. See by way of illustration, for instance, the compilation of the catalogues of the Byzantine Greek holding of biblical, patristic and liturgical manuscripts of the Synodal Library in Moscow by Archimandrite Vladimir[527]; see also the great catalogue of Slavonic manuscripts in the same library by A. Gorsky and K. Nevostruev[528].

Russian libraries, especially those in Moscow and St. Petersburg, contain large holdings of Byzantine manuscripts, reminding one physically of the Byzantine background of Russian theology. Besides this, the extant Slavonic Bible manuscripts (4.500 OT manuscripts and 10.000 NT manuscripts[529]) stem directly from the standard Byzantine prototypes (9th century and later). In comparison with Byzantine manuscript tradition of the Scriptures (estimated at ca 2005 Greek OT manuscripts – not included are the 1745 commentary and catena manuscripts[530] – and ca 5700 Greek NT manuscripts[531]), the Slavonic manuscript tradition is far more quantitative[532].

4.2 The Present State of Byzantine Manuscript Holdings in East and West

The Byzantine manuscript holdings can basically be geographically divided into three groups:

1) **The (Greek) libraries of the East.** The libraries of the Greek Orthodox monasteries and patriarchal seats, situated in the Middle East (Israel, Egypt, Turkey, Syria, Lebanon), as well as in Greece itself, are immediate descendants of the Byzantine tradition. Their language and documents, liturgical and theological thinking, are witnesses of its continuation. The national state libraries and holdings of scientific institutions and museums store today a great number of manuscripts.

2) **The libraries in Russian, other Slavic-speaking countries, Romania and Georgia.** In the Soviet period, the manuscripts were transferred to state libraries and museums and catalogued there. The pre-revolutionary collections remained intact, as did the catalogues (numbering) that already existed. Until 1917 in Russia, these collections were in the possession of ecclesiastical institutions, Orthodox hieriarchs and other private owners. The Orthodox background of the countries in this group is Byzantine, which means that this group is close to group 1. Not only have they collected Greek manuscripts, the manuscripts they have produced in their own vernacular mirror the Byzantine codices closely.

---

[524] E.E. Granstrem, 'Zur byzantinischen Minuskel', in *Op. Cit.* (Darmstadt, 1980), 76-119.

[525] Cf. N.P. Kondakov, *Histoire de l'art Byzantine considéré principalement dans les miniatures* (New York, 1970) and T. Uspenskij, *L'Octateuch de la Bibliothèque du Sérail à Constantinople* (Sofia, 1907). For the Slavonic tradition, see O. Popova, *Russian Illuminated manuscripts with 69 illustrations* (1984); Idem., *Les Miniatures Russes du Xie au Xve siècle. Russian Miniatures of the 11th to the 15th centuries* (Leningrad, 1975).

[526] For instance, Archimandrite Savva, *Specimina palaeographica codicum Graecorum et Slavonicorum bibliothecae Mosquensis synodalis saec. VI-XVIII* (Moscow, 1863).

[527] Archimandrite Vladimir, Описание славянскихъ рукописей Московской Синодальной Библиотеки [Description of Slavonic manuscripts of the Moscow Synodal Library] (Moscow, 1894 [reprint 1964]).

[528] A. Gorskij and K. Nevostruev, Описание Славянскихъ рукописей московской синодальной библиотеки [Description of Slavonic Manuscripts of the Synodal Library in Moscow] (Moscow, 1855-1869 [repr. in 5 vols., Wiesbaden, 1964]).

[529] The Slavonic manuscripts are from the 9th to the 19th century. See A.A. Alexeev, 'The Slavonic Bible and Modern Scholarship', in *ΙΟΥΔΑΪΚΗ ΑΡΧΑΙΟΛΟΓΙΑ: In Honour of Prof. Moshe Altbauer* (Jerusalem, 1995), 25 and n.1 with a reference to I.E. Evseev (1911) for the estimation of the Slavonic OT manuscripts; and the remark 'the figure for the NT is a very approximate estimation' and the note that 'among the OT Mss the Psalter takes the first place, more than 3500 Mss.'; Idem, Текстология Славяанской Библий (St. Petersburg, 1999).

[530] The Byzantine manuscripts comprise the 4th to the 15th centuries. The estimations are very rough. See B.M. Metzger, *Manuscripts of the Greek Bible. An Introduction to Greek Palaeography* (New York and Oxford, 1981), 26 n 46. The numbers are based on information from a letter of R. Hanhart, dated 24 February 1979).

[531] J.K. Elliott, *A Bibliography of Greek New Testament Manuscripts* (Cambridge, 2000), 1. The numbers are based on the *Bericht der Hermann Kunst-Stiftung zur Förderung der neutestamentlichen Textforschung* (Münster, 1998).

[532] See P.K. Grimsted, *Archives of Russia. A Directory and Bibliographic Guide to Holdings in Moscow and St. Petersburg*, 2 vols. (New York and London, 2000) for the libraries in Russia (Moscow and St. Petersburg) in which the great collections of Slavonic manuscripts are maintained.

3) **The Western libraries**. Libraries in the West (Vatican, Paris, Oxford, London, Venice, Vienna, Florence, Madrid) started gathering Byzantine Greek manuscripts at a relatively late stage[533] (beginning in the Renaissance/Reformation period), motivated by text reconstruction, translation, historical research, doctrinal disputes and purely scientific reasons. In this process, a great deal of the Byzantine manuscripts were transferred to the West, collected, catalogued and studied intensively.

Despite the loss of manuscripts or transfers to foreign regions[534] the libraries remain enormous treasure houses of Christian Byzantine books and classical literature, reaching back to the early history of Eastern Christendom. At present the monasteries of **Athos** (twenty monasteries on the Holy Mountain, sketes and kellia) have preserved approximately 16.000 Byzantine Greek manuscripts; **Sinai**: 3.141 codices (St. Catherine Monastery); **Jerusalem**: 2.000 codices (Patriarchal Library); **Patmos**: 900 codices (Monastery of St. John the Theologian); and **Istanbul**: 446 codices (Library of the Ecumenical Patriarchate), dating from the 4th to the 19th centuries. To the group of Eastern libraries belong also the libraries containing Greek manuscripts in the Slavic speaking countries: in different libraries in **St. Petersburg** (1.380 codices), in **Moscow** (881 codices), in **Kiev** (154 codices), in **Sofia** (816 codices) and in **Bucharest** (1.623 codices). The Byzantine Greek manuscripts preserved in these countries, and the Slavonic manuscripts, which are directly rooted in the Byzantine manuscript tradition, are of special value for our thesis. In Western libraries the numbers of Greek manuscripts accumulated formidably and are considerable indeed[535]: in **Paris**: *Bibliothèque Nationale de France* (4.941 codices), **Vatican City**: *Bibliotheca Apostolica Vaticana* (4.711 codices), **Oxford**: *Bodleian Library* (1.675 codices), **Florence**: *Biblioteca Medicea-Laurenziana* (1.204 codices), **Venice:** *Biblioteca Nazionale Marciana* (1204 codices), **Vienna:** *Österreichische Nationalbibliothek* (1065 codices), **Madrid:** *Biblioteca Nacional* (402 codices).

4.2.1 Virtual decentralisation of manuscript holdings

It is within the objectives of our study to pay serious attention to setting out a path of retracing the "original" or early manuscript collections of the Eastern libraries, through the study of library history and catalogue research and to provide a counter argument for the trend of centralisation, which has transposed the ancient book collections and manuscripts to the great patriarchal, state or university libraries (e.g. the Patriarchal Library in Jerusalem and Constantinople/Istanbul, the National Libraries of Athens, Moscow and St. Petersburg[536], the Bibliothèque National in Paris, the Vatican Library, the Bodleian Library in Oxford). Knowledge of the provenance of manuscripts, their scribes and their owners ("users") can contribute greatly to our comprehension of the old codices[537]. The theological and literary tradition of the Eastern Orthodox church, from which these authentic witnesses stem, is still alive in the individual churches and monasteries of the East, and their libraries are still the storehouses of these witnesses. Recent research is developing in this direction, to recover the authentic origins of the Byzantine Greek manuscripts scattered throughout the great libraries of East and West, and to decentralise them, virtually.

---

[533] B. Altaner, "Griechische Codices in abendländischen Bibliotheken des XIII. und XIV. Jahrhunderts", in *Byzantinische Zeitschrift*, 36 (1936), 32-35.

[534] Consider especially the dramatic loss of manuscripts in the Patriarchal libraries of Jerusalem, Constantinople and the library of St. Catherine at Sinai. Cf. V.N. Beneševič, *Les manuscrits grecs du Mont Sinai et le monde savant de l' Europe depuis le XVIIe siècle jusqu' à 1927* (Athens, 1937).

[535] Consult the data in Richard/Olivier, *Op. Cit.* (Turnhout, 1995); see also Omont, *Catalogue alphabétique des livres imprimés mis à la disposition des lecteurs dans la salle de travail, Département des manuscripts, Bibliothèque National: suivi de la liste des catalogues usuels du Département des manuscripts* (Paris, 1933) and V. Gardthausen, *Op. Cit.* (Leipzig, 1903) for a historical background of these libraries and their holdings (and the provenance of codices). The introductory notes of A. Ehrhard, *Op. Cit.* (Leipzig, Berlin, 1937) and A. Rahlfs, *Op. Cit.* (Berlin, 1914) are also valuable.

[536] K. Treu, ""Zu den neutestamentlichen Handschriften in der UdSSR", in *Forschungen und Fortschritte*, 38.4 (1964), 121, but compare the remark on page 120. Cf. Idem, *Die Griechischen Handschriften des Neuen Testaments in der UdSSR. Eine systematische Auswertung der Texthandschriften in Leningrad, Moskau, Kiev, Odessa, Tbilisi und Erevan* (Berlin, 1966), 2.

[537] B.L. Fonkič, "Griechische Kodikologie", in *Op. Cit.* (Darmstadt, 1980): 'fast unbekannt sind die Inventarlisten klösterlicher und kirchlicher Büchersammlungen', 20; and V. Gardthausen in *Op. Cit.* (Leipzig, 1903), 2: 'Aber auch die Bibliotheks-Cataloge von Klöstern, die natürlich keinen persönlichen Charakter haben, sondern mehr zufällig entstanden sind, haben für uns, wenn sie alt sind, ein hohes Interesse. Sie sind nicht nur beweisend für den Umfang der Sammlung, sondern zugleich auch für den geistigen Horizont ihrer Besitzer'.

Without any doubt the Greek libraries have their own history. Yet, it was not until quite recently that a real historical approach with regard to the exploration of their history, began. The more ancient catalogues were restricted to a more or less exact description of the manuscripts, mentioning only incidentally an earlier possessor, who had, by occasion, left his name in the codex. The idea of analysis of the present collections and their (original) components was alien to earlier students of manuscripts (...). Moreover, the library catalogues of the monasteries, which are of course not of a personal character, but came into being more occasionally, also have particular value for us, if they are ancient. They demonstrate not only the scope of the holding, but at the same time the intellectual horizon of the owner(s).

V. Gardthausen, Einleitung, in *Sammlungen und Cataloge Griechischer Handschriften* (Leipzig, 1903), 2-3 [trans: Ed]

4.2.2 Local and specialised library catalogues of manuscripts

There are two main types of catalogue that enumerate and/or describe the manuscripts belonging to a library of a church, monastery or Patriarchate: 1) the ancient, original, local lists or card files containing a short identification/description of the codices of the collection, handwritten or printed, with (often) incomplete and insufficient information[538]; 2) the professional, printed catalogue, with extensive and more complete descriptions of the codices. It is of importance to evaluate also the first type - the existing local catalogues of the Eastern libraries in order to build up an authentic picture of the collected codices and to learn more about the purposes of Byzantine Greek literature. Gardthausen identifies this need as follows: 'With regard to the provenance and history of a manuscript, one can profit from the accidentally incorporated historical notes; even the name of a monastery is often enough. It would be very desirable to compile an exhaustive catalogue of Greek monasteries, since we lack such a work greatly at present.'[539]

In the catalogues on location, they are organised according to special indexes (Πίνακες), classified according to a select number of categories - biblical, liturgical, patristic, hagiographic and other genres of ecclesiastical literature. One should always take into consideration a measure of discrepancy between the descriptions of holdings as found in the manuscript catalogues and the actual holdings themselves. The catalogue of the Greek Patriarchal Library of Jerusalem, compiled by A.I. Papadopoulos-Kerameus (St. Petersburg, 1891-1915 [repr. Bruxelles, 1963]) or the fundamental catalogue of the Athos Monasteries by Lambros, can serve as fine examples to provide insight in the concrete and distinctive features of the individual codices (see the indices of 'libraries and owners' and the lists of 'dated and undated' manuscripts and their precise position in the 'final state' of the holding, which is kept separately). To confuse the picture, however, there has been much swapping and transition between holdings. Codices of St. Sabas Lavra are now held in the holding of the Church of the Holy Sepulchre, and codices of the latter are now in the holding of St. Sabas. The catalogue of Papadopoulos-Kerameus also provides an overview of the 'mixed' manuscripts (Κουβαράδες), where the works of one or more writers are brought together - a codex form which is characteristic for the transmission of the Byzantine literary treasures. This codex form should not be overlooked, since there is a considerable quantity of this type preserved in Eastern libraries[540].

4.2.3 Examples of local catalogues of Greek manuscripts

Selection of frequently consulted Greek catalogues

- D.Z. Sofianos, Τὰ χειρόγραφα τῶν Μετεώρων. Κατάλογος περιγραφικὸς τῶν χειρογράφων κωδίκων τῶν ἀποκειμένων εἰς τὰς μονὰς τῶν Μετεώρων. Τόμος Δ΄: Τὰ χειρόγραφα τῆς Μονῆς Ἁγίας Τριάδος, (Ἀκαδημία Ἀθηνῶν Κέντρον Ἐρεύνης τοῦ Μεσαιωνικοῦ καὶ Νέου Ἑλληνισμοῦ), 2 vols. (Athens, 1993) [Titl. also in Fr.].

---

[538] R. Allison, 'The Libraries of Mt Athos: the case of Philotheou', in *Op. Cit.* (Variorum, 1996), 151: 'This abbreviated mode of description excluded not only a significant portion of the textual content of the service books, but also the organization of that content. If the codex is perceived of as nothing but a bearer of texts, then it is perhaps understandable that the organization of those texts is irrelevant. But if the codex is important because it is part of a manuscript tradition, then the organisation of its content is crucial, because that is an essential part of what characterizes the book, the liturgical tradition and the manuscript tradition, and what accounts for the presence of the book in the library'.

[539] V. Gardthausen in *Op. Cit.* (Leipzig, 1903), 3 [trans: Ed].

[540] Paisius Velichkovsky, *Blessed Paissy Velichkovsky, The Life and Ascetic Labors*, Ed. Schema-monk Metrophanes (Platina, Call., 1976), 198: 'A large part of the manuscripts are anthologies consisting of selections from Patristic books on dogmatic, liturgical, moral-ascetic, or canonical questions. Elder Paisius himself loved to compile such anthologies and encouraged his disciples to compile them also (...) The copying of the whole book is not always possible or necessary; often it is sufficient to copy out just the more important or interesting places so as later to have these close at hand and have the opportunity to re-read them and share them with others. In reading what various Holy Fathers wrote on the same subject, by copying out selections from them one may gain a clearer and many-sided view of the subject. Many such anthologies were made by the disciples of Elder Paisius'.

- D.Z. Sofianos, Τὰ χειρόγραφα τῶν Μετεώρων. Κατάλογος περιγραφικὸς τῶν χειρογράφων κωδίκων τῶν ἀποκειμένων εἰς τὰς μονὰς τῶν Μετεώρων. Τόμος Γ′: Τὰ χειρόγραφα τῆς Μονῆς Ἁγίου Στεφάνου, (Ἀκαδημία Ἀθηνῶν Κέντρον Ἐρεύνης τοῦ Μεσαιωνικοῦ καὶ Νέου Ἑλληνισμοῦ), 2 vols. (Athens, 1986).

- N.A. Bees, Τὰ χειρόγραφα τῶν Μετεώρων. Κατάλογος περιγραφικὸς τῶν χειρογράφων κωδίκων τῶν ἀποκειμένων εἰς τὰς μονὰς τῶν Μετεώρων ἐκδιδόμενος ἐκ τῶν καταλοίπων Νίκου Α. Βέη. Τόμος Β′: Τὰ χειρόγραφα τῆς Μονῆς Βαρλαάμ, (Ἀκαδημία Ἀθηννῶν Κέντρον Ἐρεύνης τοῦ Μεσαιωνικοῦ καὶ Νέου Ἑλληνισμοῦ) (Athens, 1984).

- N.A. Bees, Τὰ χειρόγραφα τῶν Μετεώρων. Κατάλογος περιγραφικὸς τῶν χειρογράφων κωδίκων τῶν ἀποκειμένων εἰς τὰς μονὰς τῶν Μετεώρων ἐκδιδόμενος ἐκ τῶν καταλοίπων Νίκου Α. Βέη. Τόμος Α′, (Ἀκαδημία Ἀθηνῶν Κέντρον Ἐρεύνης τοῦ Μεσαιωνικοῦ καὶ Νέου Ἑλληνισμοῦ) (Athens, 1967 [1998^2]).

- A. Tsakopoulos, Περιγραφικὸς κατάλογος τῶν χειρογράφων τῆς Βιβλιοθήκης τοῦ Οἰκουμενικοῦ Πατριαρχείου. Τόμος Γ′ (α′) Θεολογικῆς Σχολῆς Χάλκης (Istanbul, 1968); A. Tsakopoulos,, Περιγραφικὸς κατάλογος τῶν χειρογράφων τῆς Βιβλιοθήκης τοῦ Οἰκουμενικοῦ Πατριαρχείου. Τόμος Β′. Τμῆμα χειρογράφων Ἱ Μονῆς Ἁγίας Τριάδος Χάλκης (Istanbul, 1956); A. Tsakopoulos, Περιγραφικὸς κατάλογος τῶν χειρογράφων τῆς Βιβλιοθήκης τοῦ Οἰκουμενικοῦ Πατριαρχείου. Τόμος Α′. Τμῆμα χειρογράφων Παναγίας Καμαριωτίσσης (Istanbul, 1953).

- Spyridon of the Lavra and S. Eustratiades, *Catalogue of the Greek Manuscripts of the Laura on Mount Athos with notices from other libraries*. Κατάλογος τῶν κωδίκων τῆς Μεγίστης Λαύραςτῆς (ἐν Ἁγίῳ Ὄρει), Harvard Theological Studies; XII) (Cambridge, 1925).

- S. Eustratiades and Arcadios of Vatopedi, *Catalogue of the Greek Manuscripts in the Library of the Monastery of Vatopedi on Mount Athos*. Κατάλογος τῶν ἐν τῇ Ἱερᾷ Μονῇ Βατοπεδίου ἀποκειμένων κωδίκων, (Harvard Theological Studies IX) (Cambridge, 1924).

- S.P. Lambros, *Catalogue of the Greek Manuscripts on Mount Athos*. Κατάλογος τῶν ἐν ταῖς βιβλιοθήκαις τοῦ Ἁγίου Ὄρους ἑλληνικῶν κωδίκων, 2 vols. (Cambridge, 1895-1900).

- A.I. Papadopoulos-Kerameus, Ἱεροσολυμιτικὴ Βιβλιοθήκη ἤτοι κατάλογος τῶν ἐν ταῖς βιβλιοθήκαις τοῦ ἁγιωτάτου ἀποστολικοῦ τε καὶ καθολικοῦ ὀρθοδόξου πατριαρχικοῦ θρόνου τῶν Ἱεροσολύμων καὶ πάσης Παλαιστίνης ἀποκειμένων ἑλληνικῶν κωδίκων, 5 vols., (St. Petersburg, 1891-1915. [repr. Bruxelles, 1963]).

- I. Sakkelion and A. Sakkelion, Κατάλογος τῶν χειρογράφων τῆς Ἐθνικῆς Βιβλιοθήκης τῆς Ἑλλάδος (Athens, 1892).

- I. Sakkelion, Πατμιακὴ βιβλιοθήκη ἤτοι ἀναγραφὴ τῶν ἐν τῇ βιβλιοθήκῃ τῆς κατὰ τὴν νῆσον Πάτμον γεραρᾶς καὶ βασιλικῆς μονῆς τοῦ Ἁγίου Ἀποστόλου καὶ Εὐαγγελιστοῦ Ἰωάννου τοῦ Θεολόγου τεθησαυρισμένων χειρογράφων τευχῶν (Athens, 1890).

General characteristics of the Greek catalogues

- they reflect the monastic/ecclesiastical background of Byzantine codicology;
- they reflect the authentic housing of the different holdings of the libraries (in the Katholikon, in the room above the Narthex of the Church, in the Skeuophylakion annex to the Church, in a library nearby the church, in a separate tower building nearby the church);
- they reflect the liturgical function of the Byzantine codices (the majority is liturgical in the strict sense of the word);
- they reflect the authentic holdings and the arrangement of the Byzantine codices;
- they employ the authentic nomenclature of Byzantine codicology;
- they reflect the undifferentiated proximity of the biblical, patristic, liturgical and other classes of codices;
- they reflect the ongoing transmission of the same contents of the Byzantine codices up to our time;
- they reflect the authentic manuscript catalogues on which they were built (sometimes these also described).

In the box below, we present the contents of the Catalogue of Papadopoulos-Kerameus[541] to show how this catalogue presents an extremely rich pool of manuscript data, whereby the different holdings remained intact. The compiler described each manuscript in detail, indicating the whole codicological form in which he found it. He only systematised the codices into groupings in synoptic indices, not a priori. This catalogue displays attention to the historical background of the Patriarchal Library, the heritage of its holdings and previous catalogues of these holdings (see his adoption of the article by Archimandrite Kyril Athanasiades in Volume III "Ὑπόμνημα ἱστορικὸν περὶ τῶν βιβλιθηκῶν τοῦ Ὀρθοδόξου Καθολικοῦ Πατριαρχείου τῶν Ἱεροσολύμων").

Example of a Greek manuscript catalogue

The catalogue of the Library of the Greek Orthodox Patriarchate in Jerusalem

A.I. Papadopoulos-Kerameus, Ἱεροσολυμιτικὴ Βιβλιοθήκη ἤτοι κατάλογος τῶν ἐν ταῖς βιβλιοθήκαις τοῦ ἁγιωτάτου ἀποστολικοῦ τε καὶ καθολικοῦ ὀρθοδόξου πατριαρχικοῦ θρόνου τῶν Ἱεροσολύμων καὶ πάσης Παλαιστίνης ἀποκειμένων ἑλληνικῶν κωδίκων, 5 vols. (St. Petersburg, 1891-1915. repr., Bruxelles, 1963]).

T. A′ (1891):
- Πρόλογος, α′-θ
- Κατάλογος τῶν ἑλληνικῶν κωδίκων τῆς κυρίως πατριαρχικῆς βιβλιοθήκης : Codd. 1-645, *1-490*
- Κατάλογος τῶν ἑλληνικῶν κωδίκων τῆς ἐν Ἱεροσολύμοις πατριαρχικῆς βιβλιοθήκης κατὰ τὸ 1817 ἔτος , *491-500*
- Συνοπτικὸς πίναξ, *515-517*
- Κώδικες μετ' εἰκόνων ἢ κοσμημάτων, *517*
- Κώδικες ἀχρονολόγητοι, *517-520*
- Κώδικες μετὰ χρονολογίας, *520-527*
- Καλλιγράφοι ἢ ἀντιγραφεῖς καὶ αὐτόγραφα συγγραφέων τινῶν, *527-532*
- Βιβλιοδέται, *532*
- Βιβλιοθῆκαι καὶ κτήτορες, *532-537*
- Γενικὸς πίναξ, *539-619*

NB. Some sections are passed over.

T. B′ (1894):
- Πρόλογος, α′-β′
- Κατάλογος κωδίκων ἐκ τῆς λαύρας μετενεχθέντων Σάβα τοῦ ἡγιασμένου καὶ νῦν ἐν τῇ πατριαρχικῇ τῶν - Ἱεροσολύμων βιβλιοθήκῃ κατακειμένων, ἐν τόπῳ κεχωρισμένῳ : Codd. 1-706, *1-662*
- Γερμανοῦ ἐπισκόπου κατάλογος αὐτόγραφος, *663-665*
Etc.
- Συνοπτικὸς πίναξ, *755-759*
- Κώδικες ἀχρονολόγητοι, *761-764*
- Κώδικες μετ' εἰκόνων ἢ κοσμημάτων, *764*
- Κώδικες μετὰ χρονολογίας, *765-774*
- Καλλιγράφοι ἢ ἀντιγραφεῖς καὶ αὐτόγραφα συγγραφέων τινῶν, *775-782*
- Βιβλιοδέται, *783*
- Βιβλιοθῆκαι καὶ κτήτορες, *784-793*
- Γενικὸς πίναξ, *795-891*

T. Γ′ (1897):
- Πρόλογος, α′-β′
- Κατάλογος τῶν ἐκ τοῦ μοναστηρίου τοῦ τιμίου Σταυροῦ μετακομισθέντων κωδίκων εἰς τὴν ἐν Ἱεροσολύμοις πατριαρχικὴν βιβλιοθήκην : codd. 1-109, *1-175* [cf. T. E′ : Codd. 110-128]
- Κατάλογος ἑλληνικῶν κωδίκων ἀφιερωθέντων ὑπὸ τοῦ μακαριωτάτου πατριάρχου πρώην Ἱεροσολύμων Νικοδήμου τῇ κεντρικῇ βιβλιοθήκῃ τοῦ πατριαρχείου τῶν Ἱεροσολύμων : codd. 1-15, *177-192*
- Κατάλογος τῶν ἐν τῷ σκευοφυλακείῳ τοῦ ναοῦ τῆς Ἀναστάσεως φυλαττομένων ἑλληνικῶν χειρογράφων : codd. 1-22, *193-224*
- Κῶδιξ Εὐαγγελίου (ἔτους 1061-1062) ἐν τῷ Ἱεροσολυμιτικῷ μοναστηρίῳ τῷ λεγομένῳ << Μεγάλη Παναγία >> : p. 226-229
- Ἕτεροι κώδικες : codd. 1-7, *230-238*
Etc.
- Κυρίλλου Ἀθανασιάδου, ἀρχιμανδρίτου τοῦ Παναγίου Τάφου, Ὑπόμνημα ἱστορικὸν περὶ τῶν βιβλιθηκῶν τοῦ Ὀρθοδόξου Καθολικοῦ Πατριαρχείου τῶν Ἱεροσολύμων (1874-1881), *273-323*
- Συνοπτικὸς πίναξ, *353-355*
- Κώδικες ἀχρονολόγητοι, *356-357*
- Κώδικες μετ' εἰκόνων ἢ κοσμημάτων, *357*
- Κώδικες μετὰ χρονολογίας, *358-361*
- Καλλιγράφοι ἢ ἀντιγραφεῖς καὶ αὐτόγραφα συγγραφέων τινῶν, *362-364*
- Βιβλιοδέται, *364*

---

[541] Bio-bibliographical information concerning A. Papadopoulos-Kerameus is provided in t. V: А.И. Пападопуло - Керамевсъ (1855-1912 г.). Съ портретомъ, p. 5-14 and Списокъ трудовъ А.И. Пападопуло - Керамевса составленный проф. В.Н. Бенешевичемъ, p. 605-641.

- Βιβλιοθῆκαι καὶ κτήτορες, *365-369*
- Γενικὸς πίναξ, *371-433*

T. Δ' (1899):
- Πρόλογος, α'-γ'
- Κατάλογος κωδίκων (ἀριθ. 1-447), εὑρισκομένων ἐν τῇ βιβλιοθήκῃ τοῦ ἐν Κωνσταντινουπόλει Μετοχίου τοῦ Παναγίου Τάφου: codd. 1-447, *1-420*
  Etc.
- Συνοπτικὸς πίναξ, *483-486*
- Κώδικες ἀχρονολόγητοι, *487-489*
- Κώδικες μετ' εἰκόνων ἢ κοσμημάτων, *489*
- Κώδικες μετὰ χρονολογίας, *490-496*
- Καλλιγράφοι ἢ ἀντιγραφεῖς καὶ αὐτόγραφα συγγραφέων τινῶν, *497-500*
- Βιβλιοδέται, *500*
- Βιβλιοθῆκαι καὶ κτήτορες, *501-505*
- Γενικὸς πίναξ, *507-594*

T. Ε' (1915):
- Предисловие, *1-4*
- А.И. Пападопуло - Керамевсъ (1855-1912 г.). Съ портретомъ, *5-14*
- Κατάλογος κωδίκων (ἀριθ. 1-447), εὑρισκομένων ἐν τῇ βιβλιοθήκῃ τοῦ ἐν Κωνσταντινουπόλει Μετοχίου τοῦ Παναγίου Τάφου: codd. 448-890, *15-322*
- Νέα συλλογὴ κωδίκων τῆς Κεντρικῆς Πατριαρχικῆς ἐν Ἱεροσολύμοις Βιβλιοθήκης [κώδικες 1-120], *323-394*
- Ἀκολουθία καταλόγου τῶν ἐκ τοῦ μοναστηρίου τοῦ τιμίου Σταυροῦ μετακομισθέντων κωδίκων εἰς τὴν ἐν Ἱεροσολύμοις Πατριαρχικὴν Κεντρικὴν Βιβλιοθήκην [κώδικες 110-128], *394-400*
- Δύο ἕτεροι κώδικες, *401-404*
- Κατάλογος κωδίκων ἐκ τοῦ σκευοφυλακίου τοῦ ναοῦ τῆς Ἀναστάσεως καὶ νῦν εὑρισκομένων ἐν τῇ βιβλιοθήκῃ τῆς ἐγγὺς τοῦ ναοῦ τούτου μονῆς Ἀβραάμ [κώδικες 1-135], *404-457*
- Κώδικες ἐν τῇ βιβλιοθήκῃ τῆς μικρᾶς Γαλιλαίας τῆς ἐπὶ τοῦ ὄρους Ἐλεῶν [κώδικες 1-10], *460-467*
- Κώδικες ἐν τοῖς ἀρχείοις τοῦ ἐν Ἱεροσολύμοις Πατριαρχικοῦ θρόνου[κώδικες 1-9], *471-478*
- Συνοπτικὸς πίναξ, *557-558*
- Κώδικες ἀχρονολόγητοι, *559-560*
- Κώδικες μετὰ χρονολογίας, *561-565*
- Καλλιγράφοι ἢ ἀντιγραφεῖς καὶ αὐτόγραφα συγγραφέων τινῶν, *566-568*
- Βιβλιοθῆκαι καὶ κτήτορες, *569-571*
- Γενικὸς πίναξ, *572-603*
- Списокъ трудовъ А.И. Пападопуло - Керамевса составленный проф. В.Н. Бенешевичемъ, *605-641*

4.2.4 The catalogue of catalogues: the *Répertoire des Bibliothèques* (Richard/Olivier, 1995)

General entries from worldwide, regional and local libraries containing Greek Byzantine manuscripts, from the printed and handwritten catalogues and referential/historical works, can be found in the formidable manuscript databank of M. Richard and J.M. Olivier, *Répertoire des Bibliothèques et des Catalogues de Manuscrits Grecs* (Turnhout, 1995).

Arrangement of material in *Répertoire des Bibliothèques et des Catalogues de Manuscrits Grecs* (Turnhout, 1995)
- 'Table des villes et leux où sont (ou étaient) conserves des manuscripts grecs' (alphabetical list), IX-XVI;
- I. 'Bibliographie';
- II. 'Recueils de travaux';
- III. 'Catalogues spécialisés' (cf. note 1);
- IV. 'Catalogues régionaux', 29-70 (of interest are esp.: Hellas, Kypros, Romania, Turkiye, Ex-U.R.S.S.);
- V. 'Villes et autres lieux', 71-857

The catalogue is, of course, built on the work of earlier generations of catalogers. For example:

- V. Gardthausen, *Sammlungen und Cataloge Griechischer Handschriften* (Leipzig, 1903);
- O. Schissel von Fleschenberg, *Kataloge griechischer Handschriften* (Graz, 1924);
- W. Weinberger, *Wegweiser durch die Sammlungen altphilologischer Handschriften*, in *Sitzungsberichte der Akademie der Wissenschaften in Wien, Philosophisch-Historische Klasse*, v. 209, 4 (1930)
- H. Omont, *Catalogue alphabétique des livres imprimés mis à la disposition des lecteurs dans la salle de travail, Département des manuscrits, Bibliothèque National: suivi de la liste des catalogues usuels du Département des manuscrits* (Paris, 1933);
- L. Portio, *Inventarium graecorum codicum manuscriptorum a L. Portio scriptore graeco descriptum I-II* (Bibliotheca Vaticana, Sala Consultazione, manuscripts 321-322);
- D. Gkinis, "Κατάλογοι ἑλληνικῶν κωδίκων ἐν Ἑλλάδι καὶ Ἀνατολῇ" (1935).

Richard and his co-cataloguers at the *Institute des Recherches et d'Histoire des Texts* in Paris were and are still concerned with collecting catalogue data of manuscripts and entries to all libraries and holdings maintaining

Greek manuscripts for all categories (including classical literature). The actual situation of the holdings has evidently been checked, as far as is possible, through visits to libraries, consultation with librarians on location or other scholars and/or through the collection of data from catalogues with the help of literature on the holdings and the included manuscripts. Besides more elaborated descriptions of the Greek manuscripts, micro-films have also been produced. On the ground of these evaluations an estimation of the number of manuscripts has been provided. Despite this, however, the actual scope and total number of manuscripts was, and is, in many cases uncertain. The reason is simple: manuscripts appear and manuscripts disappear, which implies a constantly changing 'state of affairs'.

Rahlfs, and scholars such as Ehrhard, Gregory, Aland, von Soden set a limit at the XVIth c. passing consciously over all manuscripts of the XVIIth-XIXth c. From a codicological point of view and as explained in chapter 1, there is, in our view, no reason to adhere to this restriction. One of the great advantages of the *Répertoire des Bibliothèques et des Catalogues de Manuscrits Grecs* is the objective stand with regard to the Greek manuscripts in their totality. Nothing is excluded a priori, akin to the position of other Greek and Russian cataloguers such as Papadopoulos-Kerameus, Sakkelion, Lambros, Eustratiades, Bees, Tsakopoulos, Vladimir, Granstrem etc. Furthermore, Richard/Olivier use the original names of countries, cities, institutions, churches and monasteries.

4.2.5 Western libraries housing Byzantine Greek manuscripts

The number of Greek manuscripts that reached Western Europe is not small. A considerable part of these were preserved in the libraries of museums, universities and other academic research institutes. One can speak of a longstanding, ongoing exodus of Greek manuscripts from the East to Western Europe since the Fall of Constantinople (and earlier to Italy, for the church of Rome needed to be documented concerning the Eastern Orthodox church and its sources)[542]. Today these manuscripts are scattered all over the world. This wide distribution has had two main effects: on the one hand it has contributed to the entry of the Byzantine manuscripts and their theological heritage in the West, which was the starting point of new encounters between Western and Eastern Christendom, commencing in the 16th [543] and 17th centuries[544]. On the other hand, however, the manuscripts were received and possessed by owners who were unfamiliar with the original background of these works of Byzantine ecclesiastical literature. Since the Byzantine/Greek manuscripts are of great value for Western classical studies, they received universal scholarly attention and became a favoured good for manuscript collectors.

The orphaned manuscripts came to the West via diverse channels. Some were brought by refugees, as precious gifts to kings, others were bought or stolen in wars, or by individuals. Each manuscript has its own 'owner history' before it entered the libraries in the West. Of these libraries some possess a huge number of Byzantine/Greek manuscripts, for instance the Biblioteca Vaticana (Città del Vaticano), or the Bibliothèque Nationale (Paris), the Bodleian Library (Oxford), the Österreichische Nationalbibliothek (Vienna), the Biblioteca Medicea Laurenziana (Florence) or the Biblioteca Nacional (Madrid)[545]. This is only a small selection of the

---

[542] See the notes of V. Gardthausen, *Op. Cit.* (Leipzig, 1903), 39, concerning the ancient holdings of the 'Bibliotheca Vaticana'; and cf. Richard/Olivier, *Op. Cit..* (Turnhout, 1995), 240-245: the ancient holding *Vaticanus graecus* comprises to date 2.662 codices.

[543] G. Mastrantonis, *Augsburg and Constantinople. The Correspondence between the Tübingen Theologians and Patriarch Jeremiah II of Constantinople on the Augsburg Confession* (Brookline, Mass, 1982).

[544] J.N.W.B. Robertson, *The Acts and Decrees of the Synod of Jerusalem, sometimes called the Council of Bethlehem holden under Dositheus, Patriarch of Jerusalem in 1672* (London, 1899. [repr. New York, N.Y., 1969]).

[545] For the pre-history of the Western libraries and their holdings, see V. Gardthausen, *Op. Cit.* (Leipzig, 1903), and for the present situation, see Richard/Olivier, *Op. Cit.* (Turnhout, 1995). **Vatican (Holdings I-XVI)**: The description of the Vatican holdings started slowly. The catalogues of the library describe the collection up to No 2402, [Status quo Lilla 1990, ref in 1995]; Mercati/Franchi de'Cavalieri T. I (1923) [Codd. 1 – 329]; Devreesse T. II (1937) [Codd. 330 – 603]; Devreesse T. III (1950) [Codd. 604 – 866]; Schreiner (1988) [Codd. 867 – 932]; Giannelli (1950) [Codd. 1485 – 1683]; Gannelli/Canart (1961) [Codd. 1684 – 1744]; Canart I-II (1970-1973) [Codd. 1745 – 1962]; Lilla (1985) [Codd. 2162 – 2254]; Nicolopoulos (1966-1967) [Codd. 2401 – 2631]; Kominis (1979) [Codd. 2403 – 2596]; Lilla I-II (1987-1988) [Codd. 2644 – 2647]; Lilla (1990) [Codd. 2648 – 2651; 2658 – 2661]. See also Turyn (1964) [Codd. XIII-XIV c.]; Follieri (1969) [Codd. Selecti]. Of some importance (provenance) are, moreover: Portio: Inventarium I-II (Sala Consultazione, Mss. 321-322): codd. 1 – 992; Allaccio/Portio: Auctorum et materiarum index (Sala Cons. Mss. 421-423): codd. 1 – 1484; Portio: Initia operum: (Sala Cons. Mss. 43 [Vat. Gr. 2520]: codd. 1 – 1484; Inventarium codicum Vaticanorum Graecorum 993-2160 (Sala Cons. Mss. 323): codd. 993 – 2160; Codices olim Basiliani. Inventarium (Sala Cons. Mss. 44): codd. 1963 – 2123; Codices Vaticani graeci 1963-2053. Inventarium (Sala Cons. Mss. 326): codd. 1963 – 2053; Inventarium codicum Graecorum Bibliothecae Vaticane (Sala Cons. Mss. 324): codd. 1501 – 2402. References: V. Gardthausen, *Op. Cit.* (Leipzig, 1903), 'Bibliotheca Vaticana', 39-49; Richard/Olivier, *Op. Cit.* (Turnhout, 1995), 231-246. ‖ **Bibliothèque Nationale de France (Holdings I-V)**: I. Omont T. I-III (1886-1888) [Codd. 1-3117]; II. De Montfaucon (1715), Devreese (1945) [Codd. 1-400], Darrouzes (1949); III. Omont (1888) [codd. 1-1281], Astruc/Concasty (1960) [codd. 901-1371, with accretions to No 1386], IV. Champion (1930) [1 codex]; V. Omont (1888) [35], with accretions ? 45 codd.] References: V. Gardthausen, *Op. Cit.* (Leipzig, 1903), 'National-Bibliothek', 13-19; Richard/Olivier, *Op. Cit.* (Turnhout, 1995), 644-651. ‖ **Bodleian library (Holdings I-LVII)**: Coxe I, III, IX (1853, 1854, 1883) [Reprint I and III: 1969], Madan/Craster/Denholm-Young/Hunt/Record I-VI (I. 1953, II.1 1922, II.2 1937, III. 1895, IV. 1897, V. 1905, VI. 1924. Cf. Hutter I-III ((1977, 1978, 1982) and Wilson/Stefanovič (1963) and Dragoumi (1972).

more important libraries in Western Europe and the USA comprising Byzantine Greek codices. Here they were collected and maintained as the precious remains and treasures of human culture, and were catalogued and studied with utmost care and accurateness.

4.3 The Greek Libraries, their Catalogues and Manuscripts

4.3.1 The Greek Libraries of the Near East and Greece

The Greek libraries of the Near East and Greece include among others[546]:

- the Patriarchal Library in Jerusalem (Israel, belonging to the *Greek Orthodox Patriarchate of the Holy City of Jerusalem and of all Palestine*);
- the Holy Monastery of St. Catherine in Sinai (under the jurisdiction of the Jerusalem Greek Orthodox Patriarchate);
- the library of the Ecumenical Patriarchate of Constantinople in Istanbul (the *Great and Holy Church of Christ*);
- the library of the Holy Monastery of St. John the Theologian on Patmos (under the Ecumenical Patriarchate);
- the libraries of the Athos Monasteries (Chalchidice, Greece);
- the libraries of the Monasteries of Meteora (Thessaly, the *Church of Greece*);
- the libraries of Monasteries on Cyprus (of the *Greek Orthodox Church of Cyprus*);
- the libraries in Athens and Thessaloniki (Monasteries and other ecclesiastical and public institutions, *Church of Greece*);
- the Patriarchal Library in Alexandria (Egypt, the *Greek Orthodox Patriarchate of Alexandria and all Africa*);
- other libraries in the Near East[547].

These monasteries have inherited the ancient and rich collections of Byzantine Greek manuscripts and in many languages - Syrian, Arabic, Coptic, Armenian, Georgian, Ethiopic, Persian, Slavonic, Turkish, Polish. Latin codices are poorly represented. They contain the books of Scripture and their commentaries, the works of the fathers, and of the liturgy (including books of hymnography), asceticism and spiritual life, canon law, etc. These places continue to provide a place of study, collection and copying, in the same tradition as their Byzantine predecessors.[548]

In this paragraph we summarise the most important manuscript holdings and the actual number of manuscripts they store, according to most recent information (as far as possible), of a select group of libraries. This presentation has the aim of providing insight in the main collections of Byzantine manuscripts. Moreover, in these summaries, one can find detailed bibliographical information, which is necessary for the further codicological catalogue research we advocate. Richard/Olivier's catalogue lies at the basis of the data given, updated and augmented where possible.

References: V. Gardthausen, *Op. Cit.* (Leipzig, 1903), 'Die Bibliotheca Bodleiana', 62-63; Richard/Olivier, *Op. Cit.* (Turnhout, 1995), 605-625. ‖ **Österreichische Nationalbibliothek (Holdings I-V):** Lambeck (1665-1679), Kollar (1790), De Nessel (1690) [Pars I-V], Part I: Hunger I.1 (1961), Hunger/Kresten I.2 (1969), Hunger/Kresten I.3/1 (1976), Hunger/Kresten/Hannick I.3/2 (1984), Hunger/Lackner/Hannick I.3/3 (1992), Part II: Hunger/Hannick I. 4 (1957 replaced by 1994). See also Buberl/Gerstinger (1938), Unterkircher (1959), Hannick (1972), Bick (1920). References: V. Gardthausen, *Op. Cit.* (Leipzig, 1903), 72-73; Richard/Olivier, *Op. Cit.* (Turnhout, 1995), 832-838. ‖ **Biblioteca Medicea Laurenziana (Holdings I-XIII):** Bandini I-III (1764-1770), Rostagno/Festa (1893 and 1898) [Reprint: 1961 with suppl.] References: V. Gardthausen, *Op. Cit.* (Leipzig, 1903), 'Bibliotheca Medicea-Laurenziana', 28-31; Richard/Olivier, *Op. Cit.* (Turnhout, 1995), 294-299. ‖ **Biblioteca Nacional** (Madrid): Iriarte (1769) [codd. 1-125], Miller (1886) [codd. N. 126-141 and O 1-103], Omont (1897) [codd. O 104-106], Viellefond (1935) [codd. N. 142-175 and O 100-132], Andres (1987, 2nd ed.) [379 codd.]; and the **Real Biblioteca** (El Escorial) References: V. Gardthausen, *Op. Cit.* (Leipzig, 1903), 'Bibliotheca Medicea-Laurenziana', 8-9; 7-8; Richard/Olivier, *Op. Cit.* (Turnhout, 1995), 514-516; 286-288. ‖ **Biblioteca Nazionale Marciana:** Tomasinus (1639), Berardelli (1779) [codd. 1-88 and 401], Mittarelli (1779) [19 codd.], Mingarelli (1784), Castellani (1895) [61 codd.], Mioni I-II(1981-1985: Thesaurus Antiquus), Mioni I (Codices in classes I-V: 1967, 1972) and Mioni II-III (Codices in classes VI-VIII: 1960, IX-XI: 1972), Mioni (1986 ? Index]. References: V. Gardthausen, *Op. Cit.* (Leipzig, 1903), 'Die Biblioteca Nazionale Marciana', 53-55; Richard/Olivier, *Op. Cit.* (Turnhout, 1995), 814-820.

[546] See a more or less complete list of repositaries [places] in Greece in Richard/Olivier, *Op. Cit.* (Turnhout, 1995): 'Hellas', 44-45.

[547] Although the reference in Richard/Olivier, *Op. Cit..* (Turnhout, 1995), 256 suggests that the library of the *Greek Orthodox Patriarchate of Antioch and all the East* (in Damascus) should be of interest for Greek manuscripts, this is not affirmed by recent evidences. See the 'Patriarchate Documents Department' (official web-site of the Antiochian Patriarchate), 'The Patriarchate Library contains treasures of sourcing and rare books. Unfortunately, they are post the year 1860. These books are written in Arabic, Greek, Russian, French, English, Syrian and Romanian, of various subjects'. But also: 'The St. Lady Monastery, Balamand, Lebanon, contains a hundred and seventy manuscripts, but among these only a few are written in Greek'.

[548] Archimandrite Leontios, Foreword, in *Catalogue of Greek Manuscripts in the Library of the Monastery of St. Neophytos (Cyprus)* (Nicosia, 2002), vii: 'All the manuscripts have been restored recently, while the number of the printed books in the Library is constantly growing. This shows the Monastery's uninterrupted interest in and care of books, which is in accordance with the tradition established during the lifetime of St. Neophytos ('the Recluse' 1134-ca.1214), who himself founded a scriptorium in the Enkleistra – an enduring example for all future scribes to imitate. Besides their intellectual abilities in writing and also illuminating rare books, the scribes of that period, and later, also had a great desire to preserve them, often stressing at the end of their writings those characteristic words: 'Ἡ μὲν χεὶρ ἡ γράψασα σήπεται τάφῳ, γραφὴ δὲ μένει εἰς χρόνους ἀπεράντους'

***

(1)   Jerusalem (Israel) : Πατριαρχικὴ Βιβλιοθήκη (Patriarchal Library)[549]

The Library and its Holdings[550]

Πατριαρχικὸν Σκευοφυλάκιον		[?14 codd.]
Πατριαρχικὴ Βιβλιοθήκη		
[I.]	Πατριαρχείου [Ναὸς τοῦ Παναγίου Τάφου]	[645 codd.]
[II.]	Ἁγίου Σάββα [Λαύρα]	[706 codd.]
[III.]	Τιμίου Σταυροῦ [Μοναστήριον]	[? 129 codd.]
[IV.]	τοῦ Πατριάρχου Νικοδήμου Ι´	[15 codd.]
[V.]	Ναὸς τῆς Ἀναστάσεως	[22 codd.]
[VI]	Μονῆς Ἀβραάμ	[? 135 codd.]
[VII.]	Νέα Συλλογὴ Κωδίκων [Συλλογὴ Σ. Μετροπολίτου Ναζαρὲτ κ. Φωτίου καὶ Παρθενίου Ἀρχιμανδρίτου καὶ Καμαράση τοῦ ἡμῶν Κοινοῦ]	[? 120 codd.]
[VIII.]	Αἴθουσα τοῦ Πατριαρχείου	[3 codd.]
	Λαύρα τοῦ Ἁγίου Γεωργίου Χουζιβᾶ	[1 codex]
	Μικρὰ Γαλιλαία (Τοῦ Ἰορδάνου ἀρχιεπισκόπου Ἐπιφανίου)	[10 codd.]
	Μεγάλη Παναγία [Μοναστήριον]	[1 codex]
	Μονὴ τοῦ Ἁγίου Σάββα	[? 92 codd.]
	Ναὸς τοῦ Ἁγίου Ἰακώβου τοῦ Ἀδελφοθέου	[1 codex]
	Ναὸς τοῦ Ἁγίων Κωνσταντίνου καὶ Ἑλένης	[1 codex]
	Κώδικες ἐν τοῖς ἀρχείοις τοῦ ἐν Ἱεροσολύμοις πατριαρχικοῦ θρόνου	[9 codd.]
	[Βιβλιοθήκη τοῦ ἐν Κωνσταντινουπόλει Μετοχίου τοῦ Παναγίου Τάφου Replaced is the Library of the Metochion (Dependency of the Jerusalem Patriarchate) in Constantinople to Athens, EB]	[? 827 Codd.]

Estimated Total of Byzantine Greek manuscripts: 1.866 manuscripts.[551]

Catalogue Entries to the Holdings
Richard/Olivier (1995), 393-399; Aland [et al.] (1994), 463-465; Ehrhard (1937), xxxv-xxvi [Perria (1979), 146-148]; Rahlfs (1914), 80-87; Gregory (1908), 340-342; von Soden (1911), 75-76; Gardthausen (1903), 84-85.

Printed Catalogues of the Manuscripts
M. Smith, "Ἑλληνικὰ χειρόγραφα ἐν τῇ Μονῇ τοῦ Ἁγίου Σάββα", in Νέα Σιών, 55 (52th year) (1960), 110-125; 245-256; K.W. Clark, *Checklist of Manuscripts in the Libraries of the Greek and Armenian Patriarchates in Jerusalem microfilmed for the Library of Congress, 1949-50* (Washington, 1953); W.H.P. Hatch, *The Greek Manuscripts of the New Testament at Jerusalem. Facsimiles and Descriptions* (Paris, 1932); P. Thomsen, "Unbekannte griechische Handschriften der Patriarchatsbibliothek zu Jerusalem", in *Byzantinische Zeitschrift*, 22 (1913), 72-73; K.M. Koikylidis, Κατάλοιπα χειρογράφων Ἱεροσολυμιτικῆς βιβλιοθήκης (Jerusalem, 1899); A. Papadopoulos-Kerameus, *Op. Cit.* (St. Petersburg, 1891-1915 [repr., Bruxelles, 1963]).

Manuscript Catalogues
Codex 505: 'Alphabetical Catalogue of the Patriarchal Library' (1817), see Pap.-Ker. I: Codex 505 and the catalogue printed on pages 491-500 [111 manuscripts on paper and 23 manuscripts on parchment]; Codex 506: Κατάλογος τῶν ἐν τῇ παλαιᾷ Πατριαρχικῇ Συλλογῇ χειρογράφων τευχῶν (Jerusalem, 1865): an 'Alphabetical Catalogue of the Ancient Patriarchal Collection of manuscripts books', compiled by Kyrillos Athanasiades (Archimandrite of the Panagiou Taphou) (Jerusalem, 1865), containing descriptions of printed and manuscript books (parchment and paper) in divers languages; 412 Greek codices; Codex 507: 'Guide and Explanation concerning the catalogue of the inner library'; see Pap.-Ker. II, 1-8 (and 703); I γ´ A. 1. [manuscript catalogue of the Russian Archimandrite Antonius (Kapustin) with descriptions of 536 codices of S. Sabas Lavra].

References
Archbishop Aristarchos of Constantina, "The Mission of the Greek Orthodox Patriarchate of Jerusalem Today" (2003); J. Binns, *Ascetics and ambassadors of Christ: the monasteries of Palestine 314-631* (Oxford, 1994); D. Burton-Christie, *The Word in the Desert. Scripture and the Quest for Hoiliness in Early Christian Monasticism* (New York and Oxford, 1993); Cyril of Scythopolis, *Lives of the Monks of Palestine* (Michigan, 1991); D.J. Chitty, *The Desert a City. An Introduction to the Study of Egyptian and Palestinian Monasticism under the Christian*

---

[549] Meant is the library and holdings of the *Greek Orthodox Patriarchate of Jerusalem & All Palestine*.

[550] In the present Patriarchal Library manuscript collections were brought together from different monasteries in and around Jerusalem, which were united with the ancient holding of the Patriatchate itself. This was upon the order of the Patriarch of Jerusalem Nikodemos I in 1887 A.D.

[551] From the catalogue of A. Papadopoulos-Kerameus (Brussels, 1963), who described the different holdings which were incorporated in the Patriarchal Library in five large volumes (St. Petersburg, 1891-1915), one receives an impression of what was left of the works of these and many other ancient fathers and church leaders (in sum: 2.400 Greek codices (and in other languages), of which 850 codices were housed in Constantinople (in the library of the Metochion of Jerusalem [later transferred to Athens]) and of which the remaining are housed in the Patriarchal Library in Jerusalem (See *Ibid.*, I, Προλ, α´), Arabic, Persian and Turkian 177 codices, Georgian 143 codices, Syrian 50 codices, Ethiopian 19 codices and Slavic 22 codices; see also K.W. Clark, *Checklist of Manuscripts in the Libraries of the Greek and Armenian Patriarchates in Jerusalem* (Washington, 1953), who gives the following numbers: 1.866 Greek codices. There are also considerable collections of manuscripts in other languages: Arabic 234, Georgian 160, Syrian 50, Slavic 23, Ethiopian 21 [= 2.354]. Richard/Olivier, *Op. Cit.* (Turnhout, 1995), 399: 'En 1953, le nombre de mss grec de Jérusalem était de 1866; le nombre exact actuel est inconnu'. Archbishop Aristarchos (www..., 2003) reaffirms this number: 'with many valuable books and two thousand manuscripts (...). There are manuscripts in Greek, Slavonic, Georgian and Ethiopian, along with an Arabic collection numbering about 200'.

Empire (Crestwood, N.Y., 1966); K.W. Clark, "Exploring the Manuscripts of Sinai and Jerusalem", in *The Biblical Archaeologist*, 16 (1953), 22-44 [§ 2. The Jerusalem Greek Patriarchate, 36-40]; S. Vailhé, *"Répertoire alphab*étique *des monastères de Palestine"*, in *Revue de l'Orient Chrétien*, 4 (1899), 512-542 ; 5 (1900), 19-48, 272-292; S. Vailhé, "Le monastère de S.- Sabas", in *Echos d'Orient*, 2 (1898-1899), 332-341; 3 (1899-1900), 18-28, 168-177; S. Vailhé, "Les écrivains de Mar-Saba", in *Echos d'Orient*, 2 (1898), 1-11, 33-47; A. Ehrhard, "Das griechische Kloster Mâr-Saba in Palästina: seine Geschichte und seine literarischen Denkmäler", in *Römische Quartalschrift*, 7 (1893), 32-79; A. Ehrhard, "Der alte Bestand der griechischen Patriarchalbibliothek von Jerusalem", in *Centralblatt für Bibliothekswesen*, 9. 10-11 (1892), 441-459; A. Ehrhard, "Das Kloster zum hl. Kreuz bei Jerusalem und seine Bibliothek", in *Historisches Jahrbuch der Görresgesellschaft*, 13 (1892), 158-172; A. Ehrhard, "Die Griechische Patriarchal-Bibliothek von Jerusalem. Ein Beitrag zur Griechischen Palaeographie", in *Römische Quartalschrift*, 5 (1891), 217-265, 329-331, 383-384; J. Rendel-Harris, "The Library of the Convent of the Holy Sepulchre at Jerusalem", in *Haverford College Studies published by the Faculty of Haverford College*, no. 1 (1889), 1ff; K. Athanasiades (Archimandrite of the Panagiou Taphou), "Ὑπόμνημα ἱστορικὸν περὶ τῶν βιβλιθηκῶν τοῦ Ὀρθοδόξου Καθολικοῦ Πατριαρχείου τῶν Ἱεροσολύμων", in Papadopoulos-Kerameus, *Op. Cit.* (St. Petersburg, 1897), t. III, 273-323; K. Athanasiades, "Βιβλιοθῆκαι τοῦ Παναγίου Τάφου ἐν Κωνσταντινουπόλει καὶ ἐν Ἱερουσαλήμ", in Σωτήρ, 13 (1890), 257-266; 321-324; A. Couret, *La Palestine sous les empereurs grecs* (Grenoble, 1869).

* * *

(2)   **Sinai:** Μονὴ τῆς Ἁγίας Αἰκατερίνης (Monastery of St. Catherine)

The Library and its Holdings

        Βιβλιοθήκη τῆς Μονῆς τῆς Ἁγίας Αἰκατερίνης (Monastery of St. Catherine)
        [I.] Main holding   [2.305 manuscripts]
        [II] Formerly holding of the Sinai Metochion in Cairo   [included in I.][552]
        [III.] New findings   [836 manuscripts]

Estimated Total of Byzantine Greek manuscripts: 2.305 + 836 = 3.141 manuscripts. [VII-XIX c.][553]

Catalogue Entries to the Holdings
Richard/Olivier (1995), 746-751; Aland [et al.] (1994), 489-492; Ehrhard (1937), liii-liiii [Perria (1979), 127-132]; Rahlfs (1914), 284-293; Gregory (1908), 350-353; von Soden (1911), 79-80; Gardthausen (1903), 86.

Printed Catalogues of the Manuscripts
P.G. Nikolopoulos, Ἱερὰ Μονὴ καὶ Ἀρχειπισκοπὴ Σινᾶ. Τὰ νέα εὑρήματα τοῦ Σινᾶ (Athens, 1998); K. Weitzmann and G. Galavaris, *Op. Cit.* (Princeton, 1990); D. Harlfinger – D.R. Reinisch – J.A.M. Sonderkamp, (in Zusammenarbeit mit G. Prato), *Specimina Sinaitica. Die datierten griechischen Handschriften des Katharinen-Klosters auf dem Berge Sinai, 9. bis 12. Jahrhunderts* (Berlin, 1983); L. Politis, "Nouveaux manuscrits grecs découverts au Mont Sinaï. Rapport préliminaire", in *Scriptorium*, 34 (1980), 5-17 [pl. 1-9]; M. Kamil, *Op. Cit.* (Wiesbaden, 1970); K.W. Clark, *Op. Cit.* (Washington, 1952); W.H.P. Hatch, *Op. Cit.* (Paris, 1932); V.N. Beneševič, Описаніе греческихъ рукописей монастыря Святой Екатерины на Синаѣ. Томъ III. вып. I. Рукописи 1224-2150. *Catalogus codicum manuscriptorum graecorum qui in manasterio Sanctae Catherinae in Monte Sina asservantur. Tomi III pars I. Codices numeris 1224-2150*, (St. Petersburg, 1917); V.N. Beneševič, Описаніе греческихъ рукописей монастыря Святой Екатерины на Синаѣ. Томъ I: Замѣчательныя рукописи въ библіотекѣ Синійскаго монастыря и Синаеджуванійскаго подворья (въ Каирѣ), описанныя архимандритомъ Порфиріемъ (Успенскимъ). *Catalogus codicum manuscriptorum graecorum qui in manasterio Sanctae Catherinae in Monte Sina asservantur. Tomus I: Codices manuscripti notabiliores bibliothecae monasterii Sinaitici ejusque metochii Cahirensis, ab archimndrita Porphyrio (Uspenskio) descripti* (St. Petersburg, 1911 [repr. Hildesheim, 2 vols., 1965]); V. Gardthausen, *Catalogus codicum graecorum Sinaiticorum* (Oxford, 1886), [cod. 1-1223].

Manuscript Catalogues
Archimandrite Andronikos (Vryonides) (1924 [unpublished]), completed Gardthausen with a hand-list for the Nos 1224 to 2246 [supplemented, corrected and up-dated by Kamil in 1970 to no 2319]; Anthony Kapustin (1870) [catalogue of 1310 Greek manuscripts, 500 Arabic, 38 Slavic, and some Syriac]; Kyrillos the Librarian (of Mount Athos) (1840) [about 1500 manuscripts and printed volumes]; Archishop Kosmas (1704), (in Benesevic 1937, 25-27).

References
J. Galey, *Sinai und das Katharinen Kloster* (Stuttgart/Zürich, 1979); J.H. Charlesworth, *The New Discoveries in St. Catherine's Monastery: A Preliminary Report on the Manuscripts* (Winona Lake, IN, 1981); S. Agourides and J.H. Charlesworth, "A New Discovery of Old Manuscripts on Mt. Sinai: A Preliminary Report", in *The Biblical Archaeologist*, 41 (1978), 29-31; H. Husmann, "Die datierten griechischen Sinai-Handschriften des 9. bis 16. Jahrhunderts, Herkunft und Schreiber", in *Ostkirchliche Studien*, 27 (1978), 143-168; G.H. Forsyth and K. Weitzmann, *The Monastery of Saint Catherine at Mount Sinai. The Church and Fortress of Justinian* (Ann Arbor, [1973]); K.W. Clark, *Art. Cit.* (1953), 1. Saint Catherine's Monastery in Sinai, 22-36; M. Kamil, *Studia Egyptiaca: II. Les manuscrits du Covent Sainte Catherine au Sinai*, (Le Mardis de Dar El-Salam), Le Caire, 1952, 205-221; M. Kamil, "Die Handschriftensammlung des Sinai", in *Universitas*, 11 (Nov. 1951), 1175-1179; M.H.L. Rabino, *Le Monastère de Saint-Catherine du Mont Sinai* (Cairo, 1938); V.N. Beneševič, *Op. Cit.* (Athens, 1937);

---

[552] The return of the Library of the Metochion of the Sinai Monastery from Cairo to the main monastery must have taken place before 1903 (Gardthausen, *Op. Cit.* (Leipzig, 1903)).

[553] Richard/Olivier, *Op. Cit.* (Turnhout, 1995), for the main collection based on M. Kamil, *Catalogue of all manuscripts in the Monastery of St. Catherine on Mount Sinai* (Wiesbaden, 1970), 1-2: 'The manuscript collection consists of 3.329 manuscripts in twelve languages and a collection of Arabic and Turkish scrolle, totalling 1.742. (…) The Greek collection is possibly the most extensive of its kind in the world and contains 2.319 manuscripts'. However, see p. 61, where mention is made of 7 of lost codices from this collection and again 7 codices in other languages. The total number is, in fact: 2.305 manuscripts. For the number of 836 manuscript items (the New Findings) he refers to Archimandrite Damianos, "Εἰσήγησις ἐπὶ τῶν νεωστὶ εὑρεθέντων παλαιῶν χειρογράφων ἐν τῇ ἱερᾷ Μονῇ Σινᾶ", in *Jahrbuch der österreichischen Byzantinistik*, 32.4 (1982) [= XVI Internationalen Byzantinisten-kongress, Wien, 4.-9. Oktober, 1981, Akten, II/4], 105-115.

Prinz Johann Georg, Herzog zu Sachsen, *Das Katharinenkloster am Sinai* (Leipzig/Berlin, 1912); N. Kondakoff, *Les antiquités du monastère du Sinaï*, Ed. H. Omont, (Paris, 1882).

* * *

(3)   **Istanbul:** Βιβλιοθήκη τοῦ Οἰκουμενικοῦ Πατριαρχείου (the Library of the Ecumenical Patriarchate) and other (Public) Libraries in Istanbul

The Library and its Holdings

Πατριαρχικὸν Σκευοφυλάκιον	[20 codd.]
Πατριαρχικὴ Βιβλιοθήκη	
[I.] Μονὴ Παναγίας Καμαριωτίσσης ('Εμπορικὴ Σχολὴ)	[164 codd.]
[II.] Μονὴ τῆς 'Αγίας Τριάδος	[136 codd.]
[III.] Θεολογικὴ Σχολή	[79 codd.]
[IV.] Πατριαρχικὴ Βιβλιοθήκη [Ancient Holding]	[13 codd.]
[V.] 'Αΐθουσα τοῦ Πατριαρχείου	[? codd.]
'Εκκλησιαστικὸς Μουσικὸς Σύλλογος	[1 codex]
Τμῆμα Κωνσταντίνου 'Ανανιάδη	[6 codd.]
[VI.] Uncatalogued Codices[554]	[? 27 codd.]

Estimated Total of Byzantine Greek manuscripts: 446 manuscripts.

Replaced Holdings

Μετόχιον τοῦ Σινᾶ ἐν Κωνσταντινουπόλει → Athens [in 1966]	[?56 codd.]
Μετόχιον τοῦ Παναγίου Τάφου → Athens, Ethn. Bibl., [in ? 1940-1971?]	[?827 codd.]
Русскій Археологическій Институтв Константинополе → St. Petersburg,	
Россійская Академія Наук. Библіотека [since 1931] [See St. Petersburg]	[189 codd.]
'Ελληνικὸς Φιλολογικὸς Σύλλογος → Ankara, Türk Tarih Kurumu [in 1933]	[?127 codd.]
Μεγάλη τοῦ Γένους Σχολή → Ankara [destroyed in 1916]	[- codd.]

Catalogue Entries to the Holdings
Richard/Olivier (1995), 376-389; Aland [et al.] (1994), 462-463; Ehrhard (1937), xxxvii-xxxviii [Perria (1979), 74-77]; Rahlfs (1914), 44 [Chalki]; 89-90 [Konstantinopel]; Gregory (1908), 339 [Chalci], 343-344 [Konstantinopel]; von Soden (1911), 79-80 [Konstantinopel]; Gardthausen (1903), 82 [Chalke], 82-84.

Printed Catalogues of Manuscripts: Patriarchal Library
Unknown author, *Checklist of Greek Manuscripts in the Greek Orthodox Patriarchal Library* (Istanbul, 1962); A. Tsakopoulos, *Op. Cit.* (Istanbul, 1968); Idem, *Op. Cit.* (Istanbul, 1956); Idem, *Op. Cit.* (Istanbul, 1953); Metropolitan Athenagoras, "Περιγραφικὸς κατάλογος τῶν χειρογράφων τῆς ἐν τῇ νήσῳ Χάλκῃ ἱερᾶς μονῆς τῆς Παναγίας", in 'Επετηρὶς 'Εταιρείας Βυζαντινῶν Σπουδῶν, 10 (1933), 236-292; 11 (1935), 151-191; 12 (1936), 285-316; 13 (1937), 50-64; G.A. Soteriou, Κειμήλια τοῦ Οἰκουμενικοῦ Πατριαρχείου. Πατριαρχικὸς Ναὸς καὶ Σκευοφυλάκιον, Athens, 1937, 65-98 ; A.I. Papadopoulos-Kerameus, "'Ελληνικοὶ κώδικες ἐν τῇ Βιβλιοθήκῃ τοῦ Πατριαρχείου Κωνσταντινουπόλεως", in Византійскій временникъ, 17 (1910), 414-420.

Other Libraries and their Holdings

Γραφεῖα τῆς ἐκκλησίας Παναγίας (τῶν Εἰσοδίων)	[41 codd.]
Torkapi Sarayi [The Old Serai]	[56 codd.]
Arkeoloji Müzeleri → Topkapi Sarayi, in 1929 → Ankara, Millî Kütüphane, in 1973]	[2 codd.]
Ayasofya Müzesi	[2 codd.]

Manuscript Catalogues
Manuscript catalogue of the Theological School compiled in 1881 (Richard/Olivier, 382).
Catalogues of the 16th century, in A. Possevinus, *Apparatus sacer ad script. vet. et nov. Testamenti* (Cologne, 1608) [appendix to Catalogi mss. Graec.], t. II. , 44-49 (cf. Diehl [1892], 491 n.1); R. Förster, *De antiquitatibus et libris mss. Constantinopolitanis* (Rostock, 1877) [ancient collections according to a codex of Vienna, 9-10 and their catalogues, 14-32].
Codex Athen. 1366 9: list of Greek and Latin manuscripts of the Imperial Library Ottomane.
Inventory of the Great Church of Constantinople (October 1387), see M.M., II, No DCLXXXVI, 566-569.

References
Website of the Ecumenical Patriarchate: 'Manuscripts a spiritual testimony of many centuries'; 'Struggle for Orthodoxy in Difficult Times'; 'The Wanderings of the Patriarchate I-III; 'The Ecumenical Patriarchate in Modern Times' (www.patriarchate.org); Metropolit Maximos of Sardis, Τό Οἰκουμενικόν Πατριαρχεῖον ἐν τῇ 'Ορθοδόξῳ 'Εκκλησιᾳ (Thessaloniki, 1989); A. Pasadaiou, ΙΕΡΑ ΘΕΟΛΟΓΙΚΗ ΣΧΟΛΗ ΧΑΛΚΗΣ. ΙΣΤΟΡΙΑ, ΑΡΧΙΤΕΚΤΟΝΙΚΗΣ (Athens, 1987); T. Stavridis, "Histoire du Patriarcat œcuménique", in *Istina*, 15 (1970), 129-273 (esp. 214-221); S. Runciman, *The Great Church in captivity : a study of the Patriarchate of Constantinople from the eve of the Turkish conquest to the Greek War of Independence* (Cambridge, 1968); R. Janin, "Constantinople", in *Dictionnaire d'Histoire et de*

---

[554] In Richard/Olivier, *Op. Cit.*. (Turnhout, 1995), 384 n.2 mentions a *Checklist of Greek Manuscripts in the Greek Orthodox Patriarchal Library* (Istanbul, 1962), in which is enclosed a category "Manuscripts in the Uncatalogued Section: 27 manuscripts (information of G. Astruc). E.R. Andry, in his short "Report on microfilming the manuscripts in The Greek Orthodox Patriarchal Library, Istanbul", in *Scriptorium*, 18 (1964), 81-82, speaks of approximately 65 uncatalogued manuscripts "kept on shelves by themselves".

Géographie Ecclésiastiques, 3 (1956), 626-740; N.G. Wilson, "The Libraries of the Byzantine World", in *Greek, Roman, and Byzantine Studies*, 8.1 (1967), 53-80; E.R. Andry, "Report on microfilming the manuscripts in the Greek Orthodox Patriarchal Library, Istanbul", in *Scriptorium*, 18 (1964), 81-82; H.J. de Vleeschauwer, "The Byzantine Library to Justinian", in *Mousaion*, 74 (1964), 187-220; F. Fuchs, *Die höheren Schulen von Konstantinopel im Mittelalter* (Amsterdam, 1964); O. Volk, *Die byzantinischen Klosterbibliotheken, von Konstantinopel, Thessalonike und Kleinasien* (München, 1954); V. Burr, 'Byzantiner und Araber', in *Handbuch der Bibliothekswissenschaft*, by Eds. F. Milkau und G. Leyh (Leipzig, 1940), Kap. 2, 64-89.

* * *

(4)   Athos – The Holy Mountain: Ὁ Ἄθως - Τό Ἅγιον Ὄρος (the Monasteries, Skites and Kellia)

The Libraries and their Holdings [32 Monasteries, plus Skites and Kellia][555]

Βιβλιοθήκη τοῦ Πρωτάτου	[117 codd.]
Κελλίον Ἁγίας Τριάδος	[? 1 or 2 codd.]
Μονὴ Ἁγίου Παύλου	[? 338 codd.]
Μονὴ Βατοπαιδίου	[? 1.710 codd.]
Μονὴ Γρηγορίου	[183 codd.]
Μονὴ Διονυσίου	[832 codd.]
Μονὴ Δοχειαρίου	[? 452 codd.]
Μονὴ Ἐσφιγμένου	[354 codd.]
Μονὴ Ζωγράφου	[111 codd.]
Μονὴ Ἰβήρων	[2.120 codd.]
Μονὴ Καρακάλλου	[? 279 codd]
Μονὴ Κουτλουμουσίου	[766 codd.]
Μονὴ Κωνσταμονίτου	[111 codd.]
Μονὴ Μεγίστης Λαύρας	[2.262 codd.]
Μονὴ Ξενοφῶντος	[274 codd.]
Μονὴ Ξηροποτάμου	[426 codd.]
Μονὴ Παντελεήμονος	[? 1.318 codd.]
Μονὴ Παντοκράτορος	[335 codd.]
Μονὴ Σίμωνος Πέτρας	[? 140 codd.]
Μονὴ Σταυρονικήτα	[? 206 codd.]
Μονὴ Φιλοθέου	[? 249 codd.]
Μονὴ Χιλανδαρίου	[241 codd.]
Νέα Σκήτη Ἁγίου Παύλου	[? 39 codd.]
Σκήτη Ἁγίου Ἀνδρέου	[destroyed in 1958]
Σκήτη τῆς Ἁγίας Ἄννης	[362 codd.]
Σκήτη Προφήτου Ἠλίου	[1 ms]
Σκήτη Ἁγίου Δημητρίου	[73 codd.]
Σκήτη Ἁγίου Παντελεήμονος	[38 codd.]
Σκήτη Καυσοκαλυβίων	[272 codd.]
Σκήτη Μικρᾶς Ἁγίας Ἄννης	[37 codd.]
Σκήτη τοῦ Ξενοφῶντος	[13 codd.]
Σκήτη Τιμίου Προδρόμου	[20 codd.]

Estimated Total of Byzantine Greek manuscripts: 16.000 manuscripts.

Catalogue Entries to the Holdings
Richard/Olivier (1995), 324-349; Aland [et al.] (1994), 441-452; Ehrhard (1937), xxiii-xxvii [Perria (1979), 25-43]; Rahlfs (1914), 7-24; Gregory (1908), 318-338; von Soden (1911), 68-73; Gardthausen (1903), 80-81.

Printed Catalogues of Manuscripts
P. Soteroudis, Ἱερὰ Μονὴ Ἰβήρων. Κατάλογος Ἑλληνικῶν χειρογράφων, Α' (1-100) (Hagion Oros, 1998); R.W. Allison, *Summary Catalogue of the Greek Manuscripts of Philotheou Monastery* (Lewistin, Maine, 1995) [unpubl.]; E. Lamberz and E.K. Litsas, Κατάλογος χειρογράφων τῆς Βατοπεδινῆς Σκήτης Ἁγίου Δημητρίου (Κατάλογοι ἑλληνικῶν χειρογράφων Ἁγίου Ὄρους 1). *Catalogue of the Manuscripts of the Skete of St. Demetrius, Vatopedi, (Mount Athos)* (Thessaloniki, 1978); L. Politis, Συνοπτικὴ ἀναγραφὴ χειρογράφων ἑλληνικῶν συλλογῶν (Thessaloniki, 1976); L. Politis and M. Manousakas, Συμπληρωματικοὶ κατάλογοι χειρογράφων Ἁγίου Ὄρους (Thessaloniki, 1973); E.W. Saunders and C.G. Lahood, *A Descriptive Checklist of Selected Manuscripts in the Monasteries of Mount Athos*, (Microfilmed for the Library of Congress and the International Greek New Testament Project, 1952-53 (Washington, 1957); Spyridon of the Lavra and S. Eustratiades, *Op. Cit.* (Cambridge, 1925); S. Eustratiades and Arcadios of Vatopedi, *Op. Cit.* (Cambridge, 1924); E. Kurilas, "Κατάλογος ἁγιορειτικῶν χειρογράφων", in Θεολογία, 14 (1936), 42-52; 114-128; 330-347; 15 (1937), 239-248; 361-366; 16 (1938), 74-79; 173-180; 249-261; 350-354; 21 (1950), 269-291; 325-338; 506-525; S. Eustratiades, "ἁγιορειτικῶν κωδίκων σημειώματα", in Γρηγόριος ὁ Παλαμᾶς, 1 (1917), 49-62; 145-160; 374-384; 413-432; 457-472; 561-568; 617-624; 755-771; 2 (1918), 84-90; 167-173; S.P. Lambros, *Op. Cit.* (Cambridge, 1895-1900); S.P. Lambros, Κατάλογος τῶν ἐν ταῖς βιβλιοθήκαις τοῦ Ἁγίου Ὄρους ἑλληνικῶν κωδίκων, Ι. 1, (Athens. 1888).

---

[555] Although there are still many different numbers and uncertainties with regard to the quantities of codices in Athos libraries and holdings, it is thought useful to give some indication here at least.

Specialised Catalogues (Iconographic, Byzantine chant)
S.M. Pelekanidis, P.C. Christou, C. Tsioumis and S.N. Kadas, Οἱ θησαυροὶ τοῦ Ἁγίου Ὄρος, τόμ. : *The Treasures of Mount Athos: Illuminated Manuscripts* (1973, 1975, 1979, 1991); G.T. Stathis, Τὰ χειρόγραφα βυζαντινῆς μουσικῆς. Ἅγιον Ὄρος, τόμ. 1-3, (Athens, 1975, 1976, 1993).

Manuscript Catalogues (of the Monasteries on Athos and elsewhere)
Lit.: Sathas Mes. Bibl. I, 1872, 271-284 [Athos], 287-312 [Metochion of Jer. Taphou in Const.]; Gardthausen (Leipzig, 1903); Ehrhard (Leipzig/Berlin, 1937); Saunders (Washington, 1957); Richard/Olivier (Turnhout, 1995).
Chrysostomos of Lavra, Manuscript Catalog of the Manuscripts of the Great Lavra (1899);
Euthymios of Dionysiou, Manuscript Catalogue of the Manuscripts of Dionysiou.
Panteleimon of Lavra, Manuscript Catalogue of the Manuscripts of Great Lavra.
Chariton of Koutloumousiou, Manuscript Catalogue of the Manuscripts of Koutloumousios (1889) [with later up-datings].
[Manuscript] Catalogue of Esphigmenou.
Manuscript Catalogue of Docheiariou.
Barlaam Aggelakis, Manuscript Catalogue of Gregoriou.
Manuscript Catalogue [Inventory] of Vatopediou
Manuscript Catalogue of Hagiou Paulou.
Manuscript Catalogue of Penteleimonos.
Manuscript Catalogue of Xenophontos.
Chrysostomos (scholarc), Manuscript Catalogue of the Protaton.
Manuscript Catalogues in Paris, Bibl. Nat.: Cod. Par. Suppl. 654, 667, 675 (of the Mon. of Docheiariu), 754, 799 (of Athanasius), 1221

References
E. Litsas, "Libraries and manuscripts in Mount Athos. A survey" (Web-site of the Patriarchal Institute for Patristic Studies in Thessaloniki, December 2001); R.W. Allison, *Op. Cit* (Variorum, 1996), 135-154; E. Lamberz, "Die Handschriftenproduktion in den Athosklöstern", in *Scritture, libri e testi nelle aree provinciali Bisanzio*, by G. Cavallo, G. de Gregorio, and M. Maniaci (Eds.), (Spoleto, 1991), v. I; J. Duplacy, 'Manuscrits grecs du Nouveau Testament émigrés de la Grande Laure de l'Athos", in *Studia Codicologica*, Ed. K. Treu (Berlin, 1977), 159-178; C. Cavarnos, *Anchored in God. An inside account of Life, Art, and Thought on the Holy Mountain of Athos* (Athens, 1973); Amand de Mendieta, 'The Libraries of Athos', in *Mount Athos. The Garden of the Panaghia* (Berlin/Amsterdam, 1972), 241-251; I.P. Mamalakis, Τὸ Ἅγιον Ὄρος (Ἄθως) διὰ μέσου τῶν αἰώνων (Thessaloniki, 1971); I. Doens (Ed.), 'Bibliographie de la Sainte Montagne de l'Athos', in *Le Millénaire du Mont Athos 963-1963. Études et Mélanges* (Chevetogne, 1963-64), II, 337-495; C.G. Patrinelis, Βιβλιοθῆκαι καὶ ἀρχεῖα (Athens, 1963); S.Y. Rudberg, "Les manuscrits à contenu profane du Mont-Athos", in *Eranos*, 54 (1956), 174-185; E.W. Saunders, *Art. Cit.* (1955), 22-41; B. Krivocheine, "Mount Athos in the Spiritual Life of the Orthodox Church", in *The Christian East*, 2 (1952), 35-50; F. Dölger, 'Der Heilige Berg Athos und seine Bücherschätze', in *Bibliotheksprobleme der Gegenwart* (Frankfurt a. M., 1951), 1-15; F. Dölger, Παρασπορα. *30 Aufsätze zur Geschichte, Kultur und Sprache des byzantinischen Reiches* (Passau, 1961 [repr. 1951]), 391-409; E. Kourilas, "Athos, la vie et les institutions monacales", in *La Croix*, 1 (1947), 1-30; 2/3 (1949), 97-111; J. Thibaut, *Monuments de la notation ekphonétique et hagiopolite de l'Église Grecque: exposé documentaire des manuscrits de Jérusalem, du Sinaï et de l'Athos conservés à la Bibliothèque impériale de Saint-Pétersburg* (s.n., 1913); H. Brockhaus, *Die Kunst in den Athosklöstern* (Leipzig, 1891), 167-242, Taf. 17-27; K. Lake, "Texts from Mt. Athos", in *Studia Biblica et Ecclesiastica*, 5.2 (1902), 88-185; M.I. Gedeon, Ὁ Ἄθως (Constantinople, 1885); S. Lambros, *Op. Cit.* (Bonn, 1881).

* * *

(5)   Patmos: Μονὴ τοῦ Ἁγίου Ἰωάννου τοῦ Θεολόγου (the Monastery of St. John the Theologian)

The Library and its Holding

Μονὴ τοῦ Ἁγίου Ἰωάννου τοῦ Θεολόγου

Estimated Total of Byzantine Greek manuscripts: 900 manuscripts.

Catalogue Entries to the Holdings
Richard/Olivier (1995), 656-659; Aland [et al.] (1994), 485-486; Ehrhard (1937), xlviii [Perria (1979), 120-122]; Rahlfs (1914), 217-220; Gregory (1908), 347-348; von Soden (1911), 78; Gardthausen (1903), 85-86.

Printed Catalogues of Manuscripts
A.D. Kominis, Πατμιακὴ βιβλιοθήκη ἤτοι Νέος κατάλογος χειρογράφων κωδίκων τῆς Ἱερᾶς Μονῆς Ἁγίου Ἰωάννου τοῦ Θεολόγου Πάτμου, Τόμος Α'. Κώδικες 1-101 (Athens, 1988); A.D. Kominis, *Facsimiles of dated Patmian Codices* (Athens, 1970); Margiolos, Archimandrite Meletios, Περιγραφικὸς πίναξ τῶν χειρογράφων κωδίκων τῆς βιβλιοθήκης τῆς ἐν Πάτμῳ Ἱερᾶς Μονῆς Ἰωάννου τοῦ Θεολόγου, in Ἡ Φωνὴ τῆς Ἀποκαλύψεως, 1 (1955); 2 (1957); D. Kallimachos, "Πατμιακῆς βιβλιοθήκης συμπλήρωμα (ἄγνωστοι κώδικες)", in Ἐκκλησιαστικὸς Φάρος, 10 (1912), 246-267; 309-334; 388-404; 11 (1913), 148-160; 244-253; 12 (1913), 385-398; 525-541; 13 (1914), 256-272; 14 (1915), 68-80; 15 (1916), 357-375; 16 (1917), 98-108; 145-161; 466-484; 17 (1918), 117-128; 214-233; I. Sakkelion, *Op. Cit.* (Athens, 1890).

Manuscript Catalogues
A.D. Kominis, Πατμιακὴ βιβλιοθήκη (1988), 'παλαιοτεροὶ κατάλογοι', ιη'-κα' [not less than nine ancient catalogues before Sakkelion]. Also A.D. Kominis, see . 20.

References
S.A. Papadopoulos, *The Monastery of St. John the Theologian in Patmos*, 4th edition, [Patmos] 1974; K.T. Ware, "Patmos and its Monastery", in *Eastern Churches Review*, 1.3 (1967), 231-237; N.G. Wilson, "The Libraries of the Byzantine World", in *Greek, Roman, and*

Byzantine Studies, 8.1 (1967), 53-80 [esp. 69-71]; A.D. Kominis, "Ὁ νέος κατάλογος τῶν χειρογράφων τῆς ἐν Πάτμῳ Ἱερᾶς Μονῆς Ἰωάννου τοῦ Θεολόγου (Μέθοδος καὶ προβλήματα)", in Σύμμεικτα, 1 (1966), 17-34; C. Diehl, "Le trésor et la bibliothèque de Patmos au commencement du 13ᵉ siècle", in *Byzantinische Zeitschrift*, 1 (1892), 489-525; W. Studemund, "Das Inventar des Klosters St. Johannis auf der Insel Patmos im 16. Jahrhundert", in *Philogus*, 26 (1867), 167-173.

* * *

(6) **Meteora – Thessaly:** Μετέωρα (the Monasteries in the Meteora Mountains)

The Libraries and their Holdings

Μονὴ Ἁγίας Τριάδος	[124 codd.][556]
Μονὴ τοῦ Ἁγίου Νικολάου τοῦ Ἀναπαυσᾶ	[-]
Μονὴ Ἁγίου Στεφάνου	[147 codd.]
Μονὴ Βαρλαάμ	[290 codd.]
Μονὴ τῆς Μεταμορφώσεως	[639 codd.]
Μονὴ Ῥουσάνου	[-]

Estimated Total of Byzantine Greek manuscripts: 1.200 manuscripts [IX-XIX c.]

Catalogue Entries to the Holdings
Richard/Olivier (1995), 533-540; Aland [et al.] (1994), 474-475; Ehrhard (1937), xliv [Perria (1979), 90-92]; Rahlfs (1914), 138; Gregory (1908), - ; von Soden (1911), - ; Gardthausen (1903), 79.

Printed Catalogues of Manuscripts
D.Z. Sofianos, *Op. Cit.* (Athens, 1993); D.Z. Sofianos, *Op. Cit.* (Athens, 1986); N.A. Bees, *Op. Cit.* (Athens, 1984); N.A. Bees, *Op. Cit.* (Athens, 1967 [1998²]); N.A. Bees, Ἔκθεσις παλαιογραφικῶν καὶ τεχνικῶν ἐρευνῶν ἐν ταῖς μοναῖς τῶν Μετεώρων κατὰ τὰ ἔτη 1908 καὶ 1909, (Βυζαντιολογικὴ Ἑταιρεία ἐν Ἀθήναις. Ἀνεγνώσθη ἐν δημοσίᾳ συνεδρίᾳ τῆς Βυζαντιολογικῆς Ἑταιρείας τῇ 1 φεβρουαρίου 1910), (Athens, 1910).

References
D.Z. Sofianos, *Holy Meteora* (Kalambaka, 2002); D.Z. Sofianos, "Μετέωρα. Σύντομο ἱστορικὸ χρονικὸ τῆς Μετεωριτικῆς μοναστικῆς πολιτείας", in Νέα Ἑστια, 128 (1990), 1322-1332 and 24 pl.; D.M. Nicol, *Meteora, The Rock Monasteries of Thessaly* (London, 1963) [Bibl.: 191-199]; N.A. Bees, "Geschichtliche Forschungsresultate und Mönchs- und Volks-sagen über die Gründer der Meteorenklöster", in *Byzantinisch-Neugriechische Jahrbücher*, 3 (1922), 364-403; J. Dräseke, "Die neuen Handschriftenfunde in den Meteoraklöstern", in *Neue Jahrbücher für das klassische Altertum*, 15 (1912), 542-553; N.A. Bees, "Über zwei Codices des Alten Testaments aus den Bibliotheken von Meteoron und Megaspelaion", in *Zeitschrift für die alttestamentische Wissenschaft*, 32 (1912), 225-231; N.A. Bees, "Συμβολὴ εἰς τὴν ἱστορίαν τῶν μονῶν τῶν Μετεώρων", in Βυζαντὶς, 1 (1909), 191-331.

* * *

(7) **Athens:** Ἐθνικὴ Βιβλιοθήκη τῆς Ἑλλάδος (the National Library of Greece) and other Athenian Ecclesiastical and Public Institutions

A. The Library and its Holdings[557]

Ἐθνικὴ Βιβλιοθήκη τῆς Ἑλλάδος. Τὸ Τμῆμα Χειρογράφων	
[I.] Μετόχιον τοῦ Παναγίου Τάφου	[?]
[II.] Μεγάλη τοῦ Γένους Σχολή	[?]

Estimated Total of Byzantine Greek manuscripts (EBH only): 3.121 manuscripts. [IXth-XIXth c.]

Catalogue Entries to the Holdings
Richard/Olivier (1995), 105-110; Aland [et al.] (1994), 437-441; Ehrhard (1937), xxii-xxiii [Perria (1979), 16-24]; Rahlfs (1914), 4-7; Gregory (1908), 286-290; von Soden (1911), 66-67; Gardthausen (1903), 78.

Printed Catalogues of Manuscripts
P.G. Nikolopoulos, Περιγραφὴ χειρογράφων κωδίκων τῆς Ἐθνικῆς Βιβλιοθήκης τῆς Ἑλλάδος, Αριθ. 3122-3369 (Athens, 1996); L. Politis, Κατάλογος χειρογράφων τῆς Ἐθνικῆς Βιβλιοθήκης τῆς Ἑλλάδος, ἀρ. 1857-2500 (Athens, 1991); F. Halkin, *Op. Cit.* (Brussels, 1983); K. and S. Lake, *Monumenta palaeographica vetera. Dated Greek Minuscule Manuscripts to the year 1200*, t. 1-10, (Boston, 1934-1939) [T. 1: Manuscripts at Jerusalem, Patmos and Athens, Plates 1-6]; I. Sakkelion and A. Sakkelion, *Op. Cit.* (Athens,

---

[556] The original holdings have the numbers: Holy Trinity: 47 codices; Hagiou Nikolaou: 35 codices; Rousanou: 40 codices.

[557] The National Library of Greece is taken "pars pro toto", since it is the most representative library of Athens and of the whole of Greece, including collections of manuscripts of Greek monasteries (Μονὴ Δουσίκου near Trikkala 356 codd. and Μονὴ Μεταμορφώσεως 100 codd.), churches and other ecclesiastical instititions. Note that the foundation of The National Library of Greece came into existence quite late, with a "Deposit of Books" in 1829, and in 1832 the first catalogue was set up, see J. Demopoulos (Deputy Director, National Library of Greece), 'National Library of Greece: History, Present Status and Plans for the Future', Presentation at the Conference of the Library Congress, *Strengthening Modern Greek Collections* (1999). The Department of Manuscripts contains today a large collection of 4.500 codices, including Greek as well as codices in other languages.

1892); G.P. Kremos, Κατάλογος τῶν χειρογράφων τῆς Ἐθνικῆς καὶ τῆς τοῦ Πανεπιστημίου Βιβλιοθήκης ἀλφαβητικὸς καὶ περιγραφικὸς μετ'εἰκόνων καὶ πανομοιοτύπων κατ' ἐπιστήμας κατατεταγμένων, Τ. 1 [Θεολογία] (Athens, 1876)[558].

Special Catalogues (Iconography and Canon law)
A. Marava-Chatzinicolaou and C. Toufexi-Paschou, Κατάλογος μικρογραφιῶν βυζαντινῶν τῶν χειρογράφων τῆς Ἐθνικῆς Βιβλιοθήκης τῆς Ἑλλάδος, Τ. Γ': Ὁμιλίες Πατέρων τῆς Ἐκκλησίας καὶ Μηνολόγια 9ου-12ου αἰῶνα (Athens, 1997); A. Marava-Chatzinicolaou and C. Toufexi-Paschou, *Op. Cit.*, Τ. B: (Athens, 1985) [with parallel Eng. ed.]; A. Marava-Chatzinicolaou and C. Toufexi-Paschou, *Op. Cit.*, Τ. A: (Athens, 1978) [with parallel Eng. ed.]; A. Delatte, *Les manuscrits à miniatures et à ornements des bibliothèques d'Athènes* (Liège-Paris, 1926); P. Buberl, *Die Miniaturenhandschriften der Nationalbibliothek in Athen* (Vienna, 1917); Z. von Lingenthal, "Die juristischen Handschriften der Athener Bibliothek", in *Archiv für mittel-und neugriechischer Philologie*, 1 (Athens, 1880), 221-223.

Manuscript Catalogue
S. Lambros, 'Χειρόγραφος κατάλογος τῶν ἐν τῇ ἰδίᾳ αὐτοῦ βιβλιοθήκῃ κωδίκων', in Ἀθηναῖοι Βιβλιογράφοι (Athens, 1902).

References
J. Demopoulos, "National Library of Greece: History, Present Status and Plans for the Future", Presentation at the Conference at the Library Congress April 29-30 *Strengthening Modern Greek Collections* (1999) (www.loc.gov/rr/european/GrkColl/demop.html); L. Politis, 'Εἰσαγωγή: Τὸ Τμῆμα Χειρογράφων τῆς Ἐθνικῆς Βιβλιοθήκης and Κατάλογοι χειρογράφων τῆς Ἐθνικῆς Βιβλιοθήκης'; also 'Ἐπίμετρον: Σημείωμα περὶ τῆς προελεύσεως τῶν κωδίκων τῆς Ἐθνικῆς Βιβλιοθήκης' in *Op. Cit.* (Athens, 1991); D. Margaris, "Histoire de la Bibliothèque Nationale", in *L'Hellénisme contemporain*, 2nd series, 5 (1951), 318-326; L. Politis, "La section des manuscrits de la Bibliothèque Nationale", in *L'Hellénisme contemporain*, 1st series, 4 (1940), 242-249;

B. Other Athenian Libraries

Ἀκαδημία Ἀθηνῶν	[? 44 mss]
Ἀρχιεπισκοπὴ Ἀθηνῶν	[6 codd.]
Βιβλιοθήκη τῆς Βουλῆς Ἑλλήνων	[? 244 codd.]
Βιβλιοθήκη τῆς Ἱερᾶς Συνόδου τῆς Ἐκκλησίας τῆς Ἑλλάδοος (Μονὴ Πετράκη)	[25 codd.]
Βυζαντινὸν Μουσεῖον	[206 codd.]
[I.] [Ἑλληνικὸν Γυμνάσιον] (Part A: Edirne/Turkey, see beneath)	
[IV.] [Χριστιανικὴ Ἀρχαιολογικὴ Ἑταιρεία] (transfered in 1923)	
Γενικὰ Ἀρχεῖα τοῦ Κράτους	[? codd.]
Γεννάδειος Βιβλιοθήκη	[? 134 codd.]
Ἑταιρεία Βυζαντινῶν Σπουδῶν	[20 codd.]
Ἑταιρεία Ἑλληνικοῦ Λογοτεχνικοῦ καὶ Ἱστορικοῦ Ἀρχείου	[? 36 codd.]
Θεολογικὸ Σπουδαστήριο Πανεπιστημίου Ἀθηνῶν	[50 codd.]
Ἱστορικὸν Μουσεῖον τοῦ Νέου Ἑλληνισμοῦ [Ἱστορικὴ καὶ Ἐθνολογικὴ Ἑταιρεία]	[293 codd.]
Μορφωτικὸ Ἵδρυμα Ἐθνίκης Τραπέζης	[? 105 codd.]
Μουσεῖον Δ. Λοβέρδου	[? codd.]
Μουσεῖο Μνενάκη	
[I.] Μνενάκη + Δαμιάνος Κυριαζς	[81 + 18 codd.]
[II.] Ταμεῖο Ἀνταλλαξίμων	[326 codd.]
[III.] [Ἑλληνικὸν Γυμνάσιον] (Part B: Edirne/ Turkey)	[96 codd.]
Σιναϊτικον Μετόχιον Ἀθηνῶν	[50/51 codd.]
Σπουδαστήριον Βυζαντινῆς καὶ Νεοελληνικῆς Φιλολογίας τοῦ Πανεπιστημίου Ἀθηνῶν	[48 codd.]
Νικολάος Πολλάνης	[1 codex]

Estimated Total of Byzantine Greek manuscripts (without the EBH): 1.784 manuscripts.

B. Printed Catalogues of Manuscripts
For catalogues and reference literature, see Richard/Olivier (1995), 97-119.

* * *

(8) **Thessaloniki:** Μονὴ τῶν Βλαταίων (The Vlatadon Monastery), Πατριαρχικὸν Ἵδρυμα Πατερικῶν Μελετῶν and other Thessalonian Institutions

A. The Libraries and their Holdings

Μονὴ τῶν Βλατάδων (Βλαταίων)	[? 93 codd.]
Πατριαρχικὸν Ἵδρυμα Πατερικῶν Μελετῶν	[? 10 codd.]

Estimated Total of Byzantine Greek manuscripts (Vlatadon monastery and ΠΠΠΜ only): 103 manuscripts.

---

[558] Kremos described only 220 manuscripts. According to V. Gardthausen, *Op. Cit.*. (Leipzig, 1903, 78) the library contained 498 Greek and 267 codices in other languages. Ehrhard in 1912 had consulted an unprinted supplement to *Sakkelion* (1892) [No 1-1856] with codices 1857-2325.

Catalogue Entries to the Holdings
Richard/Olivier (1995), 782-787; Aland [et al.] (1994), 497-498; Ehrhard (1937), li-lii [Perria (1979), 134-135]; Rahlfs (1914), - ; Gregory (1908), 348-349; von Soden (1911), 78-79; Gardthausen (1903), 87.

Printed Catalogues of Manuscripts
D. Touliatos-Banker, "Εύρετήριο μικροταινιών μουσικών χειρογράφων στὸ ἀρχεῖο τοῦ Πατριαρχικοῦ Ἰδρύματος Πατερικῶν Μελετῶν ἀπὸ τὸ 1975 καὶ ἔπειτα, in Κληρονομία, 18 (1986), 431-441; S. Eustratiades, Κατάλογος ἐν τῇ μονῇ Βλατέων (Τσαοὺς Μοναστήρι) ἀποκειμένων κωδίκων (Thessaloniki, 1918); P.N. Papageorgiou, "Ἡ ἐν Θεσσαλονίκῃ μονὴ τῶν Βλαταίων καὶ τὰ μετόχια αὐτῆς", in *Byzantinische Zeitschrift*, 8 (1899), 402-428 [402-407: 18 manuscripts].

Manuscript catalogue
Manuscript catalogue of the year 1269/70 [see Usener, *Neue Jahrb. f. class. Philologie*, 107 (1873), 147 A. 2.

References
S. Lambros, "The Greek Manuscripts at Salonica", in *Athenaeum*, No 3284 (1890), 451-452.

B. The Other Thessalonian Libraries and Holdings:

Βυζαντινὸ Μουσεῖο	[1 codex]
Γυμνάσιον Ἑλληνικόν [? 146 codd.] → Athens (the National Library of Greece)	
Δημοτικὴ Βιβλιοθήκη	[5 codd.]
Κέντρο Θεολογικῶν καὶ Ἁγιολογικῶν Μελετῶν. Συλλογὴ Παν. Κ. Χρήστου	[10 codd.]
Σπουδαστήριο Κλασσικῆς Φιλολογίας τοῦ Τμήματος Φιλολογίας τῆς Φιλοσοφικῆς Σχολῆς τοῦ Πανεπιστημίου	[? 103 codd.]
Σπουδαστήριο Πρακτικῆς Θεολογίας τῆς Θεολογικῆς Σχολῆς τοῦ Πανεπιστημίου	[7 codd.]
Σύλλογος Κλεισουριέων	[1 codex]

B. Printed Catalogues of Manuscripts
For catalogues and reference literature, see Richard/Olivier (Turnhout, 1995), 780-787.

* * *

(9)   Cyprus: Ἱερὰ Μονὴ Ἁγίου Νεοφύτου (the Monastery of St. Neophytos) and other Cyprian Libraries

A. The Libraries and their Holdings

Nikosia (Levkosia):	Ἀχαιολογικὸν Μουσεῖον	[? codd.]
	Βιβλιοθήκη τῆς Ἀρχιεπισκοπῆς Κύπρου	[? 122 codd.]
	Βιβλιοθήκη Φανερωμένης	[2 codd.]
	Κέντρο Ἐπιστημονικῶν Ἐρευνῶν	[? codd.]
	Μετόχι τῆς Μονῆς Μαχαιρᾶ	[? 2 codd.]
	Μετόχι τῆς Μονῆς Παναγίας τοῦ Κύκκου	[? codd.]
	[Παγκύπριον Γυμνάσιον]	[- codd.]
Paphos:	Βυζαντινὸν Μουσεῖον	[? 2 codd.]
	Ἱερὰ Μονὴ Χρυσορρογιατίσσας	[? 21 codd.]
	Μονὴ Ἁγίου Νεοφύτου τοῦ Ἐγκλείστου	[38 codd.]

Eptakomi: Richard/Olivier, 282 [1 codex]
Kaimaki: Richard/Olivier, 400 [1 codex]
Kyrenia ? [occupation of Turcs 1974] Richard/Olivier, 449-450
Larnaka (Kition) Richard/Olivier, 452-454
Levkara (Pano Leukara): Richard/Olivier, 634-635
Kentron Epist. Erevnon
Hagios Mammas: Richard/Olivier, 350 [1 codex]
Troodos

Estimated Total of Byzantine Greek manuscripts: [38 codd. Mon. of St. Neophytos]

Catalogue Entries to the Holdings
Richard/Olivier (1995), 'Kypros', 50-52 [general], 476-482 [Leukosia], 635-639 [Paphos]; Aland [et al.] (1994), 506-507; Ehrhard (1937), xli [Perria (1979), 101]; Rahlfs (1914), 47; Gregory (1908), - ; von Soden (1911), - ; Gardthausen (1903), 84.

Printed Catalogues of Manuscripts
A. Jakovljevič, *Catalogue of Greek Manuscripts in the Library of the Monastery of St. Neophytos, Cyprus* (Nicosia, 2002); C.N. Constantinides and R. Browning, *Dated Greek Manuscripts from Cyprus to the year 1570, Washington, D.C.* (Nicosia, 1993); A. Jakovljevič, *Catalogue of Byzantine Chant Manuscripts in the Monastic and Episcopal Libraries of Cyprus* (Nicosia, 1990).

References
Official web-site of the Greek Orthodox Church of Cyprus (www.patriarchate.org); D. Serfes, "Monasticism in Cyprus", in *Cyprus Today, A Quarterly Cultural and Informative Review of the Ministry of Education and Culture*, 35.1-2 (1997), 2-15; B. Englezakis, *Studies on the*

History of the Church of Cyprus, 4th-20th centuries (Aldershot, 1995); J. Hackett, *A History of the Orthodox Church of Cyprus from the coming of the Apostles Paul and Barnabas to the commencement of the British occupation (A. D. 45-A. D. 1878)*, London, 1901.

* * *

(10) Alexandria [El-Iskandariya] (Egypt): Βιβλιοθήκη τοῦ Πατριαρχείου (the Patriarchal Library)[559]

A. The Library and its Holding

Βιβλιοθήκη τοῦ Πατριαρχείου   [530 codd.]

Estimated Total of Byzantine Greek manuscripts: 530 manuscripts.[560]

Catalogue Entries to the Holdings
Richard/Olivier (1995), 373-375 [El-Iskandariya]; Aland [et al.] (1994), 506-507; Ehrhard (1937), xli [Perria (1979), 101]; Rahlfs (1914), 47; Gregory (1908), - ; von Soden (1911), - ; Gardthausen (1903), 84 [Cairo].

Printed Catalogues of Manuscripts
T.D. Moschonas, *Catalogue of manuscripts of the Patriarchal Library of Alexandria*. Πατριαρχεῖον Ἀλεξανδρείας. Κατάλογοι τῆς πατριαρχικῆς βιβλιοθήκης. Τόμος Α'. Χειρόγραφα (Salt Lake City, 1965), [suppl. codd. 519-538; T.D. Moschonas, Πατριαρχεῖον Ἀλεξανδρείας. Κατάλογοι τῆς πατριαρχικῆς βιβλιοθήκης. Τόμος Α'. Χειρόγραφα (Alexandria, 1945), [with codd. 509-518]; N.S. Phirippides, Κατάλογος τῶν κωδίκων τῆς βιβλιοθήκης τοῦ Πατριαρχείου Ἀλεξανδρείας, in Ἐκκλησιαστικὸς Φάρος, 37 (1938), 225-240; 355-375; 445-464; 38 (1939), 74-88; 203-219; 338-357; 416-432; 39 (1940), 31-49; 183-199; 288-304; 434-440; 40 (1941), 111-128; 168-191; 355-374; 385-405; 41 (1942), 79-93 [codd. 1-380], and (completed by) T.D. Moschonas, in Ἐκκλησιαστικὸς Φάρος, 42 (1943), 289-304 [codd. 381-506]; G. Charitakis, Κατάλογος τῶν χρονολογημένων κωδίκων τῆς πατριαρχικῆς βιβλιοθήκης Καΐρου (Athens, 1927); P. van den Ven, "Inventaire sommaire des manuscrits grecs de la bibliothèque patriarcale du Caire", in *Le Muséon*, N.S. 15 (1914), [1-18?] 65-82; C. von Tischendorf, "Die Bibliothek des Sinaiklosters in Kairo", in *Wiener Jahrbücher der Literatur. Anzeigeblatt*, 112 (1845), 30-42 [description 45 codd.].

Manuscript Catalogue
A short catalogue of Germanos Maurommatis in 1895; cf. V. Gardthausen (Leipzig, 1903), 82: 'Alter Catalog der Patriarchalbibliothek zu Cairo: codex Vat. Ottob. 147'; A. Schneider, *Beiträge zur Kenntnis der griechisch-orthodoxen Kirche Ägyptens* (Dresden, 1874), 41-48 [copy of a manuscript catalogue of the year 1859]; first handwritten catalogue by Patriarch Parthenios II of Patmos (cf. Moschonas 1955).

References
The official website of the *Greek Orthodox Patriarchate of Alexandria & All Africa* (www.greekorthodox-alexandria.org); D. Burton-Christie, *Op. Cit.*, (New York and Oxford, 1993); D.J. Chitty, *Op. Cit*, (Crestwood, New York, 1966); T. Moschonas, "A Short History of the Library of the Greek Orthodox Patriarchate of Alexandria & All Africa", in *Bulletin of the Patriarchal Library* (Jan-June 1955) reprinted on the official web-site of the Patriarchate; P. van Cauwenbergh, *Étude sur les moines d'Egypte depuis le Concile de Chalcédoine jusqu'à l'invasion arabe* (Paris and Louvain, 1869-1914).

4.4 The Slavic, Romanian and Georgian Libraries, their Catalogues and Manuscripts

The Slavic speaking countries (Russia, Bulgaria, Serbia, Ukraine, Macedonia), Romania and Georgia, which are traditionally Orthodox, received Christianity from the Byzantine church. Since the 8th-9th centuries ties between the newly baptised countries and the mother church in Byzantium were close. Together with the Christian faith, these countries received the Byzantine Scriptures in the traditional codex forms of the Byzantine archetypes. They received the tradition of performing the Mysteries (the Sacraments) of the Byzantine church and the corresponding liturgical books, the writings of the Byzantine fathers, the books of the saints, influential ascetical works, the calendar of the ecclesiastical year and the cycles of the Great Feasts, the monastic traditions, the books of the canon law, iconography, church music, church architecture and many other institutions of art, science, education, and religion. Books were translated into Slavonic from the Byzantine Greek (the 9th century minuscule manuscripts) at an early stage, and in the 9th century also into Russian. Later emendations and new translations were also made from Greek.

> Greek manuscripts became known in Russia at the time of the acceptance of Christianity in the ninth century. Greek priests brought manuscripts with them to Russia and Russians acquired others during the course of their visits to the Holy Places. In Constantinople, on Mount Athos, and in Sinai Russians read and translated

---

[559] That is the Library of the Greek Orthodox Patriarchate of Alexandria and all Africa in Mancheya, Alexandria. The library was transferred to, and for a long time housed in Cairo (Kahira), from 997 A.D. until 1928, when it was brought back to Alexandria under Patriarch Meletios II Metaxakis. In 1947 a 3 volume catalogue was completed (see T. Moschonas "A Short History of the Library of the Greek Orthodox Patriarchate of Alexandria & All Africa", in *Bulletin of the Patriarchal Library*, (Jan-June 1955), comprising in Dec. 31 1955: 23.746 volumes, with 'departments of Greek manuscripts (530), rare editions (2000) and other editions, not necessarily Greek or Theological in content'.

[560] T. Moschonas, *Art. Cit.* (1955); but see also Richard/Olivier, *Op. Cit.* (Turnhout, 1995): 489 manuscripts.

Greek manuscripts. Evidence of this familiarity is provided not only by the translations themselves but also by the existence of the so-called 'Greek style' found in Russian manuscripts in the fifteenth and sixteenth centuries. In the seventeenth century Russian scribes imitated the script of documents received in Moscow from Athos and the Patriarch of Antioch.

E.E. Granstrem, "Greek Palaeography in Russia", in *Bulletin no 17 of the Institute of Classical Studies* (University of London, 1970), 125-126

In the 17th century the Muscovite monk Arseny Sukharov travelled to Athos and brought back to Moscow some 500 manuscripts, containing both classical and Byzantine texts.[561]
It is fully understandable that in Russia and also in the other Slavic countries, and Romania and Georgia, the libraries of monasteries, churches, Patriarchal/Synodal institutions and theological academies and schools collected and maintained Byzantine manuscripts and used them for translation, correction and academic study, as the basis of and parallel to their own manuscript tradition. The question of provenance of the Byzantine Greek manuscripts is, with regard to the Slavonic and Romanian collections, of special importance[562], as is the question for which reason they were brought to Russia or to the other Orthodox countries (for monasteries, churches, the holy synods, the theological academies).

A select but representative number of libraries in Russia, Ukraine, Bulgaria, Moldova, Romania and Georgia are presented below in more detail. The point of departure remains, in addition to a paragraph on the libraries, the places and repositories where the Byzantine Greek codices are presently maintained: at various locations in Moscow, St. Petersburg, Kiev, Odessa, Charkov, Sophia, Bucharest, Jassy and Tbilissi. Besides the Catalogue Entries to the Holdings, the referential works of P.K. Grimsted are useful: *Archives of Russia. A Directory and Bibliographic Guide to Holdings in Moscow and St. Petersburg* (New York and London, 2000), I: Part A. Bibliography of General Archival Reference Literature, A-7 'Greek Manuscripts', 38-39; and Idem, *Archives and Manuscripts Repositories in the USSR. Ukraine and Moldavia* (Princeton, 1988), t. I: General Bibliography and Institutional Directory, [C. 301-372]. Further: a General Bibliography to the libraries and catalogues can be found in Richard/Olivier, *Op. Cit.* (Turnhout, 1995), 'Ex-U. R. S. S.', 65-69; B.L. Fonkič, *Graeco-Russian Contacts from the Middle of the XVI Century up to the Beginning of the XVIII Century: The Greek Documents in Moscow Archives: Catalogue of Exhibition* (Moscow, 1991); B.L. Fonkič, "Греческие рукописи советских хранилищ", in *Studia Codicologica*, Ed. K. Treu (Berlin, 1977), 189-195; Z.G. Samodurova, 'Об изучении византийского рукописного наследия в СССР (1945-1971 гг.)', in *Actes du XIVe Congrès international des Études byzantines, (Bucharest, 6-12 septembre, 1971)*, Ed. M. Berza and E. Stănescu (Bucharest, 1976), t. III, 127-137; K. Treu, "Zu den neutestamentlichen Handschriften in der UdSSR", in *Forschungen und Fortschritte*, 38 (1964), 118-122; M. Richard, "Rapport sur une mission d'étude en U. R. S. S. (5 octobre – 3 novembre 1960), in *Bulletin d'information de l'Institut de Recherche et d'Histoire des Textes*, 10 (1961), 43-56; E.E. Granstrem, "Греческие рукописи в собраниях Советского Союза (дополнительные сведения)", in Византийский временник, 11 (1956), 285-291[563].

* * *

(1)   Moscow (Russia): Ecclesiastical, Public and National Institutions

Catalogue Entries to the Moscow Libraries
Grimsted (2000), II [Moscow]: H-1, G-1, H-17, H-23, H-33, H-26, G-3, B-2 [G-10, G-11]; Richard/Olivier (1995), 561-562; Aland [et al.] (1994), 475-476; Fonkič (1977), 192-194; Ehrhard (1937), xlv [Perria (1979), 95-97]; Rahlfs (1914), 141-148; Gregory (1908), 310-312; von Soden (1911), 63; Gardthausen (1903), 75-76.

The State Historical Museum: the Library and its Holdings

Государственный Исторический Музей. Отдел рукописей (State Historical Museum. Department of manuscripts)[564] [H-1]

[I.]	Музейское собрание рукописей	[17 codd.; (16)]
[II.]	Синодальное (Патриаршее) Собрание Рукописей	[514 codd.; (515)][565]

---

[561] E.E. Granstrem, "Greek Palaeography in Russia", in *Bulletin no 17 of the Institute of Classical Studies* (University of London, 1970), 126.

[562] It is curious that precisely in the Sovet period (ca 1920-1990), the time when the Orthodox (and the other Churches) were severely persecuted and monastic life nearly completely disturbed, the study of the manuscripts continued and even (in certain sense) flourished.

[563] Cf. V. Gardthausen, *Op. Cit.* (Leipzig, 1903), 'Russland', 75-77; From an 19th century Western point of view (out-dated but of some historical interest) see F. Vater, "Zur Kunde griechischer Hss. in Russland", in *Archiv für Philologie und Pädagogie*, 9 (1839), 5-49.

[564] The information and data of Richard/Olivier, *Op. Cit.* (Turnhout, 1995) and checked with other sources. Added in brackets are the estimated number of the holdings 1) Richard/Olivier; 2) Fonkič (1977).

[III]	Синодальное певчецкое	[2 codd.]
[IV.]	Собрание Рукописей Е. В. Барсова	[5 codd.; (5)]
[V.]	Собрание Рукописей А. И. Барятинского	[1 codex; (1)]
[VI.]	Собрание Рукописей Воскресенского Ново-Иерусалимского монастыря	[2 codd.; (2)]
[VII.]	Собрание Рукописей П. И. Севастьянова	[2 codd.; (1)]
[VIII.]	Собрание Рукописей А. С. Уварова	[2 codd.; (2)]
[IX.]	[Собрание Рукописей Успенского собора]	[- codd.]
[X.]	Собрание Рукописей А. И. Хлудова	[7 codd.]
[XI.]	Собрание Рукописей А. Д. Черткова	[1 cod.]
[XII.]	Собрание Рукописей П. И. Щукина	[1 cod.]
[XIII.]	Фрагменты (Fragments)	[3 codd.]

Estimated Total of Byzantine Greek manuscripts (ГИМ): 557 codices. (551 codd.) [VI-XVIII c.]

Printed Catalogues of Manuscripts

B.L. Fonkic and F.B. Poljakov, Греческие рукописи Московской Синодальной библиотеки. Палеографические, кодикологические и библиографические дополнения к каталогу архимандрита Владимира (Филантропова) (Moscow, 1993); F.G. Cereteli and S. Sobolevski, *Exempla codicum Graecorum litteris minusculis scriptorum annorumque notis instructorum*, Vol. I: Codices Mosquenses, (Moscow, 1911); Vol. II: Codices Petropolitani (Moscow, 1913); Archimandrite Vladimir (Filantropov), Систематическое описание рукописей Московской Синодальной (Патриаршей) библиотеки : Часть 1 : Рукописи греческие, (Moscow, 1894); Archimandrite Savva (Tichomirov), Палеографические снимки с греческих и славянских рукописей Московской Синодальной библиотеки VI-XVII века (*Specimina palaeographica codicum graecorum et slavonicorum bibliothecae Mosquensis Synodalis saec. vi.-xvii*) (Moscow, 1863); Archimandrite Savva (Tichomirov), Указатель для обозрения Московской Патриаршей (ныне Синодальной) ризницы и библиотеки (Moscow, 1855); C.F. Matthaei, *Accurata codicum Graecorum manuscriptorum Bibliothecarum Mosquensium Sanctissimae Synodi notitia et recensio* (Leipzig, 1805) [I. Bibliotheca Sanctissimae Synodi notitia et recensio, 1-260 (403 codd.); Bibliotheca Typographei synodalis, 261-336 (102 codd.) [Codices in folio, codices in quarto, codices in octavo]; the collections were united in 1823]; Idem, *Index codicum Graecorum Bibliothecarum Mosquensium* (St. Petersburg, 1780); Idem, *Notitia codicum manuscriptorum Graecorum Bibliothecarum* (Moscow, 1776).

The Russian State Library and its Holdings

Российская Государственная Библиотека. Отдел рукописей (The Russian State Library. Department of Manuscripts) [G-1]

[I.]	Собрание Рукописей О. М. Бодянского (Ф. 36)	[1 cod. (1)]
[II.]	Собрание Рукописей Генерального штаба (Ф. 68)	[1 cod. (1)]
[III.]	Собрание Рукописей В. И. Григоровича (Ф. 87)	[5 codd. (9)]
[IV.]	Собрани библиотеки Московской духовной академии (Ф. 173 I-IV.)	[51 codd. (64)][566]
	- Фундаментальное собрание библиотеки (Ф. 173 I.)	[27 codd. (31)]
	- Дополнительное собрание библиотеки (Ф. 173 II.)	[23 codd. (22)]
	- [по временному каталогу]	[[10 codd.]]
	- Собрани << Прочие >> библиотеки (Ф. 173 IV.)	[1 cod. (1)]
[V.]	Музейное собрание (Ф. 181)	[26 codd. (28)]
[VI.]	Собрание рукописей А. С. Норова (Ф. 201)	[15 codd. (15)]
[VII.]	Собрание рукописей В. Ф. Одоевского (Ф. 210)	[1 cod. (1)]
[VIII.]	Собрание рукописей Н. П. Румянцева (Ф. 256)	[1 cod. (1)]
[IX.]	Собрание рукописей П. И. Севастьянова (Ф. 270)	[77 codd. (189)]
[X.]	Собрание Троице-Сергиевой лавры. Собрание ризницы (Ф. 304)	[1 cod. (3)]
[XI.]	Собрание рукописей В. М. Ундольского (Ф. 310)	[8 codd. (8)]
[XII.]	Собрание рукописей Д. В. Разумовского (Ф. 379)	[13 codd. (14)]
[XIII.]	Собрание рукописей Е. И. Усова (Ф. 651)	[1 cod. (1)]

Estimated Total of Byzantine Greek manuscripts (ГИМ): 202 codices. (344 codd.) [VI-XIX c.]

Printed Catalogues of Manuscripts

K.K. Papoulidis, "Συνοπτικὴ ἀναγραφὴ ἑλληνικῶν χειρογράφων καὶ ἐγγράφων τῆς Βιβλιοθήκης Lenin τῆς Μόσχας, in Θεολογία, 52 (1981), 481-499; A. Každan, Unpublished Inventory of the Библиотеки им. В.И. Ленина [= Российская Государственная Библиотека]; A. Každan, "Греческие рукописи библиотеки им. В. И. Ленина", in Вопросы Истории, 10 (1946), 107-108 [179 codd. and 132 frgm, IX-XIX c.]; A. Viktorov, Московский Публичный и Румянцевский Музей. Собрание рукописей П. И. Севастьянова (Moscow, 1881), 1-33 [codd. 1-77].

The Other Libraries and their Holdings

[H-17]	Государственная Оружейная палата (Музеи Московского Кремля)	[2 codd.]
[H-23]	Государственная Третьяковская Галерея	[1 cod.]
[H-33]	Государственный Литературный Музей	[1 cod.]
[H-26]	Государственный Музей изобразительных искусств А. С. Пушкина. Отдел Востока	[5 codd.]
[G-3]	Научная библиотека им. А. М. Горького Московского государственного университета	[7 codd.]
[B-2]	Российский Государственный Архив Древних Актов	[? 53 codd.]
	[I.] (Ф. 181)	[28 codd.]

---

[565] See P.K. Grimsted, *Archives of Russia. A Directory and Bibliographic Guide to Holdings in Moscow and St. Petersburg* (New York and London, 2000), II: G-10, 714. Since 1987 the Patriarchal (Synodal) Library was reinstalled (it was closed in 1917 and the holdings were relocated to the State Historical Museum).

[566] See P.K. Grimsted, *Op. Cit.* (New York and London, 2000), II: G-11, 715-717.

[II.]   (Ф. 201)   [2 codd.]
[III.] (Ф. 1607 [X. Ф. Маттеи)   [23 codd.]

Estimated Total of Byzantine Greek manuscripts (Moscow): 881 codices. [557 + 202 + 122]

* * *

(2)   Sergiev Posad: Троице Сергиева Лавра

Государственный Историко-художественный Музей [1 cod. provenance: Троице Сергиева Лавра]
[4 codd. are of Lavra provenance, see above: 3 codd. in РГБ   Ф. 304/III,   Ф. 173 and and 1 cod. in ГТГ]

Московская Духовная Академия [1 cod.] [See above: РГБ   Ф. 173 I-IV]

* * *

(3)   St. Petersburg (Russia): Ecclesiastical, Public and National Institutions

Catalogue Entries to the Holdings
Grimsted (2000), II: G-15, G-16; Richard/Olivier (1995), 711-732; Aland [et al.] (1994), 494-496; Fonkič (1977), 190-192; Treu, *Griechischen Handschriften des NT/UdSSR* (1966),15-230; Richard, "Rapport Mission" (1961), 51-55; Ehrhard (1937), xlviii-xlix [Perria (1979), 80-82]; Rahlfs (1914), 220-231; Gregory (1908), 312-315; von Soden (1911), 63-64; Gardthausen (1903), 77.

Chronological Catalogue of Petersburg holdings
E.E. Granstrem, "Каталог греческих рукописей ленинградских хранилищ". 1. Рукописей IV-IX веков, in Византийский временник, 16 (1959), 216-243 [No 1-112]; 2. Рукописей X веков, in *Op. Cit.*, 18 (1961), 254-274 [No 113-184]; 3. Рукописей XI веков, in *Op. Cit.*, 19 (1961), 194-239 [No 185-297]; 4. Рукописей XII веков, in *Op. Cit.*, 23 (1963), 166-204 [No 298-426]; 5. Рукописей XIII веков, in *Op. Cit.*, 24 (1964), 166-197 [No 427-455]; *Op. Cit.*, 25 (1964), 184-211 [No 456-512]; 6. Рукописей XIV веков, in *Op. Cit.*, 27 (1967), 273-294 [No 513-556]; *Op. Cit.*, 28 (1968), 238-255 [No 557-603]; 7. Рукописей XV веков, *Op. Cit.*, 31 (1971), 132-144 [No 605-623]; 8. Добавления поправки и указатели, *Op. Cit.*, 32 (1971), 109-130 [No 623a-636 and indices].

The Russian National Library and its Holdings

Российская Национальная Библиотека [G-15]
[I.]   Собрание Греческих Рукописей   [? 713 codd.]
[II.]   Собрание Новгородской духовной семинарии   [? 13 codd.]
[III.] Собрание Общества любителей древней письменности   [15 codd.]
[IV.] Собрание рукописей И. В. Помяловского   [1 cod.]
[V.]   Собрание Русского археологического общества   [1 cod.]
[VI.] Собрание Санкт-Петербургской Духовной Академии   [? 133 codd.]
        - Александро-Невская Лавра   [Ф. I]   [? 95 codd.]
        - Софийская библиотека (Novgorod) [Ф. II]   [8 codd.]
        - Кирилло-Велозерская библиотека [Ф. III]   [? codd.]
        - New Acquisitions   [Ф. IV]   [? codd.]
[VII.] Прочие собрания   [? codd.]

Estimated Total of Byzantine Greek manuscripts: 1.025 codices.[567]

Printed Catalogues of Manuscripts
E.E. Granstrem, "Каталог греческих рукописей ленинградских хранилищ", 8. Добавления поправки и указатели, in Византийский временник, 32 (1971), 126-129 [No 1-636]; Descriptions of N°s 180-712 in Отчетъ Императорской Публичной библиотеки за 1871 годъ (St. Petersburg, 1872-1917) and no 713 in Сборник (1920); E. de Muralt, *Catalogue des manuscripts grecs de la Bibliothèque impériale publique* (St. Petersburg, 1864) [No 1-179]; E. De Muralt, *Catalogus codicum Bibliothecae Imperialis Publicae graecorum et latinorum*. Fasc. 1: Codices graeci. I. Ecclesiastici. II. Profani (St. Petersburg, 1840) [43 codd.].

The Library of the Russian Academy of Science and its holdings

Российская Академия Наук. Библиотека [G-16]
[I.]   Собрание Археографической комиссии   [1 cod.]
[II.]   Собрание А. А. Дмитриевского   [36 codd.]
[III.] Собрание иностранных рукописей   [48 codd.]
[IV.] Собрание Н. К. Никольского   [3 codd.]

---

[567] Richard/Olivier, *Op. Cit.* (Turnhout, 1995), 718: 'Le nombre exact des mss grecs est difficile à établir car l'inventaire consultable sur place mêle mss et documents; il porte 1.044 numéros, mais 24 mss ont été remis à l Pologne'; Cf. Fonkič, *Art. Cit.* (Berlin, 1977), 191: 1.025 (1020 + 5) codd. In E. Granstrem, *Art. Cit.* (1971), Index, 126-130: on the basis of 15 different holdings, are described N°s 1-636, of which 595 codd. are registered in the Index, listed according to the numberings of the original holdings; in this Index with regard to the РНБ: Собрание Греческих Рукописей, 126-129, mention is made of the library numbering: греч. 2-848, of which 474 codd actually were selected for description in the Granstrem catalogue. Between the years 1914-1938 more than 300 codd. were acquired, see Richard/Olivier, *Op. Cit.* (Turnhout, 1995), 717-718. Between the years 1872-1917, in 21 contributions of Отчетъ and 1 in Сборник (1920), the codd. 180-713 were described, continuing de Muralt (1864): codd. 1-179. Earlier de Muralt set up the catalogue in 1840 with 43 codd.

| [V.] | Собрание Русского археологического института в Константинополе [see Istanbul] | [189 codd.] |
| [VI.] | Собрание И. И. Срезневского | [2 codd.] |

Estimated Total of Byzantine Greek manuscripts: 287 codices.[568]

Printed Catalogues of Manuscripts
I.N. Lebedeva, Описание Рукописей отдела Библиотеки Академии наук СССР (Leningrad, 1973).
E.E. Granstrem, "Греческие рукописи Библиотеки Академии наук СССР", in Академии наук СССР. Библиотека. Исторический очерк и обзор фондов Рукописного отдела Библиотеки Академии наук, t. II: XIX-XX века (Moscow-Leningrad, 1958), 272-284.

The Other Libraries and their Holdings

[E-20]	Архив Российской Академии Наук	[? 2 codd.]
[H-8]	Государственный Эрмитаж. Отдел искусства Ближнего Востока	[2 codd.]
[E-28]	Институт русской литературы Российской Академии Наук (Пушкинский Дом)	[1 cod.]
	[Рукописный отдел Института народов Азии Академии наук СССР. фонд арабской графики ?]	[[3 codd.]]
[E-55]	Санкт-Петербургский государственный университет Научная библиотека	[24 codd.]
[E-24]	Санкт-Петербургский Филиал Института Российской истории Российской Академии Наук	[29 codd.]
[D-13]	Центральный государственный исторический архив [СССР ?]	[7 codd.]

Estimated Total of Byzantine Greek manuscripts (all Petersburg holdings): 1.380 codices.[569]

Specialised catalogues
E.V. Gertsman (1996) in Gr.; J.B. Thibaut.

References
P.K. Grimsted, *Op. Cit.* (New York and London, 2000), I. A-7, B-2, II, F-12, G-1, G-2, G-10, G-11, H-1, H-17, H-23, H-33, [Moscow] and II. G-15, G-16, G-26, H-88 [St. Petersburg]; B.L. Fonkič, *Op. Cit.* (Berlin, 1977), 191; M.A. Schatkin, 'Byzantine Greek Manuscripts in Leningrad – The Granstrem Catalog', in *Studia codicologica*, Ed. K. Treu (Berlin, 1977), 413-423; E.E. Granstrem, "Греческие рукописи в собраниях Советского Союза (дополнительные сведения)", in Византийский временник, 11 (1956), 192-207; B. Dudik, "Historische Forschungen in der Kaiserliche öffentliche Bibliothek zu St. Petersburg", in *Sitzungs Berichte der Wiener Akademie*, 95, phil.-hist. Cl. (1879), 329-382.

* * *

(4) Kiev (Ukraine): Ecclesiastical, Public and National Institutions

Catalogue Entries to the Holdings
Grimsted (1988), C. 301-372; Richard/Olivier (1995), 440-449; Aland [et al.] (1994), 467; Fonkič (1977), 190; Ehrhard (1937), - [Perria (1979), -]; Rahlfs (1914), 88-89; Gregory (1908), 310; von Soden (1911), 62; Gardthausen (1903), 75.

The V. Vernads'kyi National Library of Ukraine: the Manuscript Institute

Національна Бібліотека України імені В. І. Вернадського: Інститут рукопису

[I.]	Літературні матеріали (Ф. I)	4 [I] 1 [II] [5 codd.]
[II.]	Одеське товариство історії та старожитностей (Ф. V)	10 [I] 43 [II] [53 codd.]
[III.]	Архів Синоду (Ф. XIII)	6 [II] 56 [III] [62 codd.]
[IV.]	Львівська греко-католицька митрополича консисторія (Ф. XVIII)	3 [II] [3 codd.]
[V.]	Колекція грецьких рукописів (Ф. 72)	28 [I] 35 [II] [63 codd.]
[VI.]	Київська духовна академія (Ф. 72)	1 [II] [1 cod.]
[VII.]	Троїцькі Платон Олексійович і Петро (Ф. 193)	1 [I] 33 [II] [34 codd.]
[VIII.]	Київська духовна консисторія (Ф. 232)	26 [II] [26 codd.]
[IX.]	Церковно-археологічнний музей при Київській духовній академії (Ф. 301)	89 [I] 6 [II] [95 codd.]
[X.]	Київська духовна семінарія (Ф. 305)	3 [I] [3 codd.]
[XI.]	Києво-Печерська Лавра (Ф. 306)	2 [II] [2 codd.]
[XII.]	Київський Михайлівський Золотоверхий монастир (Ф. 307)	1 [I] [1 cod.]
[XIII.]	Рукописи бібліотеки Історично-Філологічного інституту князя Безбородька в Ніжині (Ф. 310)	7 [I] [7 codd.]
[XIV.]	Бібліотека Києво-Софійського собору (Ф. 312)	5 [I] [5 codd.]
[XV.]	Відділ стародруків та рідкісних видань - Фонд Гражданського друку	1 [I] [1 cod.]

Центральний державний архів України в м. Києві

---

[568] P.K. Grimsted, *Op. Cit.* (New York and London, 2000), II, 754; Fonkič, *Art. Cit.* (Berlin, 1977), 191. However, Richard/Olivier, *Op. Cit.* (Turnhout, 1995), 713-717 indicates together 279 manuscripts.

[569] P.K. Grimsted, *Op. Cit.* (New York and London, 2000), II, 725 [Quotation]. In St. Petersburg are kept the largest collections of Byzantine Greek manuscripts in Russia. There are approximately 1000 items of Greek manuscripts distributed over different libraries, brought together from ancient monasteries and other institutions of the Russian Orthodox Church into libraries of the State, the Academy of Sciences and University Institutes. However, only the Russian National Library comprises 1.025 codd.. The total number is somewhat higher.

[I.]   Колекція рукописів зісторії науки, літератури та мистецтва (1568-1918) (Ф. 228)   1 [I] [1 cod.]
[II.] Архів Коша Запорізької Січі (Ф. 229)   4 [II] [4 codd.]

Національний істрико-культурний заповідник << Киево-Печерська Лавра >> 3 [I] [3 codd.]

[See Concordance Richard-Olivier // I. Ševčenko, I. Chernukhin, and N. Cherkas'ka]

Національна Бібліотека України імені В. І. Вернадського
I :   Ф. 301 [IX.]   [a great deal of this holding comes from A. Kapustin]
II: Ф. 305 [X.]
III: Ф. 306 [XI.]
IV: Ф. 307 [XII.]
V: Ф. 312 [XIV.]
VI: Ф. 310 [XIII.]
VII: Ф. V   [II.]
VIII: Ф. I   [I.]
IX: Ф. 7   [V., VI.]
-       Ф. XIII [III.]
-       Ф. XVIII [IV.]
-       Ф. 193 [VII.]
-       Ф. 232 [VIII.]
-       Фонд Гражданського друку

Центральний державний архів України в м. Києві
-       Ф. 228 [I.]
-       Ф. 229 [II.]

Національний істрико-культурний заповідник << Киево-Печерська Лавра
-       Ф. – [I.]

Estimated Total of Byzantine Greek manuscripts: 154 codices. [VI-XIX c.]

Printed Catalogues of Manuscripts
I. Ševčenko, I. Chernukhin, and N. Cherkas'ka, Грецькі рукописи у зібраннях Києва. Каталог, (Kiev-Washington, 2000); B.L. Fonkič, "The Greek Manuscripts of A. N. Murav'ev, in *Modern Greek Studies Yearbook*, 4 (1988), 235-254; B.L. Fonkic, "Les manuscrits grecs d'Antonin Kapustin [annexe: Inventaire des manuscrits grecs d'Antonin Kapustin", in *Scriptorium*, 38 (1984), 254-271 [265-271]; A. Lebedev, Рукописы Церковно-Археологическаго Музея Императорской Киевской Духовной Академии, t. I (Saratov, 1916); N.I. Petrov, Указатель Церковно-археологическаго музея при Киевской Духовной Академии, 2nd ed. (Kiev, 1897); N.I. Petrov, Описание рукописей собрании, находящихся в городе Киеве, vols. I-III (Kiev, 1891-1904); N.I. Petrov, Описание рукописей Церковно-археологическаго музея при Киевской Духовной Академии, vols. I-III (Kiev, 1875, 1877, 1879);

References
K.E. Chernukhin, Грецькі рукописи у зібраннях Києва (Kiev, 2000); P.K. Grimsted, *Op. Cit*, t. I: General Bibliography and Institutional Directory (Princeton, 1988) [C. 301-372];

* * *

(5)   Odessa (Ukraine): Ecclesiastical, Public and National Institutions

Catalogue Entries to the Holdings
Grimsted (1988); Richard/Olivier (1995), 596-600; Aland [et al.] (1994), 478; Fonkič (1977), 194; Ehrhard (1937), - [Perria (1979), -]; Rahlfs (1914), - ; Gregory (1908), 312; von Soden (1911), - ; Gardthausen (1903), 75.

The Libraries and their Holdings
Одеська державна наукова Библиотека имени О. М. Горького
         I.   Собрание В. И. Григоровича   [16 codd.]
         II. Рукописи Греческого коммерческого училища в Одессе   [4 codd.]
         III. Рукописи А.С. Стурдзы   [2 codd.]
         IV. Рукописи, поступившие от различных владельцев, и неизвестного происхождения   [13 codd.]

Одесский Государственный историко-краеведческий   [1 cod.]

Printed Catalogues of Manuscripts
B.L. Fonkič, "Греческие рукописи Одессы" , in Византийский временник, 39 (1978), 184-200; 282-283 and 28 ill.; *Ibid.*, 40 (1979), 172-185 and 32 ill.; *Ibid.* 43 (1982), 98-101 and 6 ill.

Estimated Total of Byzantine Greek manuscripts: 36 codices.

* * *

(6)   Sofia (Bulgaria): Ecclesiastical, Public and National Institutions

Catalogue Entries to the Holdings
Richard/Olivier (1995), 758-763; Aland [et al.] (1994), 492-493; Stojanov (1973), 'Гръцки ръкописи'; Ehrhard (1937), liv-lv [Perria (1979), 133]; Rahlfs (1914), - ; Gregory (1908), - ; von Soden (1911), - ; Gardthausen (1903), - .

The St. Cyril and Methodius National Library and its Holding[570]

    Народна Библиотека "Св. Св. Кирил и Методий"[571]   [159 codd.]

The Institute for Church History

    Институт за църковна история[572]   [206 codd.]

The Ivan Dujčev Research Centre for Slavo-Byzantine Studies at the St. Kliment Ohridski University of Sofia

    Научен център за славяно-византийски проучвания "Иван Дуйчев"
    към Софийския Университет "Климент Охридски"   [451 codd.]

Printed Catalogues of Manuscripts
A. Džurova, K. Stančev, V. Atsalos, V. Katsaros, *"Checklist" de la collection de manuscrits grecs conservé au Centre de recherches slavo-byzantines "Ivan Dujčev" auprès de l'Université "Clément d'Óhrid" de Sofia* (Thessaloniki, 1994)[573]; M. Stojanov, Опис на Гръцките други чуждоезични ръкописи в Народна Библиотека "Св. Кирил и Методий" в София. *Codices graeci manuscripti Bibliothecae "Cyrilli et Methodii" Serdiciensis*, (Sofia, 1973); B. Conev [et al.], Описъ на ржкописитѣ и старопечатнитѣ книги на Народната Библиотека въ София, Vol. I (Sofia, 1910), 511-516 [Suppl. "Non Slavonic MSS."].

Estimated Total of Byzantine Greek manuscripts (holdings in Sofia): 816 codices. [X-XIX c.]

References
Official web-site of St. Cyril and Methodius National Library: 'Collection of Slavonic and Foreign Language Manuscripts', (www.nationallibrary.bg/slavezryk-en.html); B. Atsalos, B. Katsaros, Ch. Papastathis (Eds.), *Actes de la Table Ronde. << Principes et méthodes du cataloguage des manuscrits grecs de la collection du Centre Dujčev >>, (Sofia 21-23 Août 1990)* (Thessaloniki, 1992); A. Džurova, "Les manuscrits grecs du Centre Ivan Dujčev. Notes préliminaires", in *Erytheia*, 13 (1992), 117-157; M. Stojanov, 'Greek Manuscripts in the Bulgarian national Library "Cyril and Methodius" [also in Bulg.], in *Op. Cit.* (Sofia, 1973), 13-17 [very instructive concerning the provenance of the codices];

* * *

(7)   Ochrid (Macedonia): Ecclesiastical, Public and National Institutions

Catalogue Entries to the Holdings
Richard/Olivier (1995), 600-601; Aland [et al.] (1994), 478; Ehrhard (1937), xlvi [Perria (1979), 102]; Rahlfs (1914), - ; Gregory (1908), - ; von Soden (1911), - ; Gardthausen (1903), 85.

The Library of "St. Clement" of the National Museum

    Народен Музеj (Библиотека "Св. Климента")   [93 codd.]

Printed Catalogues of Manuscripts
F. Halkin, "Manuscrits byzantins d'Ochrida en Macédoine Yougoslave", in *Analecta Bollandiana*, 80 (1962), 5-21; V. Mošin, "Les manuscrits du Musée national d'Ochrida", in *Musée national d'Ohrid. Recueil de travaux. Édition spécial publié à l'occasion du Xe anniversaire de la fondation du Musée et dedié au XIIe Congrès international des études byzantines* (Ohrid, 1961), 163-243 [89 codd.]; Ohrid list, "Списокъ рукописей находящихся въ библиотекѣ "Св. Климента" въ Охрид", in Извѣстія Русскаго Археологическаго Института въ Константинополѣ, 6 (1900), 466-470 [codd.21-111].

---

[570] See the introductory note in the article 'Collection of Slavonic and Foreign Language Manuscripts (Official web-site): 'The Collection of Greek manuscripts, most of which were created for liturgical purposes, reflect the relations of Bulgarians with the Greek Patriarchate in Constantinople under whose jurisdiction the Bulgarian lands were during the time of Ottoman domination. However few, they follow the cultural traditions of Byzantium. The data about the origin of the Greek manuscripts in the Library are very scant. Most of them were written by Bulgarians and were donated or purchased from different regions of Bulgaria (Arbanasi, Bachkovo monstery, Varna, Pomorie, Sozopol etc.). There are also some manuscripts that originate from the monasteries on Mount Athos – Vatopedi, Chilandar, Zograph etc., where Bulgarian monks have lived'. For more details, cf. Stojanov, *Op. Cit.* (Sofia, 1973), 'Greek Manuscripts in the Bulgarian national Lirary "Cyril and Methodius".

[571] See Offical web-site: 'Part of the Greek manuscripts in the collection was in Ochrid from where they were brought to the Library by the enlightened public figure Eftim Sprostranov'.

[572] This collection is regrouped of two ancient holdings: the Централен църковен историко-археологически Музей and the Духовна Академия. Cf. Richard/Olivier, *Op. Cit.* (Turnhout, 1995) 758. Provenance: monasteries of Bačkovo and Xanthi.

[573] See esp. 'Appendices V-VIII: *Provenance des manuscrits grecs du centre Dujčev; Manuscrits grecs du centre Dujčevdont la provenance est inconnue; Manuscrits grecs du centre Dujčev provenant du monastère de Kosinitza; Manuscrits grecs du centre Dujčev provenant du monastère de Saint Jean Prodrome.*

References
L. Petrova, "За потеклото на Музејската библиотека во Охрид", in Лихнид. Зборник на трудови, 5 (1983), 220-227; *Blessed Paisius Velichkovsky. The Life and Ascetic Labors of Our Father, Elder Paisius, Archimandrite of the Holy Moldavian Monasteries of Niamets and Sekoul. Optina Version*, Ed. Schema-monk Metrophanes (Platina, Cal., 1976).

* * *

(8)   Bucharest (Romania): Ecclesiastical, Public and National Institutions

Catalogue Entries to the Holdings
Richard/Olivier (1995), 56-58 [România], 182-187; Aland [et al.] (1994), 454; Ehrhard (1937), xxx [Perria (1979), 49]; Rahlfs (1914), 37; Gregory (1908), - ; von Soden (1911), - ; Gardthausen (1903), 85.

The Libraries and their Holdings

Biblioteca Academiei Române	[1.566 codd.][574]
Biblioteca Naţională	[? 7 codd.]
Biblioteca Palatului Patriarhal	[? 4 codd.]
Biblioteca Sf. Sinod	[? 24 codd.]
Biblioteca Uniunii Compozitorilor - G. Breazul	[? 8 codd.]
Comisiunii Monumentelor Istorice	[1 codd.]
Directia Generala a Arhivelor Statului	[? 2 codd.]
Muzeul de Artă Religioasă	[- codd.]
Muzeul Naţional de Artă	[11 codd.]
[Seminarul Central → Biblioteca Academiei Române]	[- codd.]

Estimated Total of Byzantine Greek manuscripts: 1.623 codices.

Printed Catalogues of Manuscripts
D. Barbu, *Manuscrise bizantine în colecţii România* (Bucharest, 1984), [1523 codd.]; N. Camariano, *Biblioteca Academiei Române. Catalogul manuscriptelor greceşti*, Vol. II. (Bucharest, 1940), [codd. 831-1066]; C. Litzica, *Biblioteca Academiei Române. Catalogul manuscriptelor greceşti* (Bucharest, 1909), [codd.1-830].

Old Published Catalogue of Romanian Holdings [575]
C. Erbiceanu, in *Revista Teologica*, 3 (1885-1886).

References
C. Karanasios, "Recherche über die griechischen Handschriften in Rumänien", in *Balkan Studies*, 34 (1993), 5-16 [1566 codd.]; A. Elian, "Manuscrisele greceşti din Biblioteca Academiei", in *Studii şi cercetări de documentare şi bibliologie*, 9 (1967), 271-276 and 3 pll. [1490 codd.].

* * *

(9)   Jassy (Romania): Ecclesiastical, Public and National Institutions

Catalogue Entries to the Holdings
Richard/Olivier (1995), 56-58 [România], 362-365; Aland [et al.] (1994), 463; Ehrhard (1937), xxxv [Perria (1979), 74]; Rahlfs (1914), - ; Gregory (1908), 309; von Soden (1911), - ; Gardthausen (1903), - .

The Libraries and their holdings

Archivele Statului	[40 codd.]
Biblioteca Centrală Universitară << Mihai Eminescu >>	[? 110 codd.]
Mitropolia Moldovei şi Sucevei	[? 20 codd.]

Estimated Total of Byzantine Greek manuscripts: 170 codices.[576]

* * *

(10)   Tbilisi (Georgia): Ecclesiastical, Public and National Institutions

Catalogue Entries to the Holdings
Richard/Olivier (1995), 776-777; Aland [et al.] (1994), 497; Ehrhard (1937), - [Perria (1979), -]; Rahlfs (1914), - ; Gregory (1908), - ; von Soden (1911), - ; Gardthausen (1903), - .

---

[574] The official web-site of the Romanian Academy Library gives the number of 1.566 codices, but without catalogue information. In the same Library are: 6000 Romanian manuscripts, 860 Slavonic, 420 Oriental and 1000 Latin manuscripts.

[575] See Rahlfs (1914), 281.

[576] See Richard/Olivier (1995), 363, referring to Voicu (1969): 'près de 110 mss'. But cf. the critical remark concerning the number of 84 mss in Dossios (1902). See Rahlfs (1914), 281.

[576] See Richard/Olivier (1995).

The Library and their Holdings

Институт рукописей имени К.С. Кекелидзе Академии Наук Грузинской [ССР ?][30 codd.]

Printed Catalogues of Manuscripts
Richard/Olivier (1995), 776-777

4.5 Conclusion

This chapter was intended to conduct some groundwork for the development of a future catalogue, since for the reorganisation of the manuscripts, one must revisit the local catalogues to find the fundamental, necessary information that is missing for our purpose from the specialised catalogues (Aland, Rahlfs, Ehrhard…).
We have attempted to present the places of origin of the Byzantine manuscripts. These locations are important to show how the Byzantine libraries were originally directly linked to the church and/or monastery, thus implying their liturgical proximity. The majority of the extant manuscripts are still to be found in the Eastern libraries.

Chapter 5

The Contours of a Codico-Liturgical Model of Classification

The codico-liturgical model of classification is, in fact, an umbrella model, that is to say, it embraces all codex types of the Byzantine manuscripts, which are connected with the liturgical practice and calendar system of the Byzantine church. They are interdependent, which we assume from their liturgical function. This we can see from: 1) the codex *forms* themselves (lectionaries, homiletic text books); 2) the liturgical-patristic apparatus in the text and commentary manuscripts (lectionary equipment); 3) the biblical texts, which are included in the liturgical-ceremonial manuscripts (Euchologion, Horologion, Triodion etc.); 4) the homiletic and ascetical text components of the liturgical-ceremonial manuscripts. For those manuscripts where the liturgical function is less visible at first sight (text and commentary manuscripts without lectionary equipment; catecheses; practical and ascetical texts; biblical implications of Byzantine worship, its forms and rituals), we can still ascertain that they function in a broader sense within the same liturgical context.

The *Inner Cohesion Between the Bible and the Fathers in Byzantine Tradition*, as the title of this thesis reads, implies that there is a material connection (explicit evidence) between the biblical and patristic codices, which becomes visible when the manuscripts are "re-assessed" in their original liturgical environment, as well as an immaterial connection (implicit evidence) seen from those codices that express their liturgical function indirectly.

5.1 The setting up of a *Catalogue of Byzantine Manuscripts*

The aim of a *Catalogue of Byzantine Manuscripts* (further: the *Catalogue*) is to present *concrete* evidence for the thesis of inner cohesion between the categories of manuscripts with which we are concerned, namely biblical, patristic and liturgical codices. Behind the organisation of the proposed *Catalogue* lies the fundamental concept that the codex forms of the books and their content were compiled in such a way, that they were practical as well as appropriate for use in the churches and monasteries. From the codices themselves we can induce, beside the beauty of scribal art (the aesthetical factor), also the main purpose of the Byzantine scribes (compilers as well as commentators), which directed their editing activities, as they organised and reorganised the available theological, biblical and ascetical materials. An objective, *codicological* approach is required when revisiting the handwritten sources, directed towards the individual codices and the codex-formations in which they were transmitted to us.

> There can be no single ideal method for studying all these different manuscripts, nor can one person hope to know them all. The best approach must be to select material on some practical basis. The first step beyond the monographic treatment of a single book is to isolate a significant group.
>
> J. Lowden, *Illuminated Prophet Books. A Study of Byzantine Manuscripts of the Major and Minor Prophets* (University Park and London, 1988), 1

Our starting point is that all the Byzantine manuscripts should be revisited according to a codicological approach. This means that we want to look at:

1) the way that texts / books are *grouped* within a codex (codex-formation);
2) the exact contents of the codex (including commentary matters, lectionary equipment, added lists of lessons, material of a patristic, liturgical or hagiographical nature);
3) the form in which books are included in the codex (e.g. an Evangelion codex form);

Furthermore, we advocate that:

1) there are no pre-determined textuological criteria and/or preferences, which means that there is - at forehand - no principal demarcation line between: a) text manuscripts; b) lectionary manuscripts; and c)

commentary manuscripts (Von Soden a] and c] and Rahlfs a], b] and c]),[577] because such a principle of division did not exist in Byzantine manuscript tradition itself;

2) the actual Byzantine terminology of the manuscripts is re-appraised and used.

In general, such an endeavour should return the codices to their original, liturgical place in biblical and patristic textual history. Criticism voiced above on essential aspects of the present classifications must be transformed into new productive paradigms.

5.2 The Proposed Classification of the Byzantine Manuscripts

5.2.1 The procedure of regrouping the codices

The biblical codices are commonly divided into two main groups, that of the NT [+ comm] codices established by Gregory/Aland [Group I] and the OT [+ comm.] codices by Rahlfs [Group II]. A third group is the much neglected intermediary group of codices, in which NT and OT books and texts are combined [Group III]. Another quite unexplored group of manuscripts is that in which liturgical materials are combined with biblical and patristic texts [Group IV]. A fifth group contains the liturgical-ceremonial codices [Group V]. We then still have the as yet completely isolated group of homiletic commentary manuscripts (established by Ehrhard), which in fact belong to groups I and II.
Three further groups compete the picture: liturgical-hymnographical codices [Group VI]; liturgical-hagiographical codices [Group VII]; and liturgical/ascetical codices [Group VIII].

Groups I-II are subdivided into: 1) the lectionary manuscripts; 2) the textual manuscripts; and 3) the commentary manuscripts (which can again be sub-divided into several forms of commentary manuscripts - composed by one father, compiled from the works of many fathers, or anonymous compilations). This threefold principle of manuscript typology can also, albeit less clearly, be observed in the other distinguished groups (III-VIII).

In our structure for a *Catalogue*, we place the codex type of lectionary manuscripts (e.g. Evangelion, Apostolos, Psalterion and Prophetologion [today incorporated in the Triodion, Pentekostarion and Menaia]) first, since both the codex forms as well as the lectionary texts are considered to be of a most ancient and stable character[578], explicitly liturgical in origin and thus, one may rightfully conjecture, preserving an eminent codicological and textual condition[579], maintained by its longstanding role in the Byzantine Liturgy performed in the Eastern Orthodox Churches[580], which is still valid today.
What complicates the matter, however, is that there is no sharp demarcation line between the groups, as we saw earlier. The same applies to the text and lectionary manuscripts. The so-called text codices stem from the same period (IX-XVI c.) and approximately consist of an equal number of manuscripts as the lectionaries. They are theoretically considered to be older, as the lectionaries were derived from them. The individual texts were brought together in codex forms at a very early stage already. Slowly these codex forms acquired general acceptance. Ancient examples of this are, hypothetically, such 'proto-codex' formations as the proto-Psalterion, the proto-Prophetologion, proto-Evangelion and proto-Apostolos codex forms. A *chronological* point of view, however, an overtly quantitative argument, is ever more considered to be insufficient, and even invalid when it comes to determining the reliability or quality of the biblical text. This is true for both the NT and OT manuscripts.

---

[577] A. Rahlfs, *Op. Cit.* (Berlin, 1914), XI-XII, 'Daß die Catenenhss. mit aufgenommen werden mußten, versteht sich eigentlich von selbst. Sie sind im Grunde doch nur Bibelhss. mit hinzugefügten Erklärungen der Kirchenväter. (...) ist es am praktischten, zwischen Catenenhss. und einfachen Bibelhss. keine Scheidelinie zu ziehen'. With regard to the 'Lektionaren', see page XIII and XX.

[578] C.R. Gregory, *Textkritik des Neuen Testamentes*, I (Leipzig, 1900), 327-329, esp. 329, 'Deswegen, sowohl theoretisch, wie auch durch einige Beispiele praktisch, geleitet, erwarte ich, dass viele der Lesebücher wertvolles Zeugnis ablegen werden nicht für den jüngeren sondern für den älteren Text'.

[579] C.D. Osburn, 'The Greek Lectionaries of the New Testament', in *The Text of the New Testament in Contemporary Research. Essays on the Status Quaestionis* (Grand Rapids, Mich., 1995), 61, 'Evidence from the Greek lectionaries, however, is vital in tracing the history of the transmission of the text of the NT etc.'.

[580] F.H.A. Scrivener, *A Plain Introduction to the Criticism of the New Testament for the Use of Biblical Students* (London, 1894), 75: 'The peculiar arrangement of Lectionaries renders them very unfit for the hasty, partial, cursory collation which has befallen too many manuscripts of the other class [minuscules: Ed.], and this circumstance, joined with the irksomeness of using Service-books never familiar to the habits even of scholars in this part of Europe, has caused these documents to be so little consulted, that the contents of the very best and oldest among them have until recently been little known'. Cf. p. 327.

5.2.2 The main structure of the proposed *Catalogue*

In our proposed structure, then, the extant manuscripts are divided over eight main groups. In effect, more groups can be identified[581] (see chapter 2), but we here limit ourselves to these eight groups, since these contain, or are closely related to the biblical text in the context of our liturgical hypothesis.

Group I.	Byzantine Biblical Codices (NT)
	A. Lectionary; B. Text. C. Commentary codices
Group II.	Byzantine Biblical Codices (OT)
	A. Lectionary; B. Text. C. Commentary codices
Group III.	Byzantine Composite Codices (OT/NT)
Group IV.	Byzantine Composite Codices (Bibl/Lit)
Group V.	Byzantine Liturgical/Ceremonial Codices (Lit/Cer)
Group VI.	Byzantine Liturgical/Hymnographical Codices (Lit/Hym)
Group VII.	Byzantine Liturgical/Hagiographical Codices (Lit/Hag)
Group VIII.	Byzantine Liturgical/Ascetical Codices (Lit/Asc)

Of this extensive body of manuscripts we here concentrate on the Groups I-IV, in order to show how the proposed *Catalogue* will be structured. It is not the aim of this exercise to gather and enumerate *all* available biblical manuscripts and manuscript items, including all extant fragments (papyri), single folio's, pieces of works and incomplete codices (a procedure which is underway in Münster and Göttingen, among other places). The criterion for the inclusion of only available and complete codices (not fragments) is to be able to register the full contents of the codex, the formation/arrangement of the incorporated texts and the format of the codex.
Nor do we intend to incorporate codices of which the existence (the location or owner) is uncertain or unknown, or those that are mentioned in catalogues, but which have been destroyed or disappeared, because these cannot be verified from a codicological point of view (in order to enable this, the *Catalogue* will provide the manuscript numbers and library shelf marks of each manuscript).

Our points of departure are the catalogues of Aland (Von Soden) and Rahlfs, Ehrhard and Karo/Lietzmann. The tables we offer bring to light what is not immediately visible in these catalogues. In principle we maintain the basic catalogue information provided by Aland and Rahlfs, but we have revised and rearranged it from an explicit codicological point of view. Moreover, only those codices with complete contents have been selected (omitting fragmented codices and separate folio's), so that we can better determine the original codicological forms.

In contrast to Aland's and Rahlfs' specialised lists, the *Catalogue* will:

1) develop a new group of codex forms (Group III), in which OT & NT materials are incorporated together. We expect that this group will grow substantially as research of the group progresses;

2) profile the lectionary manuscripts, and in addition those text and commentary manuscripts which contain lectionary equipment and musical (ecphonetic) signs;

3) rearrange the codices according to their basic codex forms (Evangelion / Tetraevangelion; Apostolos / Praxapostolos / Apostoloevangelion; Psalterion; Prophetologion; Octateuch etc.);

4) profile the inclusion of commentary texts (taking Ehrhard's catalogue as a point of departure);

5) develop a new group in which the biblical, patristic and liturgical components are combined (Group IV). We expect that this group will grow substantially as research of the group progresses;

6) provide a more exact insight in the 'status quo' of the Byzantine manuscripts, in this study identified as being primarily liturgical.

---

[581] Groups: Byzantine Church History codices; Byzantine Canon Law; Theological/Dogmatic codices.

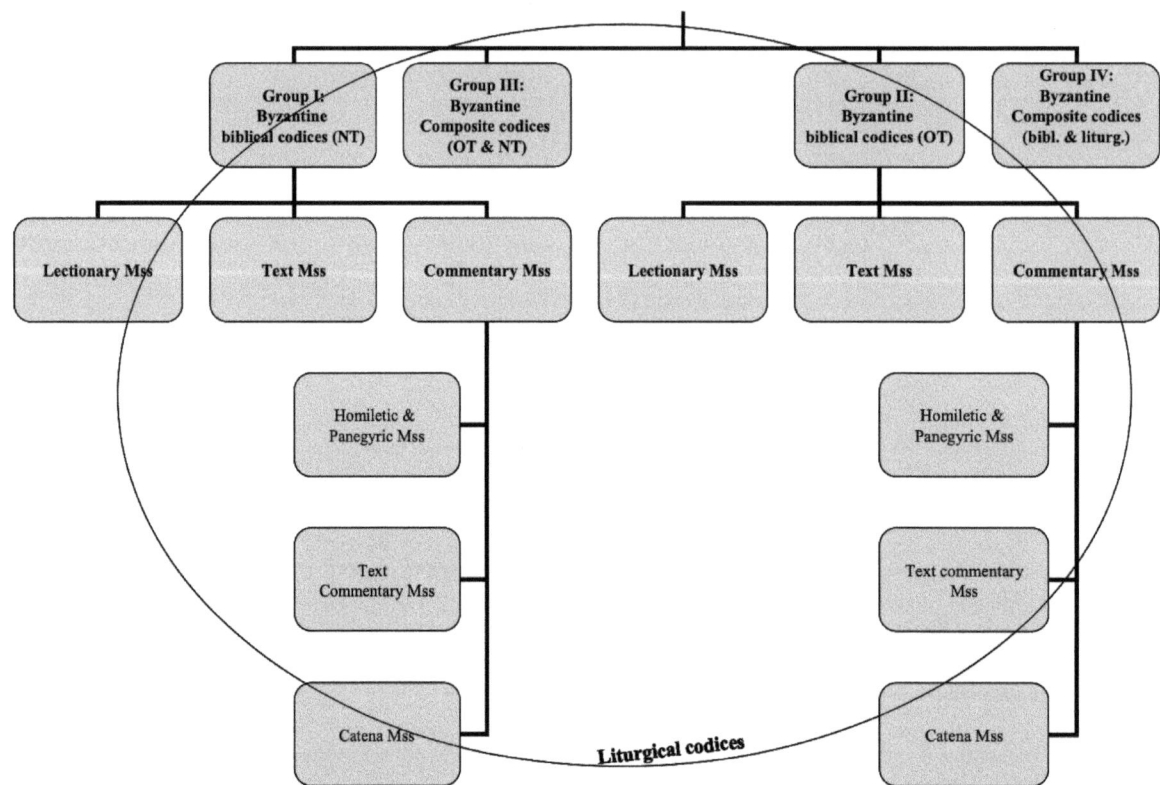

EXTANT BYZANTINE ECCLESIASTICAL CODICES: Groups I - IV

5.3 The Contours of a Typology of the Codification of the Byzantine Manuscripts

In this paragraph we intend to supply some basic, concrete insights in the codification processes behind the actual codex forms of the Byzantine manuscripts. Codicology is not only interested in the final forms of the extant codices and in providing their accurate description, but also in the formation process and the historical background of the codex types. This we cannot develop in this dissertation, but we will present the outlines of such a codicological typology in the form of a select group of examples.

5.3.1 The contents of groups one to four [I-IV]

Below we present each of the four groups [I-IV] identified earlier, presenting the sources/references used, the (distinguished) content of the group, and examples of individual codices of the groups.

Group I: Byzantine biblical codices (NT)
Group II: Byzantine biblical codices (OT)
Group III: Byzantine composite codices (OT&NT)
Group IV: Byzantine composite codices (Bibl&Lit)[582]

---

[582] This Group IV (Bibl. / Lit.) was already considered a desideratum by C.R. Gregory, *Textkritik des Neuen Testamentes*, 3 vols. (Leipzig, 1900-1909), v. 1, 333: 'Da wir aber unmöglich eine eigene Liste für jede Art von Buch aufstellen können, so wäre es richtig und praktisch, meine ich, drei Abteilungen zu machen: Evangelien, Apostel, und andere liturgische Bücher'. And again with regard to psalms and odes in codex 932, 452: 'Sie gehören kaum in diese Liste. Höchstens kämen sie in eine zukünftige "dritte" Liste der liturgischen Bücher'. In our catalogue model this "third list" is Group IV.

Sources

For the regrouping of the NT codices we used:

- K. Aland (and others), *Kurzgefasste Liste der griechischen Handschriften des Neuen Testaments, zweite, neubearbeitete und ergänzte Auflage* (2nd edition, Berlin / New York, 1994);
- C.R. Gregory, *Die Griechischen Handschriften des Neuen Testaments* (Leipzig, 1908);
- C. R. Gregory, *Textkritik des Neuen Testamentes* (Leipzig, 1900-1909) [esp. the lectionary codices];
- H.F. Von Soden, *Die Schriften des Neuen Testaments in ihrer ältesten erreichbaren Textgestalt hergestellt auf Grund ihrer Textgeschichte* (Göttingen, 1911) [esp. the lectionary equipment of the text and the text commentary codices].

For the reclassification of the OT codices we used:

- A. Rahlfs, *Verzeichnis der griechischen Handschriften des Alten Testaments für das Septuaginta Unternehmen*, in *Nachrichten der koeniglichen Gesellschaft der Wissenschaften zu Göttingen, Philolologisch Historische Klasse* (Berlin, 1914), 1-443.

For the homiletic and panegyric codices we used:

- A. Ehrhard, *Überlieferung und Bestand der hagiographischen und homiletischen Literatur der griechischen Kirche, von den Anfängen bis zum Ende des 16. Jahrhunderts*, Vol. I-III (Leipzig-Berlin, 1937-1952).

For the commentary manuscripts we used:

- K. Aland (and others), *Op. Cit.* (2nd edition, Berlin / New York, 1994);
- H.F. Von Soden, *Op. Cit.* (Göttingen, 1911);
- A. Rahlfs, *Op. Cit.* (Berlin, 1914).

5.3.1.1 Group I: Byzantine biblical codices (NT)

Group I. A: Lectionary Codices NT

- *Contents*

1. Εὐαγγέλιον

a. Evangelion Codices   [*l*e]
b. Evangelion Codices   [*l*esk]
c. Evangelion Codices   [*l*sk]
d. Evangelion Codices   [*l*k]
e. Evangelion Codices   [*l*sel]
f. Evangelion Codices   [*l*Lit]
g. Evangelion Codices   [*l*Unsp]

2. Ἀπόστολος

a. Apostolos Codices   [l^ae]
b. Apostolos Codices   [l^aesk]
c. Apostolos Codices   [l^ask]
d. Apostolos Codices   [l^ak]
e. Apostolos Codices   [l^asel]
f. Apostolos Codices   [l^aLit]
g. Apostolos Codices   [l^aUnsp.]

3. Ἀποστολοευαγγέλιον

a. Apostolo-evangelion Codices   [l^{+a}e]
b. Apostolo-evangelion Codices   [l^{+a}esk]
c. Apostolo-evangelion Codices   [l^{+a}sk]
d. Apostolo-evangelion Codices   [l^{+a}k]
e. Apostolo-evangelion Codices   [l^{+a}sel]
f. Apostolo-evangelion Codices   [l^{+a}Lit]
g. Apostolo-evangelion Codices   [l^{+a}Unsp]

- *Examples*

Ad 1a. Evangelion
Jerusalem, Patr. Libr. , Sabas 152. [Papadopoulos-Kerameus II, 236-238; Aland, *l* 1004]

Ad 1b. Evangelion
Jerusalem, Patr. Libr., Sabas 104. [Papadopoulos-Kerameus II, 178-179; Aland, *l* 1002]

Ad 2a. Apostolos
Istanbul, Patr. Libr., Pan. Kam. 57 [59]. [Tsakopoulos I, 101-102; Aland, *l* 921]

Ad 2b. Apostolos
Athos, Dochiariu, 2820 [146]. [Lambros I, 255; Aland, *l* 738]

AD 3a. Apostoloevangelion
Athens, Nat. Libr., 200 [63]. [Sakkelion/Sakkelion, 37; Aland, *l* 422]

AD 3b. Apostoloevangelion
Athens, Nat. Libr., 199 [62]. [Sakklion/Sakkelion, 37; Aland, *l* 421]

Group I. B: Text Codices NT

- Contents

1. Τετραευαγγέλιον

a. Tetraevangelion Codices *with Lect*	[e Lect]
b. Tetraevangelion Codices *without Lect*	[e]
c. Tetraevangelion Codices [Increased]	[er]

2. Πραξαπόστολος

a. Praxapostolos Codices *with Lect*	[ap Lect]
b. Praxapostolos Codices *without Lect*	[ap]
c. Praxapostolos Codices [Increased] *with Lect*	[apr Lect]
d. Praxapostolos Codices [Increased] *without Lect*	[apr]
[Praxapostolos Codices [Non-existent]][583]	[a]
e. Praxapostolos Codices [Diminished]	[p]

3. Ἀποστολοευαγγέλιον

a. Apostolo-Evangelion Codices *with Lect*	[eap Lect]
b. Apostolo-Evangelion Codices *without Lect*	[eap]

4. Ἀποκάλυψις

a. Apocalypse Codices	[r]

5. Ἀπόστολοευαγγέλιον + Ἀποκάλυψις

a. Evangelion-Apostolos-Apocalypse Codices *with Lect* [eapr/NT Lect]
b. Evangelion-Apostolos-Apocalypse Codices *without Lect* [eapr/NT]

- Examples

Ad 1a. Tetraevangelion Codex with Lect
Istanbul, Patr. Libr., H. Triad. Chalc. 9 (11). [Tsakopoulos II, 8-9; Aland, 1144]

Ad 1b. Tetraevangelion Codex without Lect
Nat. Libr. 153 [15]. [Sakkelion/Sakkelion, 30; Aland 760; von Soden, ε 475]

Ad. 2a. Praxapostolos Codex with Lect
Athos, Vatopediou, 864. [Eustratiades/Arcadios, 164; Aland, 1722; von Soden, α 384]

Ad. 2b. Praxapostolos Codex without Lect
Athos, Vatopediou, 850. [Eustratiades/Arcadios, 163; Aland, 1717; von Soden, α 487]

Ad 2c. Praxapostolos with Lect & Apocalypse Codex
Istanbul, Patr. Libr., Pan. Kam., 93 [96]. [Tsakopoulos I, 157-158; Aland, 1872; von Soden, α 209]

---

[583] A commentary form of group aK [Acts+ General Ep+Comm] does exist.

Ad 3a. Apostolo-Evangelion Codex with Lect
Athens, Nat. Libr., 130 [AKPE]. [Sakkelion/Sakkelion, 22; Aland, 801; von Soden, δ 553]

Ad 3b. Apostolo-Evangelion Codex without Lect
Athens, Nat. Libr., 130 [arr.: AKPE]. [Sakkelion/Sakkelion, 22; Aland, 801; von Soden, δ 553]

Ad 4a. Apocalypse Codex
Athos, Vatopediou, 637, f. 53^β-80^α [incorporated in a codex of Πανηγυρικοὶ Λόγοι]. [Eustratiades/Arcadios, 127; Aland, 2436][584]

Ad 5a. Evangelion-Apostolos-Apocalypse Codices with Lect
Athos, Lavra, Λ' 195. [Eustratiades/Arcadios, 298; Aland, 1075]

Ad 5a. Evangelion-Apostolos-Apocalypse Codices without Lect
Athos, Kutlumusiu, 356. [Lambros I, 312; Aland, 1704]

Group I. C: Commentary Codices NT

- Contents

1. Ὁμίλιαι / Πανηγυρικά [585]

   .1 Annual Panegyric Collections (Imm + Mov + Imm)
      Type A
      Type B
      Type C

   1.2 Semi-annual Panegyric Collections (Imm + Mov + Imm)
      Type A
      Type B
      Type C

   1.3 Italo-Greek Panegyric collections (Imm + Mov + Imm)

   1.4. Special Panegyric Collections (Imm + Mov + Imm)
      I. Panegyric collections of Movable and Immovable Feasts [of the Lord and the Theotokos]
      II. Panegyric collections of an Individual homilist (catechete)
        1. Gregory of Nazianz
        2. Gregory of Nyssa
        3. John Chrysostom
        4. Theodor of Studios
        5. Photios of Constantinopel
        6. Leo the Wise
        7. Nicetas the Paphlagonic

   1.5 Panegyric-Homiletic Collections [Ev] for the Triodion-Pentecostarion period [Mov: partial]
      I. One volume collections of homilies/panegyrika [Mov: partial]
      II. Two volume collections of homilies/panegyrika [Typus A-B]
      III. Italo-Greek collections of homilies/panegyrika
      IV. Special homiletic collections
        1. Ephrem the Syrian
        2. John Chrysostom

- Examples

Ad. 1.1 Annual Panegyrikon Collection
Type A: Moscow, Hist. Mus. Libr., Gr. 215 (V) [S 284] [Items 1-71] [Ehrhard II, *6-9*; Vladimir, *262-267*]
Type B: Athos, Iberon 658 [4778]. [Items 1-26] [Lambros II, *192*; Ehrhard II, *59-60*]
Type C: Jerusalem, Patr. Libr., Sabas 103. [Items 1-42] [Papadopoulos-Kerameus II, *175-179*; Ehrhard II, *69-72*]

Ad. 1.2 II Semi-Annual Panegyrikon Collections
Type A [Vol. I]: Vatican, Bibl. Apost. Vat., Vat. Gr. 654. [Items 1-22] [Ehrhard II, *91-93*]
Type A [Vol. II]: Moscow, Hist. Mus. Libr., Gr. 217 [S 234] [Items 1-34] [Vladimir, *270-272*; Ehrhard II, *103-104*]

---

[584] The Apocalypse codex does not exist seperately. The text is always incorporated in other codex formations, or together with commentaries (see below).

[585] For these Panegyrika and Homiletic commentaries complete insight is necessary in the whole Byzantine lection system in which these patristic readings are incorporated. See chapters 2 and 3. The panegyric/homiletic collections of the individual fathers are liturgical too and their codex formation evolved accordingly. Only a select part of the great work of Ehrhard is provided as example here.

Type B [Vol. I]:   Athos, Kutloumousiou, 28. [Item 2] [Lambros I, *276*; Ehrhard II, *113*]
Type B [Vol. II]: Vatican, Bibl. Apos. Vat., Vat. Gr. 455. [Items 1-82] [Ehrhard II, *113-119*]
Type C [Vol. I]:   Jerusalem, Patr. Libr., Met. H. Taphou in Const., 245. [Items 1-17] [Papadopoulos-Kerameus IV, *212-213*; Ehrhard II, *120-121*]

Ad. 1.4 Special Panegyric Collections: I
Sinai, Mon. St. Cath. Gr. 491. [Items 1-20]   [Ehrhard II, *195-197*]

Ad. 1.4 Special Panegyric Collections: II
1. Gregory of Nazianz : Athens, Nat. Libr., 2108 . [Items 1-16] [Ehrhard II, *211*; 2108 = Gymn. Thessal. 39, cf. Perria, *20*]
2. Gregory of Nyssa : Madrid, Archivo historico national, 163, 6. [Graux-Martin, *24-26*; Ehrhard II, *215*]
3. John Chrysostom, Type I : Paris, Bibl. Nat., Gr. 759. [Ehrhard II, *216-220*] and Type II : Patmos, St. John the Theol. 16. [Sakkelion, 87-88]

Kyriakodromion [Evangelion lessons for Triod.-Pent.+ Men]
Istanbul, Patr. Libr., Pan. Kam. 31 [Tsakopoulos I, 58-61]

Kyriakodromion [the Apostle lessons of each Sunday
Istanbul, Patr. Libr. 134 (Pan. Kam. 137) [Tsakopoulos I, 190-191]

2. Ἑρμηνεῖαι / Ὑπομνήματα - Ἑρμηνευτικαὶ Σειραί [586]

2.1.1 Tetraevangelion Commentary Codices *with Lect* (eK)
2.1.2 Tetraevangelion Commentary Codices *without Lect*
2.1.3 Individual Evangelion Commentary Codices [partial] (ePK: Mt, Mk, L, J)
2.2.1 Praxapostolos Commentary Codices (apK)
2.2.2 Praxapostolos and Apocalypse Commentary Codices [increased] (aprK)
2.2.3 Praxapostolos Codices [reduced] (aK = Acts + GenEp)
2.2.4 Praxapostolos [Pauline Epistles]Codices [reduced] (pK)
2.3.1 Praxapostolo-Evangelion Commentary Codices (eapK)
2.4.1 Apocalypse Commentary Codices (rK)
2.5.1. Evangelion-Apostolos-Apocalypse Commentary Codices (eaprK)

- Examples

Ad 2.1.1 Tetraevangelion Commentary Codices with Lect
Jerusalem, Patr. Libr. Taphu 25. [Papadopoulos-Kerameus I, *96-97*]

Ad 2.1.2 Tetraevangelion Commentary Codices without Lect
Athens, Nat. Libr., Gr. 204. [Aland 771; von Soden A^{15}]

Ad 2.1.3 Commentary to John: Cyril of Alexandria
Vatican City, Bibl. Apost. Vat., Vat. Gr. 592. [von Soden K^{i51}]

Ad 2.2.1 Commentary to the Praxapostolos: Oecumenius
Athens, Nat. Libr., Gr. 207. [von Soden O^{16}]

Ad 2.2.2 Commentary to the Praxapostolos + Apocalypse: Oecumenius
Athos, Paulu 2 [von Soden O^{11}]

Ad 2.2.3 Commentary to the Praxapostolos reduced: Andrew of Crete
Jerusalem, Staurou 25 [von Soden $A^{\pi\rho\,10}$]

Ad 2.2.4 Commentary to the Pauline Epistles
Patmos, St. John Mon., 61. [von Soden X^2]

Ad 2.3.1 Praxapostolo-Evangelion Commentary Codices (eapK)
Wien, Österr. Nat. Bibl., Theol. Gr. 79.80. [Aland 721; von Soden $Θ^{ε25}$]

---

[586] Included, but not distinguished in Aland's enumeration of Greek NT commentary mss (adopted from von Soden), are the Σειραὶ Πατέρων, the Compiled Commentaries or Catena manuscripts; there are Σειραί for each category of the NT text units: Evangelion, Acts, Epistles of Paul, General Epistles and the Apocalypse (cf. M. Faulhaber, "Katenen und Katenenforschung", in *Byzantinische Zeitschrift*, 18 (1909), 387. But also for the Apostolos (Acts, Pauline and General Epistles); the Apostolo-evangelion and the Apostolo-evangelion and Apocalypse. See Ch. 1: **Box 3**. In future research the text commentary and catena commentary forms should be distangled for reason of their original codex-formation.

Ad 2.4.1 Apocalypse Commentary Codices
Athos, Vatopediou 17. [Aland 1773; von Soden Av[404]]

Ad 2.5.1 Evangelion & Apostolos & Apocalypse commentary
Athos, Παντελεήμονος 770 [6277]. [Lambros II, 430; Aland 1678]

5.3.1.2 Group II: Byzantine biblical codices (OT)

Group II. A: Lectionary Codices OT

- *Contents*

1. Ψαλτήρια

a. Psalterion Codices (Ps.)
b. Psalterion Codices with the Nine Odes (Ps.Od.)

2. Προφητολόγια

a. Prophetologion Codices [Nativ.-Theoph + Triodion/Pentekostarion + Menologion]
b. Prophetologion Codices [Triodion part]
c. Prophetologion Codices [Triodion/Pentekostarion part]
d. Prophetologion Codices [Menologion part]
e. Prophetologion Included in Liturgical-Ceremonial codices (Group V)

- *Examples*

Ad. 1a. Psalterion & Odes
Athens, Nat. Libr. 26. [Sakkelion/Sakkelion, *4*]

Ad. 1b. Psalterion [without Odes]
Istanbul, Patr. Libr., H. Triad. (Chalci), 19 [22]. [Tsakopoulos II, *17-19*]

Ad 2a. Prophetologion [Triodion/Pentekostarion + Menologion]
Athos, Vatopediou, 626. [Eustratiades/Arcadios, *123*]

Ad 2b. Prophetologion [Triodion]
Athos, Lavra, 309 [Γ 69]. [Spyridon/Eustratiades, *42*]

Group II. B: Text Codices OT

- *Contents*

1. Ὀκτάτευχος (Octateuch codices)

a. Octateuch Codices (Gen, Ex., Lev., Num, Deut., Josh, Judg, Ruth)
b. Pentateuch Codices (Gen, Ex., Lev., Num, Deut.)
c. Extended Octateuch Codices (Gen, Ex., Lev., Num, Deut., Josh, Judg, Ruth, Esth., Tob, Jud.)
d. Incomplete Octateuch Codices

2. Τὰ Ἱστορικά / Βίβλοι Ἱστορικαί (Historical codices))

a. Historical Codices : Part 1-3 (I-IV Kgs, I-II Chr., I-II Ezra; Esth., Jud., Tob; I-IV Macc)
b. Historical Codices : Part 1-2 (I-IV Kgs, I-II Chr., I-II Ezra and Esth., Jud., Tob Esth., Jud., Tob)
c. Historical Codices : Part 1 (I-IV Kgs.; I-II Chr.; I-II Ezra)
d. Extended Historical Codices: Last three books Oct (Josh, Judg, Ruth) + Histical Codices: Part 1-3

3. Τὰ Ποητικά / Βίβλοι Στιχηραί (Sapiential codices)

a. The Sapiential Codices in one codex (Ἑξασόφιον) (Prov, Eccl., Song, Job, Eccles, Sirach)
b. The Sapiential Codices in other formations
c. Individual Sapiential Codices (Job, Prov, Eccl, Song, Eccles, Sirach)

4. Τὰ Προφητικά / Βίβλοι Προφηταί (Prophetical codices)

a. XVI Prophets Codices (οἱ δεκαὲξ προφηταί)
b. XII Prophets Codices (οἱ δώδεκα προφῆται)
c. IV Prophets Codices (οἱ τέσσαρες προφῆται)

5. Συλλογαί (Compiled codices)

a. Octateuch, Historical Codices and Sapiential Codices
b. Octateuch and Historical Codices
c. Octateuch and Prophetical Codices
d. Historical and Sapiential Codices
e. Historical and Prophetical Codices
f. Sapiential, Prophetical and Historical Codices

- *Examples*

Ad. 1a Oktateuch Codices   Athos, Lavra, 352 [Γ 112]. [Spyridon/Eustratiades, *48*; Rahlfs, *18*]

Ad. 1b Extended Oktateuch Codices (Oct + Hist [Esth., Jud., Tob., I-IV Kgs.])   Athos, Vatopediu, 598. [Eustratiades/Arcadios, *117*]

Ad. 1c Extended Oktateuch Codices (Oct + Hist [Esth., Tob., Jud.])   Athos, Vatopediu, 600. [Eustratiades/Arcadios, *118*]

Ad. 2b Historical Codices: Part 1-2   Athos, Vatopediou, 599 [512]. [Eustratiades/Arcadios, *117* ; Rahlfs 318 , *18*]

Ad. 3a Sapiential Codices (Prov, Eccl., Song, Job, Eccles, Sirach)   Paris, Bibl. Nat., Gr. 18. [Rahlfs 545]

Ad. 4a XVI Prophetical Codices   Athos, Vatopediou, 601 [514]. [Eustratiades/Arcadios, *118*; Rahlfs, *8*]

Ad. 4b XII Prophetical Codices   Sinai, St. Cat. Mon., Gr. 6. [Rahlfs 711, *285*]

Ad. 5a Octateuch, Historical and Sapiential Codices   Moscow, Hist. Mus. Libr., Syn. Libr., Gr. 30 (Vl. 3) [Rahlfs 125, *143-144*]

Group II. C: Commentary Codices OT

- *Contents*

1. Λόγοι, Ὁμίλιαι καὶ Πανηγυρικά[587]

a. Psalterion: Commentary Codices (Ps., Comm.)
b. Lessons of the Triodion (Prophetologion; Hexaemeron, Genesis, Proverbs, Jesaja, Twelve Feasts)
c. Lessons of the Menaia on the Eve of the Feasts (Prophetologion)

2. Ἑρμηνεῖαι / Ὑπομνήματα

a. Octateuch: Commentary Codices (Oct.: Gen, Ex, Lev, Num, Deut, Josh, Judg, Ruth)
b. Historical Books: Commentary Codices (I-IV Kgs, I-II Chr., I-II Ezra)
c. Historical Books: Commentary Codices (Esth, Jud, Tob)
d. Wisdom Books: Commentary Codices as a whole (Job, Prov, Eccl, Song, Wis, Eccles)
e. Wisdom Books: Commentary Codices as in parts (Job, Prov, Eccl, Song, Wis, Eccles.)
f. Wisdom and Prophets Books: Commentary Codices
g. Prophets: Commentary Codices (Proph, the XVI Prophets)
h. Prophets: Commentary Codices (Proph, the XII minor Prophets)
i. Prophets: Commentary Codices (Proph, the IV major Prophets)
j. All OT books included in one Codex

3. Ἑρμηνευτικαὶ Σειραί*

a. Psalterion [derivatives: Psalm groups]**
b. Psalterion (with Odes)
c. The Nine Odes***
d. Lessons of the Triodion (Prophetologion homiletic commentary)
e. Octateuch [derivatives: Pentateuch, Genesis etc.]
f. Prophets [the Four Great and the Twelve Minor Prophets; included are semi-canonical books/texts]

---

[587] These categories of OT commentaries need elaboration in future catalogue research.

g. Historical Books [I-IV Kgs];
h. Wisdom Books [Song, Prov, Eccles]
i. Job
j. Prooimia to biblical books

* Excluded from this category, commentaries in the form of Σειραί, are the deutero-canonical books (Faulhaber, 1909, 387)
** There are many Σειραί or Catena Mss compiled by anonymous editors (see Athens/Ethn.Bibl./Sakkelion: Index)
*** There are extensive Ms materials, see Swete III, 811-834 (Faulhaber, 1909, 387)

5.3.1.3 Group III: Byzantine Composite Codices (OT/NT)

- *In statu constructo*

This group of Byzantine codices is unexplored; presented are only some first results which invite more extensive research; no specific order or definite classification for this group is desirable for the time being (first inventarisation), but some outlines can be already recognised; there are analogies with Groups I-II. with the sub-division into lect.-text and comm codices.

- *Contents*

Group III. A: Lectionary codices (OT/NT)

1. Evangelion & Psalterion/Odes;
2. Apostolo & Evangelion & Prophetologion;

Group III. B: Text codices (OT/NT)

3. Complete Bible (OT+NT);
4. Complete NT & Psalterion;
5. Apostolo-Evangelion & Psalterion;
6. Apostolos & Psalterion;
7. Apostolo-Evangelion & Prophets;
8. Apostolo-Evangelion & Sapiental books;

Group III. C: Commentary codices (OT/NT)

9. Hist-Proph-Sapient-Apost-Apok;
10. Evangelion plus Commentary (Theophylact) & Prophets;

- *Examples*

Ad. 1. Evangelion & Psalterion/Odes Codex   Moscow, Russ. State's Libr., F. 201.18.2 (Gr. 3). [Aland, *l* 1350 (U)]

Ad. 2. Apostolos & Evangelion & Prophetologion Lessons   Athos, Φιλοθέου, 6 [1769]. [Lambros I, 1769 (items 1-6); Aland, *l* 751 (l⁺ᵃesk); Rahlfs, 1240, *23*]

Ad. 3 Complete Bible Codex (OT & NT)   London, Brit. Libr., Royal 1 D. V-VIII. [Rahlfs 1914, A, *114-116*; Fraenkel 2004, *221-226*]

Ad 4. NT & Psalterion/Odes Codex   Moscow, Hist. Mus. V. 25 , Syn. Libr. 25 [Vladimir N° 407, I, 27-229; Aland 242, *61*; von Soden δ 206; Rahlfs, 1109, *147*]

Ad 5. Psalterion & Apostoloevangelion Codex   Istanbul, Patr. Libr., Pan. Kam. 130 [133]. [Tsakopoulos I, *185-187*]

Ad 6. Apostolos & Psalterion/Odes Codex   Athos, Vatopediou 851. [Eustratiades/Arcadios, 163; Aland, 1718; Rahlfs, 655]

Ad 9. Hist. & XVI Proph & Sapient & Apost & Apoc   Paris, Bibl. Nat., Coisl. 18 (319). [Aland 2344, *182*; Rahlfs 534, *187*]

5.3.1.4 Group IV. Byzantine Composite Codices (Bibl./Lit)

- *In statu constructo (a-typical group)*

The examples of this group indicate combinations of texts and books of different sectors, biblical (OT/NT) and liturgical. The set-up was realised by Gregory I (1900) and adopted by Aland (1994) under the signs *l*Lit (27 codd), *l*ᵖLit (9 codd), and *l*⁺ᵃLit (119 codd). The precise contents of these NT-Lit codices are not given and one can only return to the succinct notes of Gregory. But a first systematisation is present (the Lit of the lectionary group). Further research can continue on this ground. In ch. 6 we will provide a specimen of the list detracted from Aland *l*Lit. We expect that the same distinctions as in Groups I-III can be followed, namely 'lectionary', 'text' and 'commentary' codices. But for the moment, since insight is too small in the state of affairs of this group, we have decided to present the examples according to their biblical contents. Below we give only some examples of *individual* codices, that could hint at other similar codices. Both the specialised catalogues (von Soden, Rahlfs) as well as the catalogues of the Eastern Libraries (Papadopoulos-Kerameus, Lambros, Spyridon-Eustratiades, Eustratiades-Arcadios, Bees/Sophianos, Sakkelion, Sakkelion/Sakkelion, Politis, Vladimir, Granstrem etc.) give the impression that many more "composite" biblical-liturgical codices exist than are presently known.

- *Sources for further research*

a) Gregory
Gregory I (1900): 'Evangelia', 387-464 and 'Apostel', 465-478.
Gregory III (1909), 'Lesebücher', 1211-1292.
b) Aland
Aland (1994): 'Lektionare', 219-370:
   *l*Lit : 27 codd
   *l*ᵃLit : 9 codd
   l⁺ᵃLit : 119 codd
c) Von Soden's *Schriften des NT I*, *passim*
d) Rahlfs' *Verzeichnis*, *passim*
e) Catalogues of Eastern libraries (Lambros, Sakkelion etc.), *passim*

- *Contents*

Group IV. A: Liturgical and NT codices (Lit/NT)

      1. Liturgical texts & inserted NT and OT lessons (*l*Lit, *l*ᵃLit, *l*⁺ᵃLit)
      2. Praxapostolos & Lit & Psalterion/Odes
      3. Psalterion & Apostoloevangelion & Lit (Trop. Euch. Kan.)

Group IV. B: Liturgical and OT codices (Lit/OT)

      4. Psalterion & parts of Horologion
      5. Psalterion + comm & Horologion
      6. Psalms & Lit & Ap/Ev lessons
      7. Euchologion & Psalterion
      8. Prophetologion Lessons & Triodion, Pentekostarion, Menaia
      9. Psalterion & Octoechos & Menaion & Triodion & Lessons of Ev/OT
     10. Job and Liturgical commentaries
     11. Triodionpropheteia

Group IV. C: Liturgical and OT/NT codices

     12. Triodion & Pentekostarion & Lessons Apostolos and Evangelion

- *Examples*

Ad. 2. Praxapostolos & Lit & Psalterion/Odes
Moscow, Russ. State's Archive, F. 1607, No 5 [Syn. Libr. 23 (341)]. [Vladimir I, 23-26; Aland, 252]

Ad. 3. Psalterion & Apostoloevangelion & Lit
Athos, Vatopediou, 762. [Spyridon-Eustratiades, *150-151*; Aland 2191; Rahlfs 610]

Ad. 4 Psalterion & Horologion parts (Hours etc.)
Istanbul, Pan. Kam. 131 [134]. [Tsakopoulos I, *187-188*]

Ad. 5. Psalterion/comm & Horologion
Athos, lavra 145 [B 25]. [Spyridon/Eustratiades, *15*]

Ad. 6 Psalms & Lit & Ap/Ev lessons & Stich
Athos, Vatopediou 625. [Eustratiades/Arcadios, *123*; Aland *l* 1556]

Ad. 9 Psalterion & Octoechos & Menaion & Triodion & Lessons NT/OT
Sinai, St. Cat. Mon., Gr. 550 [514]. [Rahlfs, 1883, *292*; Aland *l* 896, *272*]

Ad. 12 Triodion & Pentekostarion & Lessons Apostolos and Evangelion
Jerusalem, Staphrou 15. [Papadopoulos-Kerameus III, *39*; Aland, *l* 1467 (*l*⁺ᵃLit)]

5.4 Concluding Remarks

The motive for placing manuscript data from different (specialised) catalogues together in one concordant *Catalogue*, is to reunite virtually and visibly the manuscript materials, which were isolated and abstracted from their common provenance and codicological heritage. It was precisely the codex form, which guaranteed the authentic preservation of the incorporated texts, in their specific forms (continuous texts), selective collections (lectionary and catena texts) and additions (supplementary or commentary texts). It appears that the codex formations of the groups are analogous and congruent.

In the NT category the Four Gospels were codified in *three* basic forms: <u>Lect</u>: Evangelion, <u>Text</u>: Tetra-evangelion, <u>Comm</u>: Tetra-evangelion commentaries [subdivided in Homiletic, Text and Catena comm.]. The Acts, the Seven General Epistles and the Fourteen Pauline Epistles were styled in the same threefold manner: <u>Lect</u>: Apostolos, <u>Text</u>: Praxapostolos, <u>Comm</u>: Praxapostolos commentaries [subdivided in Homiletic, Text and Catena comm.]. The codex form of the combined Evangelion & Apostolos in: <u>Lect</u>: Apostolo-Evangelion, <u>Text</u>: Praxapostolo-evangelion and <u>Comm</u>: Praxapostolo-evangelion commentaries [subdivided in Homiletic, Text and Catena comm.]. In the OT category the threefold codex formation is also clearly attested: <u>Lect</u>: Psalterion/Odes and Prophetologion; <u>Text</u>: Octateuch, etc.; <u>Comm</u>: Octateuch [subdivided in: Hom., Text and Catena]. The complementarity of lectionary-text-commentary manuscripts is also found in the composite codices (groups III and IV).

Further, within the main categories of NT and OT many different codex formations were constructed and a similar tendency of diversification is seen in the composite collections (groups III and IV). The great variety of manuscripts shows many overlaps, inconsistencies, unexplained combinations, or even the unorganised heaping of materials. Manuscripts of different character: Gospel texts, Apostolos, Prophetologion and Psalterion texts, Homilies and Panegyrics, solely or collectively, in all possible variations, are to be found side by side in usage and provenance.

One conclusion is that a (codicological/textuological) gap between "text", "lectionary" and "commentary" codices is undesirable. Moreover, research of the Byzantine ecclesiastical manuscripts is brought back to the most basic elementary point of departure, namely the individual codex (with the library shelf mark which is the custodian of its 'particularity'). An important conclusion is, that each manuscript, although included in one of the categories, retains its own particular, codicological, liturgical and textual worth and relevance.

Three observations with regard to the codex formation of the OT books (group II) are relevant: 1) OT texts are incorporated between other texts, more often than NT texts are; 2) OT codex forms appear in many cases to be more "a-typical" than NT codex forms; 3) OT texts are in many cases combined with NT texts in one codex. The above reflect the ecclesiastical-patristic opinion and use of OT books.

With regard to group IV, the inclusion of biblical and liturgical materials/books in one codex is more often attested than usually presumed. This leads to the expectation that further research will reveal even more co-existence of biblical and liturgical materials in one and the same codex.

Chapter 6

The *Catalogue of Byzantine Manuscripts*
- in statu constructo -

The aim of this thesis has been to develop arguments for a new *Catalogue of Byzantine Manuscripts,* based on the hypothesis of an inner cohesion between the Bible and the fathers, and by means of a codico-liturgical model of classification. Such a catalogue will, in our view, deliver a broader overview of the actual contents of the extant Byzantine manuscripts and demonstrate that the individual manuscripts belong to, in fact, a more restricted number of basic codex "types". The whole is based on the liturgical hypothesis set out in the foregoing (chapters 2 and 3) and supported and elaborated by a codicological approach (chapter 1). The field from which material must be sourced is not only the existing manuscript catalogues we know to date, but also the libraries and library catalogues which store our resources (chapter 4).[588] The contours of a codico-liturgical model of classification have been set (chapter 5) and we will now turn to presenting the *Catalogue* itself, in a series of tabular *specimens* of data.

6.1 The Tabular Specimens

In this chapter we present 8 specimens from the first four Groups (Groups I-IV), as examples to show visually how, if the manuscripts are classified along the lines and parameters set out in chapter 5, both the biblical and patristic factors become concrete and their liturgical background evident.

The specimens also indicate how we eventually intend to form, through the *Catalogue of Byzantine Manuscripts*, a more comprehensive, all encompassing picture of the Byzantine biblical codices (NT and OT), comprising the lectionary, text and commentary manuscripts, which are known and available to scholarship.

The 8 tabular specimens of the envisaged *Catalogue* act as a demonstration, a way of working. The development of the *Catalogue* itself presupposes the efforts of a team of researchers (multidisciplinary) in the field. Here we can only provide some basic data, examples from 4 groups, to give evidence to the thesis and promote interest in the proposed *Catalogue*.

6.1.1 The specimens

Group I: Byzantine Biblical Codices (NT)

1. Evangelion codices (*le*)
2. Tetraevangelion codices (e)
3. Evangelion-Apostolos-Apocalypse codices (eapr)
4. Tetraevangelion commentary codices (eK)
5. Evangelion-Apostolos-Apocalypse commentary codices (eaprK)

Group II: Byzantine Biblical Codices (OT)

6. Prophetologion Codices (Π)

Group III: Byzantine Composite Codices (OT & NT)

7. Complete Bibles codices(OT/NT)

Group IV: Byzantine Composite Codices (Bibl & Lit)

8. Byzantine Biblical-liturgical codices (OT/NT/Lit)

---

[588] Library shelf marks preserve the most characteristic feature of an individual codex, its provenance and purpose. Serial numberings (Aland, Rahlfs, Ehrhard) abstract from the original concrete entities.

6.1.2 Criteria for the inclusion of codices in the tables

Practical guidelines for the exclusion of codices include:

- not fragments
- not single or a limited number of folio's
- not pieces or incomplete parts of works belonging to the codex type
- not codices of which the location or owner is uncertain or unknown
- not codices still mentioned in catalogues, but which are destroyed or disappeared

6.1.3 Parameters for the assessment of codices listed in the tables

Serial N^o	manuscript number of the category [NT; OT; Hom]
Place/library + Shelf Mark	identification of the codex
f	number of the folios
c	number of columns [1 or 2]
l	number of lines
format	measures of the format
Lect	lectionary information (Lect, v. Von Soden)
Comm	commentary info (v. Aland/Von Soden or Rahlfs/Fraenkel)

6.1.4 Sources of determination of the codex-contents

- descriptions of specialized catalogues
- descriptions of local library catalogues
- photographic manuscript reproductions
- descriptions based on autopsy on location

Verification of manuscript data

When compiling a new catalogue, the following should be checked:

- whether the manuscript still exists;
- the exact provenance and current location;
- the number of folio's of codices in Aland's, Rahlfs' and Ehrhard's catalogues;
- the precise descriptions of the complete contents should be checked.

NB. The total number of folio's in Aland and von Soden does not always correspond exactly.

6.2 Group I. Byzantine Biblical Codices (NT)

6.2.1 Specimen I: Evangelion (*l*e)

The Evangelion provides the four Gospels in one codex, in a nearly complete textual form (in the order of John, Matt [Mark], Luke [Mark], Mark), and basically has a threefold structure: an annual series of lessons from Pascha to Pascha, following the Byzantine calendar (movable cycle); a (parallel) annual series of lessons for fixed feasts and commemorations (immovable cycle); and a select series of additional lessons (the eleven morning resurrection evangelia, lessons for special occasions).
The whole group of εὐαγγέλια or *l* (sum total: **1.144** of selected Evangelion codices) has been subdivided into seven subgroups. The group presented here is the first of the seven. The criteria for this subdivision were adopted by Aland and his collaborators (K. Junack and M. Welte) from Gregory, *Tekstkritik* I (1900), 336 – 339. For the sub-divisions, see Ch.5.3.1.1: *Group I. A: Lectionary Codices NT* (1. Εὐαγγέλιον: *a-g*).

The reason we present this table is to show how the lectionary systems have been modelled into a codex form, namely the **Evangelion**, being a liturgical companion to the (liturgical) **Tetraevangelion**, see specimen II.

Selected from sub-group *l*e are: **458 codices**. Chronological limits: VIII - XVIII c.
In this specimen only the first 50 manuscripts of the 458 selected manuscripts are presented.

NB. We do not indicate single or a very restricted number of folios that are maintained in other libraries in the following specimens.
S= script in the form of a cross.

Table 1: Evangelion

Aland 1994[2] Serial N°	Age / Date	Place / Library + Shelf Mark	fol. [col.][589]	Gregory I 1900 Evl N°
l 2	X [U]	Paris, Bibl. Nat., Gr. 280	f. 257 [2]	Evl 2
l 7	1204 A.D.	Paris, Bibl. Nat., Gr. 301	f. 316 [2]	Evl 7
l 8	XIV	Paris, Bibl. Nat., Gr. 312	f. 309 [2]	Evl 8
l 9	XIII	Paris, Bibl. Nat., Gr. 307	f. 260 [2]	Evl 9
l 12	XIII	Paris, Bibl. Nat., Gr. 310	f. 366 [2]	Evl 12
l 14	XVI	Paris, Bibl. Nat., Gr. 315	f. 348 [2]	Evl 14
l 15	XIII	Paris, Bibl. Nat., Gr. 302	f. 310 [2]	Evl 15
l 18	XII	Oxford, Bodl. Libr., Laud. Gr. 32	f. 276 [2]	Evl 18
l 19	XIII	Oxford, Bodl. Libr., Auct. D. inf. 2. 12	f. 322 [2]	Evl 19
l 34	IX [U]	Munich, Bayer. Staatsbibl., Gr. 329	f. 430 [2]	Evl 34
l 36	X [U]	Vatican City, Bibl.Vat., Vat.Gr. 1067	f. 268 [2]	Evl 36
l 43	XIII	El Escorial, Real Bibl., X. III. 16	f. 313 [2]	Evl 43
l 48	1055 A.D.	Moscow, Гос. Ист. Музей, V. 15, S. 43	f. 250 [2]	Evl 48
l 49	X/XI	Moscow, Гос. Ист. Музей, V. 12, S. 225	f. 437 [2]	Evl 49
l 68	XII	Paris, Bibl. Nat., Gr. 285	f. 357 [2]	Evl 68
l 69	XII	Paris, Bibl. Nat., Gr. 286	f. 257 [2]	Evl 69
l 70	XII	Paris, Bibl. Nat., Gr. 288	f. 313 [2]	Evl 70
l 75	XII	Paris, Bibl. Nat., Gr. 293	f. 250 [2]	Evl 75
l 76	XII	Paris, Bibl. Nat., Gr. 295	f. 182 [2]	Evl 76
l 79	XIV	Paris, Bibl. Nat., Gr. 299	f. 126 [2]	Evl 79
l 80	XII	Paris, Bibl. Nat., Gr. 300	f. 128 [2]	Evl 80
l 83	XII	Paris, Bibl. Nat., Gr. 294	f. 245 [2]	Evl 83*
l 86	1336 A.D.	Paris, Bibl. Nat., Gr. 311	f. 382 [2]	Evl 86
l 101	XIV	Paris, Bibl. Nat., Gr. 303	f. 279 [2]	Evl 101
l 108	XI	Venice, Bibl. Naz. Marc, Gr. Z. 549 (655)	f. 292 [2]	Evl 108
l 109	XIV	Venice, Bibl. Naz. Marc., Gr. Z.550 (848)	f. 206 [2]	Evl 109
l 113	XIII	Florence, Bibl. Medicea Laur., Plutei VI. 2	f. 341 [2]	Evl 113
l 118	XIV	Florence, Bibl. Medicea Laur., Med. Pal. 243	f. 368 [2]	Evl 118
l 119	XIII	Vatican City, Bibl.Vat.,, Vat.Gr. 1155	f. 268 [2]	Evl 119
l 121	XI	Vatican City, Bibl.Vat., Vat. Gr. 1157	f. 419 [1]	Evl 121
l 126	XI	Vatican City, Bibl.Vat., Vat. Gr. 2041	f. 337 [2]	Evl 126
l 129	XII	Vatican City, Bibl.Vat., Reg. Gr. 12	f. 339 [2]	Evl 129
l 134	XIII	Vatican City, Bibl.Vat., Barb.Gr. 565	f. 343 [2]	Evl 134
l 146	XII	Cambridge, Univ. Libr., Dd. 8.23	f. 212 [2]	Evl 146
l 150	995 A.D.[U]	London, Brit. Libr., Harley 5598	f. 374 [2]	Evl 150
l 184	1319 A.D.	London, Brit. Libr., Burney 22	f. 248 [2]	Evl 184

---

[589] The complete contents of the codices should be verified (and the correctness of the number of folio's).

ℓ 185	XI	Cambridge, Christ College, GG. 1.6 (Ms. 6)	f. 218 [2]	**Evl 185**
ℓ 191	XII	London, Brit. Libr., Add. 18212	f. 297 [2]	**Evl 191**
ℓ 198	XII	Oxford, Bodl. Libr., E. D. Clarke 45	f. 276 [2]	**Evl 198**
ℓ 200	XII	Oxford, Bodl. Libr., E. D. Clarke 47	f. 292 [2]	**Evl 200**
ℓ 202	XII	Oxford, Bodl. Libr., Cromwell 27	f. 323 [2]	**Evl 202**
ℓ 203	?1067 A.D.	Oxford, Bodl. Libr., Auct. F. 6.25	f. 300 [1]	**Evl 203**
ℓ 211	XII	Oxford, Christ Church, Wake 18	f. 209 [2]	**Evl 211**
ℓ 213	XIII	Oxford, Christ Church, Wake 23	f. 256 [2]	**Evl 213**
ℓ 226	XIV	Ann Arbor, Univ. Libr., Ms. 28	f. 220 [1]	**Evl 226**
ℓ 230	XIII	London, Lambeth Palace, 1188	f. 318 [2]	**Evl 230**
ℓ 233	XI	London, Brit. Libr., Add. 39603	f. 188 [S]	**Evl 233**
ℓ 238	XI	London, Brit. Libr., Egerton 3046	f. 144 [2]	**Evl 238**
ℓ 252	XI	St. Petersburg, Росс. Нац. Библ., Gr. 69	f. 498 [2]	**Evl 252**
ℓ 262	XVII	Paris, Bibl. Nat., Suppl. Gr. 242	f. 265 [2]	**Evl 262**

Etc.

6.2.2 Specimen II. Tetraevangelion (e)

The Tetra-Evangelion comprises the complete text of the Four Gospels [Matt, Mark, Luke, John] together in one codex.
The table shows a realistic number of preserved codices of this type (not fragments, single folios etc), taken from Aland, with the shelf marks of the library where they can be found and other basic information for identification.
The Tetra-evangelion (also simply evangelion), is the most copied (used) clearly defined codex form (Sum Total: **1.312 codices**). Total : Tetraevangelion Codex items (e): **1.726**. Selected codices: **1.312**. Excluded: **414** codices. Chronological limits: IV - XVIII c.

Result: Lect evidence
Total selected: **1.312** codd.
+ Lect: **843** codd.
- Lect: **353** codd.
Insufficient data (not counted in result): **116** codd.

Key:

Insuff. Data	Not in Von Soden - mss found later than 1913
	Not in Hss-Kartei Munster
	Incomplete info in von Soden [nicht schematisiert], or little or no data
Lect	Lectionary equipment in margins
Lect[text]	Beginnings of lections in red in text
Lect[tab]	Tables of lessons provided
Lect[m.s.]	Lectionary equipment added by a second hand
Lect [Schol]	Lectionary equipment and scholia

The registered lectionary equipment, taken from Von Soden and checked against the HSS Kartei at the INTF in Munster (843 manuscripts with lect, as opposed to 353 without) is strong evidence of the thesis of liturgical heritage of the codices.
In this specimen only the first 50 manuscripts of the 1312 selected manuscripts are presented.

Table 2: Tetraevangelion

Aland 1994[2] Serial N°	Age/Date	Library ‖ Shelf Mark	fol. [col.]	Von Soden 1911[2] Lectionary equipment
E 07	VIII	Basel, Univ. Bibl., AN III 12	f. 318 [1]	ε 55 Lect
F 09	IX	Utrecht, Univ. Bibl., Ms. 1	f. 204 [2]	ε 86 Lect
G 011	IX	London, Brit. Libr., Harley 5684 [f. 251]	f. 252 [2]	ε 87 Lect
H 013	IX	Hamburg, Univ. Bibl., Cod. 91 in scrin.	f. 194 [1]	ε 88 -
K 017	IX	Paris, Bibl. Nat., Gr. 63	f. 267 [1]	ε 71 Lect[tab]
L 019	VIII	Paris, Bibl. Nat., Gr. 62	f. 257 [2]	ε 56 -
M 021	IX	Paris, Bibl.Nat. , Gr. 48	f. 257 [2]	ε 72 Lect[tab]
N 022	VI	St. Petersburg, Росс. Нац. Библ., Gr. 537 [f. 182]	f. 231 [2]	ε 19 -
S 028	949 A.D.	Vatican Library, Bibl. Vat., Vat.Gr. 354	f. 235 [2]	ε 89 Lect
U 030	IX	Venice, Bibl. Naz. Marc., Gr. 1,8 (1397)	f. 291 [2]	ε 90 -
V 031	IX	Moscow, Гос. Ист. Музей, V. 9, S. 399	f. 220 [1]	ε 75 Lect, Lect[tab]
W 032	IV/V	Washington D.C., Smithson. Inst., Freer Gall. 06274	f. 187 [1]	ε 014 -
Y 034	IX	Cambridge, Univ. Libr., Add. Mss. 6594	f. 309 [1]	ε 073 Lect
Γ 036	X	Oxford, Bodl. Libr., Auct. T. inf. 2.2 [f. 158] + St. Petersburg, Росс. Нац. Библ., Gr. 33 [f. 99]	f. 257 [1]	ε 70 -
Δ 037	IX	St. Gallen, Stifts-bibl., 48 [Gr.-Lt.]	f. 198 [1]	ε 76 -
Θ 038	IX	Tbilisi, Инст. рукописей, Gr. 28	f. 249 [2]	ε 050 -
Λ 039 + 566	IX	Oxford, Bodl. Libr., Auct. T. inf. 1. 1 + St.Petersburg, Росс. Нац. Библ., Gr. 54	f. 157 [2] + f. 122 [2]	ε 77 Lect[m.s.]
Π 041	IX	St. Petersburg, Росс. Нац. Библ., Gr. 34	f. 350 [1]	ε 73 -
Ω 045	IX	Athos, Διονυσίου (10) 55	f. 259 [2]	ε 61 Lect, Lect[tab]
047	VIII	Princeton, Univ. Libr., Med. a. Ren. Mss., Garrett 1	f. 152 [S]	ε 95 Lect
0211	IX	Tbilisi, Инст. рукописей, Gr. 27	f. 258 [2]	ε 051 -
2	XI/XII	Basel, Univ. Bibl., A. N. IV. 1	f. 248 [1]	ε 1214 Lect

4	XIII	Paris, Bibl. Nat., 84	f. 212 [1]	ε 371 Lect, Lect^{tab}
7	XII	Paris, Bibl. Nat., Gr. 71	f. 186 [1]	ε 287 Lect^{text}, Lect^{tab}
8	XI	Paris, Bibl. Nat., Gr. 49	f. 199 [2]	ε 164 Lect, Lect^{tab}
9	1167 A.D.	Paris, Bibl. Nat., Gr. 83	f. 298 [1]	ε 279 Lect^{tab}
10	XIII	Paris, Bibl. Nat., Gr. 91	f. 275 [1]	ε 372 Lect, Lect^{tab}
11	XII	Paris, Bibl. Nat., Gr. 121.122	I. f. 230 ; II. f. 274 [1]	ε 297 -
13	XIII	Paris, Bibl. Nat., Gr. 50	f. 170 [2]	ε 368 Lect, Lect^{tab}
14	X	Paris, Bibl. Nat., Gr. 70	f. 392 [1]	ε 1021 -
15	XII	Paris, Bibl. Nat., Gr. 64	f. 225 [1]	ε 283 Lect, Lect^{tab}
16	XIV	Paris, Bibl. Nat., Gr. 54 [Gr.-Lt.]	f. 361 [2]	ε 449 Lect
17	XV	Paris, Bibl. Nat., Gr. 55 [Gr.-Lt.]	f. 354 [2]	ε 525 Lect, Lect^{tab}
21	XII	Paris, Bibl. Nat., Gr. 68	f. 203 [2]	ε 286 Lect$^{m.s.}$, Lect^{tab}
22	XII	Paris, Bibl. Nat., Gr. 72	f. 232 [1]	ε 288 -
23	XI	Paris, Bibl. Nat., Gr. 77	f. 230 [1]	ε 1183 -
26	XI	Paris, Bibl. Nat., Gr. 78	f. 179 [1]	ε 165 Lect, Lect^{tab}
27	X	Paris, Bibl. Nat., Gr. 115	f. 460 [1]	ε 1023 Lect$^{tab,m.s.}$
28	XI	Paris, Bibl. Nat., Gr. 379	f. 292 [1]	ε 168 Lect, Lect^{tab}
29	X	Paris, Bibl. Nat., Gr. 89	f. 169 [1]	ε 1022 Lect^{tab}
30	XV	Paris, Bibl. Nat., Gr. 100	f. 313 [1]	ε 522 -
30^{abs}	XV	Cambridge, Univ. Libr., Kk. 5.35	f. 403 [1]	ε 520 -
31	XIII	Paris, Bibl. Nat., Gr. 94	f. 188 [1]	ε 375 -
32	XII	Paris, Bibl. Nat. , Gr. 116	f. 244 [1]	ε 296 Lect, Lect^{tab}
44	XII	London, Brit. Libr., Add. 4949	f. 259 [1]	ε 239 Lect, Lect^{tab}
45	XIII	Oxford, Bodl. Libr., Barocci 31	f. 398 [1]	ε 442 Lect
46	ca 1300 A.D.	Oxford, Bodl. Libr., Barocci 29	f. 342 [1]	ε 1285 Lect, Lect^{tab}
47	XV	Oxford, Bodl. Libr., Auct. D. 5. 2	f. 554 [1]	ε 515 -
49	XII	Oxford, Bodl. Libr., Roe 1	f. 223 [1]	ε 155 Lect
52	1285/86 A.D.	Oxford, Bodl. Libr., Laud. Gr. 3	f. 158 [1]	ε 345 -

Etc.

6.2.3 Specimen III. Evangelion-Apostolos-Apocalypse Codices (eapr/NT)

The codex form eapr (NT) should be considered as a composite corpus of an Evangelion, an Apostolos (eap) and additional to these two basic corpora, a Revelation codex. The total number eapr codex items is: **51 codd.** Selected are **45 codd.** Thus: **6** excluded codices. The Chronological limits are: X/XI - XVII c.

A great deal of these codices has lectionary equipment. The reason that we present this codex is to show that the NT should be seen primarily as a liturgical book (see the 'lectionary equipment'), instead of a so called 'text codex' and that this codex form (commenly known as 'New Testament') was anyway a standard form in Byzantine manuscript tradition. Moreover, this codex form is closely related to the **eap codex form** (a large number of which also has lectionary equipment), and should be understood as an 'extended' **apostolo-evangelion codex**.

Result: Lect evidence
Selected codices: **45** codices
+ Lect: **30** codd.
- Lect: **9** codd.
Insufficient data (not counted in result): **6** codd.

List of Excluded Codices
18 [NT+Ps/Od]
241 [loc. uncertain]
242 [NT+Ps/Od]
339 [only fragm.]
1785 [loc. uncertain](δ 405 Lect, Lect^{tab} [AKPApE])

Table 3: Evangelion-Apostolos-Apocalypse Codices [NT]

Aland 1994² Serial Nº	Age/Date	Library ‖ Shelf Mark	fol. [col.]	Von Soden 1911² Lectionary equipment
35	XI	Paris, Bibl. Nat., Coislin. Gr. 199	f. 328 [1]	δ 309 Lect, Lect^{tab}
61	XVI	Dublin, Trinity Coll., Ms. 30	f. 455 [1]	δ 603 -
69	XV	Leicester, Leicester-shire Record Office, Cod. 6 D 32/1	f. 213 [1]	δ 505 - [EPAKAp]
141	XIII	Vatican City, Bibl.Vat., Vat. Gr. 1160	I+II: f. 400 [1]	δ 408 Lect, Lect^{tab}
149	X/XI	Vatican City, Bibl.Vat., Pal. Gr. 171	f. 179 [1]	δ 503 Lect $^{beim\ Apostolos}$
175	X/XI	Vatican City, Bibl.Vat., Vat. Gr. 2080	f. 247 [1]	δ 95 -
180	e:XII + apr:1273 A.D.	Vatican City, Bibl.Vat., Borg. Gr. 18	f. 444 [1]	ε 1498 Lect, Lect^{text}, Lect^{tab} $^{m.s.}$ + α 300
201	1357 A.D.	London, Brit.Libr., Add. 11837	f. 493 [2]	δ 403 Lect, Lect^{tab}
209	eap: XIV; r: XV	Venice, Bibl. Naz. Marc., Gr. Z. 10 [394]	f. 411 [1]	δ 457 Lect + α 1581 [Ap]
296	XVI	Paris, Bibl.Nat., Gr. 123.124	I: f. 257; II: f. 303 [1]	δ 600 - [2Bd.]
367	1331 A.D.	Florence, Bibl.Medicea Laur., Conv. Soppr. 53	f. 349 [1]	δ 400 Lect, Lect^{tab}
386	XIV	Vatican City, Bibl.Vat., Ottob. Gr. 66	f. 393 [1]	δ 401 Lect, Lect^{tab}
498	XIV	London, Brit.Libr. Add. 17469	f. 186 [1]	δ 402 Lect, Lect^{tab}
506	XI	Oxford, Christ Church, Wake 12	f. 240 [2]	δ 101 Lect
517	XI/XII	Oxford, Christ Church, Wake 34	f. 201 [1]	α 214 + ε 167 Lect, Lect^{tab}; Lect
522	1515/16 A.D.	Oxford, Bodl.Libr., Canon. Gr. 34	f. 319 [1]	δ 602 -
680	XIV	New Haven, Conn./Yale Univ.Libr., Ms. 248 (Phillipps 7682)	f. 190 [2]	δ 103 -
699	XI	London, Brit.Libr., Add. 28815 [eap] Idem, Egerton 3145 [pr]	f. 302 [1] f. 67 [1]	δ 104 -
757	XIII	Athens, Ἐθν. Βιβλ. 150	f. 414 [1]	δ 304 Lect, Lect^{tab}
808	XIV	Athens, Ἐθν. Βιβλ. 2251	f. 414 [1]	δ 203 Lect, Lect^{tab}
824	XIV	Grottaferrata, Bibl. della Badia, A. α. 1	f. 366 [1]	δ 404 Lect, Lect^{tab}
922	1116 A.D.	Athos, Γρηγορίου 3	f. 405 [1]	δ 200 Lect, Lect$^{m.s.}$
935	XIV	Athos, Διονυσίου, 141 (27)	f. 410 [1]	δ 361 Lect
986	XIV	Athos, Ἐσφιγμένου 186	f. 441 [1]	δ 508 Lect, Lect^{tab}
1072	XIII	Athos, Λαύρας Γ' 80	f. 411 [2]	δ 406 Lect, Lect^{tab}
1075	XIV	Athos, Λαύρας Λ' 195	f. 348 [1]	δ 506 Lect, Lect^{tab}
1094	XIII	Athos, Παντελεήμονος 29	f. 272 [1]	δ 307 Lect, Lect $^{zum\ Apostolos}$
1248	XIV	Sinai, Μονὴ τῆς Ἁγίας Αἰκατερίνης, Gr. 267	f. 389 [1]	δ 409 Lect^{tab} [+ Patr.]
1352 + 2824	XIII	Jerusalem, Πατρ. Βιβλ., Σταυροῦ 94	f. 1-235 [eap] + f. 236-248 [r]	δ 396 Lect^{tab} [eap + r]

1384	XI	Andros, Μονὴ Παναχράντου, 13 [omm. 2 J, 3 J]	f. 296 [1]	δ 100 Lect[tab] [+ Menaion]
1503	1317 A.D.	Athos, Λαύρας Α' 99	f. 263 [2]	δ 413 Lect, Lect[tab]
1597	1299 A.D.	Athos, Βατοπαιδίου 966	f. 515 [1]	δ 308 Lect[tab], Lect [m.s.]
1617	XV	Athos, Λαύρας Ε' 157	f. 362 [2]	δ 407 Lect, Lect[tab]
1626	XV	Athos, Λαύρας Ω' 16	f. 272 [1]	δ 305 Lect, Lect[tab]
1637	1328 A.D.	Athos, Λαύρας Ω' 141	f. 294 [2]	δ 605 Lect, Lect[tab]
1652	XVI	Athos, Λαύρας Θ' 152	f. 506 [1]	δ 604 Lect, Lect[tab]
1668	XI+XVI	Athos, Παντελεήμονος 15	f. 317 [1]	δ 306 Lect, Lect[tab]
1704	1541 A.D.	Athos, Κουτλουμουσίου 356	f. 490 [1]	Insuff. Data
2136	XVII	Moscow, Гос. Ист. Музей, V. 26, S. 472 [Gr.-Sl.]	f. 479 [2]	δ 700 - [Gr.-Slav.]
2200	XIV	Elasson, Μονὴ τῆς Ὀλυμπιοτίσσης, 79	f. 286 [1]	δ 414 Lect, Lect[tab]
2201 [eapr]	XV	Elasson, Μονὴ τῆς Ὀλυμπιοτίσσης, 6	f. 245 [1]	δ 374 - [AKPE not Ap]
2352	XV	Meteora, Μεταμορφώσεως, 237	f. 389 [1]	insuff. Data
2494	1316 A.D.	Sinai, Μονὴ τῆς Ἁγίας Αἰκατερίνης, Gr.1991	f. 315 [1]	insuff. Data
2495	XV	Sinai, Μονὴ τῆς Ἁγίας Αἰκατερίνης, Gr.1992	f. 222 [1]	insuff. Data
2554	1434 A.D.	Bukarest, Bibl. Acad. Române, 3/12620[6]	f. 397 [1]	insuff. Data

6.2.4 Specimen IV. Tetraevangelion commentaries (eK)

In this table we present the Tetraevangelion commentary codex form, where Gospel text and patristic commentary text are united in the same codex: Ἑρμηνεία εἰς τὰ τέσσαρα Εὐαγγέλια (for the title, see for instance, Athens, Ἐθν. Βιβλ. Cod. 204). The whole group of eK (Evangelion commentary codices) has been subdivided into sub-groups (see Aland 1994²: 'Sigelkonkordanz II. V. Soden: Gregory', 401-405): (1) **Antiochian Ev. Comm.** (**A**: 105 cod. items [anonym]); (2) **Zigabenus Ev. Comm.** (Z^ϵ: 13 cod. items); (3) **Theophylact Ev. Comm.** (Θ^ϵ: 133 cod. items); (4) **Anonym Ev. Comm.** (E^ϵ: 1 cod. item). The group presented here is the first of the four groups. This group of commentaries affirms the tetraevangelion codex form: the four gospels are interpreted together, in their concrete interrelated fourfold form. NB. The number of tetraevangelion commentary codices differ in: v. Soden 1911: 228 cod. items; Sigelkonkordanz II in Aland 1994: 251 cod. items; the Kurzgefasste Liste: Minuskeln (eK): 314 cod. items. Total selected: **174 cod**. Excluded: 140 cod.

In this group one can also find lectionary equipment in a substantial number of codices. See Ch. 1: **Box 3**:*Tables K: NT commentary codices (Aland / von Soden)*.

In this specimen only the first 50 manuscripts of the 173 selected manuscripts are presented
NB. R= Randglossen

Table 4: Tetraevangelion commentaries

Aland 1994² Serial N°	Age/Date	Library	Shelf Mark	fol.[col.]	Von Soden 1911² Categories N°	
X 033	X	Munich, Univ. Bibl., 2° Cod. ms. 30		f. 160 [2]	A^3	-
055	XI	Paris, Bibl. Nat., Gr. 201		f. 303 [1]		-
12	XIV	Paris, Bibl. Nat., Gr. 230		f. 294 [R]	A^{137}	Lect, Lect^{tab}
19	XII	Paris, Bibl. Nat., Gr. 189		f. 387 [R]	A^{214}	-
20	XI	Paris, Bibl. Nat.,, Gr. 188		f. 274 [R]	A^{138}	Lect, m.s.Lect^{tab}
24	X	Paris, Bibl. Nat., Gr. 178		f. 240 [R]	A^{18}	m.s.Lect^{tab}
25	XI	Paris, Bibl. Nat., Gr. 191		f. 292 [R]	A^{139}	Lect passim
34	X	Paris, Bibl. Nat., Coislin. Gr. 195		f. 469 [R]	A^{19}	-
36	X	Paris, Bibl. Nat., Coislin. Gr. 20		f. 509 [R]	A^{20}	-
37	XI	Paris, Bibl. Nat., Coislin. Gr. 21		f. 357 [R]	A^{154}	Lect^{tab}
39	XI	Paris, Bibl. Nat., Coislin. Gr. 23		f. 288 [R]	A^{140}	-
40	XI	Paris, Bibl. Nat., Coislin. Gr. 22		f. 312 [R]	A^{155}	-
48	XII	Oxford, Bodl. Libr., Auct. D 2. 17		f. 145 [2]	A^{232}	-
50	XI	Oxford, Bodl. Libr., Laud. Gr. 33		f. 241 [R]	A^{152}	-
63	X	Dublin, Trinity Coll., Ms. 31		f. 1-237 [R]	A^{118}	m.s. Lect
77	XI	Vienna, Österr. Nat. Bibl., Theol. Gr. 154		f. 302 [R]	A^{143}	m.s.Lect, Lect^{tab}
100	X	Budapest, Országos Széchényi Könyvtár, Cod. Gr. 1		f. 374 [R]	A^{11}	Lect, m.s.Lect^{tab}
108	XI	Naples, Bibl. Naz., Cod. Neapol. Ex Vind. 3		f. 426 [R, I+II]	A^{144}	-
127	XI	Vatican City, Bibl.Vat., Vat. Gr. 349		f. 378 [R]	A^{124}	Lect
129	XI	Vatican City, Bibl.Vat., Vat. Gr. 358		f. 355 [R]	A^{200}	Lect^{tab}
137	XI	Vatican City, Bibl.Vat., Vat. Gr. 756		f. 300 [R]	A^{153}	Lect^{tab}
138	XI	Vatican City, Bibl.Vat., Vat. Gr. 757		f. 380 [1]	$A^{201} + C^{j24}$	-
143	XI	Vatican City, Bibl.Vat., Vat. Gr. 1229		f. 275 [R]	A^{125}	-
151	XIII	Vatican City, Bibl.Vat., Pal. Gr. 224		f. 224 [R]	A^{17}	-
154	XIII	Vatican City, Bibl.Vat., Reg. Gr. 28		f. 355 [1]	$\Theta^{\epsilon\,30}$	m.s.Lect, Lect^{tab}
168	XIII	Vatican City, Bibl.Vat., Barb. Gr. 570		f. 217 [2]	$\Theta^{\epsilon\,31}$	-
194	XI	Florence, Bibl. Medicea Laur., Plutei VI. 33		f. 258 [R]	A^{130}	-
195	XI	Florence, Bibl. Medicea Laur., Plutei VI. 34		f. 277 [R]	A^{131}	-
196	XII	Florence, Bibl. Medicea Laur., Plutei VIII. 12		f. 369 [1]	$Z^{\epsilon\,23}$	-
210	XI	Venice, Bibl. Naz. Marc., Gr. Z. 27 (341)		f. 372 [R]	A^{133}	-
215	XI	Venice, Bibl. Naz.Marc., Gr. Z. 544 (591)		f. 272 [R]	A^{134}	Lect, Lect^{tab}
222	XIV	Vienna, Österr. Nat. Bibl., Theol. Gr. 180		f. 346 [1]	A^{404}	-
233	XIII	El Escorial, Real Bibl., Y. II. 8		f. 279 [2]	A^{305}	-
237	XI	Moscow, Гос. Ист. Музей, V. 85, S. 41		f. 289 [R]	A^{13}	-
238	XI/XII	Moscow, Гос. Ист. Музей,, V. 91,S. 47 + Росс. Госуд. Архив, F. 1607, No. 3		f. 355 [1, Mt, Mk] f. 226 [1, LJ]	A^{145}	Lect
240	XII	Moskau, Гос. Ист. Музей, V. 87, S. 48		f. 411 [1]	$Z^{\epsilon\,21}$	-
244	XII	Moskau, Гос. Ист. Музей, V. 88, S. 220		f. 274 [1]	$Z^{\epsilon\,20}$	-
259	XI	Moskau, Гос. Ист. Музей, V. 86, S. 44		f. 262 [R]	A^{122}	Lect
299	X	Paris, Bibl. Nat., Gr. 177		f. 328 [R]	A^{21}	-
301	XI	Paris, Bibl. Nat., Gr. 187		f. 221 [R]	A^{156}	-
303	1255 A.D.	Paris, Bibl. Nat., Gr. 194A		f. 321 [1]	$\Theta^{\epsilon\,32}$	Lect, Lect^{tab}
305	XIII	Paris, Bibl. Nat., Gr. 195		f. 261 [1]	$Z^{\epsilon\,30}$	m.s.Lect
329	XII	Paris, Bibl. Nat., Coislin. Gr. 19		f. 321 [R]	A^{219}	-

353	XII	Milan, Bibl. Ambros., M. 93 sup.	f. 194 [R]	A ^{210}	-
370	XIV	Florence, Bibl. Riccard., 5	f.437 [1]	$\Theta^{e\,41}$	Lect
373	XV	Vatican City, Bibl.Vat., Vat. Gr. 1423	f. 221 [R]	A ^{500}	-
374	XI	Vatican City, Bibl.Vat., Vat. Gr. 1445	f. 173 [1]	A ^{204}	-
377	XVI	Vatican City, Bibl.Vat., Vat. Gr. 1618	f. 339 [1]	A ^{501}	-
379	XV	Vatican City, Bibl.Vat., Vat. Gr. 1769	f. 437 [1]	Z $^{e\,50}$	-
391	1055 A.D.	Vatican City, Bibl.Vat., Ottob. Gr. 432	f. 232 [R]	A ^{128}	-

Etc.

6.2.5 Specimen V. Evangelion-Apostolos-Apocalypse Codices (eaprK)

In addition to the **Evangelion-Apostolos-Apocalypse Codices**, this commentary form [eaprK] is rare and not a common standard Byzantine commentary form. In this codex patristic commentaries and liturgical texts are united with the text of the NT biblical books. It should be noted that, even in this commentary codex form, 'lectionary equipment' is adopted.

Table 5 Evangelion-Apostolos-Apocalypse Codices

Aland 1994[2]				Von Soden 1911[2]
Serial N°	Age/Date	Library ‖ Shelf Mark	fol. [col.]	Categories N°
886	1454?	Vatican City, Bibl.Vat., Reg.Gr. 6 [eaprPK: not Cat Ep]	f. 336 [1]	$\Theta^{\epsilon 56}$; $\Theta^{\pi\rho 50}$; $\Theta^{\pi 56}$ [+ comm. Ap]
1424	IX/X	Chicago, Jesuit Krauss-McCormick Libr., Gruber Ms. 152 [eapKr]	f. 337 [1]	δ 30 Lect [+ Schol + Komm. zu EAKP]
1678	XIV	Athos, Παντελεήμονος 770 [eaprK]	f. 334 [1]	$\Theta^{\epsilon 404}$; $A^{\pi\rho 41}$; $\Theta^{\pi 404}$; Av^{402} Lect, Lect^{tab}
1780	XIII	Durham, N.C., Duke Univ. Libr., Gr. 1	f. 198 [1]	δ 412 Lect, Lect^{tab}+ [Komm. zu Evv. + Schol zu KP]

6.3 Group II. Byzantine Biblical Codices (OT)

6.3.1 Specimen VI. Prophetologion (Π)

In this table, the Prophetologion represents the second main group of Byzantine Greek Codices. The Prophetologion should be studied parallel to another prominent liturgical codex form - the Byzantine Psalterion. The two form the two liturgical pillars of the Byzantine offices. In the Prophetologia, one observes series of OT lessons grouped together and organised according to the lectionary structure of the Byzantine Orthodox calendar. The common structure of this type of codices is threefold: (1) lessons of the feasts of Christmas and Theophany, (2) lessons of the Triodion and Pentekostarion period, (3) lessons of the fixed feasts and commemorations. This codex form is now obsolete and the series of lessons have been adopted in the Byzantine liturgical books (Triodion, Pentekostarion, Menaia). The arrangement of these three basic elements are diversified in the codices, without losing the main structure.

In this table we have updated the list of known Prophetologia compiled by Rahlfs (1914), by adding Engberg's update (1980/1981), as well as our own update. By exluding fragments and incomplete codices, this table provides a realistic picture of preserved manuscripts of this type (131 mss).

Total number of Prophetologion codices: **150 ms. items** (Rahlfs 1914). Selected Prophetologia: **95 codices** (Rahlfs 1914). Excluded are: **54 ms. items** [fragm.: 45; excl. Engberg: 8; uncertain: 1]. Additions Engberg 1980-81: 14 codices [complete or incomplete, frag. ??]. Additions Engberg 2003: 3 integral mss [incl.] + 16 [incompl.codices/fragm. not incl.]. Supplements in Present Thesis: 18 codices (catalogue research). Total of all known ms. items and mss.: **201 Mss.** Total of Selected Prophetologia Codices: 96 + 14 + 3 + 18 = **131 Mss.** Total excluded ms. items: 54 + 16 = **70 codd.** Chronological limits: IX - XVII c. NB. S. Engberg correspondence of 29/07/05, states (estimates?) that there are more than 204 ms. items. But we do not know how many fragments and incomplete manuscripts are included in this estimated sum. A complete list is not yet available, but will be published in Engberg's forthcoming book on the subject.

The reason that we present this table (in more detail than the other specimens), is that it is precisely this codex form which is of such importance in Byzantine liturgical and patristic tradition, and it has been practically ignored in Western scholarly research, beside a small group of specialists.

We have folowed the chronological order of ms-listings as set up by Rahlfs (Verzeichnis der Lectionar-Handschriften, 1914, 440-443).
The List of Rahlfs was checked by Engberg (1987).
A serial number Π′ has been introduced in the present thesis (this was not done by Rahlfs):
Not included are: (1) <u>non-prophetologia</u>; (2) <u>mss of uncertain data</u>; (3) <u>incomplete codd</u>; (4) <u>codd with a too small number of folios</u>; (5) <u>fragments.</u>

Table 6 : Prophetologion

Rahlfs (1914) *Verzeichnis*, p. 440-443				Rahlfs (1914) *Verzeichnis*, Main Part	Engberg 1980/1981
Serial N°	Age/Date	Library + Shelf Mark [ancient number]	fol. [col.]	data	Ms. code
Π 1	IX [U]	St. Petersburg, Росс. Нац. Библ., Gr. 51	f. 149	p. 223	Le [X in.]
Π 2	X	Grottaferrata, Bibl. della Badia, A. δ. II	f. 155	p. 76	δ2
Π 3	X	Vatican City, Bibl. Vat., Regin. Gr. 75	f. 101	p. 246	R [982 A. D]
Π 4	X	Venice, Bibl. Naz. Marc., Gr. 13	f. 324	p. 307	V [XI]
Π 5	X/XI	Vatican City, Bibl. Vat., Vat. Gr. 1842	f. 85. [inc.]	p. 267	V1842
Π 6	X/XI [U]	Sinai, Μονὴ τῆς Ἁγίας Αἰκατερίνης, Gr. 7	f. ?	p. 285	Sin7
Π 7	X/XI [U]	Sinai, Μονὴ τῆς Ἁγίας Αἰκατερίνης, Gr. 8	f. 299	p. 285	Sin8
Π 8	X/XI [U]	Trier, Bistumsarchiv 143. F	f. 138	p. 296	T
Π 9	1054 A.D.	St. Petersburg, Росс. Нац. Библ., Gr. 217	f. 156	p. 225-226	Len217 [XIII]
Π 10	1072 A.D.	Athens, Ἐθν. Βιβλ. 20	f. 224	p. 5	A
Π 11	1072 A.D.	Grottaferrata, Bibl. della Badia, A. δ. V	f. 162	p. 76	δ5 [XII-XIII]
Π 12	1078 A.D.	Athos, Λαύρας 190	f. 252	p. 19	L190
Π 13	XI	Athos, Φιλοθέου 6, [NT & OT Lect] [L^{+a} 751]	f. ?	p. 23	
Π 14	XI	Grottaferrata, Bibl. della Badia, A. δ. X	f. 83. (inc.)	p. 76	δ10
Π 15	XI	Jerusalem, Πατρ. Βιβλ., Σάββα Gr. 98	f. 182	p. 80	S98
Π 16	XI	Jerusalem, Πατρ. Βιβλ., Σάββα Gr. 99	f. 225	p. 80	S99 [XII]
Π 17	XI	Jerusalem, Πατρ. Βιβλ., Σάββα Gr. 143β + 147 + 704 No 12	f. 143b + 147, 45 + 172	p. 80	S143/147
Π 18	XI	Jerusalem, Πατρ. Βιβλ., Σάββα Gr. 247	f. 188	p. 81	S247
Π 19	XI	Oxford, Bodl. Libr., Laud. gr. 36	f. 275	p. 173	dz
Π 20	XI	Paris, Bibl. Nat., Gr. 372	f. 291	p. 207	
Π 21	XI	Vatican City, Bibl. Vat., Vat.. Gr. 1860	f. 120	p. 267	V1860
Π 22	XI	Sinai, Μονὴ τῆς Ἁγίας Αἰκατερίνης, Gr. 13	f. 182	p. 286	Sin13 [XIII]
Π 23	XI/XII	Sinai, Μονὴ τῆς Ἁγίας Αἰκατερίνης, Gr. 12	f. ?	p. 286	Sin12 [XIII-XIV]

Π 24	XI/XII	Sinai, Μονὴ τῆς Ἁγίας Αἰκατερίνης, Gr. 17	f. ?	p. 286	
Π 25	XI/XII?	Sinai, Μονὴ τῆς Ἁγίας Αἰκατερίνης, Gr. 18	f. ?	p. 286	
Π 26	1116 A.D.	Moscow, Гос. Ист. Музей, V. 8, S. 483	f. 200	p. 148	
Π 27	1133 A.D.	Paris, Bibl. Nat., Gr. 243	f. 219	p. 206	P243
Π 28	XII	Athos, Διονυσίου 82	f. ?	p. 10	D82
Π 29	XII	Athos, Δοχειαρίου 28	f. ?	p. 11	
Π 30	XII	Athos, Ἐσφιγμένου 46	f. 197	p. 11	Γενεσοπαροιμία
Π 31	XII?	Athos, Λαύρας 195	f. 111	p. 17	L195
Π 32	XII?	Athos, Λαύρας 196	f. 106	p. 18	
Π 33	XII	Grottaferrata, Bibl. della Badia, A.δ. I	f. 141	p. 76	δ1
Π 34	XII	Grottaferrata, Bibl. della Badia, A.δ. IIII	f. 107	p. 76	δ3
Π 35	XII	Grottaferrata, Bibl. della Badia, A.δ. IX	f. 117	p. 76	δ9
Π 36	XII	London, Brit. Mus., Add. 11 841	f. 86	p. 104	B1
Π 37	XII	London, Brit. Mus. Add. 29 715	f. ?	p. 105	B2 [175b-202b, 249a-end]
Π 38	XII	London, Brit. Mus., Add. 36 660	f. 192	p. 106	B3
Π 39	XII	Messina, Bibl. Reg. Univ., SS. Salv. 102	f. 254	p. 137	
Π 40	XII	Paris, Bibl. Nat., Gr. 272	f. 434	p. 206	P272
Π 41	XII	Paris, Bibl. Nat., Gr. 273	f. 203	p. 206	P273
Π 42	XII	Paris, Bibl. Nat., Gr. 274	f. 98. [inc.]	p. 206	
Π 43	XII	Patmos, Μονὴ τοῦ Ἰωάννου τοῦ Θεολόγου Gr. 210	f. 281	p. 218	Pt
Π 44	XII	St. Petersburg, Росс. Нац. Библ., Gr. 218	f. 130	p. 226	Len218
Π 45	XII	Vatican City, Bibl. Vat., Barb. Gr. 391	f. 138	p. 237	B(arb)391
Π 46	XII	Vatican City, Bibl. Vat., Barb. Gr. 446	f. 205	p. 238	Bb
Π 47	XII	Sinai, Μονὴ τῆς Ἁγίας Αἰκατερίνης, Gr. 10	f. ?	p. 285	Sin10 [XIV]
Π 48	XII/XIII	El Escorial, Real. Bibl., Y (lat.)-III-2	f. ?	p. 54	
Π 49	XII/XIII	Messina, Bibl. Reg. Univ., SS. Salv. 122	f. 237	p. 137	
Π 50	XII/XIII	Messina, Bibl. Reg. Univ., SS. Salv. 131	f. 198	p. 137	
Π 51	XII/XIII	Paris, Bibl. Nat., Gr. 275	f. 198	p. 206	P275
Π 52	XII/XIII	Sinai, Μονὴ τῆς Ἁγίας Αἰκατερίνης, Gr. 14	f. 124	p. 286	
Π 53	XII/XIII	Sinai, Μονὴ τῆς Ἁγίας Αἰκατερίνης, Gr. 16	f. ?	p. 286	
Π 54	1202 A.D.	Jerusalem, Πατρ. Βιβλ., Σταυροῦ Gr. 48, and → St. Petersburg, Росс. Нац. Библ., Gr. 325	f. 174 + f. 2	p. 83 + p. 230	
Π 55	1280 A.D.	Vatican City, Bibl. Vat., Vat. Gr. 770	f. 106	p. 256	V770
Π 56	XIII	Athos, Φιλοθέου 34	f. ?	p. 23	
Π 57	XIII	[Berat, [Βιβλιοθήκη τῆς Μητροπόλεως (and other Churches)]. Nr. VII]	f. ?	p. 27 [not incl.]	
Π 58	XIII	Florence, Bibl. Med. Laur., Plut. X 27	f. 168	p. 67	
Π 59	XIII	Grottaferrata, Bibl. della Badia, A.δ. IV	f. 257	p. 76	δ4
Π 60	XIII	Messina, Bibl. Reg. Univ., SS. Salv. 164	f. 187	p. 137	
Π 61	XIII	Paris, Bibl. Nat., Suppl. Gr. 805	f. 63	p. 215-216 [n.incl]	P805
Π 62	XIII	Vatican City, Bibl. Vat., Barb. Gr. 338	f. 86	p. 237	B(arb)338
Π 63	XIII	Vatican City, Bibl. Vat., Barb. Gr. 346	f. 198	p. 237	B(arb)346
Π 64	XIII	Vatican City, Bibl. Vat., Barb. Gr. 418	f. 61	p. 238	B(arb)418
Π 65	XIII	Sinai, Μονὴ τῆς Ἁγίας Αἰκατερίνης, Gr. 9	f. ?	p. 286	Sin9
Π 66	XIII	Sinai, Μονὴ τῆς Ἁγίας Αἰκατερίνης, Gr. 15	f. ?	p. 286	
Π 67	XIII	Sinai, Μονὴ τῆς Ἁγίας Αἰκατερίνης, Gr. 550	f. 489	p. 292	[Ps, Oktoe, Men, Triod, Lect V et NT]
Π 68	XIV	Amorgos, Μονὴ τῆς Χοζοβιωτίσσης 1 [Mel. S. 80]	f. 203	p. 2 [Politis1976]	
Π 69	?	Paris, Bibl. Nat., Gr. 1720	f. 193. ?	p. 211-212 [n. Incl]	
Π 70	XIV	Athos, Ἰβήρων 264	f. ?	p. 12	
Π 71	XIV	Athos, Καρακάλλου 26	f. ?	p.15	
Π 72	XIV	Athos, Καρακάλλου 119	f. ?	p. 15	
Π 73	XIV	Athos, Παντελεήμονος 48	f. ?	p. 20	
Π 74	XIV	Athos, Πρωτάτου 27	f. ?	p. 23	
Π 75	XIV	Jerusalem, Πατρ. Βιβλ., Σάββα Gr. 240	f. 272	p. 81	
Π 76	XIV	Patmos, Μονὴ τοῦ Ἰωάννου τοῦ Θεολόγου Gr. 211	f. ?	p. 218	
Π 77	XIV	St. Petersburg, Росс. Нац. Библ., Gr. 550	f. 251	p. 230	L550
Π 78	XIV	Vatican City, Bibl. Vallicell., Gr. 64	f. 124	p. 235	
Π 79	XIV/XV	Grottaferrata, Bibl. della Badia, A.δ. XIII	f. 142	p. 76	
Π 80	1449 A.D.	Zante, Κατρ. Nr. 29	f. 285	p. 325	
Π 81	XV	Athos, Φιλοθέου 170	f. ?	p. 23	
Π 82	XV	Cambridge, Clare Coll. 31	f. 206	p. 38	
Π 83	1520 A.D.	Athos, Ἰβήρων 882	f. ?	p. 14	
Π 84	1545 A.D.	Sinai, Μονὴ τῆς Ἁγίας Αἰκατερίνης, Gr. 19	f. ?	p. 286	
Π 85	1553 A.D.	Athos, Κουτλουμουσίου 303	f. 200	p. 16	

Π 86	1555 A.D.	Athos, Κουτλουμουσίου 337	f. 256	p. 16	
Π 87	1575 A.D.	Athen, 'Εθν. Βιβλ. 24	f. 346	p. 5	
Π 88	1579 A.D.	Athos, Λαύρας 207 [Rahlfs 1299 AD, p. 18?]	f. 202	p. 18	
Π 89	1593 A.D.	Athos, Διονυσίου 432 [Litur.]	f. ?	p. 10	
Π 90	XVI	Athen, 'Εθν. Βιβλ. 36	f. 137	p. 6	
Π 91	XVI	Athen, 'Εθν. Βιβλ. 37	f. 227	p. 6	
Π 92	XVI	Athos, Παντελεήμονος 454	f. 164	p. 21	
Π 93	XVI	Athos, Παντοκράτορος 179	f. ?	p. 22	
Π 94	XVI	Athos, Σταυρονικήτα 126,	f. ?	p. 23	
Π 95	XVI	Jerusalem, Πατρ. Βιβλ., Σάββα Gr. 300	f. ? [f. 216-311]	p. 81	

Additional Codices (Ed. Engberg 1980/1981)					
Π 96	IX	Athos, Παντελεήμονος 95	-	-	Ru
Π 97	IX	Moscow, Гос. Ист. Музей, V. 262	-	-	Mon
Π 98	X	Florence, Bibl. Med. Laur., Plut. IX. 15	-	-	F
Π 99	X	Athos, Λαύρας 177	-	-	L177
Π 100	X	London, Colleg. Sion., Arc. I.1	-	-	Sc
Π 101	XI	Thessaloniki, Μονὴ τῶν Βλαταίων 49	-	-	Bl
Π 102	XI	Princeton, B. Firestone, cod. De Wald	-	-	W
Π 103	XI/XII	Alexandria, Βιβλ. τοῦ Πατρ., 141	-	-	A141
Π 104	XII	Athos, Λαύρας 309	-	-	L309
Π 105	XII	Vatican City, Bibl. Vat., Vat. Gr. 768	-	-	V768
Π 106	XII/XIII	Jerusalem, Πατρ. Βιβλ., Σταυροῦ Gr. 42	-	-	St
Π 107	XII/XIII	Paris, Bibl. Nat., Gr. 372	-	-	P372
Π 108	XIII	Oxford, Bodl. Libr., Barocc. 99	-	-	Bc
Π 109	?	Florence, Bibl. Med. Laur., Plut. X. 26	-	-	Laur.X26

Additional Codices (Engberg 1988)					
Π 110	XIII	Paris, Bibl. Nat., Gr. 308	-		
Π 111	XV	Mega Spelaion 135	-		

Additonal Codices (Engberg 2003)					
Π 112	XV	Sinai, Μονὴ τῆς Ἁγίας Αἰκατερίνης, Gr. 20	-	p. 96	
Π 113	XVII	Sinai, Μονὴ τῆς Ἁγίας Αἰκατερίνης, Gr. 2042	-	p. 96	
Π 114	1285 A.D.	Oxford, Bodl. Libr., Auct. T. 3.6	[Proph. + Triodion]	p. 99	

Additonal Codices (Supplemented in the Present Thesis)			Fol. [Col.]	Ms. Catalogues
Π 115	XI	Athos, Βατοπαιδίου 626,	f. 224	Eustratiades/Arcadios
Π 116	XI	Sofia, Народна Библиотека "Св. Св. Кирил и Методий", Gr. 18	-	Stojanov (1973)
Π 117	XI/XII	Princeton, Univ. Libr., Gen. Coll., 112	-	Benett et al. (1991)
Π 118	XII	Athos, Βατοπαιδίου, 622	f. 160	Eustratiades/Arcadios
Π 119	XIV	Athos, Βατοπαιδίου, 623	f. 279	Eustratiades/Arcadios
Π 120	XIV	Kiev, Національна Бібліотека України імені В. І. Вернадського, Киево Печерська Лавра Gr. 550 [?]	-	Fonkič (1984)
Π 121	XIV	Athos, Λαύρας 746 [H 91.], [Menol. + Propheteiai]	f. 429	Spyridon/Eustratiades
Π 122	XV	Athos, Λαύρας 301 [Γ 61], [Prov. Sal. + Propheteiai]	f. 61	Spyridon/Eustratiades
Π 123	XV	Athos, Βατοπαιδίου, 624	f. 172	Eustratiades/Arcadios
Π 124	XVI	Athos, Λαύρας 1226 [I 142.], [Triodion + Prophetologion]	f. 501	Spyridon/Eustratiades
Π 125	XVI	Athos, Λαύρας 1616 [Λ 125.],	f. 187	Spyridon/Eustratiades
Π 126	XVI	Athos, Λαύρας 1617 [Λ 126.],	f. 180	Spyridon/Eustratiades
Π 127	1561 A.D.	Athos, Λαύρας 757 [H 102.],	f. 215	Spyridon/Eustratiades
Π 128	XVII	Athos, Λαύρας 599 [E 137.],	f. 226 [2]	Spyridon/Eustratiades
Π 129	XVII	Istanbul, Πατρ. Βιβλ. Μονὴ τῆς Ἁγίας Τριάδος (Chalki) 18	-	Tsakopoulos
Π 130	XVII	Athens, 'Εθν. Βιβλ. 25	f. 154	Sakkelion
Π 131	1655 A.D.	Athos, Λαύρας, 1160 [I 76.]	f. 152	Spyridon/Eustratiades
Π 132	?	Linköping, Stifts- och Landsbibl., T. 276	-	Richard/Olivier

6.4 Group III. Byzantine Composite Codices (OT & NT)

6.4.1 Specimen VII. Pandect/Complete Bibles (OT/NT)

The Byzantine Greek OT & NT codex is a composite manuscript in which the books of both Testaments (ἑξηκοντάβιβλον) are placed together in order to provide a complete collection of Christian canonical literature.
Information about both constitutive parts (OT and NT) is dispersed over both disciplines. We took the basic data from Rahlfs/Fraenkel and supplemented it with Aland, Von Soden and Gregory. Von Soden's (and Scrivener's, Bordier's, Engberg's) research indicates that several of these codexes also have lectionary equipment.
The reason for presenting the complete Bibles in this table is to demonstrate the codicological union of the manuscripts. Remarkable is that academia split their studies into two different disciplines, thus ignoring the very raison d'étre of this codex form, especially since this group contains the jewels of critical text research. It would also be interesting to notate the lectionary equipment in these complete Bibles.
It seems as if this codex form is only a small one (11 codices.), and in fact a considerable number of them are not "complete" at all. The number and arrangement of included books differ. See for precise contents of the manuscripts Rahlfs and Fraenkel.

Table 7: Pandect/ Complete Bibles (OT/NT)

Rahlfs 1914 (OT) Serial N°	Age/Date	Library	Shelf Mark	fol. [col.]	Fraenkel I 2004 (OT)	Aland 1994² (NT)	v. Soden 1911 (NT)	Gregory 1900 (NT)
S (p. 226-229)	IV [U]	St. Petersburg, Росс. Нац. Библ., Gr. 25		f. 393 [!]	p. 201-206	[א] 01	δ 2	p. 18-29
A (p. 114-116)	V [U]	London, Brit.Mus., Royal 1D V-VIII		f. 279 + 238 + 118 + 144	p. 221-226	A 02	δ 4	p. 29-32
B (p. 258-260)	IV [U]	Vatican City, Bibl.Vat. , Gr. 1209		f. 1536	p. 337-344	B 03	δ 1	p. 32-40
C (p. 193-194)	V [U]	Paris, Bibl.Nat., Coinslin. 9		f. 209	p. 313-315	C 04	δ 3	p. 40-42
V [II] (p.306 [II])	VIII	Venice, Bibl. Naz. Marc. 1 +		f. 164	p. 372-374	[NT lost]	-	-
V [I] (p. 270 [I])	VIII	Vatican City, Bibl. Vat., Gr. 2106		f. 132	p. 344-346			
55 (p. 245-246)	X	Vatican City, Bibl. Vat., Reg. gr. 1		f. 565	-	[NT lost]		
130 (p. 318-319)	XII/XIII	Vienna, Österr. Nat. Bibl., Theol. Gr. 23		f. 623	-	218	δ 300	p. 168
106 (p. 59-61)	1334 A.D.	Ferrara, Bibl.Com.187 I.II,188 II		f. 211 + 214 + 114	-	582	δ 410	p. 205
68 p. 306-307	XV	Venice, Bibl. Naz. Marc. 5		f. 441	-	205	δ 500	p. 167
122 (p. 307)	XV	Venice, Bibl.Naz. Marc. 6		f. 431	-	205^abs	δ 501	p. 167
44 (p. 325-326)	XV	Zittau, Zentralbibl. A.1		f. 775	-	664	δ 502	p. 210

6.5 Group IV. Byzantine Composite Codices (Bibl. & Lit)

6.5.1 Specimen VIII. Byzantine Biblical / Liturgical codices

This table shows the manuscripts that contain liturgical and biblical components, together in one codex. We expect that, due to the large number of unexplored liturgical manuscripts, plus the biblical and patristic manuscripts with liturgical elements, this group will grow to become a very large group.

Total selected Codices (*l* Lit): **27**
Excluded Codices: 1

Table 8: Byzantine Biblical / Liturgical codices: with Evangelion/Apostle lessons

Aland 1994 Serial N°	Age/Date	Library	Shelf Mark	fol. [col.]	Gregory I 1900 Serial N°
l 58	XVI	Paris, Bibl. Nat., Suppl. Gr. 50		f. 49	Evl 58
l 93	XVI	Paris, Bibl. Nat., Gr. 326		f. 144	Evl 93
l 487	XVII	Grottaferrata, Bibl. della Badia, Γ.α. 18		f. 170	Evl 487
l 490	IX	Grottaferrata, Bibl. della Badia, Γ.β. 7		f. 172	Evl 490
l 493	XII	Grottaferrata, Bibl. della Badia, Γ.β. 11		f. 20	Evl 493
l 496	XIII	Grottaferrata, Bibl. della Badia, Γ.β. 14		f. 54	Evl 496
l 503	XIII	Grottaferrata, Bibl. della Badia, Γ.β. 35		f. 83	Evl 503
l 507	XIV	Grottaferrata, Bibl. della Badia, Δ.γ. 7		f. 115	Evl 507
l 508	XVIII	Grottaferrata, Bibl. della Badia, Δ.γ. 26		f. 103	Evl 508
l 531	XI	Città del Vaticano, Bibl.Vat., Barg. Gr. 431		f. 145	Evl 531
l 552	XIII	Città del Vaticano, Bibl.Vat., Vat. Gr. 1813		f. 266	Evl 552
l 577	XVII	Athos, Διονυσίου, 174 [378]		f. 211	Evl 577
l 693	XV	Athos, Ἰβήρων, 847 [880]		f. 28	-
l 713	XVIII	Athos, Ξενοφῶντος, 68		f. 66	Evl 713
l 733	XVIII	Athos, Γρηγορίου, 71 [118]		f. 74	-
l 755	XV	Athos, Φιλοθέου, 1889 [125]		f. 164	Evl 755
l 896	XIII	Sinai, Μονὴ τῆς Ἁγίας Αἰκατερίνης, Gr. 550		f. 489	Evl 896
l 897	1522 A.D.	Sinai, Μονὴ τῆς Ἁγίας Αἰκατερίνης, Gr. 659		f. 397	Evl 897
l 908	1697 A.D.	Sinai, Μονὴ τῆς Ἁγίας Αἰκατερίνης, Gr. 943		f. 80	Evl 908
l 925	XVII	Venedig, Bibl. Naz. [Gr.-Lat.], Marc. Gr. II, 188 [1402]		f. 65	Evl 925
l 940	XIII	London, Brit. Libr., Eagerton 2743		f. 147	Evl 940
l 1017	XII	Jerusalem, Πατρ. Βιβλ., Σάββα 257		f. 396	Evl 1017
l 1213	XVII	Lesbos, Kalloni/Limonos, 221		f. 192	-
l 1344	XIV	Alexandria, Βιβλ. Πατρ., 104		f. 48	-
l 1361	XVIII	Athos, Ἐσφιγμένου, 237		-	-
l 1387	XVI	Moskau, Гос. Ист. Музей, V.271. S.486		f.135	-
l 1580	XVI	Ann Arbor/Univ. Libr., 130		f. 416	-

Final Conclusion and Perspective

In this work, we have attempted to demonstrate 1) the anchoring of the biblical as well as the patristic writings in the liturgy of the church; and 2) the close connection between the Scriptures and the interpretative framework of the fathers, by exploring: the codicological, liturgical forms of the Byzantine Greek manuscripts and the calendar system that regulates their use and the holdings (libraries) in the primarily Eastern Orthodox world, from which the Byzantine manuscripts stem.

A major conclusion of the thesis is the desirability of new codico-liturgical parameters to classify the manuscripts, to broaden the horizon of our knowledge of the Byzantine biblical and patristic manuscripts, as they are today. To this end we have developed an outline for a *Catalogue of Byzantine Manuscripts,* which is presented in the last part of this work. If elaborated, such a classification would contribute towards a reorganisation of the study of the Byzantine biblical and patristic codices and open new doors for cross-disciplinary research. Through the Catalogue the extant manuscripts will be presented in a new way, whereby groups of manuscripts will be placed together side by side to show new interrelationships and to reunite (visually) the manuscript materials which have been isolated and abstracted from their codicological heritage.

A future research programme could contain the following components:

1) The inauguration of a cataloguing programme in which the Byzantine ecclesiastical manuscripts are selected/collected on the basis of a codico-liturgical model, taking the existing catalogues as a point of departure (involving existing institutes from e.g. Paris, Münster, Göttingen, Thessaloniki);

2) The extension of the groups of Byzantine manuscripts [normally limited to the XV/XVI c.[590]] to include Byzantine codices up to the end of the XIX c. and, in fact, up to our own time;

3) A revisit to the local library catalogues of manuscripts (even to the local handwritten catalogues) in order to reposition the codicological identification, so as to be able to return to the individual codices themselves.

4) The publishing of new manuscript editions that are more akin to the original codex forms, e.g. a Tetra-Evangelion, or an Evangelion (cf. formerly Chicago project), and particularly a commentary manuscript such as the (anonymous) Tetraevangelion Scholion Commentary (see Migne PG 106: Scholia Palaia) or the 'standard' commentary of Theophylact of Bulgaria;

5) Fresh evaluation of the manuscript texts, on the basis of new codicological parameters of collation, including the apparatuses used in the codices by the scribes (e.g. lectionary equipment, patristic scholia and commentaries, musical notation, text-division marks, iconographic design etc);

6) Comparison of the Greek manuscript tradition, with that of the e.g. Slavonic, Romanian, Georgian Middle Eastern traditions, against the background of the one Tradition from which they all stem and one library background in which they were housed.

Moreover, it would be very interesting to attune the intended cataloguing programme to a parallel cataloguing programme for Byzantine classical manuscripts, since this type of extra-ecclesiastical Greek literature is often combined with ecclesiastical material in the codices and such a catalogue does not exist, as far as we are aware. In a similar vain, it would be relevant to compare the Jewish/rabbinical codices in the context of the study of the Byzantine Greek manuscripts.

Pointers in the direction of future research

The setting up and edition of a *Catalogue of Byzantine Manuscripts* along the principles set out in this thesis is the first task envisaged, to make the inner cohesion between Bible research and patrology fully concrete, and visible. In this process the following academic disciplines should be involved: NT and OT research, patristics, liturgical studies, hymnography, hagiography, iconography. The parameters for the structure of such a Catalogue can be found in the thesis at hand.

---

[590] This extension was never absent in the Greek & Russian scholarly and cataloguing traditions.

On the newly established ground of reclassified manuscripts, fresh investigations could be started in the field of textual research of the biblical books, according to the codicological entities in which these books and texts were transmitted. I conjecture that the model of "cohesion" will throw new light on questions of textual history and textual transmission and will have consequences for the future edition programmes.

New editions should be produced, for instance of the Prophetologion, which is very interesting from the point of view of ancient stages of textual tradition. Such a project could start with a diplomatic or phototype edition of the unique, printed edition of the Prophetologion (Venice, 1597). To our mind, such an edition should be executed according to the (codicological) viewpoints developed in this thesis.[591] Other publications could include academic editions of the Evangelion and/or Tetraevangelion, or the Apostolos, the more authentic codex forms of ancient Christianity. Most certainly, a NT (with or without the Apocalypse) could be "re-edited" according to the basic codicological forms in which it was transmitted (Evangelion/Apostolos &/or Tetraevangelion/Praxapostolos).

Codicological and liturgical manuscript research could be combined with parallel research of the biblical manuscripts in Slavonic, Romanian, etc., because in these traditions the same philological and theological approaches have been maintained.

---

[591] The existing edition of the Prophetologion produced in the context of the MMB project (Copenhagen) was not developed in correspondence to the demands of the codicological approach.

Annexes

I. Glossary of terms

II. Bibliography

III. Indices of the Byzantine Anagnosmata

Annex I

Glossary of terms

Glossary of terms

The Glossary intends to provide a quick overview and the shortest possible description of unusual expressions common to Byzantine tradition (biblical, patristic and liturgical) used in this thesis. Included are also some terms generally known in Western scholarship, but that have a different connotation from an Eastern Orthodox point of view. For more detailed information, consult the bibliographical references at the bottom of this table.

Anagnosticon	Book of [OT] lessons. Name given to the first printed edition of the Prophetologion (Venice, 1595-96).
Anaginoskomena	The books which are ordered (recommended) by the Church "to be read" besides the canonical books of holy Scripture.
Apophtegmata	Byzantine compilation of sayings of the Neptic fathers (monastic/ascetical).
Aporiai kai Luseis	A Byzantine biblical (and patristic) commentary in the form of Questions and Answers.
Apostolos	Apostle lectionary. Byzantine liturgical book intended to be read in the Liturgy (and in other offices) containing lessons of Acts, the Pauline and General Epistles, and organised according to the movable and immovable cycles of the Byzantine Orthodox calendar. Lessons for special occasions complete the book.
Apostoloi	Lessons of the Apostolos according to the Byzantine calendar.
Aprakos	Church Slavonic denotation of the Evangelion or Gospel lectionary.
Asketica	Byzantine ascetical works containing monastic rules, stories and sayings (also Gerontica, Lausaica etc.).
Byzantine ecclesiastical manuscripts	The generic denotation for the manuscripts of literary works produced (in Greek) by members of the Byzantine and Greek Orthodox Church throughout the ages and in many different places in the Middle East and Greece.
Byzantine ecclesiastical text	The generally accepted text ('koine edition") of Holy Scripture, of both the OT & NT, used in Byzantine and in later Greek Orthodox churches and monasteries, its dogmatic and philological status (authority) having been acquired through its use in the Liturgy throughout the ages. Especially refers to the text form, which was used in Constantinople/Byzantium since the $8^{th}/9^{th}$ century, predominant to other local (or inferior) text forms.
Byzantine / Eastern Orthodox Tradition	The Byzantine tradition that was set forth in the Eastern Orthodox Churches is considered to be the underlying (dynamic) basis of the contents and forms of the faith of the Church and its teachings. All Holy Scriptures, the writings of the fathers and the liturgical formulas and books are enclosed in this concept.
Byzantium after Byzantium	A relatively recent expression (used by the Romanian Byzantinist N.Jorga, 1935) indicating the continuing Byzantine tradition in the Greek Church after the Fall of Constantinople, and also the transmission/translation of that tradition to Slavonic and Romanian idioms.
Canon	The term has several meanings: a) measure of faith; b) law of the church; c) monastic rule; d) list of generally acknowledged sacred books by the Church; e) the name of a characteristic Byzantine hymnographical composition), sung by the choir in the morning service (Nine Odes based on the Nine Biblical Odes (ecclesiastical canticles), normally not chanted, only in the period of Great Lent.
Catenae (Seirai)	Byzantine compilation of chains of selected biblical commentaries by one or more fathers, provided together with the scriptural text, alternately or parallel.
Diakonikon	Byzantine liturgical book containing the celebratory texts of the deacon.
Didaskalia	The teaching of Christ, the apostles and the fathers of the Church, including biblical, dogmatic and liturgical doctrines.
Dogma	The synodal teaching of the Church, characterised by its irrevocable and absolute expression of the truth (conceptually and philologically).
Doxology	Liturgical exclamation by the priest, in which the Trinity is praised ('Glory to the Father ...'); an ancient prayer sung at the end of the morning service (Orthros) and at other offices.
Ekphonesis	Denotation for the liturgical 'exclamation' ('ekphonesis') sung loudly by the priest, and used in Byzantine hymnography to indicate the 'half sung/half recited' performance of Scripture and celebration texts in the Byzantine Liturgy.
Encomia	Hagiological composition in which a saint is praised in poetic style.
Eothina Stichira	The hymns concerning the resurrection sung in the morning service after the reading of the morning lesson of the series of eleven resurrection evangelia.
Eratopakriseis	A biblical/patristic commentary form of Questions and Answers, contained in one expression (an equivalent

for the *Aporiai kai Luseis*.

Esperinos	The evening service.
Euchologion	Fundamental Byzantine liturgical book comprising the texts for the liturgical celebrations and other mysteries and prayers for a wide spectrum of occasions. Priest's handbook.
Evangelion	Gospel lectionary. Byzantine liturgical book intended to be read in the Liturgy (and in other offices), containing the lessons of the Four Gospels, roughly in the order of John, Matthew [Mark], Luke [Mark], Mark, and organised according to the movable and immovable cycles of the Byzantine calendar. Lessons for special occasions complete the work.
Evangelia	Evangelion lessons according to the Byzantine calendar.
Evergetinos	Collection of patristic/ascetical teachings collected by Paul Evergetinos (11th c.) and edited by Nikodemos the Hagiorite (18th c.)
Gerontika	Byzantine collections of sayings and acts of the elders (of Mount Athos and other places), greatly appreciated in Orthodox monasticism and also by laymen.
Hesychasm	The word means 'inner stillness'. Considered in monastic/ascetical life as the fruit of spiritual labour and the coming of the grace of God. A mystical movement within Orthodoxy and intrinsic to its Tradition, closely related to the practice of prayer (prayer of the heart or 'Jesus prayer'). Great defenders were Gregory of Sinai, Gregory Palamas, Nikodemos the Hagiorite, Paisios Velichkosvky, Theophan the Recluse, Seraphim of Sarov and many others.
Hirmologion	Byzantine hymnological book called after the "hirmos" - the first, "leading" melody of the odes of the canon.
Horologion	Byzantine liturgical book regulating the 'prayer hours' of the daily order and containing many other liturgical texts for other occasions concerning the fixed parts of services.
Iconostasis	The wall of icons separating the main Church (Katholikon) from the Altar (Holy of Holiest).
Kathismata	The Psalterion (comprising 150 psalms) is divided into twenty sections (sittings = kathismata).
Katholikon	The main part of a Byzantine church building or the church in the middle of a monastery complex.
Kanonarion	Equivalent for Typikon.
Kontakia	Short chants in the Byzantine hymnographical repertoire, comparable with troparia.
Kyriakodromion	Book containing the Sunday homilies (Kyriake) based on the festivals and feasts of the Church according to the Byzantine Orthodox calendar.
Lausaicon	Ancient ascetical book, used in Byzantine liturgical practice.
Lectionaria	Lectionaries. Western expression for the Byzantine Evangelia and Apostoloi.
Litany	Prayer form, which consists of series of loudly exclaimed prayers by the deacon; each prayer is given a response by the congregation (Kyrie eleison, or Lord have mercy) and after the last litany - amen.
Little Entrance	The "bringing in" of Holy Scripture, represented by the precious Evangelion codex (the codex comprising the Four Gospels), from the Altar to the Katholikon, in a solemn procession, which then returns to the Altar where the Evangelion is placed on the Holy Table. This represents the coming of Christ into the world – the community.
Martyrologia	One of the forms of Byzantine hagiological compilations.
Menaia	The twelve liturgical "month" books, comprising the liturgical hymnography of the fixed feasts and commemoration days of the saints of the Orthodox Church.
Menologion	This term has two meanings: a) table of lessons (found at the beginning or end of a codex); b) the descriptions of saints in particular codices (normally more extensive than in the synaxaria in the Menaia).
Metochion	The dependence (or 'embassy') of a monastery or patriarchate in another town or country, often housing developed libraries.
Movable/immovable cycles	The basic structure of the Byzantine calendar, the movable cycle running from Pascha to Pascha, the immovable cycle starting on September 1 and accomplishing its annual 'programme' of ecclesiastical prayer and liturgy on August 31.
Mysteria	Denotation in Byzantine Tradition for the (seven) Mysteria or Sacraments and other insights given to the initiated, or baptised believers. The term also refers to the Mystery of God, of Scripture and so forth.
Mystagogy	Term indicating the initiation in the Mystery (of Faith). Another name for the Byzantine Orthodox Liturgy (and the other mysteries of salvation), apparent from the celebratory texts of the Euchologion.

Nine Odes	A select series of ancient OT and NT chants from the Psalterion, stemming from ancient liturgical practice (known in the West as the Ecclesiastical Canticles)
Octateuch	One of the standard forms of the OT codices, incorporating the first eight books of the Bible, instead of only the first five (of the Law of Moses).
Oktoechos	The Book of Eight Modes (Tones) containing hymns and hymnographical material for Saturdays and Sundays during cycles of eight weeks, after which the whole octoechos cycle starts afresh. Each day of the week has its own modal pattern ('echos'), with a appropriate melody ('ethos'), easily recognisable for the congregation. The different hymns and other chants are sung within these (melodic) modal patterns.
Orthros	The morning service.
Panegyricon	Book of homilies for feasts and commemorations according to Byzantine ecclesiastical calendar.
Paradeisos	Byzantine mystical, ascetical work, adorned with the appropriate title - the 'Garden' (meant is the Garden of God or Gladness).
Parakletike	Byzantine liturgical book. An extended version of the Octoechos (for Saturdays and Sundays), containing hymnographical material for all the days the week.
Paterika	Ascetical books containing teachings of the elders and their disciples.
Pentekostarion	Byzantine liturgical book for the Easter Period, which runs from the Paschal night service until Pentecost.
Philokalia	The great ascetical compilation entitled the 'Love of beauty', containing the literary pearls of Byzantine monastic life. Edited in the XVIIIth century by Makarios of Corinth and Nikodemos the Hagiorite, on the basis of ancient manuscripts of earlier compilations of this sort.
Propheteia(i)	Original designation used in the codices for the Prophetologion.
Prophetologion	The Byzantine liturgical compilation containing the selection of OT lessons read in the Byzantine Orthodox Church, organised according the movable and immovable cycles of the calendar.
Psalterion	The Byzantine liturgical form of the Book of Psalms, organised along twenty kathismata and completed with the Nine Odes.
Pedalion	The Rudder. The standard codex of Byzantine / Greek Orthodox Canon Law, compiled and interpreted by Nikodemos the Hagiorite.
Skeuophilakion	The treasury, located very near to the Altar in Byzantine churches and monasteries, in which precious liturgical vessels, books and other objects were stored away for use in the Liturgy.
Sticherarion	Obsolete Byzantine hymnographical book.
Sticherai	Byzantine hymnographical chant, based on biblical verses (stichoi).
Symbolon	The confession of faith of the Undivided Church (Nicea-Constantinople), maintained and sung in each divine Liturgy, in an unchanged and unviolated form. In the West called the Creed.
Synaxaria	This word has two meanings: a) the tables of lessons prefixed or appendixed in scriptural codices (tetraevangelion, praxapostolos, apostolo-evangelion), organising the biblical text into lessons according to the Byzantine Orthodox calendar (movable and immovable cycles); b) the hagiological material adopted in the liturgical books (Menaia, Triodion, Pentekostarion) to be read on the 'synaxis' (the gathering) of a feast or commemoration day.
Synod	There are two types of synod: a) the 'Ecumenical Synods', the gatherings of the bishops of the Undivided Church (Orthodoxy acknowledges Seven Synods of Ecumenical character in the true sense of the word ; b) the 'local synods' of the Orthodox Church (in ancient and more recent times. These synods tried to safeguard the dogmatic and liturgical position of the Church against heresies.
Tetraevangelion	The Byzantine liturgical book comprising the text of the Four Gospels in the customary order of Matthew, Mark, Luke, John. Often provided with lectionary equipment and other patristic apparatus.
Textus Receptus	A text edition of Scripture (especially the NT) which was developed in Western printed editions (Erasmus, Stephanus, Elzevir, Hoskier), and which acquired great authority. It was only replaced when critical editions started to appear.
Three Divine Liturgies	The three main formulas of the Byzantine Liturgy, brought together in one codex for use by the celebrating priest (the liturgies are ascribed to John Chrysostom, Basil the Great and Gregorius Dialogus).
Triodion	Byzantine liturgical book in which the particular extended liturgical texts for the Forefast and Great Lent are gathered together.
Trisagion	Angelic Hymn sung in the Liturgy ('Holy God, Holy Mighty, Holy Immortal One, Have mercy on us'), during which the congregation is prepared for the coming of Christ (by means of His Gospel).

Troparia	Short chants in Byzantine hymnography, characterising the commemoration of the liturgical day, the event, saint, always paraphrasing or alluding to a biblical text.
Typikon	The liturgical/ecclesiastical book including the rules (typikon, or 'example') of the Liturgy and services of the Byzantine / Eastern Orthodox Church, in the form of very short rubrics, indicating when and how they should be performed at each special moment of the ecclesiastical year, what should be read and done during celebrations, and what should be omitted or replaced. The Typikon is extremely complex on the level of detail; the main structure, however, is in accordance to the immovable and movable cycles.

Ref. Lit.:

Clugnet, L., *Dictionnaire grec-français des noms liturgiques en usage dans l'église grecque*, reprint, London, 1971.

Politis, L., Ὁδηγὸς καταλόγου χειρογράφων, Athens, 1961.

Prokurat, M., Golitzin, A., Peterson, M.D. (Eds.), *Historical Dictionary of the Orthodox Church* (Historical Dictionaries of religions, philosophies, and movements, 9), Lanham, MD, 1996.

Rigas, O.G.,, Τυπικόν, Thessaloniki, 1994.

Annex II

Bibliography

Aalst, G. van, "Die Bibliographie des russischen Liturgisten A.A. Dmitrievskij", in *Orientalia Christiana Periodica*, 26 (1960), 108-140.

Aalst, G. van, "Alexius Afanasevič Dmitrievskij (1856-1929): Biographische gegevens, zijn leer over het liturgisch typikon", in *Het Christelijk Oosten en Hereniging*, 7 (1955), 29-37, 212-225; 8 (1956), 163-176.

Agourides, S and Charlesworth, J.H., "A New Discovery of Old Manuscripts on Mt. Sinai: A Preliminary Report", in *The Biblical Archaeologist*, 41 (1978), 29-31.

Aland, K (and others), *Kurzgefasste Liste der griechischen Handschriften des Neuen Testaments, zweite, neubearbeitete und ergänzte Auflage*, (Arbeiten zur neutestamentlichen Textforschung, Band 1), Berlin / New York, 1994.

Aland, K., "Zur Liste der Neutestamentliche Handschriften. V.", in *Zeitschrift für die neutestamentliche Wissenschaft*, 45.1-2 (1954), 181-182.

Aland, K. and B. (et al.), *Novum Testamentum Graeca, post Eberhard et Erwin Nestle editione vicesima septima revisa, (Apparatum criticum novis curis elaboraverunt Barbara et Kurt Aland una cum Instituto Studiorum Textus Novi Testamenti Monasterii Westphaliae)*, 27th revised edition (9. corrected printing), Stuttgart, 2006.

Aland, K. and B., *The Text of the New Testament*, Leiden, 1987.

Alexeev, A.A., 'The Old Testament Lections in Orthodox Worship', in *Das Alte Testament als christliche Bibel in orthodoxer und westlicher Sicht: Zweite europäische orthodox-westliche Exegetenkonferenz, im RilaKloster vom 8-15 September 2001*, Ed. I. Dimitrov (et al.), Tübingen, 2004, 91-117.

Alexeev, A.A., Текстология Славянской Библии, St. Petersburg, 1999.

Alexeev, A.A., 'Holy Scripture and its Translation', in *The Interpretation of the Bible. The International Symposium in Slovenia*, Ed. J. Krašovec, (Journal for the Study of the Old Testament Supplement Series, 289), Sheffield, 1998, 1387-1398.

Alexeev, A.A., 'The Slavonic Bible and Modern Scholarship', in *ΙΟΥΔΑΪΚΗ ΑΡΧΑΙΟΛΟΓΙΑ: In Honour of Professor Moshe Altbauer*, (Jews & Slaws 3), ed. W. Moskovich (et al.), Jerusalem, 1995, 25-39.

Alfeyev, H., *St. Symeon the New Theologian and Orthodox Tradition*, Oxford, 2000.

Alfeyev, H., *The Spiritual World of Isaac the Syrian*, Kalamazoo, Mich., 2000.

Allison, R. W., 'The libraries of Mt Athos: the case of Philotheou', in *Mount Athos and Byzantine Monasticism*, (Papers from the Twenty-eighth Spring Symposium of Byzantine Studies, Birmingham, March 1994), Ed. A. Bryer and M. Cunningham, Variorum, 1996, 135-154.

Allison, R.W., *Summary Catalogue of the Greek Manuscripts of Philotheou Monastery*, Lewistin, Maine, 1995 [unpubl.].

Altaner, B and Stuiber, A., *Patrologie. Leben, Schriften und Lehre der Kirchenväter*, 9. Auflage, Freiburg/Basel/Wien, 1980.

Altaner, B., "Griechische Codices in abendländischen Bibliotheken des XIII. und XIV. Jahrhunderts", in *Byzantinische Zeitschrift*, 36 (1936), 32-35.

Amand de Mendieta, E., *Mount Athos. The Garden of the Panaghia*, Berlin/Amsterdam, 1972.

Andry, E.R., "Report on microfilming the manuscripts in the Greek Orthodox Patriarchal Library, Istanbul", in *Scriptorium*, 18 (1964), 81-82.

Antoniadis, S., *Place de la liturgie dans la tradition des lettres grecques*, Leiden, 1939.

Aristarchos, Archbishop of Constantina, "The Mission of the Greek Orthodox Patriarchate of Jerusalem Today", Haifa March 3rd, [on www.jerusalem-patriarchate.org/ (seen 2003)].

Arranz, M., 'Les grandes etapes de la liturgie byzantine: Palestine - Byzance - Russie. Essai d'aperçu historique', in *Liturgie de l'Église Particulière et Liturgie de l'Église Universelle*, (Bibliotheca Ephemerides Liturgicae Subsidia, 7), Rome, 1976, 43-72.

Arranz, M., "Les archives de Dmitrievsky dans la bibliothèque d'Etat de Leningrad", in *Orientalia Christiana Periodica*, 40 (1974), 61-83.

Athanasiades, K., "Βιβλιοθῆκαι τοῦ Παναγίου Τάφου ἐν Κωνσταντινουπόλει καὶ ἐν Ἱερουσαλήμ", in Σωτήρ, 13 (1890), 257-266; 321-324.

Athanasopoulos, T., Ἐκκλησία: ὁ αὐθέντικος φύλακας καὶ ἑρμηνεύτης τῆς Ἁγίας Γραφῆς, Athens, 1998.

Athenagoras, Metropolitan, "Περιγραφικὸς κατάλογος τῶν χειρογράφων τῆς ἐν τῇ νήσῳ Χάλκῃ ἱερᾶς μονῆς τῆς Παναγίας", in Ἐπετηρὶς Ἐταιρείας Βυζαντινῶν Σπουδῶν, 10 (1933), 236-292; 11 (1935), 151-191; 12 (1936), 285-316; 13 (1937), 50-64.

Atsalos, B. Katsaros, B., Papastathis, Ch. (Eds.), *Actes de la Table Ronde. << Principes et méthodes du cataloguage des manuscrits grecs de la collection du Centre Dujčev >>, (Sofia 21-23 Août 1990)*, Thessaloniki, 1994.

Backus, I. (Ed.), *Reception of the Church Fathers in the West. From the Carolingians to the Maurists*, 2 vols., Leiden, 1997.

Bakker, H.P.S., *Towards a Critical Edition of the Old Slavic New Testament. A Transparent and Heuristic Approach*, Amsterdam, 1996.

Barbu, D., *Manuscrise bizantine în colecţii România*, Bucharest, 1984.

Bardy, G., "La littérature patristique des 'Questiones et responsiones' sur l'Écriture sainte", in *Revue Biblique,* 41 (1932), 210-236; 341-369; 515-537; 42 (1933), 14-30; 211-229; 328-352.

Barrois, G., *Scripture Readings In Orthodox Worship*, Crestwood, New York, 1977.

Baumstark, A., *Liturgie comparée*, Prieuré d'Amay, 1939.

Baumstark, A., *Die Messe im Morgenland*, Kempten und München, 1906.

Bebis, G., *Nicodemos of the Holy Mountain. A Handbook of Spiritual Counsel*, Trans. P.A. Chamberas, NY, Mahwah, 1989.

Beck, H.G., *Kirche und Theologische Literatur im byzantinischen Reich*, (Byzantinisches Handbuch, II Teil, Bd.1), München, 1959.

Bees, N.A., Τὰ χειρόγραφα τῶν Μετεώρων. Κατάλογος περιγραφικὸς τῶν χειρογράφων κωδίκων τῶν ἀποκειμένων εἰς τὰς μονὰς τῶν Μετεώρων ἐκδιδόμενος ἐκ τῶν καταλοίπων Νίκου Α. Βέη. Τόμος Β΄: Τὰ χειρόγραφα τῆς Μονῆς Βαρλαάμ, (Ἀκαδημία Ἀθηνῶν Κέντρον Ἐρεύνης τοῦ Μεσαιωνικοῦ καὶ Νέου Ἑλληνισμοῦ), Athens, 1984.

Bees, N.A., Τὰ χειρόγραφα τῶν Μετεώρων. Κατάλογος περιγραφικὸς τῶν χειρογράφων κωδίκων τῶν ἀποκειμένων εἰς τὰς μονὰς τῶν Μετεώρων ἐκδιδόμενος ἐκ τῶν καταλοίπων Νίκου Α. Βέη. Τόμος Α΄ : Μονὴ Μεταμορφώσεως (Ἀκαδημία Ἀθηνῶν Κέντρον Ἐρεύνης τοῦ Μεσαιωνικοῦ καὶ Νέου Ἑλληνισμοῦ), Athens, 1967 [repr. 1998].

Bees, N.A., "Geschichtliche Forschungsresultate und Mönchs- und Volks-sagen über die Gründer der Meteorenklöster", in *Byzantinisch-Neugriechische Jahrbücher*, 3 (1922), 364-403.

Bees, N.A., "Über zwei Codices des Alten Testaments aus den Bibliotheken von Meteoron und Megaspelaion", in *Zeitschrift für die alttestamentische Wissenschaft*, 32 (1912), 225-231.

Bees, N.A., Ἔκθεσις παλαιογραφικῶν καὶ τεχνικῶν ἐρευνῶν ἐν ταῖς μοναῖς τῶν Μετεώρων κατὰ τὰ ἔτη 1908 καὶ 1909, (Βυζαντιολογικὴ Ἐταιρεία ἐν Ἀθήναις. Ἀνεγνώσθη ἐν δημοσίᾳ συνεδρίᾳ τῆς Βυζαντιολογικῆς Ἐταιρείας τῇ 1 φεβρουαρίου 1910), Athens, 1910.

Bees, N.A., "Συμβολὴ εἰς τὴν ἱστορίαν τῶν μονῶν τῶν Μετεώρων", in Βυζαντὶς, 1 (1909), 191-331.

Behr, J., Louth, A., Conomos, D. (Eds.), *Abba. The Tradition of Orthodoxy in the West*, (Festschrift for Bishop Kallistos (Ware) of Diokleia), Crestwood, New York, 2003.

Belting, H and Cavallo, G., *Die Bibel des Niketas, Ein Werk der höfischen Buchkunst in Byzanz und sein antikes Vorbild*, Wiesbaden, 1979.

Beneševič, V.N., *Les manuscrits grecs du Mont Sinai et le monde savant de l'Europe depuis le XVIIe siècle jusqu' à 1927*, (Texte und Forschungen Zur Byzantinisch-neugriechischen Philologie; Nr. 21), Athens, 1937.

Beneševič, V.N., Описаніе греческихъ рукописей монастыря Святой Екатерины на Синаъ. Томъ III:

вып. I. Рукописи 1224-2150. *Catalogus codicum manuscriptorum graecorum qui in monasterio Sanctae Catherinae in Monte Sina asservantur.* Tomi III pars I. Codices numeris 1224-2150, St. Petersburg, 1917.

Beneševič, V.N., Описаніе греческихъ рукописей монастыря Святой Екатерины на Синаъ. Томъ I: Замѣчательныя рукописи вь библіотекъ Синийскаго монастыря и Синаеджуванійскаго подворья (въ Каиръ), описанныя архимандритомъ Порфиріемъ (Успенскимъ), (*Catalogus codicum manuscriptorum graecorum qui in monasterio Sanctae Catharinae in Monte Sina asservantur*, I), St. Petersburg, 1911 [repr. Hildesheim, 1965].

Bentley, J.H., *Humanists and Holy Writ. New Testament Scholarship in the Renaissance,* Princeton, 1983.

Binns, J., *Ascetics and ambassadors of Christ: the monasteries of Palestine 314-631*, Oxford, 1994.

Birdsall, J.N., 'The Recent History of New Testament Textual Criticism (from Westcott and Hort, 1881, to the Present)', in *Aufstieg und Niedergang der römischen Welt,* Part II: Principate, Vol. 26.1, Ed. W. Haase and H. Temporini, Berlin / New York, 1992, 99-197.

Blowers, P.M. (Ed. and Trans.), *The Bible in Greek Christian Antiquity,* Notre Dame, Indiana, 1997.

Bollandists, *Acta Sanctorum,* 67 vols, Brussels/Venice/Paris, 1643-1940.

Bompaire, J and Irigoin, J. (Eds.), *La paléographie grecque et byzantine (Paris, 21-25 octobre 1974),* (Actes du Colloque international sur la paléographie grecque et byzantine organisé dans le cadre des colloques internationaux du Centre National de la Recherche Scientifique à Paris du 21 au 25 octobre 1974), Paris, 1977.

Bordier, H.I., *Description des peintures et autres ornaments contenu dans les Manuscrits Grecs de la Bibliothèque Nationale,* Paris, 1883.

Bornert, R., *Les commentaires byzantines de la divine liturgie du VIIe au XVe siècle,* (Archives de l'Orient Chrétien 9), Paris, 1966.

Bouhot, J.P., 'Pentateuque chez les Pères', in *Dictionnaire de la Bible, Supplément,* 7, (Paris, 1966), 687-708.

Braithwaite, W.C., "The Lection-System of the Codex Macedonianus", in *The Journal of Theological Studies,* 5 (1904), 265-274.

Bratsiotis, P. (Ed.), Ἡ Ἁγία Γραφή - Παλαιὰ Διαθήκη καὶ ἡ Καινὴ Διαθήκη, 15th edition, Athens, 1999.

Brightman, F.E., *Liturgies Eastern and Western.* Vol. I. Eastern Liturgies, Oxford, 1896.

Brockhaus, H., *Die Kunst in den Athos-Klöstern,* Leipzig, 1891.

Brooke, A.E. and McLean, N., *The Old Testament in Greek According to the Text of the Codex Vaticanus,* Vol. I-IX, Cambridge, 1906-1940.

Bryner, E., "Bible Translations in Russia", in *The Bible Translator,* 25.3 (July 1974), 318-331.

Buberl, P. and Gerstinger, H., *Die byzantinischen Handschriften II: Die Handschriften des X bis XVIII Jahrhunderts. Die illuminierten Handschriften und Inkunabeln der Nationalbibliothek in Wien,* Leipzig, 1938.

Buberl, P., *Die byzantinischen Handschriften I: Die Wiener Dioskurides und die Wiener Genesis. Beschreibendes Verzeichnis der illuminierten Handschriften in Österreich,* 2 vols., Leipzig, 1937-1938.

Buberl, P., *Die Miniaturenhandschriften der Nationalbibliothek in Athen,* Vienna, 1917.

Buchthal, H. and Belting, H., *Patronage in Thirteenth-Century Constantinople: An Atelier of Late Byzantine Book Illumination and Calligraphy* (Dumbarton Oaks Studies, 16), Washington, 1978.

Burns, Y., 'The Lectionary of the Patriarch of Constantinople', in *Studia Patristica,* 15 (1984), 515-520.

Burns, Y., 'The Historical Events that Occassioned the Inception of the Byzantine Gospel Lectionaries', in *Jahrbuch der österreichischen Byzantinistik 32/4* (Akten II/4, XVI Internationaler Byzantinistenkongress Wien, 4-9 Oktober, 1981), Vienna, 1982, 119-127.

Burr, V., 'Byzantiner und Araber', in *Handbuch der Bibliothekswissenschaft,* Ed. F. Milkau und G. Leyh, Dritter Band: Geschichte der Bibliotheken, Leipzig, 1940, Kap. 2, 64-89.

Burton-Christie, D., *The Word in the Desert. Scripture and the Quest for Holiness in Early Christian Monasticism*, New York and Oxford, 1993.

Camariano, N., *Biblioteca Academiei Române. Catalogul manuscriptelor greceşti*, Vol. II., Bucharest, 1940.

Casel, O., *The Mystery of Christian Worship and other Writings*, Ed. B. Neunheuser, Westminster, Md., 1962.

Casey, R.P., "A Russian Orthodox View of New Testament Textual Criticism", in *Theology*, 60.439 (1957), 50-54.

Cauwenbergh, P. van, *Étude sur les moines d'Egypte depuis le Concile de Chalcédoine jusqu'à l'invasion arabe*, Paris and Louvain, 1869-1914.

Cavallera, F., *Patrologiae cursus completus accurante J.P. Migne, Series graeca, Indices*, Paris, 1912.

Cavarnos, C., *Anchored in God. An inside account of Life, Art, and Thought on the Holy Mountain of Athos*, Athens, 1973.

Cereteli, F.G. and Sobolevski, S., *Exempla codicum Graecorum litteris minusculis scriptorum annorumque notis instructorum*, Vol. I : Codices Mosquenses, Moscow, 1911; Vol. II : Codices Petropolitani, Moscow, 1913.

Charitakis, G., Κατάλογος τῶν χρονολογημένων κωδίκων τῆς πατριαρχικῆς βιβλιοθήκης Καΐρου, Athens, 1927.

Charlesworth, J.H., *The New Discoveries in St. Catherine's Monastery: A Preliminary Report on the Manuscripts*, Winona Lake, In, 1981.

Chatzedaniel, D., "'Η Καινὴ Διαθήκη (ἐγκρίσει τῆς μεγάλης τοῦ Χριστοῦ ἐκκλησίας)", in Ἐκκλησίας Ἀλληθεία, ΚΕ/29 (1905), 458-461.

Chitty, D.J., *The Desert a City. An Introduction to the Study of Egyptian and Palestinian Monasticism under the Christian Empire*, Crestwood, New York, 1966.

Chrestou, P.K., *Greek Orthodox Patrology. An Introduction to the Study of the Church Fathers*, Ed. and Trans. G.D. Dragas, Rollinsford, New Hampshire, 2005.

Chrestou, P.K., Ἑλληνικὴ Πατρολογία, Vol. I-V, Thessaloniki, 1976-1992.

Chrestou, P.K. and others (Eds.), Ἕλληνες Πατέρες τῆς Ἐκκλησίας (Gr.-NGr.), Thessaloniki, 1953 -.

Clark, K.W., *Checklist of Manuscripts in the Libraries of the Greek and Armenian Patriarchates in Jerusalem microfilmed for the Library of Congress, 1949-50*, Washington, 1953.

Clark, K.W., "Exploring the Manuscripts of Sinai and Jerusalem", in *The Biblical Archaeologist*, 16 (1953), 22-44.

[**Clement VIII**, Official edition of the Vulgate under the auspices of Clement VIII], *Biblia Sacra vulgatae editionis Sixti Quinti Pont. Max. iussu recognita adque edita ("Sixtine-Clementine" or "Clementine Bible")*, Rome, 1592.

Clugnet, L., *Dictionnaire grec-français des noms liturgiques en usage dans l'église grecque*, reprint, London, 1971.

Collins, N.L., *The Library in Alexandria and the Bible in Greek*, Leiden/Boston/Köln, 2000.

Conev, B [et al.], Описъ на ръкописитѣ и старопечатнитѣ книги на Народната Библиотека въ София [Description of the manuscripts and old printed books in the National Library of Sofia], Vol. I, Sofia, 1910.

Conomos, D.E., *Byzantine Trisagia and Cheroubika of the Fourteenth and Fifteenth Centuries: A Study of Late Byzantine Liturgical Chant*, Thessaloniki, 1974.

Constantelos, D.J., "The Holy Scriptures in Greek Orthodox Worship (A Comparative and Statistical Study)", in *The Greek Orthodox Theological Review*, 12.1 (1966), 7-83.

Constantinides, C.N. and Browning, R., *Dated Greek Manuscripts from Cyprus to the year 1570*, Washington, D. C., Nicosia, 1993.

Conticello, C and Conticello, V. (Eds.), *La Théologie Byzantine et sa Tradition XIIIe-XIXe s.*, Vol. II, Turnhout, 2002.

Couret, A., *La Palestine sous les empereurs grecs*, Grenoble, 1869.

Cozza–Luzi, G. (Ed.), *Vetus Testamentum iuxta LXX interpretum versionem e codice omnium antiquissimo Graeco Vaticano 1209 phototypice repraesentatum*, 4 vols., Rome, 1890.

Cozza–Luzi, G. (Ed.), *Novum Testamentum e codice Vaticano 1209 nativi textus graeci primo omnium*, Rome, 1889.

Cramer, J.A., *Catenae Graecorum Patrum in Novum Testamentum*, 8 vols., Oxford, 1838-1844. [Repr. Hildesheim, 1967].

Cutler, A., *The Aristocratic Psalters in Byzantium*, Paris, 1981.

Cyril of Scythopolis, *Lives of the Monks of Palestine*, Trans: R.M. Price, Kalamazoo, Michigan, 1991.

Dain, A., "Rapport sur la codicologie byzantine", in *Berichte zum XI. Internationaler Byzantinisten-Kongress* (München, 1958), 1-22.

Dain, A., *Les manuscrits*, Paris, 1949 [3rd edition, 1975].

Damianos, Archimandrite, "Εἰσήγησις ἐπὶ τῶν νεωστὶ εὑρεθέντων παλαιῶν χειρογράφων ἐν τῇ ἱερᾷ Μονῇ Σινᾶ", in *Jahrbuch der österreichischen Byzantinistik*, 32.4 (1982) [XVI Internationalen Byzantinistenkongress, Wien, 4.-9. Oktober, 1981, Akten, II/4], 105-115.

Darlow, T.H. and Moule, H.F. (Eds.), *Historical Catalogue of the Printed Editions of Holy Scripture in the Library of the British and Foreign Bible Society*, in 2 volumes, Vol. II: *Polyglots and Languages Other Than English*, New York, reprint, 1963. [1st ed. London, 1903-1911].

Day, P.D., *The Liturgical Dictionary of Eastern Christianity*, Collegeville, MN., 1991.

Delatte, A., *Les manuscrits à miniatures et à ornements des bibliothèques d'Athènes*, (Bibliothèque de la Faculté de Philosophie et Lettres de l'Université de Liège, 34), Liège-Paris, 1926.

Delehaye, H., *Synaxarium ecclesiae Constantinopolitanae*, Leuven, 1954.

Delehaye, H., "Catalogus codicum hagiographicorum graecorum bibliothecae Scholae theologicae in Chalce insula", in *Analecta Bollandiana*, 44 (1926), 5-63.

Delicostopoulos, A., 'Major Greek Translations of the Bible', in *The Interpretation of the Bible. The International Symposium in Slovenia*, (Journal for the Study of the Old Testament Supplement Series; 289), Ed. J. Krašovec, Sheffield, 1998, 297-316.

Demetrakopoulos, A., Προσθῆκαι καὶ διορθώσεις εἰς τὴν Νεοελληνικὴν Φιλολογίαν Κωνστ. Σάθα, Leipzig, 1871.

Demopoulos, J., 'National Library of Greece: History, Present Status and Plans for the Future' (Presentation at the Conference of the Library Congress, *Strengthening Modern Greek Collections*, April 29-30, 1999), [www.loc.gov/rr/european/GrkColl/demop.html (seen 14.12.2005)].

Devreesse, R., *Les anciens commentateurs grecs de l'Octateuque et des Rois. Fragments tirés des chaînes*, (Studi e testi, 201), Cité du Vatican, 1959.

Devreesse, R., *Introduction à l'Étude des Manuscrits Grecs*, Paris, 1954.

Devreesse, R., 'Chaines Exégétiques Grecques', in *Dictionnaire de la Bible, Supplément*, 1 (Paris, 1928), 1096-1099.

Diehl, C., "Le trésor et la bibliothèque de Patmos au commencement du 13e siècle", in *Byzantinische Zeitschrift*, 1 (1892), 489-525.

Dimitrievsky, A.A., Описание литургическихъ рукописей хранящихся въ библиотекахъ православнаго востока, I. Kiev, 1895; II. Kiev, 1901; III. Petrograd, 1917.

Dimitrov, I., 'The Relationship Between the Old and the New Testament', in *Das Alte Testament als christliche Bibel in orthodoxer und westlicher Sicht: Zweite europäische orthodox-westliche Exegetenkonferenz, im Rilakloster vom 8-15 September 2001*, Ed. I. Dimitrov (et al.), Tübingen, 2004, 145-153.

Dix, G., *The Shape of the Liturgy*, San Francisco, 1982.

Doens, I. (Ed.), 'Bibliographie de la Sainte Montagne de l'Athos', in *Le Millénaire du Mont Athos 963-1963. Études et Mélanges*, 2 vols., Chevetogne, 1963-64, II, 337-495.

Dölger, F., Παρασπορα. *30 Aufsätze zur Geschichte, Kultur und Sprache des byzantinischen Reiches,* Passau, 1961. [reprint]

Dölger, F., 'Der Heilige Berg Athos und seine Bücherschätze', in *Bibliotheksprobleme der Gegenwart,* Frankfurt a. M., 1951, 1-15.

Doreval, G., *Les Chaines exegetiques greques sur les Psaumes: contributions à l'étude d'une forme litteraire,* (Spicilegium Sacrum Lovaniense. Études et Documents; fasc. 43-46), 4 volumes, Leuven, 1986-1995.

Doreval, G., 'Des Commentaires de l'Écriture aux les chaînes', in *Le monde grec ancien et la Bible,* (Bible de tous les temps, 1), Paris, 1984, 361-386.

Dorotheos Scholarios, Κλεὶς Πατρολογίας καὶ Βυζαντινῶν συγγραφέων, Athens, 1879. [Migne, PG, T. 162].

Dräseke, J., "Die neuen Handschriftenfunde in den Meteoraklöstern", in *Neue Jahrbücher für das klassische Altertum,* 15 (1912), 542-553.

Drobner, R., *Lehrbuch der Patrologie,* Freiburg / Basel / Vienna, 1994.

Drozdov, P. (Metropolitan Philaret of Moscow), "О догматическом достоинстве и охранительном употреблении греческого семидесяти толковников и славянского переводов священного писания 1845 год", in Прибавления к изданию творении Святих Отцов Церкви в русском переводе, 17, (Moscow, 1858), 452-484. [Reprint in Metropolitan Philaret, избранные творения, 2nd ed., Moscow, 2004, 355-373.

Dudik, B., "Historische Forschungen in der Kaiserliche öffentliche Bibliothek zu St. Petersburg", in *Sitzungs Berichte der Wiener Akademie 95,* phil.-hist. Cl. (1879), 329-382.

Dunn, J.D.G. et al. (Eds.), *Auslegung der Bibel in orthodoxer und westlicher Perspektive,* (Akten des west-östlichen Neutestamentler/innen-Symposiums von Neamţ vom 4.-11. September 1998), Tübingen, 2000.

Duplacy, J., 'Manuscripts grecs du Nouveau Testament émigrés de la Grande Laure de l'Athos', in *Studia Codicologia,* Ed. K. Treu, Berlin, 1977, 159-178.

Džurova, A., *Byzantinische Miniaturen. Schätze der Buchmalerei vom 4. bis zum 19. Jahrhundert,* Regensburg, 2002.

Džurova, A., Stančev, K., Atsalos, V., Katsaros, V., *"Checklist" de la collection de manuscrits grecs conservé au Centre de recherches slavo-byzantines "Ivan Dujčev" auprès de l'Université "Clément d'Óhrid" de Sofia,* Thessaloniki, 1994.

Džurova, A., "Les manuscrits grecs du Centre Ivan Dujčev. Notes préliminaires", in *Erytheia,* 13 (1992), 117-157.

Ehrhard, A., *Überlieferung und Bestand der hagiographischen und homiletischen Literatur der griechischen Kirche, von den Anfängen bis zum Ende des 16. Jahrhunderts,* Vols. I-III, Leipzig-Berlin, 1937-1952.

Ehrhard, A., 'Theologie', in, *Geschichte der byzantinischen Litteratur von Justinian bis zum Ende des oströmischen Reiches (527-1453),* Ed. K. Krumbacher, 2nd ed., München, 1897, 37-218.

Ehrhard, A., "Das griechische Kloster Mâr-Saba in Palästina: seine Geschichte und seine literarischen Denkmäler", in *Römische Quartalschrift,* 7 (1893), 32-79.

Ehrhard, A., "Der alte Bestand der griechischen Patriarchalbibliothek von Jerusalem", in *Centralblatt für Bibliothekswesen,* 9. 10-11 (1892), 441-459.

Ehrhard, A., "Das Kloster zum hl. Kreuz bei Jerusalem und seine Bibliothek", in *Historisches Jahrbuch der Görresgesellschaft,* 13 (1892), 158-172.

Ehrhard, A., "Die Griechische Patriarchal-Bibliothek von Jerusalem. Ein Beitrag zur Griechischen Palaeographie", in *Römische Quartalschrift,* 5 (1891), 217-265, 329-331, 383-384.

Ehrman, B.D. and Holmes, M.W. (Eds.), *The Text of the New Testament in contemporary research: essays on the status questionis* (Studies and Documents; vol. 46), Grand Rapids, Mich., 1995.

Ehrman, B.D., "The text of Mark in the Hands of the Orthodox", in *Lutheran Quarterly,* 5.1 (1991), 143-156.

Elian, A., "Manuscrisele greceşti din Biblioteca Academiei", in *Studii şi cercetări de documentare şi bibliologie,* 9 (1967), 271-276.

Elliott, J.K., *A Bibliography of Greek New Testament Manuscripts,* Cambridge, 2000.

Engberg, S.G., 'Les lectionnaires grecs', in *Les manuscrits liturgiques, cycle thématique 2003-2004 de l'IHRT*, Ed. O. Legendre and J.B. Lebigue, Paris, 2005.

Engberg, S.G., "Prophetologion Manuscripts in the << New Finds >> of St. Catherine's at Sinai", in *Scriptorium*, 57.1 (2003), 94-109.

Engberg, S.G., "The Greek Old Testament Lectionary as a Liturgical Book", in *Cahiers de l'Institut du Moyen Âge grec et latin*, 54 (1987), 39-48.

Engberg, S.G., *Prophetologium. Pars altera: Lectiones anni immobilis (Fasc. I-II)*, (Monumenta Musicae Byzantinae. Lectionaria. Vol. I), Copenhagen, 1980-1981.

Englezakis, B., *Studies on the History of the Church of Cyprus, 4th-20th centuries*, Trans. N. Russell, Ed. S. and M. Ioannou, Aldershot, 1995.

Ephraim of Mount Athos, *Counsels from the Holy Mountain. Selected from the Letters and Homilies of Elder Ephraim.* Florence, Arizona, 1999.

[Ephraim the Syrian], *A Spiritual Psalter or Reflections on God, excerpted by Bishop Theophan the Recluse from the works of our Holy Father Ephraim the Syrian*, Trans. [from the Russian] A. Janda, St. John of Kronstadt Press, 1997.

Epp, E.J., *Perspectives on New Testament Textual Criticism. Collected Essays, 1962-2004*, Leiden / Boston, 2005.

Epp, E.J., "The Multivalence of the Term 'Original Text' in New Testament Textual Criticism", in *Harvard Theological Review*, 42 (1999), 245-281.

Erbiceanu, C., "Manuscrise vechi aflate în biblioteca sf. Metropolii a Moldovei", in *Revista Teologica*, 3 (1885-1886).

Estienne, R. (Ed.), *Biblia*, Paris, 1528.

Eusebius of Caesarea, *The Ecclesiastical History*, Trans. K. Lake, 2 vols., Cambridge, Mass. & London, 1980. [1st edition 1926].

Eustratiades, S. and Arcadios of Vatopedi, *Catalogue of the Greek Manuscripts in the Library of the Monastery of Vatopedi on Mount Athos. Κατάλογος τῶν ἐν τῇ Ἱερᾷ Μονῇ Βατοπεδίου ἀποκειμένων κωδίκων*, (Harvard Theological Studies IX), Cambridge, 1924.

Eustratiades, S., Κατάλογος ἐν τῇ μονῇ Βλατέων (Τσαοὺς Μοναστήρι) ἀποκειμένων κωδίκων, Thessaloniki, 1918.

Eustratiades, S., "Ἁγιορειτικῶν κωδίκων σημειώματα", in Γρηγόριος ὁ Παλαμᾶς, 1 (1917), 49-62; 145-160; 374-384; 413-432; 457-472; 561-568; 617-624; 755-771; 2 (1918), 84-90; 167-173.

Faulhaber, M., "Katenen und Katenenforschung", in *Byzantinische Zeitschrift*, 18 (1909), 383-395.

Faulhaber, M., "Die Katenenhandschriften der spanischen Bibliotheken", in *Biblische Zeitschrift*, 1 (1903), 151-159, 246-255, 351-371.

Fiedrowicz, M., 'Homily', in *Dictionary of Early Christian Literature*, Ed. S. Döpp and W. Geerlings, Trans. M. O' Connell, New York, 2000, 290.

(Filantropov), Archimandrite Vladimir, Систематическое описание рукописей Московской Синодальной (Патриаршей) библиотеки: Часть 1: Рукописи греческие, Moscow, 1894.

Fischer, B., *Lateinische Bibelhandschriften im frühen Mittelalter*, Freiburg im Breisgau, 1985.

Florovsky, G., *Bible, Church, Tradition: An Eastern Orthodox View*, (Collected Works, Vol. I), Belmont, 1972.

Florovsky, G., *Ways of Russian Theology*, Trans. R.L. Nichols, 2 vols., (The Collected Works, Vol. V-VI), Belmont, Mass., 1979 & Vaduz, 1987.

Florovsky, G., *The Eastern Fathers of the IVth Century*, Trans. C. Edmunds, (The Collected Works of Georges Florovsky; Vol.VII), Vaduz, 1987.

Florovsky, G., *The Byzantine Fathers of the Vth Century,* Trans. R. Miller, A-M. Dollinger-Labriolle, H.W. Schmiedel, (The Collected Works, Vol. VIII), Belmont, Mass., 1987.

Florovsky, G., *The Byzantine Fathers of the VIth – VIIIth Centuries,* Trans. R. Miller, A-M. Dollinger-Labriolle, H.W. Schmiedel, (The Collected Works, Vol. IX), Belmont, Mass., 1987.

Florovsky, G., *The Byzantine Ascetic and Spiritual Fathers,* (The Collected Works, Vol. X), Belmont, MA, 1987.

Florovsky, G., Пути Русского Богословия, Paris, 1937. [3rd ed. 1983]

Florovsky, G., Византийские Отцы V-VIII, Paris, 1933.

Florovsky, G., Восточные Отцы IV-го Вѣка, Paris, 1931.

Fonkic, B.L. and Poljakov, F.B., Греческие рукописи Московской Синодальной библиотеки. Палеографические, кодикологические и библиографические дополнения к каталогу архимандрита Владимира (Филантропова), Moscow, 1993.

Fonkič, B.L., *Graeco-Russian Contacts from the Middle of the XVI Century up to the Beginning of the XVIII Century: The Greek Documents in Moscow Archives: Catalogue of Exhibition,* Moscow, 1991.

Fonkič, B.L., "The Greek Manuscripts of A.N. Murav'ev", in *Modern Greek Studies Yearbook*, 4 (1988), 235-254.

Fonkič, B.L, "Les manuscrits grecs d'Antonin Kapustin [annexe: Inventaire des manuscrits grecs d'Antonin Kapustin", in *Scriptorium*, 38 (1984), 254-271.

Fonkič, B.L, 'Griechische Kodikologie', in *Griechische Kodikologie und Textüberlieferung,* Ed. D. Harlfinger, Darmstadt, 1980, 14-21.

Fonkič, B.L, "Греческие рукописи Одессы", in Византийский временник, 39 (1978), 184-200; 282-283.

Fonkič, B.L, 'Греческие рукописи советских хранилищ', in *Studia Codicologica*, Ed. K. Treu, Berlin, 1977, 189-195.

Forsyth, G.H. and Weitzmann, K., *The Monastery of Saint Catherine at Mount Sinai. The Church and Fortress of Justinian*, Ann Arbor, 1973.

Fraenkel, D., *Verzeichnis der griechischen Handschriften des Alten Testaments von Alfred Rahlfs. Die Überlieferung bis zum VIII Jahrhundert*, Bd. 1, 1, (Septuaginta Supplement), Göttingen, 2004.

Fragkiskos, E.N., *La Bibliothèque de Patmos. Catalogue d'imprimés (XVe-XIXe s.): introduction, description des imprimés, annexes, index*, 2 vols., Athens, 1995-1996.

Fuchs, F., *Die höheren Schulen von Konstantinopel im Mittel Alter*, Amsterdam, 1926 [repr. 1964].

Fuhrer, T.F., 'Commentary', in *Dictionary of Early Christian Literature*, Ed. S. Döpp and W. Geerlings, Trans. M. O'Connell, New York, 2000, 138-139.

Galey. J., *Sinai und das Katharinen Kloster*, Stuttgart/Zürich, 1979.

Gamble, H.Y., *Books and Readers in the Early Church. A History of Early Christian Texts*, New Haven and London, 1995.

Gardner, J. von, *Russian Church Singing, Volume 1: Orthodox Worship and Hymnography*, Crestwood, NY, 1980.

Gardthausen, V., *Griechische Palaeographie*, 2. Aufl., 2 vols., Leipzig, 1911-1913.

Gardthausen, V., *Sammlungen und Cataloge Griechischer Handschriften*, Leipzig, 1903.

Gardthausen, V., *Catalogus codicum graecorum Sinaiticorum*, Oxford, 1886.

Garzaniti, M., *Die altslavische Version der Evangelien: Forschungsgeschichte und zeitgenössische Forschung*, Köln-Weimar-Wien, 2001.

Gastoué, A., *Introduction à la paléographie musical byzantine. Catalogue du MSS. De musique byzantine*, Paris, 1907.

Gedeon, M.I., Ὁ Ἄθως, Constantinople, 1885.

Geerard, M. and Noret, J. (Eds.), *Clavis Patrum Graecorum*, 6 vols., Turnhout, 1974-1998.

Géhin, P., *Evagre le Pontique, Scholies aux Proverbes*, (Sources Chretien; 340), Paris, 1987.

Genest, J., 'Books and Libraries in Byzantium', published on www. geocities. com/TimesSquare/Labyrinth/2398/bginfo/social/books.html) [Seen 05.12.2005].

Gennadios of Heliopolis, "Πῶς οἱ Ἀμερικανοὶ Θεολογοὶ ἐκφράζονται περὶ τῆς Πατριαρχικῆς ἐκδόσεως τῆς Καίνης Διαθήκης", in Ὀρθοδοξία, 13 (1938), 74-76.

Ginsburg, C.D., *Introduction to the Massoretico-Critical Edition of the Hebrew Bible*, London, 1897 [Repr. New York, 1966].

Gkinis, D., "Κατάλογοι ἑλληνικῶν κωδίκων ἐν Ἑλλάδι καὶ Ἀνατολῇ", in Ἐπιτηρὶς Ἑταιρείας Βυζαντινῶν Σπουδῶν, 11 (1935), 361-382.

Gorskij, A. and Nevostruev, K., Описание Славянскихъ рукописей московской синодальной библиотеки, 3 parts in 6 vols., Moscow, 1855-1869. [repr. in 5 vols., (Monumenta Linguae Slavicae Dialecti Veteris Fontes et Dissertationes; Tom. II), Wiesbaden, 1964]. [Register: E.M. Vitosinskij, Wiesbaden, 1966]

Grabe, C. (Ed.), "Scholia Gregoriana" (Joh. Gregorius) in *Novum Testamentum una cum scholiis Graecis e Graecis scriptoribus tam ecclesiasticis quam exteris maxima ex parte desumptis*, Oxford, 1703.

Granstrem, E.E., 'Zur byzantinischen Minuskel', in *Griechische Kodikologie und Textüberlieferung*, Ed. D. Harlfinger, Darmstadt, 1980, 76-119.

Granstrem, E.E., "Greek Palaeography in Russia", in *Bulletin no 17 of the Institute of Classical Studies*, University of London (1970), 124-135.

Granstrem, E.E., "Каталог греческих рукописей ленинградских хранилищ", in Византийский временник (1959 - 1971).

Granstrem, E.E., "Греческие рукописи Библиотеки Академии наук СССР", in Академии наук СССР. Библиотека. Исторический очерк и обзор фондов Рукописного отдела Библиотеки Академии наук, t. II: XIX-XX век, Moscow-Leningrad, 1958.

Granstrem, E.E., "Греческие рукописи в собраниях Советского Союза (дополнительные сведения)", in Византийский временник, 11 (1956), 285-291.

Grégoire, R., 'Homéliaires orientaux', in *Dictionnaire de Spiritualité*, 7 (Paris, 1969), 606-617.

Gregory, C.R., *Die Griechischen Handschriften des Neuen Testaments*, Leipzig, 1908.

Gregory, C.R., *Textkritik des Neuen Testamentes*, 3 vols., Leipzig, 1900-1909.

Grimsted, P.K., *Archives of Russia. A Directory and Bibliographic Guide to Holdings in Moscow and St. Petersburg*, 2 vols., New York and London, 2000.

Grimsted, P.K., *Archives and Manuscripts Repositories in the USSR. Ukraine and Moldavia*. Princeton, 1988.

Gutenberg, J. (Ed.), *Biblia Latina*, Mainz, 1454-1455.

Hackett, J., *A History of the Orthodox Church of Cyprus from the coming of the Apostles Paul and Barnabas to the commencement of the British occupation (A.D. 45-A.D. 1878)*, London, 1901.

Hakkert, A.M. (Ed.), *Byzanz après Byzanz: Aufsätze Symposion Byzantinon*, Amsterdam, 1991.

Halkin, F., *Catalogue des manuscrits hagiographiques de la Bibliothèque Nationale d'Athènes* (Subsidia hagiographica, 66), Brussels, 1983.

Halkin, F., *Manuscrits grecs de Paris. Inventaire hagiographique* (Subsidia hagiographica, 44), Brussels, 1968.

Halkin, F., "Manuscrits byzantins d'Ochrida en Macédoine Yougoslave", in *Analecta Bollandiana*, 80 (1962), 5-21.

Halkin, F., *Bibliotheca Hagiographica Graeca*, 3 vols. (Subsidia Hagiographica 8, 3rd ed., Brussels, 1957.

Hanhart, R., *Septuaginta. It est Vetus Testamentum graece iuxta lxx interpretes edidit Alfred Rahlfs*, Editio altera quam recognovit et emendavit Robert Hanhart, (Duo volumina in uno), Stuttgart, 2006.

Hannick, C., 'Das Neue Testament in altkirchenslavischer Sprache: Der gegenwärtige Stand seiner Erforschung und seine Bedeutung für die griechische Textgeschichte', in *Die alten Übersetzungen des Neuen Testaments, die Kirchenväterzitate und Lektionare*, Ed. K. Aland, Berlin/New York, 1972, 403-435.

Hapgood, I.F. (Ed.), *Service Book of the Holy Orthodox-Catholic Apostolic Church, compiled, translated, and arranged from the Old Church-Slavonic service books of the Russian Church and collated with the service books of the Greek Church*, revised [sixth] edition, Englewood, New Jersey, 1983.

Harl, M. and Lange, N. de, *Origène: Philocalie, 1-20 sur les écritures*, introd., texte, trad. [du grec] et notes. *La lettre à Africanus sur l'histoire de Suzanne*, introd., texte, trad. [du grec] et notes, (SC 302), Paris, 1983.

Harlfinger, D. and Prato, G. (Eds), *Paleografia e Codicologia Greca* (Atti del II Colloquio internazionale [Berlino-Wolfenbüttel, 17-21 ottobre 1983]), 2 vols., Allesandria, 1991.

Harlfinger, D., Reinisch, D.R., Sonderkamp, J.A.M. (in Zusammenarbeit mit Prato, G.), *Specimina Sinaitica. Die datierten griechischen Handschriften des Katharinen-Klosters auf dem Berge Sinai, 9. bis 12. Jahrhunderts*, Berlin, 1983.

Harnack, A. von, *Der Scholien-Kommentar des Origenes zur Apokalypse Johannis*, (Texte und Untersuchungen; 38.3), Leipzig, 1911.

Hatch, W.H.P., "An Early Edition of the New Testament in Greek", in *Harvard Theological Review*, 34.2 (1941), 69-78.

Hatch, W.H.P., *The Greek Manuscripts of the New Testament at Jerusalem. Facsimiles and Descriptions* (American Schools of Oriental Research. Publications of the Jerusalem School, I), Paris, 1932.

Hausherr, I., *Spiritual Direction in the Early Christian East*, Kalamazoo, MI., 1990.

Heine, R.E., 'The Introduction to Origen's Commentary on John compared with the Introductions to the ancient philosophical commentaries on Aristotle', in *Origeniana Sexta: Origène et la Bible/Origen and the Bible*, Ed. Alain de Boulluec and Gilles Dorival, (Actes du Colloquium Origenianum Sextum, Chantilly, 30 août – 3 septembre 1993), Leuven, 1995, 3-12.

Heinrici, G., 'Zur Patristischen Aporienliteratur', in *Abhandlungen der philologisch-historischen Klasse der königlichen sächsischen Gesellschaft der Wissenschaften*; Bd. XXVII, No xxiv, Leipzig, 1909, 843-860.

Heinrici, G., 'Scholien', in *Realencyklopädie für protestantische Theologie und Kirche*, 3.17 (1906), 732-741.

Heinrici, G., 'Catenen', in *Realencyklopädie für protestantische Theologie und Kirche*, 3 (1897), 754-767.

Hengel, M., *The Septuagint as Christian Scripture: Its Prehistory and the Problem of Its Canon*, with the assistance of R. Deines, Trans: M.E. Biddle, Edinburgh & New York, 2002.

Hennephof, H., *Das Homilar des Patriarchen Neilos und die chrysostomische Tradition. Ein beitrag zur Quellengeschichte der spätbyzantinischen Homiletik*, Leiden, 1963.

Hesseling, D.-C., *Miniatures de l'Octateuque Grec de Smyrne manuscrit de l'école évangélique de Smyrne, édition phototypique*, (Codices Graeci et Latini; Supplementum VI), Leiden, 1909.

Hobson, A., *Große Bibliotheken der Alten und der Neuen Welt*, München, 1970.

Hoeck, J.M., "Der Nachlass Albert Ehrhards und seine Bedeutung für die Byzantinistik", in *Byzantion*, 21.1 (1951), 171-178.

Høeg, C., Zuntz, G., Engberg, G. (Eds.), *Prophetologium I-II* (Monumenta Musicae Byzantinae. Lectionaria. Vol. I), Copenhagen, 1939-1981.

Holmes, R. and Parsons, J., *Vetus Testamentum Graecum cum variis lectionibus*, I-V, Oxford, 1798-1827.

Holton, D. et al.(Eds.), Κωδικογράφοι, συλλέκτες, διασκευαστές, και εκδότες. Χειρόγραφα και εκδόσεις της όψιμης βυζαντινής και πρώιμης νεοελληνικής λογοτεχνίας. *Copyists, collectors, redactors and editors: manuscripts and editions of late Byzantine and early modern Greek literature* (Papers given at a Conference held at the Danish Institute at Athens, 23-26 May 2002, in honour of H. Eideneier and A. van Gemert), Heraklaeion, 2005.

Holy Apostles Convent and Dormition Skete (Ed.), *The Apostolos. The English New Testament Text is based on The Orthodox New Testament*, Buena Vista, Colorado, 2000.

Holy Apostles Convent and Dormition Skete (Ed.), *The Evangelion. The English New Testament Text is based on The Orthodox New Testament*, Buena Vista, Colorado, 2000.

Holy Transfiguration Monastery (Trans.), *The Psalter According to the Seventy, of St. David, the Prophet and King, together with the Nine Odes and an Interpretation of how the psalter should be recited throughout the whole year*, Boston, Mass., 1987.

Holy Transfiguration Monastery (Trans.), *The Pentecostarion*, Boston, Mass., 1990.

Hunger, H., *Schreiben und Lesen in Byzanz. Die byzantinische Buchkultur*, München, 1989.

Husmann, H., "Die datierten griechischen Sinai-Handschriften des 9. bis 16. Jahrhunderts, Herkunft und Schreiber", in *Ostkirchliche Studien*, 27 (1978), 143-168.

Isaac of Nineveh, *Mystic Treatises*, Trans from Syrian by A.J. Wensinck, Amsterdam, 1923.

Ivanov, A., "Новое критическое издание Греческого текста Нового Завета", in Журнал Московской Патриархии, 12 (1954), 69; 3 (1956), 49-58; 4 (1956), 49-58; 5 (1956), 43-52.

Ivanov, A., "К вопросу о восстановлении первоначального греческого текста нового завета", in Журнал Московской Патриархии, 3 (1954), 38-50.

Jacob, A., "Les euchologes du fonds Barberini grec de la Bibliothèque Vaticane", in *Didaskalia*, 4 (1974), 131-222.

Jacob, A., 'La Tradition Manuscrite de la Liturgie de Saint Jean Chrysostome', in *Eucharisties d'orient en d'occident*, II, ED. B. Botte, H. Cazelles, K. Hruby, Paris, 1970, 109-138.

Jacob, A., *Histoire du formulaires grecs de la liturgie de Saint Jean Chrysostome*, Louvain, 1968 [unpubl. diss.]

Jakovljevič, A., *Catalogue of Greek Manuscripts in the Library of the Monastery of St. Neophytos (Cyprus)*, Nicosia, 2002.

Jakovljevič, A., *Catalogue of Byzantine Chant Manuscripts in the Monastic and Episcopal Libraries of Cyprus* (Publications of the Cyprus Research Centre, 15), Nicosia, 1990.

Janin, R., "Constantinople", in *Dictionnaire d'Histoire et de Géographie Ecclésiastiques*, 3 (1956), 626-740.

Jobes, K.H. and Silva, M., *Invitation to the Septuagint*, Grand Rapids, Michigan, 2001.

Johann Georg (Prinz), Herzog zu Sachsen, *Das Katharinenkloster am Sinai*, Leipzig und Berlin, 1912.

John Climacus, *The Ladder of Divine Ascent*, Ed. Holy Transfiguration Monastery, Trans. L. Moore, Boston, Mass., 1991.

Jorga, N., *Byzance après Byzance: Continuation de l'Histoire de la vie Byzantine*, Bucharest, 1935 [cf. the edition of 1971 with an avant-propos of M. Berza].

Junod, É., 'Que savons-nous des <<Scholies>> (ΣΧΟΛΙΑ - ΣΗΜΕΙΩΣΕΙΣ) d' Origène', in *Origeniana Sexta: Origène et la Bible/Origen and the Bible*, Ed: A. de Boulluec and G. Dorival (*Actes du Colloquium Origenianum Sextum, Chantilly, 30 août – 3 septembre 1993*), Leuven, 1995, 133-149.

Junod, É., 'Wodurch unterscheiden sich die Homilien des Origenes von seiner Kommentaren?', in *Predigt in der Alten Kirche*, Ed: E. Mühlenberg, Kampen, 1993, 50-81.

Kallimachos, D., "Πατμιακῆς βιβλιοθήκης συμπλήρωμα (ἄγνωστοι κώδικες)", in ’Εκκλησιαστικὸς Φάρος, 10 (1912), 246-267; 309-334; 388-404; 11 (1913), 148-160; 244-253; 12 (1913), 385-398; 525-541; 13 (1914), 256-272; 14 (1915), 68-80; 15 (1916), 357-375; 16 (1917), 98-108; 145-161; 466-484; 17 (1918), 117-128; 214-233.

Kallinikos, K., ῾Υπόμνημα εἰς τὸν ἱερὸν ψαλτῆρ, 2 vols., Alexandria, 1929.

K. Kallinikos, Εἰσαγωγὴ εἰς τὸν ἱερὸν ψαλτῆρ, Alexandria, 1927.

Kamil, M., *Catalogue of all manuscripts in the Monastery of St. Catherine on Mount Sinai*, Wiesbaden, 1970.

Kamil, M., *Studia Egyptiaca: II. Les manuscrits du Covent Sainte Catherine au Sinai*, (Le Mardis de Dar El-Salam), Le Caire, 1952, 205-221.

Kamil, M., "Die Handschriftensammlung des Sinai", in *Universitas*, 11 (Nov. 1951), 1175-1179.

Kannengieser, C., *Handbook of Patristic Exegesis,* 2 Vols., Leiden / Boston, 2004.

Karabinov, I.A., Тріодъ постная [The Lenten Triodion], St. Petersburg, 1910.

Karanasios, C., "Recherche über die griechischen Handschriften in Rumänien", in *Balkan Studies*, 34 (1993), 5-16.

Karavidopoulos, I.D., "The Interpretation of the New Testament in the Orthodox Church", in *Jesus Christus als die Mitte der Schrift* etc., Berlin/New York, 1997.

Karavidopoulos, I.D., "The Origin and History of the Terms >>Evangelistarion<< and >>Evangeliarion<<", in *Orthodox Forum*, 7.2 (1993), 177-183.

Karavidopoulos, I.D., "L'Édition Patriarchale du Nouveau Testament (1904). Problems de Texte et de Traduction dans le monde Orthodoxe", in *Kleronomia,* 20 (1988), 195-204.

Karayannopoulos, J., 'Bericht über Paläographie, Kodikologie und Diplomatik im Rahmen der Byzantinistik', in *Actes du XIVe Congrès International des Études Byzantines* (Bucarest, 6-12 septembre, 1971), by M. Berza and E. Stănescu (Eds.), Bucharest, 1976, III, 13-21.

Karo, G. und Lietzmann, H., 'Catenarum Graecorum Catalogus', in *Nachrichten der Gesellschaft der Wissenschaften zu Göttingen, Philol. hist. Klasse*, Göttingen, 1902, 1-66; 299-350; 559-620.

Každan, A., "Греческие рукописи библиотеки им. В.И. Ленина", in Вопросы Истории, 10 (1946), 107-108.

Kniazeff, A., 'La lecture de l'Ancien et du Nouveau Testament dans le rite byzantin', in *La Prière des Heures*, Eds. C. Bezobrazof and B. Botte, Paris, 1963, 201-251.

Koikylides, K.M., Κατάλοιπα χειρογράφων Ἱεροσολυμιτικῆς βιβλιοθήκης, Jerusalem, 1899.

Kominis, A.D., Πατμιακὴ βιβλιοθήκη ἤτοι Νέος κατάλογος χειρογράφων κωδίκων τῆς Ἱερᾶς Μονῆς Ἁγίου Ἰωάννου τοῦ Θεολόγου Πάτμου, Τόμος Α'. Κώδικες 1-101, Athens, 1988.

Kominis, A.D., *Facsimiles of dated Patmian Codices. With an Introduction by D. A. Zakythinos*, Eng. version by M. Naoumides, Athens, 1970 [Gr. 1968].

Kominis, A.D., " Ὁ νέος κατάλογος τῶν χειρογράφων τῆς ἐν Πάτμῳ Ἱερᾶς Μονῆς Ἰωάννου τοῦ Θεολόγου (Μέθοδος καὶ προβλήματα)", in Σύμμεικτα, 1 (1966), 17-34.

Kondakov, N.P., *Histoire de l'art byzantin considéré dans les miniatures*, edition française originale, publ. par l'auteur, sur la traduction de M. Trawinski, Tom. 1-2, Paris/London, 1886-1891 [Repr. New York, 1970].

Kondakoff, N.P., *Les antiquités du monastère du Sinaï*, Ed. H. Omont, Paris, 1882.

Kotsonis, H. (Archimandrite), 'Die Griechische Theologie', in *Die Orthodoxe Kirche in Griechischer Sicht*, Vol. 2, Ed. P. Bratsiotis, 1960, 7-37.

Kourilas, E., "Athos, la vie et les institutions monacales", in *La Croix*, 1 (1947), 1-30; 2/3 (1949), 97-111.

Kovalchuk, F. (Ed.), *Abridged Typicon*, 2nd edition, South Canaan, 1985.

Krasnoseltsev, N.F., Материалы для истории чинопоследования литургии св Иоанна Златоустаго, Kazan, 1889.

Krasnoseltsev, N.F., Сведения о некоторых литургических рукописях Ватиканской библиотеки, Kazan, 1885.

Krašovec, J. (Ed.), *The Interpretation of the Bible. The International Symposium in Slovenia*, (Journal for the Study of the Old Testament Supplement Series; 289), Sheffield, 1998.

Kremos, G.P., Κατάλογος τῶν χειρογράφων τῆς Ἐθνικῆς καὶ τῆς τοῦ Πανεπιστημίου Βιβλιοθήκης ἀλφαβητικὸς καὶ περιγραφικὸς μετ' εἰκόνων καὶ πανομοιοτύπων κατ' ἐπιστήμας κατατεταγμένων, Τ. 1 [Θεολογία], Athens, 1876.

Krikonis, C.T., "Περὶ ἑρμηνευτικῶν σειρῶν (Catenae)", in *Byzantina*, 8 (1976), 91-139 [Πιν.1-26].

Krikonis, C.T., Συναγωγὴ Πατέρων εἰς τὸ κατὰ Λουκᾶν Εὐαγγέλιον ὑπὸ Νικήτα Ἡρακλείας (κατὰ τὸν κώδικα Ἰβήρων 371), Thessaloniki, 1973.

Krivocheine, B., "Mount Athos in the Spiritual Life of the Orthodox Church", in *The Christian East*, 2 (1952), 35-50.

Krumbacher, K. (Ed.), *Geschichte der Byzantinischen Litteratur von Justinian bis zum Ende des oströmischen Reiches (527-1453)*, 2nd ed., München, 1897.

Kucharek, K., *The Byzantine-Slav Liturgy of Saint John Chrysostom*, Ontario, 1971.

Kurilas, E., "Κατάλογος ἁγιορειτικῶν χειρογράφων", in Θεολογία, 14 (1936), 42-52; 114-128; 330-347; 15 (1937), 239-248; 361-366; 16 (1938), 74-79; 173-180; 249-261; 350-354; 21 (1950), 269-291; 325-338; 506-525.

Lake, H. and K. (Eds.), *Codex Sinaiticus Petropolitanus. The Old Testament preserved in the public library of Petrograd, in the library of the Society of Ancient Literature in Petrograd, and in the Library of the University of Leipzig, now reproduced in facsimile from photographs, with a description and introduction to the history of the Codex*, Oxford, 1922.

Lake, H. and K. (Eds.), *Codex Sinaiticus Petropolitanus: the New Testament, the Epistle of Barnabas and the Shepherd of Hermas*, Oxford, 1911.

Lake, H. and K. (Eds.), *Monumenta palaeographica vetera. Dated Greek Minuscule Manuscripts to the year 1200*, t. 1-10, Boston, 1934-1939.

Lake, K., "Texts from Mt. Athos", in *Studia Biblica et Ecclesiastica*, 5.2 (1902), 88-185.

Lambertsen, I. (Trans.), *The Complete Menaion, providing the services for the feasts of Our Lord Jesus Christ, of the Most Holy Theotokos, and of the Saints for Every Day of the Year, set to the meter of the original Byzantine melodies*, vols. 1-12, Boston, Mass., 2005.

Lamberz, E., "Die Handschriftenproduktion in den Athosklöstern", in *Scritture, libri e testi nelle aree provinciali Bisanzio* (Atti del seminario di Erices, 18-25 Settembre 1988), by G. Cavallo, G. de Gregorio, and M. Maniaci (Eds.), Spoleto, 1991.

Lamberz, E. and Litsas, E.K., Κατάλογος χειρογράφων τῆς Βατοπεδινῆς Σκήτης Ἁγίου Δημητρίου (Κατάλογοι ἑλληνικῶν χειρογράφων Ἁγίου Ὄρους 1). *Catalogue of the Manuscripts of the Skete of St. Demetrius, Vatopedi, (Mount Athos)*, Thessaloniki, 1978.

Lambros, S.P. (Trans.), Ἐγχειρίδιον ἑλληνικῆς καὶ λατινικῆς παλαιογραφίας, by E. Thompson, Athens, 1903 [reprint 1973].

Lambros, S.P., 'Χειρόγραφος κατάλογος τῶν ἐν τῇ ἰδίᾳ αὐτοῦ βιβλιοθήκῃ κωδίκων', in Ἀθηναῖοι Βιβλιογράφοι (Athens, 1902).

Lambros, S.P., *Catalogue of the Greek Manuscripts on Mount Athos*. Κατάλογος τῶν ἐν ταῖς βιβλιοθήκαις τοῦ Ἁγίου Ὄρους ἑλληνικῶν κωδίκων, 2 vols., Cambridge, 1895-1900.

Lambros, S.P., "The Greek Manuscripts at Salonica", in *Athenaeum*, No 3284 (1890), 451-452.

Lambros, S.P., Κατάλογος τῶν ἐν ταῖς βιβλιοθήκαις τοῦ Ἁγίου Ὄρους ἑλληνικῶν κωδίκων, I. 1, Athens, 1888.

Lambros, S.P., *Die Bibliotheken der Klöster des Athos*, Trans: A. Boltz, Bonn, 1881.

Lash, E., Archimandrite (Ed.), *Prophetologion/The Lectionary*, [on http://web.ukonline.co.uk/ephrem/prophetologion.htm.]

Lash, E., Archimandrite (Ed.), 'Saint Ephrem the Syrian: Ascetical and other Writings extant only in Greek', [on http://web.ukonline.co.uk/ephrem/prophetologion.htm].

Laurence, rassaphor-monk (Ed.), *The Unabbreviated Horologion*, revised edition, n.l., 1984.

Lebedev, A., Рукописи Церковно-Археологическаго Музея Императорской Киевской Духовной Академии, t. I, Saratov, 1916.

Lebedeva, I.N., Описание Рукописей отдела Библиотеки Академии наук СССР, Leningrad, 1973.

Leclercq, H., 'Montfaucon (Dom Bernard de)', in *Dictionnaire d'Archéologie Chrétienne et de Liturgie*, 11 (Paris, 1934).

Leclercq, H., 'Bibliothèques', in *Dictionnaire d'Archéologie Chrétien et de Liturgie*, 2.1 (Paris, 1925), 842-904.

Legrand, E. and Pernot, H., *Bibliographie Ionienne. Description raisonnée des ouvrages publiés par des Grecs des sept-îles ou concernant ces îles du XVe siècle à l'année 1900*, t. I-II, Paris, 1910.

Legrand, E., *Bibliographie Hellénique ou Description raisonnée des ouvrages publiés par des Grecs aux dix-septième siècle*, 5 tom., Paris, 1894-1903 [Repr. Paris, 1975].

Legrand, E., *Bibliographie Hellénique ou Description raisonnée des ouvrages publiés par des Grecs aux dix-huitième siècle*, oevre posthume complétée et publiée par L. Petit et H. Petit, 2 tom., Paris, 1918-1928 [Repr. Paris, (ca. 1975)].

Legrand, E., *Bibliographie Hellénique des XVe et XVIe siècles ou Description raisonnée des ouvrages publiés en Grec [ou] par des Grecs aux XVe et XVIe siècles*, 4 tom., Paris, 1885-1906 [Repr. 1962].

Lemaire, J., *Introduction à la Codicologie*, Louvain-la-neuve, 1989.

Archimandrite Leontios (Abbot of the Monastery of St. Neophytos, Cyprus), 'Foreword', in *Catalogue of Greek Manuscripts in the Library of the Monastery of St. Neophytos (Cyprus)*, by A. Jakovljevič, Nicosia, 2002.

Lietzmann, H., *Catenen. Mitteilungen über ihre Geschichte und handschriftliche Überlieferung*, mit einem Beitrag von H. Usener, Freiburg/Leipzig/Tübingen, 1897.

Lingenthal, Z. von, "Die juristischen Handschriften der Athener Bibliothek", in *Archiv für mittel-und neugriechischer Philologie*, 1 (Athens. 1880), 221-223.

Litsas, E., "Libraries and manuscripts in Mount Athos. A survey", *Mount Athos Manuscripts Digital Library*, [(Web-site of the Patriarchal Institute for Patristic Studies in Thessaloniki, seen Dec 2001)].

Litzica, C., *Biblioteca Academiei Române. Catalogul manuscriptelor grecești*, Bucharest, 1909.

Logachev, K.I., 'Greek Lectionaries and Problems in the Oldest Slavonic Gospel Translations', in *New Testament Textual Criticism. Its Significance for Exegesis*, (Essays in Honour of Bruce M. Metzger), Ed. E.J. Epp and G.D. Fee, Oxford, 1981, 345-348.

Logachev, K.I., "The Problem of the Relationship of the Greek Text of the Bible to the Church Slavonic and Russian Text", in *The Bible Translator*, 25.3 (1974), 313-318.

Logachev, K.I., "Критические издания текстов Священного Писания", in Журнал Московской Патриархии, 6 (1971), 78 ff.; 2 (1972), 79 ff.; 9 (1972), 76-80.

Logachev, K.I., "Русский перевод Нового Завета (к 150-летию изданию)", in Журнал Московской Патриархии, 11 (1969), 61-68.

Lossky, V., *The Mystical Theology of the Eastern Church*, Trans: Fellowship of St. Alban and St. Sergius, Cambridge & London, 1973.

Lowden, J., *The Octateuchs. A Study in Byzantine Manuscript Illustration*, University Park, Pennsylvania, 1992.

Lowden, J., *Illuminated Prophet Books. A Study of Byzantine manuscripts of the Major and Minor Prophets*, University Park and London, 1988.

Macarius the Great, *Fifty Spiritual Homilies, St. Macarius the Great, St*, Trans: A.J. Mason, with The Life of St. Macarius and the Teachings of St. Macarius by I.M. Kontzevich, Willits, Cal., 1974.

Mai, A. (Ed.), Σχόλια παλαιὰ εἰς τοὺς Εὐαγγελιστάς, in *Classici Auctores*, 10 vols., Rome, 1828-1838, volumes 6 and 9. [Migne PG 106, 1077-1290]

Makarios (Hieromonk) of Simonos Petra, *The Synaxarion. The Lives of the Saints of the Orthodox Church*, Trans. from French by C. Hookway, Vol. I, Ormylia (Chalkidike), 1998.

Mamalakis, I.P., Τὸ Ἅγιον Ὄρος (Ἄθως) διὰ μέσου τῶν αἰώνων, Thessaloniki, 1971.

Manley, J., *The Bible and the Holy Fathers for Orthodox. Daily Scripture Readings and Commentary for Orthodox Christians*, Crestwood, NY, 2003.

Manley, J. (Ed.), *Grace for Grace: The Psalter and the Holy Fathers*, Menlo Park, CA, 1992.

Mantzaridis, G., "Universality and Monasticism", in *Precious Vessels of the Holy Spirit. The Lives and Counsels of Contemporary Elders of Greece*, Ed. H.A. Middleton, 2nd ed. (Thessalonica & Asheville, NC, 2004), 25-36.

Marava-Chatzinicolaou, A. and Toufexi-Paschou, C., Κατάλογος μικρογραφιῶν βυζαντινῶν τῶν χειρογράφων τῆς Ἐθνικῆς Βιβλιοθήκης τῆς Ἑλλάδος, T. Γ': Ὁμιλίες Πατέρων τῆς Ἐκκλησίας καὶ Μηνολόγια 9ου-12ου αἰῶνα, Athens, 1997.

Marava-Chatzinicolaou, A. and Toufexi-Paschou, C., Κατάλογος μικρογραφιῶν βυζαντινῶν τῶν χειρογράφων τῆς Ἐθνικῆς Βιβλιοθήκης τῆς Ἑλλάδος, T. B: Χειρόγραφα Καινς Διαθήκης ΙΓ' - ΙΕ' αἰῶνος, *Catalogue of Illuminated Byzantine Manuscripts of the National Library of Greece. Vol. II: Manuscripts of New Testament Texts 13th – 15th Century*, Athens, 1985.

Marava-Chatzinicolaou, A. and Toufexi-Paschou, C., Κατάλογος μικρογραφιῶν βυζαντινῶν τῶν χειρογράφων τῆς Ἐθνικῆς Βιβλιοθήκης τῆς Ἑλλάδος, T. A: Χειρόγραφα Καινς Διαθήκης Ι' - ΙΒ' αἰῶνος, *Catalogue of Illuminated Byzantine Manuscripts of the National Library of Greece. Vol. I: Manuscripts of New Testament Texts 10th – 12th Century*, Athens, 1978.

Marcos, N.F., *The Septuagint in Context. Introduction to the Greek Versions of the Bible,* Trans: W.G.E. Watson, Leiden/Boston/Köln, 2000.

Margaris, D., "Histoire de la Bibliothèque Nationale", in *L'Hellénisme contemporain*, 2nd series, 5 (1951), 318-326.

Mary, Mother and Ware, Archimandrite Kallistos (Trans.), *The Lenten Triodion*, London & Boston, 1978.

Mary, Mother and Ware, Archimandrite Kallistos (Trans.), *The Festal Menaion*, London, 1977.

Meletios, Archimandrite (Margiolos), Περιγραφικὸς πίναξ τῶν χειρογράφων κωδίκων τῆς βιβλιοθήκης τῆς ἐν Πάτμῳ Ἱερᾶς Μονῆς Ἰωάννου τοῦ Θεολόγου, in Ἡ Φωνὴ τῆς Ἀποκαλύψεως, 1 (1955); 2 (1957).

Masai, F., "La paléographie et la codicologie", in *Scriptorium*, 4 (1950), 270-293.

Mastrantonis, G., *Augsburg and Constantinople. The Correspondence between the Tübingen Theologians and Patriarch Jeremiah II of Constantinople on the Augsburg Confession*, Brookline, Mass., 1982.

Mateos, J. (Ed), *Le Typicon de la grande Église: ms. Saint-Croix no. 40, Xe siècle* (introd., texte critique, trad.), v. I-II, Rome, 1977, [reprint, 1962-1963].

Mateos, J., *La célébration de la parole dans la liturgie byzantine*, (OCA 191), Rome, 1971.

Mateos, J., "La psalmodie dans la rite byzantin", in *Periodica Orientalia Christiana*, 15 (1965), 107-126.

Matthaei, C.F., *Accurata codicum Graecorum manuscriptorum Bibliothecarum Mosquensium Sanctissimae Synodi notitia et recensio*, 2 vols., Leipzig, 1805.

Matthaei, C.F., *Novum Testamentum Graece... Iterum recensuit, sectiones maiores et minores Eusebii, Euthalii et Andreae Caesariensis notavit, primum quoque lectiones ecclesiasticas ex usu Ecclesiae Graecae designavit ac synaxaria Evangeliarii et Praxapostoli addidit et criticis interpositis animadversionibus edidit*, Ed. Hof, Ronneburg, 1803-1807.

Matthaei, C.F. (Ed.), *Novum Testamentum XII Tomis distinctum Graece et Latine, Textum denuo recensuit, varias lectiones numquam antea vulgates ex centum codicibus mss*, 12 vols., Riga, 1782-1788.

Matthaei, C.F., *Index codicum Graecorum Bibliothecarum Mosquensium*, St. Petersburg, 1780.

Matthaei, C.F., *Notitia codicum manuscriptorum Graecorum Bibliothecarum*, Moscow, 1776.

Metropolit Maximos of Sardis, Τὸ Οἰκουμενικόν Πατριαρχεῖον ἐν τῇ Ὀρθοδόξῳ Ἐκκλησια, 2nd ed, Thessaloniki, 1989.

Mazal, O., *The Keeper of Manuscripts*, Trans: T.J. Wilson, in collaboration with M. McNamara, Turnhout, 1992.

Mazal, O., *Jozua-Rolle. Vollständige Faksimile-Ausgabe im Original-Format des Codex Vaticanus Palatinus Graecus 431 der Biblioteca Apostolica Vaticana*, Graz, 1983-84.

Meester, P. De, 'Grecques (Liturgies)', in *Dictionnaire d'Archéologie Chrétienne et de Liturgie*, 6, (1925), 1591-1662.

Metzger, B.M. and Ehrman, B.D., *The Text of the New Testament. Its Transmission, Corruption and Restoration*, 4th edition, New York/Oxford, 2005.

Metzger, B.M., *Manuscripts of the Greek Bible. An Introduction to Greek Palaeography*, New York and Oxford, 1981.

Metzger, B.M., 'Greek lectionaries and a critical edition of the Greek New Testament', in *Die alten Übersetzungen*, by K. Aland (Ed.), Berlin/New York, 1972, 479-497.

Meyendorff, J., *Byzantine Theology. Historical Trends and Doctrinal Themes*, Oxford, 1983.

Meyer, P., *Die Theologische Literatur der griechischen Kirche im sechzehnten Jahrhundert*, Leipzig, 1899.

Migne, J.P., *Patrologiae Cursus Completus, Series Graeca*, vols. 1 – 161, Paris, 1857-1866.

Milasch, N., *Das Kirchenrecht der morgenländischen Kirche. Nach den allgemeinen Kirchenrechtsquellen und nach den in den autokephalen Kirchen geltenden Spezial-Gesetzen*, 2. Aufl., Mostar, 1905.

Milkau, F. and Leyh, G. (Eds.), *Handbuch der Bibliothekswissenschaft*, 5 vols., Leipzig, 1931-1940.

Milne, H.J.M. and Skeat, T.C., *Scribes and Correctors of Codex Sinaiticus*, London, 1938.

Mitrevski, T., "Die kanonische Geltung der deuterokanonischen Bücher der Hl. Schrift in der orthodoxen Kirche nach den Konzilsentscheidungen", in *Kyrios*, 13 (1973), 49-58.

Moraitis, D.N., "Οἱ ἐν τῇ Ἐθνικῇ Βιβλιοθήκῃ τῶν Παρισίων Ἑλληνικοὶ λειτουργικοὶ κώδικες", in Θεολογία, 24 (1953), 536-542.

Morcelli, S.A., Μηνολόγιον τῶν εὐαγγελίων ἑορταστικόν, sive Kalendarium ecclesiae Constantinopolitanae. Accedunt quattuor evangeliorum lectiones in codice variantes, 2 vols., Rome, 1788.

Moschonas, T.D., *Catalogue of manuscripts of the Patriarchal Library of Alexandria*. Πατριαρχεῖον Ἀλεξανδρείας. Κατάλογοι τῆς πατριαρχικῆς βιβλιοθήκης. Τόμος Α'. Χειρόγραφα, [Studies and Documents edited by Jacob Geerlings, 26], Salt Lake City, 1965.

Moschonas, T.D., "A Short History of the Library of the Greek Orthodox Patriarchate of Alexandria & All Africa", in *Bulletin of the Patriarchal Library* (Jan-June 1955, reprinted on the official web-site of the Patriarchate; www.greekorthodox-alexandria.org). [seen 2-12-2005].

Moschonas, T.D., Πατριαρχεῖον Ἀλεξανδρείας. Κατάλογοι τῆς πατριαρχικῆς βιβλιοθήκης. Τόμος Α'. Χειρόγραφα, Alexandria, 1945.

Mošin, V., "Les manuscrits du Musée National d'Ochrida", in *Musée National d'Ohrid. Recueil de travaux. Édition spécial publié à l'occasion du Xe anniversaire de la fondation du Musée et dedié au XIIe Congrès international des études byzantines*, Ohrid, 1961, 163-243.

Mühlenberg, E., 'Katenen', in *Theologische Realenzyklopädie*, 18, 1989, 14-21.

Mühlenberg, E., *Psalmenkommentare aus der Katenenüberlieferung*, 3 vols., Berlin, 1975-1978.

Moutsoula, E.D. and Papachristopoulos, K.G. (Eds.), Βιβλιοθήκη Ἑλλήνων Πατέρων καὶ Ἐκκλησιαστικῶν Συγγραφέων, t. 1-82, Athens, 1955- .

Müller, M., *The First Bible of the Church. A Plea for the Septuagint* (Journal for the Study of the Old Testament Supplement Series: 206), Sheffield, 1996.

Muralt, E. de, *Catalogue des manuscripts grecs de la Bibliothèque impériale publique*, St. Petersburg, 1864.

Muralt, E. de, *Catalogus codicum Bibliothecae Imperialis Publicae graecorum et latinorum*, St. Petersburg, 1840.

Neale, J.M., *A History of the Holy Eastern Church, Part 1: General Introduction*, 2 vols, London, 1850.

Nees, L., "An Illuminated Byzantine Psalter at Harvard University", in *Dumbarton Oaks Papers*, 29 (1975), 207-224.

Nersessian, S. Der, "A Psalter and New Testament Manuscript at Dumberton Oaks", in *Dumberton Oaks Papers*, 19 (1965), 153-183.

Nestle, E., 'Early History of the Septuagint', in *A Dictionary of the Bible*, 4 (1906), 437-454.

Nestle, E., *Septuagintastudien*, Ulm, 1886.

Nicodemos of the Holy Mountain, *A Handbook of Spiritual Counsel*, Trans: P. A. Chamberas, New York, Mahwah, 1989.

Agapios the Peloponnesian and Nicodemos the Hagiorite (Eds.), Πηδάλιον, Leipzig, 1800, [reprint Thessaloniki, 2003].

Nicol, D.M., *Meteora, The Rock Monasteries of Thessaly*, London, 1963.

Niebuhr, K.W., 'Zu den Ergebnissen des Rila-Symposiums', in I. Dimitrov (Ed. et al.), *Das Alte Testament als christliche Bibel in orthodoxer und westlicher Sicht: Zweite europäische orthodox-westliche Exegetenkonferenz, im Rila Kloster vom 8-15 September 2001, Tübingen*, 2004.

Nikephoros Theotokos Ieromonachos, Σειρὰ ἑνὸς καὶ πεντήκοντα ὑπομνηματιστῶν εἰς τὴν Ὀκτάτευχον καὶ τὰ τῶν Βασιλειῶν, t. I-II, Leipzig, 1772-1773.

Nikolopoulos, P.G., Ἱερὰ Μονὴ καὶ Ἀρχειπισκοπὴ Σινᾶ. Τὰ νέα εὑρήματα τοῦ Σινᾶ, Athens, 1998.

Nikolopoulos, P.G., Περιγραφὴ χειρογράφων κωδίκων τῆς Ἐθνικῆς Βιβλιοθήκης τῆς Ἑλλάδος, Ἀριθ. 3122-3369, Athens, 1996.

Nilles, N., *Kalendarium Manuale*, 2 vols, Innsbruck, 1896-1897.

Oikonomos, E., 'Die Bedeutung der deuterokanonischen Schriften in der orthodoxen Kirche', in *Die Apokryphen-Frage im ökumenischen Horizont*, Ed. S. Meurer, Stuttgart, 1989, 26-40.

Oikonomos, K., Περὶ τῶν Ο′ Ἑρμηνευτῶν τς παλαιᾶς θείας Γραφς, Athens, 1849.

Ohrid list, "Списокъ рукописей находящихся въ библіотекѣ "С&. Климента" въ Охрид", in Извѣстія Русскаго Археологическаго Института въ Константинополѣ, 6 (1900), 466-470.

Old, H.O., *The Reading and Preaching of the Scriptures in the Worship of the Christian Church*, 3 vols., Grand Rapids, Mich./Cambridge, U.K., 1998-1999.

Omont, H., *Catalogue alphabétique des livres imprimés mis à la disposition des lecteurs dans la salle de travail, Département des manuscripts, Bibliothèque National: suivi de la liste des catalogues usuels du Département des manuscripts*, Paris, 1933.

Onasch, K., *Das Weinachtsfest im orthodoxen Kirchenjahr. Liturgie und Ikonographie*, Berlin, 1958.

Onasch, K., "Der Psalter in der byzantinisch-slavischen Orthodoxie", in *Wissenschaftliche Zeitschrift der Martin-Luther-Universität Halle-Wittenberg*, 7.1 (1957), 145-168.

Origen, 'A Letter from Origen to Africanus', in *The Writings of Origen*, Trans: F. Crombie, Vol 1, Edinburgh, 1868.

Orthodox Monastery of the Veil of Our Lady (Trans.), *The Octoechos. Saturday and Sunday Offices Tones 1 – 8*, Bussy-en-Othe, n.d.

Osburn, C.D., 'The Greek Lectionaries of the New Testament', in *The Text of the New Testament in Contemporary Research. Essays on the Status Quaestionis*, Ed. B.D. Ehrman and M.W. Holmes, Grand Rapids, Mich., 1995, 61-74.

Panagopoulos, J., Ἡ ἑρμηνεία τῆς Ἁγίας Γραφῆς στὴν Ἐκκλησία τῶν Πατέρων· Οἱ τρεῖς πρῶτα αἰῶνες καὶ ἡ ἀλεξανδρινὴ ἐξηγητικὴ παράδοση ὥς τὸν πέμπτο αἰῶνα, t. 1, Athens, 1991.

Pani, G., 'Un centenaire rappeler: L'édition sixtine des Septante', in *Théorie et pratique et l'exégèse*, Ed. I. Bakus and F. Higman, Geneva, 1990, 413-428.

Pantelakis, E.G., "Les Livres ecclésiastiques de l'Orthodoxie. Étude Historique", in *Irénikon*, 13.5 (1936), 521-557.

Papadopoulos, S.A., *The Monastery of St. John the Theologian in Patmos*, 4th edition, Patmos, 1974.

Papadopoulos-Kerameus, A.I., "Ἑλληνικοὶ κώδικες ἐν τῇ Βιβλιοθήκῃ τοῦ Πατριαρχείου Κωνσταντινουπόλεως", in Византийский Временникъ, 17 (1910), 414-420.

Papadopoulos-Kerameus, A.I., Ἱεροσολυμιτικὴ Βιβλιοθήκη ἤτοι κατάλογος τῶν ἐν ταῖς βιβλιοθήκαις τοῦ ἁγιωτάτου ἀποστολικοῦ τε καὶ καθολικοῦ ὀρθοδόξου πατριαρχικοῦ θρόνου τῶν Ἱεροσολύμων καὶ πάσης Παλαιστίνης ἀποκειμένων ἑλληνικῶν κωδίκων, 5 vols., St. Petersburg, 1891-1915 [Repr., Bruxelles, 1963].

Papadopoulos-Kerameus, A.I., "Σχεδίασμα περὶ τῶν λειτουργικῶν Μηναίων", in Βυζαντινὰ Χρονικά [Византийский Временникъ], 1 (1894), 341-388.

Papoudopoulos Vretos, A., Νεοελληνικὴ Φιλολογία ἤτοι κατάλογος τῶν ἀπὸ πτώσεως τῆς βυζαντινῆς αὐτοκρατορίας μέχρι ἐνκαθιδρύσεως τῆς ἐν Ἑλλάδι βασιλείας τυπωθέντων βιβλίων παρ' Ἑλλήνων εἰς τὴν ὁμιλουμένην, ἢ εἰς τὴν ἀρχαίαν ἑλληνικὴν γλῶσσαν συνεθεὶς, 2 vols., Athens, 1854-1857.

Papageorgiou, P.N., "Ἡ ἐν Θεσσαλονίκῃ μονὴ τῶν Βλαταίων καὶ τὰ μετόχια αὐτῆς", in *Byzantinische Zeitschrift*, 8 (1899), 402-428.

Papoulidis, K.K., "Συνοπτικὴ ἀναγραφὴ ἑλληνικῶν χειρογράφων καὶ ἐγγράφων τῆς Βιβλιοθήκης Lenin τῆς Μόσχας, in Θεολογία, 52 (1981), 481-499.

Pasadaiou, Α., ΙΕΡΑ ΘΕΟΛΟΓΙΚΗ ΣΧΟΛΗ ΧΑΛΚΗΣ. ΙΣΤΟΡΙΑ, ΑΡΧΙΤΕΚΤΟΝΙΚΗΣ, Athens, 1987.

Patrinelis, C.G., Βιβλιοθῆκαι καὶ ἀρχεῖ, Athens, 1963.

Pattie, T.S., 'The Creation of the Great Codices', in *The Bible as Book. The Manuscript Tradition*, Ed. by J.L. Sharpe and K. Van Kampen, London, Newcastle, 1998, 61-72.

Pelekanides, S.M., Christou, P.C., Mavropoulos–Tsioumis, C., Kadas, S.N. (Eds.), Οἱ θησαυροὶ τοῦ Ἁγίου Ὄρος, *The Treasures of Mount Athos: Illuminated Manuscripts*, 4 vols., Athens, 1973, 1875, 1979, 1991.

Pelikan, J.J., *The Reformation of the Bible. The Bible of the Reformation*, Catalogue of the Exhibition by V. Hotchkiss and D. Price, New Haven and London, 1996.

Percival, H.R. (Ed.), *The Seven Ecumenical Councils of the Undivided Church, their Canons and Dogmatic Decrees, together with the canons of all the local synods which have received ecumenical acceptance*, (A Select Library of Nicene and Post-Nicene Fathers of the Christian Church, Second Series, XIV), Reprint: Grand Rapids, Michigan, 1977.

Perria, L., *I Manoscritti Citati da Albert Ehrhard, Indice di: A. Ehrhard, Überlieferung und Bestand der hagiographischen und homiletischen Literatur der griechischen Kirche, I-III*, Leipzig-Berlin, 1937-1952 [Roma 1979].

Perrone, L., 'Perspectives sur Origène et la literature patristique des 'Quaestiones et Responsiones'', in *Origeniana Sexta: Origène et la Bible/Origen and the Bible*, Eds: A. de Boulluec and G. Dorival (Actes du Colloquium Origenianum Sextum, Chantilly, 30 août – 3 septembre 1993), Leuven, 1995.

Petit, F., *La chaîne sur la Genèse. Édition intégrale*, t. I-II, Louvain, 1991-1993.

Petit, F., *Catenae graecae in Genesim et in Exodum. II: Collectio Coisliniana in Genesim*, (CCSG 15), Turnhout and Louvain, 1986.

Petit, F., *Catenae graecae in Genesim et in Exodum. I: Catena Sinaitica* (CCSG 2), Turnhout and Louvain, 1977.

Petras, D.M., "The Gospel Lectionary of the Byzantine Church", in *St Vladimir's Theological Quarterly*, 41.2-3 (1997), 113-140.

Petrov, N.I., Указатель Церковно-археологическаго музея при Киевской Духовной Академии, 2nd ed., Kiev, 1897.

Petrov, N.I., Описание рукописей собрании, находящихся в городе Киеве, vols. I-III, Kiev, 1891-1904.

Petrov, N.I., Описание рукописей Церковно-археологическаго музея при Киевской Духовной Академии, vols. I-III, Kiev, 1875, 1877, 1879.

Petrova, L., "За потеклото на Музејската библиотека во Охрид", in Лихни*. Зборник на трудови, 5 (1983), 220-227.

Phirippides, N.S., Κατάλογος τῶν κωδίκων τῆς βιβλιοθήκης τοῦ Πατριαρχείου Ἀλεξανδρείας, in Ἐκκλησιαστικὸς Φάρος, 37 (1938), 225-240; 355-375; 445-464; 38 (1939), 74-88; 203-219; 338-357; 416-432; 39 (1940), 31-49; 183-199; 288-304; 434-440; 40 (1941), 111-128; 168-191; 355-374; 385-405; 41 (1942), 79-93, and completed by T.D. Moschonas, in Ἐκκλησιαστικὸς Φάρος, 42 (1943), 289-304.

Plümacher, E., 'Bibliothekswesen', in *Theologische Realenzyklopädie*, 6, (1980), 413-426.

Politis, L., Κατάλογος χειρογράφων τῆς Ἐθνικῆς Βιβλιοθήκης τῆς Ἑλλάδος, ἀρ. 1857-2500, Athens, 1991.

Politis, L., "Nouveaux manuscripts grecs découverts au Mont Sinaï. Rapport préliminaire", in *Scriptorium*, 34 (1980), 5-17 [pl. 1-9].

Politis, L., Συνοπτικὴ ἀναγραφὴ χειρογράφων ἑλληνικῶν συλλογῶν, Thessaloniki, 1976.

Politis, L., *Paléographie et littérature byzantine et néo-grecque: recueil d'études*, London, 1975.

Politis, L. and Manousakas, M., Συμπληρωματικοὶ κατάλογοι χειρογράφων Ἁγίου Ὄρους, Thessaloniki, 1973.

Politis, L., Ὁδηγὸς καταλόγου χειρογράφων, Athens, 1961.

Politis, L., "La section des manuscrits de la Bibliothèque Nationale", in *L'Hellénisme contemporain*, 1st series, 4 (1940), 242-249.

Popova, O., *Russian Illuminated manuscripts with 69 illustrations*, 48 in color. Trans: K. Cool, V. Ivanov and L. Sorokina, London, 1984.

Popova, O., *Les Miniatures Russes du XIe au XVe siècle. Russian Miniatures of the XIth to the XVth centuries*, Leningrad, 1975.

Prokurat, M., Golitzin, A., Peterson, M.D. (Eds.), *Historical Dictionary of the Orthodox Church* (Historical Dictionaries of religions, philosophies, and movements, 9), Lanham, MD, 1996.

Quasten, J., *Patrology*, 4 vols, Utrecht, 1962-1986.

Rabino, M.H.L., *Le Monastère de Saint-Catherine du Mont Sinai*, Cairo, 1938.

Rahlfs, A., *Psalmi cum Odis*, Göttingen, 1931 [repr. 1967 and 1979].

Rahlfs, A., 'Die alttestamentlichen Lektionen der griechischen Kirche', in *Mitteilungen des Septuaginta-Unternehmens*, Heft V, Berlin, 1915, 120-230.

Rahlfs, A., 'Verzeichnis der griechischen Handschriften des Alten Testaments für das Septuaginta Unternehmen', in *Nachrichten der koeniglichen Gesellschaft der Wissenschaften zu Göttingen, Philolologisch Historische Klasse*, (Beiheft), Berlin, 1914, 1-443.

Rallis, G.A. and Potlis, M., Σύνταγμα τῶν Θείων καὶ Ἱερῶν Κανόνων τῶν τε ἁγίων καὶ πανευφήμων Ἀποστόλων καὶ τῶν ἱερῶν Οἰκουμενικῶν καὶ Τοπικῶν Συνόδων καὶ τῶν κατὰ μέρος ἁγίων Πατέρων (...), ἐκδοθὲν μετὰ τῶν ἀρχαίων ἐξηγητῶν, t. I-VI, Athens, 1852-1859.

Rendel-Harris, J., "The Library of the Convent of the Holy Sepulchre at Jerusalem", in *Haverford College Studies published by the Faculty of Haverford College*, no. 1 (1889), 1ff.

Renoux, C., 'The Reading of the Bible in the Ancient Liturgy of Jerusalem', in *The Bible in Greek Christian Antiquity*, Trans. and Ed. by P.M. Blowers, Notre Dame, Indiana, 1997, 389-414.

Richard, M. and Olivier, J.M., *Répertoire des Bibliothèques et des Catalogues de Manuscrits Grecs*, troisième édition, Turnhout, 1995.

Richard, M., "Rapport sur une mission d'étude en U.R.S.S. (5 octobre-3 novembre 1960)", in *Bulletin d'information de l'Institut de recherche et d'histoire des textes*, 10 (1961), 43-56.

Riddle, D.W., 'The Use of Lectionaries in Critical Editions and Studies of the New Testament Text', in *Prolegomena to the Study of the Lectionary Text of the Gospels*, Ed. E.C. Colwell and D.W. Riddle, Chicago, Illinois, 1933, 67-77.

Rife, J.W., 'The Antonides Greek New Testament', in *Prolegomena to the Study of the Lectionary Text of the Gospels*, Ed: E.C. Colwell and D.W. Riddle, Chicago, Illinois, 1933, 57-66.

Rigas, O.G., Τυπικόν, Thessaloniki, 1994.

Robertson, J.N.W.B. (Trans), *The Acts and Decrees of the Synod of Jerusalem, sometimes called the Council of Bethlehem holden under Dositheus, Patriarch of Jerusalem in 1672*, London, 1899. [Repr. New York, N.Y., 1969]

Roloff, H., 'Die Katalogisierung', in *Handbuch der Bibliothekswissenschaft*, Ed: G. Leyh, vol. II, Wiesbaden, 1961.

Rudberg, S.Y., "Les manuscripts à contenu profane du Mont-Athos", in *Eranos*, 54 (1956), 174-185.

Runciman, S., *The Great Church in captivity : a study of the Patriarchate of Constantinople from the eve of the Turkish conquest to the Greek War of Independence*, Cambridge, 1968.

Sakkelion, I. and Sakkelion, A.I., Κατάλογος τῶν χειρογράφων τῆς Ἐθνικῆς Βιβλιοθήκης τῆς Ἑλλάδος, Athens, 1892.

Sakkelion, I., Πατμιακὴ βιβλιοθήκη ἤτοι ἀναγραφὴ τῶν ἐν τῇ βιβλιοθήκῃ τῆς κατὰ τὴν νῆσον Πάτμον γεραρᾶς καὶ βασιλικῆς μονῆς τοῦ Ἁγίου Ἀποστόλου καὶ Εὐαγγελιστοῦ Ἰωάννου τοῦ Θεολόγου τεθησαυρισμένων χειρογράφων τευχῶν, Athens, 1890.

Samodurova, Z.G., 'Об изучении византийского рукописного наследия в СССР (1945-1971)', in *Actes du XIVe Congrès international des Études byzantines*, (Bucharest, 6-12 septembre, 1971), Ed. M. Berza and E. Stănescu, Bucharest, 1976, t. III, 127-137.

Sathas, K.N., Νεοελληνικὴ Φιλολογία, Athens, 1868.

Saunders, E.W. and Lahood, C.G., *A Descriptive Checklist of Selected Manuscripts in the Monasteries of Mount Athos*, (Microfilmed for the Library of Congress and the International Greek New Testament Project, 1952-53), Washington, 1957.

Saunders, E.W., "Operation Microfilm at Mt. Athos", in *The Biblical Archaeologist*, 18.2 (1955), 22-41.

Scanlin, H.P., "The Old Testament Canon in the Orthodox Churches", in *New Perspectives on Historical Theology: Essays in Memory of John Meyendorff*, Ed. B. Nassif, Grand Rapids, 1996, 300-312.

Schatkin, M.A., 'Byzantine Greek Manuscripts in Leningrad – The Granstrem Catalog', in *Studia codicologica*, Ed. K. Treu (in cooperation with J. Dummer, J. Irmscher and F. Paschke; TU 124), Berlin, 1977, 413-423.

Schmemann, A., *The Eucharist. Sacrament of the Kingdom*, Crestwood, New York, 1988.

Schmemann, A., *Great Lent*, rev. ed., Crestwood, N.Y., 1974.

Schmemann, A., *Russian Theology 1920-1965. A Bibliographical Survey*, Crestwood, NY, 1969.

Schmemann, A., *Introduction to Liturgical Theology*, Trans: A.E. Moorehouse, London/Portland, 1966.

Schneider, A., *Beiträge zur Kenntnis der griechisch-orthodoxen Kirche Ägyptens*, Dresden, 1874.

Schneider, H., [I] "Die Biblischen Oden im Christlichen Altertum", [II] "Die Biblischen Oden Seit dem Sechsten Jahrhundert", [III] "Die Biblischen Oden in Jerusalem und Konstantinopel", [IV] "Die Biblischen Oden in Mittelalter", in *Biblica*, 30 (1949), 28-65, 239-272, 433-452, 479-500.

Scholz, J.M.A., *Novum Testamentum Graece*, I-II, Leipzig, 1830-1836.

Schulz, H.J., *The Byzantine Liturgy: Symbolic Structure and Faith Expression*, Trans: M.J. O'Connell, New York., 1986.

Scrivener, F.H.A., *A Plain Introduction to the Criticism of the New Testament for the Use of Biblical Students*, 4th ed. Ed. E. Miller, 2 Vols., London, 1894.

Serfes, D., "Monasticism in Cyprus", in *Cyprus Today, A Quarterly Cultural and Informative Review of the Ministry of Education and Culture*, 35.1-2 (1997), 2-15.

Ševčenko, I., Chernukhin, I., and Cherkas'ka, N., Грецькі рукописи у зібраннях Києва. Каталог, Kiev-Washington, 2000.

Smith, M., "Ἑλληνικὰ χειρόγραφα ἐν τῇ Μονῇ τοῦ Ἁγίου Σάββα", in Νέα Σιών, 55 (52th year) (1960), 110-125, 245-256.

Smolitsch, I., *Leben und Lehre der Starzen*, Wien, 1936.

Soden, H. von, *Die Schriften des Neuen Testaments in ihrer ältesten erreichbaren Textgestalt hergestellt auf Grund ihrer Textgeschichte*, 2 vols, Göttingen, 1911.

Sofianos, D.Z., *Holy Meteora*, Kalambaka, 2002.

Sofianos, D.Z., "Μετέωρα. Σύντομο ἱστορικὸ χρονικὸ τῆς Μετεωριτικῆς μοναστικῆς πολιτείας", in Νέα Ἑστια, 128 (1990), 1322-1332 and 24 pl.

Sofianos, D.Z., Τὰ χειρόγραφα τῶν Μετεώρων. Κατάλογος περιγραφικὸς τῶν χειρογράφων κωδίκων τῶν ἀποκειμένων εἰς τὰς μονὰς τῶν Μετεώρων. Τόμος Δ': Τὰ χειρόγραφα τῆς Μονῆς Ἁγίας Τριάδος, (Ἀκαδημία Ἀθηνῶν Κέντρον Ἐρεύνης τοῦ Μεσαιωνικοῦ καὶ Νέου Ἑλληνισμοῦ), 2 vols., Athens, 1993.

Sofianos, D.Z., Τὰ χειρόγραφα τῶν Μετεώρων. Κατάλογος περιγραφικὸς τῶν χειρογράφων κωδίκων τῶν ἀποκειμένων εἰς τὰς μονὰς τῶν Μετεώρων. Τόμος Γ': Τὰ χειρόγραφα τῆς Μονῆς Ἁγίου Στεφάνου, (Ἀκαδημία Ἀθηνῶν Κέντρον Ἐρεύνης τοῦ Μεσαιωνικοῦ καὶ Νέου Ἑλληνισμοῦ), 2 vols., Athens, 1986.

Soteriou, G.A., Κειμήλια τοῦ Οἰκουμενικοῦ Πατριαρχείου. Πατριαρχικὸς Ναὸς καὶ Σκευοφυλάκιον, Athens, 1937.

Soteroudis, P., Ἱερὰ Μονὴ Ἰβήρων. Κατάλογος Ἑλληνικῶν χειρογράφων, Α' (1-100), Hagion Oros, 1998.

Spyridon of the Lavra and Eustratiades, S., *Catalogue of the Greek Manuscripts of the Laura on Mount Athos with notices from other libraries.* Κατάλογος τῶν κωδίκων τῆς Μεγίστης Λαύρας (ἐν Ἁγίῳ Ὄρει), (Harvard Theological Studies; XII), Cambridge, 1925.

Stählin, O., 'Christliche Schriftsteller', in *Wilhelm von Christs Geschichte der Griechischen Litteratur,* München, 1924.

Staikos (Kotinos), K.S., "Libraries: History (Byzantine)", on www.libraries.gr/nonmembers/en/history_bizadinos.htm (seen December 2005)

Staikos, K.S., *The Great Libraries. From Antiquity to the Renaissance (3000 B.C. to A.D. 1600),* Newcastle DE/London, 2000.

Stathis, G.T., Τὰ χειρόγραφα Βυζαντινῆς μουσικῆς Ἅγιον Ὄρος. Κατάλογος περιγραφικὸς τῶν χειρογράφων κωδίκων Βυζαντινῆς μουσικῆς τῶν ἀποκείμενων ἐν ταῖς βιβλιοθήκαις τῶν ἱερῶν μονῶν καὶ σκητῶν τοῦ Ἁγίου Ὄρους, τ. 1-3, Athens, 1975, 1976, 1993.

Stavridis, T., "Histoire du Patriarcat œcuménique", in *Istina,* 15 (1970), 129-273.

The Stavropegic Monastery of St. John the Baptist, Essex (Ed.), *The Orthodox Liturgy being The Divine Liturgies of S. John Chrysostom and S. Basil the Great and the Divine Office of the Presanctified Gifts,* Oxford, 1982.

Stojanov, M., Опис на Гръцките други чуждоезични ръкописи в Народна Библиотека "Свё Кирил и Методий" в София. Codices graeci manuscripti Bibliothecae "Cyrilli et Methodii" Serdiciensis, Sofia, 1973.

Stroth, F.A., "Versuch eines Verzeichnisses der Handschriften der LXX", in *Repertorium für Biblische und Morgenländische Litteratur,* 5 (1779), 94-134; 8 (1781), 177-205; 11 (1782), 45-72. [Cod. 1-269]

Strzygowski, J., *Der Bilderkreis des griechischen Physiologus des Kosmas Indikopleustes und Oktateuch nach Handschriften der Bibliothek zu Smyrna,* Leipzig, 1899.

Studemund, W., "Das Inventar des Klosters St. Johannis auf der Insel Patmos im 16. Jahrhundert", in *Philogus,* 26 (1867), 167-173.

Stylianopoulos, T.G., *The New Testament: An Orthodox Perspective* (Vol.1: Scripture, Tradition, Hermeneutics), Brookline, Mass., 1999.

Stylianopoulos, T.G., "Historical Studies and Orthodox Theology or the Problem of History for Orthodoxy", in *The Greek Orthodox Theological Review,* 12.3 (1967), 394-419.

Swete, H.B. and Ottley, R.R., *An Introduction to the Old Testament in Greek,* Peabody, Mass., 1989 [repr. 1914].

Synodal Press of the Russian Patriarchate (Ed.), Святое Евангелие, Moscow, 1994.

Taft, R.F., *The Byzantine Rite. A Short History* (American Essays in Liturgy), Collegeville, 1992.

Taft, R.F., *The Great Entrance,* Rome, 1978.

Talley, T.J., *The Origins of the Liturgical Year,* Second, emended Edition, Collegeville, Minnesota, 1991.

Tanner, T.M., "A History of Early Christian Libraries from Jesus to Jerome", in *The Journal of Library History, Philosophy and Comparative Librarianship,* 14.1 (1979), 407-435.

M. Tarchnischvili, M. (Ed.), *Le Grand Lectionnaire de l'Église de Jérusalem (Ve-VIIIe siècle),* (Corpus Scriptorum Christianorum Orientalium; vol. 188-189, 204-205), Louvain, 1959-1960.

Themeles, T. Archimandrite, Τὰ Μηναῖα ἀπὸ τοῦ ΙΑ'- ΙΓ' αἰῶνος, Alexandria, 1931.

Theophylact of Bulgaria, *Theophylacti Archiepiscopi Bulgariae, Commentarii in quatuor Euangelia. Opus nunc primum Graece et Latine editum*, Paris, 1631.

Thibaut, J., *Monuments de la notation ekphonétique et hagiopolite de l'Église Grecque: exposé documentaire des manuscrits de Jérusalem, du Sinaï et de l'Athos conservés à la Bibliothèque impériale de Saint-Pétersburg*, s.n., 1913.

Thibaut, J., "Etude de Musique byzantine: Le chant ekphonétique", in *Byzantinische Zeitschrift*, 8 (1899), 122-147.

Thompson, E.M., *Facsimile of the Codex Alexandrinus*, Ed. with introductions to vols. 1 and 4, London, 1879-1883.

Thomsen, P., "Unbekannte griechische Handschriften der Patriarchatsbibliothek zu Jerusalem", in *Byzantinische Zeitschrift*, 22 (1913), 72-73.

Thomson, F.J., 'The Slavonic Translation of the Old Testament', in *The Interpretation of the Bible. The International Symposium in Slovenia*, by J. Krašovec (Ed.), (Journal for the Study of the Old Testament Supplement Series; 289), Sheffield, 1998, 605-920.

[Tichomirov], Archimandrite Savva, Палеографические снимки с греческих и славяанских рукописей Москов ской Московской Синодальной библиотеки VI-XVII век" (Specimina palaeographica codicum graecorum et slavonicorum bibliothecae Mosquensis Synodalis saec. vi.-xvii), Moscow, 1863.

[Tichomirov], Archimandrite Savva, Указатель для обозрения осковской Патриаршей (ныне Синодальной) ризницы и библиотеки, Moscow, 1855.

Tillyard, H.J.W., *Byzantine Music and Hymnography*, London, 1923 [repr. New York, 1976].

Tischendorf, C. von, "Die Bibliothek des Sinaiklosters in Kairo", in *Wiener Jahrbücher der Literatur. Anzeigeblatt*, 112 (1845), 30-42.

Tomadakis, N.B., Κλεὶς τῆς Βυζαντινῆς Φιλολογίας, Thessaloniki, 1993. [4th edition]

Touliatos-Banker, D., "Εὑρετήριο μικροταινιῶν μουσικῶν χειρογράφων στὸ ἀρχεῖο τοῦ Πατριαρχικοῦ Ἱδρύματος Πατερικῶν Μελετῶν ἀπὸ τὸ 1975 καὶ ἔπειτα, in Κληρονομία 18 (1986), 431-441.

Trebolle Barrera, J.C., *The Jewish Bible and the Christian Bible. An Introduction to the History of the Bible*, Trans: W.G.E. Watson, Leiden/New York/ Köln and Grand Rapids/ Cambridge, U.K., 1998.

Tregelles, S.P., *An Account of the Printed Text of the Greek New Testament with Remarks on Its Revision upon Critical Principals: Together with a Collation of Critical Texts of Griesbach, Scholtz, Lachmann and Tischendorf, with That in Common Use*, London, 1854.

Trempelas, P.N., Αἱ τρεῖς λειτουργίαι κατὰ τοὺς ἐν ἀθήναις κώδικας, Athens, 1935.

Treu, K., "Zu den neutestamentlichen Handschriften in der UdSSR", in *Forschungen und Fortschritten*, 38.4 (1964), 118.

Treu, K., *Die Griechischen Handschriften des Neuen Testaments in der UdSSR. Eine systematische Auswertung der Texthandschriften in Leningrad, Moskau, Kiev, Odessa, Tbilisi und Erevan*, Berlin, 1966.

Troelsgerd, C. (Ed.), *Monumenta Musicae Byzantinae: Collection of Microfilms and Photographs*, [Website publication: www.igl.ku.dk/MMB/mmb.html], Institute for Greek and Latin, University of Copenhagen, [seen 30.12.2005].

Tsakopoulos, A., Περιγραφικὸς κατάλογος τῶν χειρογράφων τῆς Βιβλιοθήκης τοῦ Οἰκουμενικοῦ Πατριαρχείου. Τόμος Γ' (α') Θεολογικς Σχολς Χάλκης, Istanbul, 1968.

Tsakopoulos, A., Περιγραφικὸς κατάλογος τῶν χειρογράφων τῆς Βιβλιοθήκης τοῦ Οἰκουμενικοῦ Πατριαρχείου. Τόμος Β'. Τμῆμα χειρογράφων Ἱ Μονῆς Ἁγίας Τριάδος Χάλκης, Istanbul, 1956.

Tsakopoulos, A., Περιγραφικὸς κατάλογος τῶν χειρογράφων τῆς Βιβλιοθήκης τοῦ Οἰκουμενικοῦ Πατριαρχείου. Τόμος Α'. Τμῆμα χειρογράφων Παναγίας Καμαριωτίσσης, Istanbul, 1953.

Tsurkan, R.K., Славянский перевод Библии: Происхождение, история текста и важнейшие издания, St. Petersburg, 2001.

Turner, C.H., "Patristic Commentaries on the Gospel of St. Matthew", in *The Journal of Theological Studies*, 12 (1910-1911), 99-112.

Turner, C.H., 'Greek Patristic Commentaries on the Pauline Epistles', in *A Dictionary of the Bible, Extra Volume*, Ed. J. Hastings, Edinburgh, 1906, 484-531.

Unknown author, *Checklist of Greek Manuscripts in the Greek Orthodox Patriarchal Library*, Istanbul, 1962.

Uspenskij, T., *L'Octateuch de la Bibliothèque du Sérail à Constantinople*, Sofia, 1907. [+ un album avec 47 pl. in folio].

Uthemann, K., 'Was verraten die Katenen über die Exegese ihrer Zeit?', in *Stimuli: Exegese und ihre Hermeneutik in Antike und Christentum*, (Festschrift für E. Dassmann), Ed. G. Schöllgen and C. Scholten, Münster Westfalen, 1996, 284-296.

Vailhé, S., "Répertoire alphabétique des monastères de Palestine", in *Revue de l'Orient Chrétien*, 4 (1899), 512-542 ; 5 (1900), 19-48, 272-292.

Vailhé, S., "Le monastère de S.- Sabas", in *Echos d'Orient*, 2 (1898-1899), 332-341; 3 (1899-1900), 18-28, 168-177.

Vailhé, S., "Les écrivains de Mar-Saba", in *Echos d'Orient*, 2 (1898), 1-11, 33-47.

Vater, F., "Zur Kunde griechischer Hss. in Russland", in *Archiv für Philologie und Pädagogie*, 9 (1839), 5-49.

Velichkovsky, P., *Blessed Paisius Velichkovsky. The Life and Ascetic Labors of Our Father, Elder Paisius, Archimandrite of the Holy Moldavian Monasteries of Niamets and Sekoul*. Optina Version, Ed. Schema-monk Metrophanes, Platina, Cal., 1976.

Ven, P. van den, "Inventaire sommaire des manuscrits grecs de la bibliothèque patriarcale du Caire", in *Le Muséon*, N.S. 15 (1914), [1-18?] 65-82.

Vercellone, C. et Cozza–Luzi, G. (Eds.), *Bibliorum Sacrorum.Graecus: codex Vaticanus, auspice Pio IX. Pontifice Maximo collatis studiis etc.*, 6 tom., Rome, 1868-1881.

Vikan, G., 'Walters Lectionary W.535 (A.D. 1594) and the Revival of Deluxe Greek Manuscript Production after the Fall of Constantinople', in *The Byzantine Tradition after the Fall of Constantinople*, Ed. J.J. Yiannias, Charlottesville / London, 1991, 181-268.

Vikan, G. (Ed.), *Illuminated Greek Manuscripts from American Collections*, Princeton, 1973.

Viktorov, A., Московский Публичныйи Румянцевский Музей. Собрание рукописей П.И. Севастьянова, Moscow, 1881.

Archimandrite Vladimir, Описание славянскихъ рукописей Московской Синодальной Библиотеки, Moscow, 1894. [reprint 1964]

Vleeschauwer, H.J. de, "The Byzantine Library to Justinian", in *Mousaion*, 74 (1964), 187-220.

Vleeschauwer, H.J. de, "Encyclopaedia of Library History", in *Mousaion*, 2 (1955), 1-44, 46-95.

Volk, O., *Die byzantinischen Klosterbibliotheken von Konstantinopel, Thessalonike und Kleinasien*, Diss., München, 1954.

Vries, I.M. De, "The Epistles, Gospels and Tones of the Byzantine Liturgical Year [I-IV]", in *The Eastern Churches Quarterly*, 10 (1953-1954), 41-49; 85-95; 137-149; 192-195.

Wald, E.T. De, *Psalms and Odes, 1. Vaticanus graecus 1927; 2. Vaticanus graecus 752* (The Illustrations in the Manuscripts of the Septuagint; v. 3), The Hague, 1941-1942.

Ware, T (Bishop Kallistos of Diokleia), *The Inner Kingdom*, (Collected Works; Vol. 1), Crestwood, New York, 2004.

Ware, T (Bishop Kallistos of Diokleia), *The Orthodox Church*, [n.l.], 1997.

Ware, T (Bishop Kallistos of Diokleia), 'Lectionary', in *The Orthodox Study Bible (New Testament and Psalms)*, Nashville, Tennessee 1993, 771-780.

Ware, T (Bishop Kallistos of Diokleia), "Patmos and its Monastery", in *Eastern Churches Review*, 1.3 (1967), 231-237.

Weitzmann, K. and Bernabò, M., *The Byzantine Octateuchs*, 2 vols., Princeton, 1999.

Weitzmann, K. and Galavaris, G., *The Monastery of Saint Catherine at Mount Sinai. The Illuminated Greek Manuscripts*, Volume I: From the ninth to the twelfth century, Princeton, New Jersey, 1990.

Weitzmann, K. and Essler, H.L.K., *The Cotton Genesis: British Library Codex Cotton Otho B. VI.* (Illustrations in the Manuscripts of the Septuagint I.), Princeton, 1986.

Weitzmann, K., *Byzantine Liturgical Psalters and Gospels*, London, 1980.

Weitzmann, K., *Illustrations in Roll and Codex. A study of the origin and method of text illustration*, Princeton, 1947. [sec. ed. 1970]

Wellesz, E., *A History of Byzantine Music and Hymnography*, 2nd ed., Oxford, 1971.

Wellesz, E., "Die byzantinischen Lektionszeichen", in *Zeitschrift für Musikwissenschaft*, 11 (1929), 513-534.

Wendel, C., "Die erste kaiserliche Bibliothek in Konstantinopel", in *Zentralblatt für das Bibliothekswesen*, 5 (1942), 193-209.

Wendel, C., 'Das griechisch-römische Altertum', in *Handbuch der Bibliothekswissenschaft*, Ed. F. Milkau und G. Leyh, Dritter Band: Geschichte der Bibliotheken, Leipzig, 1940, Kap. 1, 1-63.

Wensinck, A.J., *Mystic Treatises by Isaac of Nineveh*, translated from Bedjan's Syriac text with an introduction and registers, (Verhandelingen der koninklijke Akademie van Wetenschappen te Amsterdam, Afdeeling Letterkunde Nieuwe Reeks, Deel XXIII No. 1), Amsterdam, 1923.

Werner, E., *The Sacred Bridge. The Interdependence of Liturgy and Music in Synagogue and Church during the First Millennium*, London / New York, 1959.

Werner, E., "The Origin of Psalmody", in *Hebrew Union College Annual*, 25 (1954), 327-345.

Wettstein, J. (Ed.), ‛Η Καινὴ Διαθήκη. *Novum Testamentum Graecum editionis receptae cum lectionibus variantibus Codicum MSS., editionum aliarum, versionum et Patrum, nec non Commentario pleniore ex Scriptoribus veteribus Hebraeis, Graecis et Latinis historiam et vim verborum illustrante opera et studio*, 2 vols., Amstelaedami, 1751-1752.

Wikren, A., "Chicago Studies in the Greek Lectionary of the New Testament", in *Biblical and Patristic Studies, (in Memory of Robert Pierce Casey)*, Ed. J.N. Birdsall and R.W. Thomson, Freiburg-Basel-Barcelona-New York-Roma-São Paulo-Wien, 1963, 96-121.

Wilson, N.G., *Scholars of Byzantium*, London, 1983.

Wilson, N.G., "A Chapter in the History of Scholia" in *Classical Quarterly*, 17 (1967), 244-256.

Wilson, N.G., "The Libraries of the Byzantine World", in *Greek, Roman, and Byzantine Studies*, 8.2 (1967), 53-80.

Würthwein, E., *Der Text des Alten Testaments*, Stuttgart, 1973.

Yiannias, J.J. (Ed.), *The Byzantine Tradition after the Fall of Constantinople*, Charlottesville, 1991.

Zabiras, G.I., Νέα ‛Ελλὰς ἢ ‛Ελληνικὸν Θέατρον, Ed. G.P. Kremos, Athens, 1872. [Reprint of the first edition, Athens, 1972]

Zervos, S. (Archimandrite of the Ecumenical Throne), Εὐχολόγιον τὸ Μέγα τῆς κατὰ ᾽Ανατόλας ᾽Ορθοδόξου ᾽Εκκλησίας, 4th ed., Athens, 1992.

Annex III

Indices of the Byzantine Anagnosmata

The Anagnosmata of the Evangelion

Evangelion according to John[592]

Kephalaia	Stichoi	Anagnosmata	Synaxarion/Menologion	Kin	Akin
1	1-17	α′	Sunday of Pascha	A 1	
	18-28	β′	2nd day of the week of the Renewing	A 2	
	29-34	γ′	7 Jan Synaxis of John the Baptist		B 34
	35-52	δ′	4th day of the week of the Renewing	A 4	
	43-52	ε′	Sunday of the 1st week of Great Lent	A 310	
2	1-11	ς′	2nd day of the 2nd week (after Pascha)	A 9	
	12-22	ζ′	Friday of the week of the Renewing	A 6	
	23-25				
3	1-15	η′	5th day of the week of the Renewing	A 5	
	13-17	θ′	Sunday before the Exaltation of the Cross		X
	16-21	ι′	3rd day of the 2nd week (after Pascha)	A 10	
	22-33	ια′	Saturday of the week of the Renewing	A 7	
	34-36				
4	1-4				
	5-42	ιβ′	Sunday of the 5th week (after Pascha)	A 29	
	43-45				
	46-54	ιγ′	2rd day of the 3rd week (after Pascha)	A 16	
5	1-15	ιδ′	Sunday of the 4th week (after Pascha)	A 22	
	17-24	ιε′	4th day of the 2nd week (after Pascha)	A 11	
	24-30	ις′	5th day of the 2nd week (after Pascha)	A 12	
	30-47	ιζ′	Friday of the 2nd week (after Pascha)	A 13	
6	1-2	Continued	Cont.	Cont.	
	3-4				
	5-14	ιη′	4th day of the 5th week (after Pascha)	A 32	
	14-27	ιθ′	Saterday of the 2nd week (after Pascha)	A 14	
	27-33	κ′	3rd day of the 3rd week (after Pascha)	A 17	
	34				
	35-39	κα′	4th day of the 3rd week (after Pascha)	A 18	
	40-44	κβ′	5th day of the 3rd week (after Pascha)	A 19	
	45-47				
	48-54	κγ′	Friday of the 3rd week (after Pascha)	A 20	
	55				
	56-69	κδ′	2nd day of the 4th week (after Pascha)	A 23	
	70-71				
7	1-13	κε′	3rd day of the 4th week (after Pascha)	A 24	
	14-30	κς′	4th day of Mid-Pentecost (after Pascha)	A 25	
	31-36				
	37-52 [8, 12]	κζ′	Sunday of Pentecost	A 50	
	53				
8	1-2				
	3-11	κη′	1 April Mary of Egypt		X
	12-20	κθ′	5th day of the 4th week (after Pascha)	A 26	
	21-30	λ′	Friday of the 4th week (after Pascha)	A 27	
	31-42	λα′	Saturday of the 4th week (after Pascha)	A 28	
	42-51	λβ′	2nd day of the 5th week (after Pascha)	A 30	
	51-59	λγ′	3rd day of the 5th week (after Pascha)	A 31	

---

[592] The Index follows the order of books according to the Evangelion (the arrangement of the Anagnoseis), i.e John, Matthew, Luke, Mark. Only registered are passages the first time they occur in the Tables of Anagnosmata; later repetitions (and/or overlaps) are not indexed.

9	1-38	λδ′	Sunday of the 6th week (after Pascha)	A 36	
	39-41	λε′	5th day of the 5th week (after Pascha)	A 33	
10	1-9	Continued	Cont.	Cont.	
	9-16	λς′	13 November John Chrysostom		X
	17-28	λζ′	Friday of the 5th week (after Pascha)	A 34	
	27-38	λη′	Saturday of the 5th week (after Pascha)	A 35	
	39-42				
11	1-45	λθ′	Saturday of the 6th week of Great Lent (Lazarus)	A 343	
	46				
	47-54	μ′	2nd day of the 6th week (after Pascha)	A 37	
	55-57				
12	1-18	μα′	Palm Sunday	A 344	
	17-50	μβ′ [μγ′]	Great Fourth Day (Holy Week)	A 347	
13	1-2				
	3-11	μδ′	Great Fifth day (Holy Week) (Washing of the Feet)	A 349	
	12-17	με′	Great Fifth day (Holy Week) (Washing of the Feet)	A 349	
	18-30				
	31	μς′	Passion of the Lord (Holy Week) (Evangelion 1)	A 350	
14	1-9	μζ′	Continued	Cont.	
	10-26	μη′	Continued	Cont.	
	27-31	μθ′	Continued	Cont.	
15	1-7	ν′	Continued	Cont.	
	8-16	να′	Continued	Cont.	
	17-27	νβ′	Continued	Cont.	
16	1-14	νγ′	Continued	Cont.	
	15-22	νδ′	Continued	Cont.	
	23-33	νε′	Continued	Cont.	
17	1-17	νς′	Continued	Cont.	
	18-26 [18, 1]	νζ′	Continued	Cont.	
18	1-28	νη′	Passion of the Lord (Holy Week) (Evangelion 2)	A 350	
	28-40 [19, 16]	νθ′	Passion of the Lord (Holy Week) (Evangelion 4)	A 350	
19	1-5				
	6-11	ξ′	14 Sept Exaltation of the Cross		B 4
	12				
	13-20	Continued	Cont.		Cont.
	21-24				
	25-28	Continued	Cont.		Cont.
	29				
	30-35	Continued	Cont.		Cont.
	25-37	ξα′	Passion of the Lord (Evangelion 9)	A 350	
	38-42	ξβ′	Passion of the Lord (Evangelion 11)	A 350	
20	1-10	ξγ′	Eothinon Evangelion 7		
	11-18	ξδ′	Eothinon Evangelion 8		
	19-31	ξε′	Eothinon Evangelion 9		
21	1-14	ξς′	Eothinon Evangelion 10		
	15-25	ξζ′	Eothinon Evangelion 11		

Evangelion according to Matthew

Kephalaia	Stichoi	Anagnosmata	Synaxarion/Menologion	Kin	Akin
1	1-25	α′	Sunday before the Nativity of Jesus Christ		B 26
	18-25	β′	25 Dec Nativity of Jesus Christ (Morning office)		B 29
2	1-12	γ′	25 Dec Nativity of Jesus Christ (Liturgy)		B 29
	13-23	δ′	Sunday after the Nativity of Jesus Christ		X
3	1-6	ε′	Saturday before Theophany		X
	7-12				
	13-17	ϛ′	6 Jan Theophany		B 33
4	1-11	ζ′	Saturday after Theophany		X
	12-17	η′	Sunday after Theophany		X
	18-23	θ′	2nd Sunday (after Pentecost)	A 64	
	23-25	ι′	3rd day of the 1st week (after Pentecost)	A 52	
5	1-13	Continued	Cont.	Cont.	
	14-19	ια′	18 Jan Archbishops of Alexandria		B 37
	20-26	ιβ′	4th day of the 1st week (after Pentecost)	A 53	
	27-32	ιγ′	5th day of the 1st week (after Pentecost)	A 54	
	33-41	ιδ′	Friday of the 1st week (after Pentecost)	A 55	
	42-48	ιε′	Saturday of the 1st week (after Pentecost)	A 56	
6	1-13	ιϛ′	Saturday of the cheesefare week (36th week)	A 301	
	14-21	ιζ′	Sunday of the cheesefare week (36th week)	A 301	
	22-33	ιη′	Sunday of the 3rd week (after Pentecost)	A 71	
	31-34 [7, 9-11]	ιθ′	2nd day of the 2nd week (after Pentecost)	A 58	
7	1-8	κ′	Saturday of the 2nd week (after Pentecost)	A 63	
	9-11				
	12-21	κα′	13 Oct Commemoration of martyrs		X
	15-21	κβ′	3rd day of the 2nd week (after Pentecost)	A 59	
	21-23	κγ′	4th day of the 2nd week (after Pentecost)	A 60	
	24-29	κδ′	Saturday of the 3rd week (after Pentecost)	A 70	
8	1-4	Continued	Cont.	Cont.	
	5-13	κε′	Sunday of the 4th week (after Pentecost)	A 78	
	14-23	κϛ′	Saturday of the 4th week (after Pentecost)	A 77	
	23-27	κζ′	5th day of the 2nd week (after Pentecost)	A 61	
	28-34	κη′	Sunday of the 5th week (after Pentecost)	A 85	
9	1	Continued	Cont.	Cont.	
	1-8	κθ′	Sunday of the 6th week (after Pentecost)	A 92	
	9-13	λ′	Saturday of the 5th week (after Pentecost)	A 84	
	14-17	λα′	Friday of the 2nd week (after Pentecost)	A 62	
	18-26	λβ′	Saturday of the 6th week (after Pentecost)	A 91	
	27-35	λγ′	Sunday of the 7th week (after Pentecost)	A 99	
	36-38	λδ′	2nd day of the 3rd week (after Pentecost)	A 65	
10	1-8	Continued	Cont.	Cont.	
	9-15	λε′	3rd day of the 3rd week (after Pentecost)	A 66	
	16-22	λϛ′	4th day of the 3rd week (after Pentecost)	A 67	
	23-31	λζ′	5th day of the 3rd week (after Pentecost)	A 68	
	32-36 [11, 1]	λη′	Friday of the 3rd week (after Pentecost)	A 69	
	37-42	λθ′	Saturday of the 7th week (after Pentecost)	A 98	
11	1	Continued	Cont.	Cont.	
	2-15	μ′	2nd day of the 4th week (after Pentecost)	A 72	
	16-20	μα′	3rd day of the 4th week (after Pentecost)	A 73	
	20-26	μβ′	4th day of the 4th week (after Pentecost)	A 74	
	27-30	μγ′	5th day of the 4th week (after Pentecost)	A 75	

223

12	1-8	μδ′	Friday of the 4th week (after Pentecost)	A 76	
	9-13	με′	2nd day of the 5th week (after Pentecost)	A 79	
	14-16 [22-30]	μϛ′	3rd day of the 5th week (after Pentecost)	A 80	
	17-21				
	30-37	μζ′	Saturday of the 8th week (after Pentecost)	A 105	
	38-45	μη′	4th day of the 5th week (after Pentecost)	A 81	
	46-50	μθ′	5th day of the 5th week (after Pentecost)	A 82	
13	1-3	Continued	Cont.	Cont.	
	3-9	ν′	Friday of the 5th week (after Pentecost)	A 83	
	10-23	να′	2nd day of the 6th week (after Pentecost)	A 86	
	24-30	νβ′	3rd day of the 6th week (after Pentecost)	A 87	
	31-36	νγ′	4th day of the 6th week (after Pentecost)	A 88	
	36-43	νδ′	5th day of the 6th week (after Pentecost)	A 89	
	44-54	νε′	Friday of the 6th week (after Pentecost)	A 90	
	54-58	νϛ′	2nd day of the 7th week (after Pentecost)	A 93	
14	1-13	νζ′	3rd day of the 7th week (after Pentecost)	A 94	
	14-22	νη′	Sunday of the 8th week (after Pentecost)	A 106	
	22-34	νθ′	Sunday of the 9th week (after Pentecost)	A 113	
	35-36	ξ′	4th day of the 7th week (after Pentecost)	A 95	
15	1-11	Continued	Cont.	Cont.	
	12-21	ξα′	5th day of the 7th week (after Pentecost)	A 96	
	21-28	ξβ′	Sunday of the 17th week (after Pentecost)	A 169	
	29-31	ξγ′	Friday of the 7th week (after Pentecost)	A 97	
	32-39	ξδ′	Saturday of the 9th week (after Pentecost)	A 112	
16	1-6	ξε′	2nd day of the 8th week (after Pentecost)	A 100	
	6-12	ξϛ′	3rd day of the 8th week (after Pentecost)	A 101	
	13-19	ξζ′	29 June The Apostles Peter and Paul		B 57
	20-24	ξη′	4th day of the 8th week (after Pentecost)	A 102	
	24-28	ξθ′	5th day of the 8th week (after Pentecost)	A 103	
17	1-9	ο′	6 August Metamorphosis		B 67
	10-18	οα′	Friday of the 8th week (after Pentecost)	A 104	
	14-23	οβ′	Sunday of the 10th week (after Pentecost)	A 120	
	24-27	ογ′	Saturday of the 10th week (after Pentecost)	A 119	
18	1-4	Continued	Cont.	Cont.	
	1-11	οδ′	2nd day of the 9th week (after Pentecost)	A 107	
	10-20	οε′	2nd day of the 1st week (after Pentecost)	A 51	
	18-22 [9, 1-2, 13-15]	οϛ′	3rd day of the 9th week (after Pentecost)	A 108	
	23-35	οζ′	Sunday of the 11th week (after Pentecost)	A 127	
19	1-2				
	3-12	οη′	Saturday of the 11th week (after Pentecost)	A 126	
	13-15				
	16-26	οθ′	Sunday of the 12th week (after Pentecost)	A 134	
	27-30				
20	1-16	π′	4th day of the 9th week (after Pentecost)	A 109	
	17-28	πα′	5th day of the 9th week (after Pentecost)	A 110	
	29-34	πβ′	Saturday of the 12th week (after Pentecost)	A 133	
21	1-11 [15-17]	πγ′	Palm Sunday (Morning office)	A 345	
	12-14 [17-20]	πδ′	Friday of the 9th week (after Pentecost)	A 111	
	18-22	πε′	2nd day of the 10th week (after Pentecost)	A 114	
	23-27	πϛ′	3rd day of the 10th week (after Pentecost)	A 115	
	28-32	πζ′	4th day of the 10th week (after Pentecost)	A 116	
	33-42	πη′	Sunday of the 13th week (after Pentecost)	A 141	
	43-46	πθ′	5th day of the 10th week (after Pentecost)	A 117	

22	1-14	λ′	Sunday of the 14th week (after Pentecost)	A 148
	15-22	λα′	Saturday of the 13th week (after Pentecost)	A 140
	23-33	λβ′	Friday of the 10th week (after Pentecost)	A 118
	35-46	λγ′	Sunday of the 15th week (after Pentecost)	A 155
23	1-12	λδ′	Saturday of the 14th week (after Pentecost)	A 147
	13-22	λε′	2nd day of the 11th week (after Pentecost)	A 121
	23-28	λϛ′	3rd day of the 11th week (after Pentecost)	A 122
	29-39	λζ′	4th day of the 11th week (after Pentecost)	A 123
24	1-13	λη′	Saturday of the 15th week (after Pentecost)	A 154
	13-28	λθ′	5th day of the 11th week (after Pentecost)	A 124
	27-33 [42-51]	ρ′	Friday of the 11th week (after Pentecost)	A 125
	34-37 [42-44]	ρα′	Saturday of the 16th week (after Pentecost)	A 161
	36-51	ρβ′	Great Third Day (Holy Week) (Liturgy)	A 346
	42-47	ργ′	30 Sept Gregory of Great Armenia	X
25	1-13	ρδ′	Saturday of the 17th week (after Pentecost)	A 168
	14-30	ρε′	Sunday of the 16th week (after Pentecost)	A 162
	31-46	ρϛ′	Sunday of the Last Judgement (35th week)	A 295
26	1			
	2-20	ρζ′	Great Fifth Day (Holy Week) (Liturgy)	A 349
	21-39	Continued	Cont.	Cont.
	40-75	Continued	Cont.	Cont.
	6-16	ρη′	Great Fourth Day (Holy Week) (Liturgy)	A 347
	57-75	ρθ′	Passion of the Lord (Holy Week) (Evangelion 3)	A 350
27	1-2			
	3-32	ρι′	Passion of the Lord (Holy Week) (Evangelion 5)	A 350
	33-54	ρια′	Passion of the Lord (Holy Week) (Evangelion 7)	A 350
	55-61	ριβ′	Passion of the Lord (Holy Week) (Evening office)	A 352
	62-66	ριγ′	Passion of the Lord (Holy Week) (Evangelion 12)	A 350
28	1-20	ριδ′	Great Saturday (Holy Week) (Liturgy)	A 354
	16-20	ριε′	Eothinon Evangelion 1	

Evangelion according to Luke

Kephalaia	Stichoi	Anagnosmata	Synaxarion/Menologion	Kin	Akin
1	1-25 [57-68, 76, 80]	α′	24 June Nativity of John the Baptist		B 56
	5-25	β′	23 Sept Conception of John the Baptist		B 5
	24-38	γ′	25 March Annunciation of the Theotokos		B 46
	39-49 [56]	δ′	25 March Annunciation of the Theotokos		B 46
2	1-20	ε′	Preparation day of the Nativity of Christ (3rd Great Hour)		B 27
	20-21, [40-52]	ϛ′	1 Jan Circumcision of the Lord		B 30
	22-40	ζ′	2 Febr Meeting of Our Lord (Liturgy)		B 41
	40-52	η′	1 Jan Circumcision of the Lord		B 30
3	1-18	θ′	Preparation day of Theophany (9th Great Hour)		B 31
	19-22	ι′	2nd day of the 1st week (18th week)	A 170	
	23-38 [4,1]	ια′	3rd day of the 1st week (18th week)	A 171	
4	1-15	ιβ′	4th day of the 1st week (18th week)	A 172	
	16-22	ιγ′	5th day of the 1st week (18th week)	A 173	
	22-30	ιδ′	Friday of the 1st week (18th week)	A 174	
	31-36	ιε′	Saturday of the 1st week (18th week)	A 175	
	37				
	38-44	ιϛ′	2nd day of the 2nd week (19th week)	A 177	
5	1-11	ιζ′	Sunday of the 1st week (18th week)	A 176	
	12-16	ιη′	3rd day of the 2nd week (19th week)	A 178	
	17-26	ιθ′	Saturday of the 2nd week (19th week)	A 182	
	27-32	κ′	Saturday of the 3rd week (20th week)	A 189	
	33-39	κα′	4th day of the 2nd week (19th week)	A 179	
6	1-10	κβ′	Saturday of the 4th week (21st week)	A 196	
	11				
	12-19	κγ′	5th day of the 2nd week (19th week)	A 180	
	17-23	κδ′	Friday of the 2nd week (19th week)	A 181	
	24-30	κε′	2nd day of the 3rd week (20th week)	A 184	
	31-36	κϛ′	Sunday of the 2nd week (19th week)	A 183	
	37-45	κζ′	3rd day of the 3rd week (20th week)	A 185	
	46-49 [7,1]	κη′	4th day of the 3rd week (20th week)	A 186	
7	1-10	κθ′	Saturday of the 5th week (22nd week)	A 203	
	11-16	λ′	Sunday of the 3rd week (20th week)	A 190	
	17-30	λα′	5th day of the 3rd week (20th week)	A 187	
	31-35	λβ′	Friday of the 3rd week (20th week)	A 188	
	36-50	λγ′	2nd day of the 4th week (21st week)	A 191	
8	1-3	λδ′	3rd day of the 4th week (21st week)	A 192	
	4				
	5-15	λε′	Sunday of the 4th week (21st week)	A 197	
	16-21	λϛ′	Saturday of the 6th week (23rd week)	A 210	
	22-25	λζ′	4th day of the 4th week (21st week)	A 193	
	26				
	27-39	λη′	Sunday of the 6th week (23rd week)	A 211	
	40				
	41-56	λθ′	Sunday of the 7th week (24th week)	A 218	
9	1-6	μ′	Saturday of the 7th week (24th week)	A 217	
	7-11	μα′	5th of the 4th week (21st week)	A 194	
	12-18	μβ′	Friday of the 4th week (21st week)	A 195	
	18-22	μγ′	2nd of the 5th week (22nd week)	A 198	
	23-27	μδ′	3rd of the 5th week (22nd week)	A 199	

	28-36	με′	6 August Metamorphosis (Morning office)		B 67
	37-43	μϛ′	Saturday of the 8th week (25th week)	A 224	
	44-50	μζ′	4th day of the 5th week (22nd week)	A 200	
	49-56	μη′	5th day of the 5th week (22nd week)	A 201	
	57-62	μθ′	Saturday of the 9th week (26th week)	A 231	
10	1-15	ν′	Friday of the 5th week (22nd week)	A 202	
	16-21	να′	8 Nov Synaxis of the Archangels (Liturgy)		B 16
	22-24	νβ′	2nd day of the 6th week (23th week)	A 205	
	25-37	νγ′	Sunday of the 8th week (25th week)	A 225	
	38-42 [11, 27-28]	νδ′	8 Sept Nativity of the Theotokos (Liturgy)		B 2
11	1-10	νε′	3rd day of the 6th week (23rd week)	A 206	
	9-13	νϛ′	4th day of the 6th week (23rd week)	A 207	
	14-23	νζ′	5th day of the 6th week (23rd week)	A 208	
	23-26	νη′	Friday of the 6th week (23rd week)	A 209	
	29-33	νθ′	2nd of the 7th week (24th week)	A 212	
	34-41	ξ′	3rd of the 7th week (24th week)	A 213	
	42-46	ξα′	4th of the 7th week (24th week)	A 214	
	47-54	ξβ′	5th of the 7th week (24th week)	A 215	
12	1	Continued	Cont.	Cont.	
	2-12	ξγ′	Friday of the 7th week (24th week)	A 216	
	8-12	ξδ′	6 Nov Archbishop Paul of Constantinople		X
	13-15 [22-31]	ξε′	2nd of the 8th week (25th week)	A 219	
	16-21	ξϛ′	9th Sunday (26th week)	A 232	
	22-31				
	32-40	ξζ′	Saturday of the 11th week (28th week)	A 245	
	41				
	42-48	ξη′	3rd of the 8th week (25th week)	A 220	
	48-59	ξθ′	4th of the 8th week (25th week)	A 221	
13	1-9	ο′	5th day of the 8th week (25th week)	A 222	
	10-17	οα′	Sunday of the 10th week (27th week)	A 239	
	18				
	19-29	οβ′	Saturday of the 12th week (29th week)	A 252	
	30				
	31-35	ογ′	Friday of the 8th week (25th week)	A 223	
14	1-11	οδ′	Saturday of the 13th week (30th week)	A 259	
	1, 12-15	οε′	2nd day of the 9th week (26th week)	A 226	
	16-24	οϛ′	Sunday of the 11th week (28th week)	A 246	
	25-35	οζ′	3rd of the 9th week (26th week)	A 227	
15	1-10	οη′	4th day of the 9th week (26th week)	A 228	
	11-32	οθ′	17th Sunday (34th week) (Prodigal Son)	A 288	
16	1-9	π′	5th day of the 9th week (26th week)	A 229	
	10-15	πα′	Saturday of the 14th week (31st week)	A 266	
	15-18 [7, 1-4]	πβ′	Friday of the 9th week (26th week)	A 230	
	19-31	πγ′	Sunday of the 5th week (22nd week)	A 204	
17	1-2				
	3-10	πδ′	Saturday of the 15th week (32nd week)	A 273	
	11				
	12-19	πε′	Sunday of the 12th week (29th week)	A 253	
	20-25	πϛ′	2nd of the 10th week (27th week)	A 233	
	26-37 [18, 8]	πζ′	3rd of the 10th week (27th week)	A 234	
18	1				
	'2-8	πη′	Saturday of the 16th week (33rd week)	A 280	
	9				
	10-14	πθ′	Sunday of the 16th week (33rd week)	A 281	

226

	15-17 [26-30]	λ′	4th day of the 10th week (27th week)	A 235
	18-27	λα′	Sunday of the 13th week (30th week)	A 260
	28-30			
	31-34	λβ′	5th day of the 10th week (27th week)	A 236
	35-43	λγ′	Sunday of the 14th week (31st week)	A 267
19	1-10	λδ′	Sunday of the 15th week (32rd week)	A 274
	11			
	12-28	λε′	Friday of the 10th week (27th week)	A 237
	29-40 [22, 7-39]	λϛ′	2nd day of the Meatfare week (36th week)	A 296
	37-44	λζ′	2nd day of the 11th week (28th week)	A 240
	45-48	λη′	3rd day of the 11th week (28th week)	A 241
20	1-8	λθ′	4th day of the 11th week (28th week)	A 242
	9-18	ρ′	5th day of the 11th week (28th week)	A 243
	19-26	ρα′	Friday of the 11th week (28th week)	A 244
	27-44	ρβ′	2nd day of the 12th week (29th week)	A 247
	45			
	46-47	ργ′	Saturday of the 17th week (34th week)	A 287
21	1-4			
	5-7 [10-11, 20-24]	ρδ′	4th day of the 12th week (29th week)	A 249
	8-9 [25-27, 33-36]	ρε′	Saturday of the Last Judgement (35th week)	A 294
	10-11			
	12-19	ρϛ′	3rd day of the 12th week (29th week)	A 248
	28-33	ρζ′	5th day of the 12th week (29th week)	A 250
	37-38	ρη′	Friday of the 12th week (29th week)	A 251
22	1-8	Continued	Cont.	Cont.
	[19, 29-40] 7-39		2nd day of the Meatfare week (36th week)	A 296
	43-44			
	39-42 [45-71; 23,1]	ρθ′	3rd day of the Meatfare week (36th week)	A 297
23	1-31 [33, 44-56]	ρι′	5th day of the Meatfare week (36th week)	A 299
	32-49	ρια′	Passion of the Lord (Holy Week) (Evangelion 8)	A 350
24	1-12	ριβ′	Eothinon Evangelion 4	
	12-35	ριγ′	Eothinon Evangelion 5	
	36-53	ριδ′	Eothinon Evangelion 6	

228

Evangelion according to Mark

Kephalaia	Stichoi	Anagnosmata	Synaxarion/Menologion	Kin	Akin
1	1-8	α′	Sunday before Theophany		X
	9-15	β′	2nd day of the 12th week of Matthew	A 128	
	16-22	γ′	3rd day of the 12th week of Matthew	A 129	
	23-28	δ′	4th day of the 12th week of Matthew	A 130	
	29-35	ε′	5th day of the 12th week of Matthew	A 131	
	35-44	ς′	Saturday of the 2nd week of Great Lent	A 315	
	45				
2	1-12	ζ′	Sunday of the 2nd week of Great Lent	A 316	
	13				
	14-17	η′	Saturday of the 3rd week of Great Lent	A 322	
	18-22	θ′	Friday of the 12th week of Matthew	A 132	
	23-28	ι′	Saturday of the 1st week of Great Lent	A 308	
3	1-5	Continued	Cont.	Cont.	
	6-12	ια′	2nd day of the 13th week of Matthew	A 135	
	13-21	ιβ′	3rd day of the 13th week of Matthew	A 136	
	20-27	ιγ′	4th day of the 13th week of Matthew	A 137	
	28-35	ιδ′	5th day of the 13th week of Matthew	A 138	
4	1-9	ιε′	Friday of the 13th week of Matthew	A 139	
	10-23	ις′	2nd day of the 14th week of Matthew	A 142	
	24-34	ιζ′	3rd day of the 14th week of Matthew	A 143	
	35-41	ιη′	2nd day of the 16th week of Matthew	A 144	
5	1-20	ιθ′	5th day of the 14th week of Matthew	A 145	
	21				
	22-24 [35-43; 6,1]	κ′	Friday of the 14th week of Matthew	A 146	
	24-34	κα′	2nd day of the 15th week of Matthew	A 149	
6	1-7	κβ′	3rd day of the 15th week of Matthew	A 150	
	7-13	κγ′	4th day of the 15th week of Matthew	A 151	
	14-30	κδ′	29 August Beheading of John the Baptist		B 71
	30-45	κε′	5th day of the 15th week of Matthew	A 152	
	45-53	κς′	Friday of the 15th week of Matthew	A 153	
	54-56	κζ′	2nd day of the 16th week of Matthew	A 156	
7	1-8	Continued	Cont.	Cont.	
	5-16	κη′	3rd day of the 16th week of Matthew	A 157	
	14-24	κθ′	4th day of the 16th week of Matthew	A 158	
	24-30	λ′	5th day of the 16th week of Matthew	A 159	
	31-37	λα′	Saturday of the 4th week of Great Lent	A 329	
8	1-10	λβ′	Friday of the 16th week of Matthew	A 160	
	11-21	λγ′	2nd day of the 13th week of Luke	A 254	
	22-26	λδ′	3rd day of the 13th week of Luke	A 255	
	27-31	λε′	Saturday of the 5th week of Great Lent	A 336	
	30-34	λς′	4th day of the 13th week of Luke	A 256	
	34-38	λζ′	Sunday of the 3rd week of Great Lent	A 323	
9	1	Continued	Cont.	Cont.	
	2-9	λη′	7 Aug Afterfeast of Metamorphosis		X
	10-15	λθ′	5th day of the 13th week of Luke	A 257	
	16				
	17-31	μ′	Sunday of the 4th week of Great Lent	A 330	
	33-41	μα′	Friday of the 13th week of Luke	A 258	
	42-50	μβ′	2nd day of the 14th week of Luke	A 261	

10	1	Continued	Cont.	Cont.
	2-12	μγ′	3rd day of the 14th week of Luke	A 262
	11-16	μδ′	4th day of the 14th week of Luke	A 263
	17-27	με′	5th day of the 14th week of Luke	A 264
	23-32	μς′	Friday of the 14th week of Luke	A 265
	32-45	μζ′	Sunday of the 5th week of Great Lent	A 337
	46-52	μη′	2nd day of the 15th week of Luke	A 268
11	1-11	μθ′	2nd day of the Last Judgement (35th week)	A 289
	11-23	ν′	3rd day of the 15th week of Luke	A 269
	23-26	να′	4th day of the 15th week of Luke	A 270
	27-33	νβ′	5th day of the 15th week of Luke	A 271
12	1'-12	νγ′	Friday of the 15th week of Luke	A 272
	13-17	νδ′	2nd day of the 16th week of Luke	A 275
	18-27	νε′	3rd day of the 16th week of Luke	A 276
	28-37	νς′	4th day of the 16th week of Luke	A 277
	38-44	νζ′	5th day of the 16th week of Luke	A 278
13	1-9	νη′	Friday of the 16th week of Luke	A 279
	9-13	νθ′	2nd day of the 17th week of Luke	A 282
	14-23	ξ′	3rd day of the 17th week of Luke	A 283
	24-31	ξα′	4th day of the 17th week of Luke	A 284
	31-37	ξβ′	5th day of the 17th week of Luke	A 285
14	1-2	Continued	Cont.	Cont.
	3-9	ξγ′	Friday of the 17th week of Luke	A 286
	10-42	ξδ′	3rd day of the Last Judgement (35th week)	A 290
	43-72 [5, 1]	ξε′	4th day of the Last Judgement (35th week)	A 291
15	1-15	ξς′	5th day of the Last Judgement (35th week)	A 292
	16-32	ξζ′	Passion of the Lord (Holy Week) (Evangelion 6)	A 350
	[20, 22, 25] 33-41 42	ξη′	Friday of the Last Judgement (35th week)	A 293
	43-47	ξθ′	Passion of the Lord (Holy Week) (Evangelion 10)	A 350
16	1-8	ο′	Eothinon Evangelion 2	
	9-20	οα′	Eothinon Evangelion 3	

The Anagnosmata of the Apostolos

The Acts of the Apostles[593]

Kephalaia	Stichoi	Anagnosmata	Synaxarion/Menologion	Kin	Akin
1	1-8	α′	Sunday of Pascha	A 1	
	1-12	β′	Ascension of the Lord (6th week after Pascha)	A 40	
	12-17 [21-26]	γ′	2nd day of the week of the Renewing	A 2	
	18-20				
2	1-11	δ′	Sunday of Pentecost	A 50	
	12-13				
	14-21	ε′	3rd day of the week of the Renewing	A 3	
	22-36	ς′	4th day of the week of the Renewing	A 4	
	37				
	38-43	ζ′	5th day of the week of the Renewing	A 5	
	44-47				
3	1-8	η′	Friday of the week of the Renewing	A 6	
	9-10				
	11-16	θ′	Saturday of the week of the Renewing	A 7	
	17-18				
	19-26	ι′	2nd day of the 2nd week (after Pascha)	A 9	
4	1-10	ια′	3rd day of the 2nd week (after Pascha)	A 10	
	11-12				
	13-22	ιβ′	4th day of the 2nd week (after Pascha)	A 11	
	23-31	ιγ′	5th day of the 2nd week (after Pascha)	A 12	
	32-37				
5	1-11	ιδ′	Friday of the 2nd week (after Pascha)	A 13	
	12-20	ιε′	Sunday of Antipascha (2nd week after Pascha)	A 8	
	21-32	ις′	Saturday of the 2nd week (after Pascha)	A 14	
	33-42				
6	1-7	ιζ′	Sunday of the 3rd week the Myrrhbearing Women	A 15	
	8-15	ιη′	2nd day of the 3rd week (after Pascha)	A 16	
7	1-5 [47-60]	Continued	Cont.	Cont.	
	6-46				
8	5-17	ιθ′	3rd day of the 3rd week (after Pascha)	A 17	
	18-25	κ′	4th day of the 3rd week (after Pascha)	A 18	
	26-39	κα′	5th day of the 3rd week (after Pascha)	A 19	
	40	κβ′	Friday of the 3rd week (after Pascha)	A 20	
9	1-18	Continued	Cont.	Cont.	
	19-31	κγ′	Friday of the 3rd week (after Pascha)	A 21	
	32-42	κδ′	Sunday of the 4th week the Paralytic (after Pascha)	A 22	
	43				
10	1-16	κε′	2nd day of the 4th week (after Pascha)	A 23	
	17-20				
	21-33	κς′	3rd day of the 4th week (after Pascha)	A 24	
	34-43	κζ′	5th day of the 4th week (after Pascha)	A 26	
	44-48	κη′	Friday of the 4th week (after Pascha)	A 27	
11	1-10	Continued	Cont.	Cont.	
	11-18				
	19-30	κθ′	Sunday of the 5th week Samaritan Woman	A 29	

---

[593] The Index follows the order of books according to the Apostolos, i.e the Acts, the Epistles of Paul, the General Epistles.

12	1-11	λ′	Saturday of the 4th week (after Pascha)	A 28	
	12-17	λα′	2nd day of the 5th week (after Pascha)	A 30	
	18-24				
	25	λβ′	3rd day of the 5th week (after Pascha)	A 31	
13	1-12	Continued	Cont.	Cont.	
	13-24	λγ′	4th day of the 5th week (after Pascha)	A 32	
	25-32	λδ′	29 Aug Beheading of John the Baptist		B 71
	33-52				
14	1-5				
	6-18	λε′	4th day of the 4th week (after Pascha)	A 25	
	19				
	20-28	λϛ′	5th day of the 5th week (after Pascha)	A 33	
15	1-4	Continued	Cont.	Cont.	
	5-12	λζ′	Friday of the 5th week (after Pascha)	A 34	
	13-34				
	35-41	λη′	Saturday of the 5th week (after Pascha)	A 35	
16	1-15				
	16-34	λθ′	Sunday of the 6th week Blind Man (after Pascha)	A 36	
	35-40				
17	1-9	μ′	2nd of the 6th week (after Pascha)	A 37	
	10-15				
	16-34	μα′	3 Oct Dionysius the Areopagite		X
	19-28	μβ′	3rd of the 6th week (after Pascha)	A 38	
18	'1-21				
	22-28	μγ′	4th of the 6th week (after Pascha)	A 39	
19	1-8	μδ′	Friday of the 6th week (after Pascha)	A 41	
	9-41				
20	1-6				
	7-12	με′	Saturday of the 6th week (after Pascha)	A 42	
	13-15				
	16-18 [28-36]	μϛ′	Sunday of the 7th week Fathers of Nicea I	A 43	
	19-27				
	37-38				
21	1-7				
	8-14	μζ′	2nd day of the 7th week (after Pascha)	A 44	
	13-25				
	26-32	μη′	3rd day of the 7th week (after Pascha)	A 45	
	33-40				
22	1-30				
23	1-11	μθ′	4th day of the 7th week (after Pascha)	A 46	
	12-35				
24	1-27				
25	1-12				
	13-19	ν′	5th day of the 7th week (after Pascha)	A 47	
	20-27				
26	1-11				
	12-20	να′	21 May Constantine and Helena		X
27	1-44 [28, 1]	νβ′	Friday of the 7th week (after Pascha)	A 48	
28	1-31	νγ′	Saturday of the 7th week (after Pascha)	A 49	

The Epistles of the Apostle Paul (incl. Hebrews)

Kephalaia	Stichoi	Anagnosmata	Synaxarion/Menologion	Kin	Akin
Romans					
1	1-7 [13-17]	α'	3rd day of the 1st week (after Pentecost)	A 52	
	7-12	β'	Saturday of the 1st week (after Pentecost)	A 56	
	18-27	γ'	4th day of the 1st week (after Pentecost)	A 53	
	28-32	δ'	5th day of the 1st week (after Pentecost)	A 54	
2	1-9	Continued	Cont.	Cont.	
	10-16	ε'	Sunday of the 2nd week (after Pentecost)	A 64	
	14-28	ς'	Friday of the 1st week (after Pentecost)	A 55	
	28-29	ζ'	2nd day of the 2nd week (after Pentecost)	A 58	
3	1-18	Continued	Cont.	Cont.	
	19-26	η'	Saturday of the 2nd week (after Pentecost)	A 63	
	27				
	28-31	θ'	Saturday of the 3rd week (after Pentecost)	A 70	
4	1-3	Continued	Cont.	Cont.	
	4-12	ι'	3rd day of the 2nd week (after Pentecost)	A 60	
	13-25	ια'	4th day of the 2nd week (after Pentecost)	A 61	
5	1-10	ιβ'	Sunday of the 3rd week (after Pentecost)	A 71	
	10-16	ιγ'	5th day of the 2nd week (after Pentecost)	A 61	
	17-21	ιδ'	Friday of the 2nd week (after Pentecost)	A 62	
6	1-2	Continued	Cont.	Cont.	
	3-11	ιε'	Great Saturday (Holy Week) (Liturgy)	A 354	
	12-17				
	18-23	ις'	Sunday of the 4th week (after Pentecost)	A 78	
7	1-13	ιζ'	2nd day of the 3rd week (after Pentecost)	A 65	
	14-25	ιη'	3rd day of the 3rd week (after Pentecost)	A 66	
8	1-2	Continued	Cont.	Cont.	
	2-13	ιθ'	4th day of the 3rd week (after Pentecost)	A 67	
	14-21	κ'	Saturday of the 5th week (after Pentecost)	A 84	
	22-27	κα'	5th day of the 3rd week (after Pentecost)	A 68	
	28-39	κβ'	2 Sept John the Faster		X
9	1-5	κγ'	Saturday of the 6th week (after Pentecost)	A 91	
	6-19	κδ'	Friday of the 3rd week (after Pentecost)	A 69	
	18-33	κε'	2nd of the 4th week (after Pentecost)	A 72	
10	1-10	κς'	Sunday of the 5th week (after Pentecost)	A 85	
	11-21	κζ'	3rd day of the 4th week (after Pentecost)	A 73	
11	1-2	Continued	Cont.	Cont.	
	2-12	κη'	4th day of the 4th week (after Pentecost)	A 74	
	13-24	κθ'	5th day of the 4th week (after Pentecost)	A 75	
	25-36	λ'	Friday of the 4th week (after Pentecost)	A 76	
12	1-3	λα'	Saturday of the 7th week (after Pentecost)	A 98	
	4-5 [15-21]	λβ'	2nd day of the 5th week (after Pentecoste)	A 79	
	6-14	λγ'	Sunday of the 6th week (after Pentecost)	A 92	
13	1-10	λδ'	Saturday of the 8th week (after Pentecost)	A 105	
	11-14	λε'	Sunday of the Cheesefare week	A 302	
14	1-4	Continued	Cont.	Cont.	
	5				
	6-9	λς'	Saturday of the 9th week (after Pentecost)	A 112	
	9-18	λζ'	3rd day of the 5th week (after Pentecost)	A 80	

	19-23 [16, 25-27]	λη′	Saturday of the cheesefare week (36th week)	A 301	
	24-26				
15	1-7	λθ′	Sunday of the 7th week (after Pentecost)	A 99	
	7-16	μ′	4th day of the 5th week (after Pentecost)	A 81	
	17-29	μα′	5th day of the 5th week (after Pentecost)	A 82	
	30-33	μβ′	Saturday of the 1st week (after Pentecost)	A 119	
16	1-16	μγ′	Friday of the 5th week (after Pentecost)	A 83	
	17-24	μδ′	2nd day of the 6th week (after Pentecost)	A 86	

I Corinthians

1	1-9	α′	3rd day of the 6th week (after Pentecost)	A 87	
	3-9	β′	Saturday of the 11th week (after Pentecost)	A 126	
	10-17	γ′	Sunday of the 8th week (after Pentecost)	A 106	
	18-24	δ′	14 Sept Exaltation of the Cross		B 4
	26-31	ε′	Saturday of the 12th week (after Pentecost)	A 133	
2	1-5	Continued	Cont.	Cont.	
	6-9	ϛ′	Saturday of the 13th week (after Pentecost)	A 140	
	9-16	ζ′	4th day of the 6th week (after Pentecost)	A 88	
3	1-8	Continued	Cont.	Cont.	
	9-17	η′	Sunday of the 9th week (after Pentecost)	A 113	
	18-23	θ′	5th day of the 6th week (after Pentecost)	A 89	
4	1-5	ι′	Saturday of the 14th week (after Pentecost)	A 147	
	5-8	ια′	Friday of the 6th week (after Pentecost)	A 90	
	9-16	ιβ′	Sunday of the 10th week (after Pentecost)	A 120	
	17-21	ιγ′	Saturday of the 15th week (after Pentecost)	A 154	
5	1-5	Continued	Cont.	Cont.	
	6-8 [Gal 3, 13-14]	ιδ′	Great Saturday (Holy Week) (Morning office)	A 354	
	9-13	ιε′	2nd day of the 7th week (after Pentecost)	A 93	
6	1-11	Continued	Cont.	Cont.	
	12-20	ιϛ′	Sunday of the 34th week (after Pentecost)	A 288	
	20	ιζ′	3rd day of the 7th week (after Pentecost)	A 94	
7	1-12	Continued	Cont.	Cont.	
	12-24	ιη′	4th day of the 7th week (after Pentecost)	A 95	
	24-35	ιθ′	5th day of the 7th week (after Pentecost)	A 96	
	35-40	κ′	Friday of the 7th week (after Pentecost)	A 97	
8	1-7	Continued	Cont.	Cont.	
	8-13	κα′	Sunday of the Meatfare week (35th week)	A 295	
9	1-2	Continued	Cont.	Cont.	
	2-12	κβ′	Sunday of the 11th week (after Pentecost)	A 127	
	13-18	κγ′	2nd day of the 8th week (after Pentecost)	A 100	
	19-27	κδ′	5 Jan Eve of Theophany (Evening office)		B 32
10	1-4	κε′	5 Jan Eve of Theophany (Great Blessing of Water)		B 32
	5-12	κϛ′	3rd day of the 8th week (after Pentecost)	A 101	
	12-22	κζ′	4th day of the 8th week (after Pentecost)	A 102	
	23-28	κη′	Saturday of the 16th week (after Pentecost)	A 161	
	28-33	κθ′	5th day of the 8th week (after Pentecost)	A 103	
11	1-8	Continued	Cont.	Cont.	
	8-23	λ′	Friday of the 8th week (after Pentecost)	A 104	
	23-32	λα′	Great Fifth Day (Holy Week) (Evening office)	A 349	
	31-34	λβ′	2nd day of the 9th week (after Pentecost)	A 107	
12	1-6	Continued	Cont.	Cont.	
	7-11	λγ′	17 Nov Gregory Thaumaturgus		X
	12-26	λδ′	3rd day of the 9th week (after Pentecost)	A 108	
	27-31	λε′	1 July the Martyrs Cosmas and Damian		X

13	1-8	Continued	Cont.	Cont.	
	4-13	λϛ′	4th day of the 9th week (after Pentecost)	A 109	
14	1-5	Continued	Cont.	Cont.	
	6-19	λζ′	5th day of the 9th week (after Pentecost)	A 110	
	20-25	λη′	Saturday of the 17th week (after Pentecost)	A 168	
	26-40	λθ′	Friday of the 9th week (after Pentecost)	A 111	
15	1-11	μ′	Sunday of the 12th week (after Pentecost)	A 134	
	12-19	μα′	2nd day of the 10th week (after Pentecost)	A 114	
	20-28	μβ′	the 5th day (Commemoration of the Reposed)		X
	29-38	μγ′	3rd day of the 10th week (after Pentecost)	A 115	
	39-45	μδ′	Saturday of the 18th week (after Pentecost)	A 175	
	46				
	47-57	με′	Saturday (Commemoration of the Reposed)]		X
	58	μϛ′	Saturday of the 19th week (after Pentecost)	A 182	
16	1-3	Continued	Cont.	Cont.	
	4-12	μζ′	4th day of the 10th week (after Pentecost)	A 116	
	13-24	μη′	Sunday of the 13th week (after Pentecost)	A 141	

II Corinthians

1	1-7	α′	5th day of the 10th week (after Pentecost)	A 117	
	8-11	β′	Saturday of the 20th week (after Pentecost)	A 189	
	12-20	γ′	Friday of the 10th week (after Pentecost)	A 118	
	21-24	δ′	Sunday of the 14th week (after Pentecost)	A 148	
2	1-4	Continued	Cont.	Cont.	
	3-15	ε′	2nd day of the 11th week (after Pentecost)	A 121	
	14-17	ϛ′	3rd day of the 11th week (after Pentecost)	A 122	
3	1-3	Continued	Cont.	Cont.	
	4-11	ζ′	4th day of the 11th week (after Pentecost)	A 123	
	12-18	η′	Saturday of the 21st week (after Pentecost)	A 196	
4	1-12	θ′	5th day of the 11th week (after Pentecost)	A 124	
	6-15	ι′	Sunday of the 15th week (after Pentecost)	A 155	
	13-18	ια′	Friday of the 11th week (after Pentecost)	A 125	
5	1-10	ιβ′	Saturday of the 22nd week (after Pentecost)	A 203	
	10-15	ιγ′	2nd day of the 12th week (after Pentecost)	A 128	
	15-21	ιδ′	3rd day of the 12th week (after Pentecost)	A 129	
6	1-10	ιε′	Sunday of the 16th week (after Pentecost)	A 162	
	11-16	ιϛ′	4th day of the 12th week (after Pentecost)	A 130	
	16-18	ιζ′	Sunday of the 17th week (after Pentecost)	A 169	
7	1	Continued	Cont.	Cont.	
	1-10	ιη′	5th day of the 12th week (after Pentecost)	A 131	
	10-16	ιθ′	Friday of the 12th week (after Pentecost)	A 132	
8	1-5	κ′	Saturday of the 23rd week (after Pentecost)	A 210	
	6				
	7-15	κα′	2nd day of the 13th week (after Pentecost)	A 135	
	16-24	κβ′	3rd day of the 13th week (after Pentecost)	A 136	
9	1-5	Continued	Cont.	Cont.	
	6-11	κγ′	Sunday of the 18th week (after Pentecost)	A 176	
	12-15	κδ′	4th day of the 13th week (after Pentecost)	A 137	
10	1-7	Continued	Cont.	Cont.	
	7-18	κε′	5th day of the 13th week (after Pentecost)	A 138	
11	1-6	κϛ′	Saturday of the 24th week (after Pentecost)	A 217	
	5-21	κζ′	Friday of the 13th week (after Pentecost)	A 139	
	21-33	κη′	29 June The Apostles Peter and Paul		B 57

12	1-9	Continued	Cont.	Cont.	
	10-19	κθ′	2nd day of the 14th week (after Pentecost)	A 142	
	20-21	λ′	3rd day of the 14th week (after Pentecost)	A 143	
13	1-2	Continued	Cont.	Cont.	
	3-13	λα′	4th day of the 14th week (after Pentecost)	A 144	

Galatians

1	1-3 [20-24; 2, 1-5]	α′	5th day of the 14th week (after Pentecost)	A 145	
	3-10	β′	Saturday of the 25th week (after Pentecost)	A 224	
	11-19	γ′	Sunday of the 20th week (after Pentecost)	A 190	
	20-24				
2	1-5				
	6-10	δ′	Friday of the 14th week (after Pentecost)	A 146	
	11-16	ε′	2nd day of the 15th week (after Pentecost)	A 149	
	16-20	ς′	Sunday of the 21st week (after Pentecost)	A 197	
	21	ζ′	3rd day of the 15th week (after Pentecost)	A 150	
3	1-7	Continued	Cont.	Cont.	
	8-12	η′	Saturday of the 26th week (after Pentecost)	A 231	
	13-14	θ′	Great Saturday (Holy Week) (Morning office)	A 353	
	15-21	ι′	4th day of the 15th week (after Pentecost)	A 151	
	22-26	ια′	Saturday of the 27th week (after Pentecost)	A 238	
4	1-2	Continued	Cont.	Cont.	
	[3, 23-29] 1-5	ιβ′	5th day of the 15th week (after Pentecost)	A 152	
	4-7	ιγ′	25 Dec Nativity of the Lord Jesus Christ		B 29
	8-21	ιδ′	Friday of the 15th week (after Pentecost)	A 153	
	22-27	ιε′	23 Sept Conception of John the Baptist		B 5
	28-31	ις′	2nd day of the 16th week (after Pentecost)	A 156	
5	1-10	Continued	Cont.	Cont.	
	11-21	ιζ′	3rd day of the 16th week (after Pentecost)	A 157	
	22-26	ιη′	Saturday of the 27th week (after Pentecost)	A 238	
6	1-2	Continued	Cont.	Cont.	
	2-10	ιθ′	4th day of the 16th week (after Pentecost)	A 158	
	11-18	κ′	Sunday of the 22nd week (after Pentecost)	A 204	

Ephesians

A 159

1	1-9	α′	5th day of the 16th week (after Pentecost)		
	7-17	β′	Friday of the 16th week (after Pentecost)	A 160	
	16-23	γ′	Saturday of the 28th week (after Pentecost)	A 245	
	22-23	δ′	2nd day of the 17th week (after Pentecost)	A 163	
2	1-3	Continued	Cont.	Cont.	
	4-10	ε′	Sunday of the 23rd week (after Pentecost)	A 211	
	11-13	ς′	Saturday of the 29th week (after Pentecost)	A 252	
	14-22	ζ′	Sunday of the 24th week (after Pentecost)	A 218	
	19-22	η′	3rd day of the 17th week (after Pentecost)	A 164	
3	1-7	Continued	Cont.	Cont.	
	8-21	θ′	4th day of the 17th week (after Pentecost)	A 165	
4	1-7	ι′	Sunday of the 25th week (after Pentecost)	A 225	
	7-13	ια′	25 July Dormition of Anna		B 65
	14-17	ιβ′	5th day of the 17th week (after Pentecost)	A 166	
	17-25	ιγ′	Friday of the 17th week (after Pentecost)	A 167	
	25-32	ιδ′	2nd day of the 18th week (after Pentecost)	A 170	
5	1-8	ιε′	Saturday of the 30th week (after Pentecost)	A 259	
	8-19	ις′	2nd day of the 1st week (after Pentecost)	A 51	
	20-25	ιζ′	3rd day of the 18th week (after Pentecost)	A 171	

235

	25-33	ιη′	4th day of the 18th week (after Pentecost)	A 172	
	33	ιθ′	5th day of the 18th week (after Pentecost)	A 173	
6	1-9	Continued	Cont.	Cont.	
	10-17	κ′	Sunday of the 27th week (after Pentecost)	A 239	
	18-24	κα′	Friday of the 18th week (after Pentecost)	A 174	

Philippians

1	1-7	α′	2nd day of the 19th week (after Pentecost)	A 177	
	8-14	β′	3rd day of the 19th week (after Pentecost)	A 178	
	12-20	γ′	4th day of the 19th week (after Pentecost)	A 179	
	20-27	δ′	5th day of the 19th week (after Pentecost)	A 180	
	27-30	ε′	Friday of the 19th week (after Pentecost)	A 181	
2	1-4	Continued	Cont.	Cont.	
	5-11	ϛ′	8 Sept Nativity of the Theotokos		B 2
	12-16	ζ′	2nd day of the 20th week (after Pentecost)	A 184	
	16-23	η′	3rd day of the 20th week (after Pentecost)	A 185	
	24-30	θ′	4th day of the 20th week (after Pentecost)	A 186	
3	1-8	ι′	5th day of the 20th week (after Pentecost)	A 187	
	8-19	ια′	Friday of the 20th week (after Pentecost)	A 188	
	20-21	ιβ′	24 Nov Commemorations of martyrs		X
4	1-3	Continued	Cont.	Cont.	
	4-9	ιγ′	Palm Sunday	A 344	
	10-23	ιδ′	2nd day of the 21st week (after Pentecost)	A 191	

Collossians

1	1-3 [6-11]	α′	3rd day of the 21st week (after Pentecost)	A 192	
	1-6	β′	Saturday of the 31st week (after Pentecost)	A 266	
	12-18	γ′	Sunday of the 28th week (after Pentecost)	A 246	
	18-23	δ′	4th day of the 21st week (after Pentecost)	A 193	
	24-29	ε′	5th day of the 21st week (after Pentecost)	A 194	
2	1	Continued	Cont.	Cont.	
	1-7	ϛ′	Friday of the 21st week (after Pentecost)	A 195	
	8-12	ζ′	1 Jan Circumcision of the Lord		B 30
	13-20	η′	2nd day of the 22nd week (after Pentecost)	A 198	
	20-23	θ′	3rd day of the 22nd week (after Pentecost)	A 199	
3	1-3	Continued	Cont.	Cont.	
	4-11	ι′	Sunday of the 29th week (after Pentecost)	A 253	
	12-16	ια′	Sunday of the 30th week (after Pentecost)	A 260	
	17-25	ιβ′	4th day of the 22nd week (after Pentecost)	A 200	
4	1	Continued	Cont.	Cont.	
	2-9	ιγ′	5th day of the 22nd week (after Pentecost)	A 201	
	10-18	ιδ′	Friday of the 22nd week (after Pentecost)	A 202	

I Thessalonians

1	1-5	α′	2nd day of the 23rd week (after Pentecost)	A 205	
	6-10	β′	3rd day of the 23rd week (after Pentecost)	A 206	
2	1-8	γ′	4th day of the 23rd week (after Pentecost)	A 207	
	9-14	δ′	5th day of the 23rd week (after Pentecost)	A 208	
	14-20	ε′	Friday of the 23rd week (after Pentecost)	A 209	
	20	ϛ′	2nd day of the 24th week (after Pentecost)	A 212	
3	1-8	Continued	Cont.	Cont.	
	8-13	ζ′	3rd day of the 24th week (after Pentecost)	A 213	
4	1-12	η′	4th day of the 24th week (after Pentecost)	A 214	
	13-17	θ′	Saturday (Commemoration of the Reposed)		X

		18	ι′	5th day of the 24th week (after Pentecost)	A 215	
	5	1-10	Continued	Cont.	Cont.	
		9-13 [24-28]	ια′	Friday of the 24th week (after Pentecost)	A 216	
		14-23	ιβ′	Saturday of the 32nd week (after Pentecost)	A 273	
II Thessalonians						
	1	1-10	α′	2nd day of the 25th week (after Pentecost)	A 219	
		10-12	β′	3rd day of the 25th week (after Pentecost)	A 220	
	2	1-2	Continued	Cont.	Cont.	
		1-12	γ′	4th day of the 25th week (after Pentecost)	A 221	
		13-17	δ′	5th day of the 25th week (after Pentecost)	A 222	
	3	1-5	Continued	Cont.	Cont.	
		6-18	ε′	Friday of the 25th week (after Pentecost)	A 223	
I Timothy						
	1	1-7	α′	2nd day of the 26th week (after Pentecost)	A 226	
		8-14	β′	3rd day of the 26th week (after Pentecost)	A 227	
		15-17	γ′	Sunday of the 31st week (after Pentecost)	A 267	
		18-20 [2, 8-15]	δ′	4th day of the 26th week (after Pentecost)	A 228	
	2	1-7	ε′	1 Sept Beginning of the Indiction		B 1
	3	1-13	ς′	5th day of the 26th week (after Pentecost)	A 229	
		13-16	ζ′	Saturday before Theophany		X
	4	1-5	Continued	Cont.	Cont.	
		4-8 [16]	η′	Friday of the 26th week (after Pentecost)	A 230	
		9-15	θ′	Sunday of the 32nd week (after Pentecost)	A 274	
		16				
	5	1-10	ι′	2nd day of the 27th week (after Pentecost)	A 233	
		11-21	ια′	3rd day of the 27th week (after Pentecost)	A 234	
		22-25	ιβ′	4th day of the 27th week (after Pentecost)	A 235	
	6	1-11	Continued	Cont.	Cont.	
		11-16	ιγ′	Saturday of the 34th week (after Pentecost)	A 287	
		17-21	ιδ′	5th day of the 27th week (after Pentecost)	A 236	
II Timothy						
	1	1-2 [8-18]	α′	Friday of the 27th week (after Pentecost)	A 237	
		3-9	β′	22 Jan The Apostle Timotheos		X
	2	1-10	γ′	26 Oct Martyr Demetrios the Myrrhgusher		X
		11-19	δ′	Saturday of the 33rd week (after Pentecost)	A 280	
		20-26	ε′	2nd day of the 28th week (after Pentecost)	A 240	
	3	1-9				
		10-15	ς′	Sunday of the 33rd week (after Pentecost)	A 281	
		16-17	ζ′	3rd day 28th week (after Pentecost)	A 241	
	4	1-4	Continued	Cont.	Cont.	
		5-8	η′	Sunday before Theophany		X
		9-22	θ′	4th day 28th week (after Pentecost)	A 242	
Titus						
	1	1-5 [2, 15; 3, 1-2, 12-15]	α′	25 Aug Bartholomeos and Titus		X
			β′			
		15-16	γ′	Friday of the 28th week (after Pentecost)	A 244	
	2	1-10	Continued	Cont.	Cont.	
		11-14 [3, 4-7]	δ′	6 Jan Theophany		B 33
	3	8-15	ε′	11 Oct The Holy Fathers		X

237

Philemon

	1-25	α′	22 Nov The Apostle Philemos		X

Hebrews

1	1-12	α′	Saturday of the 1st week of Great Lent	A 310	
	'10-14	β′	Sunday of the 2nd week of Great Lent	A 316	
2	1-3	Continued	Cont.	Cont.	
	2-10	γ′	8 Nov Synaxis of the Archangels		B 16
	11-18	δ′	Great Friday (Holy Week) (6th Hour)	A 351	
3	1-4	ε′	13 Sept Founding Church of Resurrection (Jerusalem)		B 3
	5-11 [17-19]	ς′	2nd day of the 29th week (after Pentecost)	A 247	
	12-16	ζ′	Saturday of the 2nd week of Great Lent	A 315	
4	1-13	η′	3rd day of the 29th week (after Pentecost)	A 248	
	14-16	θ′	Sunday of the 3rd week of Great Lent	A 323	
5	1-6	Continued	Cont.	Cont.	
	4-10	ι′	2 Jan Silvester of Rome		X
	11-14	ια′	4th day of the 29th week (after Pentecost)	A 249	
6	1-8	Continued	Cont.	Cont.	
	9-12	ιβ′	Saturday of the 4th week of Great Lent	A 329	
	13-20	ιγ′	Sunday of the 4th week of Great Lent	A 330	
7	1-6	ιδ′	5th day of the 29th week (after Pentecost)	A 250	
	7-17	ιε′	2 Febr Meeting of the Lord		B 41
	18-25	ις′	Friday of the 29th week (after Pentecost)	A 251	
	26-28	ιζ′	13 Nov John Chrysostom		B 18
8	1-2	Continued	Cont.	Cont.	
	1-6	ιη′	6 Nov Paul of Constantinople		X
	7-13	ιθ′	2nd day of the 30th week (after Pentecost)	A 254	
9	1-7	κ′	21 Nov Entry of the Theotokos into the Temple		B 19
	8-23	κα′	3rd day of the 30th week (after Pentecost)	A 255	
	11-14	κβ′	Sunday of the 5th week of Great Lent	A 337	
	24-28	κγ′	Saturday of the 5th week of Great Lent	A 336	
10	1-18	κδ′	4th day of the 30th week (after Pentecost)	A 256	
	19-31	κε′	Great Friday (Holy Week) (9th Hour)	A 351	
	32-38	κς′	Saturday of the 3rd week of Great Lent	A 322	
	35-39	κζ′	5th day of the 30th week (after Pentecost)	A 257	
11	1-7	Continued	Cont.	Cont.	
	8-16	κη′	Friday of the 30th week (after Pentecost)	A 258	
	17-31	κς′	2nd day of the 31th week (after Pentecost)	A 261	
	[24-26] 32-40	κζ′	Sunday of the 1st week of Great Lent	A 309	
12	1-10	κη′	9 March Forty Martyrs of Sebaste		B 45
	6-29	κθ′	26 Oct Earthquake of Constantinople A.D. 740		B 14
	28-29	λ′	Saturday of the 6th week of Great Lent (Lazarus)	A 343	
13	1-8	Continued	Cont.	Cont.	
	7-16	λα′	18 Jan Athanasius and Cyril of Alexandria		B 37
	17-21	λβ′	6 Dec Nicholas of Myra		B 24
	22-25				

238

The General Epistles

Kephalaia	Stichoi	Anagnosmata	Synaxarion/Menologion	Kin	Akin
James					
1	1-18	α′	4th day of the 31st week (after Pentecost)	A 263	
	19-27	β′	5th day of the 31st week (after Pentecost)	A 264	
2	1-13	γ′	Friday of the 31st week (after Pentecost)	A 265	
	14-26	δ′	2nd of the 32nd week (after Pentecost)	A 268	
3	1-10	ε′	3rd of the 32nd week (after Pentecost)	A 269	
	11-18	ς′	4th of the 32dt week (after Pentecost)	A 270	
4	1-6	Continued	Cont.	Cont.	
	7-17	ζ′	5th of the 32nd week (after Pentecost)	A 271	
5	1-9	Continued	Cont.	Cont.	
	10-20	η′	20 July The Prophet Elias		B 64
I Peter					
1	1-25	α′	Friday of the 32nd week (after Pentecost)	A 272	
2	1-10	Continued	Cont.	Cont.	
	11-19				
	21-25	β′	2nd of the 33rd week (after Pentecost)	A 275	
3	1-9	Continued	Cont.	Cont.	
	10-22	γ′	3rd of the 33rd week (after Pentecost)	A 276	
4	1-11	δ′	4th of the 33rd week (after Pentecost)	A 277	
	12-19	ε′	5th of the 33rd week (after Pentecost)	A 278	
5	1-5	Continued	Cont.	Cont.	
	6-14	ς′	25 April The Apostle Mark		B 49
	15-20				
II Peter					
1	1-10	α′	Friday of the 33rd week (after Pentecost)	A 279	
	10-19	β′	6 Aug Metamorhosis		B 67
	20-21	γ′	2nd day of the 34rd week (after Pentecost)	A 282	
2	1-9	Continued	Cont.	Cont.	
	9-22	δ′	3rd day of the 34rd week (after Pentecost)	A 283	
3	1-18	ε′	4th day of the 34rd week (after Pentecost)	A 284	
I John					
1	1-7	α′	8 May The Apostle John		B 51
	8-9	β′	5th day of the 34rd week (after Pentecost)	A 285	
2	1-6	Continued	Cont.	Cont.	
	7-17	γ′	Friday of the 34rd week (after Pentecost)	A 286	
	18-29	δ′	2nd day of Meatfare week (35th week)	A 289	
3	1-8	Continued	Cont.	Cont.	
	9-22	ε′	3rd day of Meatfare week (35th week)	A 290	
	21-24	ς′	4th day of Meatfare week (35th week)	A 291	
4	1-11	Continued	Cont.	Cont.	
	12-19	ζ′	26 Sept Repose of the Apostle John		B 6
	20-21	η′	5th day of Meatfare week (35th week)	A 292	
5	1-21	Continued	Cont.	Cont.	

II John
| | 1-13 | α′ | Friday of Meatfare week (35th week) | A293 |

III John
| | 1-15 | α′ | 2nd day of Cheesefare week (36th week) | A 296 |

Jude
| | 1-10 | α′ | 3rd day of Cheesefare week (36th week) | A 297 |
| | 11-25 | β′ | 5th day of Cheesefare week (36th week) | A 299 |

The Anagnosmata of the Prophetologion (according to the Triodion, Pentekostarion, Menaia)[594]

Prophetologion

Kephalaia	Stichoi	Anagnosmata	Synaxarion/Menologion	Kin	Akin
Genesis					
1	1-13	α′	2nd day of the 1st week of Great Lent	A 303	
	14-23	β′	3rd day of the 1st week of Great Lent	A 304	
	24-31	γ′	4th day of the 1st week of Great Lent	A 305	
2	1-3	Continued	Cont.	Cont.	
	4-19	δ′	5th day of the 1st week of Great Lent	A 306	
	20-25	ε′	Friday of the 1st week of Great Lent	A 307	
3	1-20	Continued	Cont.	Cont.	
	21-24	ς′	2nd day of the 2nd week of Great Lent	A 310	
4	1-7	Continued	Cont.	Cont.	
	8-15	ζ′	3rd day of the 2nd week of Great Lent	A 311	
	16-26	η′	4th day of the 2nd week of Great Lent	A 312	
5	1-24	θ′	5th day of the 2nd week of Great Lent	A 313	
	32	ι′	Friday of the 2nd week of Great Lent	A 314	
6	1-8	Continued	Cont.	Cont.	
	9-22	ια′	2nd day of the 3rd week of Great Lent	A 317	
7	1-5	ιβ′	3rd day of the 3rd week of Great Lent	A 318	
	6-9	ιγ′	4th day of the 3rd week of Great Lent	A 319	
	11-24	ιδ′	5th day of the 3rd week of Great Lent	A 321	
8	1-3	Continued	Cont.	Cont.	
	4-21	ιε′	Friday of the 3rd week of Great Lent	A 321	
	21-22	ις′	2nd day of the 4th week of Great Lent	A 324	
9	1-7	Continued	Cont.	Cont.	
	8-17	ιζ′	3rd day of the 4th week of Great Lent	A 325	
	18-28	ιη′	4th day of the 4th week of Great Lent	A 326	
10	1	Continued	Cont.	Cont.	
	32	ιθ′	5th day of the 4th week of Great Lent	A 327	
11	1-9	Continued	Cont.	Cont.	
12	1-7	κ′	Friday of the 4th week of Great Lent	A 328	
13	12-18	κα′	2nd day of the 5th week of Great Lent	A 331	
14	14-20	κβ′	7th Sunday of Pascha (Fathers of Nicea)	A 43	
15	1-15	κγ′	3rd day of the 5th week of Great Lent	A 332	
17	1-9	κδ′	4th day of the 5th week of Great Lent	A 333	
	15-17, 19	κε′	24 June Nativity of John the Baptist		B 56 (1)
18	11-14 [21, 1-2, 4-8]	Continued	Cont.	Cont.	
	20-33	κς′	5th day of the 5th week of Great Lent	A 334	
22	1-18	κζ′	Friday of the 5th week of Great Lent	A 335	
27	1-11	κη′	2nd day of the 6th week of Great Lent	A 338	
28	10-17	κθ′	8 Sept Nativity of the Theotokos		B 2 (1)
31	3-16	λ′	3rd day of the 6th week of Great Lent	A 339	
32	1-10	λα′	6 Jan Eve of Theophany		B 32 (8)
43	25-30	λβ′	4th day of the 6th week of Great Lent	A 340	

---

[594] The Index provides the lessons of the OT books in chronological order, including only the selected passages of the Octateuch (Gen, Ex, Lev, Num, Deut, Josh, Judg, Ruth) and Kings III-IV, the Wisdom books (Prov, Iob, Eccl., Wis, Eccless) and the Prophets (Minor and Major), that are included in the Prophetologion (i.e. in the Triodion, Pentekostarion and Menaia), without indicating the lacunae in the continuous text.

45	1-16	Continued	Cont.	Cont.	
46	1-7	λγ′	5th day of the 6th week of Great Lent	A 341	
49	1-2 [8-12]	λδ′	6th Sunday of Pascha (Palmsunday)	A 344 (1)	
	33	λε′	Friday of the 6th week of Great Lent	A 342 (1)	
50	1-26	Continued	Cont.	Cont.	

Exodus

1	1-20	α′	Great Second Day (Holy Week) (Evening office)	A 345 (1)	
2	5-10	β′	Great Third Day (Holy Week) (Evening office)	A 346 (1)	
	11-23	γ′	Great Fourth Day (Holy Week) (Evening office)	A 347 (1)	
12	1-11	δ′	Great Saturday (Holy Week) (Evening office)	A 354 (3)	
13	20-22	ε′	Great Saturday (Holy Week) (Evening office)	A 354 (6)	
14	1-31	Continued	Cont.	Cont.	
15	1-19	Continued	Cont.	Cont.	
	22-27	ς′	14 Sept Exaltation of the Cross		B 4 (1)
16	1	Continued	Cont.	Cont.	
19	10-19	ζ′	Great Fifth Day (Holy Week) (Evening office)	A 349 (1)	
24	12-18	η′	6 Aug Metamorphosis		B 67 (1)
33	11-23	θ′	Great Friday (Holy Week) (Evening office)	A 352 (1)	
34	[3, 11-23] 4-6, 8	ι′	6 Aug Metamorphosis		B 67 (2)
40	1-5, 7, 9, 14, 28-29	ια′	21 Nov Entry of the Theotokos in the Temple		B 19 (1)
40	15-32	ιβ′	25 Oct The Protecting Veil of the Theotokos		B 15 (2)

Leviticus

12	2-4, 6-8	α′	2 Febr Meeting of Our Lord		B 41(1b)
26	3-5, 7-8, 9-12, 14-17, 19-20, 22, 33, 23-24	β′	1 Sept Beginning of the Indiction		B 1 (2)

Numeri

8	16-17	α′	2 Febr Meeting of Our Lord		B 41 (1c)
9	15-23	β′	28 Oct The Protecting Veil of the Theotokos		B 15 (1)
11	16-17, 24-29	γ′	Sunday of Pentecost (Evening office)	A 50 (1)	
24	2-3, 5-9, 17-18	δ′	24 Dec Eve of the Nativity of the Lord		B 28 (2)

Deuteronomy

1	8-11, 15-17	α′	Sunday of the Fathers of the Council of Nicea I	A 43 (2)	
10	14-18, 20-21	β′	Sunday of the Fathers of the Council of Nicea I	A 43 (2)	

Joshua

3	7-8, 15-17	α′	5 Jan Eve of Theophany		B 32 (4)
5	10-15	β′	Great Saturday (Holy Week) (Evening office)	A 354 (5)	
	13-15	γ′	8 Nov Synaxis of the Archangels		B 16 (1)

Judges

6	2, 7, 11-24	α′	8 Nov Synaxis of the Archangels		B 16 (2)
	36-40	β′	5 Nov Eve of Theophany		B 32 (10)
13	2-8, 13-14, 17-18, 21	γ′	24 June Nativity of John the Baptist		B 56 (2)

III Kings

8	1, 3, 9, 10-11	α′	21 Nov Entry of the Theotokos in the Temple		B 19 (2)
8	22-23, 27-30	β′	13 Sept Founding of the Resurrection Church (Jerusalem)		B 3 (1)
17	1-24	γ′	20 July The Prophet Elias the Thesbite		B 64 (1)
17	8-24	δ′	Great Saturday (Holy Week) (Evening office)	A 354 (8)	
18	1, 17-46 [19, 1-6]	ε′	20 July The Prophet Elias the Thesbite		B 64 (2)

18	30-39	ς'	5 Jan Eve of Theophany		B 32(11)
19	3-9, 11-13, 15-16	ζ'	6 Aug Metamorphosis		B 67 (3)
19	19-21 [IV Kings 2, 1, 6-14]	η'	20 July The Prophet Elias the Thesbite		B 64 (3)

IV Kings

2	19-22	α'	5 Jan Eve of Theophany		B 32 (12)
2	6-14	β'	5 Jan Eve of Theophany		B 32 (5)
4	8-37	γ'	Great Saturday (Holy Week)	A 354 (12)	
5	9-14	δ'	5 Jan Eve of Theophany		B 32 (6)

Proverbs

1	1-20	α'	2nd day of the 1st week of Great Lent	A 303 (2)	
	20-33	β'	3rd day of the 1st week of Great Lent	A 304 (2)	
2	1-22	γ'	4th day of the 1st week of Great Lent	A 305 (2)	
3	1-18	δ'	5th day of the 1st week of Great Lent	A 306 (2)	
	19-34	ε'	Friday of the 1st week of Great Lent	A 307 (2)	
	34	ς'	2nd day of the 2nd week of Great Lent	A 310 (2)	
4	1-22	Continued	Cont.	Cont.	
5	1-15	ζ'	3rd day of the 2nd week of Great Lent	A 311 (2)	
	15-23	η'	4th day of the 2nd week of Great Lent	A 312 (2)	
6	1-3	Continued	Cont.	Cont.	
	3-20	θ'	5th day of the 2nd week of Great Lent	A 313 (2)	
	20-35	ι'	Friday of the 2nd week of Great Lent	A 314 (2)	
7	1	Continued	Cont.	Cont.	
8	1-21	ια'	2nd day of the 3rd week of Great Lent	A 317 (2)	
	22-30	ιβ'	1 Jan Circumcision of Our Lord		B 30 (2)
	32-36	ιγ'	3rd day of the 3rd week of Great Lent	A 318 (2)	
9	1-11	Continued	Cont.	Cont.	
	12-18	ιδ'	4th day of the 3rd week of Great Lent	A 319 (2)	
10	1-22	ιε'	5th day of the 3rd week of Great Lent	A 320 (2)	
	31-32	ις'	Friday of the 3rd week of Great Lent	A 321 (2)	
11	1-12	Continued	Cont.	Cont.	
	19-31	ιζ'	2nd day of the 4th week of Great Lent	A 324 (2)	
12	1-6	Continued	Cont.	Cont.	
	8-22	ιη'	3rd day of the 4th week of Great Lent	A 325 (2)	
	23-27	ιθ'	4th day of the 4th week of Great Lent	A 326 (2)	
13	1-9	Continued	Cont.	Cont.	
	19-25	κ'	5th day of the 4th week of Great Lent	A 327 (2)	
14	1-6	Continued	Cont.	Cont.	
	15-26	κα'	Friday of the 4th week of Great Lent	A 328 (2)	
	27-35	κβ'	2nd day of the 5th week of Great Lent	A 331 (2)	
15	1-4	Continued	Cont.	Cont.	
	7-19	κγ'	3rd day of the 5th week of Great Lent	A 332 (2)	
	20-33	κδ'	4th day of the 5th week of Great Lent	A 333 (2)	
16	1-9	Continued	Cont.	Cont.	
	17-33	κε'	5th day of the 5th week of Great Lent	A 334 (2)	
17	1-17	Continued	Cont.	Cont.	
	17-28	κς'	Friday of the 5th week of Great Lent	A 335 (2)	
18	1-5	Continued	Cont.	Cont.	
19	16-25	κζ'	2nd day of the 6th week of Great Lent	A 338 (2)	
21	3-21	κη'	3rd day of the 6th week of Great Lent	A 339 (2)	
	23-31	κθ'	4th day of the 6th week of Great Lent	A 340 (2)	
22	1-4	Continued	Cont.	Cont.	

23	15-35	λ'	5th day of the 6th week of Great Lent	A 341 (2)	
24	1-5	Continued	Cont.	Cont.	
31	8-31	λα'	Friday of the 6th week of Great Lent	A 342 (2)	
	10-20, 25	λβ'	19 Febr Philothei of Athens		B 44 (1)

Iob

1	1-12	α'	Great Second Day (Holy Week)	A 345 (2)
	13-22	β'	Great Third Day (Holy Week)	A 346 (2)
2	1-10	γ'	Great Fourth Day (Holy Week)	A 347 (2)
38	1-21	δ'	Great Fifth Day (Holy Week)	A 348 (2)
42	1-5	Continued	Cont.	Cont.
	12-17	ε'	Great Friday (Holy Week)	A 351 (2)

Wisdom

3	1-9	α'	1st week after Pentecost	A 57 (2)
4	7-15	β'	1 Sept Beginning of the Indiction	B 1 (3)
4	7, 16-17, 19-20	γ'	29 Aug Beheading of John the Baptist	B 71 (3)
5	1-7	Continued	Cont.	Cont.
5	15-23	δ'	1st week after Pentecost	A 57 (3)
6	1-3	Continued	Cont.	Cont.

Micah

4	2-3, 5	α'	4th week after Pascha	A 25 (1)
5	2-5, 8	Continued	Cont.	Cont.
	1-3	β'	23 Dec Preparation day of the Nativity of the Lord	B 27

Joel

2	12-26	α'	4th day of th 36th week (after Pentecost)	A 298
2	23-32	β'	Pentecost	A 50 (2)
3	1-5	Continued	Cont.	Cont.
4	12-21	γ'	4th day of th 36th week (after Pentecost)	A 298

Jonah

1-4		α'	Great Saturday (Holy Week)	A 354 (4)

Zephaniah

3	8-15	α'	Great Saturday (Holy Week)	A 354 (7)
3	14-19	β'	Saturday of the 6th week of Great Lent (Lazarus)	A 343 (2)

Zechariah

8	7-17	α'	Friday of the 36th week (after Pentecost)	A300
8	19-23	β'	Friday of the 36th week (after Pentecost)	A300
9	9-15	γ'	Saturday of the 6th week of Great Lent	A 343 (3)
11	10-13	δ'	Great Friday (Holy Week)	A 351
14	1, 4, 8-11	ε'	5th day of the 6th week (after Pascha) (Ascension)	A 40 (3)

Malachi

3	1-3, 5-7, 12, 18	α'	29 Aug Beheading of John the Baptist		B 71 (2)
4	4-6	Continued	Cont.	Cont.	

Isaiah

1	1-20	α'	2nd day of the 1st week of Great Lent	A 303
	19-31	β'	3rd day of the 1st week of Great Lent	A 304
2	1-3	Continued	Cont.	Cont.

	3-11	γ'	4th day of the 1st week of Great Lent	A 305
	11-21	δ'	5th day of the 1st week of Great Lent	A 306
3	1-14	ε'	Friday of the 1st week of Great Lent	A 307
4	2-6	ς'	2nd day of the 2nd week of Great Lent	A 310
5	1-7	Continued	Cont.	Cont.
	7-16	ζ'	3rd day of the 2nd week of Great Lent	A 311
	16-25	η'	4th day of the 2nd week of Great Lent	A 312
6	1-12	θ'	5th day of the 2nd week of Great Lent	A 313
7	1-14	ι'	Friday of the 2nd week of Great Lent	A 314
	10-16	ια'	Preparation day of the Nativity of the Lord	B 27
8	1-4, 9-10	Continued	Cont.	Cont.
	13-22	ιβ'	2nd day of the 3rd week of Great Lent	A 317
9	1-7	Continued	Cont.	Cont.
	9-20	ιγ'	3rd day of the 3rd week of Great Lent	A 318
10	1-4	Continued	Cont.	Cont.
	12-20	ιδ'	4th day of the 3rd week of Great Lent	A 319
11	1-10	ιε'	24 Dec Eve of the Nativity of the Lord	B 28 (4)
	11-16	ις'	5th day of the 3rd week of Great Lent	A 320
12	1-2	Continued	Cont.	Cont.
	3-6	ιζ'	Preparation day of Theophany (6th Hour)	B 31
13	2-13	ιη'	Friday of the 3rd week of Great Lent	A 321
14	24-32	ιθ'	2nd day of the 4th week of Great Lent	A 324
19	1, 3-5, 12, 16, 19-21	κ'	2 Febr Meeting of Our Lord	B 41 (3)
25	1-9	κα'	3rd day of the 4th week of Great Lent	A 325
26	21	κβ'	4th day of the 4th week of Great Lent	A 326
27	1-9	Continued	Cont.	Cont.
28	14-22	κγ'	5th day of the 4th week of Great Lent	A 327
29	13-23	κδ'	Friday of the 4th week of Great Lent	A 328
35	1-10	κε'	5 Jan Preparation day of Theophany	B 31
37	33-38	κς'	2nd day of the 5th week of Great Lent	A 331
38	1-6	Continued	Cont.	Cont.
40	18-31	κζ'	3rd day of the 5th week of Great Lent	A 332
41	4-14	κη'	4th day of the 5th week of Great Lent	A 333
42	5-16	κθ'	5th day of the 5th week of Great Lent	A 334
43	9-14	λ'	Sunday of All Saints	A 57 (1)
45	11-17	λα'	Friday of the 5th week of Great Lent	A 335
48	17-22	λβ'	2nd day of the 6th week of Great Lent	A 338
49	1-4	Continued	Cont.	Cont.
49	8-15	λγ'	5 Jan Preparation day of Theophany	B 31
50	4-11	λδ'	Great Fifth Day (Holy Week)	A 349 (3)
	6-10	λε'	3rd day of the 6th week of Great Lent	A 339
52	13-15	λς'	Great Friday (Holy Week)	A 351
53	1-12	Continued	Cont.	Cont.
54	1	Continued	Cont.	Cont.
55	1-3, 6-13	λζ'	4th day of the 4th week after Pascha	A 25 (2)
58	1-11	λη'	4th day of the 6th week of Great Lent	A 340
60	1-16	λθ'	Great Saturday (Holy Week)	A 354 (2)
61	1-10	μ'	Great Saturday (Holy Week)	A 354 (11)
	10-11	μα'	Great Saturday (Holy Week)	A 354 (9)
62	1-5	Continued	Cont.	Cont.
	10-12	μβ'	5th day of the 6th week of Great Lent	A 40 (2)
63	1-3, 7-9	Continued	Cont.	Cont.
	15-19	μγ'	26 Oct Demetrius the Myrrhgusher	B 14 (1)
64	1-5, 8-9	Continued	Cont.	Cont.

65	8-16	μδ′	5th day of the 6th week of Great Lent	A 341	
66	10-24	με′	Friday of the 6th week of Great Lent	A 342	

Jeremiah

2	1-12	α′	26 Oct Demetrius the Myrrhgusher		B 14 (2)
11	18-23	β′	Great Fifth Day (Holy Week)	A 348	
12	1-5, 9-11, 14-15	Continued	Cont.	Cont.	
38	31-34	γ′	Great Saturday (Holy Week)	A 354 (14)	

Baruch

3	35-38	α′	23 Dec Preparation day of the Nativity of the Lord		B 27
4	1-4	Continued	Cont.	Cont.	

Ezekiel

1	1-20	α′	Great Second Day (Holy Week)	A 345	
	21-28	β′	Great Third Day (Holy Week)	A 346	
2	3-10	γ′	Great Fourth Day (Holy Week)	A 347	
3	1-3	Continued	Cont.	Cont.	
36	24-28	δ′	Pentecost	A 50 (3)	
37	1-14	ε′	Great Saturday	A 353	
43	27	ς′	8 Sept The Nativity of the Theotokos		B 2 (2)
44	1-4	Continued	Cont.	Cont.	

Daniel

2	31-36, 44-45	α′	24 Dec Eve of the Nativity of the Lord		B 28 (6)
3	1-23	β′	Great Saturday (Holy Week)	A 354 (15)	
			(including: the Hymn of the Holy Children, 1-33)		
10	1-21	γ′	8 Nov Synaxis of the Archangels		B 16 (3)

www.ingramcontent.com/pod-product-compliance
Lightning Source LLC
LaVergne TN
LVHW071637080526
838199LV00095BA/6736